St. Joseph Catholic Church

GALVESTON, TEXAS

Baptismal, Confirmation,
Marriage and Death Records

- 1860-1952 -

Published under the auspices

of

The Galveston County Genealogical Society

Book Publishers

Southern Historical Press, Inc.
Greenville, South Carolina

Please direct all correspondence and orders to:

www.southernhistoricalpress.com
or
SOUTHERN HISTORICAL PRESS, Inc.
PO BOX 1267
375 West Broad Street
Greenville, SC 29601
southernhistoricalpress@gmail.com

ISBN #0-89308-344-5

Printed in the United States of America

TABLE OF CONTENTS

Chapter   Page

I   Confirmation Records   1860-1922   1
II   First Communions   1893-1933   11
III   Marriage Records   1860-1900   19
IV   Marriage Records   1900-1952   45
V   Funeral Records   1860-1899   69
VI   Funeral Records   1900-1952   89
VII   Baptismal Records   1860-1900   117
      Index   219

FOREWORD

    The Galveston County Genealogical Society was organized
April 19, 1979 with twenty-eight members. We are small in number
but most eager to make available material to perpetuate and
preserve our heritage for the present and future generations.

    The entire membership has been very supportive in this
endeavor to make these records available.

HISTORY

By the 1850's Galveston was the port of entry for most goods
shipped to inland Texas as well as to other points north. Very
important to the growth of Galveston and particularly to the
building trades were the immigrants, especially the Germans who
made Galveston their point of entry. Many of them chose either
to settle in the city or at least remain long enough to accumu-
late some capital before moving inland. The skilled German
craftsmen made a major contribution to the architecture of the
city.

By the mid-fifties, the more or less permanent population
of Galveston was composed of from 1/3 to 1/2 Germans. The
Bishop of the Catholic Diocese of Texas thought it advisable
to build a church to celebrate the service in the German language.
In 1859 three lots were purchased from J.L. Darraugh and a
church was erected in the same year at a cost of nearly $4,000.

On April 23, 1860 this simple Gothic Revival church was
dedicated under the patronage of St. Joseph, the patron saint
of laborers. Bishop Odin officiated, assisted by several other
clergymen, including Father Ansata, St. Joseph's first pastor.

In 1968 after 109 years as a place of worship, the Diocese
closed the church and sold its contents at public auction. Due
to the efforts of interested citizens and the Galveston Historical Foundation, the Galveston-Houston Roman Catholic Diocese
decided to lease the building to the Galveston Historical
Foundation under whose auspices it still remains. The Historical Foundation was successful in finding most of the auctioned
furnishings which were either donated or brought back returning
the church to its original state.

Most of the original records were written in the German
language but have since been transcribed to English. Copies
of baptism, marriage and death records from St. Joseph are
kept in Galveston at St. Mary's Cathedral. St. Mary's has
generously furnished the Galveston County Genealogical Society
copies for publication as opportunity permits.

ARCHITECTURE OF ST. JOSEPH'S

The architect-contractor for St. Joseph's Church was
Joseph Bleicke, born in Germany. Bleicke immigrated with his
family to Texas in November, 1850.

The church is a simple wood Gothic Revival building, rec-
tangular in shape with a central square bell tower. The windows and doors are painted, the windows are protected by
shutters and the front double door is unadorned. A trefoil
window is placed in the tower which intersects the gable end
of the pitched roof.

The interior is unique and after seeing the exterior,
unexpected. A central aisle separates the original pews which
are made of cedar and grained. The pews can seat about 250

people. It is believed the kneelers, located behind each of
the wooden, slatted backed seats, retain the original hardware
and are very novel. An altar rail carved in Gothic Revival
motif divides the sanctuary from the congregation. The enormous
statue of the crucifixion   which rests atop the main altar
is original with the building, as is the one of the Sacred Heart.

Adorning the walls of the nave are the Stations of the Cross
which are made of plaster with German lettering. The ceiling
is coffered and painted with quatrefoils and other Gothic
Revival symbols in soft, muted colors. The pulpit, the altars
and the reredos are believed to be original.

ST. JOSEPH'S SCHOOL

St. Joseph's Catholic Church established Galveston's first
non-private high school in 1887 beginning five years prior to
the establishment of Galveston's public school system. The
school operated in a building adjacent to the church until it
closed in 1926.

PARISHIONERS

The parishioners at St. Joseph's were primarily of the work-
ing class, with such occupations as carpenter, printer, pipeman
and clerk being common. Most lived south of Broadway in comfor-
table yet unimposing houses.

Probably the best known member of St. Joseph's Church during
its formative years was Peter Gengler, an immigrant from
Bohlendorff, Germany. He and his brother founded a food emporium
which became, under his son, one of the "best stocked and
equipped food emporiums in the United States."

The first recorded marriage at St. Joseph's was performed
June 6, 1860 between David Herzog and Mary Branden. The first
baptisms were Frederick P. and Peter Schneider, sons of William
A. Schneider and Adolphine Gruendel. In a touch of irony,
the first funeral was that of Joseph Bleicke, architect and
contractor of the church on June 15, 1860.

CONFIRMATION
1860 - 1922

CONFIRMATION 1860

Rt. Rev. John M. Odin
Dom. infra October Corp. Christi

Ferdinand Sommer	Mathew Herrmann	Euphemia Roeper
Frank Sammet	Joseph Elbert	Josephine Niemeyer
Andrew Mayer	Anthony Herrmann	Mary Adelaide Antonia
Charles Boeddeker	Philomene Dircks	Joseph Aull
Charles Lang	Anne Tschaeke	Wm. Bern. Oppermann
Charles Juersig	Mary Elizabeth Aull	Celestine . . . . .

CONFIRMATION 1861

Rt. Rev. John M. Odin
Ascension Feast

John Mayer	John Spann	Joan Moser
Michael Lang	Kaniel Mitchell	Caroline Kircher
Joseph Kraus	Mary Joseph Pelerise	Caroline Werdehausen
John Kircher	Mary Heimann	Caroline Maurer

CONFIRMATION January 6, 1864

Rt. Rev. Claud M. Dubuis

Mary Koehler	Scholastica Elbert	Gertrude Bergenbusch

CONFIRMATION December 8, 1864

ab eodem Ep.

August Sommer	Elizabeth Allen	Josephine Bleike
Joseph (John) Heimann	Catherine Lang	Anne Kimley
Josephine Niemeyer	Cecile Aull	Sophie Weyers

CONFIRMATION November 1, 1865

Rt. Rev. C. M. Dubuis

Joseph Hollinghaus	August Niebling	Ann Edwards
Joseph Cryacker	Mary Hermann	Magdalen Lydia Bernard
Herman Victor Lang	Mary Kleinmann	Mary Ann Oppermann
Patrick Gane	Rose Elbert	

CONFIRMATION January 17, 1866

John H. Stoner (convert)

CONFIRMATION March 25, 1866

Rt. Rev. C. M. Dubuis

Henry Schaefer	Amalia Heimann	Elizabeth Bleike
Anthony Aull	Margaret Werdehausen	Mary Verberne
Anthony Sommer	Catherine Elbert	Caroline Kimley
Joseph Paul Dumesney	Caroline Hagemann	Anne Philips
Hermann Maurer	Caroline Jung	Regina Ticks
William Tschocke	Mary Tavenet	Mary Lang
John Henry Moser	Adolphine Bergenbusch	Mary Jarmann
Louis Joseph	Teresa Schroeder	Joan Ricke Jensky
von Struve	Terese Bleike	

1

CONFIRMATION April 14, 1867

Rt. Rev. C. M. Dubuis

Dominic Morgan
Theodore Brinkhof
Catherine Ritzler
  (Michels)

Clement Stanislaus Portier
Catherine Rosalie Floeck
Emily Angela Kirker
Catherine Mary Agnes Siringo

Mary Magdalen Davis
Angela Aloysia Smith
Margaret Josephine
  Haley

CONFIRMATION April 19, 1868

Rt. Rev. C. M. Dubuis

Ferdinand Andler
Frederic Bleike
Henry Dircks
John Hagemann
Joseph Jersig
Emil Leinbach
Sarah Allen
Frances Dircks

Teresa Dircks
Antonia Bergmann
Aloysia Philipps
William F. Shetley
Philip Morgan
Victor Philipps
Alexander Weyers
William Michels

Benjamin Berrmann
Cecile Adam Shetley
Leopold Blondeau
Amalia Fink (Kallus)
Agnes Kallus
Wilhelmine Juergens
Edward Hergot

CONFIRMATION May 6, 1869

Rt. Rev. C. M. Dubuis

Elisabeth Moser
Caroline Elbert
Mary Sammet
Anne Schreiber
Terese Rohrmann

Elisabeth Dalmer
Anne Gengler
Terese Juette
Catherine Kaloe

John Maurer
John Weber
David Hermann
John Schmidt

CONFIRMATION January 14, 1872

Frank Anthony Koch
John Joseph Krauss
Henry George
  Stoppelberg
John Joseph Peine
Charles Sommer
John William Schocke
Joseph Milliany
Joseph Trost
Frank Anthony Koch

Henry Schultz
Clara Laura . . . .
Augusta Bertha Dalien
Emily Tillwitz
Mary Hergot
Caroline Vogt
Louise Young
Wilhelmine Muller
Dorthy Augusta
  Stoppelberg

Helen Agnes Clarke
Henrietta Werdehausen
Ida Ricke
Sophie Trost
Bertha Abel
Louise Brosig

CONFIRMATION April 30, 1875

Frederic Kraus
John Janssen
Joseph Werdehausen
Joseph Anderson
Joseph Werdehausen
Peter Joseph Lancton
Albert Demonet (?)
Martin Henry Flake

Ernest Fiebel
August Weber
James Bauhans
Mary Schocke
Augusta Mary Olive
  Heymann
Mary Agness Koehler
Mary Demonet

Mathilda Caroline Dinter
Helen Spieker
Anne Brokhof
Caroline Schneider
Terese Hofbek
Mary Bergmann
Catherine Josephine Young

CONFIRMATION May 18, 1876

Frank Edward Bruecher
Joseph Lang
Philip Helfrich
Joseph Matt
William Werdehausen
Germanicus Dinter
Ernestine Rose
  Dallmer

Margaret Elbert
Emma Anne Kimley
Mary Elisabeth Heymann
Mary Magdalen Ricke
Mary Elisabeth Moser
Emma Sophe Rose Pierre
Helen Mary Haehnlein
John Hermann

Mary Elisabeth Helfrich
Mary Elisabeth Steymann
Mary Elisabeth Schromer
Wilhelmine Elisabeth
  Winslow
Sophie Bauhans
Ann Louise Bleike
Emma Terese Mary Verberne

A. D. 1881, die ... Rmus ac Illmus C. M. Dubuis confirmavit in Ecclesia
Sti. Josephi ....

CONFIRMATION May 13, 1883

Rt. Rev. N. A. Gallagher

Frederic Wm. Buerger
John Frank Trost
John Herman Hofbeck
Henry Joseph
    Schwerdtfeger
George Joseph Edwards
Joseph Marion Buerger
Frank G. M. Brunner
George Alfred Henckel
William John Mueller
Martha I. C. Leman

Ann Mary Sommer
Catherine Mary Mueller
Frances Augusta Grey
Mary Augusta Moor
Margaret C. Bullascher
Clara T. E. Bullascher
Helen Celestine Drew
Rosalie Mary Leman
Rosalie Helen Bild
Elisabeth Brigid Ricke
Anne C. H. Leinbach

Clara Mary Flaig
Agnes Louise Pflueger
Mary Terese Maurer
Margaret Mary Kelley
Emma M.A. Van den Ende
Mary Gertrude Moor
Catherine Mary Mueller
Charles John Mueller
Otto Albert Jance
Louis Niederreuther
Frank Theo. Reicherzer

God-father for boys: Michael Maurer
God-mother for girls: Mary Emes
Signed: Rev. Jac. F. Lauth C. S. C., Rector

CONFIRMATION June 1, 1884

Rt. Rev. N. A. Gallagher

John Frederic Gruenroth
William Kampe
Geo. Adelbert Alois
    Buerger
Donatus Clement Victor
    Lerous
John Joseph Schulte
Frederic William Flaig
John Peter Lenz
Joseph Anthony Sommer
Joseph Corn. Poplier
Anna Mary Maurer
Louise Barb. Wilh. Seel
Mary Ann Magd. Jung
Frances Mary Byron
Pauline Ambrosia Leroux
Catherine Cecile Keegan
Louise Josephine
    Hoffmann

Terese Carol. Elis.
    Leinbach
Mary Ann Wilson
Mary Catherine Ward
Christine Mary Marx
Rose Mary Marx
Mary Eliz. Kraus
Mary Terese Lachmund
Louise Jos. Spieker
Augusta Terese Dom
Louise Mathilda Masse
Mary Buhl
Christian Voigt
Chas. Wm. Henry
    Scheider
John Joseph Neis
Bernard Peter Gautier
Henry Ferdinand
    Stechmann

George Conrad Fluehr
Frank Joseph Ressel
Charles Joseph Buesmuel-
    ler
Joseph Triacker
Thomas John Dayle
Otto John Mangeliers
Mary Elisabeth Keegan
Hedwig Mary Henkel
Helen Margaret Engelke
Emma Clara Franke
Gertrude Bonn
Catherine Hogan
Caroline Anna Ant.
    Boesmueller
Barbara Helen Mary
    Kaiser
Mary McWaters

God-father for boys: Christian Emes
God-mother for girls: Margaret Neis
Signed: Rev. Jac. F. Lauth C. S. C., Rector

CONFIRMATION May 24, 1885

Rt. Rev. N. A. Gallagher

Victor Joseph Loth-
    ringer
Hubert Alois Butcher
William John Fluehr
Richard Joseph Elsner
Albert Michael Browns
Frederic Thomas Henckel
Aug. Rudolf Ferd.
    Stechmann
Henry Peter Mueller
August John Bauer
William Lawrence
    Heimann
Joseph Paul Day
Charles Louis Best
John Daniel Doyle

Catherine Lucie Fowler
Anne Catherine Haeknlein
Wilhelmine Elisabeth
    Pflueger
Emily Hoffmann
Mary Elisabeth Mueller
Ann Mary Barb. Duffard
Elisabeth Mary Magd.
    Schocke
Magdalen Segnanovicz
Hedwig Mary Boes-
    mueller
Elisabeth Van den
    Ende
Anne Heinze

Angeline Mary Justine
    Goyes
Rose Magdalene Fluehr
Cecile Eliz. Magd.
    Gengler
Catherine Cecile
    Triacker
Sarah Isabelle Bock
Mary Agnes Day
Mary Helen O'Keefe
Martha Agnes Henkel
Mary Terese Eve
Rosine Agnes Michels
Mary Magdalen Hartwig
Catherine Elizabeth
    Sweeney

3

Ann Mary Theilmann   Mary Caroline Seraphine   Adelaide Mary Kirker
Ann Elisabeth Kelley   Boesmueller

God-father for boys: John Ricke
God-mother for girls: Fides Gruenroth
Signed: Rev. Jac. F. Lauth C. S. C., Rector

CONFIRMATION June 13, 1886

Rt. Rev. N. A. Gallagher

John Emes	Mary Frances Maurer	Aline Mary Lauve
William Frederic Ricks	Henrietta Heimann	Wilhelmine Mary Schmidt
Ferdinand Jos. Jung	Mary Ann Arnold	Alice Koerner
Wm. Joseph Meyer	Sophie Mary Windmeyer	Anna Koerner
Miles Frank Breen	Laura Mary Bleike	Catherine Best
William Aull-Noun	Teresa Mary Schulte	Emma Augusta Heimann
Louis David Wenzel	Adine Mary Lauve	Mary Magdalen Aull
Chas. Joseph Kampe	Bernard Bohn Held	Helen Mary McCauley
Monroe Julius Heimann	Frederic Caesar Gleich	Mary Fages
Adolph John Leutsch	Ernest Raphael Schultz	Mary Trevinio
Frank Claud Smith	William Krieger	Mary Gilbert
Wm. John Ressel	George Kriger, Jr.	Mary Anne Augusta Blank
George Krieger, Sr.	Cecile Clementine	Louise Ernestine McNally
	Leroux	

God-father for boys: James Gengler
God-mother for girls: Mary Peine
Signed: Rev. Jac. F. Lauth, C. S. C., Rector

CONFIRMATION May 1, 1887

Rt. Rev. N. A. Gallagher

Octavius Balez	Herman Krieger	Elisabeth Melville
Dominic Puppo	Theodore Eggert	Helen Dwane (Divane?)
Herman Joseph Brendler	Joseph Cornelius Shannon	Mary Anne Neuhaus
Charles Hartwight	Mary Amalia Henckel	Mary Truchard
Adolf Goyes	Caroline Spieker	Charles Louis Bee
Anthony Poplier	Ann Elis. Antonovich	James Joseph Seawell
John Joseph Wendel	Ann Mary Sommer	Henry Rinker
Joseph Michael Maurer	Emma Marx	Christian Louis Beckmann
Martin Rud. Chas. Jos.	Anastasia McCauley	Michael Reeb
Hock	Ann Mary Leutsch	John Kellermeier
John Cornelius Barthel	Helen Cecile Killeen	Joseph Auxin
John Joseph Lordan	Mary Virginia	George Andrew Aull
Charles Pflueger	Seguanovicz	James Joseph McGinnis
Mich. Alex. Aug.	Mary Joan Doyle	William Megson
Duffard	Aldia Clara Douroux	Bertha Mary Yilge
Peter Jos. Wilricx	Mary Angela Boedecker	Agnes Mary Moser
Frank Theodor Buerger	Pauline Celestine Neis	Alice McManus
Sidney Eugene	Rosalie Lenz	Catherine Frances
Loustaunau	Helen Terese Schocke	McGuire
William Joseph Doyle	Mary Elis. Mueller	Rose Anne Collins
Joseph Aull	Dorothy Rose Mueller	
William Foster	Daisy Falconieri Bonn	
Chs. Philip Wolff	Elis. Anne Smith	
Chs. Wm. Dolye	Adelaide Elis. Watts	
Adolf Gustave Yilge	Terese Ramaker	
Charles Wm. Coleman	Rita Victoria Trahan	

God-father: Geo. Leinbach
God-mother: Terese Maurer
Signed: Rev. Jac. F. Lauth, C. S. C., Rector

CONFIRMATION May 20, 1888

Rt. Rev. N. A. Gallagher

Max James Hendel
John Jos. Christian
  Stumf
Ida Rosalie Menzel

William Henry Colsberg
Caroline Celestine
  Brosig
Margaret Ritzler

Ferdinand Joseph Schaer
Elis. Terese Doyle
Josephine Kraus
Anne Mary Marg. Sattler

Signed: Rev. V. Gury, Rector

CONFIRMATION June 2, 1889

Rt. Rev. N. A. Gallagher

Charles Jos. Henkel
Mary Gertrude Brosig
Rudolf Alois Bullascher
John Jos. Balderachi
Clara Veronica Cavitt
Joan Mary Mueller
Terese Helen Fleuhr
Albertine Cecile
  Stechmann
Mary Aloysia Fiake

Adolf Joseph Ressel
Frederic Joseph
  Speaker
Mary Veronica Martin
Geo. Joseph Sgitowich
Elisabeth Anne Elsler
Julia Aloysia Meurie
Terese Ignatia Sommer
Susan Agnes Seel
Mary Gertrude
  Bullasher

Augusta Cecile Brosig
Camille Mary Macera
Terese Agnes Windmeyer
Edward Aloysius Macera
Susan Mary Hahn
Agnes Mary Popular
Antonia Helen Joung
Angeline Mary Coudage
Anne Elis. Gibbs

Signed: Rev. V. Gury, Rector

CONFIRMATION May 25, 1890

Rt. Rev. N. A. Gallagher

Hedwig Beck
Charles Joseph Sommer
Joseph Philip Arnold
Joan Montfort
Ferdinand Aloysius
  Lordan
Pelego Stephen Puppo
Cora Terese Mengel
Joseph Ferdinand
  Praker

Maurice Baumann
Anne Baumann
Ambrose Montfort
Edw. Sebastian Garth
Chs. Philip Menzel
Sebastian Neiss
Elis. Mary Gautier
Peter Joseph Traverso
Fanny Mary Johnson
Odile Agnes Heimann

Joseph Ignatius Breen-
  rood
James Herman Dolan
Fr. Joseph Triaccar
Odilia Mary Keats
Caroline Joan Young
Emil Michael Dantin
Mary Elis. Lenz
Frank James Hahn
Michael John Lang

Signed: Rev. J. Grabinger, Rector

CONFIRMATION June 4, 1893

Claud Ignatius Burnett
Terese Ferd. Mary
  Eggert
Michael Aloysius Heck
Emma Aloysia Kindt
Jos. Sebastian Imhoff
Charles Michael Lenz
Clemens Paul Martin
Ann Mary Barbara
  Stechmann

Carolije Agnes Abels
James Leo Alois Dantin
Charles John Ehlert
Frederice Cecile Heck
Wm. Jos. Heimann
Alma Helen Ernestine
  Schneider
Helen Margaret Sommer

Edw. Ignatius McCarthy
Mary Magdalen Fideli
Estelle Mary Eliz. Hahn
Leo Jos. Alois Flieller
Eugenia Mary Rosalia
  Regini
Margaret Josepha Selenki
Jules Joseph Tacquard

Signed: Rev. J. B. Weimer, Rector

5

CONFIRMATION May 1894

Edmund John Greenrood
Joan Mary Bohn
George Joseph Lordan
Julia Elizabeth Gleich
Joseph Aloysius Paysse
Eliz. Margaret Moni
Henry Joseph Windmeyer
Emma Agnes Wevlla (?)

Agnes Elizabeth Beck
Edward John Leutsch
Terese Margaret Gay
Wm. Aloysius Moffith
Ann Mary Malloy
Anthony Joseph Schocke
Elenore Mary Seel

William Joseph Herr
Louise Mary Bohn
Otto Michael Menzel
Mary Catherine Lang
Leo John Schneider
Marietta Lucia Puppo
James Joseph Jent

Signed: Rev. J. B. Weimer, Rector

CONFIRMATION June 9, 1895

John Joseph Dinter
Mary Agnes Gay
Richard Aloysius Smith
Agnes Mary Mueri
Anne Agnes Stumpf
Beatrice Flora

Lucia Catherine Dantin
Wm. James Rowan
Anne Veronica McCracken
Charles Aloysius
    Zimmermann

James Aloysius McNally
Catherine Agnes Kraus
John Joseph Selenki
Louise Mary Regini
Angelica Ignatia Cordero

Signed: Rev. J. B. Weimer, Rector

CONFIRMATION May 31, 1896

John Joseph Barlemann
Rose Catherine Moni
Jerome Stephen Lordan
Leonida Catherine
    Schocke
Louise Aloysia
    Schulte ad.

Louise Mary Martini
John George Lang
Elizabeth Agnes Smith
George Joseph Wolff
Sarah Catherine Breen
Rose Agnes Ehlert
Lillian Veronica Liberto

John Joseph Gilbert
Lena Terese Schmidt
Seymour Joseph Moffith
Louise Margaret
    Stechmann
Anne Mary Selenski, ad.
Catherine Agnes Wehmeyer

Signed: Rev. J. B. Weimer, Rector

CONFIRMATION June 13, 1897

Louise Joseph Engelke
Clara Cath. Gaschen
Wm. Frank Gilbert
Mary Catherine Menzel
Charles Aloysius Stumpf
Augusta Eliz. Pavell
Angelina Genevieve
    Arnold
Anne Mary Flake

Magdalen Eliz. Fivel
Charles Aloysius Gery
Mary Helen McNally
Joseph Anthony Lenz
Margaret Mary Neis
Theobald Frand Wolff
Anne Elenore Sommer
..... Elsner
Frieda Mary Wolff

Joseph Peter Flake
Mary Terese Gleich
Martin Joseph Hock
Amelia Elenore Moni
Joseph John Windmeyer
Bernardette Angelica
    Payssee
Sophie Cecile Sommer

Signed: Rev. J. B. Weimer, Rector

CONFIRMATION April 30, 1899

John James Carroll
Susan Mary Lang
Joseph Aloysius Roch
Anne Cecile Stechmann
Barbara Agnes Beekmann
Chatherine Mary Biering
Peter Chas. Jos.
    Boergershausen
Frank Picture
Anne Mary Hausen

Fay Mary Lang
John Joseph McNally
Mary Helen Marg. Mess
Barthalomew Joseph
    Vuletich
Eve Eliz. Mary
    Boergershausen
Christian Frank Schocke
Mary Aline Granguard
Leo Bernard Hury

Herman John Dircks
Mary Terese Mees
Anthony Frank Sommer
Cecile Agnes Sommer
Louise Emma Walsh
Agnes Margaret Breen
Elizabeth Anne Breen
Vivian Mary Prendergast
Joseph Charles Ricke
Julia Leontine Moth

Signed: Rev. J. B. Weimer, Rector

6

CONFIRMATION May 6, 1900

Rt. Rev. N. A. Gallagher

Joseph Aloysius
   Barlemann
Anne Cecile Barlemann
Max Aloysius Eisenbach
Catherine Cecile Malloy
Wendolin Joseph Maurer
Josephine Cecile
   Stechmann
Martin Aloysius Ricke
Adele Catherine
   Lothringer, ad.

Frank Clement Mees, ad.
L. W. Louis Senechal
James Anthony Brammer
Mathilde Eliz. Kirchem
Herman Anton Lenz
Cecile Odile Schocke
Thomas Henry Payne
Chs. Peter Priesmuth
P. Sarah Delomel, ad.
J.P. John Caninenberg,
   ad.

Louis Joseph Beckmann
George Frank Bohn
Anne Antonia Bendixen
Adolph Joseph Hopf
Marg. Catherine Mees
Innocent John Moser
Clara Terese Weber
Laetitia Mary Boyd, ad.
F.J. James Allen, ad.
J.J. Terese Ann Stumpf,
   ad.

Signed: Rev. Geo. A. Rittmeyer, S. J.

CONFIRMATION May 18, 1902

Rt. Rev. N. A. Gallagher

Henry Anthony Eckenfels
Benno Aloysius Engelke
Bridid Ann Hoefer
James Aloysius Fuchs
Ethel Mary Gertrude
   Lordan
Herman Anthony Schocke
Alice Cecile Ressel
Laura Agnes Crittenden

Mary Josephine Fiesel
Augustine Alois Fiesel
Edw. Aloysius Franz
Mary Cathr. Lasserre
Otto Aloysius Jordan
Daniel Aloysius Lordan
Marg. Catherine Ricke
Anna Bohn (Agnes)

Wilhelmine Cecile Got-
   tlob
Jeanette Celestine Jacobs
Theodore Aloysius Gottlob
Caroline Cecil Maurer
Mary Agnes Monshausen
Michael Peter Walsh
Elizabeth Cecile Sommer

Signed: Rev. J. B. Weimer, Rector

CONFIRMATION May 31, 1903

Rt. Rev. N. A. Gallagher

Herman Lang
Helen Rose Helfenstein
Mary Elenore
   Helfenstein
Josephine Dom

Alphonse Aloysius Arnold
Charles Ressel
Aemilian Weber
Marg. Frederice Dau
Mrs. Mary Gotllob

Magdalen Josephine
   Gaschen
Cecile Helmer
Eliz. Wilhelmine Lott

Signed: Rev. J. B. Weimer, Rector

CONFIRMATION May 29, 1904

Rt. Rev. N. A. Gallagher

Albert Joseph Brammer
Sophie Cecile Heinze
Jos. Aloysius Selenski
Dora Eliz. Andrea
Edna Agnes Baehr
Teresa Mary Sommer
Ethel Marg. Flake

Mary Agnes Gottlob
Walter Aloysius
   Schoellmann
Bertha Agnes Schocke
Louise Cecile Beckmann
Emma Agnes Fiessel
Xenia Gertrude Wilke

John Joseph Caulking
Gertrude Mary Lordan
Rose Mary Ratzmann
Fides Wilhelmine
   Senechal
Frances Cath. Selenski

Signed: Rev. J. B. Weimer, Rector

7

CONFIRMATION June 3, 1906

Rt. Rev. N. A. Gallagher

Wm. Aloysius Barlemann
Mary Terese Barlemann
Ernest Aloysius Fivel
Ruth Teresa Dom
Mabel Cecile Flake
Bernard John Junker
Mary Eliz. Ricke
Clarence Anthony Maurer
Rose Eliz. Traverso
Ruth Terese Dom
Joseph Aloysius
    Schocke

Audrey Agnes Baehr
Edw. Drescher, ad.
Angeline Josephine
    Dircks
Wm. Peter Helfenstein
Edelgard Cath. Lang
Louis Aloysius Leonard
Henriette Bernadette
    Roubion
May Eliz. Wickes

Robert Joseph Bohn
Gertrude Agnes Brammer
John Paul Gottlob
Victor Bernard Heinrich
Anne Marg. Fuessel
Charles Joseph Laine
Edna Catherine Ritzler
Ernest Aloysius Ratzmann
Louis Andrew Ricke
George James Selenski

CONFIRMATION May 26, 1907

Frank Carroll
Helen Haxthausen
Kimey Nichols
Teresa Jung
Herman Weber
Mildred Delz

William Korte
George Maurer
Josephine Kampe
Dorthy Nichols
Wilhelmine Schocke
Florence Wilke

Irene Marg. Haussinger
Mathew Monshausen
    (Mathias)
Frances Louise Monshau-
    sen
Lillian Eliz. Eckenfels

Signed: Rev. J. B. Weimer, Rector

CONFIRMATION May 22, 1910

Harold Murphree
Ida Ricke
Ethel Hausinger
Myrtle Thielen

Harry Wicks
Clara Dues
Rose May Tickle
Anita Viscovich

Helen Nichols
Mary Skarke
Angelina Monshausen

Signed: Rev. Amatus J. Snebelen, S. J.

CONFIRMATION April 28, 1912

John Tickle
Wilbur Steinbrink
Willie Briggs
Joan Monshausen
Robert Finn
Georgie Wicks
Frida Duley
Clarence Weber

Cecile Gottlob
Beuhla Schembre
Florence Junker
Peter Lera
Ellerine Baehr
Henry Skarke
Joe Rohde
Helen Ritzler

Wilfred Gilbert
Josephine Briggs
John Monshausen
Anita Skarke
Joe Schembre Willie
    Kampe
Helen Burger
Louise Lassen

The following names were struck out on the list; no reason given.

Earl Thompson
Frank Roemer
A.... Surral

Frank Gilbert
Charles Gross

Lee Steinbrink
Anthony Rass

CONFIRMATION Juen 4, 1922

James Carroll
Henry Broers
Fred Kameyer
Fred Croft

Julia Schmidt
Bertha Belbaze
Nemera Pilsen
Jane Bujan (Buchan)

Catherine Kameyer
Annie Harris
Florene Schocke
Emil Puciarello

CONFIRMATION May 20, 1934

Charles Howard (Albert) Mildred Ruth (Anne)   Vincent Mazzara
  Herman   Herman   Mary Josephine Mazzara

Rev. A. M. Maechler

CONFIRMATION May 22, 1934

James Ryan (Jerome)   James Hudnall (Michael)   Joseph Aaron Broussard
Joseph Hudnall   Joseph Norris (John)   (Paul)
  (Patrick)   James Hughes (Francis)   Dallas Felix Sonnier
Eliz. Hudnall (Magdal- Anna Mae Norris (Rita)   (Peter)
  en)   Elodie Dugus (Cecile)   Ida Mae Kahla (Cecile)
Stella Roberts   Rorvena Vincent (Lucia) Leona Bautte (Cecile)
  (Theresa)   Paul Norris (Joseph)   Mary Silva (Cruasbassia)
Natalie Champagne   Eljie Broussard (Rila)   Mrs. Willie May
  (Catherine)   Hungerford (Agnes)

Signed: Rev. A. M. Maechler

CONFIRMATION June 7, 1943

Port Bolivar

Phelsie Julia Gary, born July 13, 1895, Angela
Evelyn Aleen Schexnaider (née Bouse), born August 26, 1919, bapt.
  June 5, 1943, Anna
Warren Jerome Conceaux, born July 23, 1925, bapt. Biloxi, Miss., Autonius
Arnold James Conceaux, born March 20, 1927, bapt. Biloxi, Miss., Joseph
Abdon Norris, born July 30, 1928, bapt. Cathederal, James
Darby Joseph Mouton, born August 8, 1928, bapt. September 4, 1928 Coulee
  Croche, La., Paul
Dorothy Teresa Segura, born March 6, 1929, bapt. Port Arthur, Texas, Rita
Evelyn Rita Roberts, born June 23, 1929, bapt. Cathederal, Teresa
Jane Lois Hudnall, born August 6, 1929, bapt. St. Anthony, Beaumont, Tx.
  Teresa
Janet Marie Comeaux, born March 8, 1929, bapt. Cathedral, Bernadette
Loretta Marie Lauuier, born June 22, 1930, bapt. Cathedral, Bernadette
Cecil Warren Kohla, born September 6, 1930, bapt. Cathedral, Paul
Aarace Joseph Norris, born October 20, 1930, bapt. Cathedral, Anthony
Arthurine Cecile Mouton, born November 21, 1931, bapt. Coulee Croche, La.
  January 19, 1932, Mary
Ralph Paul Segura, born September 4, 1930, bapt. Cathedral, Joseph
Patrick Huduall, born November 18, 1931, bapt. Cathedral, Joseph
Leroy Anthony Coneaux, born October 10, 1931, bapt. Bolivar, James
Shirley Marie Norris, born December 24, 1932, bapt. Bolivar, Rita
Alice Marie Gary, born July 4, 1932, bapt., Cecile
Duffy Lee Jos. Segura, born June 19, 1932, bapt. Bolivar, Paul

Most Rev. C. E. Byrne: Rev. A. M. Maechler

CONFIRMATION May 20, 1956

Sacred Heart

Comeaux, Yvonne; Name, Gertude; Sponcer, Mrs. Trollney
Delafonte, Patricia Ann A.; Name, Cecilia; Sponcer, Rudy Silva
Norris, Gloria Jean; Name, Theresa
Norris, Uyless Paul; Name, Paul
Schexnaider, Dalton John; Name; Joseph
Schexnaider, Wilton Lee Joseph; Name; John
Simpton, Rita Maric; Name, Monica

Rev. A. M. Maechler

FIRST HOLY COMMUNIONS
(1893 - 1933)

FIRST COMMUNION June 14, 1893

Claud Burnett
Caroline Abels
John Ehlert
William Heimann
Jules Taquart
Emma Kindt
Helen Sommer

Edward McCarthy
James Bantin
Michael Heck
Charles Lenz
Estelle Mary Hahn
Eugenia Mary Regini
Anne Mary Stechmann

Terese Ferdinanda Eggert
Mary Fideli
Leo Fliehler
Clement Martin
Frederice Heck
Alma Schneider

Signed: Rev. J. B. Weimer, Rector

FIRST COMMUNION May 1894

Edmund Greenrood
George Lordan
William Moffith
Anthony Schocke
Joan Bohn
Julia Gleich
Elizabeth Moni
Emma Werlla

William Herr
James Jos. Jent ad.
Joseph Paysse
Henry Windmeyer
Louise Bohn
Mary Lang
Marietta Puppo

Edward Leutsch
Otto Menzel
Leo Schneider
Agnes Beck
Terese Gay
Anne Malloy
Elenore Seel

Signed: Rev. J. B. Weimer, Rector

FIRST COMMUNION June 9, 1895

John Dinter
Angelica Cordero
Mary Gay
Agnes Meuri

James McNally
Lucia Dantin
Catherine Kraus
Louise Regini

William Rowan
Richard Smith (Schmidt)
Anne McCracken
Anna Stumpf

Signed: Rev. J. B. Weimer, Rector

FIRST COMMUNION May 31, 1896

John Gilbert
Jerome Lordan
Sarah Breen
Louise Martini
Elisabeth Smith

John Barlemann
Seymour Moffith
Rose Ehlert
Rose Moni
Leonida Schocke

John Lang
George Wolff
Lillian Liberto
Lena Schmidt
Louise Stechmann

Signed: Rev. J. B. Weimer, Rector

FIRST COMMUNION June 13, 1897

Louis Engelke
William Gilbert
Clara Gaschen
Mary Menzel
Joseph Windmeyer
Hedwig Elsner
Margaret Neis
Anna Sommer

Joseph Flake
Martin Hock
Mary Gleich
Joseph Lenz
Theobald Wolff
Magdalen Fivel
Augusta Pavell
Sophie Sommer

Charles Gery
Anna Flake
Mary McNally
Charles Stumpf
Angelina Arnold
Amelia Moni
Bernardette Paysse
Frieda Wolff

Signed: Rev. J. B. Weimer, Rector

FIRST COMMUNION June 5, 1898

Leo Hury
Joseph Ricke
Mary Anne Mees
Anne Barbara Stechmann

Paschalis Douroux
Robert K. Whitty
Mary Helen Mess

Frank Picture
Frederice Mary Heck
Cecile Emma Sommer

Signed: Rev. J. B. Weimer, Rector

13

FIRST COMMUNION April 30, 1899

John Carroll
John McNally
Bartholomew Vuletich
Agnes Breen
Anne Hansen
Susan Lang

Herman Dircks
Joseph Roch
Barbara Beckmann
Vivian Prendergast
Julia Moth

Elisabeth Breen
Anthony Sommer
Catherine Biering
Mary Granguard
Jay Lang

Signed: Rev. J. B. Weimer, Rector

FIRST COMMUNION May 6, 1900

Joseph Barlemann
Louise Beckmann
Herman Lenz
Thomas Payne
Anne Barlemann
Catherine Malloy
Clara Weber

George Bohn
Max Eisenbach
Wendelin Maurer
Martin Ricke
Anne Bendixen
Cecile Schocke

James Brammer
Adolph Hopf
Innocent Moser
Charles Priesmuth (Roch)
Mathilde Kirchem
Josephine Stechmann

Signed: Rev. Geo. A. Rittmeyer, S. J.

FIRST COMMUNION Juen 2, 1901

Theodore Gottlob
Charles Kais, ad.
Laura Crittenden
Alice Ressel

August Fiesel
Frederic Mueller
Mary Fiesel
Margaret Ricke

James Fuchs
Herman Schocke
Minna Gottlob

Signed: Rev. J. B. Weimer, Rector

FIRST COMMUNION May 18, 1902

Benno Joseph Engelke
Anne Marg. Bohn
Michael Walsh
Anne Mary Monshausen

Otto Joseph Jordan
Caroline Wilhelmine
    Maurer
Elizabeth Sommer

Henry Lawrence Eckenfels
Lily Mary Eliz. Laserre
Daniel Baptist Lordan

Signed: Rev. J. B. Weimer, Rector

FIRST COMMUNION May 31, 1903

Alphonse Alois Arnold
Charles Ressel
Marg. Fred. Dau
Mary Elenore Helfenstein
Elis. Wilhelmine Lott

Herman Lang
Aemilian Peter Weber
Josephine Dom

Magdalen Josephine
    Gaschen
Helen Rose Helfenstein
Cecile Helmer

Signed: Rev. J. B. Weimer, Rector

FIRST COMMUNION May 29, 1904

Albert Brammer
Dora Andrea
Emma Fiesel
Sophie Heinze
Bertha Schocke
Terese Sommer

John Caulking
Edna Baehr
Ethel Flake
Gertrude Lordan
Fanny Selenski
Xenia Wilke

Walter Schoellmann
Louise Beckmann
Mary Gottlob
Rose Ratzmann
Fides Senechal

Signed: Rev. J. B. Weimer, Rector

FIRST COMMUNION 1905

Louis Leonard
Edna Ritzler

Angelina Dircks

...... Ricke

Signed: Rev. J. B. Weimer, Rector

14

FIRST COMMUNION June 3, 1905

William Barlemann	Robert Bohn	Edw. Drescher, ad.
Ernest Fivel	John Gottlob	Victor Heinrich
Wm. Helfenstein	Bernard Junker	Charles Lauie
Clarence Maurer	Ernest Ratzmann	Louis Ricke
George Selensky	Joseph Schocke	Audrey Baehr
Mary Barlemann	Gertrude Brammer	Ruth Dom
Mabel Flake	Anne Fuessel	Edelgard Lang
Henrietta Rubion	Rose Traverso	Mary Wickes

Signed: Rev. J. B. Weimer, Rector

FIRST COMMUNION May 26, 1907 (?)

Frank Carroll	William Korte	Irene Marg. Hausinger
Helen Haxthausen	Geroge Maurer	Terese Jung
Mathias Monshausen	Josephine Kampe	Kinney Nichols
Herman Weber	Mildred Delz	Lillian Elis. Eckenfels
Dorothy Nichols	Wilhelmine Schocke	Frances Louise Monshau-
Florence Wilke		sen

Signed: Rev. J. B. Weimer, Rector

FIRST COMMUNION June 14, 1908

Agnes Cross	Ruth Dantin	May Belle Helfenstein
Cecile Dircks	Rosalie Lenz	Clara Schocke
Ursula Wickes	Fred Kraus	

Signed: Rev. J. B. Weimer, Rector

FIRST COMMUNION April 18, 1909

Edwin Dantin	Thomas Finn	Alfert Kampe
Carl Mueller	Frank Ratzmann	John Roubion
Arthur Schoellmann	Terese Ahrens	Ruth Dolan
Eve Dreydoppel	Leona Franz	Sophie Leonard
Eliz. Monshausen	Anna Ricke	Marcelline Scher
Rose Senechal		

Signed: Rev. Amatus J. Snebelen, S. J.

FIRST COMMUNION 1910

John Tickle	Wilfred Gilbert	Wilbur Steinbrink
Cecile Gottlob	Beulah Schembre	Josephine Briggs
Willie Briggs	John Monshausen	Peter Lera
Robert Finn	Joe Schembre	Willie Kampe
Henry Skarke	Joe Rohde	Clarence Weber
Florence Junker	Joan Monshausen	Anita Skarke
Ellerine Baehr	Georgie Wicks	Frida Duley
Helen Burger	Helen Ritzler	Louise Lassen

FIRST COMMUNION April 23, 1922

James Carroll	Henry Broers	Fred Kameyer
Fred Croft	Emil Puciarello	Julia Schmidt
Catherine Kameyer	Bertha Belbaze	Annie Harris
Nemera Pilsen	Florene Schocke	Jane Bujan (Buchan)

FIRST COMMUNION April 18, 1923

Evelyn Josephine	Henry Aymes	Martha Mitchell
Monford	Helen Leimer	

FIRST COMMUNION April 27, 1924

Marcus Pierson
Curtis Erwin
Thomas Decoito
Elisabeth Sabatiere

Joseph Decoito
Ivonetta Lelsz
Mary Isabelle Buck

Louis Geo. Hasselmeier
Mary Lassin
Wm. John Corker (Carker)

FIRST COMMUNION April 19, 1925

Bennie Bendixen Miles
Gale Hasselmeier
Mary L. K. Lassin

Gaschen Hasselmeier
Dorothy Martin
Elisabeth Sabetier

Mary Martha Marg. Devito
    (Devoti)

FIRST COMMUNION April 11, 1926

Marian Boening
Anne Kameyer

Joseph Waidhofer
Margaret Ecret

Viola Boedecker

FIRST COMMUNION April 15, 1928

Brobert Leimer

Frank Leimer

Ellis Buck

FIRST COMMUNION May 28, 1933

Vincent Mazzara
Charles Howard Heuman

Mary Josephine Mazzara
Mildred Ruth Heuman

Mary Anne Miles

FIRST COMMUNIONS June 18, 1933

Port Bolivar, Texas (Mission)

Rowena Mae Vincent
James Ryan
James Hudnall

Anna Mae Norris
Mary Louise Champagne
Eliz. Sue Hudnall

Elodie Rita Dugas
Eugene Champagne

Signed: Rev. A. M. Maechler, Rector

FIRST COMMUNION 1934

Port Boliver, Texas

Rudolph Silva
Abdow Norris
Reua Norris
Lillie Mae Segura
Juanita Silva

William McCarthy
Arnold Comeaux
Margie Ryan
Ruth McCarthy
Desomeaux Gerald

(Paul) Hardy Nagnin
Warren Comeaux
Nolia Naguin (May)
Genevieve Desomieary
Malvin Landry

Signed: Rev. A. M. Maechler

FIRST COMMUNION May 1, 1938

Port Boliver, Texas

Evelyn Roberts
Lois Jane Hudnall
Norma Sue Frugé
Jasper Bergeron

Loretta Sauiner
Dorothy Segira
Ollie Ruth Frugé
John Dugas

Janet Corneaux
Hazel Champagne
Wallace Bugeron

Signed: Rev. A. M. Maechler

PRIVATE FIRST COMMUNION April 5, 1942

Luella Johnson (H.I.) Born October 17, 1829; Orange Texas; bap.
    August 26, 1934 by Rev. A. Viehl at Church Point, La.

FIRST COMMUNION June 14, 1942

Port Bolivar

Ferryline Mary Segura, born December 21, 1934, bapt. January 13, 1935
Ralph Paul Segura, born September 4, 1930, bapt. September 27, 1930
Leroy Authony Comeaux, born October 10, 1931, bapt. November 15, 1931
Gerald Michael Naguin, born January 20, 1935, bapt. March 3, 1935
Horace Joseph Norris, born November 20, 1930, bapt. December 8, 1930
Shirley Marie Norris, born December 24, 1931, bapt. February 7, 1932
David Edward Naquim, born July 26, 1932, bapt. February 12, 1933
Edna Louise Maubaules, born..., bapt... 1929
Cecile Warren Kahla, born September 6, 1930, bapt. October 5, 1930
Dell William Guidry, born February 19, 1934, bapt. November 4, 1934
Alice Marie Garrie, born July 4, 1932, bapt. July 15, 1932 (Sour Lake)
Duffy Lee Joseph Segura, born June 19, 1932, bapt. July 10, 1932
Pat Walton Hudnall, born November 18, 1931, bapt. May 18, 1932
Mary Catherine Hudnall, born August 19, 1934, bapt. October 28, 1934
Anthony Everett Jr. "Skippy" Meyers, born November 1, 1934, bapt. Dec. 9,
   1934

Rev. A. M. Maechler

FIRST COMMUNION June 3, 1943

Joseph Darby Mouton, born August 8, 1928, bapt. September 4, 1928 at
   Coulee Crocke, La.
Arthuisue Cecile Moriton, born November 21, 1931, bapt. January 19, 1932
   at Coulee Crocke, La.

FIRST COMMUNION June 6, 1943

Mrs. Evelyn Aleen (Bouse née) Schexnaider, born August 26, 1919, bapt.
   June 5, 1943

FIRST COMMUNION 1946

Mrs. Flora Brooks (Surnin)
Mrs. Fiesel

FIRST COMMUNION 1967

Margaret Maiy Paetz, age 7, (Parents: Mr. and Mrs. Chas. J. Paetz,
   3127-0), February 12, (with permission)

FIRST COMMUNION June 25, 1939

High Island

Bergeron, Betty Ann, born December 7, 1930, bapt. December 21, 1930,
   Deaumont, Texas
Desormeaux, Gertude, born December 24, 1929, bapt. Nederland, Texas,
   March 16, 1930
La Bauve, Junior, born December 26, 1923, bapt. Galveston, Texas, June
   23, 1939
La Bauve, Wilbur, born August 30, 1929, bapt. Beaumont, Texas, September,
   1929
Loepz, Earl, born December 20, 1922, bapt. Port Arthur

Rev. A. M. Maechler

MARRIAGE RECORDS
1860 - 1890

141 ABELS, HENRY - WILSON, OLIVE; John Schulte, E. Abels, Witnesses;
    March 5, 1874, date; Rev. Ch. Ch. Greyenbuehl, Minister

305 AHREUS, JOSEPH EMANUEL - LEINBACH, MARY; August Ahreus and Augusta
    Heinze, John Leinbach and Theresa Hagemann, Parents; Augusta
    Ahreus, Witness; November 8, 1893, date; Rev. J. B. Weimer,
    Minister

42 ALBERTSON, CHARLES - CLAIR, CATHERINE (Widow); Peter Richard and
    Rev. John Bigat, Witnesses; February 2, 1866 - Disp. Mix rel.,
    Date and Remarks; Rev. J. Anstaett, Minister

103 ALFSON, CHARLES - EISEN, THERESA; H. Reinbuhr and Catherine Eisen,
    Witnesses; February 1, 1871 - Disp. Mix Rel., Date and Remarks;
    Rev. Ch. Ch. Greyenbuehl, Minister

165 ALLEN, C. J. - WEGMER, WILHELMINE; H. Trube, F. Mauser, E. Meibour,
    E. Weniburg, Witnesses; August 22, 1881 - Disp. Mix Rel., Date
    and Remarks; Rev. J. J. Leonard, Minister

    AMBRUSTER, ANTHONY - LEMMAL, HENRIETTA (n.c.); Peter _elfrich,
    Alphonse Kleiber, Witnesses; April _4, 1873, Date; Rev. Ch.
    Ch. Greyenbuehl, Minister

239 ANDERSON, JOHN - _SEPMSON, ADELEID; Ferdinand F. Heigel, Jos.
    W. Anderson, Witnesses; September 29, 1886, Date; Rev. Jac.
    F. Lauth, C. S. C., Minister

285 ANDERSON, JOSEPH WILLIAM - DAHM, SELINA ANNA; John Anderson,
    Catherine Rothmund, John Grahm, Mary Ann Schantz, Parents;
    Catherine Anderson, Mary Anna Dahm, Witnesses; September 21,
    1892, Date; Rev. J. B. Weimer, Minister

250 ANDERSON, THEOPILO - BOCK, ROSE; Two Nuns, Witnesses; April 30,
    1887, Date; Rev. Jac. F. Lauth, C. S. C., Minister

    (Anonymous), THEOPHILE - ....; J. Jacobs, M. Greyenbuehl,
    Witnesses; March 18, 1875, Date; Rev. Ch. Ch. Greyenbuehl,
    Minister

    ANTONOVICH, LAZARUS - THAVENET, MARY; Two Nuns, Witnesses; May
    19, 1884, Date; Rev. Jac. F. Lauth, C. S. C., Minister

    AULL, ANTHONY - NOUN, THERESA; David Aull and Catherine Aull,
    Witnesses; August 27, 1881 - Disp. Mix Rel., Date and Remarks;
    Rev. J. N. Leonard, Minister

    AVINEY, E. E. - HOFBECK, MARY; J. M. Lepeyre and Elizabeth
    Stechmann, Witnesses; March 1, 1881, Date; Rev. J. N. Leonard,
    Minister

58 BAKER, DANIEL M. - HARRINGTON, MARY WINIFRED (alias Murphy);
    Louis Emil Fleury and Joseph Ferra, Witnesses; January 3, 1867-
    Dispensation dispar. cultus, Date and Remarks; Rev. Jos.
    Anstaett, Minister

183 BARLEMANN, CHARLES - RICKE, THERESA; September 14, 1882, Date;
    Rev. J. N. Leonard, Minister

94 BARMANN, FREDERIC (n.c.) - MEIER, JOSEPHINE; Timothy Gulden and
    Anna Gengler, Witnesses; June 7, 1870 - Dispensation of mixed
    religion, Date and Remarks; Rev. N. Gaellweiler, Minister

260 BARRY, R. H. - WEBER, MATHILDA; Arthur Weber and Mary Arnold,
    Witnesses; July 17, 1889, Date; Rev. V. Gury, Minister

252   BATJE, OTTO (n. c.) - WOLFF, AMALIA (widow) (see Schlosser);
       Dietrich Batje and Rebecca Batje, Rudolph Schlosser, Parents;
       Latharius Becker, John Fark, Witnesses; June 12, 1887 --
       Dispensation of mised religion, Date and Remarks; Rev. V. Gury,
       Minister

253   BAUMANN, CHRISTIAN - BROKOF, AGNES; George Baumann and Joan Emes,
       Joseph Brokof and Thecla Jensky, Parents; P. William Braeutigam,
       Geo. Diehl, Rose Picture, Witnesses; July 2, 1887, Date;
       Rev. V. Gury, Minister

187   BECKMAN, LOUIS C. - STECHMANN, ANNA, ELIZABETH; Mr. and Mrs.
       Stechmann, Witnesses; October 12, 1882, Date; Rev. J. N.
       Leonard, Minister

221   BENDIXEN, GOERGE CHRISTIAN (n. c.) - HAEHNLEIN, MARY APPOLLONIA;
       Richard Uger and Mary Frances, Witnesses; October 20, 1885,
       Date; Rev. Jac. F. Lauth, C. S. C., Minister

298   BERGMANN, WILLIAM - MASONET, MARIE; John Bergmann and Mary Hoffs-
       child, John Michael Masonet and Margaret Liefrich, Parents;
       Sr. Mary and Sr. Ignatius, Witnesses; September 2, 1893, Date;
       Rev. J. B. Weimer, Minister

104   BEST, JOHN GEORGE - CLARK, ELIZABETH; P. H. Moser and M. Whitaker,
       Witnesses; February 5, 1871, Date; Rev. Ch. Ch. Greyenbuehl,
       Minister

 33   BEST, LOUIS - TSCHAEKE, ANNA; John Jos. Best and Marg. Bender
       (Hillschieden, Nassua), Frank Tschaeke and Catherine Herrmann
       (Albendorf, Silesia), Parents; Maximilian Best and Joseph
       Ricke, Witnesses; October 24, 1865, Date; Rt. Rev. C. M. Dubuis,
       Baptist Galveston, Minister

 52   BEST, WILLIAM - RITZLER, CATHERINE; Jos. Ricke, Anna Tschaeke and
       Louis Best, Witnesses; August 12, 1866, Date; Rev. Jos.
       Anstaett, Minister

127   BIERMANN, HERNY (n. c.) - HAGEMANN, CAROLINE; Henry Schneider and
       Rev. E. Fleury, Witnesses; October 15, 1872 - Dispensation of
       mixed religion, Date and Remarks; Rev. Ch. Ch. Greyenbuehl,
       Minister

193   BIERMANN, HENRY - BAKER, ELENORE NELLIE; Joseph Drndull and Mary
       Drndull, Witnesses; December 3, 1883, Date; Rev. Jac. F. Lauth,
       C. S. C., Minister

170   BIERMAN, PETER - MUELLER, CATHERINE; Joseph Peine and Mary Yardem,
       Witnesses; July 31, 1880, Date; Rev. H. Reiffert, Minister

185   BLOCKE, JACOB - MC BRIDE, HELEN; John Michels and Marie Giminski,
       Witnesses; September 28, 1882, Date; Rev. J. N. Leonard,
       Minister

 63   BOCARD, ANTHONY - GROSS, MARY A.; Anthony Oberle, John Peter
       Lasserre and Jos. Blum, Witnesses; May 21, 1867, Date; Rev.
       Jos. Anstaett, Minister

121   BOCK, PETER (n. c.) - SCHWERTFEGER, SUSAN; Peter Bock Jr. and
       Ernest Schwertfeger, Witnesses; August 17, 1872 - Dispensation
       of mixed religion, Date and Remarks; Rev. Ch. Ch. Greyenbuehl,
       Minister

277   BOCKELMAN, ADOLPH (n. c.) - BUHL, MARY; Julian Thernat and Mary
       Anna Haehnlein, Witnesses; October 21, 1891 - Dispensation of
       mixed religion, Date and Remarks; Rev. Michael Heinzelmann,
       Minister

93   BODEKER, FRANCIS - FOLDEMAYER, MARY; John Bodeker, Jos. Bodeker
      and Mary Verberne, Witnesses; May 5, 1870, Date; Rev. N.
      Gaellweiler, Minister

51   BODEN, LAMBERT - SPAITH, LEOPOLDINE (alias Reissner); Rev. Thomas
      J. Johnston, Witness; July 17, 1866, Date; Rev. Jos. Anstaett,
      Minister

336   BOENING, FRANK - HENRICK, MARY; Frank Boening and Mary Gottlob,
      Henry Kainer and Mary Kainer, Parents; Rudolph Boening and
      ...... Kainer, Witnesses; November 16, 1898, Date; Rev. J. B.
      Weimer, Minister

216   BOHN, EMIL (n. c.) - RICKE, MARY; Joseph Ricke Jr. and Caroline
      Ricke, Witnesses; April 21, 1885 - Dispensation of mixed
      religion, Date and Remarks; Rev. Jac. F. Lauth, C. S. C.,
      Minister

48   BRAEUTIGAM, PETER W. - HEINSOHN, HENRIETTA M. (n. c.); Anthony
      Braeutigam and Catherine Themann and Frederic Heinsohn and
      Augusta Oering, Parents; William Heinsohn and William Pans,
      Witnesses; December 21, 1887 -- Dispensation of mixed religion,
      Date and Remarks; Rev. V. Gury, Minister

23   BRAUN, JOHN - RIED, LOUISE; George H. McGruder and W. K. Foster,
      Witnesses; February 1, 1863, Date; Rev. Jos. Anstaett,
      Minister

128   BREEN, MARTIN - LANG, CATHERINE; J. A. Doil and Catherine Wheeling,
      Witnesses; January 21, 1873, Date; Rev. Ch. Ch. Greyenbuehl,
      Minister

304   BRENNAN, MICHAEL - GRONE, MARY (n. c.); November 6, 1893 --
      Dispensation of mixed religion, Date and Remarks; Rev. J. B.
      Weimer, Minister

325   BRINK, CORNELIUS (widower) - HEIDET, MARGARET (widow) (nee
      Werdehausen); Mrs. Werdehausen and Rev. George Apel, Witnesses;
      October 28, 1890, Date; Rev. J. B. Weimer, Minister

317A BROOKS, EDDIE - SCHOECKE, ELIZABETH; George Herrick Brooks and
      Helen Eddy, Christian Schoecke and Theresa Muehe, Parents;
      Lena Schoecke, Witness; January 16, 1895, Date; Rev. J. B.
      Weimer, Minister

278   BROWN, MICHAEL - HOLM, CAROLINA (n. c.); Martin Smith and Mary
      Smith, Witnesses; December 20, 1891 -- Dispensation of mixed
      religion, Date and Remarks; Rev. Michael Heinzelmann, Minister

15   BRUCH, OTTO - SHAW, PHILIPPINE; Theodore Quitsch, Gustave
      Prellwitz and Frank Shaw, Witnesses; May 7, 1861, Date;
      Rev. Jos. Anstaett, Minister

100   BRUNNER, CHARLES - KALLUS, AGNES; William Koch and Mary Koch,
      Witnesses; November 30, 1870 -- Dispensation of two bans,
      Date and Remarks; Rev. Ch. Ch. Greyenbuehl, Minister

82   BULLACHER, RUDOLPH (n. c.) - HERRMANN, MARY; Paul Heins and
      Lena Hagemann, Witnesses; May 29, 1869 -- Dispensation of mixed
      religion, Date and Remarks; Rev. N. Gaellweiler, Minister

68   BURNER, NEWTON B. - GORMAN, MARGARET; Louis Duerr, Salomon
      Peterson, Mary Gorman and Cath. Nass, Witnesses; November 7,
      1867, Date; Rev. Jos. Anstaett, Minister

29   BURNS, JOSEPH - MILLER, JOSEPHINE; John G. Frerich and James
      Watzlavick, Witnesses; February 7, 1865 -- Dispensation of
      three bans, Date and Remarks; Rev. Jos. Anstaett, Minister

2   CHANDLER, P. H. (n. c.) - EISEN, JOSEPHINE; Nicholas Eisen and
Catherine Weidenbach (Linz, Prussia), Parents; Ann Mary Leonard,
John Jos. Weidenbach, Anna McGreal, Pauline Hutchins and
Nicholas Eisen, Witnesses; June 7, 1860, Date; Rev. Jos.
Anstaett, Minister

150   CHEVARRI, RAMON - DELTZ, AUGUSTA (n. c.); W. Hans and Mrs. A.
Hans, Witnesses; April 28, 1875, Date; Rev. Ch. Ch. Greyenbuehl,
Minister

6   CLOSSON, JOHN - KARLINE, MARY; Clemence Baudenon, Michael C. Spann
and Frances Bleike, Witnesses; July 18, 1860, Date; Rev. Jos.
Anstaett, Minister

101   CONLEY, CORNELIUS - WHITNEY, ANNA; John Dowley and Mary Warren,
Witnesses; November 30, 1870 - Disp. three banns, Date and
Remarks; Rev. Ch. Ch. Greyenbuehl, Minister

3   COOPER, W. S. (n. c.) - SOMMERS, CATHERINE; Capt. H. D. Garretsom,
Caroline Clementine Guenard and Capt. A. Wilson, Witnesses;
June 14, 1860, Date; Rev. Jos. Anstaett, Minister

192   COUSINS, JOSEPH - BERLETH, THERESA; Thomas Cousins and Mary
Berleth, Witnesses; November 28, 1883, Date; Rev. Jac. F.
Lauth, S. C. S., Minister

86   COYLE, JAMES - LANGE, MARY (widow)(nee Werdehausen); Martin Davy
and Anna Edwards, Witnesses; February 1, 1870, Date; Rev. N.
Gaellweiler, Minister

316   CROSS, CHAS. WELSH - LENZ, ROSE; Thomas L. Cross and Ellen Walsh,
Anthony Lenz and Elizabeth Hornung, Parents; William Sheihan
and Mary Lenz, Witnesses; January 9, 1895, Date; Rev. J. B.
Weimer, Minister

49   CROSSMAN, WILLIAM J. - PESKE, MARY ANN; Edmund Logre Jr. and
Henrietta Peske, Witnesses; May 30, 1866, Date; Rev. J.
Anstaett, Minister

156A   CRY, JAMES - DENOIS, ...; August 19, 28, 1876 - Disp. of Banns,
Date and Remarks

162   CUSHMAN, W. D. - KESSAN, E. M.; Joseph Peine, Witness; June 21,
1881 - Disp. Mixed religion, Date and Remarks; Rev. J. N.
Leonard, Minister

83   DAM, CHRISTOPHER - SCHMIDT, WILHELMINA; Wilhelmin Homburg, Mary
Ehlinger and Henry Homburg, Witnesses; June 2, 1869 - Disp.
mixed religion, Date and Remarks; Rev. N. Gaellweiler, Minister

190   DANGELESEN, HENRY ANDREW - WERDEHAUSEN, HENRIETTA; James Drew and
Caroline Lang, Witnesses; May 4, 1883, Date; Rev. Jac. F.
Lauth, C. S. C., Minister

287   DARNEY, PATRICK F. - MERCER, CLARA E.; Maurice Darney and Ellen
Morrissy, Oscar H. Mercer and Ottilia Jaeka, Parents; October
12, 1892, Date; Rev. L. Ph. Keller, Minister

49   DAU, FRANK LEONARD (n. c.) - SCHMITZ, ANNA; Jurgen Dau and
Augusta Dau, Anton Schmitz and Mary Schmitz, Parents; C. B.
Anderson and George Lang, Witnesses; October 6, 1888 - Disp.
mixed religion, Date and Remarks; Rev. V. Gury, Minister

186   DAVIDSON, HENRY - SCHMERBER, ALBERTA; Mollie McMullin and John
McCluskey, Witnesses; Ocotber 7, 1882, Date; Rev. J. N.
Leonard, Minister

49   DEBNER, THEODORE - VAN DE ENDE, EMMA; William Van den Ende and
      Mary Beckmann, Parents; J. E. Taylor and John C. Nordstrom,
      Witnesses; April 25, 1885 - Disp. mixed religion, Date and
      Remarks; Rev. V. Gury, Minister

292   DELZ, JOHN JOSEPH (n. c.) - LEUTSCH, MARY; Michael Delz and
      Theresa Prockhoff, Adolph Leutsch and Emma Weidenmann, Parents;
      April 20, 1893, Date; Rev. J. B. Weimer, Minister

173   DINTER, JOHN HERMAN - HOFBECK, THERESA; John Krause and Philippine
      Deiks, Witnesses; October 22, 1881 - Disp. of bans, Date and
      Remarks; Rev. J. N. Leonard, Minister

207   DIRKS, THEODORE - FRANZ, EMMA; John Koehler and Anna Hoch, Witnes-
      ses; May 4, 1885, Date; Rev. Jac. F. Lauth, C. S. C., Minister

288   DORECK, FRANK - DUFFARD, EMMA; Laurence Doreck and Josephine
      Schneider, Alexander Duffard and Caroline Kuemely, Parents;
      Robert Miller, Michael Duffard and John Deltz, Witnesses;
      November 30, 1892, Date; Rev. J. B. Weimer, Minister

328   DORECK, LAWRENCE - LEUTSCH, EMMA (wodow) (nee Weidemann); Frank
      Hubert Doreck and Josephine Schneider, Christopher Weidemann
      and Barbara Gross, Parents; William Vanderpool and Elizabeth
      Vanderpool, Witnesses; January 20, 1897, Date; Rev. J. B.
      Weimer, Minister

67   DOYLE, THOMAS - CURTIS, HANNA; Michael E. Spann, Jos. Blum and
      H. Schaefer, Witnesses; October 27, 1867 - Disp. 3 bans, Date
      and Remarks; Rev. Jos. Anstaett, Minister

64   DUCROS, ELIAS - RENANT, MARY FRUMENTIA (widow); John Baptist Riat
      and Joan Riat (Menne), Witnesses; May 26, 1867, Date; Rev.
      Jos. Anstaett, Minister

73   DUERR, LOUIS - GORMANN, MARY; Chas. Anglehoffer, Lena Hagemann
      and Helen Jordan, Witnesses; February 4, 1868, Date; Rev. Jos.
      Anstaett, Minister

120   DUFARE, ALEXANDER - KIMLEY, CAROLINE MARIE; J. B. Madison and
      Theresa Lecrose, Witnesses; August 15, 1872 - Disp. 2 Banns,
      Date and Remarks; Rev. Ch. Ch. Greyenbuehl, Minister

28   DUMESNEY, WILLIAM ADOLPH (widower) - ARNOLD, AGATHA; ....
      (Hamburg, German), Anton Arnold and Agatha Fischer (Krueth,
      Alsace), Parents; John Smith, Xavier Bilharts and Mary Aull,
      Witnesses; July 28, 1864, Date; Rev. Jos. Anstaett, Minister

46   DUNKLACKER, WILLIAM P. - MOSER, PHILOMEN; William and Sophy
      Bleicke and E. Anstaett, Witnesses; April 23, 1866, Date;
      Rev. J. Anstaett, Minister

197   DURST, FRIDOLIN - DIRKS, JOSEPHINE; Two nuns, Witnesses; January
      26, 1884, Date; Rev. Jac. F. Lauth, C. S. C., Minister

224   DREW, JAMES J. - LANG, CAROLINE M.; Jos. Werdehausen and Mary
      Bleicke, Witnesses; November 25, 1885, Date; Rev. Jac. F.
      Lauth, C. S. C., Minister

49   ECKENFELS, HENRY - BAUHHANS, CATHERINE; Lawrence Eckenfels and
      Rose Kuhens, John Bauhhans and Elizabeth Ritzles, Parents;
      Otto H. Lott and Henry Ritzler, Witnesses; February 14, 1888,
      Date; Rev. V. Gury, Minister

297   ECKERSKORN, JOSEPH - ZUBER, EMILIA (widow) (nee Gelpke); Patrick
      Eckerskorn and Elizabeth Schaeffer, Christian Gelpke and Mary
      Franke, Parents; Mathilde Kanyser and Louis Zeller, Witnesses;
      August 9, 1893, Date; Rev. J. B. Weimer, Minister

223   EDMISTON, ROBERT (n. c.) - HINRICKS, HELEN; T. A. Burke and
      Margaret Bateman, Witnesses; November 19, 1885, Date; Rev.
      Jac. F. Lauth, C. S. C., Minister

 22   EDWARDS, HENRY - BERGMANN, ANNA; ....., Anton Bergmann and Ann
      Elsner (Bohemia), Parents; Anthony Bergmann, Herman Marvitz,
      Bertha Marvitz and Louis Genard, Witnesses; October 29, 1862,
      Date; Rev. Jos. Anstaett, Minister

126   EHBERT, CHARLES HY. ALBERT (n. c.) - WEYERS, SOPHIE; B. Wilson,
      Olive Wilson and Henry Abler, Witnesses; October 8, 1872 --
      Dispensation of mixed religion, Date and Remarks; Rev. Ch. Ch.
      Greyenbuehl, Minister

281   EHRHOLD, JOSEPH (n. c.) - JUNG, MARY; Joseph Nutt and Frank Ressel,
      Witnesses; April 28, 1892 -- Dispensation of mixed religion,
      Date and Remarks; Rev. Michael Heinzelmann, Minister

179   EISENBACH, E. - FEICHMANN, L.; Edward Eisenbach, Helen Feichmann,
      August Feichmann and Julius Feichmann, Witnesses; March 1,
      1882, Date; Rev. J. N. Leonard, Minister

191   ELBERT, BENJAMIN - SOMMERS, CAROLINE; Q. P. Kirk and Rose Elbert,
      Witnesses; August 18, 1883, Date; Rev. Jac. F. Lauth, C. S. C.,
      Minister

135   EMIS, CHRISTIAN - NORDMANN, ELIZABETH MARY (n. c.); Mrs. Elbert
      per Nicholas Elbert and B. D. Davis, Witnesses; July 10, 1873,
      Date; Rev. Ch. Ch. Greyenbuehl, Minister

240   ENGLAND, GEORGE (n. c.) - SOMMERS, JULIA; Benjamin Elbert and
      Caroline Elbert, Witnesses; October 4, 1886, Date; Rev. Jac.
      F. Lauth, C. S. C., Minister

167   EUCUDI, BASIL - RICHTER, HENRIETTA; Charles Bouryes and Albertina
      Vernert, Witnesses; September 5, 1881 -- Dispensation of mixed
      religion, Date and Remarks; Rev. J. N. Leonard, Minister

195   FAGAN, STANISLAUS - BEST, ANN MARGARET; William Lott and Sophy
      Bauhans, Witnesses; December 13, 1883, Date; Rev. Jac. F.
      Lauth, C. S. C., Minister

163   FALLON, LEORGE, F. - RUTHERFORD, DORA; Louis S. Sawson and Mary
      Fallon, Witnesses; March 18, 1879, Date; Rev. Em. Fleury,
      Minister

 76B FELINK, JOSEPH - HOSPAEKY, THERESA; Anthony Grote and Joseph Kupsa,
      Witnesses; August 25, 1868, Date; Rev. Theo. Grunkner, Minister

 70   FINK, PETER - KALLUS, AMALIA; Anthony Fink and Mary Kraemer
      (Erbach, Nassau), Philip Kallus and Joan Theimer (Frankstadt,
      Moravia) (Austria), Parents; Charles Moser, Magdalene Fink and
      Joseph Blum, Witnesses; December 2, 1867, Date; Rev. Jos.
      Anstaett, Minister

 84B FINK, PETER - KREMER, CATHERINE (n. c.); John Kremer, Margaret
      Gengler and Theresa Rehrmann, Witnesses; November 14, 1869 --
      Disp. mix religion, Date and Remarks; Rev. N. Gaellweiler,
      Minister

324   FINN, PATRICK - SCHOECKE, THERESA; Thomas Finn and Mary Kenna,
      Christian Schoecke and Theresa Muehe, Parents; James Degen
      and Mary Martin, Witnesses; July 1, 1896, Date; Rev. J. B.
      Weimer, Minister

180   FLAKE, OTTO - CHIFTON, L. E.; April 18, 1882, Date; Rev. J. N.
      Leonard, Minister

88   FLUEHR, GEORGE - SCHREIBER, ROSINA; John Joseph Kraus and Catherine
      Kraus, Witnesses; February 28, 1870 - Disp. consanguinity first
      and second grade, Date and Remarks; Rev. N. Gaellweiler,
      Minister

212   FLYNN, JOHN W. - HARRIS, CATHERINE A.; Thomas Pendergast and
      Elizabeth Harris, Witnesses; November 19, 1884, Date; Rev. Jac.
      F. Lauth, C. S. C., Minister

107   FORD, HUGO - DOYLE, ANNA; Jacob Kitty (Rickett), Anna Maggarthy
      and Ann McGorigan, Witnesses; April 5, 1871 - Disp. three banns,
      Date and Remarks; Rev. Ch. Ch. Greyenbuehl, Minister

140   FOREST, EDWIN (n. c.) - MAGKONSKY, ELIZABETH; M. Greyenbuehl and
      Sophie Magkonsky, Witnesses; February 14, 1874 - Disp. Dispar.
      Cultus, Date and Remarks; Rev. Ch. Ch. Greyenbuehl, Minister

124   FRANCISCO, EMMANUEL - DONOHOE, CATHERINE; Mrs. Schmidt and M.
      Midleton, Witnesses; September 18, 1872, Date; Rev. Ch. Ch.
      Greyenbuehl, Minister

71   FRANKLIN, JOSEPH - DIRKS, THERESA; .... Ramacker, ... Leblani
      and .... Rossignol, Witnesses; December 28, 1867 - Disp. three
      Banns, Date and Remarks; Rev. Jos. Anstaett, Minister

315   FRANZ, HERMAN - KUHN, FRANCES; William Franz and Ferdinand Leck,
      John William Kuhn and Elizabeth Richard, Parents; George
      Pendergast and Sister Veronica C. P., Witnesses; March 17,
      1895, Date; Rev. J. B. Weimer, Minister

9   FROHNE, CHARLES - DIERS, CAROLINA; Jos. Bruecher, Caroline
      Bruecher and Victor Krahn, Witnesses; October 24, 1860, Date;
      Rev. Jos. Anstaett, Minister

30   FUGGER, (THAVENET), JOSEPH, born September 29, 1842 - SOMMER, ANNA,
      born September 1, 1845; Joseph Thavenet and Julianne Thavenet
      (Lekenik, Croatia), Ferdinand Sommers and Catherine Senft
      (Budhesheim, Hessia), Parents; McCarte Steinhoff, Henry
      Steinhoff, Susan Little and Lucy Webb, Wittnesses; August 7,
      1865, Date; Rev. Jos. Anstaett, Minister

37   FUNDENBERG, STANLEY B. (n. c.) - AHERN, MARY; Rev. J. B. Ballaclas,
      Mary Ann Lewis and Mrs. Carson, Witnesses; December 19, 1865 -
      Disp. Dispar. Cultus, Date and Remarks; Rev. J. Anstaett,
      Minister

16   FUNK, JOSEPH FRANK - SEEL, SOPHIE; Frank Charles Funk and Susan
      Monger, John Seel and Catherine Wagner, Parents; Andrew Mayer,
      Elizabeth Mayer and Mary Seel, Witnesses; June 3, 1861, Date;
      Rev. Jos. Anstaett, Minister

123   GALVIN, JOHN - HAVARTY, MARY; Rev. E. Fleury and J. Jacobs,
      Witnesses; August 29, 1872, Date; Rev. Ch. Ch. Greyenbuehl,
      Minister

204   GARNIER, GEORGE (n. c.) - BROWNING, ANNA T. (nee Killeen); Two
      Nuns, Witnesses; June 4, 1884 -- Dispensation of mixed religion,
      Date and Remarks; Rev. Jac. F. Lauth, C. S. C., Minister

95   GEBNEY, JOHN - COX, CATHERINE; Mathias Ford and Anna Ford,
      Witnesses; August 2, 1870, Date; Rev. N. Gaellweiler, Minister

302   GENGLER, PETER MATTHEW - SCHULTE, THERESA; John Gengle and
      Margaret Schreiber, Henry Schulte and Clara Moeller, Parents;
      James C. Gengler and Joseph Schulte, Witnesses; September 18,
      1893, Date; Rev. J. B. Weimer, Minister

105   GERBNER, JOHN - MILLER, BARBARA; Severus Jung and Anna Miller,
        Witnesses; February 7, 1871, Date; Rev. Ch. Ch. Greyenbuehl,
        Minister

129   GERHARDT, HENRY (n. c.) - HEINE, MARY (widow); H. Biermann and
        Guido Buehl, Witnesses; January, February (?) 12, 1873 --
        Dispensation dispar. cultus, Date and Remarks; Rev. Ch. Ch.
        Greyenbuehl, Minister

257   GLASS, PAUL (n. c.) - MAYER, ELIZABETH; Louis Glass and Caroline
        Glass, Fridolin Mayer and Anna Frei, Parents; Michael Lang and
        Catherine Lang, Witnesses; March 4, 1889 -- Dispensation of
        mixed religion, Date and Remarks; Rev. V. Gury, Minister

 10   GLOECKNER, ANTHONY - ILGEN, WILHELMINE; .... (ex Neustadtel,
        Bohemia), (ex Schweighatten, Hessia), Parents; Gottlieb Ilgen
        and Stephen Lang, Witnesses; January 4, 1861, Date; Rev. Jos.
        Anstaett, Minister

156B GOEDECKE, CHARLES OSCAR EMIL - MURRAY, MRS. MARY (nee Bock);
        Charles Oscar Emil Goedecke and ..... Meyer, Peter Bock and
        Susan Gengler, Parents; Helen Sommer, Witness; December 18,
        1876, Date, Rev. Ch. Ch. Greyenbuehl per Rev. J. B. Weimer,
        Minister

318   GOMBERT, ANDREW THOMAS - BURGER, ESTELLA; M. Theodore Gombert and
        Margaret Schuell, Frederic William Burger and Gertrude Backen-
        bush, Parents; William Moffeth and James Dantin, Witnesses;
        May 3, 1895, Date; Rev. J. B. Weimer, Minister

264   GOMBERT, JOHN B. - LACHMUND, HEDWIG; Ricka Lachmund and Mr.
        Lachmund, Witnesses; February 13, 1890, Date; Rev. L. Ph.
        Keller, Minister

247   GOTTLOB, JOHN - FRIEDRICH, MARY (n. c.); Theodore Gottlob and
        Louise Friedrich, Witnesses; April 12, 1887, Date; Rev. Jac.
        F. Lauth, C. S. C., Minister

282   GREEN, SAMUEL (n. c.) - TAIT, LOUISE; William Green and Indiana
        Griffith, Charles William Tait and Louise M. Tait, Parents;
        Walter Jones and ...... Jones, Witnesses; June 23, 1892, Date;
        Rev. J. B. Weimer, Minister

175   GROSS, KILIEN - MITZ, MARY; January 14, 1882, Date; Rev. J. N.
        Leonard, Minister

 61   GRUENROOD, HENRY O ELBERT, FIDES; Henry Gruenrodd and Mary Wolken
        (Bossel, Oldenburg), Joseph Elbert and Christine Hoffmann
        (Trenfuth, Bavaria), Parents; Joseph Elbert Sr., Scholastica
        Elbert, Joseph Elbert Jr. and Rosina Lemke, Witnesses; January
        29, 1867, Date; Rev. Jos. Anstaett, Minister

145   GRUNDELL, JOSEPH - BEARMANN, MARY; A. Karper and Mrs. E. Heymann,
        Witnesses; November 7, 1874, Date; Rev. Ch. Ch. Greyenbuehl,
        Minister

 85   HAHAN, WILLIAM (n. c.) - LAUBENGEIGER, MARGARET; Edward Mecki and
        Mary Heimer, Witnesses; November 28, 1869 -- Dispensation of
        mixed religion, Date and Remarks; Rev. N. Gaellweiler,
        Minister

222   HANSEN, ALFRED (n. c.) - BAUMANN, ROSINA; Joseph J. Kraus and
        Catherine Kraus, Witnesses; November 5, 1885, Date; Rev. Jac.
        F. Lauth, C. S. C., Minister

241   HARRIS, DANIEL J. - BOOTH, SARA RENET; Henry F. Harris and Sara
       Harris, Witnesses; December 6, 1886, Date; Rev. Jac. F.
       Lauth, C. S. C., Minister

 50   HARTMAN, ANDREW - BLEICKE, FRANCES (nee Bergenbusch); ...... (ex
       Meyhof, Bavaria), (ex Erwitte, Westphalia), Parents; Fred
       Bleicke and Elizabeth Nuese, Witnesses; July 12, 1866, Date;
       Rev. Jos. Anstaett, Minister

 98   HARTWIGT, CHARLES - FROBOSEN, LEOPOLDINE; John Ricke and Theresa
       Schoecke, Witnesses; August 28, 1870, Date; Rev. N. Gaellweiler,
       Minister

177   HEER, WILLIAM - VERBERNE, EMMA; B. H. Elbert and Joan Verberne,
       Witnesses; February 15, 1882, Date; Rev. J. N. Leonard,
       Minister

131   HEIDET, FRANK JOHN - WERDEHAUSEN, MARGARET; E. Jordan and R.
       Forest, Witnesses; March 21, 1873, Date; Rev. Ch. Ch. Greyen-
       buehl, Minister

205   HEIMANN, HENRY - HUGHES, ELIZABETH; Henry Heimann Sr. and Mary
       Heimann, Witnesses; July 2, 1884, Date; Rev. Jac. F. Lauth,
       C. S. C., Minister

235   HEIMANN, WALTER - MC CORMICK, DATHULA; Henry Heimann and Mary
       Heimann, Witnesses; May 7, 1886 (at Smith's Point), Date and
       Remarks; Rev. Jac. F. Lauth, C. S. C., Minister

234   HEIMANN, WILLIAM - MC CORMICK, HENRIETTA; Henry Heimann and Mary
       Heimann, Witnesses; May 6, 1886 (at Smith's Point), Date and
       Remarks; Rev. Jac. F. Lauth, C. S. C., Minister

  5   HEINE, WILLIAM - COERS, MARY; John Henry Coers and .... Hagemann,
       Parents; Frederic Wagner, Adelle Richers, Adam Link and Augusta
       Boyken, Witnesses; June 28, 1860, Date; Rev. Jos. Anstaett,
       Minister

 49   HELFENSTEIN, JOHN - SCHREIBER, ELISA; Louis Helfenstein and Helen
       O'Brien, Herman Schreiber and Rosina Fleuhr, Parents; Emile
       Weber and Mary Schreiber, Witnesses; February 14, 1888, Date;
       Rev. V. Gury, Minister

258   HELFERICH, PHILIP (widower) - HOCK, MARGARET; John Helferich and
       Susan Schvirnn, George Hock and Margaret Meithof, Parents;
       Martin Ricke and Maggie Delahunty, Witnesses; May 6, 1889
       (at Spring Creek), Date and Remarks; Rev. V. Gury, Minister

 75   HERBERT, JOHN J. - PHILLIPS, THERESA; John Sawyer, Henry Gorsen,
       Anna Philips and Daniel Phillips, Witnesses; March 4, 1868,
       Date; Rev. Jos. Anstaett, Minister

146   HERMANN, DAVID - BLOODGOOD, LAURA (n. c.); .... 1875 -- Dispensa-
       tion of mixed religion, Date and Remarks; Rev. Ch. Ch.
       Greyenbuehl, Minister

114   HERMANN, MATHIAS - EGGERT, AUGUSTA (n. c.); David Hermann and
       Julius Schaeffer, Witnesses; March 26, 1872 -- Dispensation of
       mixed religion, Date and Remarks; Rev. Ch. Ch. Greyenbuehl,
       Minister

  1   HERZOG, DAVID - BRANDES, BERNARDINE; Joseph Herzog and Anna Ebner
       (Thiengen, Baden), ... (Brunswick), Parents; John Henry
       Coers, Henry Steinbrink, Mary Coers and Augusta Carsch,
       Witnesses; June 6, 1860, Date; Rev. Jos. Anstaett, Minister

112   HEYMAN, ANTHONY - BIEHLER, AUGUSTA (n. c.); M. Biehler and Mrs.
      Lassen, Witnesses; December 21, 1871 -- Dispensation of mixed
      religion, Date and Remarks; Rev. Ch. Ch. Greyenbuehl, Minister

261   HEYMAN, JOHN ALBERT - CLLER, MARY; Anthony Heyman and Minnie
      Koerner, Joseph Cleer and Catherine Frey, Parents; J. T.
      Heymann and William Ebourg, Witnesses; September 5, 1889,
      Date; Rev. V. Gury, Minister

194   HILL, JACOB - STEINHART, ANNA; Herman Kraus and Linus Schueler,
      Witnesses; December 4, 1883, Date; Rev. Jac. F. Lauth, C. S. C.,
      Minister

 80   HILL, MELVIN - WETTENHAUSEN, CARRIE; Henry Loenring and Charles
      Brink, Witnesses; January 2, 1869, Date; Rev. Theo. Grundner,
      Minister

117   HOERNER, CHARLES - MUELLER, ANNA; Theodore Koch and Martha Haller,
      Witnesses; June 2, 1872, Date; Rev. Ch. Ch. Greyenbuehl,
      Minister

  4   HOFBECK, JOHN - TROST, CAROLINE; Michael Hofbeck and Theresa
      Freisternen (Ruedershofen, Bavaria), Louis Trost and Anne Mary
      Rothemeyer (Rooesebeck, Westphalia), Parents; Herman Trost,
      Theresa Hofbeck, Anton Rehrmann and Mrs. Schober, Witnesses;
      June 16, 1860, Date; Rev. Jos. Anstaett, Minister

330   HOGAN, THOMAS - ROSKOPF, ROSE MARGARET; Patrick Hogan and Margaret
      Corbet, Joseph Roskopf and Margaret Batzler, Parents; Rev.
      George Apel and Veronica Apel, Witnesses; June 28, 1897, Date;
      Rev. J. B. Weimer, Minister

102   HOMRIGHANS, CHRISTIAN - KELLEY, CATHERINE; Rev. Tairier, John
      Krone and Theresa Rehrman, Witnesses; December 11, 1870, Date;
      Rev. Ch. Ch. Greyenbuehl, Minister

 12 HOWARD, HARRISON BENJAMIN - RISTOE, FLORENCE (n. c.); Joseph
      Laverdy, Caroline Bockling and J. B. Anstaett, Witnesses;
      February 23, 1861 -- Dispensation dispar. cultus, Date and
      Remarks; Fev. Jos. Anstaett, Minister

342   HOWLETT, ROBERT H. - RICKE, ELIZABETH; Robert Howle-t and Mary
      Doyle, John Ricke and Mary Muehe, Parents; Frederic Pierce,
      Joseph Ricke, Mary Martin and Theresa Barlemann, Witnesses;
      November 29, 1899, Date; Rev. George A. Rittmeyer, S. J.,
      Minister

308   HOYLE, GEORGE EDWARD - QUESTED, SARAH; Richard E. Hoyle and Sarah
      Doulding, William George Quested and Helen (Ellen) Richardson,
      Parents; Vincent Bryan O'Rourke and Clara Hoyle, Witnesses;
      January 24, 1894 -- Dispensation of mixed religion, Date and
      Remarks; Rev. J. B. Weimer, Minister

340   HUEBNER, RUDOLPH MICHAEL (n. c.) - SCHNEIDER, ANTONIA MARGARET;
      Theodore Huebner and Augusta Heinze, Joseph Schneider and Hedwig
      Buchmann, Parents; A. Mohr and Dr. A. Sund, Witnesses; April
      13, 1899, Date; Rev. J. B. Weimer, Minister

154   HUGHES, HENRY SAMUEL - HEIMANN, ERNESTINE; Mr. and Mrs. Poplar,
      Witnesses; July 3, 1876, Date; Rev. Ch. Ch. Greyenbuehl,
      Minister

275   JACKSON, JOHN - BURNS, ALICE; October 15, 1891, Date; Rev.
      Mich. Heinzelman, Minister

116   JACOBS, JACOB - HEIMANN, AMALIA; A. Heimann, F. Samed, Theresa
      Hoermann and Anna Gengler, Witnesses; June 1, 1872, Date;
      Rev. Ch. Ch. Greyenbuehl, Minister

168   JAGER, WALTER H. - SCHWARZBACH, ELIZABETH; Cato Schwarzback,
      George Koehler, Charles Schaeffer, Mary Elizabeth Jaeger,
      Helen Schwarzbach and Martha Hak, Witnesses; October 4, 1881,
      Date; Rev. J. N. Leonard, Minister

326   JOHNSTON, JAMES FRANK - PICTURE, ROSALIA HELEN; William Henry
      Johnston and Margaret Anna Hoffmann, William Henry Picture and
      Mathilda Louise Vieweger, Parents; William James Steinbrink
      and Leahr Schmalm, Witnesses; November 22, 1896, Date; Rev.
      J. B. Weimer, Minister

202   JORDAN, CHRISTIAN - KRAMER, MARY; Two Nuns, Witnesses; May 25,
      1884, Date; Rev. Jac. F. Lauth, C. S. C., Minister

317A KAMPE, WILLIAM - FOWLER, CATHERINE J.; Charles Kampe and Mathilda
      Franke, James Fowler and Mary Heimann, Parents; Frank Roessel
      and Charles Kampe, Witnesses; April 24, 1895, Date; Rev. J. B.
      Weimer, Minister

11   KANDER, FRANK NICHOLAS - HARRIS, ANNA ELIZABETH (widow); John
      Anthony Scherffins, Theodore Dryaker and Mrs. E. A. Speers,
      Witnesses; February 2, 1861, Date; Rev. Jas. Anstaett, Minister

74   KASSMEIER, GEORGE - PAUL, CHRISTINA; Jos. Blum, Peter C. Spann,
      Anthony Aull, Witnesses; Rebruary 25, 1868, Date; Rev. Jos.
      Anstaett, Minister

59   KEHNE, CHARLES (September 1, 1837) - BYRNE, JOAN (July 25, 1847);
      Fred. Kehne and Cressy Hornung (Baltimore, Maryland), John
      Byrne and Margaret Donevan, Parents and Origin; Frederic Mille
      and Jos. Ferra, Witnesses; January 4, 1867, Date; Rev. Jos.
      Anstaett, Minister

8   KEISS, JOHN - SCHLEHUBER, FRANCES; John Keiss and Veronica Hutte
      (Dantzig, Prussia), ... and Dorothy Schlehuber (Furth,
      Bavaria), Parents and Origin; Herman Schneider, Wilhelmina
      Schneider and Wilhelmina Kerner, Witnesses; October 4, 1860,
      Date; Rev. Jos. Anstaett, Minister

92   KELLEGHEN, PHILIP - HENDREN, ANN; William Sullivan and Anna
      Flanigan, Witnesses; April 29, 1870, Date; Rev. N. Gaellweiler,
      Minister

213   KELLEY, JOHN I. - SCHULTZ, ANN ELIZABETH (nee Schuchardt); Two
      Nuns, Witnesses; February 27, 1885, Date; Rev. Jac. F. Lauth,
      C. S. C., Minister

198   KESSLER, JOHN JOSEPH - BONIFACE, CATHERINE; Herman Schocke and
      Mary Schocke, Witnesses; February 15, 1884, Date; Rev. Jac. F.
      Lauth, C. S. C., Minister

323   KETTLER, RUDOLPH - SOMMER, THERESA; Frederic Kettler and Mary
      Schwendinger, Ferdinand Sommer and Anna Glasser, Parents;
      Charles Sommer and Anthony Brock, Witnesses; April 29, 1896,
      Date; Rev. J. B. Weimer, Minister

229   KILLIAN, MICHAEL N. - EYTH, EUGENIA STANLEY (n.c.); James Cassidy
      and Mrs. Eyth, Witnesses; Jamuary 6, 1886, Date; Rev. Jac. F.
      Lauth, C. S. C., Minister

14   KIMLEY, AUGUST - GLOECKNER, MARY; Ambrose Martin and John Capde
      Ville, Witnesses; March 21, 1861, Date; Rev. Jos. Anstaett,
      Minister

31

225 KIRSCHNER, GEORGE (n. c.) - EICHLER, ALICE; William Eichler and
     Mary Kirschner, Witnesses; December 2, 1885, Date; Rev. Jac.
     F. Lauth, C. S. C., Minister

  7 KLENK, FREDERIC MICHAEL - ARNOLD, PAULINE; John Rheinleender and
     Ann Jackson, Witnesses; July 25, 1860, Date; Rev. Jos.
     Anstaett, Minister

199 KOCH, HENRY - SULLIVAN, HELEN; Theresa Verberne and Mary Burke,
     Witnesses; March 7, 1884, Date; Rev. Jac. F. Lauth, C. S. C.,
     Minister

200 KOCH, LOUIS DAVID - LINNETT, ANNA; Therese Verbarne and two nuns,
     Witnesses; April 5, 1884, Date; Rev. Jac. F. Lauth, C. S. C.,
     Minister

 25 KOESTER, JOSEPH - DIRKS, WILHELMINA; John Koester and Mary Rose
     Meumann (Roerde, Westphalia), Frank Dirks and Catherine
     Franken (Galveston), Parents and Origin; Frank Dirks and
     William Muehe, Witnesses; April 21, 1864, Date; Rev. Jos.
     Anstaett, Minister

332 KRATZER, ANTHONY - STETTING, ELIZABETH MARGARET (widow) (n. c.)
     (nee Starke); David Kratzer and Amalia Behringer, Charles
     Henry Stetting and Frederica Kahlenberg, Parents; ...... Wilryks
     and Catherine Kraus, Witnesses; November 16, 1897, Date;
     Rev. J. B. Weimer, Minister

189 KRAUS, JOHN - HEIMANN, LILLIE; Michael Maurer and Sophie Bauhans,
     Witnesses; April 14, 1883, Date; Rev. Jac. F. Lauth, C. S. C.,
     Minister

208 KRAUS, JOHN FREDERIC - CASEY, AMALIA ELENORE; Herman Kraus and
     Catherine Kraus, Witnesses; August 27, 1884, Date; Rev. Jac.
     F. Lauth, C. S. C., Minister

 87 KRAUS, JOHN JOSEPH - KRAUS, MRS. CATHERINE; George Fluehr and
     Rosina Schreiber, Witnesses; February 28, 1870 -- Disp.
     affinity first and second grade, Date and Remarks; Rev. N.
     Gaellweiler, Minister

 90 KRAUS, F. JOSEPH - BUSCH, ELIZABETH; Frank Busch, J. Jacobs and
     Mary Kleinmann, Witnesses; April 19, 1870, Date; Rev. N.
     Gaellweiler, Minister

174 KREPE, ARNOLD - BUNZEL, THERESA; Theodore Eggert and Rosale Bunzel,
     Witnesses; November 24, 1881, Date; Rev. J. N. Leonard,
     Minister

220 KRIEGER, GEORGE - HENDERSON, MARGARET (nee Dooley); Parker Annon
     and Mary Foster, Witnesses; October 1, 1885, Date; Rev. Jac.
     F. Lauth, C. S. C., Minister

 55 KRONE, WILLIAM - SCHWAB, MARY; Rev. Anthony M. Micouleau, Thomas
     Kromer, Anna Schwab and James McDonald, Witnesses; November 8,
     1866, Date; Rev. Jos. Anstaett, Minister

284 KUEMMELE, MICHAEL - FALCO, PHILOMINA; Michael Kuemmele and Anna
     Barbara Froeber, Joseph Falco and Philomine Pechler, Parents;
     Felix Dever and Josephine Artisan, Witnesses; September 3, 1892,
     Date; Rev. J. B. Weimer, Minister

211 LAHRSEN, HENRY (n. c.) - KOENIG, JOAN; Alexander Thomfohrden and
     Catherine Thomfohrden, Witnesses; November 8, 1884 -- Dispen-
     sation of mixed religion, Date and Remarks; Rev. Jac. F. Lauth,
     C. S. C., Minister

286 LAINE, ALBERT - HAENLEIN, ANNA; Ossemy Laine and Eulie Pluff,
     Henry Haenlein and Lena Hildebrandt, Parents; October 12, 1892,
     Date; Rev. Ph. Keller, Minister

231 LAMATHE, ALTO - AUGUSTIN, THERESA; Henry Mathews and Anna Clinton,
     Witnesses; May 2, 1886, Date; Rev. Jac. F. Lauth, C. S. C.,
     Minister

 91 LAMERS, FRANK - BERKENBUSCH, ADOLPHINE; A. Stein, Arthur Dege
     and Mr. and Mrs. Nuesse, Witnesses; April 19, 1870, Date;
     Rev. N. Gaellweiler, Minister

322 LANG, HERMAN VICTOR (widower) - FREY, MARTHA; Michael Lang and
     Susan Hermann, Anthony Frey and Martha Braden, Parents; Michael
     Reeb and Catherine Eckstrom, Witnesses; April 26, 1896 --
     (civil marriage before), Date and Remarks; Rev. J. B. Weimer,
     Minister

338 LANG, MICHAEL - BROUSSARD, NELLIE LILLIAN; Michael Lang and ....,
     Parents; Martha Lang and Lucie Carragin, Witnesses; March 18,
     1899, Date; Rev. J. B. Weimer, Minister

 35 LANG, PETER A. - FINCH, EMMA J.; Joachin ....., Witness; November
     29, 1865, Date; Rev. Jos. Anstaett, Minister

 21 LANGE, STEPHEN (30 years) - STEHLIN, HELEN (29 years); Frank Lange
     and Apollina Walter (ex Bernsdofr, Bohemia), Sebastian Stehlin
     and Mary Anne Metzger (Niederhausen, Baden), Parents and Origin;
     Ferdinand Marchand, Margaret McKimley and J. B. Capde Ville,
     Witnesses; May 6, 1862, Date; Rev. Jos. Anstaett, Minister

 48 LANGE, STEPHEN - WERDEHAUSEN, MARY; Frank Lange and Apollonia
     Walter (Berensdorp, Austria), Philip Werdehausen and
     Bernardine Neumann (Oberhausen, Prussia), Parents and Origin;
     Adam Nahm, Caroline Werdehausen and Caroline Hagermann,
     Witnesses; May 24, 1866, Date; Rev. Jos. Anstaett, Minister

157 LASSERRE, LOUIS - BASTIT, JOAN; December 22, 1877, Date; Rev. M.
     Weinzaepflen, Minister

143 LEATHEREN, LOUIS - MOORE, ELIZABETH (widow); Joseph Ricke and
     Caroline Ricke, Witnesses; September 28, 1874 -- Dispensation
     of mixed religion, Date and Remarks; Rev. Ch. Ch. Greyenbuehl,
     Minister

 20 LEANTAND, ANTHONY - SHAUGHNESSY, CATH. FITZERGALD (widow); .....
     (ex Marseilles, France), ... (ex Cork, Ireland), Parent's
     Origin; George Fluegel and J. B. Cap de Ville, Witnesses;
     March 12, 1862, Date; Rev. Jos. Anstaett, Minister

148 LEGATOS, CHARLES - WERNERT, VIRIGINIA; W. Young and S. Wernert,
     Witnesses; April 2, 1875 -- Dispensation of ......, Date and
     Remarks; Rev. Ch. Ch. Greyenbuehl, Minister

 96 LEONARD, HENRY (n. c.) - MARY, MARIA; T. H. Ramacker and Cornelius
     Conley, Witnesses; August 7, 1870 -- Dispensation of mixed
     religion, Date and Remarks; Rev. N. Gaellweiler, Minister

 89 LEUTSCH, ADOLPH - WEIDEMAN, EMMA; Charles Johnson and
     Clementine Tribout, Witnesses; March 9, 1870, Date; Rev.
     N. Gaellweiler, Minister

227 LEWIS, JAMES (n. c.) - REAGAN, CATHERINE; John Reagan and Lottie
     Jones, Witnesses; December 12, 1885, Date; Rev. Jac. F. Lauth,
     C. S. C., Minister

106   LIEBREICH, ALBERT (n. c.) - BERGMANN, ANNA (widow); Anthony
       Heimann and Odelia Heimann, Witnesses; March 9, 1871 --
       Dispensation of mixed religion, Date and Remarks; Rev. Ch. Ch.
       Greyenbuehl, Minister

113   LOESCHLER, CHARLES - BLONDEAU, MARY PHILOMENE; Eugene Blondeau
       and Emily Blondeau, Witnesses; February 28, 1872 -- Dispensation
       of three bans, Date and Remarks; Rev. Ch. Ch. Greyenbuehl,
       Minister

138   LONG, JOHN GEORGE - PLATTOW, CATHERINE; M. Greyenbuehl and Ch.
       Roehrmann, Witnesses; December 24, 1873, Date; Rev. Ch. Ch.
       Greyenbuehl, Minister

243   LOTT, FREDERIC W. (n. c.) - BAUHANS, SOPHIE; Henry Eckenfels and
       Elixabeth Bauhans, Witnesses; January 12, 1887, Date; Rev.
       Jac. F. Lauth, C. S. C., Minister

 38   LYONS, THOMAS J. - O'CONNELL, JEAN; George Reeves and Brigid
       Reeves, Witnesses; January 14, 1866 -- Dispensation of three
       bans, Date and Remarks; Rt. Rev. C. M. Dubuis, Bp. Galveston,
       Minister

335   MACERA, JULIUS - FLAKE, MARY; James Macera and Julia Caddoue,
       Otto Flake and Laura Hofmann, Parents; October 12, 1898, Date;
       Rev. J. B. Weimer, Minister

149   MAGADIEN, PAUL - KUNTZ, CATHERINE; Magdalene Greyenbuehl and
       ..... Dufoure, Witnesses; December 31, 1875, Date; Rev. Ch.
       Ch. Greyenbuehl, Minister

296   MAGNA, MICHAEL - ROSELLI, LUCIE; Joseph Magna and Crocifisca
       Annello, Dominic Roselli and Angelica Hil, Parents; Joseph
       Darras and Joan Magna, Witnesses; July 6, 1893, Date; Rev.
       J. B. Weimer, Minister

265   MAGUIRE, GEORGE M. - MARX, CUNIGUNDE; Miss Emma Marx and Sam
       Carter, Witnesses; April 23, 1890, Date; Rev. L. Ph. Keller,
       Minister

 48   MANGLIER, OTTO - KRESTA, ROSE; Henry Manglier and Theresa Tengler,
       Anton Kresta and Anna Friedel, Parents; John Emis and Charles
       Hock, Witnesses; January 8, 1888, Date; Rev. V. Gury, Minister

182   MAURER, JAMES - BENDER, MINA; Michael Maurer and Paula Moser,
       Witnesses; September 14, 1882, Date; Rev. J. N. Leonard,
       Minister

228   MAURER, MICHAEL - TISCHENDORF, MARY FRANCES; John Maurer and Ida
       Tischandorf, Witnesses; December 30, 1885, Date; Rev. Jac. F.
       Lauth, C. S. C., Minister

 17   MAYER, JOHN BAPTIST - LUEDIGE, HENRIETTA; Xavier Mayer and Mary
       Ann Mayer (Freiburg, Baden), Christian Luedige and Frederica
       Moritz (Anhalt, Dessau), Parents and Origin; Andrew Mayer and
       J. B. Anstaett, Witnesses; January 9, 1862, Date; Rev. Jos.
       Anstaett, Minister

230   MC CARRON, HENRY - CLUEN, ALICE EDWARDS; Gilbert McCarron and
       Belle Melville, Witnesses; February 17, 1886, Date; Rev. Jac.
       F. Lauth, C. S. C., Minister

MC DONALD, JAMES - NEITSCH, AMALIA; Henry Neitsch and Elizabeth C.
       Taylor, Witnesses; December 15, 1873 -- Disp. 2 bans, Date and
       Remarks; Rev. L. Glynn, Minister

218   MC MANUS, THOMAS - BRANDT, ALICE (nee Rittmus); J. P. Jenkens,
       Mary Buhl and two Nuns, Witnesses; Rev. Jac. F. Lauth, C. S.
       C., Minister

238   MC NALLY, JAMES - WECKERT, LOUISE ERNESTINE; Two Nuns, Witnesses;
       September 16, 1885, Date; Rev. Jac. F. Lauth, C. S. C.,
       Minister

153A   MENZEL, CHARLES (n. c.) - HORNUNG, ANNA MARY; Frederic Wolff and
       Rosa Wolff, Witnesses; March 23, 1876 -- Disp. dispar. Cultus,
       Date and Remarks; Rev. Ch. Ch. Greyenbuehl, Minister

262B   MILLIANI, JOSEPH J. - MC NAB, JOAN FRANCES; Frank J. Milliani and
       Emily Williams, Witnesses; October 24, 1889 -- Disp. two banns,
       Date and Remarks; Rev. V. Gury, Minister

48   MILLINIANEY (Mellen), GOERGE J. - REINEKE, MINN; Frank Millen,
       Frank Tiernan, Catherine Fundling and Perle Compton, Witnesses;
       November 22, 1887 -- Disp. Dispar. Cultus, Date and Remarks;
       Rev. V. Gury by Rev. J. Blum, Minister

242   MITCHELL, JOHN E. (n. c.) - HARRIS, ELIZABETH M.; George Riesel
       and Sara Harris, Witnesses; January 5, 1887, Date; Rev. Jac.
       F. Lauth, C. S. C., Minister

49   MITCHELL, PHILIP - STEINBACH, GERTRUDE; Sr. Mary and Sr. ....,
       Witnesses; September 8, 1888 - Marriage Revalidated, Date and
       Remarks; Rev. V. Gury, Minister

134   MONDRIK, JOSEPH - KUHLHANECH, CECIL; Ed. Gnesik and Jos. Gulhanik,
       Witnesses; February 19, 1873, Date; Rev. Ch. Ch. Greyenbuehl,
       Minister

31   MORIARTY, EUGENE - HASSET, JOAN; Thomas Bricks and Honoria Scott,
       Witnesses; October 12, 1865, Date; Rev. Jos. Anstaett, Minister

226   MOSER, JOHN H. - NIEDENFUEHR, AGNES; J. Hourigan and Anna Moser,
       Witnesses; December 12, 1885, Date; Rev. Jac. F. Lauth, C. S.
       C., Minister

245   MOTH, JAMES SAMUEL - DANTIN, LEONTINE; Geo. Golden and Julia
       Dantin, Witnesses; February 5, 1887, Date; Rev. Jac. F. Lauth,
       C. S. C., Minister

18   MUELLER, JOHN PETER - RADEMACHER, CAROLINE; Herman Mueller and
       Christine Vollmer (Halberbracht, Prussia), Frank Geo.
       Rademacher and Ann Mary Rose (Roesebeck, Westphalia), Parents
       and Origin; Mathias Weber and Joseph Paine, Witnesses;
       February 8, 1862, Date; Rev. Jos. Anstaett, Minister

77   MUELLER, PETER - LAND, MAGDALENE; September 26, 1868, Date;
       Rev. Theo. Grundner, Minister

334   MULLEN, JOHN - BUERGER, MATHILDA; Paul Fitton Mullen and Ellen
       Morat, William Buerger and Gertrude Berkenbusch, Parents;
       Claude Mullen and Mary Nolan, Witnesses; February 2, 1898,
       Date; Fev. Geo. Apel per Rev. J. B. Weimer, Minister

246   MULROY, JAMES P. - JOHNSON, JOSEPHINE; W. H. Finclair and
       Lorraine Finclair, Witnesses; February 20, 1887, Date; Rev.
       Jac. F. Lauth, C. S. C., Minister

171   NAGNOBER, CHARLES - OPPERMANN, AMANDA; H. E. Wolcott, Jos.
       Oppermann, Laura Oppermann and Emily Oppermann, Witnesses;
       October 12, 1881 -- Disp. mixed rel., Date and Remarks;
       Rev. J. N. Leonard, Minister

45   NAHM, ADAM - STEHLING, ANNA; L. C. M. Chambodut and Paul Kraus,
     Witnesses; Rt. Rev. C. M. Dubuis, Ep. Galveston, Minister;
     March 2, 1866, Date

311 NELSON, ARNOLD - PRADIER, AUGUSTA; John Nelson and Mina Anderson,
     August Pradier and Armance Enoch, Parents; Albert N. Brauns
     and Theresa Margaret ...., Witnesses; Rev. J. B. Weimer,
     Minister

248 NEUHANS, JOSEPH - KUHN, MARY ANN; Two Nuns (Sr. Mary and Sr. M.
     Peloyia), Witnesses; April 23, 1887, Date; Rev. Jac. F. Lauth,
     C. S. C., Minister

237 NIEDERGANG, ANTON - FRICKER, CATHERINE; Two Nuns, Witnesses;
     July 11, 1886, Date; Rev. Jac. F. Lauth, C. S. C., Minister

56   OBERLE, ANTHONY - FISCHEL, THERESA; ..... (ex Dahl, Alsace),
     ..... (ex Bohemia), Origin of Parents; Nicholas Gaellweiler,
     Frances Hartmann and ...... Nuese, Witnesses; December 14, 1866;
     Rev. Jos. Anstaett, Minister

333 OLLIS, WILLIAM FREDERIC (n. c.) - MAURER, MINNA (widow) (nee
     Bender); James Ballis and Sara Colleger, Peter Bender and
     Elizabeth Kettner, Parents; John Theobald and Minna Theobald,
     Witnesses; November 21, 1897, Date; Rev. J. B. Weimer, Minister

259 ORY, S. JOHNSON LOUIS - MARX, ROSE MARY; Ledger Ory and Celina
     Merique, Anthony Marx and Emma Faber, Parents; George McGuire
     and Kerney Marx, Witnesses; June 4, 1889, Date; Rev. V. Gury,
     Minister

293 OSER, GEORGE WILLIAM - ARNOLD, MARY ANN; William Oser and Anna
     Hoffmann, Isidor Arnold and Mary Ann Hug, Parents; Joseph
     Arnold and August Schultz, Witnesses; June 7, 1893 -- Two bans
     omitted, Date and Remarks; Rev. J. B. Weimer, Minister

48   PETTERSON, ANDREW (n. c.) - BITTEL, ANNA C.; Erasonic Petterson
     and Singar Jenson, Frank Jos. Bittel and Mary Harting, Parents;
     Stephan Bittel and John Nelson, Witnesses; December 14, 1887--
     Dispensation of mixed religion, Date and Remarks; Rev. V. Gury,
     Minister

254 PLITT, EDWARD - WEINRECHT, CAROLINE (CORA) A.; George Plitt and
     Margaret Sommer, Frederic P. Weinrecht and Ellen McCarthy,
     Parents; Henry Hubele and Walter Reiffel, Witnesses; October
     17, 1887, Date; Rev. V. Gury, Minister

62   POPULIER, ANTHONY (May 14, 1845) - HEIMANN, MARY JOAN; Rudolph
     Populier and Wilhemina Vaneker (ex Offenhausen, Prussia), Henry
     Heimann and Mary Walters (ex Anahuac, Texas), Parents and
     Origin; Anthony Heimann Jr., Charles Bodeker, Mary Heimann
     and Sophie Weyers, Witnesses; April 22, 1867, Date; Rev. Jos.
     Anstaett, Minister

331 PORITZ, MAX - JASINKA, APOLLONIA; Herman Poritz and Louise Neumann,
     Thomas Jasinka and Mary Anna Cicmnoczlowska, Parents; James
     Grueningn and Ann Andrycryk, Witnesses; August 1, 1897, Date;
     Rev. J. B. Weimer, Minister

251 POUEIGH, THEOPHILO ANTON - DREW, MARY ANN; James Drew and
     Caroline Drew, Witnesses; May 6, 1887, Date; Rev. Jac. F.
     Lauth, C. S. C., Minister

115 POULSON, CHARLES - RAMSEY, BARBARA; Magdalen Greyenbuehl and
     Mrs. Roehrmann, Witnesses; March 4, 1872, Date; Rev. Ch. Ch.
     Greyenbuehl, Minister

341 PRESTON, CHARLES HENRY - STECHMAN, MARGARET ANN; Jon Preston and
Mary Wakefield, August Ferdinand Stechman and Ann Barbara
Hiller, Parents; Charles Heck, John Elfstrom, Albertine
Stechman and Frederica Swanson, Witnesses; July 5, 1899, Date;
Rev. George A. Rittmeyer, S. J., Minister

169 RAKEL, ALBERT - WAGENBRETT, MATHILDA (n. c.); Gerhard Rakel and
P. Moser, Witnesses; July ... 1880 -- Dispensation dispar.
cultus, Date and Remarks; Rev. H. Reiffert, Minister

188 RAMAKER, THEODORE - WALSH, MARY; Two Nuns, Witnesses; January 24,
1883, Date; Rev. Jac. F. Lauth, C. S. C., Minister

337 RAMEAU, JOHN BAPTIST - LOCE, LEONIDA; Joseph Rameau and Mary
Ducasse, August Loce and Martha Artique, Parents; Frank Offer
and Mary Offer, Witnesses; January 11, 1899, Date; Rev. J. B.
Weimer, Minister

 19 RATISSEAU, AUGUST ANSELM - KRETZSCHMAR, JOAN CAMILLE F. MARY
(convert); .... (ex Paris, France), ... (ex Dresden, Saxony),
Parent's Origin; Joseph Vigne and Mary Thalia Ratisseau,
Witnesses; March 11, 1862 -- Dispensation of three bans,
Date and Remarks; Rev. Jos. Anstaett, Minister

321 RHODE LOUIS GEORGE (n. c.) - WINDMEYER, SOPHIE L.; Theodore Henry
Rhode and Mary Krausse, William Windmeyer and Mary ....,
Parents; William Windmeyer and Theresa Windmeyer, Witnesses;
April 14, 1896, Date; Rev. J. B. Weimer, Minister

 41 RICKE, ANTHONY - JENSKY, JOAN; Charles Ricke and Elizabeth Lueke
(Roesebeck, Westphalia), August Jensky and Agatha Neigebauer
(Glaaz, Silesia), Parents; Martin Ricke, Joan Moser and P. K.
Moser, Witnesses; January 30, 1866, Date; Rev. Jos. Anstaett,
Minister

276 RICKE, JOSEPH - SANASKI, LEO CASIA; M. Ricke and F. Sanaski,
Witnesses; October 7, 1891 -- Dispensation of one ban, Date and
Remarks; Rev. Michael Heinzelmann, Minister

 69 RICKE, MARTIN - MISPEL, IDA; Charles Ricke and Elizabeth Luecke
(Rosebeck, Westphalia), Robert Mispel and Caroline Heimann
(Kabneik, Silesia) (Bruecher), Parents and Origin; Frank
William Burger, Mary Herrmann and Anthony Ricke, Witnesses;
November 23, 1867, Date; Rev. Jos. Anstaett, Minister

196 RICKE, MARTIN - HOCK, MARY; Joseph Ricke and Anna Hock, Witnesses;
January 8, 1884, Date; Rev. Jac. F. Lauth, C. S. C., Minister

295 RINGH, EDWARD - GOLDEN, ANNA; Ernest Ringh and Louise ....,
Timothy Golden and Josephine Parmer, Parents; Otto Schneider
and Lizzie Fitzpatrick, Witnesses; June 28, 1893, Date; Rev.
J. B. Weimer, Minister

 43 RINGH, ERNEST GODFREY (n. c.) - DOEMMERMUTH, ANN; Charles George
Ringh and Emily Pfister (Schaffhausen, Switzerland), Nicholas
Doemmermuth and Eliz. Gilles (Neudof, Nassau), Parents and
Origin; Michael Lang, Geo. Herzog, Anna Kimley and Wilhelmine
Ochs, Witnesses; February 13, 1866 -- Dispensation of mixed
religion, Date and Remarks; Rev. Jos. Anstaett, Minister

262A RINZ, JULIUS - POPULAR, THERESA; Emil Rinz and Helen Walker,
Anton Popular and Mary Joan Heimann, Parents; Mr. and Mrs.
Popular, Anthony Popular and M. Joan Popular, Witnesses;
September 15, 1889 -- Dispensation of two bans, Date and
Remarks; Rev. V. Gury, Minister

181   RINZ, P. W. - WOLKARS, ZOE; Blanche Guerin and P. M. Dumont,
      Witnesses; July 20, 1882, Date; Rev. J. N. Leonard, Minister

269   RITZLER, HENRY - GEBBERT, MARY; William Miller and Frances
      Gebbert, Witnesses; October 22, 1890, Date; Rev. J. Grabinger,
      Minister

 53   RITZLER, VALENTINE - MICHELS, CATHERINE; David Ritzler and Susan
      Ruder (Mosbach, Nassau), Henry Michels and Emily Huehhold
      (Houston, Texas), Parents and Origin; Ferdinand Geilfuss, H.
      Michels, Dorothy Erickson and Mathilde Kose, Witnesses; October
      4, 1866, Date; Rev. Jos. Anstaett, Minister

266   ROFTOPOLA, JOHN - AULL, MARY; Anton Aull and Theresa Aull, Witnes-
      ses; May 25, 1890, Date; Rev. J. Grabinger, Minister

244   ROGERS, JOHN M. - DISUBADORA, ALICE V. (Nee McCrohan); Two Nuns,
      Witnesses; January 16, 1887, Date; Rev. Jac. F. Lauth, C. S.
      C., Minister

274   ROUBION, BERNARD - PAYSSE, ANNIE; Eugene Paysse, James Roubion
      and Victor Dantin, Witnesses; August 15, 1891, Date; Rev.
      Michael Heinzelmann, Minister

312   RUDA, FLORIAN - FERIC, ANNA; Gottob Ruda and Anna Schrina,
      William Feric and Barbara Falesky, Parents; Charles Lentz
      and Otto Menzel, Witnesses; August 27, 1894 -- Dispensation
      of three bans, Date and Remarks; Rev. J. B. Weimer, Minister

268   RUEMBUEHL, E. - MOORE, MARY; Mrs. Parish and Mrs. Mary Aull,
      Witnesses; September 1, 1890, Date; Rev. J. Grabinger, Minister

130   RUMBUEHL, HENRY (n. c.) - GILLET, ANNA (widow); V. G. Bollard
      and Rev. E. Fleury, Witnesses; February 10, 1873 -- Dispensation
      dispar. cultus, Date and Remarks; Rev. Ch. Ch. Greyenbuehl,
      Minister

136   SEBELL, N. S. - PALLIAS, MARY; Jos. Blum, Henry Schan and M. Blum,
      Witnesses; September 24, 1873 - Disp. three banns, Date and
      Remarks; Rev. Ch. Ch. Greyenbuehl, Minister

309   SCARF, HERMAN - HERTH, THERESA; Irvin Scarf and Carline Marhold,
      Raymond Herth and Caroline Schmidt, Parents; Adolph Lepfel
      and Anna Hedwig, Witnesses; April 2, 1894, Date; Rev. J. B.
      Weimer, Minister

155   SCHAEFFER, HENRY C. - GENGLER, ANNIE SUSAN; Tony Sommer, Annie
      Schneider, Ida Schan, Lena Gengler and Miss Perle, Witnesses;
      July 18, 1876, Date; Rev. Ch. Ch. Greyenbuehl, Minister

263   SCHEELE, HENRY (n. c.) - ZEITLER, FRANCES; Michael Lang and C.
      Scheele, Witnesses; January 16, 1890 -- Disp. mixed religion,
      Date and Remarks; Rev. L. Ph. Keller, Minister

144   SCHERIDAN, PATRICK - KENNY, MARY; Thaddeus Mannaghan and Mary
      Kenny, Witnesses; Ocotber 25, 1874, Date; Rev. Ch. Ch.
      Greyenbuehl, Minister

139   SCHERR, STEPHEN - CHRISTIANS, ANNA (n. c.); A. Sommer and Mary
      Haggerti, Witnesses; January 17, 1874 -- Disp. Dispar. Cultus,
      Date and Remarks; Rev. Ch. Ch. Greyenbuehl, Minister

161   SCHMIDT, B. - SCHREIBER, LILLIE; F. Young, William G. Schmidt,
      Catherine Erouan and El. Schreiber, Witnesses; March 8, 1881--
      Disp. mixed religion, Date and Remarks; Rev. J. N. Leonard,
      Minister

203   SCHMIDT, JOHN JOSEPH - GALLASHAW, BERTHA; Brigid Gallashaw and
          Helen Ross, Witnesses; May 29, 1884, Date; Rev. Jac. F. Lauth,
          C. S. C., Minister

172   SCHOCKE, J. - MC GRAW, CATHERINE; Joseph McGraw and Mary Schocke,
          Witnesses; October 17, 1881 -- Disp. Mixed religion, Date and
          Remarks; Rev. J. N. Leonard, Minister

151   SCHOCKE, WILLIAM - ROEHRMANN, THERESA; Henry Schaeffer and
          Theresa Ricke, Witnesses; April 6, 1875 -- Disp. of bans,
          Date and Remarks; Rev. Ch. Ch. Greyenbuehl, Minister

290   SCHOECKE, JOHN - HAHNREITER, OTTILIA; Christian Schocke and
          Theresa Mihr, Anthony Hahnreiter and Anna Weitzmann, Parents;
          Anthony Schoecke and Theresa Schoecke, Witnesses; April 2,
          1893, Date; Rev. J. B. Weimer, Minister

214   SCHOELLER, HENRY - PETER, MARTINA; Sebastian Hifinger and Anna
          Hifinger, Witnesses; March 23, 1885, Date; Rev. Jac. F. Lauth,
          C. S. C., Minister

280   SCHOELLMAN, WILLIAM - WINDMEIER, PHILIPPINE; Alice Boucher and
          William Windmeier, Witnesses; February 7, 1892, Date; Rev.
          Mich. Heinzelmann, Minister

255   SCHOKE, HERMAN - MARX, CHRISTINA; Christian Schoke and Theresa
          Mihr, Anthony Marx and Emma Faber, Parents; Joseph Ricke and
          Cunigunda Marx, Witnesses; October 17, 1888, Date; Rev. V.
          Gury, Minister

 27   SCHOLIBO, HENRY - HERRMANN, MARGARET; Mathias Herrmann and Mary
          Becker, Parents; Frank Sommer, Mathias Herrmann, Anne Drouet
          and Sara Kelse, Witnesses; July 26, 1864, Date; Rev. Jos.
          Anstaett, Minister

271   SCHREIBER, FRANK - CASTELLO, ADA; Victor Gillett and Rosa Fleuhr,
          Witnesses; May 20, 1891, Date; Rev. L. Ph. Keller, Minister

110   SCHULTE, HENRY - WEBER, CLARA; M. Weber and Mrs. Weber, Witnesses;
          May 7, 1871, Date; Rev. Ch. Ch. Greyenbuehl, Minister

320   SCHULTE, JOSEPH J. - VIEHMANN, LOUISE; Henry Schulte and Clara
          Mueller, Frederic Viehmann and Mina Herwig, Parents; April 8,
          1896, Date; Rev. J. B. Weimer, Minister

236   SCHULTZE, JOSEPH - BUCHOLTZ, ELIZABETH (nee Lange); Two Nuns,
          Witnesses; June 20, 1886, Date; Rev. Jac. F. Lauth, C. S. C.,
          Minister

215   SCHWARZBACH, THEODORE - VOGT, MARY; William Koehler and Elizabeth
          Schreiber, Witnesses; March 25, 1885, Date; Rev. Jac. F. Lauth,
          C. S. C., Minister

118   SCHWENDINGER, JOSEPH - NUTT, MARY; John Peine and Charles Sommer,
          Witnesses; June 22, 1872, Date; Rev. Ch. Ch. Greyenbuehl,
          Minister

 84A   SEEL, LOUIS - KIKS, REGINA; Peter Loiselle and Josephine Doebbner,
          Witnesses; August 30, 1869, Date; Rev. N. Gaellweiler, Minister

 48   SEIBERT, GEORGE W. (n. c.) - MC KESSON, EMMA; Louis Seibert and
          Anna M. Bensel, David McKesson and Mary Cook, Parents; M. J.
          Walsh, Mrs. M. J. Walsh and Thomas Keats, Witnesses; October
          18, 1887 - Disp. mixed religion, Date and Remarks; Rev. V.
          Gury, Minister

306   SEIHULSKY, STEPHEN - STEGEL, JOSEPHA; Gabriel Seihulsky and
      Bertha Tulae, (Mathias Fogler) and Frances Stegel, Parents;
      Charles Tries and Emma Giesel, Witnesses; January 4, 1894,
      Date; Rev. J. B. Weimer, Minister

289   SELENSKI, JOHN - MARGARET LUTZ; John Selenski and Mary Schaeffer,
      Adam Lutz and Caroline Goetz, Parents; Agnes McDonald and
      Caspar Selenski, Witnesses; January 15, 1893, Date; Rev. J.
      B. Weimer, Minister

267   SENECHAL, LOUIS W. - GRUENROOD, ROSE; Jos. Matt and Mary Leinbach,
      Witnesses; August 15, 1890, Date; Rev. J. Grabinger, Minister;

      SHERIDAN, vide Scheridan

 76A SHETLEY, WILLIAM FRANKLIN - SAUNDERSON, CECIL ADA; Martin
      McDermoth and Mary E. McDermoth, Witnesses; April 17, 1868,
      Date; Rev. Jos. Anstaett, Minister

209   SIGRIST, JOHN - CONNOR, SARA; Two Nuns, Witnesses; November 4,
      1884, Date; Rev. Jac. F. Lauth, C. S. C., Minister

344   SIMPSON, JAMES T. (n. c.) - SIEBERT, ANNA M.; Jos. C. Sheldon
      and Henry Gayton, Witnesses; May 20, 1900 - Disp mixed religion
      (marriage blessed after 5 years civil marriage), Date and
      Remarks; Rev. Geo. A. Rittmeyer, S. J., Minister

 60   SMITH, DANIEL C. - BERNARD, LYDIA; Martha Bernard, Thomas J. Munn,
      Chas. Brock and Margaret Munn, Witnesses; January 23, 1867,
      Date; Rev. Jos. Anstaett, Minister

314   SMITH, GEORGE - ENGELHARDT, LOUISE; Geo. Smith and Laura Hall,
      Werner Engelhardt and Caroline Halshorn, Parents; Rev. Ph.
      Keller and Chas. Sommer, Witnesses; November 14, 1894, Date;
      Rev. J. B. Weimer, Minister

158   SOMMER, ANTHONY - GENGLER, HELEN; Peter Gengler, John Gengler
      and Chas. Sommer, Witnesses; Rev. M. Weinzaepflen, Minister

109   SOMMER, FERDINAND = GLASER, ANNA; August Sommer, Caroline Kimley,
      Richard Drew and Anna Gengler, Witnesses; July 6, 1871, Date;
      Rev. J. William Ruthmann, S. S. C., Minister

 66   SOMMER, FRANK - SCHROEDER, THERESA;   Frank Sommer and Theresa
      Krause (Bulendorf, Bohemia), James Schroeder and Christine
      Gloeckner (Galveston, Texas), Parents and Origin; July 16, 1867,
      Date; Rev. Jos. Anstaett, Minister

303   SOMMER, JOSEPH ANTHONY - HEIMAN, ODILIA; Ferdinand Sommer and
      Anna Glass, Anthony Heiman and Augusta Biehler, Parents;
      Joseph Lang and Robert Mueller, Witnesses; October 7, 1893,
      Date; Rev. J. B. Weimer, Minister

272   STECHMANN, CARL W. - MONFORD, JOAN L.; James F. Johnston and Miss
      Margaret Stechmann, Witnesses; Rev. L. Ph. Keller, Minister;
      June 27, 1891, Date

249   STEINHOFF, JOHN HENRY (n. c.) - WINN, ANNA BUTLER; William
      Nettelton and Emma Johnson, Witnesses; April 27, 1887, Date;
      Rev. Jac. F. Lauth, C. S. C., Minister

 26   STENZEL, CHARLES - HAZELHORST, JOAN; John Bigat and Pauline Lewis,
      Witnesses; June 12, 1864 -- Children legitimatized by disp;
      Otto, Chas., William, Ann, Geo., Mary., Date and Remarks;
      Rev. Jos. Anstaett, Minister

153B STENZLER, AUGUST - KAUFFMANN, LENA; John Fabian and Mrs. Fabian, Witnesses; June 19, 1876 -- Disp. 3 banns, Date and Remarks; Rev. Ch. Ch. Greyenbuehl, Minister

256 STEWARD, JOHN LAWRENCE - PHLUEGER, HENRIETTA; Peter Wallace Steward and Georgia Escher, Geo. Pflueger and Elizabeth Schneider, Parents; G. T. Joseph and Charles Doran, Witnesses; January 23, 1889, Date; Rev. V. Gury, Minister

39 STONER, JOHN H. - HART, HELEN; January 17, 1866 - Disp. 3 bans, Date and Remarks; Rev. Jos. Anstaett, Minister

343 STUMPF, JOHN JOSEPH - BULLINGTON, ANN THERESA; William Stumpf and Mary Sattler, Jaspar, William Bullington, Parents; Mary Theresa and Ann Cahterine Stumpf, Witnesses; April 24, 1900, Date; Rev. Geo. A. Rittmeyer, S. J., Minister

57 SULLEY, JOHN - STEIN, MARY; Mary Sweeney, E. Magdalene Rohleder and Henry Schaefer, Witnesses; January 3, 1867, Date; Rev. Jos. Anstaett, Minister

206 SWARBRICK, JAMES - DUNN, DELIA (nee Burke); Walter Quested and Helen Quested, Witnesses; July 23, 1884, Date; Rev. Jac. F. Lauth, C. S. C., Minister

176 TACQUARD, J. - BOUTHERY, FAUSTINE; D. H. Beguin and H. Perthuis, Witnesses; January 15, 1882, Date; Rev. J. N. Leonard, Minister

294 TACQUART, JULIUS - HENCKEL, HEDWIG; Henry Tacquart and Pauline Moeller, Chas. Henckel and Anna Baer, Parents; Henry Seibel and Frederic Henckel, Witnesses; June 21, 1893, Date; Rev. J. B. Weimer, Minister

273 TANBUSH, STEPHAN - HEIMAN, ANNA; Joseph Sommer and Mary Sommer, Witnesses; July 29, 1891, Date; Rev. Mich. Heinzelman, Minister

111 THIELEN, CHAS. F. - KRAUSE, ANTONIA; August Bernard B. Krause and Catherine Alfson, Witnesses; October 28, 1871 - Disp. three bans, Date and Remarks; Rev. Ch. Ch. Greyenbuehl, Minister

142 THOMPSON, WILLIAM - SCHAEPER, JOAN; Caroline Ricke and Magdalen Greyenbuehl, Witnesses; August 2, 1874 -- Disp. mixed religion, Date and Remarks; Rev. Ch. Ch. Greyenbuehl, Minister

159 THORMAHLEY, A. E. - PIASECKA, MARY; April 27, 1878 -- Disp. dispar. cultus, Date and Remarks; Rev. M. Weinzaepflen, Minister

283 TICKLE, JOSEPH BERNARD - MAURER, THERESA; James Tickle and Anna Mary Benett, John Maurer and Lena Scherer, Parents; James Tickle Jr. and Ann Maurer, Witnesses; June 29, 1892, Date; Rev. J. B. Weimer, Minister

339 TRALLE, ERNEST - SMITH, HENRIETTA; Julius Trolle and Ann Healy, John F. Smith and Joan Smith, Parents; Rev. Gustaf Wiese and A. Nun, Witnesses; April 8, 1899 -- Disp. mixed religion, Date and Remarks; Rev. J. B. Weimer, Minister

79 TREACCAR, THEODORE - SCHMID, ELIZABETH; Frederic Findling and Wilhelmina Bleicke, Witnesses; November 28, 1868, Date; Rev. Theo. Grundner, Minister

47 TROST, HERMAN - WEDEMEYER, SOPHY; Frederic Wedemeyer and Wilhelmin Rheinfeld (Kellerberg, Hanover), Parents and Origin; Anna Dina and Margaret Potthoff, Witnesses; April 28, 1866, Date; Rev. J. Anstaett, Minister

34   VARGA, JOSEPH HENRY - TSCHAEKE, JOSEPHINE SOPHIE; Benjamin Varga
       and Magdalen Nida (Boez, Hungary), Frank Tschaeke and Catherine
       Herrmann (Albendorf, Silesia), Parents and Origin; Joseph
       Ricke and Caroline Ricke, Witnesses; November 14, 1865, Date;
       Rev. Jos. Anstaett, Minister

40   VERBERNE, ANDREW - HILDEBRAND, THERESA; August Gardet and Rev.
       Peter Richard, Witnesses; January 31, 1866 -- legitimatized,
       Date and Remarks; Rev. Jos. Anstaett, Minister

78   VOGT, CONRAD - RICHTER, HENRIETTA MARIE; P. Hartmann, Witness;
       October 29, 1868, Date; Rev. Theo. Grundner, Minister

44   WAGENFUEHRER, FREDERIC - MAURER, CAROLINE; Henry Loewing, O. B.
       Chapin, Mary Werdehausen and Caroline Werdehausen, Witnesses;
       February 19, 1866 -- Dispensation of mixed religion, Date and
       Remarks; Rev. Jos. Anstaett, Minister

72   WALSH, PATRICK - WALDSCHMIDT, MARGARET (widow Warren); Patrick
       Walsh, Parent; Eugene O'Meara, Patrick August Walsh, John E.
       Mahoney and Catherine Cowan, Witnesses; January 30, 1868,
       Date; Rev. Jos. Anstaett, Minister

32   WAPPLER, FREDERIC THEOPHILUS - DALLMER, SOPHIE; Frederic Theophilus
       Wappler and Christina Wappler (ex Saxony), James Dallmer and
       Mary Ann Zeiser (ex Baden, Germany), Parents and Origin;
       Clemence Evers and Helen Schwarzbach, Witnesses; October 14,
       1865 -- Dispensation of mixed religion, Date and Remarks;
       Rev. Jos. Anstaett, Minister

54   WARREN, JOHN (n. c.) - SCHULTZ, MARY (alias Arnold); Rev.
       Micouleau, H. Terheum, Thomas Pugh and Theo. Arnold, Witnesses;
       November 7, 1866, Date; Rev. Jos. Anstaett, Minister

217   WATT, JOSEPH - RINGELER, VICTORIA; Two Nuns, Witnesses; May 27,
       1885, Date; Rev. Jac. F. Lauth, C. S. C., Minister

210   WEBER, AUGUST - PENDERGAST, MARY; Emil Weber and Isabella
       Pendergast, Witnesses; November 5, 1884, Date; Rev. Jac. F.
       Lauth, C. S. C., Minister

270   WEBER, EMIL - SCHREIBER, MARY; William Weber and Henry Schulte,
       Witnesses; April 29, 1891, Date; Rev. J. Grabinger, Minister

13   WEBER, JOHN - INGERMANN, PETRONELLA; William Weber and Catherine
       Oleschlaeger (Dueren, Prussia), Alexander Ingermann and
       Margaret Nipp (Dueren, Prussia), Parents and Origin; Mathias
       Weber and .... Ingermann, Witnesses; March 15, 1861, Date;
       Rev. Jos. Anstaett, Minister

178   WEBER, WILLIAM J. - STEPHENS, NETTIE A.; Paul A. Auerbach and H.
       Meyer, Witnesses; February 10, 1882, Date; Rev. J. N. Leonard,
       Minister

329   WEBSTER, THOMAS - VAN DEN ENDE, ELIZABETH; Edward Webster and
       Juliette Knight, William Van den Ende and Dorothea Beckmann,
       Parents; Frank Quinn and Casey McKenna, Witnesses; June 9,
       1897, Date; Rev. J. B. Weimer, Minister

65   WEINBERG, LOUIS - BECKER, CATHERINE; Joseph Blum and M. C. Spann,
       Witnesses; July 11, 1867, Date; Rev. Jos. Anstaett, Minister

97   WEYHER, HENRY - KLEIMAN, MARY; Henry Gottwald and Joan Henrietta
       Moser, Witnesses; August 25, 1870, Date; Rev. N. Gaellweiler,
       Minister

279   WICKES, HENRY (n. c.) - LEINBACH, MAGDALEN; Anna Leinbach and
        Mary Leinbach, Witnesses; December 27, 1891 -- Dispensation
        of mixed religion, Date and Remarks; Rev. Michael Heinzelmann,
        Minister

119   WILD, CHARLES HENRY - KIMLEY, ANNA SUSAN; J. B. Madison and August
        Zeinmer, Witnesses; August 14, 1872, Date; Rev. Ch. Ch.
        Greyenbuehl, Minister

 24   WINDMEYER, FLORENCE WILLIAM - SEEL, ANNE MARY; Frank Funk, P.
        Loiselle, August Kleinecke, Henrietta Gay and Lena Kleinecke,
        Witnessess; November 8, 1863, Date; Rev. Jos. Anstaett,
        Minister

125   WINKELBACH, HENRY (n. c.) - BLEICKE, ELIZABETH; August Winkel-
        bach, Caroline Gillet and E. Flake, Witnesses; October 8, 1872-
        Dispensation of mixed religion, Date and Remarks; Rev. Ch. Ch.
        Greyenbuehl, Minister

307   WOLFF, FERDINAND - SELENSKI, ANNA MARY; Ferdinand Wolff and
        Crescentia Maurath, Joseph Selenski and Helen Stengle, Parents;
        Nicholas Malsam and Peter Selenski, Witnesses; January 14, 1894,
        Date; Rev. J. B. Weimer, Minister

319   WOLF, FERDINAND - BRAUNNAGEL, EVA; Ferdinand Wolf and Crescentia
        Maurath, Joseph Braunnagel and Margaret Oxmann, Parents;
        Martin Heck and Caspar Selenski, Witnesses; November 26, 1895,
        Date; Rev. J. B. Weimer, Minister

108   WILFF, FREDERIC - ARNOLD, PAULINE (widow); Frederic Robert and
        Louis Balcet, Witnesses; May 7, 1871 -- Dispensation of mixed
        religion, Date and Remark; Rev. Ch. Ch. Greyenbuehl, Minister

122   ZABEL, FERDINAND - LUTZ, THERESA; A. Schuetz and Magdalene
        Greyenbuehl, Witnesses; August 20, 1872 -- Disp. three banns,
        Date and Remarks; Rev. Ch. Ch. Greyenbuehl, Minister

184   ZIEGLER, AUGUST HENRY - LYNCH, WILHELMINE E.; September 21, 1882,
        Date; Rev. J. N. Leonard, Minister

        DAU, FRANK LEONARD (n. c.) - ANNA SCHMITZ; Jurgen Dau and Augusta
        Dau, Anton Schmitz and Mary Schmitz, Parents; C. B. Anderson
        and George Lang, Witnesses; October 6, 1888, Date; Rev. V.
        Gury, Minister; Page 49

        DORECK, FRAON - EMMA DUFFARD; Lawrence Doreck and Josephine
        Schneider, Alexander Duffard and Caroline Kuemely, Parents;
        Robert Miller, Michael Duffard and John Deltz, Witnesses;
        November 30, 1892, Date; Rev. J. B. Weimer, Minister

        RICKE, MARTIN - IDA MISPEL; Charles Ricke and Elizabeth Luecke
        (Rosebeck, Westphalia), Robert Mispel and Caroline Heimann
        (Kabneik, Silesia) (Bruecher), Parents and Origin; Frank
        William Burger, Mary Hermmann and Anthony Ricke, Witnesses;
        November 23, 1867, Date; Page 69

MARRIAGE RECORDS
1900 - 1952

77   ALLEN, FRED GUY, Sealy, Texas aged 31 to WELLINGTON, BEATRICE
     MARGARET, Kentucky aged 23; William John Allen and Mary Jane
     Erdman, Thomas Wellington and Catherine Martin, Parents;
     Thomas Finn, Mrs. Cath. Bargong and Chas. Engelking, Witnesses;
     June 1, 1909, Date; Rev. J. B. Weimer, Minister

141 ANDERS, PAUL ROBERT, Galveston, Texas aged 19 to MARY SKARKE,
     Galveston; Paul Robert Anders and Mary Hampel, Henry Skarke
     and Mary Yaneska, Parents; Patrick Kiernan and Max Eisenbach,
     Witnesses; June 23, 1918, Date; Rev. P. M. Lennartz, Minister

43   ANDERSON, BURT WILBUR, Dixie Ill. to LANG, SUSAN CATHERINE,
     Galveston; James Henry Anderson, Toronto, Canada and Clara
     A. Clark, Chicago, Ill., Michael Lang, Galveston and Catherine
     Pfeiffer, Oberwiesen, Pfalz, Parents; Michael Lang and
     Catherine Barbong, Witnesses; December 22, 1906 -- disp. mixed
     religion, Date and Remarks; Rev. J. B. Weimer, Minister

73   ANDERSON, JOHN OSCAR, aged 24 to FOURBEY, MARY AGNES, aged 20;
     John P. Andrson, Sweden and ......, John Fourbey, Canada and
     Mary Parham, Parents; John Fourbey and John Hopkins, Witnesses;
     February 20, 1909, Date; Rev. J. B. Weimer, Minister

133 ANDREWS, JOHN BENJAMIN, Galveston to MEYERS, LENA, Galveston;
     Ww. Peter Andrews and Mary Grimshaw, Emil Koebelen and
     Theresa Hans, both from Ellinger, Texas, Parents; August
     Ltznich and Theresa Letznich (nee Koebelen), Witnesses;
     February 8, 1917, Date; Rev. P. M. Lennartz, Minister

91   BABIK, SIMON to VYORAL, ROSA; Note: no other information; July
     21, 1911, Date

101 BARONCINI, JOHN ANTON TH., Island of Elba, Italy, aged 24 to
     RICKE, CHRISTINE M., Galveston; Ippolito Baroncini and
     Cath. Paoli, both from Italy, Martin Ricke and Mary Hock,
     both from Galveston, Parents; George William Plitt and Mary
     Ricke, Witnesses; July 10, 1912, Date; Rev. P. M. Lennartz,
     Minister

120 BARTHELME, AUGUST, San Antonio to MATHIS, LOUISE, immigrate:
     Muehlhausen, Elsace; Ludwig Barthelme and Louisa Lenz,
     Grafenstaden, Elsace, Ludwig Mathis and Louise Sicka,
     Muelhausen, Elsace, Parents; John Leotand and Anna H.
     Kirkpatrick, Witnesses; April 29, 1914, Date; Rev. P. M.
     Lennartz, Minister

3   BASMAISON, PIERRE, France to SCHANDREIN, EMILY, Lothringen,
     Germany; Gilbert Basmaison, Alliers, France and Mary
     Bosmembren, Thiers, France, Paul Schandrein and Mary Paulus,
     Parents; Ottilia Heimann and Sr. Mary, Div. Prov., Witnesses;
     January 8, 1901 -- disp. Trib bannis, Date and Remarks;
     Rev. J. B. Weimer, Minister

54   BATES, JOSEPH THOMAS, Galveston to DUFFARD, CECILE, Galveston,
     John Mifflin Bates and Lucinda Tegade, Alexander Duffard
     and Caroline Kimmele, Parents; testes ......, Witnesses;
     October 2, 1907 -- disp. duob bannis, Date and Remarks;
     Rev. J. B. Weimer, Minister

144 BAUTSCH, FRANK CHARLES, Galveston, n.c., aged 24 to JUNKER,
     FLORENCE FRANCES, Galveston, aged 18; Henry Bautsch and Mary
     Kramer, William Peter Junker and Julia Meuri, Parents; Earl
     Thomson and Mary Ervin, Witnesses; January 2, 1919 -- disp
     mixed religions, Date and Remarks; Rev. P. M. Lennartz,
     Minister

149   BECKER, ADOLF C., Galveston, aged 25 to FIESEL, EMMA, Galveston,
      age 26; Fred Richard Becker and Mary Vehm, August Fiesel and
      Antonia Chiedel, Parents; Fred Richard Becker and Anna Fiesel,
      Witnesses; March 4, 1920 -- disp dispar cult, Date and Remarks;
      Rev. P. M. Lennartz, Minister

168   BECKER, FRED WILLIAM RICHARD, Galveston, n.c., age 35 to FIESEL,
      ANNA, Galveston, age 25; John Fred Hy Becker and Mary Ohme,
      August Fiesel and Antonia Schiedel, Parents; Leonard John
      Becker and Alice Ressel, Witnesses; December 4, 1922 -- disp
      mixed religion, Date and Remarks; Rev. P. M. Lennartz,
      Minister

103   BERGMANN, ROBERT JOS., n.c., Germany to KAMPE, MATHILDE EMILY,
      Glaveston, age 34; John Bergmann, Germany and Louise Hoffschild,
      George Kampe and Mathilda Franke, Parents; testes..., Witnesses;
      February 19, 1913 -- disp. mixed religion, Date and Remarks;
      Rev. P. M. Lennartz, Minister

204   BLUME, VIRGIL ALBERT n.c., Cedar Bayou, Texas age 20 to ROBERTS,
      STELLA, Baldwin, La. age 20; Neal Blume, Boliver and
      Natalie Lipscomb, Alabama, Gaston Roberts and Alma Thibodaux,
      both from Abbeville, La., Parents; James L. Hughes and Anna
      Mae Norris, Witnesses; November 12, 1938 -- disp. dispar cult
      and mixed religion, Date and Remarks; Rev. A. M. Maechler,
      Minister

128   BOCKELMANN, ADOLF JULIUS, Galveston age 23 to LANDRY, BENITA,
      Abbeville, La. age 20; Adolf Hy Bockelmann and Mary Marg.
      Buhl, Nicholas Landry and Marie Broussard, both Abbeville,
      La., Parents; Charles Linus Lane and Ethel May Bockelmann,
      Witnesses; May 28, 1916, Date; Rev. P. M. Lennartz, Minister

  1   BOENING, RUDOLF ALFRED, Steele/Ruhr, Rheinland age 26 to MARY
      LENZ, Galveston age 20; Frank Boening and Mary Gottlob,
      Steele a/Ruhr, Anton Lenz, Coblentz, Prussia and Elizabeth,
      Hornung, Bavaria, Parents; John Lenz and Mary Mentzel,
      Witnesses; January 7, 1901, Date; Rev. J. B. Weimer, Minister

108   BOENING, WILLIAM PAUL, Galveston to SENECHAL, MARY FIDES,
      Galveston; Frank A. Boening and Mary Gertrude Gottlob, Louis
      Senechal and Rose Grenrodd, Parents; Henry Boening and Rose
      Senechal, Witnesses; April 24, 1913 -- disp banns, Date and
      Remarks; Rev. P. M. Lennartz, Minister

 96   BOGUSKI, MARCEL, Russ. Poland, age 26 to SZEZYREK, VICTORIA,
      Galicia, Poland, age 24; Casimir Boguski and Frances Chojnoska,
      Stanislaus Szezurek and Victoria Tlehanek, both from Austria,
      Parents; John Smith and Henry Kessl, Witnesses; February 14,
      1912, Date; Rev. P. M. Lennartz, Minister

146   BOHN, ROBERT JOHN, Galveston age 26 to TAYLOR, LYDIA MATHILDA,
      Galveston, n.c., age 19; George Leonard Bohn and Emma
      Ernestine Julia, Thomas S. Taylor and Agnes Schroeder (Cering),
      Parents; Benard C. Prosch and Myrtle Taylor, Witnesses;
      September 25, 1919 -- disp dispar cult, Date and Remarks;
      Rev. P. M. Lennartz, Minister

161   BOLLER, GEORGE CARL, Galveston, bapt. Luth., age 24 to
      HAUSINGER, ETHEL CECIL, Galveston age 23; William Boller and
      Mathilda Wertpfal, George Henry Hausinger and Anna Maurer,
      Parents; Frederic Pratali and Florence Campbell, Witnesses;
      June 29, 1921 -- disp mixed religion, Date and Remarks;
      Rev. P. M. Lennartz, Minister

49   BONNO, JOHN, Sicily, Italy to RUSSO, ALPHONSA, Sicily, Italy;
      Kate Fitzmorris, Witness; April 28, 1907, Date; Rev. J. B.
      Weimer, Minister

153   BOREN, WILLIAM ARCHIC, Knoxville, Ia. age 28 to RITZLER, HELEN
      PAULINE, Galveston, Texas; Lenis T. A. Boren and Jessie
      Leggitt, Henry Ritzler and Mary Gubbert, Parents; Henry
      Ritzler and Mrs. Mary Ritzler (nee Gubbert), Witnesses;
      September 28, 1920, Date; Rev. P. M. Lennartz, Minister

65   BORIK, FRANK, Zinkau, Bohemia age 22 to NEUMANN, ANNA, Chlum,
      Bohemia age 21; Jos. Boric, Zinkau, Bohemia and Catherine
      Burg, Cernice, Bohemia, Joseph Neumann, Chlum, Bohemia and
      Mary Silhanek, Zelesny, Brod, Bohemia, Parents; Joseph
      Ovesney and Edward Denke, Witnesses; November 2, 1908 --
      disp. three banns, Date and Remarks; Rev. J. B. Weimer,
      Minister

178   BOUDREAUX, JOSEPH OSCAR, Beaumont, Texas age 41 to AMMABELL
      DUPLANTIS nee Bowler, Houston, Texas, n.c., age 27; Theodor
      Boudreaux and Angela A. Guidry, John Henry Bowles and Ida
      E. Johnson, Parents; Henry Ritzler and Adolph Perthuis,
      Witnesses; June 28, 1924 -- disp mixed religion, Date and
      Remarks; Rev. P. M. Lennartz, Minister

203   BOURGEOIS, WILFRED, New Iberia, La. age 22 to CHAMPAGNE,
      NATALIE, Broussard, La. age 16½; Odilon Bourgeois, New
      Iberia, La. and Oliveda Rodriguz, Abbeville, La., Paul
      Champagne, Abbeville, La. and Leonida Romero, New Iberia,
      La., Parents; Loveless Norris and Leona Boutte, Witnesses;
      May 5, 1938, Date; Rev. A. M. Maechler, Minister

224   BRADFORD, PERCY AULCIE, Gena, La., n.c., age 27 to CLEVELAND,
      CATHERINE ELIZABETH, Alpine, Texas, age 21; J. D. Bradford
      and Rosina Crook, both N.C., O. D. Cleveland and Catherine
      S. Rooney, Parents; Walter R. Rooney and Mrs. J. Edwards,
      Witnesses; November 6, 1948 -- disp. dispar. cult, Validatio,
      Date and Remarks; Rev. A. M. Maechler, Minister

139   BREITSCHOPF, HENRY A., Moulton, Texas age 26 to PELZEL, OTTILIA
      nee Podzemny, Moulton, Texas age 24; Emmanuel Breitschopf
      and Barbara Feschinger, Joseph Podzemny and Anna Juenger,
      Parents; William Breitschopf and Barbara Feschinger,
      Witnesses; April 14, 1918, Date; Rev. P. M. Lennartz,
      Minister

152   BRIGGS, FREDERIC WILLIAM, Galveston age 21 to FUENTES, DOLORES,
      Elmendorf, Texas age 22; Harry Briggs and Catherine Seiler,
      Luziano Fuentes and Lucille Saludo, Parents; George Hurlberto
      and Lucille Saludo, Witnesses; September 6, 1920, Date;
      Rev. P. M. Lennartz, Minister

19   BROS, FRANCIS, near Schulenburg, Texas to SITZVANZ, SOPHIE, near
      Schulenburg, Texas; Father from Bohemia, mother from near
      Schulenburg, Texas (groom), Father and Mother from Bohemia
      (bride), Parents; Testes....., Witnesses; March 31, 1903 -
      Married on shipboard, all dispensations obtained, Date and
      Remarks; Rev. J. B. Weimer, Minister

215   BROUSSARD, JOSEPH AARON, Maurice, La. age 20 to NORRIS, RENA,
      Biloxi, Miss. age 17; Alpha Broussard, Lafayette, La. and
      Eloge Broussard, Abbeville, La., Avnel Norris, New Iberia,
      La. and Aspasie Langlinais, Youngsville, La., Parents and
      Origins; Paul Wylie Norris and Elvira Garcia, Witnesses;
      September 19, 1942, Date; Rev. A. M. Maechler, Minister

202   BROWN, GLENNON DOWNEY, Charleston, Mo. age 21 to TAVENER, EVELYN
MYRTLE, Rosenberg, Texas, n.c., age 18; Marck C. Brown,
Charleston, Mo. and Minnie Hay, Cape Girardeau, Mo., Bert E.
Tavener, Fiarbury, Ill. and Agnes Foytik, Schulenburg, Texas,
Parents and Origin; Mr. and Mrs. Marion J. Brown, Witnesses;
February 12, 1938 -- disp. dispar cult and mixed religion,
Date and Remarks; Rev. A. M. Maechler, Minister

174   BRUNTON, JOHN JOSEPH, Galveston age 36 to JUNKER, RUTH CATHERINE,
Galveston, age 20; James Brunton and Mrs. Birdie Brunton,
William P. Junker and Mrs. Julia Mary Junker, Parents; Emmet
Jones and Anita Junker, Witnesses; September 26, 1923, Date;
Rev. P. M. Lennartz, Minister

39   BURGESS, JOHN EDWARD (n.c.) to FLAKE, ETHEL; August 3, 1906 --
Disp mixed religion, Date and Remarks; Rev. J. B. Weimer,
Minister

117   BURIC, JOHN, Houston, Texas to PENCE, BOZINA, Rudolfstadt, Bohemia;
Joseph Buric and Veronica Dvorak, John Pence and Mary Rybola,
Parents; T. Winderwolf M. D., Mathias Muzur and Mary Chalke,
Witnesses; February 7, 1914, Date; Rev. P. M. Lennartz,
Minister

98   BURSUM, HENRY SIGFRIED, Germany to PETERS, ERNESTINE MARY, Germany
age 18; Herman Bursum and Anna Mary Raimer, both Germany,
Carl Ww Chr Peters and Lanira Marki, both Germany, Parents;
Henry Ritzler and Mary Koch, Witnesses; May 1, 1912 -- disp.
mixed religion, Date and Remarks; Rev. P. M. Lennartz,
Minister

220   CANNON, FREDERIC JOSEPH, Galveston age 29 to HEUMAN, EDITH
CATHERINE, Galveston age 30; John Cannon and Clara Schug,
Chas. Howard Heuman, n.c. and Edith Cath. Cordray, Parents;
John Marion Cannon and Lois M. Crothers, Witnesses; February
20, 1946 - Wedding at Sacred Heart, Date and Remarks; Rev.
A. M. Maechler, Minister

50   CANNON, JOHN J., Galveston age 30 to SCHUG, CLARA, Philadelphia,
Penna age 21; Andrew Cannon, Raguna, Austria and Elizabeth
Hinsey, Limerick, Ireland, Fred Schug, Wurtemberg and Ida
Kaist, Schaffhausen, Switzerland, Parents and Origins; James
Fuchs and Susan Stelzel, Witnesses; June 3, 1907, Date;
Rev. J. B. Weimer, Minister

187   CARLESON, OSCAR M., New York age 57 to BERNER, CATHERINE (nee
Maier) age 58; Rudolph A. Boening and Charlotte Maier,
Witnesses; January 9, 1929, Date; Rev. P. M. Lennartz,
Minister

68   CARRAGUE, JOHN JOSEPH age 23 to CARSTEN, ELIZABETH, Galveston
age 20; George and Marguerite Carrague, Henry Carsten and
Elizabeth Schneider, Parents; George Carrague and Frieda
Carsten, Witnesses; February 3, 1909 -- disp mixed religion,
Date and Remarks; Rev. J. B. Weimer, Minister

126   CARTER, JAMES LOUIS, Bastrop, Texas to HAUSINGER, IRENE
MARGARET, Galveston; A. H. Carter, Bastrop and ...., Geo.
Henry Hausinger and Anna Maurer, Parents and Origin; Joseph
Michael Maurer and Sydney Ernest Carter, Witnesses; October
27, 1915 -- disp mixed religion, Date and Remarks; Rev. P. M.
Lennartz, Minister

225 COMEAUX, WARREN JEROME, Biloxi, Miss. age 23 to STEPHENSON, NORMA
LEE, n.c., Boliver age 20; Delano Comeaux, New Iberia, La. and
Celest Thibodaux, Erath, La., E. J. Stephenson and Agnes Blume,
Parents and Origin; P. M. Schexnaider and Mrs. Virgil Blume,
Witnesses; February 18, 1949 -- disp mixed religion and disp
cult, Date and Remarks; Rev. A. M. Maechler, Minister

26 CORDRAY, GEORGE C., Harrisburg to MOBERG, HANNA C., n.c., New
Mexico; Thomas Jules Cordray and Catherine Fox, Henry Olsen
and Julia Moberg, Parents; Julius Herbst and Carrie Cordray,
Witnesses; April 18, 1904 -- disp of mixed marriage, Date and
Remarks; Rev. J. B. Weimer, Minister

196 CORNELIUS, WILLIAM, n.c., Galveston age 20 to CONSTANTINE, DOLORES
M., Mobile Alabama age 19; Conrad C. Constantine and Evadna
Johnson, Parents; June 3, 1936 -- disp mixed religion, Date
and Remarks; Rev. A. M. Maechler, Minister

136 CRONHOLM, CARL REUBEN, n.c., Galveston to ANDERSEN, ELIZABETH
CHRISTINE, Galveston; Gustave Cronholm and Christine Johnson,
Andrew Andersen and Sarah Parker, Parents; Milton George
Sampson and Evelyn Kassel, Witnesses; August 15, 1917 -- disp
mixed religion, Date and Remarks; Rev. P. M. Lennartz, Minister

175 CROTHERS, WILLIAM HARRISON, n.c., Galveston age 33 to CROSS, MARY
AGNES, Galveston age 28; Samuel Crothers and Angeline Sweam,
George Cross and Rosa Lenz, Parents; Charles Lee Cross and
Mrs. Rosa Cross, Witnesses; January 19, 1924 -- disp dispar
cult, Date and Remarks; Rev. P. M. Lennartz, Minister

116 CZERKAS, BRANISLAV, Bonajewsky, Poland to KASINSKI, SOPHIE
CATHERINE, Russia; Clement Czerkas and Mary Novak, Constantin
Kasinski and Avalina Denika, Parents; Mathias Mucas and
Guadelupe Valot, Witnesses; December 23, 1913, Date; Rev.
P. M. Lennartz, Minister

218 DAFONTE, BENITO, Rebareda, Spain age 41 to SILVA, MARY, Beaumont,
Texas age 23; Ramon Dafonte, Spain and Mary Dabano, Spain,
Jesus de la Luz Silva and Elbadocia Garcia, Parents and
Origin; John W. Young and Juanita Silva, Witnesses; June 13,
1943 -- disp banns - Revalidatio, Date and Remarks; Rev. A. M.
Maechler, Minister

195 DAILEY, PERCY AROND, High Island age 31 to TRUMP, TRALICE NORMA,
Egan, La. age 24; John S. Dailey, Alabama and Lilly Patton,
High Island, Arthur Trump, Crowley, La. and Loretta Youse,
N.O., La., Parents and Origin; Ven Sr M. Daniel and Ven Sr M.
Justice (Hosp), Witnesses; May 24, 1936 -- disp banns -
Revalidatio at Hospital, Date and Remarks; Rev. A. M. Maechler,
Minister

38 DANIEL, JAMES LYNN to KRAUS, VIOLA MARY; James Thomas Daniel,
Georgia and Sybil Estelle Poole (Mrs. Ruther) Texas, Frederic
Kraus, Galveston and Emily Casey, Galveston, Parents and
Origins; Fred Kraus, George Kaiser and Mary Mentzel, Witnesses;
June 13, 1906, Date; Rev. J. B. Weimer, Minister

6 DANTIN, VICTOR, Galveston to CRITTENDEN, SADIE L.; Joseph Matt
and .... Dantin, Witnesses; April 29, 1901, Date; Rev. J. B.
Weimer, Minister

182   DARRAS, GEORGE HECTOR, Galveston age 22 to CARROLL, HERMA HELEN,
      Galveston age 17; George Darras and Nellie Moore, John M.
      Carroll and Anna Sommer, Parents; Russel L. Wallace and James
      Carroll, Witnesses; June 24, 1925 - disp mixed religion, Date
      and Remarks; Rev. P. M. Lennartz, Minister

  2   DARRAS, JULIUS, Galveston to STEGER, CELIA, New Braunfels, Texas;
      Peter Darras and Cecile Hector, John Steger and Mary Brossive,
      Parents; Basil Steger and Felicitas Darras, Witnesses; October
      10, 1900, Date; Rev. J. B. Weimer, Minister

 64   DECOITO, CASIMIR, Portugal age 28 to GILBERT, ROSE, Galveston age
      23; Joseph Decoit, Portugal and Rita Maria de Jesu (ibid),
      Thomas Gilbert and Anna Crayeroft, Parents and Origins;
      John Gilbert and Elizabeth Gilbert, Witnesses; August 26,
      1908, Date; Rev. J. B. Weimer, Minister

 95   DEUTSCHER, CHARLES, Moravia to NAVRATIL, STEPHANIE, Moravia;
      Joseph Deutscher and Mary Bak, both Moravia, August Navratil
      and Theresa Behr, both Moravia, Parents and Origin; Rev.
      John Ed Reifschneider and Rudolf Anton, Witnesses; November 13,
      1911, Date; Rev. P. M. Lennartz, Minister

143   DIRCKS, HERMAN JOHN, Galveston age 32 to PETERSON, LOUISE REBECCA,
      Galveston, n.c. age 27; Tho Geo Dircks and Emma Franz,
      Gustave Peterson and Caroline Cossman, Parents; October 15,
      1918, Date; Rev. P. M. Lennartz, Minister

105   DOBBERSTEIN, PAUL, Germany to RIEMER, HEDWIG, Germany; Paul
      Dobberstein and Martha Helmich, Paul Riemer and Amalia Miethe,
      Parents; R. J. Miller and Hedwig Brendle, Witnesses; December
      6, 1912, Date; Rev. P. M. Lennartz, Minister

223   DOERFLER, ROBERT ALOYSIUS, Kenosha, Wis. age 23 to CONSTANTINE,
      MARY MARGARET, Mobile, Ala. age 21; Andrew Doerfler, Kenosha
      and Helen Schilz, Conrad Constantine, Mobile and Evanda
      Johnson, Parents and Origin; John C. Constantine, Witness;
      May 22, 1948, Date; Rev. A. M. Maechler, Minister

 75   DOREE, CHARLES JAMES, Mentz, Texas to JACOBS, CLARA JOSEPHINE,
      Mentz, Texas; Jacob Doree and ....., James Jacob, Hesse
      Darmstadt and Emily Heiman, Franz, Parents and Origin; Edwin
      Franz and Rudolph Gloger, Witnesses; April 28, 1909, Date;
      Rev. J. B. Weimer, Minister

154   DOWDY, JAMES THOMAS, Texas City age 25 to MONSHAUSEN, ANNA ANGELA,
      Galveston age 21; Nicholas Dowdy and Mary Richmond, John
      Monshausen and Selma Pflum, Parents; John Maurice Howard and
      Joan Monshausen, Witnesses; October 12, 1920, Date; Rev. P. M.
      Lennartz, Minister

170   DOWNEY, JOHN WILLIAM, Galveston age 30 to GILLET, PEARL EVELYN,
      Galveston age 21; William A. Downey and Margaret Smith, Victor
      Andrew Gillet and Elizabeth Sullivan, Parents; Victor W.
      Gillet and Dorothy Biggs, Witnesses; June 11, 1923, Date;
      Rev. P. M. Lennartz, Minister

 30   DREYDOPPEL, CHARLES, Galveston to LAINE ANNA, nee Haenlein,
      Galveston; Charles Dreydoppel, Hessen and Louise Stork,
      Henry Haenlein, Bavaria and Helen Hildebrandt, ibid, Parents
      and Origin; J. Gaschen and Anna Bendixen, Witnesses; May 3,
      1905 - disp two banns, Date and Remarks; Rev. J. B. Weimer,
      Minister

148   DUES, EDWARD HERMAN, Dickinson, Texas age 31 to MULLER, EDELLA,
      n.c.; Dickinson; George H. Dues and Catherine Hagedorn,
      Louis Muller and Bertha Symank, Parents; Anthony John Dues
      and Ella Muller, Witnesses; October 29, 1919 -- disp obt.
      Date and Remarks; Rev. P. M. Lennartz, Minister

 63   DYDA (DYDER), ILKO, Austrian Poland age 25 to AMBROSE, NASKA,
      Austrian Poland age 21; Jos. Dyda and Paranka Senkovolwowirki,
      both Austrian Poland, Andrew Ambrose and Catherine Tupil,
      both ibid, Parents and Origins; Adam Fuchs and Agnes Fuchs,
      Witnesses; May 31, 1908 -- disp two banns, Date and Remarks;
      Rev. J. B. Weimer, Minister

173   ECKENFELS, HENRY LAWRENCE, Galveston to DAEHNE, LUCILLE CATHERINE,
      Galveston; Henry Eckenfels and Catherine Bauhans, Louis Daehne
      and Anna Josephine Kampe, Parents; William Martin and Anna
      Daehne, Witnesses; July 4, 1923, Date; Rev. P. M. Lennartz,
      Minister

119   EIMER, MARTIN, Electra, Texas to HANSA, MATHILDS, Salzburg,
      Austria; Blase and Anna Eimer, Wenzel Hansa and Josephine
      Reisinger, Parents; Mathias Muzar and Mrs. Chas Lasalinier,
      Witnesses; April 11, 1914, Date; Rev. P. M. Lennartz, Minister

107   FENETY, CARL LESTER, n.c., Houston age 30 to ARNOLD, MARY EDNA,
      Galveston age 24; Edward W. Fenety and Alice Williams, Abbott
      Lawrence Arnold and Anna F. Garey, Parents; Abbott Lawrence
      Arnold and Bian J. Arnold, Witnesses; April 3, 1913 -- disp
      mixed religion, Date and Remarks; Rev. P. M. Lennartz,
      Minister

150   FIELDS, ROY HOWARD, n.c., Galveston to MONSHAUSEN, ELIZABETH
      BARBARA, Galveston; William Harrison Fields and Esena Statton,
      John Monshausen and Selma Pflum, Parents; John Crossman and
      Frances Monshausen, Witnesses; June 9, 1920 -- disp dispar
      cult, Date and Remarks; Rev. P. M. Lennartz, Minister

208   FINN, JAMES WALTER, Galveston age 34 to CORDRAY, ALICE LOUISE,
      Orange Texas age 38; Patrick Finn and Theresa Schocke, Thomas
      J. Cordray Sr. and Caroline M. Heuman, Parents; Thomas P. Finn
      and Lillian Heuman, Witnesses; September 18, 1940, Date; Rev.
      A. M. Maechler, Minister

226   FINN, ROBERT WILLIAM, Galveston age 50 to KAMEYER, MARIE THERESA,
      Galveston age 45; Patrick Finn and Theresa Schocke, Fred Ww
      Kameyer and Anna C. Stumpf, Parents; James W. Finn and Catherine
      F. Kameyer, Witnesses; August 11, 1952, Date; Rev. A. M.
      Maechler, Minister

159   FLACK, GORDON REX, n.c., San Antonio age 22 to BRIGGS, JOSEPHINE
      CATHERINE, Galveston age 22; Thomas Jefferson Flack and Alice
      Bell Crittenden, William Harry Briggs and Catherine Seiler,
      Parents; Fred William Briggs and Corinne Agnes Gittry,
      Witnesses; April 15, 1921, Date; Rev. P. M. Lennartz, Minister

 51   FLORS, ABRAHAM, San Antonio age 27 to BERGER, LENA (Mrs. Erick),
      Russia age 26; Dionysius Flores and Adele Trevino, both of
      San Antonio, Joseph Berger and Martha Zink, both of Russia,
      Parents; Adele Flores, nee Trevino and Sr M Mary, Div. Prov.,
      Witnesses; June 15, 1907 -- disp three banns, Date and
      Remarks; Rev. J. B. Weimer, Minister

61   FRANK, JOSEPH PHILIP, League City, Texas to ROURKE, PEARL CECILE,
     Galveston; Frank Ignaz Frank, Houston and Marg. Brown, Ireland,
     J. M. Rourke and Mathilda Riesener, Brazoria County, Parents
     and Origin; Walter Frank and Agnes Rourke, Witnesses; June 24,
     1908 -- disp three banns, Date and Remarks; Rev. J. B. Weimer,
     Minister

15   FRIEDENBURG, CHARLES, n.c., Galveston to BARLEMANN, MARY,
     Galveston; Henry Friedenburg and Louise Ripchi, Charles
     Barlemann and Theresa Ricke, Parents; E. C. Woodman and
     William Barlemann, Witnesses; December 13, 1914 - Validatio,
     Date and Remarks; Rev. P. M. Lennartz, Minister

52   FREUDENBURG, HENRY AUGUST, n.c., Galveston age 33 to BARLEMANN,
     ANNA CATHERINE, Galveston age 24; Henry Aug. Freudenburg and
     Aloysia Ripke, Charles Barlemann, Bavaria and Theresa Ricke,
     Parents and Origins; Louis Schmidt and May Garthar, Witnesses;
     July 3, 1907 - disp for mixed marriage, Date and Remarks;
     Rev. J. B. Weimer, Minister

44   FUCHS, ADAM J., Unterfranken, Bavaria age 49 to RULOFF, AGNES
     (nee Babacki), Russian Poland, age 40; Henry Fuchs, Bavaria
     and Gertr. Fischer, Bavaria, Geo. Babacki and Marianne Banach,
     both Russian Poland, Parents and Origins; James Fuchs and
     Minnie Gottlob, Witnesses; January 21, 1907, Date; Rev. J. B.
     Weimer, Minister

37   GARLAND, THOS. J. BARTHOLOMEW to NELSON, BERTHA, n.c., Galveston;
     Peter Garland, Ireland and Mary Ann Hort, New Orleans, La.,
     Christ. Nelson, Denmark and Irene ..., Germany, Parents and
     Origins; William Johnson and Bartholomew Hort, Witnesses;
     August 25, 1906 -- disp pro mixed religions, Date and Remarks;
     Rev. J. B. Weimer, Minister

27   GARINGS, JERRY JOSEPH to BARRY, FRANCES MC CARTHY, Ireland;
     Garings Joseph Jeremiah, Ireland and Anice Cavanaugh, John
     McCarthy Barry and ...., Ireland, Parents and Origin;
     James Reagan and Mrs. Lucas ..., Witnesses; June 29, 1904 --
     disp. three banns, Date and Remarks; Rev. J. B. Weimer,
     Minister

41   GERE (JERRY), CHARLES BURKHART, Galveston to BENNOT, OLIVE G.,
     Galveston; Jules Ernest Gere, N.O., La. and Frances Haar,
     Albert Bennot, France and Alice White, Parents and Origins;
     Joseph Keppler and May Johnson, Witnesses; September 18, 1906--
     disp mixed religion, Date and Remarks; Rev. J. B. Weimer,
     Minister

83   GILMAN, FREDERIC HERBERT, Ithake, n.c. to TROY, LOUISE C., Ithaka;
     Geo. L. Gilman, Winterport, Me. and Flora Holmes, ibid, John
     Troy, Limerick, Ireland and Elizabeth McAlister, Loud, Ireland,
     Parents and Origins; John P. Troy, Witness; September 3, 1910--
     disp mixed religion, Date and Remarks; Rev. J. B. Weimer,
     Minister

93   GLOWACKI, VINCENT to POKORSKA, HELEN; Felix Glowacki and Catherine
     Kalokovski, Frank Pokorska and Marianne Boyorska, Parents;
     September 16, 1910, Date; Rev. J. B. Weimer, Minister

124 GOODMAN, OSCAR J.,n.c., Galveston to HEINTZ, CAROLINE (nee
     Heyerman), Galveston; Adam Fuchs and Henry Ritzler, Witnesses;
     October 28, 1914 -- disp obtt, Date and Remarks; Rev. P. M.
     Lennartz, Minister

129   GORDON, JOHN RALPH, Mexico to PERALTA, MANUELA, New Mexico; John
        Bertrand A. Gordon and Mary Cohalen, John Peralta, New Mex.
        and Vincenta Lopez, Parents and Origins; Frank Black, Mrs.
        Black, nee Emily Peralta, Witnesses; July 1, 1916 -- disp
        dispar cult, Date and Remarks; Rev. P. M. Lennartz, Minister

151   GOTTSELIG, ALLARD BARKAL (adopted) age 20 to HARTMAN, ETHEL NELL,
        New Iberia, La. age 21; John Gottselig and Eugenia Heinz,
        Roger John Hartman and Ida Elizabeth Hanschett, Parents;
        Martin Mitchell Kovis and Ida Gottseling, Witnesses; August
        7, 1920, Date; Rev. P. M. Lennartz, Minister

 21   GRINROOD, JOSEPH J., Galveston age 24 to JACOBS, JOANETTE, E.,
        Bernardo, Texas age 19; Henry Grinrood, Prussia and Fides
        Elbert, Parents; John Jacobs and Minnie Gottlob, Witnesses;
        May 20, 1903, Date; Rev. J. B. Weimer, Minister

190   GUIDRY, ANTHONY, Lafayette, La. age 26 to HUGHES, MILDRED,
        Beaumont, Texas age 19; Alb. Guidry, Lafayette and Anice
        Domaine, Ibid, William Hughes, Beaumont and Eloise Monteau,
        Parents and Origins; Enis T. Champagne and Dilta Vincent,
        Witnesses; October 16, 1932 -- disp from banns, Dates and
        Remarks; Rev. A. M. Maechler, Minister

 72   GUOKAS, ANTHONY, Lithuania age 32 to KOVAL, MARY, Vienna, Austria,
        age 19; Anton Guokas, Lithuania and Elizabeth Shukes, John
        Koval, Bohemia and Elizabeth Radlec, Parents and Origins;
        Arthur Schoelmann and Sr. M. De Pazzi, Div. Prov., Witnesses;
        February 17, 1909, Date; Rev. J. B. Weimer, Minister

104   HACKER, FRANK, Bavaria age 29 to JETZELSPEREGER, THERESA, Bavaria
        age 28; Michael Hacker and Frances Benscova, Joseph Jetzels-
        perger and Louise Stoller, Parents; H. A. Kirkpatrick and
        Alma Kirkpartrick, Witnesses; March 4, 1913, Date; Rev.
        P. M. Lennartz, Minister

114   HACKER, OSWALD PAUL, n.c., Brownsville, Texas to ROSENBAUM,
        MAGDALEN, Rommerskirchen, Koeln; Gottlieb Hacker and Amalia
        Hacker, Bernard and Marie Rosenbaum, Parents; Dr. L.
        Bahrenbert, T. Hartman and Dr. Burosse, Witnesses; October 10,
        1913 -- disp obt., Date and Remarks; Rev. P. M. Lennartz,
        Minister

138   HAND, ROBERT, Houston Harbor age 36 to FRITCH, ANNE, Houston Harbor
        age 23; Robert Hand and Esther Murray, Frederic Fritch and
        Minnie Barwik, Parents; Ellis Ritzler and Harold Daily,
        Witnesses; January 26, 1918, Date; Rev. P. M. Lennartz,
        Minister

 28   HANSEN, WILLIAM HERMAN TOWALD, Kademinde, Denmark, n.c., age 25
        to LANG, FELICITAS, Galveston age 18; Neil Hansen, Denmark and
        Sophie Aarensdorf, ibid, Herman Lang, Baden and Cath. Seipels,
        Wiesbaden Hess-Nassau, Parents and Origins; Herman Lang Jr.
        and Edelgard Lang, Witnesses; January 16, 1905 -- disp for
        mixed marriage, Date and Remarks; Rev. J. B. Weimer, Minister

217   HARDKING, FREDERIC JACKSON, n.c., Double Bayou, Texas age 25 to
        KAHLA, IDA MAE, Stowell, Texas age 22; L. J. Harding and
        Mattie Tremell, Frank W. Kahla and M. Elizabeth Hughes,
        Parents; Cecil W. Kahla and Mrs. Evelyn Schexnaider, Witnesses;
        June 8, 1943 -- desp mixed religion and disp cult Revalidatio,
        Date and Remarks; Rev. A. M. Maechler, Minister

123   HARREL, HUGH, n.c., San Antonio, Texas to RICKE, MARY, Galveston;
       Taylor Harrel and Samia Peacock, Martin Ricke and Mary Hock,
       Parents; Otto Onken and Annie Ricke, Witnesses; October 14,
       1914 -- disp obt., Date and Remarks; Rev. P. M. Lennartz,
       Minister

199   HARRYMAN, VIRGIL, n.c., Galveston age 24 to DECOITO, MARY ANN,
       Galveston age 22; T. G. Harryman, Norman, Okla. and Omah Hobbs,
       Okla., Casimir Decoito, Azores, Portugal and Rose Gilbert,
       Galveston, Parents and Origins; Joseph Decoito and Rosalie
       Croft, Witnesses; June 7, 1937 -- disp dispar cult, instructions
       given, Date and Remarks; Rev. A. M. Maechler, Minister

59   HASSELMEIER, FRED MAURY, n.c., age 20 to GASCHEN, MATTIE age 18;
       Louis Geo Hasselmeyer and Mary Lyons, Matthew Gaschen and
       Helen Haenlein, Parents; William Hasselmeyer and Anna Bendixen,
       Witnesses; January 29, 1908 -- disp mixed religion, Date and
       Remarks; Rev. J. B. Weimer, Minister

22   HAYMANN, ANTON A., Galveston age 23 to WHITE, AMELIA, Galveston
       age 19; Anton Haymann, Prussia and Minnie Koerner, ibid,
       Chas White, England and Ann Joan Boken, Parents and Origins;
       Anna Spalding and Joan Hancock, Witnesses; June 11, 1903 --
       disp three banns, Date and Remarks; Rev. J. B. Weimer,
       Minister

40   HEINRICH, JOSEPH P., Schulenburg, Texas to SANDERS, RHEA, n.c.,
       LaPorte; August 7, 1906 -- disp mixed religion, Date and
       Remarks; Rev. J. B. Weimer, Minister

171   HEINS, GEORGE, Galveston age 27 to ECKENFELS, ROSALIE MARY,
       Galveston age 21; Charles Heins and Charlotte Hein, Henry
       Eckenfels and Cath. Bauhans, Parents; Albert William Heins
       and Mrs. Valentine Lott, Witnesses; June 27, 1923 -- disp
       dispar cult, Date and Remarks; Rev. P. M. Lennartz, Minister

36   HEINTZ, GEORGE, Plantersville, Texas age 58 to SCHLOSSER, BARBARA,
       Russia age 55; Daniel Heintz and Barbara Epp, Clemens Schwan
       (sic) and Cath. Homann, both from Russia, Parents and Origin;
       Casper Selenski and Edna Ritzler, Witnesses; May 14, 1906 --
       disp three banns, Date and Remarks; Rev. J. B. Weimer,
       Minister

79   HEINZE, EMMANUEL, Muensterberg, Breslau age 61 to BIERMANN (nee
       Hagemann), CAROLINE age 57; Robert Heinze and Anna Glabach,
       both Breslau, Henry Hagemann and Eliz. Koss, both from
       Hildesheim, Hanover, Parents and Origin; Mary Wicks, Witness;
       June 23, 1909, Date; Rev. J. B. Weimer, Minister

16   HERMANN, RUDOLF MATTHIAS, Galveston to SOMMER, CECILE AGNES,
       Galveston age 18; Matthias Hermann, Trier Prussia and Augusta
       Eggert, Parents and Origin; Zedock Pratt Mott Jr. and Louisa
       Sommer, Witnesses; June 4, 1902 -- disp three banns, Date and
       Remarks; Rev. J. B. Weimer, Minister

216   HESLOP, FRANCES, Columbus, Ohio age 23 to SEGURA, LILLIE MAE,
       Port Bolivar, age 17; Frank Heslop and Flora Hullett, Eloi
       Segura and Rose Champagne, Parents; Arnold Comeaux and Dorothy
       Theresa Segura, Witnesses; March 21, 1943, Date; Rev. A. M.
       Maechler, Minister

55   HILLERS, FRED HENRY MARION, Duelman, Westphalen to WALTHER, ANITA
     ELIZABETH, Austin, Texas; Anton Hillers, Velen, Westph and
     Elizabeth Hollweg, Muenster, Westph, Alfred Walther, Graubunden,
     Switzerland and Emma Gimbel, San Antonio, Texas, Parents and
     Origins; Ven Sisters Elizabeth and Pius, Div Prov, Witnesses;
     October 25, 1907 -- disp three banns, Date and Remarks; Rev.
     J. B. Weimer, Minister

15   HINDS, WALTER ROBERT to STOWEL (nee Kraus), CATHERINE AGNES:
     Edward Lawrence Kraus and Elizabeth Kraus, Witnesses; September
     21, 1914, Revalidatio, Date and Remarks; Rev. P. M. Lennartz,
     Minister

42   HONCHERA, STANISLAUS age 20 to BLASSKIEWICZ, ANTONIA, Polish
     Russia age 21; John Honchera and Louise Carnekoswrsa, Warsaw,
     Jos. Blasskiewicz and Frances Siahouwicz, both from Polish
     Russia, Parents and Origins; Adam J. Fuchs and Agnes Ruloff,
     Witnesses; November 4, 1906 -- disp three banns, Date and
     Remarks; Rev. J. B. Weimer, Minister

106 HORACK, LEOPOLD, Bohemia, Austria age 33 to PALLA, ANNE, Bohemia,
     Austria age 26; Frank Horack and Caroline Stasni, Joseph Palla
     and Anna Neubauer, Parents; Reneker Gheyer and Hugo Hettner,
     Witnesses; March 28, 1913, Date; Rev. P. M. Lennartz, Minister

222 HORNER, LESTER GEORGE, n.c., Hyde Park, Vermont age 23 to
     CONSTANTINE, ROSE ANN, Mobile, Alabama age 22; Arkley Horner
     and Eunice Louise Perry, Conrad C. Constantine and Evadna
     Dean Johnson, both from Mobile, Alabama, Parents and Origin;
     John Constantine and Mary Constantine, Witnesses; June 21,
     1947 -- disp dispar cult and mixed religion, Date and Remarks;
     Rev. A. M. Maechler, Minister

176 HOWARD, WALTER EARL, n.c., Galveston age 19 to MONSHAUSEN, JOAN
     THERESA, Galveston age 23; Roger Howard and Callie Pearl
     Doodman, John Monshausen and Selma Pflum, Parents; John
     Monshausen and Mrs. Nick Colombo (nee Howard), Witnesses;
     May 28, 1924 -- disp dispar cult, Date and Remarks; Rev. P. M.
     Lennartz, Minister

156 HUEPERS, AUGUST EDWARD, Convert, Galveston age 22 to RAMMER,
     MARGARET, Alta Loma, Texas age 19; Geo William Huepers and
     Mary Selzer, John J. Rammer and Mary Wiegeshing, Parents;
     William B. Jones and Alice Rammer, Wintesses; January 22, 1921,
     Date; Rev. P. M. Lennartz, Minister

211 HUGHES, JAMES LESLIE, Port Arthur, Texas age 21 to NORRIS, ANNA
     MAY, Bayou Baker, La. age 17; William Lawr Hughes and Elvira
     Reilly, both Port Arthur, Dave Norris, Delcambre, La. and
     Electa Rodriguez, New Iberia, La., Parents and Origin;
     Lawrence Hughes and Leona Boutte, Witnesses; August 26, 1941,
     Date; Rev. A. M. Maechler, Minister

41   JERRY, see GERE

191 JONES, EDGAR HARDING, n.c. age 24 to DORIAN, LENORA CATHERINE,
     Galveston age 27; William Penn Jones, Rockdale, Texas and
     Margaret Cartwell, Charles B. Dorian and Agnes Pfluger,
     Parents and Origin; William P. Jones and Mrs. Elizabeth
     Dalney, Witnesses; September 13, 1934 -- disp mixed religion
     and disp cult, Date and Remarks; Rev. A. M. Maechler, Minister

8   KAIS, CHARLES JOSEPH, Galveston to EHLERT, MARY SOPHIE, Galveston;
     John Joseph Kais and Frances Reisser, ... and ..., Germany,
     Parents and Origin; John Ehlert and Anna Weyer, Witnesses;
     June 11, 1901 -- disp two banns, Date and Remarks; Rev. J. B.
     Weimer, Minister

89   KALA, ALOYSIUS, Bohemia to TULIS, JOSEPHINE, Bohemia; Frank Vance
      and Bliss Morton, Witnesses; May 26, 1911 -- disp three banns,
      Date and Remarks; Rev. J. B. Weimer, Minister

18   KALBEY, CHARLES, age 22 to FLAKE, ANNA, Galveston age 18; August
      Kalbey and Pauline Schroeder, Otto Flake and ...., Parents;
      Jules J. Tribout and Otto Flake, Witnesses; September 22, 1902--
      disp dispar cult, Date and Remarks

33   KAMEYER, FREDERIC W., n.c. age 28 to STUMPF, ANNA CATHERINE age 23;
      Frederick Kameyer and Frances Herthal, William Stumpf and
      Mary Sattler, Parents; January 10, 1906 -- disp mixed religion,
      Date and Remarks; Rev. J. B. Weimer, Minister

31   KAMEYER, HERMANN, Galveston to BIERING, CATHERINE, Galveston;
      F. W. Kameyer and Frances Herthal, E. J. Biering and Joan
      Sattler, Parents; F. Kameyer Jr. and Anna K. Stumpf, Witnesses;
      September 27, 1905 -- disp mixed religion, Date and Remarks;
      Rev. L. J. Bashnal, S. J., Minister

110   KANEWSKI, AUGUSTIN HENRY, Galveston to COOK, ANITA, Galveston;
      Sylvester Kanewski and Catherine Cartler (Castles?), Geo. Cook
      and Minnie Schmidt, Parents; Mrs. Elsa Furby, Ella Mae Cook
      and Lillie Pendergast, Witnesses; July 1, 1913, Date; Rev.
      P. M. Lennartz, Minister

131   KISSINGER, JOHN CHARLES, n.c., Galveston to CHASSANIOL, EDNA,
      Galveston; John James Kissinger and Ida Elbert, George
      Chassaniol and Minnie Keis, Parents; Charles Elbert and
      Celeste Day, Witnesses; August 23, 1916 -- disp mixed
      religion, Date and Remarks; Rev. P. M. Lennartz, Minister

14   KLEINECKE, HERMANN EMIL, n.c., Galveston to SOMMER, HELEN
      THERESA, Galveston; Hermann Ferd. Kleinecke and Emily Huebele,
      Anton Sommer and Helen Gengler, Parents; Charles Sommer,
      Witness; April 23, 1902 -- disp. mixed religion, Date and
      Remarks; Rev. J. B. Weimer, Minister

48   KONECNY, JAMES, Bruenn, Austria age 22 to NAKWASIL, THERESA,
      Bruenn, Austria age 24; John Konecny and Mary Ann Gardase,
      Paul Nakwasil, Bruem, Austria and Theresa Koutila, Parents;
      Michel ...., Witness; April 8, 1907, Date; Rev. J. B. Weimer,
      Minister

86   LACHINE, GEORGE, France to MRS. ELIZABETH DENIKE, nee Brockhard,
      Rhein Prov.; sponsi ex Gallia, sponsae ex Germania, Parents;
      Mrs. E. Davie and Mrs. A. Sands, Witnesses; February 18, 1911 --
      Validatio, Date and Remarks; Rev. J. B. Weimer, Minister

163   LAGLER, STEPHAN, Hungary age 28 to KARLOVITZ, CATHERINE, Hungary
      age 27; Henry Lagler and Martha Blasvitz, Paul Karlovitz and
      Anna Blasvitz, Parents; Andrew Michael Garvey and Mary Darlitz,
      Witnesses; October 20, 1921, Date; Rev. P. M. Lennartz,
      Minister

186   LAHRRSEN, GEORGE FREDERIC, Galveston age 41 to DAVENPORT, LORRAINE
      age 31; Henry Lahrrsen and Joan Lahnen, James Robt Davenport
      and Emma Conway, Parents; February 14, 1928, Date; Rev. P. M.
      Lennartz, Minister; Parents were Witnesses

23   LARSON, JOHN, Galveston to WEBER, LILLIAN, Bremen, Germany;
      Frank D. Larson and Maggie Hart, John Weber, Breman and Cath.
      Schnabel, Germany, Parents and Origins; Mabel Ehrends (Mrs.)
      (soror uxoris), Witness; August 20, 1903 -- disp mixed
      religion, Date and Remarks; Rev. J. B. Weimer, Minister

181   LASSEN, OTTO GODFREY, Germany age 55 to BOHN, LOUISE IDA,
       Galveston age 43; Mr. and Mrs. John Ricke, Witnesses;
       February 8, 1925 -- Validatio, Date and Remarks; Rev. P. M.
       Lennartz, Minister

 66   LEIMER, FERDINAND, Styria, Austria age 39 to JEDLIKA, ANTONIA,
       Styria, Austria age 21; Michael Leimer and Mary Seidelhufer,
       Austria, Anton Jedlika and Julianne Hoedl, all Austria,
       Parents and Origins; Rev. Phil. Keller and Florian Amsehl,
       Witnesses; November 20, 1908 - disp banns, Date and Remarks;
       Rev. J. B. Weimer, Minister

 76   LELSZ, PETER, Holland to GOTTLOB, WILHELMINE CAROLINE, Galveston;
       Murk Lelsz and Janieka Van der Werff, both Holland, John
       Gottlob, Rheinland and Marie Friederich, Saxony, Parents and
       Origins; June 2, 1909, Date; Rev. J. B. Weimer, Minister

177   LERA, THOMAS, Galveston age 31 to BRICK, CATHERINE U., Galveston
       age 28; Alfred Lera and Palmira Menicucci, Thomas Dubois
       Brick and Catherine Dumschen, Parents; Jerry C. Brick and Mrs.
       Earl Yeadacken, Witnesses; June 26, 1924, Date; Rev. P. M.
       Lennartz, Minister

 56   LINTNER, FRANK, Kirrweiler, Bavaria to HUND, ELIZABETH ....;
       Frank Lintner, Altbergen and Cath. Zeller, Kirrweiler,
       Henry Hund and Elizabeth Keiler, both Kirrweiler, Parents and
       Origins; Ven Sr M. Elizabeth and Xenia Wilke, Witnesses;
       October 26, 1907, Date; Rev. J. B. Weimer, Minister

  7   LORENTZ, HUGH, n.c., Holstein to SCHOMERS, LOUISE, Sealy, Texas;
       sponsi ex Schleswig - Holstein, sponsae: John Schomers, Trier,
       Prussia and Mrs. Schomers ex Hacine, Wis., Parents and Origin;
       John and Mary Schomers, Witnesses; May 6, 1901, Date; Rev.
       J. B. Weimer, Minister

145   LOWRY, CHARLES C., Clarksburg, West Virginia age 26 to ROURKE,
       LILLIAN ETTA, Galveston, Texas age 26; Lloyd Lowry and
       Eugenia Doyle, John Rourke and Mathilda Reisner, Parents;
       Dudley Thomas Rourke and Mrs. Joseph Frank, Witnesses;
       September 18, 1919, Date; Rev. P. M. Lennartz, Minister

188   MAHR, ALBERT JOSEPH, St. Louis, Mo. age 48 to MARSCHNER, FLORENCE
       (nee Wertrop); Philip Mahr and Emily Hammerle, William
       Wertrop and Mary Bailey, Parents; August 5, 1929, Date; Rev.
       P. M. Lennartz, Minister

 25   MARTIN, LOUIS, Strassburg, Germany to CONBOY, AGNES, Canada;
       John Martin, Constanz, Baden and Ernestine Steinbach, ibid,
       Parents; Walter Schoelmann and Mary Moffeth, Witnesses;
       January 1904, Date; Rev. J. B. Weimer, Minister

 67   MARTIN, LOUIS JOSEPH, Alsace age 30 to FLEIDER, CAROLINE, n.c.,
       Galveston age 18; John Martin, Baden and Ernestine Steinbach,
       .... Fleider and Sophie Davis, Parents and Origin; Charles
       Straub and Dottie Nichols, Witnesses; January 27, 1909 --
       disp. mixed religion, Date and Remarks; Rev. J. B. Weimer,
       Minister

 92   MASAR, DIVIS, Horney Lhota age 21 to JANEK, FRANCES, Moravia age
       18; .. Masar, Horney Lhota and Mary Keccherova, Kutlova,
       Frank Janek, Dobokovici and Frances Novosad, Provodovge,
       Parents and Origin; Mr. Hamplon, Witness; July 27, 1911 --
       disp banns, Date and Remarks; Rev. J. B. Weimer, Minister

17   MATYOWSKY, THEODORE to PAYSSE, BERNADETTE, Galveston; Henry
     Matyowski, Poland and Mary Rose, Germaine Paysse, France and
     Marie Angelice Pairis, France, Parents and Origins; John
     Bapt. Paysse and Mr. Matyowsky (father), Witnesses;
     September 25, 1902 -- disp two banns, Date and Remarks;
     Rev. J. B. Weimer, Minister

57   MATELA, JOSEPH, Moravia, Austria to SCHESTA, SOPHIE, Moravia,
     Austria; Ignatius Matela and Rosalie Pospical, Joseph
     Schestak and Catherine Waslavik, all from Moravia, Parents
     and Origin; Ven Sr M. Elizabeth and Xenia Wilke, Witnesses;
     October 26, 1907, Date; Rev. J. B. Weimer, Minister

172 MATELSKY, HENRY HERMAN, Houston or Bremond age 22 to POLKA,
     LOUISE ELLA, Houston or Bremond age 24; Frank Matelsky and
     Catherine Snider, Albert Polka and Anna Maducia, Parents;
     John Peine and Otto Jos Jordan, Witnesses; July 8, 1923, Date;
     Rev. P. M. Lennartz, Minister

198 MATTE, WILSON, Eunice, La. age 35 to GARY, MABEL MARIE, Sulphur,
     La. age 20; Jean Baptiste Matte and Melanie Lebeauf, both
     Eunice, La., Erville Gary and Phelian Rodriguez, both Erath,
     La., Parents and Origins; Francis J. Pameri and Mary Garrie,
     Witnesses; March 31, 1937 -- Validatio, Date and Remarks;
     Rev. A. M. Maechler, Minister

100 MATYSEK, CHARLES, Moravia, Austria age 22 to MYLCOVA, HEDWIG,
     Moravia, Austria age 18; Frank Matysek and Anna Tchakovan,
     Ignaz Mylkova and Barbara Kuhalova, all from Moravia, Parents
     and Origin; Gregory Vanek and Frances Kamikova, Witnesses;
     May 30, 1912 -- disp two banns, Date and Remarks; Rev. P. M.
     Lennartz, Minister

5   MAURER, JOSEPH M., Galveston age 25 to HAMELIN, INEZ ELOISE,
     Galveston age 18; John Maurer, Baden and Caroline Scheer,
     Austria, Parents; Frank Ressel and Mary Biron, Witnesses;
     April 9, 1901, Date; Rev. J. B. Weimer, Minister

214 MC INERNEY, EDWARD, Galveston age 25 to CORNETT, WILLEWA MARY,
     Galveston age 19; Daniel B. McInerney and Catherine Dana,
     James Cornett and Almeda Eddy, Parents; Frank Lyle and
     Ethel Mae Lyle, Witnesses; December 27, 1941, Date; Rev. A. M.
     Maechler, Minister; Validatio

213 MEIERS, EUGENE FRED., San Diego, Calif. age 29 to PINKENBURG
     (nee Allwood), MARY, Galveston age 30; Louis Ly. Meiers,
     Germany and Kathleen Naylor, Holland, Sidney Allwood, England
     and Louise Porterhouse, Galveston, Parents and Origins;
     Julus Magnani and Sisie Magnani, Witnesses; November 23, 1941,
     Date; Rev. A. M. Maechler, Minister

165 MERSINGEN (?), EDW. LAWRENCE, Galveston age 39 to BREEN, ALICE,
     Galveston age 26; Lawrence Mersinger and Agnes Duffy, Martin
     Breen and Catherine Lang, Parents; Mr. and Mrs. William
     Stevens (ux. nee Breen), Witnesses; February 8, 1922, Date;
     Rev. P. M. Lennartz, Minister

118 MILES, LAWRENCE ABBOTT, n.c., Galveston to BENDIXEN, ANNA MARY,
     Galveston; F. J. Miles and Elva Willoughby, George Bendixen
     and Mary Heinlein, Parents; George and Pauline Bendixen,
     Witnesses; April 2, 1914 -- disp obt., Date and Remarks;
     Rev. P. M. Lennartz, Minister

12 MUELLER (MILLER), CHARLES AUGUST, n.c., Germany to BOLTON, MARY
   ELIZABETH, Galveston; John Henry Bolton and Anna Fagan,
   Parents; parentes uxoris ut supra, Witnesses; December 14, 1901
   -- disp mixed religion, Date and Remarks; Rev. J. B. Weimer,
   Minister

47 MILLER, ROBERT, Galveston to MENZEL, IDA, Galveston; April 1, 1907,
   Date; Rev. J. B. Weimer, Minister

167 MONSHAUSEN, JOHN, Germany age 50 to ZERNA, METHA JOAN (nee Mueller)
    Germany age 38; Henry Jaeckel and Mary Berginius, Witnesses;
    August 2, 1922, Date; Rev. P. M. Lennartz, Minister

    MUELLER, CHAS. see above Number 12

121 NEUSTAPA, ..., Ennis, Texas to PATEROVA, SOPHIE, Shotakova,
    Moticin, Austria; Matthias Neustapa and Anna Velels, Joseph
    Paterova and Emily Shotakova, Parents; June (sic) E. Green
    and Matth. Muzar, Witnesses; June 6, 1914, Date; Rev. P. M.
    Lennartz, Minister

46 NIGHTWINE, CHARLES KANE, Missouri age 43 to MC CLEERY, JENNIE
   LOUISE, Missouri age 31; Chas Aug Nightwine, Penna. and
   Elizabeth Jane O'Kane, Ireland, Samuel McClerry, Topeka, Kan.
   and Mary Levering, Parents and Origin; Catherine Barbong,
   Xenia Wilke, Witnesses; January 1907 -- disp. mixed religion,
   Date and Remarks; Rev. J. B. Weimer, Minister

81 NOWROSKI, JOSEPH, Germany to KULIKOWSKA, FRANCES, Germany;
   Parentes amborum ex Germania, Parents; John Thiem and W.
   Figoski, Witnesses; April 3, 1910, Date; Rev. A. J. Snebelen,
   S. J., Minister

221 O'DONOHOE, CLARENCE W., Galveston age 26 to MILES, MARY ANN,
    Galveston age 23; Th. O'Donohoe and Rachel L. Williams,
    Lawrence A. Miles and Anna M. Bendixen, Parents; Ben D. Miles
    and Mrs. Paul Gamble, Witnesses; January 11, 1947, Date;
    Rev. A. M. Maechler, Minister

166 OSTERMAYER, LOUIS, Galveston age 23 to WAGNER, ALICE H., California
    age 17; Arthur Ostermayer and Lillian Hasselmeyer, Truitt
    Wagner and Clara Saeschen, Parents; Fred Maury Hasselmeyer
    and Mattie Hasselmeyer, Witnesses; June 21, 1922 -- disp obt.,
    Date and Remarks; Rev. P. M. Lennartz, Minister

200 OWENS, BENNIE F. JR., Galveston age 23 to SCHOCKE, FLORINE LUCILLE,
    Galveston age 23; Bennie F. Owens, Dallas and Mary Elizabeth
    Ryan, Galveston, Ww F. Schocke, Galveston and Annie Lee
    Williams, New Orleans, La., Parents and Origins; Marvin Owens
    and Lois Schocke, Witnesses; September 4, 1937, Date; Rev.
    A. M. Maechler, Minister

60 PETERSEN, ANTON CHRISTIAN, Denmark age 24 to HANSEN, ANNA
   JOSEPHINE, Galveston age 21; Rasmus Chr. Petersen, Denmark and
   Anna Christine Andersdatter, ibid, Alfr Christina Hansen,
   Denmark and Rosina Baumann, Wuertemberg, Parents and Origins;
   April 22, 1908 -- disp mixed religion, Date and Remarks;
   Rev. J. B. Weimer, Minister

109 PIERSEN, MARY ANDREW, Galveston age 28 to GOTTLOB, MARY FRANCES,
    Galveston age 22; Andrew Luke Piersen and Margaret Williams,
    John Gottlob and Mary Friederich, Parents; June 4, 1913, Date;
    Rev. P. M. Lennartz, Minister

29   PINKENBURG, FREDERIC to STUMPF, MARY THERESA, Galveston; William
      Stumpf and Wallduren Baden, Parents; John Earls and Walter
      Moore, Witnesses; January 18, 1905 -- disp for mixed marriage,
      Date and Remarks; Rev. J. B. Weimer, Minister

162   PLUMMER, JAMES TUCKER, Galveston age 23 to MONSHAUSEN, FRANCES
      LOUISE, Galveston age 25; Vemes Willis Plummer and Louise
      Raubshaulz, John Monshausen and Selma Pflum, Parents;
      Douglas Plummer and Joan Monshausen, Witnesses; June 29, 1921,
      Date; Rev. P. M. Lennartz, Minister

20   POTTER, WILLIAM, Houston age 25 to NONUS, LYDIA MARY, Galveston
      age 20; Leo William Potter and Martha Anderson, Emmanuel
      Jackson Nonus and Angela Pinto, Parents; Charles Ressel and
      Magdalen Gaschen, Witnesses; May 18, 1903 -- disp dispar cult,
      Date and Remarks; Rev. J. B. Weimer, Minister

111   POUR, JAROSLAV, Bohemia, Austria to PACAL, MARY, Croatia;
      Joseph Pour and Anna Rehak, Aloysius Pacal and Barbara Rayer,
      Parents; Carl Westerfeld and Manuel T. Astrow, Witnesses;
      July 17, 1913, Date; Rev. P. M. Lennartz, Minister

201   PRETS, STEVE, Gerisdorf, Austria age 57 to REPOSE (nee Kovacs),
      THERESA, San Nikolia, Badapest, Hungary age 58; Thomas Prets,
      Gerisdorf and Anna ...., Borisdorf, Austria, Joseph Kovacs and
      Regina Lapat, both Budapest, Parents and Origins; Mr. and Mrs.
      John Prets, Witnesses; November 10, 1937 -- disp from Banns,
      Date and Remarks; Rev. A. M. Maechler, Minister

94   PRETS, THOMAS, Hungary to LAGLER, CECILE, Hungary; Thomas Prets
      and Anna Crissmanik, both Hungary, Henry Lagler and Martha
      Blasovic, both Hungary, Parents and Origins; Stephan Lagler
      and John Joseph Stumpf, Witnesses; November 12, 1911, Date;
      Rev. P. M. Lennartz, Minister

164   PUSKER, MICHAEL, Hungary age 33 to TURBA, JULIA, Hungary; Louis
      Pusker and Anna Kirz, Charles Turba and Julia Glockner,
      Parents; Louis Kerpel and Erick Eggeling, Witnesses; November
      5, 1921, Date; Rev. P. M. Lennartz, Minister

115   RASNOWSKY, ALOIS, Ryshaltice, Austria to CADAN, JULIA, Mirtek,
      Austria; Vincent Rasnowsky and Mary Kous, Anton Cadan and
      Antonia Seibert, Parents; F. Veuil and Mary Hackel, Witnesses;
      November 26, 1913, Date; Rev. P. M. Lennartz, Minister

130   RATLIFF, LESLIE ALFRED, Galveston to KIRK, MARGARET ELIZABETH,
      Galveston; Henry Alfred Ratliff and Minnie Pink, Thomas
      Joseph Kirk and Elizabeth Moser, Parents; Edward George Seale
      and Flora Seale (Kirk), Witnesses; August 2, 1916 -- disp
      mixed religion, Date and Remarks; Rev. P. M. Lennartz,
      Minister

85   RICKE, JOSEPH CHARLES, Galveston age 24 to FLECKENSTEIN, ROSA,
      Caldwell, Texas age 23; Parentes sponsi ex westphalia, Bavaria,
      sponsae ex Bavaria ambo, Parents; Jacob Fuchs and Mary Ricke,
      Witnesses; January 30, 1911, Date; Rev. J. B. Weimer, Minister

70   RIVAUX, GEORGE, Galveston age 21 to WERDEHAUSEN, AGNES LOUISE,
      Galveston age 20; Louis Rivaux, France and Caroline Kaufmann,
      William Werdehausen and Agnes Smith, Parents and Origins;
      D. J. Sweeney and Edna M. Werdehausen, Witnesses; February 10,
      1909, Date; Rev. J. B. Weimer, Minister

53   ROBERTSON, OSCAR, Galveston to WILRYCX, LEONA, Galveston;
      Samuel Robertson and Catherine Burke, Charles and Regina
      Wilrycx, Holland, Parents and Origins; Edmund Dorthy and
      Rosaline Dorothy, Witnesses; October 1, 1907 -- renovatio
      consensus, Date and Remarks; Rev. J. B. Weimer, Minister

192   RODRIGUEZ, CLIFTON JOHN, New Iberia, La. age 23 to VINCENT, MARY
         DILTA, Delcambre, La. age 22; Hubert Rodriguez, Jeanerette, La.
         and Laura Lyon, Lognion, ibid, Eugene Vincent, Youngsville,
         La. and Rosina Perez, Lafayette, La., Parents and Origins;
         J. E. Champagne and Mrs. David Norris, Witnesses; February 10,
         1935 -- Validatio, Date and Remarks; Rev. A. M. Maechler,
         Minister

193   ROGERS, HOWARD A., New Orleans, La. age 24 to CORCA, GRACE MARIE,
         New Orleans, La. age 20; Carles Rogers, Jeanerette, La. and
         Euola Aucoin, Eratha, La., Joseph Corca and Edna Wood, both
         New Orleans, La., Parents and Origin; E. J. Rogers and Elva
         Rhodes, Witnesses; June 2, 1935, Date; Rev. A. M. Maechler,
         Minister

183   ROTHSPRACK, HENRY WILLIAM, Galveston age 29 to SENESCHAL, ROSE
         HENRIETTE, Galveston age 30; Louis Ww Seneschal and Rose
         Grenrood, Fred Ww Rothsprack and Frances Cath. Sensen,
         Parents; John Patrick Mullen and Cecile Dircks, Witnesses;
         September 11, 1926, Date; Rev. P. M. Lennartz, Minister

205   RUNFOLA, JOSEPH, New Orleans, La. age 34 to AUGUSTINE, JENNY,
         Los Angeles, Calif. age 32; Gabriel Runfola, Italy and Mary
         Russo, Sicily, Salvatore Augustine, Italy and Rosalie Trainer,
         Parents and Origins; Gabrile Gulotta and Rosalie Palermo,
         Witnesses; September 24, 1939, Date; Rev. A. M. Maechler,
         Minister

 62   RUSSI, CHARLES, Houston age 21 to CONLIN, MATTIE, Houston age 18;
         Michael Russi and Mary Heine, Frank Conlin and Jenny Jinkens,
         Parents; Adam Fuchs and Mrs. Agnes Fuchs, Witnesses; July 15,
         1908 -- disp mixed religion, Date and Remarks; Rev. J. B.
         Weimer, Minister

125   SABATIER, JEAN GEORGE CHARLES, New Orleans, La. age 26 to
         SCHOCKE, MINNIE ANNA WILHELMINE, Galveston; Charles and Mary
         Sabatier, New Orleans, La., John and Ottilia Schocke, Galveston,
         Parents; Thomas Brown and Cecilia Schocke, Witnesses; March 4,
         1915, Date; Rev. P. M. Lennartz, Minister

219   SCHEXNAYDER, PHILIMIER M., Henry La. age 31 to BOUSE, EVELYN,
         Port Bolivar age 23; Romuald Schexnayder and Agnes Rodriguez,
         John Bouse and Mattie Lane, Parents; Ambrose Trahan and Mrs.
         Lola S. Viator, Witnesses; June 20, 1943 -- Revalidatio --
         disp banns, Date and Remarks; Rev. A. M. Maechler, Minister

122   SCHIESSEL, IGNATIUS, Muellersbert z/d Schlag, Moravia, Austria
         to ANDRASCHKA, MARY - same place; Lawrence Schiessel and
         Catherine Kahlenberger, Peter Kinsey and Barbara Andraschka,
         Parents; Mrs. Henrietta Rau and Catherine Rupprecht,
         Witnesses; June 8, 1914, Date; Rev. P. M. Lennartz, Minister

 84   SCHINDLER, THOMAS, Weimar, Texas to HUVER, ANNA, Weimar, Texas;
         Anton Schindler, Austria and Mary Warne, Bernardo, Texas,
         Francis Huver and Mary Haine, Parents and Origin; Elizabeth
         Lenz and Rose Senechal, Witnesses; January 11, 1911 -- disp
         three banns, Date and Remarks; Rev. J. B. Weimer, Minister

134   SCHMIDT, JULIUS WILLIAM, Galveston to SMITH, MARGARET LOUISE,
         Galveston; Gustave Schmidt and Julia Lowenstein, James Smith
         and Brigid Duffy, Parents; Henry Ritzler and Ferdinand Berner,
         Witnesses; February 18, 1917 -- disp mixed religion, Date and
         Remarks; Rev. P. M. Lennartz, Minister

9   SCHMUCK, REINHOLD, Galveston to MELVILLE, ELIZABETH, Galveston;
        Frank Schmuck and Theresa Prillwitz, Parents; William Prouse
        and Mary Sullivan, Witnesses; July 17, 1901 -- disp for mixed
        marriage, Date and Remarks; Rev. J. B. Weimer, Minister

112   SCHOCKE, HERMAN ALOYSIUS, Galveston to RATZMAN, ROSALIE WILHELMINE,
        Galveston; Herman Martin Schocke and Christine Mar, Fred W.
        Ratzman and Josephine Ring, Parents; Max Eisenbach and Bertha
        Schocke, Witnesses; August 6, 1913, Date; Rev. P. M. Lennartz,
        Minister

10   SCHWARZ, MATTHIAS, Boerne, Texas to BEHRENS (nee Schneider),
        LOUISE, San Antonio, Texas; Michael Schwarz, Bavaria and
        Marguerite Hoff, Jacob Schneider, Hesse-Darmstadt and
        Catherine Steiner, Nassau, Parents and Origins; Ven Sr. M.
        Wilhelmine, div pr and Susan Stelzel, Witnesses; August 10,
        1901 -- banns omitted, Date and Remarks; Rev. J. B. Weimer,
        Minister

137   SCOTT, CHARLES BENJAMIN, Galveston age 30 to SCHOCKE, CLARA
        MARGARET Galveston age 21; Charles Fred Scott and Grace
        Elizabeth Kyle, William Fred Schocke and Theresa Rehmann,
        Parents; William Fred Schocke and Anna Schocke, nee Williams,
        Witnesses; January 9, 1918, Date; Rev. P. M. Lennartz, Minister

58   SEIBEL, GEORGE, Hessen age 27 to MENTZEL, MARY ELIZABETH Galveston
        age 23; James Seibel, Hessen and ....., Charles Mentzel,
        Breslau, Silesia and Mary Anna Hornung, Rheinpfalz, Parents
        and Origins; Anton Lenz and Charles Mentzel, Witnesses;
        December 24, 1907 -- disp mixed religion, Date and Remarks;
        Rev. J. B. Weimer, Minister

132   SHUKANES, STEPHAN ANDREW, Hungary to VILLENEUVE, CECILE J.,
        Galveston; Jura and Catherine Shukanes, John Villeneuve and
        Anna Banner, Parents; Robert W. Finn and Mary Margaret
        Villeneuve, Witnesses; September 20, 1916, Date; Rev. P. M.
        Lennartz, Minister

147   SIKICH, WALTER Galveston age 22 to ROACH, ALICE Galveston age 20;
        Robert and Louise Sikich, Arthur and Lannie Roach, Parents;
        George Schroth and Leana Poetz, Witnesses; October 8, 1919,
        Date; Rev. P. M. Lennartz, Minister

97   SIMONIZ, MARK, Austria age 27 to KRASIVIZ, MARY Austria; Matthias
        Simoniz and Kostiliz Anna Mettlika, Mark Krasiviz and Anna
        Neniniz, all from Austria, Parents and Origins; B. Morton
        and Rev. J. E. Reifschneider, Witnesses; March 7, 1912, Date;
        Rev. P. M. Lennartz, Minister

160   SIMPSON, NEAL CAVITT, Galveston age 31 to STUMPF, ANNA MAY,
        Galveston age 18; Charles Neal Simpson and Mary Ann Conway,
        John Joseph Stumpf and Anna Mary Ballington, Parents;
        Chas. William Stuart and Emma Th. Hanson, Witnesses; June 2,
        1921 -- disp mixed religion, Date and Remarks; Rev. P. M.
        Lennartz, Minister; *(Divorced and married a Price, J.L.)*

212   SIMPTON, ERNEST EUGENE, Kaplen, Texas age 30 to BROUSSARD, ELJIE,
        Maurice, La.; Leslie Fern Simpton and Anna Laura Kahla, both
        from Bolivar peninsula, Alphie Broussard, Lafayette, La. and
        Eloge Broussard, Vermilion parish, La., Parents and Origins;
        Aaron Broussard and Reina Norris, Witnesses; October 29, 1941--
        disp mixed religion and disp cult, Date and Remarks; Rev.
        A. M. Maechler, Minister

140   SKARKE, HERBERT OSCAR, Galveston age 21 to WEAVER, JIMMIE
       ELIZABETH, Galveston; Chas. Joseph Skarke and Anna Boehm,
       Leonard Weaver and Ella Griffon, Parents; Ernest Marrart
       and Beulah Weaver, Witnesses; May 13, 1918, Date; Rev. P. M.
       Lennartz, Minister

74   SKROBANEK, ADOLF, Amansville, La. age 25 to TILL, THERESA, Weimar,
       Texas age 19; John Skrobanek and Anna Paula, both Bohemia,
       Stephan Till and Theresa Beyer, Parents and Origins; Frank
       Chwostek and Anthony Vasla, Witnesses; April 26, 1909, Date;
       Rev. J. B. Weimer, Minister

90   SMETANA, FRANK CHARLES, Bohemia age 21 to WEVERKOVA, FRANCES,
       Prague age 19; Joseph Smetana, Aussig and Frances Weverkova,
       ..... and Medo Ugesdo, Praha, Bohemia, Parents and Origins;
       Matthias Muzar and Raymond Miller, Witnesses; May 29, 1911 --
       disp consang primi grad, Date and Remarks; Rev. J. B. Weimer,
       Minister

189   SONNIER (SOULNIER), OLLIE age 21 to NAQUIN, URSULA URA age 18;
       Valcin Sonnier, Lafayette, La. and Laura Savois, ibid, Adam
       Naquin and Sarah Lemaire, both Abbeville, La., Parents and
       Origins; N. D. Broussard and Amelia Naquin, Witnesses;
       August 7, 1932 -- disp banns - Validatio, Date and Remarks;
       Rev. A. M. Maechler, Minister

35   SPRINGER, CAJUS, Demark to BOENING (nee Heinrich), MARY, High
       Hill, Texas; Fred Majus Springer and Anna Mary Juergersen,
       both Denmark, Joseph Heinrich and Mary Kainer, both Austria,
       Parents and Origin; Charles Springer and Charles Skarke,
       Witnesses; February 20, 1906, Date; Rev. J. B. Weimer,
       Minister

69   STANSFILED, CHARLES BONART, Galveston age 23 to ROBINIUS, MARTHA
       MARY, Saarbruecken age 20; James Ww Stansfiled, W. Va. and
       Caroline Moors, John Jos. Robinius, Saarbruecken and Mary
       Marcion, Parents and Origins; Andrew Smith and Caroline
       Stansfield, Witnesses; February 3, 1909 -- disp mixed religion,
       Date and Remarks; Rev. J. B. Weimer, Minister

4   STEGER, BASIL, New Braunsfels, Texas to DARRAS, FELICITAS,
       Galveston; John Steger and Mary Brosovic, Parents; Henry
       Winker and Julius Darras, Witnesses; March 19, 1901, Date;
       Rev. J. B. Weimer, Minister

24   STELZEL, RICHARD WIGAND, Roxheim, Germany to MARTIN, MARY,
       Strassburg, Alsace; John Stelzel, Prussia and Barbara Weimer,
       Coblentz, John Martin, Constanz, Baden and Ernestine Steinbach,
       Baden, Parents and Origins; John Schorpp and Ella Powell,
       Witnesses; January 1904, Date; Rev. J. B. Weimer, Minister

142   STINES, WILLIAM JAMES, Galveston age 42 to FIESEL, MARY, Galveston
       age 30; Marion Smith Stines and Mary Ellen, August Fiesel and
       Antonia Schiedel, Parents and Origins; Adolf C. Becker and
       Emma Fiesel, Witnesses; September 9, 1918, Date; Rev. P. M.
       Lennartz, Minister

127   STRICKLAND, JOSEPH A., Galveston to SENA, DELPHINE, El Paso, Texas;
       Joseph Strickland and Susan Adams, Emmanuel Sena, Albuquerke,
       New Mexico and Nora Hartez, ibid, Parents and Origins; Adam
       Fuchs and James Fuchs, Witnesses; January 30, 1916 -- disp
       dispar cult, Date and Remarks; Rev. P. M. Lennartz, Minister

155   STUBBS, FRANK SPENCER, Galveston to GOTTLOB, CECILE, Galveston;
       John Adam Stubbs and Virginia McDonald, John Gottlob and Mary
       Friederich, Parents; Walter Eggers and Thomas Shaw, Witnesses;
       November 25, 1920, Date; Rev. P. M. Lennartz, Minister

102   STUMPF, JOHN JOSEPH, Galveston to HERMANN, CATHERINE HELEN,
      Galveston; William Stumpf and Mary Sattler, Ferdinand
      Hermann and Catherine Ahl, Parents; Joseph Keppler and Anna
      Bridges, Witnesses; October 3, 1912 -- disp two banns, Date
      and Remarks; Rev. P. M. Lennartz, Minister

179   SWEENEY, JAMES JOSEPH, Galveston age 19 to JUNKER, ANITA MARY,
      Galveston age 17; John Joseph Sweeney and Brigid O'Connor,
      T. William Junker and Julia Murray, Parents; John Parker and
      Mary Agnes Holmes, Witnesses; September 16, 1924, Date;
      Rev. P. M. Lennartz, Minister

209   TAX, NICHOLAS ALOYSIUS, Hitchcock, Texas age 23 to SANDERS,
      THELMA LEE, Atoka, Okla. age 20; Joseph Frank Tax, Brenham
      and Isabel Joan Yeager, Geo. Ww. Snaders and Zula Rogers,
      both Okla., Parents and Origins; Joe Frank Tax Jr. and
      Loretta Tax, Witnesses; October 26, 1940 -- disp mixed
      religion and disp cult, Date and Remarks; Rev. A. M. Maechler,
      Minister

 80   THELE, AUGUST JOSEPH, Cape Girardeau, Mo. age 38 to KAPROLAT,
      AUGUSTA, Nausenden, E. Prussia age 35; William Thele and
      Antonia Breekmann, both Hannover, Fred Kaprolat and Wilhelmine
      Lucat, Parents and Origins; H. F. Weber and Kate Barbona,
      Witnesses; December 20, 1909 -- disp (?) from Dallas chancery,
      Date and Remarks; Rev. J. B. Weimer, Minister

197   THIEM, RICHARD, Galveston age 23 to FORDER, ELLEN LEONTINE, age
      21; Emil Thiem, Germany and May Simmons, Pt. Isabel, Texas,
      Fred Alb. Forder, London, England and Julia Moth, Galveston,
      Parents and Origins; Nyman Stetter and Dolores M. Chassaniol,
      Witnesses; January 30, 1937 -- disp mixed religion, Date and
      Remarks; Rev. A. M. Maechler, Minister

 11   TISCHENDORF, GEO. CONSTANTINE, Galveston to ABADIE, CECILE,
      Galveston; Constantine Tischendorf and Caroline Hummel,
      August Abadie and Chlothilde Monteaut, Parents; Charles
      Holzworth and Leah Abadie, Witnesses; October 9, 1901 -- disp
      mixed religion, Date and Remarks; Rev. G. A. Rittmeyer, S. J.,
      Minister

135   TOBLEMAN, HARRY REINHARD, Galveston age 29 to SOMMER, THERESA G.,
      Galveston age 25; John Reinhard Tobleman and Anna Widdemeyer,
      August Sommer and Mary Hergott, Parents; Norman Clarence
      Tobleman and Pauline A. Carroll, Witnesses; May 23, 1917 --
      disp. mixed religion, Date and Remarks; Rev. P. M. Lennartz,
      Minister

210   TRAHAN, AMBROSE, Maurice, La. age 30 to DUBOIS, THELESSIA, Lake
      Arthur, La. age 31; Francois Trahan and Emma Simon, both
      Lafayette, La., Israel Dubois, Gedon, La. and Duprea Trahan,
      Parents and Origins; Antoine Guidry and Mrs. Gaston Roberts,
      Witnesses; August 17, 1941 -- Validatio, Date and Remarks;
      Rev. A. M. Maechler, Minister

194   TRAMONTE, JOSEPH J., Galveston age 24 to PERRICONE, MARY CAMILLE,
      Alta Loma, Texas age 23; Sam Tramonte and Frances Messia, both
      from Ghibellina, Italy, Alphonse Perricone and Josephine
      Rosario Amaro, both Rhibeda, Italy, Parents and Origins;
      Dominic and Dinah Tramonte, Witnesses; June 15, 1935 -- disp.
      banns - Validatio, Date and Remarks; Rev. A. M. Maechler,
      Minister

180   VALUSEK, FERDINAND, Caldwell, Texas age 26 to WIHLANDER, ALICE,
      Galveston age 17; John Valusek and Emily Slavik, Henry
      Wihlander and Bertha Usnarsch, Parents; Louis Macik and Moli
      Macik, nee Valucek, Witnesses; October 29, 1924 -- disp mixed
      religion, Date and Remarks; Rev. P. M. Lennartz, Minister

15 VAN DEN ENDE, CATHOLICUS (sic), Galveston age 60 to NIEDERMANN
    (nee Patron), SOPHIE, Denmark age 52; ... Van den Ende and Mary
    Beckmann, Peter Patron and Mary Anderson, Parents; John Maurer
    and Caroline Scher, Witnesses; April 26, 1902, Date; Rev. J. B.
    Weimer, Minister

99 VANEK, GREGORY, Moravia, Austria age 25 to KARINKOVA, FRANCES,
    Moravia, Austria age 16½; Martin Vanek and Anna Clavikova,
    .... Karinkova and Mary Sdanice, all Moravia, Parents and
    Origins; Charles Matysek and Hedwig Milkova, Witnesses;
    May 30, 1912, Date; Rev. P. M. Lennartz, Minister

113 VORAUER, LUDWIG, Wallbach, Austria to HICKNER, CAROLINE,
    Reichensperg, Austria; John Vorauer and Mary Aigner, Frank
    Hickner and Catherine Arnold, Parents; George Monahan and Mary
    Chalker, Witnesses; September 4, 1913 - (Validatio?), Dates
    and Remarks; Rev. P. M. Lennartz, Minister

206 VOIGT, CARL HERMAN, Galveston age 24 to SCHOCKE, LOIS MARGUERITE,
    Galveston age 22; Herman Voigt and Martha Schroeder, both
    Germany, William Schocke and Anna Lee Williams, Parents and
    Origins; Bennie F. Owens, Jr. and Norma Lee Schocke, Witnesses;
    August 14, 1940 -- disp mixed religion and disp cult, Date and
    Remarks; Rev. A. M. Maechler, Minister

13 WAGNER, TRUE EATON, Illinois to GASCHEN, CLARA, Galveston; Paul
    Wagner and Alice Wise, ... Gaschen and Lena Haehnlein,
    Parents; April 8, 1902 -- disp mixed religion, Date and Remarks;
    Rev. J. B. Weimer, Minister

87 WANNEMACHER, CHARLES, Vienna, Austria age 22 to SPIES, HERMINE,
    Vienna, Austria age 23; Aloysius Wannemacher and Aloysia
    Wistermeier, Joseph Spies and Gabrielle Olaeu, all from
    Austria, Parents and Origins; John Gottlob and Lyda Walker,
    Parents; March 6, 1911 -- banns omitted, Date and Remarks;
    Rev. J. B. Weimer, Minister

    WEBSTER, see appendix, #228

34 WEIHAUSEN, CLAUS AUGUST to CRITTENDEN, LILLIAN LEONA, Galveston;
    Sidney Kraus and Evelyn Masey, Witnesses; January 31, 1906 --
    disp mixed religion, Date and Remarks; Rev. J. B. Weimer,
    Minister

185 WENZEL, ALPHONSE, New Braunfels, Texas to CASANEK, FRANCES, La
    Grange, Texas; Ferdinand Wenzel and Helen Liab, Joseph
    Casanek and Anna Baron, Parents; September 11, 1927, Date;
    Rev. P. M. Lennartz, Minister

158 WILSON, PAUL, St. Louis, Mo. age 22 to GOTTSELIG, IDA (adopted),
    Galveston age 18; Benjamin Wilson and Mabel ...., John
    Gottselig and Eugenia Heinz, Parents; George Wilson and
    Theresa Wolf, Witnesses; April 9, 1921, Date; Rev. P. M.
    Lennartz, Minister

78 WIRTH, OTTO. Wernigerode, N. Germany age 27 to SCHNEIDER, AGATHA,
    Pfaffenhausen, Wuertemberg age 24; August Wirth and Louise
    Becker, both Braunschweig, Germany, Jos. Schneider and
    Crescentia Steinle, both Wuertemberg, Parents and Origins;
    ... Harry and Mrs. Clover, Witnesses; June 13, 1909, Date;
    Rev. J. B. Weimer, Minister

82 WISCINSKI, WLADISLAS, Poland to ZACHARKS, ROSIE, Austria; John
    Wiscinski and Catherine Chokada, Russ. Poland, John and Anne
    Agnes Zacharks, Austria, Parents and Origins; Joe Smith and
    Steve Shouk (sic), Witnesses; May 8, 1910, Date; Rev. A. J.
    Snebelen, S. J., Minister

32   WOLFF, GEORGE JOSEPH, Galveston age 24 to JOHNSON, LUCILLE ROSE,
      Galveston age 20; Fred Wolff, Alsace and Rose Hornung, Bavaria,
      Geo. William Johnson and Emily Duly, Parents and Origins;
      Frederic and Frieda Wolff, Witnesses; July 19, 1905 -- disp
      dispar cult, Date and Remarks; Rev. Joseph J. Mack, Minister

157   WOODS, ALBERT, age 45 to SCHOCKE, CECILE C. T. O., Galveston age
      34; John Schocke and Catherine Schubert, Parents; Robert
      William Finn and Leonida Schocke, Witnesses; February 6, 1921,
      Date; Rev. P. M. Lennartz, Minister

88   YURKOVICH, MARK, Autovich, Dalmatia age 52 to MOSSER, ROSA,
      Spital a/a/ Drau, age 32; Grooms parents from Autovich,
      Dalmatia, Brides parents from Karnthen - Baldramsdorf, Parents
      Origins; ... Baehr and Homan Simpson, Witnesses; May 25, 1911
      -- disp banns, Date and Remarks; Rev. J. B. Weimer, Minister

169   ZAESKE, OSCAR F., Galveston age 26 to BUCKLEY, MYRTLE, Galveston
      age 17; Albert Zaeske, Germany and Mary Frieser, Thomas
      Buckley and Ida Lothringer, Parents and Origins; Fred Henry
      Becker and (Mrs.) Mildred Becker (nee Buckley), Witnesses;
      May 15, 1923, Date; Rev. P. M. Lennartz, Minister

184   ZECELICH, JOHN age 32 to KRECOVA, LIDA age 25; John and Mary
      Zecelich, Crossmarestaff, Austria, Jos. Krecova and Barbara
      Sheorlavin, Frankstadt a/Rh. ?, Parents and Origins; J.
      Kopecky and A. von Rotc, Witnesses; May 21, 1927, Date; Rev.
      P. M. Lennartz, Minister

207   ZIDEK, JOHN, Poth, Texas age 30 to WAGNER, CATHERINE M., Lincoln,
      Nebr. age 29; John Zidek and Mary Kuban, both Moulton, Texas,
      Herman Wagner and Christine Schmid, both Germany, Parents and
      Origin; Thomas P. Finn and Martha Meza, Witnesses; August 18,
      1940 - disp banns -- delegation from S. Heart, San Antonio,
      Date and Remarks; Rev. A. M. Maechler, Minister

45   ZINGELMANN, LOUIS F. C., Strelitz, Mecklenburg to MITCHELL
      (nee Kimmele), EMMA, Galveston; William Zingelmann and
      Christine Bengelsdorf, both Mecklenburg, George Michael
      Kimmele and Anna Barbara Froeber, both Bavaria, Parents and
      Origins; Frederic Duffard and Ida May Shotwell, Witnesses;
      February 6, 1907 -- disp mixed religion, Date and Remarks;
      Rev. J. B. Weimer, Minister

227   WALDRON, RICHARD LLOYD, Shreveport, La. age 22 1/3 to KNOPP,
      CLAUDIA ANN age 23½, San Antonio, Texas; Ww. Harold Waldron
      and Anna Belle Ferguson, Claude Knopp and Pauline Hasselmeier,
      Parents; E. S. Whitley and Elanor Sabatimo, Witnesses;
      November 26, 1958 -- disp mixed religion et disp cults ad
      cautelum obtenta, married at ...... rail by permission, V. PM.,
      Date and Remarks; Rev. A. M. Meachler, Minister

228   WEBSTER, LUDON GERALD, Port Arthur Texas age 19 to GANGI, JO ANN
      Galveston age 20; Kenneth B. Webster, Okla. and Louise Marg.
      Juneau, La., Jos. C. Gangi, Italy and Theresa Pistone, Alta
      Loma, Texas, Parents and Origins; Fred Cappadona and Jo Ann
      Marullo, Witnesses; Sunday, July 26, 1964, 10 a.m. mass,
      no disp. needed, Date and Remarks; Rev. A. M. Meachler,
      Minister

FUNERAL RECORDS
1860 - 1899

150   ALDRIDGE, ...   March 30, 1868; Rev. N. N., Minister

321   AMADEO, CECIL   October (?) 27, 1893; age 3½; Ignatius Amadeo and
      Louise Vitter, Parents; Rev. J. B. Weimer, Minister

198   ANDERSON, WILLIAM JAMES   July 17, 1872; age 15 months; Rev. Ch.
      Ch. Greyenbuehl, Minister

 18   ANONYMOUS, ...   September 22, 1861; Bavaria, Germany, Origin;
      Rev. Jos. Anstaett, Minister

  8   ANONYMOUS, ...   October 29, 1860; Rev. Jos. Anstaett, Minister

 42   ANONYMOUS, EDWARD   April 19, 1864; Rev. Jos. Anstaett, Minister

104   ANONYMOUS, LOUIS   November 2, 1866; From Switzerland, Origin;
      Rev. Jos. Anstaett, Minister

123   ANONYMOUS, MARCUS   August 12, 1867; Rev. Jos. Anstaett, Minister

 82   ANONYMOUS, ROBERT (orphan)   December 24, 1865; Rev. Jos. Anstaett,
      Minister

281   APPEL, ANNA (nee Wiechert)   February 23, 1889; about 39 years
      old; Rev. V. Gury, Minister

287   ARNOLD, ROSINA MATHILDA   November 7, 1889; age 2; Isidor Arnold
      and Mary Ann ...., Parents; Rev. V. Gury, Minister

124   AUCLAIR, CYRIL   August 12, 1867; Rev. Jos. Anstaett, Minister

 40   AULL, JAMES GEORGE   January 29, 1864; born July 25, 1863; Rev.
      Jos. Anstaett, Minister

148   BAIL, MARY   March 5, 1868; Rev. Jos. Anstaett, Minister

290   BATTI, MARGARET (Mrs.)   December 15, 1889; Rev. N. N., Minister

239   BAUHANS, ... (infant)   July 13, 1875; age 22 days; Rev. Ch.
      Ch. Greyenbuehl, Minister

371   BAUMANN, MARY MAGDALEN   February 28, 1897; age 10 months and
      16 days; Christian Baumann and Agnes Brockhoff, Parents;
      Rev. J. B. Weimer, Minister

181   BECKER, JOHN   April 7, 1871; Rev. Ch. Ch. Greyenbuehl, Minister

 94   BEERMANN, JOHN   August 15, 1866; Rev. Jos. Anstaett, Minister

318   BENDIXEN, GEORGE A.   August 11, 1893; age 23 months; Rev. J. B.
      Weimer, Minister

258   BENEDIXEN, GEORGE THOMAS (infant)   May 23, 1887; age 9 months;
      George Benedixen and Mary Haehnlein, Parents; Rev. V. Gury,
      Minister

141   BERGEN, JAMES   September 22, 1867; Rev. J. Anstaett, Minister

131   BERGMANN, ANTHONY   September 3, 1867; Rev. J. Anstaett, Minister

 43   BERGMANN, AUGUST   April 20, 1864; age 5 months; Rev. J. Anstaett,
      Minister

172   BEST, LOUIS JOHN   July .., 1870; age 8 months; Louis Best and
      Anna Tschaecke, Parents; Rev. N. Gaellweiler, Minister

322   BILLIGMANN, FREDERIC   February 22, 1894; age 67 years; Prussia,
      Germany, Origin; Rev. J. B. Weimer, Minister

28   BLEICKE, CAROLINE   October 17, 1862; age 4; Rev. Jos. Anstaett,
      Minister

1   BLEICKE, JOSEPH   June 15, 1860; West Phalia, Germany, Origin;
      first juneral; architect of church, Remarks; Rev. Jos. Anstaett,
      Minister

63   BLEICKE, JOSEPH G. M.   October 11, 1864; born November 10, 1860;
      Jos. Bleicke and Frances Bergenbusch, Parents; Rev. Jos.
      Anstaett, Minister

34   BLEICKE, THEODORE   March 9, 1863; Rev. Jos. Anstaett, Minister

11   BLEICKE, WILHELMINE   December 20, 1860; Rev. Jos. Anstaett,
      Minister

279   BOCK, PETER   December 8, 1888; age 58; Rev. V. Gury, Minister

69   BOCK, ...   October 7, 1865; Rev. Jos. Anstaett, Minister

301   BODDEKER, ANGELINA   February 6, 1891; age 83; Rev. J. Grabinger,
      Minister

199   BODDEKER, JOSEPH LEONARD   July 30, 1872; age 12 hours; Rev. Ch.
      Ch. Greyenbuehl, Minister

255   BONG, DOROTHY   July 26, 1880; age 76; Rev. H. Reiffert, Minister

362   BONN, HENRY   December 18, 1896; age 59; Rev. J. B. Weimer,
      Minister

151   BOUNCIL, ROSALE   July 24, 1868; Rev. Theo. Grundner, Minister

50   BOWDEN, CATHERINE   September 13, 1864; age 15; Ophaven, Prussia,
      Origin; Quirin Bowden and Sibyl Wend, Parents; Rev. L. C. M.
      Chambodut, Minister

284   BRAEUTIGAM, EDWARD   June 29, 1889; age 5 months; Peter and
      Henrietta Braeutigam, Parents; Rev. V. Gury, Minister

372   BRAMMER, PETER   March 8, 1897; age 7 months; Albert Brammer and
      Mary Schocke, Parents; Rev. J. B. Weimer, Minister

355   BRINK, ERNESTINE   June 3, 1896; age 66; Rev. J. B. Weimer,
      Minister

29   BROECKELMANN, THERESA   October 17, 1862; Rev. N. N., Minister

322   BROKHOF, FRANK   September 9, 1894; age 43; Rev. J. B. Weimer,
      Minister

293   BROKHOF, JOSEPH   June 28, 1890; Rev. J. Grabinger, Minister

129   BROCKHOF, JOSEPH   August 25, 1867; Rev. J. Anstaett, Minister

300   BROKHOF, THECLA   December 1, 1890; age 69; Rev. J. Grabinger,
      Minister

389   BROSING, AUGUSTA   October 2, 1898; age 24; Hugo Brosig and
      Louise Bloviar, Parents; Rev. J. B. Weimer, Minister

110   BROSIG, EMILY CATHERINE HENRIETTA   February 1, 1867; born
      December 1, 1866; Chas. Brosig and Mary Louise Koester,
      Parents; Rev. Jos. Anstaett, Minister

158   BROSIG, HUGO   February 7, 1869; age 4 years and 7 months;
      Rev.

158   BROSIG, HUGO   February 7, 1869; Age 4 years and 7 months;
      Rev. Thoe. Grundner, Minister

 59   BUCHMANN, JOSEPH   September 23, 1864; Age, about 30; Neudorf,
      Bohemia, Origin; Rev. Jos. Anstaett, Minister

109   BUCKLEY, JAMES   January 30, 1867; Age 14 days; Edward Buckley
      and Emily Spann, Parents; Rev. J. Anstaett, Minister

345   BUERGER, FREDERIC   July 24, 1895; Age 55; Westphalia, Germany,
      Origin; Rev. J. B. Weimer, Minister

286   BUERGER, GERTRUDE   October 12, 1889; Age 39; First wife of
      Frank W. Buerger, Remarks; Rev. V. Gury, Minister

341   BURKITT, JOHN THOMAS   March 28, 1895; Andrew John Burkitt and
      Cath. Blake, Parents; Rev. J. B. Weimer, Minister

366   BUSCH, MARGARET   January 22, 1897; Age 9; Rev. J. B. Weimer,
      Minister

149   BYRNE, TIMOTHY   March 15, 1868; Rev. N. N., Minister

143   CHARLOTTE, PETER   October 14, 1867; Age 34; Rev. Jos. Anstaett,
      Minister

296   CLAIRE, MARGARET   September 23, 1890; Age 5 days; Rev. J.
      Grabinger, Minister

325   CONNOR, MARGARET LOUISE   June 26, 1894; Age 29; Rev. J. B.
      Weimer, Minister

 21   CONRAD, ...   December .., 1861; Rev. Jos. Anstaett, Minister

358   COONEY, THOMAS FRANK   August 5, 1896; Age about 30; Rev. J. B.
      Weimer, Minister

307   CORK, ANGELIS   March 20, 1892; Age 9; Rev. Michael Heinzelmann,
      Minister

 47   DALLMER, ANN MARY   June 27, 1864; Age 6; George Dallmer and
      Ann Mary Schaub, Parents; Rev. L. C. M. Chambodut, Minister

 45   DALLMER, ERNEST A.   June 20, 1864; Born March 14, 1862; George
      Dallmer and Ann Mary Schaub, Parents; Rev. Jos. Anstaett,
      Minister

 97   DALLMER, GREGORY   September 6, 1866; Age 7 days; Rev. Jos.
      Anstaett, Minister

 19   DALLMER, PETER ALBERT   November 17, 1861; Born April 8, 1860;
      George Dallmer and Ann Mary Schaub, Parents; Rev. Jos.
      Anstaett, Minister

 26   DAVIS, MATHIDA B.   August 24, 1862; Age 44; Montreal, Canada,
      Origin; Rev. Jos. Anstaett, Minister

357   DE BARBIERIS, MARY   July 3, 1896; Age 79; Rev. J. B. Weimer,
      Minister

137   DECROS, FRUMENTIA   September 12, 1867; *) wife of Eli Decros,
      Remarks; Rev. Jos. Anstaett, Minister

361   DELZ, HAZEL DOROTHY LOUISE   November 9, 1896; Age 5 weeks;
      Rev. J. B. Weimer, Minister

113   DEMESY, ...   April .., 1867; Age 1; *) privately baptized,
       Remarks; Rev. Jos. Anstaett, Minister

347   DEROUX, CLARA   September 15, 1895; Age 85; Rev. J. B. Weimer,
       Minister

207   DINTER, EMMA   July 3, 1873; Age 9; Rev. Ch. Ch. Greyenbuehl,
       Minister

368   DINTER, HERMAN   January 30, 1897; Age 38; Rev. J. B. Weimer,
       Minister

223   DIRCKS, ANNA MARY (infant)   October 15, 1874; Rev. Ch. Ch.
       Greyenbuehl, Minister

107   DIRKS, GEORGE   January 13, 1867; Rev. Jos. Anstaett, Minister

231   DIRKS, JOSEPH   April 1875; Age 17; Rev. Ch. Ch. Greyenbuehl,
       Minister

 80   DIRKS, MARY ANN   November 5, 1865; Age 85; Rev. Jos. Anstaett,
       Minister

310   DIRKS, MARY CATHERINE (nee Franklin)   September 14, 1892; Age 62;
       Rev. J. B. Weimer, Minister

166   DORECK, JOSEPHINE (nee Schneider)   July 17, 1869; Rev. N.
       Gaellweiler, Minister

146   DORNIACK, PAULINE   January 10, 1868; Rev. Jos. Anstaett, Minister

295   DRAMMAN, ALBERT   August 5, 1890; Rev. J. Grabinger, Minister

262   DUBOIS, FREDERIC (infant)   November 17, 1887; Aage 8½; Rev. V.
       Gury, Minister

192   EDWARDS, ELIZABETH   May 14, 1872; Rev. Ch. Ch. Greyenbuehl,
       Minister

241   EDWARDS, JOSEPH   November 3, 1875; Age about 40; *) baptised
       conditionally on death bed, Remarks; Rev. Ch. Ch. Greyenbuehl,
       Minister

242   EGGERT, ...   January 3, 1876; Age about 96; Rev. Ch. Ch.
       Greyenbuehl, Minister

183   EGGERT, EMMA   May (?) 27, 1871; Age 8 days; Rev. Ch. Ch.
       Greyenbuehl, Minister

170   EGGERT, THEODORE RUDOLPH   June 28, 1870; Theodore Eggert and
       Rosalee Bunzel, Parents; Rev. N. Gaellweiler, Minister

268   EISENBACH, GEORGE EDWARD   February 14, 1888; Age 5; Baltazar
       Louis Ed. Eisenbach and Lena Teuchman, Parents; Rev. V. Gury,
       Parents; Rev. V. Gury, Minister

391   ELBERT, CHRISTINA   December 30, 1898; Age 83; Frankfort, Germany,
       Origin; Rev. J. B. Weimer, Minister

  3   ELBERT, JOHN   June 29, 1860; Rev. Jos. Anstaett, Minister

238   ELLINGER, EMMA   July 13, 1875; Age 11 months; G. Ellinger and
       ...., Parents; Rev. Ch. Ch. Greyenbuehl, Minister

271   ELSLER, JOSEPH (infant)   May 15, 1888; Age 4 months; Benjamin
       Elsler and Frances Franke, Parents; Rev. V. Gury, Minister

382   ELZNER, BENJAMIN   October 26, 1897; Age 49; Rev. J. B. Weimer,
       Minister

   7   EMILIANI, JOSEPHINE   October 21, 1860; Age 5½; Joseph Emiliani
       and Barbara Wagner, Parents; Rev. Jos. Anstaett, Minister

364   ERHOLD, MICHAEL   January 11, 1897; Age 65; Rev. J. B. Weimer,
       Minister

201   EYT, M.   .. 26, 1872; Age 73; Rev. Ch. Ch. Greyenbuehl, Minister

145   FALDERMEYER, BARBARA (alias Mayer)   December 19, 1867; Rev. J.
       Anstaett, Minister

377   FALKE, LOUISE   June 15, 1897; Age 36; Rev. Geo. Apel (per J. B.
       W.), Minister

121   FARREN, ELIZABETH   August 8, 1867; Rev. J. Anstaett, Minister

154   FINK, AMALIA   October 14, 1868; Age 23; Rev. Theo. Grundner,
       Minister

240   FINK, MARY ANN (GENGLER)   September 13, 1875; Rev. Ch. Ch.
       Greyenbuehl, Minister

 33   FISCHER, ANTHONY   January 2, 1863; Rev. J. Anstaett, Minister

283   FISHER, JOHN J.   June 17, 1889; Age 41; Rev. V. Gury, Minister

269   FIVEL, ALEXANDER F.   March 1, 1888; Age 13 months; Leopold
       Fivel and Elizabeth Marchand, Parents; Rev. V. Gury, Minister

384   FIVEL, ELIZABETH   April 10, 1898; Age 7; Leopold Fivel and
       Elizabeth Marchand, Parents; Rev. J. B. Weimer, Minister

392   FIVEL, LEOPOLD   January 26, 1899; Age about 9; Rev. Gus. Wiese,
       Minister

266   FLAKE, LAURA BERTHA   January 21, 1888; Age 16 months; Rev. V.
       Gury, Minister

213   FLUEHER, CONRAD   November 17, 1873; Age about 70; Rev. Ch. Ch.
       Greyenbuehl, Minister

 12   FOUNDLING, JOHN HENRY   December 23, 1860; Age 4 months; Rev. J.
       Anstaett, Minister

117   FRANKE, ...   July 29, 1867; Rev. J. Anstaett, Minister

243B   FRANKLIN, ... (infant)   March 18, 1876; Rev. Ch. Ch. Greyenbuehl,
       Minister

 53   FREEMAN, PATRICK   September 19, 1864; Rev. Jos. Anstaett, Minister

180   FREI, PAUL   April 19, 1871; Age 24; Reiselfingen, Baden, Origin;
       Rev. Ch. Ch. Greyenbuehl, Minister

373   FROHNE, ANN MARGARET MARY   March 20, 1897; Age 3½ months;
       Rev. H. B. Weimer, Minister

 44   FROSCH, CATHERINE   June 18, 1864; Age 6 months; George Frosch
       and ...., Parents; Rev. J. Anstaett, Minister

305   FUNK, MARY   January 27, 1892; Age 84; Rev. Mich. Heinzelman,
       Minister

 93   GAERTNER, CHARLES   August 10, 1866; Rev. Jos. Anstaett, Minister

119   GARMANN, JAMES   August 5, 1867; Rev. Jos. Anstaett, Minister

118   GARMAN, THEODORE   August 1, 1867; Rev. Jos. Anstaett, Minister

315   GARTH, DOROTHY AUGUSTA (Mrs.)   April 16, 1893; Age 36; Rev. J. B. Weimer, Minister

273   GARTH, JOHN LOUIS EMIL   June 14, 1888; Age 1; A. E. Garth and Dora Augusta Stoppelberg, Parents; Rev. V. Gury, Minister

187   GENGLER, CATHERINE   October 25, 1871; Age 74; Rev. Ch. Ch. Greyenbuehl, Minister

156   GENGLER, NICHOLAS   December 14, 1868; Age 79; Rev. Theo. Grundner, Minister

363   GENGLER, JOHN   January 3, 1897; Age 7; Rev. J. B. Weimer, Minister

259   GERTNER, PETER (infant)   July 11, 1887; Born October 7, 1886; Rev. V. Gury, Minister

 81   GINGLER, HERMAN   November 18, 1865; Age 3 years and 3 months; Rev. Jos. Anstaett, Minister

308   GLEICH, JOHN   June 8, 1892; Age 21; August Gleich and Mary O'Connor, Parents; Rev. J. B. Weimer, Minister

  9   GLOECKNER, ...   November 8, 1860; Rev. Jos. Anstaett, Minister

179   GRABSCH, AMALIA   November 27, 1870; Age 2 years and 1 month; Charles Grabsch and Amalia Ansen, Parents; Rev. Ch. Ch. Greyenbuehl, Minister

189   GRABSCH, CHARLES   November 27, 1871; Age 29; Rev. Ch. Ch. Greyenbuehl, Minister

247   GRAY, CAROLINE   August 26, 1876; Rev. Ch. Ch. Greyenbuehl, Minister

224   GRAY, JOHN (infant)   October 17, 1874; Age 9 days; William Gray and Caroline Young, Parents; Rev. Ch. Ch. Greyenbuehl, Minister

218   GRAY, WILLIAM   June 28, 1874; Age 16; William Gray and Caroline Young, Parents; Rev. H. Pefferkorn, Minister

263   GRUENROOD, MARY   January 2, 1888; Age 75; Rev. V. Gury, Minister

196   GUMINISKI, BRUNO   July 11, 1872; Rev. Ch. Ch. Greyenbuehl, Minister

       HAEHNLEIN, ...   April 1875; Rev. Ch. Ch. Greyenbuehl, Minister

205   HAENLEIN, ANNA URSULA   June 8, 1873; Henry Haenlein and Helen Haenlein, Parents; Rev. Ch. Ch. Greyenbuehl, Minister

184   HAENLEIN, HENRY   .. 29, 1871; Age 2½; Rev. J. Wm. Ruthman, S. S. C., Minister

204   HAGEMANN, HENRY   May 29, 1873; Rev. Ch. Ch. Greyenbuehl, Minister

311   HAMBURG, GERTRUDE   November 9, 1892; Age 14; Henry Hamburg and Barbara ..., Parents; Rev. J. B. Weimer, Minister

365   HANSEN, CATHERINE BARBARA   January 21, 1897; Age 3 years and 3 months; Rev. J. B. Weimer, Minister

233 HARDWIG, MARY (infant) April 25, 1875; Rev. Ch. Ch. Greyenbuehl, Minister

 35 HARRIS, ANNE ELISABETH March 23, 1863; Age 13; Adopted by Frances M. Kauder; Rev. Jos. Anstaett, Minister

346 HARTWIG, CHARLES August 1895; Age 57; Westphalia, Origin; Rev. J. B. Weimer, Minister

342 HEIDET, FRANK May 31, 1895; Age 48; Rev. J. B. Weimer, Minister

270 HEIMANN, ALICE April 18, 1888; Age 5½; Anthony Heimann and ..., Parents; Rev. V. Gury, Minister

245 HEYMANN, ANNA February 19, 1876; Age 10; Rev. Ch. Ch. Greyenbuehl, Minister

264 HEIMANN, ANTHONY January 3, 1888; Rev. V. Gury, Minister

 37 HEIMANN, FRANK September 1863; Age 3 months; Rev. J. Anstaett, Minister

285 HELFENSTEIN, MARY ELIZABETH July 23, 1889; Age 9 months; John and Elizabeth Helfenstein, Parents; Rev. V. Gury, Minister

277 HEMMES, PETER October 5, 1888; Age 58; Homerich, Lothringen, Origin; Rev. V. Gury, Minister

369 HERRGOTT, CECIL February 1, 1897; Age 76; Rev. J. B. Weimer, Minister

 48 HERRGOTT, JOSEPHINE August 1, 1864; Born September 1863; August Herrgott and Cecile ...., Parents; Rev. Jos. Anstaett, Minister

 68 HERRMANN, JOSEPH September 23, 1865; Born April 15, 1862; Rev. J. Anstaett, Minister

350 HERMANN, MATHIAS October 20, 1895; Age 74; Rev. J. B. Weimer, Minister

228 HIFFINGER, LOUIS November 12, 1874; Born in 1872; Bohemia, Origin; Rev. Ch. Ch. Greyenbuehl, Minister

215 HILDENBRAND, FRANZ BERNARD May 28, 1874; Age 69; Rev. H. Pefferkorn, Minister

 70 HOFBECK, ... October 12, 1865; Rev. J. Anstaett, Minister

246 HOFBECK, JOHN August 4, 1876; Rev. Ch. Ch. Greyenbuehl, Minister

125 HUSSEY, MICHAEL JR. August 13, 1867; Rev. J. Anstaett, Minister

138 HUSSEY, MICHAEL September 14, 1867; Rev. Jos. Anstaett, Minister

209 HUTCHISON, ANNA August 28, 1873; Age 53; Rev. Ch. Ch. Greyenbuehl, Minister

  2 HUTTER, LOUIS HERMAN June 27, 1860; Born April 15, 1860; Rev. Jos. Anstaett, Minister

 27 HUTZ, MARY September 5, 1862; Age 8; Rev. Jos. Anstaett, Minister

378 JACOBER, JOSEPH July 2, 1897; Age 29; Rev. George Apel (per Rev. J. B. W.), Minister

114   JAMISON, JOHN (convert)   May 26, 1867; Rev. Jos. Anstaett,
       Minister

165   JANSEN, CHARLES ROBERT   July 30, 1869; John Jansen and Frances
       Jersig, Parents; Rev. N. Gaellweiler, Minister

115   JANSEN, FRANCES   May 29, 1867; Born December 2, 1865; Rev. Jos.
       Anstaett, Minister

  5   JANSEN, JOAN WILHELMINE AEMILIA   September 28, 1860; Born
       December 11, 1859; John Jansen and Frances Jersig, Parents;
       Rev. Jos. Anstaett, Minister

306   JANSEN, JOHN   January 28, 1892; Age 56; Rev. Michael Heinzelmann,
       Minister

320   JERSIG, CHARLES   September 30, 1893; Age about 46; Rev. J. B.
       Weimer, Minister

206   JERSIG, JOHN   June 11, 1873; Born in 1805; Rev. Ch. Ch.
       Greyenbuehl, Minister

334   JOERGENS, AUGUSTA   November 7, 1894; Age 77; Rev. J. B. Weimer,
       Minister

326   JOHNSON, SOPHIE (nee Frohne)   July 29, 1894; Rev. J. B. Weimer,
       Minister

144   JOHNSON, ... (infant)   November 10, 1867; Rev. Jos. Anstaett,
       Minister

390   JORDAN, CHRISTIAN   December 26, 1898; Age 43; Rev. J. B. Weimer,
       Minister

153   JOSEPH, ELENORE JOSEPHINE   September 17, 1868; Age 8 days;
       Frank Joseph and Mary Ann Recheltlock, Parents; Rev. Theo.
       Grundner, Minister

 20   JUERSIG, MAGDALEN   December 4, 1861; Age 50; Rev. L. C. M.
       Chambodut, Minister

 96   JUNG, LOUIS   August 24, 1866; Age 10; Gustave Jung and Frances
       Schneider, Parents; Rev. Jos. Anstaett, Minister

134   JURGENS, WILLIAM   September 5, 1867; Rev. Jos. Anstaett, Minister

163   KAUDER, FRANK NICHOLAS   July 11, 1869; Age 35; Rev. N. Gaellweiler,
       Minister

280   KESSLER, PHILIP WALTER   January 5, 1889; Born November 16, 1887;
       Joseph Kessler and Carrie Primrose, Parents; Rev. V. Gury,
       Minister

 22   KIMLEY, AUGUST   June 24, 1862; Age 30; Rheinland, Origin;
       Rev. Jos. Anstaett, Minister

 51   KIMLEY, GEORGE   September 17, 1864; Born November 8, 1856;
       Michael Kimley and Anna Froeber, Parents; Rev. Jos. Anstaett,
       Minister

 57   KIMLEY, LOUISE CAROLINE   September 21, 1864; Age 2; Rev. Jos.
       Anstaett, Minister

 56   KIMLEY, MARY   September 20, 1864; Born January 21, 1859;
       Rev. Jos. Anstaett, Minister

17   KIMLEY, MARY (nee Gloeckner)   September 17, 1861; Rev. Jos.
        Anstaett, Minister

252   KIMMICK, ANDREW JAMES   May 11, 1879; Age 11 months; Andrew
        Kimmick and ..., Parents; Rev. Em. Fleury, Minister

202   KIRKER, JOHN   February 25, 1873; Rev. Ch. Ch. Greyenbuehl,
        Minister

275   KIRKPATRICK, CLINTON LEOPOLD   July 12, 1880; Age 20 months;
        Clinton Kirkpatrick and Octavia Marchand, Parents; Rev. V.
        Gury, Minister

171   KLOEPPER, ...(widow)   December 7, 1869; Rev. N. Gaellweiler,
        Minister

108   KNOPIER, JOHN   January 29, 1867; Lothringen, Germany, Origin;
        Rev. Jos. Anstaett, Minister

299   KOCH, ANNA   November 14, 1890; Age 3; Rev. J. Grabinger, Minister

298   KOCH, EMMA   October 9, 1890; Age 6; Rev. J. Grabinger, Minister

256   KOCH, HENRY   January 14, 1881; Rev. J. N. Leonard, Minister

335   KOCH, MARTIN BRUNO   December 17, 1894; Age 2 years and 10 months;
        Adam Koch and ... Koehler, Parents; Rev. J. B. Weimer,
        Minister

67   KOEHLER, ...   August 28, 1865; Rev. G. Berthet, Minister

222   KOESTER, WILHELMINA CAROLINE   October 17, 1874; Age 27; Rev.
        Ch. Ch. Greyenbuehl, Minister

62   KRAUS, CATHERINE   October 5, 1864; Age 60; Herbolsheim, Baden,
        Origin; Rev. Jos. Anstaett, Minister

100   KRAUS, FRANK   October 3, 1866; Born February 18, 1822;
        Herbolsheim, Baden, Origin; Rev. Jos. Anstaett, Minister

276   KRAUS, FRANK CORNELIUS   September 4, 1888; Age 11 months;
        Frederic John Kraus and ..., Parents; Rev. V. Gury, Minister

52   KRAUS, MARY HELEN   September 18, 1864; Born May 22, 1857; Frank
        Kraus and Catherine Kirchgaessner, Parents; Rev. Jos.
        Anstaett, Minister

36   KRONE, CATHERINE (nee Linnmann)   August 22, 1863; Age 66;
        Oldenburg, Germany, Origin; Rev. Jos. Anstaett, Minister

297   KUEHNE, THEODORE   October 6, 1890; Age 65; Rev. J. Grabinger,
        Minister

160   KUEMLIN, CAROLINE WALBURGA   May 18, 1869; Age 13 months; Rev.
        Theo. Grundner, Minister

257   KUFFNER, FRANCIS XAVIER   September 5, 1883; Rev. Jac. F. Lauth,
        C. S. C., Minister

351   KURPITEZ, LOUIS   January 7, 1896; Age 32; Rev. J. B. Weimer,
        Minister

112   LABADIE, NICHOLAS D.   March 13, 1867; Age 67; Canada, Origin;
        Rev. Jos. Anstaett, Minister

348   LAINE, ALBERT   September 15, 1895; Age 2 years and 2 months;
        Rev. J. B. Weimer, Minister

339   LANG, CATHERINE (nee Horn)   February 17, 1895; Age 83; Rev. J. B.
      Weimer, Minister

 31   LANG, ELIZABETH   October 21, 1862; Age 3; Rev. J. Anstaett,
      Minister

272   LANG, HERMAN CHARLES   May 23, 1888; Age 4 months; Michael Lang
      and Caroline Pfeifer, Parents; Rev. V. Gury, Minister

147   LANG, STEPHEN   January 31, 1868; Rev. J. Anstaett, Minister

 60   LANGE, HELEN (nee Stehlin)   September 29, 1864; Born May 20, 1833;
      Niederhausen, Baden, Origin; Sebastian Stehlin and Mary Ann
      Metzger, Parents; Rev. J. Anstaett, Minister

374   LASSOW, LOUIS RICHARD   March 25, 1897; Age 3 months; Rev. J. B.
      Weimer, Minister

 15   LATER, MARY   May 10, 1861; Born May 20, 1860; Rev. Jos. Anstaett,
      Minister

261   LEATHERN, JOHN   October 15, 1887; Age 14; Louis Leathern and
      ..., Parents; Rev. V. Gury, Minister

 83   LEINBACH, ELIZABETH   January 21, 1866; Rev. J. Anstaett, Minister

177   LEINBACH, ELIZABETH   September 21, 1870; Age 11; Rev. N.
      Gaellweiler, Minister

302   LONG, SUSAN   April 26, 1891; Age 75; Rev. J. Grabinger, Minister

274   LORDAN, MARY HORTENSE   July 12, 1888; Age 4; Jeremiah Lordan
      and M. Hortense Martial, Parents; Rev. V. Gury, Minister

338   LUDWIG, ANNA (nee Bergmann)   February 1895; Age 51; Rev. J. B.
      Weimer, Minister

 13   MALZBURGER, CATHERINE   February 8, 1861; Rev. Jos. Anstaett,
      Minister

265   MANSER, MARY   January 10, 1888; Age 44; Rev. V. Gury, Minister

343   MARCHAND, ERNEST   June 2, 1895; Age 8 months; Julius Marchand
      and Mary Fivel, Parents; Rev. J. B. Weimer, Minister

317   MARCHAND, FERDINAND HENRY   July 12, 1893; Age 9 months;
      Rerdinand Marchand and Lillie Rentsch, Parents; Rev. J. B.
      Weimer, Minister

381   MARKE, ANN (Mrs.)   September 20, 1897; Age 76; Rev. Geo. Apel
      (per J. B. W.), Minister

169   MATHISON, MELVIN   June 24, 1870; Malvin Mathison and Caroline
      Werdehausen, Parents; Rev. N. Gaellweiler, Minister

359   MATT, JOSEPH   September 9, 1896; Age 66; Rev. J. B. Weimer,
      Minister

356   MAURER, FREDERIC   July 1, 1896; Age 12½; James Maurer and
      Wilhelmin Bender, Parents; Rev. J. B. Weimer, Minister

313   MAURER, JAMES   January 8, 1893; Age 38; Baden, Germany, Origin;
      Rev. J. B. Weimer, Minister

292   MAURER, JOHN   February 8, 1890; Age 34; Peter Maurer and Lucia
      ..., Parents; Rev. L. Ph. Keller, Minister

16   MAURER, LOUISE   September 17, 1861; Age 2 years and 6 months;
      Peter Maurer and Lucie ..., Parents; Rev. J. Anstaett, Minister

191   MAURER, PETER   March 3, 1872; Rev. Ch. Ch. Greyenbuehl, Minister

193   MAURER, WENDELIN   June 6, 1872; Age 52; Rev. Ch. Ch. Greyenbuehl,
      Minister

367   MAYER, FRIDOLIN   January 29, 1897; Age 55; Rev. J. B. Weimer,
      Minister

111   MAYER, WILLIAM   March 8, 1867; Argentorato, Alsace, Origin;
      Rev. J. Anstaett, Minister

316   MC KAWENE, ANNA   May 27, 1893; Age 3 years and 1 month; Edward
      McKawere and Mary Hofbeck, Parents; Rev. J. B. Weimer, Minister

159   MEIER, JOSEPH   March 2, 1869; Age 40; Rev. Theo. Grundner,
      Minister

106   MICHALICK, ...   December 8, 1866; Rev. Jos. Anstaett, Minister

328- MICHEL, PHILIP JAMES   August 9, 1894; Age 35; Rev. J. B. Weimer,
      Minister

176   MICHEL, WILLIAM   September 15, 1870; Age 16; Henry Michel and
      ..., Parents; Rev. N. Gaellweiler, Minister

379   MEIBACH, CHARLES   July 15, 1897; Age 39; Rev. J. B. Weimer,
      Minister

182   MILLER, MARY   May 5, 1871; M. Miller and ..., Parents; Rev. Ch.
      Ch. Greyenbuehl, Minister

99   MITCHOULI, AGNES   September 10, 1866; Age 2; Rev. J. Anstaett,
      Minister

188   MOORE, LOUISE   November 6, 1871; Age 30; Rev. Ch. Ch. Greyenbuehl,
      Minister

200   MOSBAUER, JOHN   August 2, 1872; Age 49; Rev. Ch. Ch. Greyenbuehl,
      Minister

250   MOSER, ANNA   April 6, 1879; Age 81; Rev. Em Fleury, Minister

14   MOSER, ANNA CAROLINE   February 10, 1861; Age 11 months; Rev. Jos.
      Anstaett, Minister

289   MOSER, CAROLINE   November 30, 1889; Age 85; Rev. V. Gury, Minister

278   MOSER, URSULA   November 20, 1888; Age 7 weeks; John Moser and
      Agnes ..., Parents; Rev. V. Gury, Minister

291   MOSER, WILLIAM   January 1, 1890; Age 5 months; Rev. L. Ph.
      Keller, Minister

385   MOTH, LEONTINE (nee Dantin)   ... 17, 1898; Age 29; Rev. J. B.
      Weimer, Minister

103   MUEHE, ELIZABETH   October 29, 1866; Rev. J. Anstaett, Minister

234   MUEHE, WILLIAM   May 28, 1875; Age 75; Rev. Ch. Ch. Greyenbuehl,
      Minister

190   MUEHEL, HENRY   February 8, 1872; Age 66; Westphalia, Germany,
      Origin; Rev. Ch. Ch. Greyenbuehl, Minister

86   MUELLER, ANTHONY JOSEPH   March 22, 1866; Born November 18, 1866;
     Peter Mueller and ..., Parents; Rev. Jos. Anstaett, Minister

130 MUELLER, AUGUST   August 29, 1867; Rev. Jos. Anstaett, Minister

135 MUELLER, CAROLINE   September 1867; Rev. J. Anstaett, Minister

386 MUELLER, LULA   July 17, 1898; Age 5½; Rev. J. B. Weimer,
     Minister

65   MULHERN, TERENCE   November 13, 1864; Ireland, Origin; Rev. Jos.
     Anstaett, Minister

128 NAGLE, STEPHEN   August 16, 1867; Rev. Jos. Anstaett, Minister

309 NEIS, PAULINE   August 1, 1892; Age 16; James Neis and Margaret
     Kirchem, Parents; Rev. J. B. Weimer, Minister

235 NEISS, JAMES   July 6, 1875; Born October 1, 1874; Rev. Ch. Ch.
     Greyenbuehl, Minister

23   NONNENMACHER, ROSINA   June 28, 1862; Age 66; Alsace, Germany,
     Origin; Rev. Jos. Anstaett, Minister

248 NUESSE, ELIZABETH   August 1876; Age about 46; Rev. Ch. Ch.
     Greyenbuehl, Minister

127 OBERLE, ANTHONY   August 14, 1867; Steigen, Alsace, Origin;
     Rev. Jos. Anstaett, Minister

142 OEHLRICH, EDWARD   October 14, 1867; Age 5½; Rev. Jos. Anstaett,
     Minister

139 OEHLSCHLAEGER, MAGDALEN   September 1867; Age 94; Rev. Jos.
     Anstaett, Minister

393 OLLIS MAURER, MINNA (nee Bender)   February 24, 1899; Age 37;
     Rev. J. B. Weimer, Minister

344 OSER, GEORGE WILLIAM   July 15, 1895; Age 15; George William
     Oser and Mary Ann Arnold, Parents; Rev. J. B. Weimer, Minister

91   OSBURG, DANIEL   May 31, 1866; Born May 24, 1866; George Osburg
     and Augusta Lese, Parents; Rev. Jos. Anstaett, Minister

49   PAINE, JOSEPH HERMAN   September 3, 1864; Born April 13, 1862;
     Rev. Jos. Anstaett, Minister

211 PARIS, EDWARD   September 24, 1873; Age 40; Rev. Ch. Ch.
     Greyenbuehl, Minister

337 PAYSSE, EUGENE BERNARD   February 1, 1895; Age 3 months and 15
     days; Rev. J. B. Weimer, Minister

333 PAYSSE, GERMANUS   September 14, 1894; Rev. J. B. Weimer, Minister

349 PEINE, ANNA   December 30, 1895; Age 36; Joseph Peine and
     Margaret Rose, Parents; Rev. J. B. Weimer, Minister

217 PEINE, MARGARET (nee Rose)   June 8, 1874; Age 46; Rev. H.
     Pefferkorn, Minister

157 PLANCHET, CAROLINE   January 13, 1869; Age 5; Rev. Theo.
     Grundner, Minister

360 POHL (POOLE), MARGARET   November 6, 1896; Age 89½; Trier,
     Germany, Origin; Rev. J. B. Weimer, Minister

254   POLASCHE, ELIZABETH   June 11, 1880; Age 2 days; Rev. H.
       Reiffert, Minister

102   POPULIER, WILHELMINE   October 17, 1866; Rev. Jos. Anstaett,
       Minister

152   PORTSCHER, JOSEPH ANTHONY   July 26, 1868; Age 26; Rev. Theo.
       Grundner, Minister

178   PREISS, ELIZABETH   November 25, 1870; Germany, Origin; Rev. Ch.
       Ch. Greyenbuehl, Minister

319   PUPPO. STEPHEN   September 2, 1893; Age 9; Bartholomew Puppo and
       Rosalina Maitré, Parents; Rev. J. B. Weimer, Minister

331   RAKEL, ALBERT   August 13, 1894; Age 50; Rev. J. B. Weimer,
       Minister

383   RAKEL, HENRY   December 17, 1898; Age 20; Gerhardt Rakel and Mary
       Schneider, Parents; Rev. J. B. Weimer, Minister

 46   REHRMANN, ANTHONY   June 23, 1864; Age 39; Rev. L. C. M.
       Chambodut, Minister

 89   REISS, ...   April 27, 1866; Rev. Jos. Anstaett, Minister

340   REITZE, MARY CAROLINE (nee Lang)   March 1, 1895; Age about 85½;
       Rev. J. B. Weimer, Minister

324   RESSEL, WILHELMINE   April 25, 1894; Age 20½; Frank Joseph Ressel
       and Caroline Tschiedal, Parents; Rev. J. B. Weimer, Minister

164   RICKE, AGNES   July 13, 1869; Martin Ricke and Ida Misbel,
       Parents; Rev. N. Gaellweiler, Minister

236   RICKE, ANNA   July 7, 1875; Born June 10, 1875; Rev. Ch. Ch.
       Greyenbuehl, Minister

175   RICKE, ANN LEOPOLDINE   July 17, 1870; Age 14 months; John Ricke
       and Mary Muehe, Parents; Rev. N. Gaellweiler, Minister

221   RICKE, IDA (infant)   September 26, 1874; Martin Ricke and Ida
       Ricke, Parents; Rev. Ch. Ch. Greyenbuehl, Minister

136   RICKE, MARY   September 10, 1867; Rev. Jos. Anstaett, Minister

195   RICKE, ODILIA   June 23, 1872; Age 16 months; Rev. Ch. Ch.
       Greyenbuehl, Minister

251   RIESENBACK, GEORGE   April 25, 1879; Rev. Em. Fleury, Minister

155   RINGH, ANN OLGA   November 12, 1868; Age 29; Rev. Theo. Grundner,
       Minister

226   RITZLER, ...; Rev. Ch. Ch. Greyenbuehl, Minister
227

376   RITZLER, LOUIS VALENTIN   June 27, 1897; Age 2½; Henry Ritzler and
       Mary Gebbert, Parents; Rev. J. B. Weimer, Minister

375   RITZLER, MARGARET JOSEPHINE   April 23, 1897; Aage 3 years and
       7 months; Rev. J.~B. Weimer, Minister

253   RITZLER, SUSAN WILHELMINE   May 29, 1880; Age 3; Rev. H. Reiffert,
       Minister

303   ROEMER, JOSEPH   May 8, 1891; Age 10; J. B. Roemer and ...,
       Parents; Rev. L. Ph. Keller, Minister

282   ROEMER, LEO EMIL   May 27, 1889; Age 7 months; John B. Roemer
       and ... Moser, Parents; Rev. V. Gury, Minister

388   ROHDE, LOUIS GEORGE   August 21, 1898; Age about 2; Louis George
       Rohde and Sophie Windmeyer, Parents; Rev. J. B. Weimer, Minister

 30   ROHLEDER, VICTOR   October 18, 1862; Bavaria, Germany, Origin;
       Rev. Jos. Anstaett, Minister

173   SANDERSON, ... (infant)   July 10, 1870; Oliver Sanderson and
       Nelly Lyons, Parents; Rev. N. Gaellweiler, Minister

 25   SANTERS, JOHN A.   August 25, 1862; Age 21; Galveston, Texas,
       Origin; Rev. Jos. Anstaett, Minister

260   SCHAEFER, MARY   August 31, 1887; Age 80; Rev. V. Gury, Minister

225   SCHMITZ, NICHOLAS   November 3, 1874; Age 27; Rev. Ch. Ch.
       Greyenbuehl, Minister

249   SCHNEIDER, ...   September (?) 13, 1876; Rev. Ch. Ch.
       Greyenbuehl, Minister

  4   SCHNEIDER, PETER   July 25, 1860; Age 10 months; Adolph Schneider
       and Adolphine Gruendel, Parents; Rev. Jos. Anstaett, Minister

 41   SCHNEIDER, THERESA JOSEPHINE JOAN   January 30, 1864; Born
       November 4, 1863; Rev. J. Anstaett, Minister

194   SCHOBER, JOHN   June 17, 1872; Rev. Ch. Ch. Greyenbuehl, Minister

312   SCHOCKE, THERESA (nee Muehe)   November 10, 1892; Age 65; Rev.
       J. B. Weimer, Minister

126   SCHREIBER, HERMAN   August 14, 1867; Rev. Jos. Anstaett, Minister

212   SCHREIBER, JOHN   October 1873; Age about 9; Rev. Ch. Ch.
       Greyenbuehl, Minister

122   SCHREYER, MARY   August 9, 1867; Rev. Jos. Anstaett, Minister

243A   SCHULTE, H. (infant)   March 12, 1876; Rev. Ch. Ch. Greyenbuehl,
       Minister

304   SCHULTE, JOHN   August 18, 1891; Age 33; Henry Schulte and ...,
       Parents; Rev. Mich Heinzelmann, Minister

336   SCHUPPERT, SUSAN (nee Riether)   January 19, 1895; Age 81; Rev.
       J. B. Weimer, Minister

132   SCHUTZI, JOHN   September 3, 1867; Rev. Jos. Anstaett, Minister

174   SEEL, SOPHIE MARY JOSEPHINE   July 15, 1870; Louis Seel and
       Regina Ticks, Parents; Rev. N. Gaellweiler, Minister

203   SELLER, AUGUST HERMAN   May 24, 1873; Born May 4, 1873; Herman
       Seller and Terese ..., Parents; Rev. Ch. Ch. Greyenbuehl,
       Minister

387   SKARKE, ANNA (nee Melcher)   August 18, 1898; Age 25; Rev. J. B.
       Weimer, Minister

329   SOMMER, ANTHONY   August 15, 1894; Age 42; Rev. J. B. Weimer,
       Minister

 66   SOMMER, FRANK   June 18, 1865; Germany, Origin; Rev. Jos.
       Anstaett, Minister

61   SOMMER, JOHN BAPTIST   October 2, 1864; Born January 16, 1862;
      Frank Sommer and Theresa Kraus, Parents; Rev. Jos. Anstaett,
      Minister

54   SOMMER, JOSEPH   September 18, 1864; Rev. J. Anstaett, Minister

267   SOMMER, MARY AGNES   February 4, 1888; Age 5; Anthony Sommer and
      Helen Gengler, Parents; Rev. V. Gury, Minister

90   SPANN, FRANCIS SALES   May 24, 1866; Rev. Jos. Anstaett, Minister

133   SPANN, JOHN F.   September 3, 1867; Rev. J. Anstaett, Minister

210   SPEAKER, JOSEPHINE (infant)   September 17, 1873; Age 1½; Rev.
      Ch. Ch. Greyenbuehl, Minister

288   SPEAKER, THEODORE   November 22, 1889; Age 63; Westphalia, Germany,
      Origin; Rev. V. Gury, Minister

105   SPETH, ...   November 24, 1866; Age 13; Rev. J. Anstaett, Minister

64   STEHLE, MAXIMILIAN   October 14, 1864; Baden, Origin; Rev. J.
      Anstaett, Minister

186   STENZEL, ...   October 7, 1871; Age 50; Rev. Ch. Ch. Greyenbuehl,
      Minister

98   STENZEL, ANN   September 9, 1866; Age 6½; Rev. Jos. Anstaett,
      Minister

214   STENZEL, HELEN   November 22, 1873; Age 4; Rev. Ch. Ch. Greyen-
      buehl, Minister

95   STENZEL, JOAN (nee Hasselhorst)   August 23, 1866; Rev. J.
      Anstaett, Minister

314   STEVENET, SIMON STEPHEN   January 25, 1893; Age 58; France,
      Origin; Rev. J. B. Weimer, Minister

92   STOPPELBERG, CHARLES   August 8, 1866; Rev. Jos. Anstaett,
      Minister

162   STUBENRAUCH, LOUISE   June 2, 1869; Adam Stubenrauch and Catherine
      Blatz, Parents; Rev. N. Gaellweiler, Minister

237   STUMPF, M. H. (infant)   July 19, 1875; Rev. Ch. Ch. Greyenbuehl,
      Minister

55   THAVENET, JOHN   September 20, 1864; Rev. Jos. Anstaett, Minister

161   TOOK, MARY DAVIDA   May 27, 1869; Age 14 months; David Took and
      Anna Took, Parents; Rev. N. Gaellweiler, Minister

197   TRIACCAR, WILLIAM   July 17, 1872; Age 9 months; Rev. Ch. Ch.
      Greyenbuehl, Minister

208   TROST, ANNA MARY CECIL   August 24, 1873; Age about 8 months;
      Rev. Ch. Ch. Greyenbuehl, Minister

229   VERBENA, ANDREW   February 27, 1875; Age 42; Rev. Ch. Ch.
      Greneybuehl, Minister

116   VERBERNE, ...   June 29, 1867; Rev. Jos. Anstaett, Minister

294   VERBERNE, CAMILLE   June (?) 31, 1890; Age 4 months; Rev. J.
      Grabinger, Minister

327   VOLLERT, CATHERINE (nee Franz)   August 5, 1894; Rev. J. B.
        Weimer, Minister

 39   WAGNER, JOSEPH   January 15, 1864; Age 30; Rev. Jos. Anstaett,
        Minister

 84   WAPPLER, SOPHIE (alias Dallmer)   February 20, 1866; Rev. Jos.
        Anstaett, Minister

354   WASNA, CATHERINE   May 10, 1896; Age 3 weeks; Michael Wasna and
        Victoria Madalinska, Parents; Rev. J. B. Weimer, Minister

352   WASNA, VOCTORIA (nee Madalinski)   May 2, 1896; Age 23; Rev. J. B.
        Weimer, Minister

  6   WEBER,HELEN   October 14, 1860; Age 16 months; William Weber and
        Teresa Schulte, Parents; Rev. Jos. Anstaett, Minister

 88   WEBER, HENRY   March 28, 1866; Born November 22, 1860; Mathias
        Weber and Clara Mueller, Parents; Rev. Jos. Anstaett, Minister

 85   WEBER, JOHN EMIL   March 18, 1866; Born November 9, 1864; Mathias
        Weber and Clara Mueller, Parents; Rev. Jos. Anstaett, Minister

330   WEBER, MARY (nee Pendergast)   August 25, 1894; Age 32; Rev. J. B.
        Weimer, Minister

 58   WEBER, MATHIAS   September 22, 1864; Rev. Jos. Anstaett, Minister

 87   WEBER, OSCAR   March 27, 1866; Born June 13, 1858; Mathias Weber
        and Mary Wilhelm, Parents; Rev. Jos. Anstaett, Minister

353   WEBER, THERESA   May 7, 1896; Age 58; Rev. J. B. Weimer, Minister

230   WEBER, WILLIAM   March 23, 1875; Rev. Ch. Ch. Greyenbuehl,
        Minister

 38   WEBER, WILLIAM OTTO   September 24, 1863; Born January 18, 1863;
        Mathias Weber and Clara Mueller, Parents; Rev. Jos. Anstaett.
        Minister

 32   WEYERS. HENRY J.   October 22, 1862: Age 57: Rev. Jos. Anstaett.
        Minister

244   WEYERS. SOPHIE   March 23. 1876: Age 64: Rev. Ch. Ch. Grevenbuehl.
        Minister

323   WERDEHAUSEN. PHILIPP   April 5. 1894: Westphalia. Germany. Origin:
        Rev. J. B. Weimer. Minister

168   WEYHER. ALEXANDER BERNARD   October 24. 1869: Born June 13, 1852;
        John Henry Weyher and Sophie Magd. Engel, Parents; Rev. N.
        Gaellweiler, Minister

220   WIEDEMANN, BARBARA   September 1, 1874; Age about 69; Rev. H.
        Pefferkorn, Minister

140   WIENERS, ANTHONY   September 20, 1867; Rev. Jos. Anstaett,
        Minister

 10   WILSON, CATHERINE   November 26, 1860; Buedesheim, Hessen-
        Darmshadt, Origin; Rev. Jos. Anstaett, Minister

101   WINDMEYER, JOSEPHINE CAROLINE SOPHIE   October 13, 1866; Born
        July 29, 1866; William Windmeyer and Mary Seel, Parents;
        Rev. Jos. Anstaett, Minister

370   WOLFGANG, WILLIAM   February 18, 1897; Age 74; Rev. J. B. Weimer,
       Minister

216   WUIHL, APOLLONIA   June 3, 1874; Age 72; Rev. H. Pefferkorn,
       Minister

185   YOUNG, ...   October 5, 1871; Age 50; Rev. Ch. Ch. Grevenbuehl,
       Minister

219   YOUNGE, ANNA MARY   August 9, 1874; Age 4; Rev. Ch. Ch.
       Greyenbuehl, Minister

 24   Z..., ANDREW   August 4, 1862; Age 28; Prussia, Origin; Rev. J.
       Anstaett, Minister

120   ZARALLA, ... (infant)   August 6, 1867; Rev. Jos. Anstaett,
       Minister

380   ZCHIEDEL, FERDINAND   August 31, 1897; Age about 36; Rev. J. B.
       Weimer, Minister

167   ZWICKEL, PAUL   October 13, 1869; Rev. N. Gaellweiler, Minister

       FREUDENBURG, CHARLES R.   December 21, 1967; Age 79 and 9 months;
       Galveston, Texas, Origin; Born February 27, 1888; Rev. J. B.
       Jones, Minister

FUNERAL RECORDS
1900 - 1952

245   ABELS, HENRY   April 18, 1927; Age 78; Germany *12-12-49, Origin;
       Divorced, died in rail road accident on April 18, 1927,
       Remarks; Buried Old Cathlic Cemetery on April 19; Rev. P. M.
       Lennartz, Minister

       ALBERT, FIDES   see Mrs. Grenrood #194

289   ANDERSON, O. A.   June 24, 1934; Bolivar Peninsula, Origin;
       Buried June 25 - Levy at Galveston Cemetery; Rev. A. M.
       Maechler, Minister

332   ANDERSON, MRS. SARAH (nee Parker)   June 1, 1947; Age 89;
       Galveston, Texas, Origin (3-12-58); Buried June 3 - Levy at
       Old Cathlic Cemetery; Rev. A. M. Maechler, Minister

       ARNOLD, ANNA MARY   see Mrs. Huch #14

 15   ARTO, MRS. CAROLINE (nee Elbert)   February 25, 1902 in Houston;
       Age 46; Buried February 26; Rev. J. B. Weimer, Minister

 76   AULL, MRS. CATHERINE (widow)   December 24, 1907; Age 80; Buried
       December 25; Rev. J. B. Weimer, Minister

279   BAGBY, CECILE KING   August 23, 1932; Age 56; S. Heart, Edinburg,
       Texas; Died of heart ailment; Buried August 25 from local
       depot, Calvary cemetary; Rev. A. M. Maechler, Minister

 86   BALDRI, MRS. MARY ANNA (widow)   May 22, 1909; Age 82; Buried May
       23; Rev. J. B. Weimer, Minister

117   BARBONG, MRS. BARBARA CATHERINE (nee Weimer)   July 8, 1913;
       Born 7-15-1840 soror Rev. Weimer; Married 7-15-1871; Buried
       July 9 in Calvary cemetery; Rev. P. M. Lennartz, Minister

315   BARLEMANN, CHARLES   May 31, 1940; Age 80; Alsace-Lorraine, 7-15-
       59, Origin; Buried June 1 with Mass - Malloy, Calvary cemetery;
       Rev. A. M. Maechler, Minister

219   BARLEMANN, CHARLES ANDREW   November 7, 1923; Age 42; Galveston
       11-10-81, Origin; Charles Barlemann and Theresa Ricke, Parents;
       Married Clemona Perthuis on 2-21-190_; Buried November 9,
       1923 in Hitchcock, Texas; Rev. P. M. Lennartz, Minister

172   BARLEMANN, JOHN ALOIS   October 26, 1918; Age 35; *5-14-83;
       Chas. Barlemann and Theresa Ricke, Parents; Buried October 27
       in Calvary cemetery; Rev. P. M. Lennartz, Minister

       BARLEMANN, WILLIAM FREDERIC   October 19, 1917; Age 24; *12-20-93;
       Chas. Barlemann and Theresa Ricke, Parents; Buried October 21;
       Rev. P. M. Lennartz, Minister

297   BARROW, VERNA (child)   June 13, 1935; Age 11; High Island, Origin;
       Private bapt. Hospital; Buried June 14 - Malloy; Rev. A. M.
       Maechler, Minister

       BAUER, FLORA   see Mrs. Brooks #337

206   BAUHANS, MRS. ELIZABETH (nee Ritzler)   March 6, 1922; *11-26-1936;
       Born in Germany, immigrant 1848; Married Geo. Bauhans in 1851;
       Buried March 7 in Cahil cemetery (sic); Rev. P. M. Lennartz,
       Minister

 18   BAUHENS, JAMES   June 27, 1902; Age 41; Buried June 28; Rev.
       J. B. Weimer, Minister

151   BAUHENS, WILLIAM GEORGE   December 28, 1917; Age 58, born .., 24,
       1859; Buried December 29; Rev. P. M. Lennartz, Minister

       BAUMANN, ROSINA see Mrs. Hansen #159

 37   BECKMANN, LOUIS   January 18, 1904; Age 45; Died suddenly;
       Buried January 21; Rev. J. B. Weimer, Minister

       BENDIXEN, ANNA MARY CATHERINE see Mrs. Miles #339

105   BENDIXEN, MRS. MARY (nee Haenlein)   April 28, 1912; Age 45, born
       3-16-1867; Married 10-24-1884; Buried in Calvary Cemetery;
       Rev. P. M. Lennartz, Minister

 73   BERGER, MRS. MARQUERITE (nee Selenski)   October 17, 1907; Age 29;
       Married George Berger; Buried on October 18; Rev. J. B. Weimer,
       Minister

270   BERNARD, MRS. MARTHA (nee Baroness von Stimfried)   February 25,
       1931; Age 71, born 8-19-1860; Nutonez, Breslau, Origin; Married
       Johann Bernard; Buried February 26; Rev. P. M. Lennartz, Min.

233   BERNER, FERDINAND C.   May 19, 1925; Age 60, born 10-9-1864;
       Schleswig-Holstein, Germany, Origin; Married Catherine Maier
       in 1901; Buried May 20 in Calvary Cemetery; Rev. P. M. Lennartz,
       Minister

346   BETHSCHEIDER, NICHOLAS EDW.   February 21, 1961; Age 70, born July
       26, 1891; Hebron, Nebr., Origin; Died suddenly at 3717 N.,
       his residence; Buried February 24, 1961, with mass, at Mt.
       Olivet Cemetery in Dickinson, Texas; Wife, (Roberts); Under-
       taker, Broadway Funeral Home; Rev. A. M. Maechler, Minister

292   BINAR, AUGUST   August 2, 1934; Born in Switerland; Buried from
       Sacred Heart, Galveston

       BLANEY, FLORENCE see Mrs. Ivey #331

       BLANTZ, ELIZABETH see Mrs. Morgan #221

 23   BLEIKE, FREDERIC PETER   December 9, 1902; Age 74; Westphalia,
       Germany, Origin; Buried December 10; Rev. J. B. Weimer, Minister

 65   BOCKELMANN, HERMAN CHARLES (infant 1 year)   May 1907; Adolph
       Bockelmann and Mary Buhl, Parents; Rev. J. B. Weimer, Minister

348   BOCKELMANN, MRS. MARY BOHL   December 24, 1961; Born Jan. 12, 1872;
       Residence at 3418 Ave. Q; New Orleans, La., Origin; Buried
       at New City Cemetery - J. Levy; Rev. A. M. Maechler, Minister

 24   BOENING, FRANK   December 22, 1902; Age 30; Prussia, Germany, Origin;
       Buried December 23; Rev. J. B. Weimer, Minister

227   BOENING, MRS. MARY AMALIA (nee Lenz)   September 29, 1924; Age 46;
       Born 1-31-78 in Galveston, Tx.; Married Rudolf Alfred Boening
       1-7-01; Buried September 30 in Calvary Cemetery; Rev. P. M.
       Lennartz, Minister

165   BOENING, MARY ROSE (infant, 13 months)   June 5, 1918; Born 5-4-
       17; W. T. Boening and Fides Senechal, Parents; Buried June 6 in
       Calvary Cemetery; Rev. P. M. Lennartz, Minister

 69   BOENING, RAYMOND   July 2, 1807; Age 22 months; Rudolph Boening and
       Mary Lenz, Parents; Buried July 3; Rev. J. B. Weimer, Minister

       BOHN, LOUISE IDA see Mrs. Lassen #298

281 BOHN, NICHOLAS   December 12, 1932; Bronch. Pheumonia, Origin;
     Buried December 13 - Malloy, Evergreen Cemetery; Rev. A. M.
     Maechler, Minister

114 BOWMAN, MRS. HELEN (nee Haenlein)   February 1, 1913; Age 50
     *1863; Married widower Matthew Gaschen 6-19-00; Widow of
     George Bowman; Buried February 3, City Cemetery; Rev. P. M.
     Lennartz, Minister

128 BRANDSTETTER, LEOPOLD (infant 1 year)   June 4, 1914; Tyrol,
     Austria, Origin; Born June 11, 1913; Leopold Brandstetter
     and Cath. Lengauer, immigrants in May 1914, Parents; Buried
     June 5, Calvary cemetery; Rev. P. M. Lennartz, Minister

201 BREEN, MRS. CATHERINE MAGDALEN (nee Lang)   July 12, 1921; Age 61;
     Born July 30, 1860; Married Martin Charles Breen in 1878;
     Buried July 15 in Calvary Cemetery; Rev. P. M. Lennartz,
     Minister

241 BREEN, MARTIN C.   September 1, 1926; Age 76 *May 3, 1850;
     Buried September 2; Rev. P. M. Lennartz, Minister

125 BREEN, MARY MAGDALEN (adopted), infant   March 29, 1914; Real
     parents unknown; Martin Breen and Cath Lang, sponsors and
     adoptive parents; Buried March 30 in Calvary Cemetery; Rev.
     P. M. Lennartz

183 BREEN, MILES FRANCIS   November 11, 1919; Age 46, *8-14-73;
     Martin Chas. Breen and Cath. Magd. Lang, Parents; Married
     Laura Marshal; Buried November 12 in Calvary Cemetery;
     Rev. P. M. Lennartz, Minister

     BRICE, CATHERINE   see Mrs. Seiler #158

     BRIGGS, JOSEPHINE CATHERINE   see Mrs. Flack #222

340 BROOKE, MRS. CAROLINE MARIE   June 13, 1952; Age 89½; Born
     November 16, 1862 in Louisiana; Buried June 14 - Levy,
     Evergreen Cemetery; Rev. A. M. Maechler, Minister

337 BROOKS, MRS. FLORA (nee Bauer)   November 7, 1950; Age 60,
     *12-23-90; Died in convalescent home; Buried November 9 with
     Mass - Broadway, Lakeview Cemetery; Rev. A. M. Maechler,
     Minister

156 BRUENING, MRS. PAULINE   May 3, 1917; Age 54, *1863 New York;
     Widow of Herman John Bruening (d. 1916); Buried May 4, 1917
     in City Cemetery; Rev. P. M. Lennartz, Minister

164 BUECHNER, MRS. WILHELMINA (widow)   March 29, 1918; (nee Van
     Rochon); Age 74; Born October 25, 1844 in Neustrelitz, Germany;
     Married Chas Fred Buechner in 1859; Buried March 31 in Calvary
     Cemetery; Rev. P. M. Lennartz, Minister

 13 BUERGER, LOE   January 20, 1902; Age 18; Buried January 21;
     Rev. J. B. Weimer

276 BUHL, MRS. MARGARET (widow)   March 7, 1932; Age 79; Born
     January 16, 1953; Spier, Germany, Origin; Married Fritz Buhl;
     Died of old age; Buried March 8 in Evergreen Cemetery

191 BURDA, JOHN FRANK   August 24, 1920; Age 33; Died of accidental
     drowning; Born 1887; Skorkan, Bohemia, Origin; John Burda
     and Mary Beska, Parents; Immigrant in 1906; Buried August 26
     in Lakeview Cemetery; Rev. P. M. Lennartz, Minister

     BURLINGTON, ANNA   see Mrs. J. Stumpf #90

231   BURGER, GEORGE ADALBERT ALOYSIUS   February 4, 1925; Age 52, born
           1873; Galveston, Tx., Origin; Fred William Burger and
           Gertrude Berkenhurst, Parents; Married Mary Keis, September
           1894; Buried February 5 in Calvary Cemetery; Rev. P. M.
           Lennartz, Minister

78F   CANNON, ANDREW JOHN   May 9, 1908; Infant of 6 months; Buried May
           10; Rev. J. B. Weimer, Minister

           CAREY, EMILY E. see Mrs. Kraus #239

332A   CARROLL, MRS. ANNA S. (widow)(nee Sommer)   March 11, 1948; Age
           79, born January 4, 1869; Galveston, Origin; Died of old age;
           Buried March 13 at Calvary Cemetery- J. Levy; Rev. A. M.
           Maechler, Minister

54   CARROLL, EMILY IRWIN   January 15, 1906; Age 71; Alsace, Origin;
           Buried January 17; Rev. J. B. Weimer, Minister

287   CARROLL, JOHN M.   May 14, 1934; Age 71; New Orleans, La., Origin;
           Died of intestinal operation; Buried May 16 at Calvary Cemetery,
           Malloy; Rev. A. M. Maechler, Minister

152   CASSEY, CORLEIUS J.   June 27, 1916; Age 70, born 5-21-1846;
           Noew Orleans, La., Origin; Married Lizzie Dean (drowned 1900);
           Buried June 28 at Cahil Cemetery; Rev. P. M. Lennartz, Minister

291   CHAMPAGNE, MRS. PAUL   July 17, 1934; Age 46; Died of Diabetes;
           Buried July 19 in St. Martinville, La.

336   CONSTANTINE, JOHN C.   June 4, 1949; Age 20, born 6-22-1929;
           Mobile, Ala., Origin; Burned in explosion, died in hospital;
           Married Ann Louise Reifel; Buried June 6 with mass - J. Levy
           and Brothers; Buried at Old Cathlic Cemetery; Rev. A. M.
           Maechler, Minister

350   CONSTANTINE, MRS. EVAILNA (Jobeson)   April 11, 1965; Age 69;
           Mobile, Ala., Origin; Born 1-22-1896; Funeral at St. Josephs
           at 9 am with mass on 4-13-1965; Buried at Old Cathlic Cemetery;
           Services by Rt. Rev. Jos. McArdle of Montgomery, Alabama;
           Undertaker, James Crawper, La Marque at Malloys; Rev. A. M.
           Maechler, Minister

268   COOPER, REBECCA RUBI   May 18, 1930; Age 7 months, born October 4,
           1929; Died of child's disease; Henry Cooper and Ramona Izagmire,
           Parents; Buried May 19 at Calvary Cemetery; Rev. P. M.
           Lennartz, Minister

326   CORDRAY, MRS. CAROLINE MAGDALEN (nee Heuman)   August 3, 1945;
           Age 65, born July 23, 1880; Galveston, Origin; Buried August
           4 with mass - Malloy and Son, at Calvary Cemetery; Rev. A. M.
           Maechler, Minister

314   CORDRAY, THOMAS J. SR.   March 20, 1940; Age 69, born 11-8-1870;
           Buried March 21 - Malloy and Son, at Calvary Cemetery; Rev.
           A. M. Maechler, Minister

           COSTELLA, ADA see Mrs. Lenz #243

34   CRITTENDEN, LAURA V.   November 1, 1903; Age 18; Buried November 2;
           Rev. J. B. Weimer, Minister

345   COURAGE, MISS MARGARET JEAN   October 12, 1958; Born October 20,
           1875; Cuero, Texas, Origin; Buried October 14, with mass at
           St. Josephs, at Calvary Cemetery; Rev. A. M. Meachler,
           Minister

353   CROSS, MRS. ROSA LENZ   July 18, 1966; Age 90, born October 12,
        1875; Galveston, Texas, Origin; Died at 701 Sealy Avenue,
        Residence; Buried on July 22, 1966, mass by Rev. Vrana,
        Cathedral, sermon, Rev. Jos. Broussard, Cathedral, at Old
        Cathlic Cemetery; Rev. A. M. Maechler, Minister

265   CRITTENDEN, MRS. LEONA JOSEPHINE (nee Shasolm)   April 24, 1930;
        Age 75, born July 4, 1855; Galveston, Origin; Married Frank
        Crittenden; Buried April 26 at Old Cathlic Cemetery; Rev.
        P. M. Lennartz, Minister

251   CROFT, DANIEL HELLER (adopted)   January 25, 1928; St. John Croft
        and Lillian Krueger, adoptive Parents; Buried January 26 at
        Evergreen Cemetery; Rev. P. M. Lennartz, Minister

179   DAHN, MRS. ANNA JOSEPHINE (nee Kampe)   January 26, 1919; Age. 54,
        Born September 7, 1865; Charles Kampe and Mathilda Frank,
        Parents; Married Louis Dahn, April 23, 1886; Buried (post
        multos dies, propter magnam pluviam) at Calvary Cemetery;
        Rev. P. M. Lennartz, Minister

        DALLMER, MARY EVA see Mrs. Koehler #3

        DAMANI, HELEN CAROLINE see Mrs. Daxberger #116

244   DANIEL, MRS. VIOLA (nee Kraus)   February 1, 1927; Age 41, born
        June 1885; Died of Pneumonia; Buried February 2 at Calvary
        Cemetery; Rev. P. M. Lennartz, Minister

  7   DAU, FREDERIC   April 27, 1901; Age 6; Fred Leonard Dau and
        Mary Schmitz, Parents; Buried April 28; Rev. J. B. Weimer,
        Minister

186   DAVIS, MRS. URSULA MARY EMILY (nee Lenz)   February 9, 1920;
        Age 22, born November 4, 1897; Married Birschie Scott Davis
        12-28-1913; Buried February 15 at Calvary Cemetery; Rev. P. M.
        Lennartz, Minister

116   DAXBERGER, MRS. HELEN CAROLINE (nee Damani)   March 8, 1913;
        Schoehnach, Bavaria, Origin; Age 36, born January 2, 1877;
        Lawr Francis Damani and Mary ..., Parents; Married John
        Daxberger April 30, 1903 in Munich, St. Peter's; Buried March
        9 at Calvary, Paradise #951; Rev. P. M. Lennartz, Minister

126   DAXBERGER, JOHN   May 11, 1914; Age 44, born 3-12-1870; Ottachin,
        Bavaria, Origin; John Daxberger and Theresa Rumi, Parents;
        Married Helen Carol. Damani on 4-30-1903; Buried May 12 at
        Calvary Cemetery, Paradise #952; Rev. P. M. Lennartz, Minister

305   DECOITO, MRS. ROSETTA (nee Gilbert)   May 6, 1937; Age 59;
        Galveston, Origin; Died of heart disease; Buried May 7 by
        Levy; Rev. A. M. Maechler, Minister

288   DELZ, MRS. THERESA (nee Prockhoff)   May 30, 1934; Age 84, born
        February 19, 1850; Schlesia, Germany, Origin; Buried June 1,
        by Malloy in Calvary Cemetery; Rev. A. M. Maechler, Minister

174   DIRCKS, ANGELINA MARY CATHERINE   October 27, 1918; Age 26, born
        ... 6, 1892; Theodore George Dircks and Emma Franz, Parents;
        Buried October 30 at Calvary Cemetery; Rev. P. M. Lennartz,
        Minister

269   DIRCKS, EMMA   June 23, 1930; Age 76; Died of heart trouble;
        Buried June 24; Rev. P. M. Lennartz, Minister

250   DIRCKS, HERMAN JOHN   January 3, 1928; Age 40; Died of Pneumonia;
        Buried January 4; Rev. P. M. Lennartz, Minister

271   DIRCKS, THEODORE GEORGE   July 26, 1931; Age 80; Married; Died
        of old age; Buried July 27 at Calvary Cemetery; Rev. P. M.
        Lennartz, Minister

187   DITTMAN, MRS. CLARA VICTORIA (nee Gree)   March 26, 1920; Age
        50, born April 10, 1870; Married Thomas Freeman and (later)
        Francis Dittman, May 27, 1910; Buried March 27 at Calvary
        Cemetery; Rev. P. M. Lennartz, Minister

        DORECK, EMMA see Mrs. Leutsch #83

 78C   DORECK, LAWRENCE; Age 73; Husband of Widow Emma Leutsch; Buried
        April 23, 1908; Rev. J. B. Weimer, Minister

   1   DOUROUX, LILLIAN   January 1, 1901; Age of about 5; Lucian
        Douroux and Roselle Isabel Glenn, Parents; Buried January 2;
        Rev. J. B. Weimer, Minister

216   DREW, WILLIAM   August 6, 1923; Age 68, born 1-8-1855; Single;
        Buried August 7 at Old Cathlic Cemetery; Rev. P. M. Lennartz,
        Minister

329   DREYDOPPEL, MRS. ANNIE (nee Haenlein)   January 18, 1947; Age 73,
        Born September 25, 1873; Galveston, Origin; Died at a nursing
        home; Buried January 21 with mass - Malloy, at Old Catholic
        Cemetery; Rev. A. M. Maechler, Minister

267   DREYDOPPEL, CHARLES E.   May 5, 1930; Age 63, born 11-6-1867;
        Married Anna Haenlein in 1905; Died of heart failure; Buried
        May 6 at Old Catholic Cemetery; Rev. P. M. Lennartz, Minister

221   DREYDOPPEL, EVA LOUISE (adopted)   January 1, 1924; Age 28, born
        September 27, 1896; Single; Chas. Edw. Dreydoppel and Emma
        Haenlein, adoptive parents; Buried January 3 at non-Catholic
        Cemetery; Rev. P. M. Lennartz, Minister

312   DUGAS, MRS. LOLA   July 26, 1939; Age 46; Bolivar, Texas, Origin;
        Killed in auto accident; Buried O. L. of Mercy church in
        Bolivar on July 27, 1939, Malloy, in the Bolivar Cemetery;
        Rev. A. M. Maechler, Minister

 92   ECKENFELS, HENRY   September 4, 1910; Age 48; Married Catherine
        Bauhans; Buried September 5; Rev. J. B. Weimer, Minister

162   ECKSTEIN, MRS. CATHERINE (nee Oelschlaeger)   January 5, 1918;
        Age 95, born ...23, 1823; Duesen, Germany, Origin; Widow of
        Peter Abels (first husband), Widow of Moritz Brann (second
        husband), Widow of Theodore Eckstein (third husband); Buried
        January 6 in Old Catholic Cemetery; Rev. P. M. Lennartz,
        Minister

351   EDWARDS, MRS. JOSEPHINE (nee Courage)   February 2, 1966; Born
        September 18, 1876; Galveston, Origin; Died in Commerce, Texas;
        Widow; Buried February 4, 1966 with mass at Calvary Cemetery;
        Rev. A. M. Maechler, Minister

 35   EGGERT, ROSALIE   January 17, 1904; Age 60; Widow; Buried January
        18, 1904; Rev. J. B. Weimer, Minister

163   EISENBACH, BALTHASAR LOUISE EDWARD   March 3, 1918; Age 67,
        born August 9, 1851; San Goas, Germany, Origin; John
        Eisenbach and Elizabeth Loyan, Parents; Immigaret in 1870
        (January 28); Married Lena Teichmann on March 1, 1881; Buried
        March 4 at Old Catholic Cemetery; Rev. P. M. Lennartz,
        Minister

        ELBERT, CAROLINE see Mrs. Arto #15

ELIA, ESTELLE see Mrs. Gaschen #223

91 ELZNER, FRANCES   January 8, 1910; Age 62; Buried January 9;
     Rev. J. B. Weimer, Minister

ENGELKE, JULIA see Mrs. Linke #47

67 ERHOLD, LOUISE; Age 17; Joseph Erhold and Mary Junge, Parents;
     Buried June 1907 (between 5th and 24th); Rev. J. B. Weimer,
     Minister

48 EVERLING, MARY LOUISE JOSEPHINE   January 17, 1905; Age 20
     months; Buried January 18; Rev. J. B. Weimer, Minister

256 FERNANDEZ, LOUISE   June 12, 1929; Age 52; Buried June 13; Rev.
      P. M. Lennartz, Minister

296 FIESEL, MRS. ANTONIA (nee Tschiedl)   March 12, 1935; Age 77;
      Bullendorf, Germany, Origin; Buried March 13, Malloy at Lake-
      view Cemetery; Rev. A. M. Maechler, Minister

257 FINN, PARTRICK   July 10, 1929; Age 72, born 6-3-1857; Married
      Theresa Schocke in Galveston; Died of old age; Buried July 12
      in Calvary Cemetery; Rev. P. M. Lennartz, Minister

     FINN, THERESA   March 6, 1964; Age 97; Buried from Sacred Heart
      Church on March 9, 1964, Malloy, at Calvary Cemetery; Rev.
      Jos. O'Sullivan (Sacred Heart), Minister

222 FLACK, MRS. JOSEPHINE CATHERINE (nee Briggs)   January 31, 1924;
      Born October 15, 1899; W. H. Briggs and Catherine Seiler,
      Parents; Married Gordon Rex Flack on 4-15-1921; Buried
      February 2 at Calvary Cemetery; Rev. P. M. Lennartz, Minister

262 FLAKE, LAURA EMMA (nee Halfman)   January 27, 1930; Age 68;
      Galveston, Origin; Married Adolf Flake; Died of old age;
      Buried January 28 at Old Catholic Cemetery; Rev. P. M.
      Lennartz, Minister

220 FLAKE, OTTO   November 23, 1923; Age 64, born May 8, 1859;
      Married Laura Hoffman 4-19-1892; Buried November 25 at Old
      Catholic Cemetery; Rev. P. M. Lennartz, Minister

166 FLUEHR, GEORGE   April 21, 1918; Age 47, born 12-30-1870; George
      and Rosa Fluehr, Parents; Buried April 23 at Lake View
      Cemetery; Rev. P. M. Lennartz, Minister

     FLUEHR, MRS. ROSINA see Mrs. Schreiber #110

217 FRENCH, DORA   August 11, 1923; Age 82, born 1841; Nonau,
      Germany, Origin; Single; Christian French and Marie Schmidt,
      Parents; Buried August ... in Calvary Cemetery; Rev. P. M.
      Lennartz, Minister

343 FREUDENBURG, MRS. MARIE M.   February 4, 1955; Age 61, born
      December 12, 1893; Galveston, Origin; Died of strock or heart
      attack; Mr. and Mrs. Charles Barlernarer (?), Parents;
      Funeral with mass on February 7, 1955; Buried at Calvary
      Cemetery

144 FROEHLICH, JOSEPH   July 26, 1916; Age 45, born March 25, 1871;
      Widower; Married Theresa Prenihsl in Berg Reichenstein,
      Bohemia; Rohrbrunn, Hungary, Origin; Buried July 30 in
      Calvary Cemetery; Rev. P. M. Lennartz, Minister; Note:
      Three daughters, Mary, Ernestine and Pauline, placed in St.
      Mary's Orphanage

78 FROEHLICH, MRS. THERESA; Age 37; Buried February 2, 1908; Rev.
    J. B. Weimer, Minister

39 FROHNE, CAROLINE   April 27, 1904; Age 88; Bavaria, Origin;
    Buried April 28; Rev. J. B. Weimer, Minister

189 FUCHS, ADAM   July 23, 1920; Buried July 24 in Calvary Cemetery;
     Rev. P. M. Lennartz, Minister

GASCHEN, CLARA see Mrs. Wagner #78A

GASCHEN, MRS. HELEN see Mrs. Bowmann #114

GASCHEN, MATTIE see Mrs. Hasselmayer #260

223 GAESCHEN, MRS. ESTELLE (nee Elia)   May 18, 1924; Age 25, born
     August 18, 1899; Houma, La., Origin; Married Frederic Matthew
     Gaeschen on August 16, 1922; Died in Houma, La.?; Buried May
     19 at Lake View Cemetery; Rev. P. M. Lennartz, Minister

GENGLER, ANNIE SUSAN see Mrs. Schaefer #307

GENGLER, HELEN see Mrs. Sommer #316

8 GENGLER, HENRY   June 16, 1901; Age 21 months; Peter Gengler and
   Theresa Schulte, Parents; Buried June 17; Rev. J. B. Weimer,
   Minister

278 GENGLER, MRS. THERESA MARY (nee Schulte)   August 2; Age 57;
     Born in Galveston, Origin; Married Peter M. Gengler; Died
     of Cerebral Hemorrhage; Buried August 3 at Calvary Cemetery;
     Rev. A. M. Maechler, Minister

190 GILBERT, MRS. ANNA (nee Young)   August 7, 1920; Age 76, born
     January 1844; Married to Thomas David Gilbert in 1860;
     Buried August 8 in Calvary Cemetery; Rev. P. M. Lennartz,
     Minister

129 GILBERT, CATHERINE   June 5, 1914; Age 1, born May 27, 1913;
     Don Gilbert and Minnie Frank, Parents; Buried June 6; Rev.
     P. M. Lennartz, Minister

229 GILBERT, DAVID THOMAS   December 28, 1924; Age 56, born 10-10-
     1868; Galveston, Origin; Married Winiford Frank on 10-26-1898;
     Buried December 29 at Calvary Cemetery; Rev. P. M. Lennartz,
     Minister

169 GILBERT, JOHN J.   July 24, 1918; Age 36, born 7-16-1882; Died
     in railroad accident; Thomas David Gilbert and Anna Graycroft,
     Parents; Buried July 25 in Old Catholic Cemetery; Rev. P. M.
     Lennartz, Minister

266 GILBERT, MARY ELLEN   May 7, 1930; Age 59, born 10-14-1870;
     Thomas David Gilbert and Anna Jung, Parents; Died of heart
     trouble; Buried May 9 at Old Catholic Cemetery; Rev. P. M.
     Lennartz, Minister

GILBERT, ROSETTA see Mrs. Decoito #305

120 GILBERT, ELIZABETH FRANCES   September 9, 1913; Age 35, born
     October 4, 1878; Single; Thomas D. Gilbert and Anna ...,
     Parents; Buried September 10 at Old Catholic Cemetery;
     Rev. P. M. Lennartz, Minister

130 GILBERT, ...   January 23, 1914; Age infant, one hour old;
     Don Gilbert and Minnie Frank, Parents; Privately baptized;
     Buried January ... at Old Catholic Cemetery; Rev. P. M.
     Lennartz, Minister

101   GLEICH, JULIA MAUD   December 5, 1911; Age 26, born July 25, 1885;
      Single; Augustin Gleich and Mary O'Connor, Parents; Buried
      December 7 at Calvary Cemetery; Died in Houston; Rev. P. M.
      Lennartz, Minister

 38   GOLKE, LOUISE   March 6, 1904; Age 79; Widow; Buried March 7;
      Rev. J. B. Weimer, Minister

 16   GOMBERT, MRS. CATHERINE   March 24, 1902; Age 56; Widow; Buried
      March 25; Rev. J. B. Weimer, Minister

264   GOODMAN, MRS. CAROLINE   March 7, 1930; Age 75, born 10-16-1854;
      Married Martin Emm. Heintze (died 1909), first husband;
      Married Oscar John Goodman on 10-28-1915; Died of old age;
      Buried March 9 at Old Catholic Cemetery; Rev. P. M. Lennartz,
      Minister

255   GOTTLOB, JOHN ANTON   February 24, 1929; Age 68, born December 6,
      1860; Steele, Westphalia, Origin; Anton Gottlob and Mary
      Dornhoff, Parents; Immigrant (via New York) in 1877; Married
      Mary Friederich of Galveston; Died of old age; Buried February
      26 at Old Catholic Cemetery; Rev. P. M. Lennartz, Minister

181   GOTTSELIG, LEO   August 18, 1919; Age 8 months; Michael Gottselig
      and Anna Mock, Parents; Buried August 19 at Calvary Cemetery;
      Rev. P. M. Lennartz, Minister

338   GRASSMUCK, MRS. LINDA MELANIE   September 2, 1951; Age 75, born
      February 2, 1876; St. Louis, Mo., Origin; Married W. H.
      Grassmuck 8-30-1900; Died after long illness; Buried September
      4, Levy, at Memorial Park in Hitchcock, Texas; Rev. A. M.
      Maechler, Minister

      GREE, CLARA VICTORIA see Mrs. Dittman #187

194   GRENROOD, MRS. FIDES (nee Albert)   November 17, 1920; Age 76,
      born in 1844; Married to Henry Grenrood; Widow; Buried
      November 18 at Calvary Cemetery; Rev. P. M. Lennartz, Minister

173   GRENROOD, MRS. LAURA BESSIE   October 16, 1918; Age 34, born 1884;
      Married Christopher Kelley, first husband; Married Edward
      Aloysius Grenrood, November 14, 1910, second husband; Buried
      October 17 at Calvary Cemetery; Rev. P. M. Lennartz, Minister

 77   GRINROOD, HENRY   January 21, 1908; Age 72; Married to Fides
      Elbert; Buried January 23; Rev. J. B. Weimer, Minister

259   GUNTER, EDITH MRS. (nee Menzel)   September 11, 1929; Age 53, born
      January 19, 1876; Galveston, Origin; Married H. Gunter;
      Buried September 13 at Calvary Cemetery; Died of Paralysis;
      Rev. P. M. Lennartz, Minister

      HAENLEIN, ANNA see Mrs. Dreydoppel #329

 40   HAENLEIN, MRS. HELEN   July 3, 1904; Age 65; Bavaria Rhenana,
      Origin; Died of Dropsy (rupture); Buried July 4; Rev. J. B.
      Weimer, Minister

      HAENLEIN, HELEN see Mrs. Bowmann #114

      HAENLEIN, MARY see Mrs. Bendixen #105

 57   HAGEMANN, ELIZABETH   April 9, 1906; Age 83; Hanover, Germany,
      Origin; Buried April 10; Rev. J. B. Weimer, Minister

      HAGEMANN, THERESA see Mrs. Leinbach #212

238   HAHN, MRS. EVE (nee Lang)   February 15, 1926; Age 78, born
      in 1848; Germany, Origin; Married to Frank Hahn; Buried
      February 16 at Old Catholic Cemetery; Rev. P. M. Lennartz,
      Minister

      HAHNREITER, OTTILIA see Mrs. J. Schocke #302

      HALFMAN, LAURA EMMA see Mrs. Flake #262

      HAMILTON, ANICE see Mrs. Maurer #28

      HANSEN, ANNE JOSEPHINE see Mrs. Peterson #115

159   HANSEN, MRS. ROSINA (nee Bauman)   November 14, 1917; Age 55,
      born May 14, 1862; Germany, Origin; Married to Alfred
      Christian Hansen; Buried November 15 in Calvary Cemetery;
      Rev. P. M. Lennartz, Minister

 44   HARVEY, MARY   September 27, 1904; Age 4; Buried September 28;
      Rev. J. B. Weimer, Minister

 89   HARVEY, MARY THERESA   November 6, 1909; Age 14 months; Buried
      November 7; Rev. J. B. Weimer, Minister

209   HASSELMEIER, MRS. MARY AGNES (nee Lyons)   May 29, 1922; Age 66,
      born July 26, 1856; New Orleans, La., Origin; Married Louis
      Geo Hasselmeier (died 1914) in September 15, 1874; Buried
      May 30 at Lake View Cemetery; Rev. P. M. Lennartz, Minister;
      Note: Left 6 children, 30 grandchildren and 82 great-
      grandchildren

260   HASSELMEYER, MRS. MATTIE (nee Gaschen)   October 30, 1929; Age 39,
      Born March 19, 1890; Galveston, Origin; Married Fred. M.
      Hasselmeyer 1-29-1908; Buried November 2; Rev. P. M. Lennartz,
      Minister

106   HAUER, CHARLES BORROMEO   May 28, 1912; Age 38, born 9-1-1874;
      Austria, Origin; Leopold Hauer and Agnes Mueller, Parents;
      Buried May 29 at Calvary Cemetery; Rev. P. M. Lennartz,
      Minister

      HEIMAN, EMILY E. see Mrs. Hughes #325

 27   HEIMANN, JOHN   February 19, 1903; Age 52; Galveston, Origin;
      Buried February 20; Rev. J. B. Weimer, Minister

  5   HEIMAN, MRS. OTTILIA   March 3, 1901; Age 78; Widow; Married
      Anton Heiman; Buried March 5; Rev. J. B. Weimer, Minister

113   HEINKELE, RUDOLPH ADALBERT   January 14, 1913; Born September 28,
      1874; Germany, Origin; Joseph and Rosa Heinkele, Parents;
      Immigrant 1896; Married Mathilda Ruitz; Buried January 15 in
      Calvary Cemetery; Rev. P. M. Lennartz, Minister

121   HEINRICH, VICTOR BERNARD   October 31, 1913; Age 19, born May 24,
      1894; Schulenburg, Texas, Origin; Joseph Heinrich and Mary
      Kainer, Parents; Buried November 1 at Calvary Cemetery;
      Rev. P. M. Lennartz, Minister

      HEINTZE, MRS. CAROLINE see Mrs. Goodman #264

 87   HEINZE, EMMANUEL   July 4, 1909; Age 62; Husband of Mrs. Caroline
      Biermann, widow (nee Hageman); Buried July 5; Rev. J. B.
      Weimer, Minister

46A   HEINZE, PAULINE   December 12, 1904; Age 12; ... Heinze and Lena
      Hagemann, Parents; Buried December 16; Rev. J. B. Weimer,
      Minister

49   HEINZE, SOPHIE   April 25, 1905; Age 16; Emmanuel Heinze and
        Lena Hagemann, Parents; Buried April 26; Rev. J. B. Weimer,
        Minister

26   HELMER, ALBERT MAGNUS   January 14, 1903; Age 19; Died suddenly;
        Buried January 18; Rev. J. B. Weimer, Minister

81   HELMER, JOHN EDWARD   January 7, 1909; Age 68 years and 9 months;
        Buried January 9; Rev. J. B. Weimer, Minister

247   HERMAN, DAVID   June 7, 1927; Age 70; Died of old age; Buried
        June 8; Rev. P. M. Lennartz, Minister

196   HERRMANN, MATTHIAS   December 28, 1920; Age 73, born March 20,
        1847; Alsace, France, Origin; Married Augusta Eggert;
        Buried December 29 at Calvary Cemetery; Rev. P. M. Lennartz,
        Minister

      HERRGOTT, MARY see Mrs. Sommer #215

      HEUMAN, CAROLINE MAGDALEN see Mrs. Cordray #326

      HILLS, MARY see Mrs. Speaker #148

      HOCK, ANNA MARY see Mrs. Ricke #167

132   HOFBECK, CAROLINE JOSEPHINE   September 12, 1914; Age 83; Buried
        September 13 in Calvary Cemetery; Rev. P. M. Lennartz, Minister

      HORNUNG, ELIZABETH MARY see Mrs. Lenz #272

      HORNUNG, MARY ELIZABETH see Mrs. Menzel #134

      HORNUNG, ROSE see Mrs. Wolff #119

14   HUCK, MRS. ANNA MARY (nee Arnold)   February 21, 1902; Buried
        February 22; Rev. J. B. Weimer, Minister

207   HUEBERT, FRANK   May 7, 1922; Age 63, born August 13, 1859;
        Galveston, Origin; John Huebert and Anna Haze, Parents; Married
        Carlotta Welshans 5-12-1896; Buried May 9 at Cahill Cemetery;
        Rev. P. M. Lennartz, Minister

325   HUGHES, EMELEN (Emily) E. (nee Heiman)   June 17, 1945; Age 90,
        Born November 11, 1854; Smith's Point, Texas, Origin; Buried
        June 18 at Bolivar Cemetery, Levy; Died in Port Bolivar;
        Rev. A. M. Maechler, Minister

      HUMMEL, CAROLINE see Mrs. Tischendorf #170

      IRWIN, EMILY see Carroll #54

331   IVEY, MRS. FLORENCE (nee Blaney)   April 25, 1947; Age 86, born
        February 26, 1861; Independence, Cal., Origin; Lived at 2112
        Ave. M.; Died at Sealy Hospital; Buried April 28 with mass
        (J. Levy Bro.); Rev. A. M. Maechler, Minister

79   JACOBS, LESTER EMIL   April 20, 1908; Age 8 months; John Jacobs
        and Regina Gloger, Parents; Buried Arpil 21; Rev. J. B. Weimer,
        Minister

2   JANSSENS, WILLIAM GODFREY HENRY   January 15, 1901; Age 35;
        Died while traveling; Buried January 16; Rev. J. B. Weimer,
        Minister

      JERSIG, FRANCES see Mrs. Johnson #84 (below)

84   JOHNSON, MRS. FRANCES (nee Jersig)   February 15, 1909; Age 70;
      Widow; Buried February 16; Rev. J. B. Weimer, Minister

85   JOHNSON, JOSEPH CHARLES   March 5, 1909; Age 8 months; ... Johnson
      and Leona Wilrycz, Parents; Buried March 6; Rev. J. B. Weimer,
      Minister

205   JOHNSTON, MRS. ROSALIE (nee Picture)   January 5, 1922; Age 51,
      born June 7, 1871; Galveston, Origin; William Henry Picture
      and Louise Furwagen, Parents; Grotkam, Austria, Parents
      Origin; Buried January 6 in Calvary Cemetery; Married James
      Frank Johnston in 1896; Rev. P. M. Lennartz, Minister

309   JORDAN, MRS. MARY (nee Kramer)   July 13, 1938; Age 84, born
      January 3, 1854; Soests, Westphalia, Origin; Buried July 14,
      1938 with Mass (Malloy) at Old Catholic Cemetery; Rev. A. M.
      Maechler, Minister

284   JUNG, MRS. ANNA (nee Tschiedl)   October 30, 1933; Age 83; Died
      of Cardio-Renal disease at Old Women's Home; Buried October
      31 (J. Levy) at Calvary Cemetery; Rev. A. M. Maechler, Minister

200   JUNG, FERDINAND   July 12, 1921; Age 70, Born November 1, 1850;
      Tolendorf, Austria, Origin; Married Anna Schiedel 7-20-1870;
      Buried July 14 at Calvary Cemetery; Rev. P. M. Lennartz,
      Minister

237   JUNGE, RICHARD (adopted, nee Kelly)   February 14, 1926; Age 15,
      Born December 29, 1910; San Antonio, Texas, Origin; John T.
      Kelly and Theresa Junge, Parents; Adopted by grandmother;
      Buried February 16 at Calvary Cemetery; Rev. P. M. Lennartz,
      Minister

168   JUNKER, MRS. JULIA (nee Meury)   July 4, 1918; Age 42, born
      October 17, 1876; Married W. T. Junker; Buried July 15 at
      Calvary Cemetery; Rev. P. M. Lennartz, Minister

175   KAMEYER, MRS. ANNA (nee Stumpf)   October 30, 1918; Age 36½,
      Born April 1882; Married Frederic William Kameyer 1-20-1906;
      Buried October 31 at Calvary Cemetery; Rev. P. M. Lennartz,
      Minister

323   KAMEYER, FREDERIC WILLIAM SR.   October 9, 1944; Age 67, born
      February 13, 1877; San Antonio, Texas, Origin; Convert; Buried
      October 12 with Mass (J. Levy and Brother) at Calvary
      Cemetery; Rev. A. M. Maechler, Minister

      KAMPE, ANNA JOSEPHINE see Mrs. Dahn #179

103   KAMPE, WILLIAM HERMAN   March 2, 1912; Age 41, born 3-19-1871;
      Shot accidentally; Buried at Calvary Cemetery; Rev. P. M.
      Lennartz, Minister

242   KEAGHEY, KELLIE   December 3, 1926; Age 75; Ireland, Origin;
      Widower; Immigrant 4 years of age; Married Catherine Lang;
      Died of old age; Buried December 4 at Calvary Cemetery;
      Rev. P. M. Lennartz, Minister

      KELLY, MRS. C., LAURA BESSIE see Mrs. Grenrood #173

      KELLY, RICHARD see Junge #237

185   KETTLER, RUDOLPH   January 23, 1920; Age 47, born 9-3-1873;
      Ferdinand Kettler and Mary Schwendinger, Parents; Married
      Theresa Lammer 4-29-1996; Buried January 26 at Calvary
      Cemetery; Rev. P. M. Lennartz

55   KIMMELY, MRS. GEO. M., ANNA BARBARA   January 28, 1906; Age 79;
       Widow; Buried January 29; Rev. J. B. Weimer, Minister

42   KIMMLEY (KIMMLE), GEORGE MICHAEL   July 5, 1904; Age 91; Bavaria
       Rhenana, Germany, Origin; Died of paralysis; Buried July 6;
       Rev. J. B. Weimer, Minister

74   KIMMELE, JOSEPH   December 8, 1907; Age 41; Buried December 9;
       Rev. J. B. Weimer, Minister

141   KIRK, MRS. ELIZABETH (nee Moser)   February 19, 1916; Age 58,
       Born October 12, 1857; Galveston, Origin; Married Thomas
       Joseph Kirk 2-12-1877; Buried February 20 at Calvary Cemetery;
       Rev. P. M. Lennartz, Minister

146   KISSINGER, JOHN CHARLES   September 25, 1916; Died at birth;
       John Charles Kissinger and Edna Chassaniol, Parents; Buried
       September at Calvary Cemetery; Rev. P. M. Lennartz, Minister

45   KOCH, ADAM   November 25, 1904; Age 49; Husband of Lina Koehler;
       Buried November 26; Rev. J. B. Weimer, Minister

344   KNOPP, MRS. PAULINE (nee Hasselmeier)   March 23, 1958; Born
       August 11, 1907; Wife of Claude C. Knopp; Son, Paul J. Knopp,
       Sr.; Daughter, Claudia; Died of Cancer at St. Mary's Inf.;
       Funeral, Levy, at 9 a.m. at St. Josephs with mass, March 25,
       1955; Buried at Mt. Olivet Cemetery in Dickinson, Texas;
       Rev. A. M. Maechler, Minister

75   KOCH, JOSEPH   December 1907;   Age 27; Adam Koch and Lina
       Koehler, Parents; Died between the 9th and 24th; Buried day
       after; Rev. J. B. Weimer, Minister

64   KOCH, MARGARET   February 24, 1907; Age 3 years and 9 months;
       Adam Koch and Lina Koehler, Parents; Buried February 25; Rev.
       J. B. Weimer, Minister

63   KOCH, MARY   November 20, 1906; Age 24 years and 7 months;
       Adam Koch and Lina Koehler, Parents; Buried November 21; Rev.
       J. B. Weimer, Minister

41   KOCH, WILMA ANITA   July 3, 1904; Age 4 years and 2 months;
       Adam Koch and Lina Koehler, Parents; Died of Pneumonia; Buried
       July 4; Rev. J. B. Weimer, Minister

36   KOEHLER, JOHN   January 22, 1904; Age 37; Galveston, Origin;
       Buried January 23; Rev. J. B. Weimer, Minister

3   KOEHLER, MRS. MARY EVE (nee Dallmer)   January 17, 1901; Age 68;
       Buried January 18; Rev. J. B. Weimer, Minister

66   KORTE, WILLIAM   June 5, 1907; Age 13; Buried June 6; Rev. J. B.
       Weimer, Minister

58   KRAEMER (METZGER ?), ANTON; Died between April and July 1906;
       Buried day after; Rev. J. B. Weimer, Minister

       KRAEMER, MARY see Mrs. C. Jordan #309

248   KRAUS, MRS. ELIZABETH   June 28, 1927; Age 80, born in 1852;
       Married Frank Joseph Kraus in Galveston; Widow; Died of old
       age in San Francisco; Buried July 7 at Calvary Cemetery;
       Rev. P. M. Lennartz, Minister

239   KRAUS, MRS. EMILY E. (nee Carey)   March 23, 1926; Age 59, born
       January 1, 1867; Married John Fred Kraus; Died of Pneumonia;
       Buried March 24 at Calvary Cemetery; Rev. P. M. Lennartz,
       Minister

135   KRAUS, FRANK JOSEPH   March 31, 1915; Age 68; Buried April 1 at
       Calvary Cemetery; Rev. P. M. Lennartz, Minister

218   KRAUS, JOHN   October 28, 1923; Age 60, born 10-31-1863; Frank
       Kraus and Catherine Herschgaensner, Parents; Buried October
       29 at Calvary Cemetery; Rev. P. M. Lennartz, Minister

       KRAUS, MARY see Mrs. Lutz #118

       KRAUS (?), VIOLA see Mrs. Daniel #244

 78E   KRYENEN, PETRONELLA   May 6, 1908; Age 28; Buried same day;
       Rev. J. B. Weimer, Minister

228   KUEBELER, JOSEPH ALPHONSE   December 12, 1924; Age 76, born
       2-29-1849; Married 1) in 1876; Married 2) in 1897; Buried
       December 14 at Lake View Cemetery; Rev. P. M. Lennartz, Minister

  9   LAINE, ALBERT   October 5, 1901; Age 33; Married Anna Haehnlein;
       Buried October 6; Rev. J. B. Weimer, Minister

236   LAMMER, LOUISE (SOMMER?)   December 31, 1925; Age 46, born
       December 11, 1879; Galveston, Origin; August Lammer and Mary
       Hergott, Parents; Died of Pneumonia; Buried January 1, 1926 at
       Calvary Cemetery; Rev. P. M. Lennartz, Minister

       LANG, CATHERINE MAGDALEN see Mrs. Breen #201

       LANG, EVA see Mrs. Hahn #238

226   LANG, LOUIS   September 24, 1924; Age 95, born in 1829; Single;
       Frankfurt, Germany, Origin; Frank Lang and Catherine Horn,
       Parents; Buried September 26 at Old Catholic Cemetery; Rev.
       P. M. Lennartz, Minister

192   LANG, MICHAEL   September 20, 1920; Age 72, Born February 13, 1848;
       Galveston, Origin; Married Catherine Pfeifer June 1877;
       Buried September 21 in Old Catholic Cemetery; Rev. P. M.
       Lennartz, Minister

249   LASSEN, JOSEPH CHARLES   August 16, 1927; Age 21; Died in
       Springfield, Mo. of Typhoid; Buried August 19 at Calvary
       Cemetery; Rev. P. M. Lennartz, Minister

298   LASSEN, MRS. LULA LOUISE (nee Bohn?)   June 29, 1935; Age 53, Born
       January 3, 1882; Galveston, Origin; Died at John Sealy
       Hospital; Buried July 1, 1935 with Mass, Malloy at Calvary
       Cemetery; Rev. A. M. Maechler, Minister

294   LANGE, MRS. CATHERINE   December 3, 1934; Buried December 5; Rev.
       A. M. Maechler, Minister

212   LEINBACH, MRS. THERESA (nee Hageman)   January 5, 1923; Age 95,
       Born May 22, 1828; Widow; Hildesheim, Germany, Origin; Married
       John Leinbach; Buried January 7 at Old Catholic Cemetery;
       Rev. P. M. Lennartz, Minister

243   LENZ, MRS. ADA (nee Costella)   December 18, 1926; Age 43; Married
       Charles A. Lenz; Buried December 19 at Calvary Cemetery;
       Rev. P. M. Lennartz, Minister

193   LENZ, ANTON   October 1, 1920; Age 72, born 1848; Married Mary
       Hornung; Buried October 2 at Calvary Cemetery; Rev. P. M.
       Lennartz, Minister

301   LENZ, CHARLES A.   February 19, 1936; Age 52; Galveston, Origin;
       Buried February 21 with Mass, Malloy at Calvary Cemetery;
       Died at John Sealy Hospital; Rev. A. M. Maechler, Minister

272   LENZ, MRS. ELIZABETH MARY   August 13, 1931; (nee Hornung); Age 79,
       Born October 30, 1851; Schleswig-Holstein, Origin; Died of
       old age; Buried August 15 at Calvary Cemetery; Rev. P. M.
       Lennartz, Minister

33   LENZ, ERNESTINE M.   October 1903; Age 2; Mr. and Mrs. John Lenz,
       Parents; Buried day after; Rev. J. B. Weimer, Minister

109   LENZ, JOHN PETER   August 13, 1912; Age 39; Anton Lenz and Mary
       Hornung, Parents; Buried August 14 at Calvary Cemetery; Rev.
       P. M. Lennartz, Minister

       LENZ, MARY AMALIA see Mrs. Boening #227

       LENZ, URSULA MARY EMILY see Mrs. Davis #186

208   LENZ, VICTOR FRANK   May 22, 1922; Age 26, Born 11-6-1896; Married
       Ottilia ...; John Peter Lenz and Mathilde Voulk, Parents;
       Buried May 23 at Calvary Cemetery; Rev. P. M. Lennartz, Minister

83   LEUTSCH, MRS. EMMA (nee Doreck ?)   February 14, 1909; Age 60;
       Died suddenly; Buried February 16; Rev. J. B. Weimer, Minister

286   LEWIS, THOMAS H.   December 9, 1933; Age 83, Born February 26,
       1850; Brooklyn, New York, Origin; Died of Cancer; Buried
       December 10 at Evergreen Cemetery, Levy; Rev. A. M. Maechler,
       Minister

       LIEBISCH, MATHILDE see Mrs. Schaefer #240

47   LIMKE, MRS. JULIA (nee Engelke)   December 16, 1904; Age 51; Wife
       of Henry Limke; Buried December 18; Rev. J. B. Weimer, Minister

184   LIZA, JOSEPH   December 2, 1919; Age 43, Born October 28, 1876;
       Magyarad, Hungary, Origin; Married Louise Markovich; Frank
       and Mary Liza, Parents; Buried December ... at Lake View
       Cemetery; Rev. P. M. Lennartz, Minister

118   LUTZ, MRS. MARY (nee Kraus)   August 6, 1913; Age 40, Born April
       21, 1873; Galveston, Origin; Married John Lutz 4-22-1891;
       Buried August 7 at Calvary Cemetery; Rev. P. M. Lennartz,
       Minister

       LYONS, MARY AGNES see Mrs. Hasselmeier #209

210   LYONS, WILLIAM GEORGE   September 30, 1922; Widower; Age 72,
       Born October 26, 1850; New Orleans, La., Origin; Married
       Mary Tidings in Galveston; Buried September 31 at Calvary
       Cemetery; Rev. P. M. Lennartz, Minister

70   MACHIN, MRS. JOSEPHINE (nee Mayer)   July 29, 1907; Age 47;
       Died in Pittsburgh, Pa.; Buried August 2; Rev. G. J. Dane,
       S. J., Minister; Note: was daughter of Andrew Mayer and Eliz.
       Sell

53   MACK, REV. JOSEPH J.   September 1905; Pfalheim (Ellwangen),
       Wuertemberg, Origin; Former pastor of Whitelow, Wis. (Diocese
       of Greenbay); Buried day after; Rev. L. G. Bashnal, S. J.,
       Minister

78D   MARTIN, AGNES ERNESTINE   April 24, 1908; Age 5 months; Louis
       Martin and Agnes Conboy, Parents; Buried April 25; Rev. J. B.
       Weimer, Minister

94   MARTIN, CAROLINE ELIZABETH   November 3, 1910; Age 1; Louis Martin
       and Agnes Conboy, Parents; Buried November 4; Rev. J. B.
       Weimer, Minister

203   LUTHER, WILLIAM LOUIS   November 4, 1921; Age 59, Born 9-18-1862;
       Bremen, Germ., Origin; Andrew Luther and Augusta Polsfuss,
       Parents; Married Nellie Miller on 10-30-1901; Buried November
       5 at Calvary Cemetery; Rev. P. M. Lennartz, Minister

274   MARTIN, JOHN   October 14, 1931; Age 81, Born March 30, 1850;
       Germany, Origin; Married Ernestine Steinbach; Died in Houston;
       Buried October 16 at Calvary Cemetery; Rev. P. M. Lennartz,
       Minister

 50   MARTIN, LOUIS DANIEL   June 1, 1905; Age 6 months; Louis Martin
       and Agnes Conboy, Parents; Buried June 2; Rev. Jos. Mack per
       Rev. J. B. Weimer, Minister

       MARTIN, MARGUERITE see Mrs. Neis #154

 98   MATT, JOSEPH   March 14, 1911; Buried March 15; Rev. J. B. Weimer,
       Minister

295   MAUBAULES, ETHEL MARY   December 16, ____; Age 2; Port Bolivar,
       Origin; Died of Pneumonia; Buried December 17 at Bolivar
       Cemetery; Rev. A. M. Maechler, Minister

290   MAUBAULES, JACKLIN CECILE   November 7, 1934; Age 4 months;
       Bolivar, Origin; Born June 27, 1934; Buried same day at
       Bolivar Cemetery; Rev. A. M. Maechler, Minister

293   MAUBAULES, JOHNNY FAY   November 18, 1934; Age 3; Bolivar,
       Origin; Died of Pneumonia; Buried November 19 at Bolivar
       Cemetery; Rev. A. M. Maechler, Minister

 28   MAURER, AMIZE MRS. (nee Hamilton)   July 4, 1903; Age 26; Wife of
       Joseph Maurer; Buried July 5; Rev. J. B. Weimer, Minister

155   MAURER, MRS. CAROLINE (nee Schaer)   May 22, 1917; Age 68; Widow
       of John Maurer; Buried May ... in Calvary Cemetery; Rev. P. M.
       Lennartz, Minister

147   MAURER, GEORGE   November 14, 1916; Age 21, Born 10-18-1895;
       Michael Maurer and Frances Tischendorf, Parents; Buried
       November 15 at Calvary Cemetery; Rev. P. M. Lennartz, Minister

150   MAURER, JOHN   February 15, 1917; Age 65, Born October 6, 1851;
       Runenberg, Germany, Origin; Married Caroline Schaer; Buried
       February 17; Rev. P. M. Lennartz, Minister

       MAURER, THERESA MARIE see Mrs. Tickle #176

178   MAURER, WENDELIN   January 22, 1919; Age 32, Born April 25, 1887;
       Michael Maurer and Frances Tischendorf, Parents; Buried
       January 24; Rev. P. M. Lennartz, Minister

 32   MAYER, MRS. ELIZABETH   October 4, 1903; Age 84; Widow; Bavaria,
       Origin; Buried October 5; Rev. J. B. Weimer, Minister

       MAYER, JOSEPHINE see Mrs. Machin #70

335   MC GOWAN, MRS. BRIDGET   March 11, 1949; Age 80½, Born September
       11, 1868; Widow; Ireland, Origin; Buried March 12 with Mass,
       J. Levy & Brother at Old Catholic Cemetery; Rev. A. M.
       Maechler, Minister

349   EUGENE MEIERS   May 30, 1962; Age 52, Born January 17, 1910;
       San Diego, Calif., Origin; Residence at 2114 M½; Mary
       Pinkerberg's husband; Funeral at 10:00 a.m. with mass, J.
       Levy; Buried at Oleander, family plot

127   MENZEL, CHARLES   May 14, 1914; Age 75; Buried May 15 at
       Calvary Cemetery; Rev. P. M. Lennartz, Minister

       MENZEL, EDITH see Mrs. Gunter #259

134   MENZEL, MRS. MARY ELIZABETH   February 3, 1915; Widow; Age ca.
       69, Born Mary Eliz. Hornung; Wife of Charles Menzel (late)
       #127; Buried February 4 at Calvary Cemetery; Rev. P. M.
       Lennartz, Minister

 51   MENZEL, OTTO FREDERIC   June 19, 1905; Age 23; Buried June 22;
       Rev. Jos. Mack per Rev. J. B. Weimer, Minister

       METZGER, ANTON see Kraemer #58

 43   METZGER, MRS. MARY   September 17, 1904; Age 73; Wife of Anton
       Metzger; Buried September 18; Rev. J. B. Weimer, Minister

       MEURY, JULIA see Mrs. Junker #168

122   MEYER, ANNA   November or December 3, 1913; Age 70; Buried 4th
       of same month at Calvary Cemetery; Rev. P. M. Lennartz,
       Minister

 31   MEYER, MRS. MARY   August 17, 1903; Widow; Age 77; Buried August
       18; Rev. J. B. Weimer, Minister

352   MEZA, MRS. JOHN (OLGA INEZ)   March 10, 1966; Age 71, Born
       September 29, 1894; Residence 1911 Ave. L.; Died at St. Mary's
       Hospital; Funeral on March 12, 10:00 a.m. at St. Josp. with
       mass; Buried at Calvary Cemetery, Malloy and Son; Note: Rev.
       N. Perusina said the Mass; Rev. J. Perusina conducted the
       body from Molloys and at cemetery; Rev. A. M. Maechler,
       Minister

354   MEZA, JOHN F.   August 27, 1966; Widower; Residence 1911 Ave. L;
       Born May 30. 1891; Mexico, Origin; Died at residence, sudden,
       heart; Funeral on August 29 at 10:00 a.m. with mass at St.
       Josephs; Buried at Calvary Cemetery, Malloy and Son; Rev.
       A. M. Maechler, Minister

234   MICHALIK, VINCENT   September 1, 1925; Age 41, Born 1884;
       Grosmarasdorf, Austria, Origin; Anton Michalik and Rose
       Bintiger, Parents; Died of Heart failure; Buried September 4
       at Calvary Cemetery; Rev. P. M. Lennartz, Minister

339   MILES, MRS. ANNA MARY (nee Bendixen)   November 6, 1951; Age 64,
       Born April 20, 1888; Married Lawrence A. Miles; Died at John
       Sealy Hospital; Buried November 8, with mass, J. Levy and
       Brothers, at New City Cemetery; Rev. A. M. Maechler, Minister

       MONSHAUSEN, MARY see Pflum #29

202   MONSHAUSEN, MRS. SELMA   July 15, 1921; Age 54, Born August 16,
       1867; Steinhofen, Hohenzollern, Origin; Immigrant 1890;
       Married John Monshausen in 1893; Buried July 16 at Calvary
       Cemetery; Rev. P. M. Lennartz, Minister

211   MORGAN, MRS. ELIZABETH (nee Blantz)   November 7, 1922; Age 68,
       Born June 17, 1854; Studgard, (New Orleans), Origin; Married
       William Morgan 9-19-1875; Buried November 8 at Calvary
       Cemetery; Rev. P. M. Lennartz, Minister

       MOSER, ELIZABETH see Mrs. Kirk #141

104   MOSER, JOHN HENRY   March 19, 1912; Widower; Age 59, Born
       October 3, 1853; Born on board ss Star of Republic (Mallory
       Line); Married Agnes Niedenfeur on 12-12-1885; Buried March
       20 at Old Catholic Cemetery; Rev. P. M. Lennartz, Minister

       MUEHE, MARY SOPHIE see Mrs. Ricke #254

341   MOSER, MISS PAULA   October 18, 1953; Age 90, Born October 17,
       1863; Galveston, Origin; Died of old age complications; Peter
       Hysinth Moser and Elizabeth Schnmacher, Parents; Buried
       October 20, 1953 at Old Catholic Cemetery, Malloys; Rev.
       A. M. Maechler, Minister

       MUELLER, CLARA see Mrs. Schulte #180

198   MUELLER, HENRY   April 1, 1921; Age 87, Born 1834; Widower;
       Buried April 2 at Calvary Cemetery; Rev. P. M. Lennartz,
       Minister

 12   MULHOLLAND, MARGUERITE   January 1902; Age 3; Buried January 17;
       Rev. J. B. Weimer, Minister

347   MUNN, MRS. HELEN (nee Nichols)   March 9, 1961; Age 64, Born
       2-17-1897; Galveston, Origin; Widow; Died of Hemmoriging
       ulcers; Funeral March 11, 1961 with mass, 9:00 a.m., Malloy;
       Buried at Old Catholic Cemetery, Rev. Anton Frank went to
       Cemetery; Rev. A. M. Maechler, Minister; Note; Mrs. Munn
       was not a parishiner, though see attended services almost
       regularly

 93   NEIS, JAMES   September 24, 1910; Age 70; Husband of Margaret
       Kirchem; Buried September 25; Rev. J. B. Weimer, Minister

154   NEIS, MARGUERITE   May 11, 1917; Age 74; Widow; Married John
       Neis; Buried May 12 at Calvary Cemetery; Rev. P. M. Lennartz,
       Minister

333   NICHOLS, MRS. CATHERINE   August 27, 1948; Widow; Age 78, Born
       April 6, 1870; Galveston (Philipson), Origin; Died at John
       Sealy Hospital; Buried August 28 with mass, Malloy at Old
       Catholic Cemetery; Rev. A. M. Maechler, Minister

 97   NUESE, LAWRENCE   February 28, 1911; Age 90; Buried March 1;
       Rev. J. B. Weimer, Minister

108   OEHLERT, MRS. MAUD (nee Siler)   August 6, 1912; Age 25, Born
       September 1887; Married John Fred Oehlert on 4-20-1908; Buried
       August 7; Rev. P. M. Lennartz, Minister

       OEHLSCHLAEGER, CATHERINE see Mrs. Eckstein #162

306   ORTLON, N. N.   June 12, 1937; Age 5 hours; Bolivar, Origin;
       Mr. and Mrs. Jim Ortlon of Patton, Texas, Parents; Baptized
       privately; Born June 12, 1937; Buried June 13 at Bolivar
       Cemetery, Malloy; Rev. A. M. Maechler, Minister

235   OSTERMAYER, LOUIS ARTHUR   October 5, 1925; Age 5 days;
       Born September 30, 1925; Buried October 6 at Lakeview
       Cemetery; Rev. P. M. Lennartz, Minister; Louise Arthur
       Ostermayer and Alice Wagner, Parents

       PARKER, SARAH see Mrs. Anderson #332

313   PEINE, JOHN   January 31, 1940; Age 81, born December 9, 1858;
       Galveston, Origin; Single; Buried February 2 with Mass at
       Old Catholic Cemetery; Rev. A. M. Maechler, Minister

10   PEINE, JOSEPH   December 27, 1901; Age 75; Widower; Husband of
      Margaret Rose (deceased); Buried December 30; Rev. J. B.
      Weimer, Minister

246   PEINE, MARTIN   April 29, 1927; Age 61, Born November 3, 1865;
      Single; Galveston, Origin; Joseph Peine and Margaret Bore,
      Parents; Died of Tuberculosis; Buried May 1 at Old Catholic
      Cemetery; Rev. P. M. Lennartz, Minister

334   PEINE, MARY J.   February 9, 1949; Age 81½, Born June 3, 1867;
      Single; Galveston, Origin; Died at St. Mary's Inf.; Buried
      February 10 with Mass, Malloy, at Old Catholic Cemetery;
      Rev. A. M. Maechler, Minister

30   PETERS, HENRY   August 16, 1903; Age 52; Married; Austria,
      Origin; Buried August 17; Rev. J. B. Weimer, Minister

115   PETERSEN, MRS. ANNA JOSEPHINE (nee Hansen)   February 6, 1913;
      Age 45, Born July 27, 1868; Married Anthony Christian
      Peterson, n.c., on April 22, 1908; Buried February 7 at
      Calvary Cemetery; Rev. P. M. Lennartz, Minister

204   PFLUEGER, MRS. ELIZABETH (nee Schneider)   January 19, 1920;
      Age 78, Born April 5, 1842; Immigrant in 1846; Married George
      Pflueger 11-3-1860; Buried January 21 at Lake View Cemetery;
      Rev. P. M. Lennartz, Minister

282   PFLUGER, CHARLES GEORGE   March 7, 1933; Age 56, Born July 14,
      1876; Galveston, Origin; George and Elizabeth Pfluger,
      Parents; Attended by chaplain at St. Mary's Inf. upon death;
      Buried March 8 at Lakeview Cemetery, Malloy; Rev. A. M.
      Maechler, Minister

29   PFLUM, MARY (Monshausen)   July 25, 1903; Age 13; Buried July 26;
      Rev. J. B. Weimer, Minister

      PHILIPSON, CATHERINE see Mrs. Nichols #333

62   PHILIPPSON, ROBERT   September 13, 1906; Age 72; Buried September
      14; Rev. J. B. Weimer, Minister

277   PHILIPSON, THOMAS   June 19, 1932; Age 63; Died of heart
      trouble; Buried June 20 at Old Catholic Cemetery; Rev. A. M.
      Maechler, Minister

52   PICTURE, FRANK   July 20, 1905; Age 21; Buried July 21; Rev. Jos.
      Mack per Rev. J. B. Weimer, Minister

149   PICTURE, MRS. LOUISE   January 25, 1917; Age 69; Nee Viewerger;
      Germany, Origin; Buried January 26 at Calvary Cemetery; Rev.
      P. M. Lennartz, Minister

      PICTURE, ROSALIE see Mrs. Johnston #205

342   PICTURE, WILLIAM H.   June 20, 1953; Died at St. Mary's Inf.;
      Buried June 22 with Mass at Calvary Cemetery, Levy; A. M.
      Maechler, Minister

138   PINKENBERG, MRS. THERESA MARY (nee Stumpf)   September 20, 1915;
      Age 38, Born August 7, 1877; Married Fred Pinkerberg, n.c.,
      1894; Buried September 21 at Calvary Cemetery; Rev. P. M.
      Lennartz, Minister

      PROCKOFF, THERESA see Mrs. Delz #288

285   PROSPER, LEO JOSEPH   November 4, 1933; Age 57; Attended by
      chaplain at St. Mary's Inf.; Cause of death chronic myocarditis
      and nephritis; Buried November 5, 1933 O. L. of Mercy Church
      (Bol) and Bolivar Cemetery; Rev. A. M. Maechler, Minister

283   QUINN, MRS. MARY A.   July 25, 1933; Age 86; Greenland, Scotland,
      Origin; Died of fracture of femur at St. Mary's Infirmary;
      Buried July 26 with mass, Malloy and Son, at Calvary Cemetery;
      Rev. A. M. Maechler, Minister

      RALLEY, EMMA see Mrs. Rogano #261

310   RANKIN, MYRL   August 21, 1938; Age 11, Born August 16, 1927;
      First Communion and Extr Unct August 15, 1938 at St. Mary's
      Inf.; Buried August 23 with Mass, Malloy, at Memorial Park,
      Hitchcock, Texas; Rev. A. M. Maechler, Minister

161   RATLIFF, N. N.   December 2, 1917; Died at birth; Leslie
      Ratliff and Margaret Kirk, Parents; Buried December 3 at
      Calvary Cemetery; Rev. P. M. Lennartz, Minister

107   REIN, ANNA   July 25, 1912; Age 2½, Born January 20, 1910;
      William Rein and Mary Brown, Parents; Died of Tetanus;
      Buried July 27 at Calvary Cemetery; Rev. P. M. Lennartz,
      Minister

321   RESSEL, MRS. CAROLINE (nee Tschiedl)   August 1, 1942; Age 88,
      Born August 20, 1853; Germany, Origin; Died of old age;
      Buried August 2 at Calvary Cemetery, Malloy; Rev. A. M.
      Maechler, Minister

300   RESSEL, EMMA   December 14, 1935; Single; Buried December 16 at
      Calvary Cemetery; Rev. A. M. Maechler, Minister

137   RESSEL, FRANK JOSEPH   June 25, 1915; Age 64; Married; Buried
      June 26; Rev. P. M. Lennartz, Minister

275   RESSEL, CHARLES AUGUST   January 18, 1932; Age 43, Born July 17,
      1888; Galveston, Origin; Frank Jos. Ressel and Caroline
      Tschiedl, Parents; Died of Diabetes; Buried January 19 at
      Calvary Cemetery; Rev. P. M. Lennartz, Minister

167   RICKE, MRS. ANNA MARY   July 1, 1918; Age 59, Born September 22,
      1859; Balvaria, Origin; Nee Hock; George Hock and Margaret
      Maindhoff, Parents; Immigrant April 21, 1881; Married Martin
      Ricke 1-7-1884; Buried July 2 at Calvary Cemetery; Rev. P. M.
      Lennartz, Minister

 95   RICKE, MARTIN   February 15, 1911; Husband of Mary Hock; Buried
      February 16; Rev. J. B. Weimer, Minister

254   RICKE, MARY SOPHIE (nee Muehe)   December 29, 1928; Age 94,
      Born April 21, 1834; Married John Joseph Ricke; Died of old
      age; Buried December 31 at Old Catholic Cemetery; Rev. P. M.
      Lennartz, Minister

 68   RICKE, WILLIAM FREDERIC   June 24, 1907; Age 33; Son of John
      Ricke; Died a violent death; Buried June 25; Rev. J. B.
      Weimer, Minister

153   RIESENHUBER, ALOYSIUS FRANK   March 11, 1917; Age 10 months;
      Born May 3, 1916; Frank and Mary Riesenhuber, Parents;
      Buried March 12 at Calvary Cemetery; Rev. P. M. Lennartz,
      Minister

      RITZLER, ELIZABETH see Mrs. Bauhans #206

273   RITZLER, ELLIS F.   January 16, 1931; Age 28, Born September 15,
      1903; Buried January 17 at Lakeview Cemetery; Henry Ritzler
      and Mary Goebhart, Parents; Rev. P. M. Lennartz, Minister

324   RITZLER, HENRY   October 23, 1944; Age 77, Born July 28, 1867;
      Galveston, Origin; Buried October 25 at Lakeview Cemetery,
      J. Levy and Brothers; Rev. A. M. Maechler, Minister

  6   ROEHRMANN, THERESA   March 28, 1901; Age 82; Widow; Buried
      March 29; Rev. J. B. Weimer, Minister

 19   ROEMER, MRS. ANNA MARY   September 7, 1902; Age 76; Widow of
      Christopher Roemer; Buried September 8; Rev. J. B. Weimer,
      Minister

261   ROGANO, MRS. EMMA RALLEY   December 23, 1929; Age 36, Born
      December 25, 1893; Missouri, Origin; Married Antonio Rogano
      (civil marriage) on July 5, 1924; Buried December 26 at
      Hitchcock, Texas; Rev. P. M. Lennartz, Minister

139   ROHDE, JOSEPH HENRY   November 10, 1915; Age 17, Born November
      26, 1898; Louis George Rhode and Sophie Louise Windmeyer,
      Parents; Buried November 11 at Calvary Cemetery; Rev. P. M.
      Lennartz, Minister

327   ROONEY, FRANCIS   September 14, 1945; Age 78, Born March 4, 1867;
      Ireland, Origin; Buried September 17 with mass, J. Levy and
      Brothers, at Memorial Park, Hitchcock, Texas; Rev. A. M.
      Maechler, Minister

 21   RUBION, EUGENE   October 16, 1902; Age 10; Buried October 17;
      Rev. J. B. Weimer, Minister

      RUEHRMAN, THERESA see Mrs. Schocke #199

322   RYAN, MRS. GEORGIANA   November 26, 1943; Age 70; Port Bolivar,
      Origin; Buried November 27 in Bolivar Cemetery, Froberg,
      Alvin; Rev. A. M. Maechler, Minister

177   SABATIER, CHARLES   December 9, 1918; Married Wilhelmina Schocke,
      3-4-1915; Died instantly on Dry Dock; Buried December 11 at
      Calvary Cemetery; Rev. P. M. Lennartz, Minister

111   SAMMET, FRANK   October 8, 1912; Age 66, Born in 1846; Single;
      Buried October 9 at City Cemetery; Rev. P. M. Lennartz,
      Minister

307   SCHAEFER, MRS. ANNIE SUSAN (nee Gengler)   March 15, 1938; Age 82,
      Born June 24, 1855; Galveston, Origin; Died of Cerebral
      Hemorrhage; Buried March 16 at Calvary Cemetery; Rev. A. M.
      Maechler, Minister

160   SCHAEFER, HENRY CHARLES   December 17, 1917; Age 64, Born April
      24, 1853; Christian Schaefer and Mary Anne Wunder, Parents;
      Married Anna Susan Gengler 7-18-1876; Buried December 18 at
      Calvary Cemetery; Rev. P. M. Lennartz, Minister

240   SCHAEFER, MATHILDA (nee Liebisch)   April 30, 1926; Age 70, Born
      January 1, 1856; Austria, Origin; David and Helen Liebisch,
      Parents; Married Joseph Schaefer in 1881; Immigrant to Galveston
      in 1911; Died of old age; Buried May 1; Rev. P. M. Lennartz,
      Minister

133   SCHEELE, MRS. ANNA   January 2, 1915; Age 76, Born October 4,
      1838; Seidler by first marriage; Franfurt a/M, Germany,
      Origin; Married January 16, 1889; Buried January 3 at Calvary
      Cemetery; Rev. P. M. Lennartz, Minister

145   SCHIEBEL, MARTIN   September 15, 1916; Buried September 16 at
      Calvary Cemetery; Rev. P. M. Lennartz, Minister

124   SCHMIDT, ADAM WILLIAM   February 7, 1914; Age 2 years, 4 months,
      Born October 17, 1911; Adolf Henry Schmidt and Josephine
      Cath ..., Parents; Buried February 9 at Calvary Cemetery;
      Rev. P. M. Lennartz, Minister

 72   SCHMIDT, MARY ELLEN   October 1, 1907; Age 22; Buried October 2;
      Rev. J. B. Weimer, Minister

136   SCHMIDT, WILLIAM   April 27, 1915; Age 67, Born November 11, 1847;
      Married Catherine Donaghan (Donovan); Buried April 18 at
      Calvary Cemetery; Rev. P. M. Lennartz, Minister

      SCHNEIDER, ELIZABETH see Mrs. Pfluger #204

 60   SCHNEIDER, JOHN   July 30, 1906; Age 3½ months; Buried July 31;
      Rev. J. P. Weimer, Minister

112   SCHOCKE, CHRISTIAN CHARLES   December 23, 1912; Age 92, Born
      March 17, 1820; Widower; Married Theresa Muehe, about 1850;
      Buried December 24 at Calvary Cemetery; Rev. P. M. Lennartz,
      Minister

 56   SCHOCKE, HELEN   February 20, 1906; Age 30; Buried February 21;
      Rev. J. B. Weimer, Minister

182   SCHOCKE, JOHN   August 29, 1919; Age 61, Born December 2, 1858;
      Christian Schocke and Theresa Muehe (Hanover, Germany), Parents;
      Buried August 30 at Calvary Cemetery; Rev. P. M. Lennartz,
      Minister

 82   SCHOCKE, JOSEPH   February 14, 1909; Age 15; Sudden death, no
      last sacr.; Son of Herman and Christina Schocke, Parents;
      Buried February 15; Rev. J. B. Weimer, Minister

302   SCHOCKE, MRS. OTTILIA (nee Hahnreiter)   February 25, 1936; Age 73,
      Born November 27, 1862; Munich, Germany, Origin; Resided here
      45 years; Died at home; Buried February 26 with Mass, Malloy,
      at Calvary Cemetery; Rev. A. M. Maechler, Minister

199   SCHOCKE, THERESA (nee Roehrman by adoption)   April 16, 1921;
      Age 62, Born December 2, 1858 of John Shubert and wife; Married
      William Frederic Schocke 4-6-1875; Buried April 17 at Calvary
      Cemetery; Rev. P. M. Lennartz, Minister

258   SCHOCKE, WILLIAM FREDERIC   July 15, 1929; Age 75; Died of old
      age; Buried July 16; Rev. P. M. Lennartz, Minister

303   SCHOCKE, WILLIAM FREDERIC   March 8, 1936; Age 51, Born February
      3, 1885; Galveston, Origin; Died after long illness; Buried
      March 9 at Calvary Cemetery, Malloy; Rev. A. M. Maechler,
      Minister

      SCHOER, CAROLINE see Mrs. Maurer #155

317   SCHOLZE, JOHN   January 20, 1941; Age 78; Buried January 21, J.
      Levy and Brother at Galveston Memorial Park in Hitchcock,
      Texas; Rev. A. M. Maechler, Minister

      SCHREIBER, MARY see Mrs. Weber #330

110   SCHREIBER, MRS. ROSINA (Mrs. Fluer)   October 14, 1912; Age 76,
      Born February 24, 1836; Baden, Germany, Origin; Married
      Herman Schreiber in 1856; Married George Fluer in 1896;
      Buried October 15 at Old Catholic Cemetery; Rev. P. M.
      Lennartz, Minister

180   SCHULTE, MRS. CLARA (nee Mueller)   August 13, 1919; Age 84, Born
       July 15, 1835; Widow; Married three times - 1) Weber, 2) John
       Schulte, 3) Henry Schulte; Buried August 15 at Calvary
       Cemetery; Rev. P. M. Lennartz, Minister

 59   SCHULTE, JOHN HENRY   July 22, 1906; Age 23; La Grange, Texas,
       Origin; Buried July 24; Rev. J. B. Weimer, Minister

       SCHULTE, THERESA MARY see Mrs. Gengler #278

 25   SCHWARZBACH, MRS. HELEN   January 1, 1903; Age 63; Widow; Baden
       Germany, Origin; Buried January 2; Rev. J. B. Weimer, Minister

188   SCHWARTZER, JOSEPH   June 1920; Age 44; Single; Drowned on dredge
       boat; Buried June 7 at Lakeview Cemetery; Rev. P. M. Lennartz,
       Minister

       SEIDLER, ANNA see Mrs. Scheele #133

158   SEILER, MRS. CATHERINE (nee Brice)   November 4, 1917; Widow;
       Age 59, Born December 13, 1858; Married Frederic Seiler
       (died 1892); Buried November 5 at Calvary Cemetery; Rev. P.
       M. Lennartz, Minister

       SELENSKI, MARGARET see Mrs. Berger #73

213   SENECHAL, LOUIS WILLIAM   March 15, 1923; Age 60, Born April 15,
       1863; Married Rosa Grenrood; Buried March 16 at Calvary
       Cemetery; Rev. P. M. Lennartz, Minister

       SHASOLM, LEONA JOSEPHINE see Mrs. Crittenden #265

319   SHAW, WILLIAM JAMES   November 16, 1941; Age 52, Born November
       29, 1888; Sydney, Australia, Origin; Died in U. S. Marine
       Hospital; Buried November 17 at Memorial Park, Hitchcock,
       Malloy; Rev. A. M. Maechler, Minister

195   SIKICH, WALTER PAUL   December 13, 1920; Age 3½ months, Born
       August 27, 1920; Walter Paul Sikich and Alice Roark (Roach?),
       Parents; Buried December 14 at Calvary Cemetery; Rev. P. M.
       Lennartz, Minister

102   SILER, LAURA   January 19, 1912; Age 21, Born November 3, 1890;
       Frederic Siler and Catherine Brice, Parents; Died in San
       Marcos, Texas; Buried January 21 at Calvary Cemetery; Rev.
       P. M. Lennartz, Minister

       SILER, MAUD see Mrs. Oehlert #108

311   SILVA, JESSIE   February 13, 1939; Age 1 month; Port Bolivar,
       Origin; Born January 13, 1939; Bapt priv St. Mary's Inf. on
       February 12; Buried February 14 at Bolivar Cemetery, Malloy;
       Rev. A. M. Maechler, Minister

 80   SKARKE, ADELE ANNA MARY   November 19, 1908; Age 1 week;
       Frederic Skarke and Pauline Blaschka, Parents; Buried
       November 20; Rev. J. B. Weimer, Minister

140   SKARKE, JOSEPH   January 8, 1916; infant still-born; Charles
       Skarke and Anna Malcher, Parents; Buried January 9 at Calvary
       Cemetery

308   SKARKE, MARY ROSALIE   June 24, 1938; Age 74; Single; Died of
       Chronic Nephritis; Buried June 27 at Catholic Cemetery at
       Schulenburg, Texas, Malloy; Rev. A. M. Maechler, Minister

       SOMMER, ANNA MARY see Mrs. Carroll #332 a

232   SOMMER, AUGUST   May 7, 1925; Age 75, Born September 26, 1849; Austria, Origin; Immigrant in 1853; Married Mary Herrgott 1876; Buried May 9 at Calvary Cemetery; Rev. P. M. Lennartz, Minister

123   SOMMER, CHARLES LOUIS   January 7, 1914; Age 56, Born March 13, 1858; Galveston, Origin; Frank and Theresa Sommer, Parents; Married Louise Keveny on April 30, 1879; Buried January 8 at Lakeview Cemetery; Rev. P. M. Lennartz, Minister

316   SOMMER, MRS. (A. L.) HELEN (nee Gengler)   August 17, 1940; Age 82, Born June 25, 1858; Liverpool, Texas, Origin; Died of Coronary Thrombosus; Buried August 18 at Old Catholic Cemetery (Malloy); Rev. A. M. Maechler, Minister

SOMMER (?), LOUISE see Lammer #236

215   SOMMER, MRS. MARY (nee Herrgott)   June 2, 1923; Age 66, Born February 20, 1857; Galveston, Origin; Married August Sommer in 1876; Buried June 4 at Calvary Cemetery; Rev. P. M. Lennartz, Minister

304   SOSBY, JOHN   December 22, 1936; Age 67; Port Bolivar, Origin; Died Chronic Myocarditis at St. Mary's Infirmary; Buried December 23 at Bolivar Cemetery, Levy; Rev. John Doyle, SSJ (Rev. A. M. Maechler), Minister

148   SPEAKER, MRS. MARY (nee Hills)   November 24, 1916; Widow; Age 81, Born April 15, 1835; Germany, Origin; Immigrant with parents in 1861; Buried November 25 at Calvary Cemetery; Rev. P. M. Lennartz, Minister

 46   STELZEL, MARY   December 14, 1904; Age 13 days; Richard Wigand Stelzel and Mary Martin, Parents; Buried December 15; Rev. J. B. Weimer, Minister

328   STELZEL, SUSIE   April 16, 1876; Age 70, Born April 16, 1876; Single; Caberland, Germany, Origin; John Stelzel and Barbara Weimer, Parents; Died in State Hospital, San Antonio; Buried November 6 at Calvary Cemetery, Malloy; Rev. A. M. Maechler, Minister

280   STEWART, JOHN LAWRENCE   September 3, 1932; Age 72, Born November 17, 1859; Died suddenly, heart trouble, in John Sealy Hospital; Buried September 5 at Old City Cemetery, Malloy; Rev. A. M. Maechler, Minister

STUMPF, ANNA see Mrs. Kameyer #175

 90   STUMPF, MRS. ANNA (nee Burlington)   December 20, 1909; Age 30; Wife of John Stumpf; Buried December 21; Rev. J. B. Weimer, Minister

42A   STUMPF, EMMA WILHELMINE   September 6, 1904; Age 3 months; John Joseph Stumpf and Anna Theresa (Burlington), Parents; Buried September 7; Rev. J. B. Weimer, Minister

214   STUMPF, LOUISE CATHERINE   December 15, 1922; Age 17, Born January 29, 1906; John Jos. Stumpf and Anna Theresa Burlington, Parents; Buried December 17 at Calvary Cemetery; Rev. P. M. Lennartz, Minister

 17   STUMPF, MARY MARTHA   March 25, 1902; Age 1 year and 6 days; Buried March 26; Rev. J. B. Weimer, Minister

STUMPF, THERESA MARY see Mrs. Pinkenberg #138

 20   STUMPF, WILLIAM   October 3, 1902; Age 68; Buried October 6; Rev. J. B. Weimer, Minister

176   TICKLE, THERESA MARY (Mrs.) (nee Maurer)   November 23, 1918;
       Age 46, Born May 12, 1872; John and Caroline Maurer, Parents;
       Married Joseph Bennet Tickle 6-29-1892; Buried November 25 at
       Calvary Cemetery; Rev. P. M. Lennartz, Minister

170   TISCHENDORF, MRS. CAROLINE   August 29, 1918; Widow; Age 73,
       Born (Hummel) February 2, 1845; Baden-Baden, Origin; Married
       Constantine Tischendorf in 1864; Buried September 4 in a
       mausoleum in a non-Catholic cemetery; Rev. P. M. Lennartz,
       Minister

131   TREACCAR, ALVIN JOSEPH   July 5, 1914; Age 6 months, Born
       February 2, 1914; Alvin William Treaccar and Rose Gloger,
       Parents; Buried July 6 at Calvary Cemetery; Rev. P. M.
       Lennartz, Minister

230   TREACCAR, GERTRUDE MARY   February 9, 1922; Age 79, Born in 1843;
       Single; Frank William and Margaret Treaccar, Parents; Buried
       February 10 at City Cemetery; Rev. P. M. Lennartz, Minister

224   TREACCAR, FRANK WILLIAM   September 2, 1924; Age 48, Born August
       6, 1876; Joseph Treaccar and Lissie Heiman, Parents; Married
       Rose Gloger; Buried September 3 at City Cemetery; Rev. P. M.
       Lennartz, Minister

 61   TROST, HERMAN   August 20, 1906; Age 78; Buried August 22; Rev.
       J. B. Weimer, Minister

       TSCHIEDL (?), ANNA see Mrs. Jung #284

       TSCHIEDL, ANTONIA see Mrs. Fiesel #296

       TSCHIEDL, CAROLINE see Mrs. Ressel #321

318   VALENZUELA, ANN MARIE MARGUERITE   Ocotber 31, 1941; Age 2 days;
       Mr. and Mrs. Angelo Carlos Valenzuela; Born October 29, 1941;
       Died at St. Mary's Inf.; Buried October 31 at Old Catholic
       Cemetery, Levy; Rev. A. M. Maechler, Minister

       VAN ROCHON, WILHELMINE see Mrs. Buechner #164

 99   VIEWEGER, CHARLES AUGUST   April 6, 1911; Age 60; Buried August 7;
       Rev. J. B. Weimer, Minister

       VIEWEGER, LOUISE see Mrs. Picture #149

225   VON DEN ENDEN, WILLIAM SIMON HUBERT   September 23, 1924; Born
       January 19, 1842; Ruhrost, Germany, Origin; Widower; Arnold
       Von den Enden and Marg. Harstman, Parents; Immigrant in 1867;
       Married ...; Buried September 25 at Calvary Cemetery; Rev. P.
       M. Lennartz, Minister

       VON STIMFRIED, BARONESS MARTHA see Mrs. Bernard #270

 78A   WAGNER, MRS. CLARA (nee Gaschen)   March 28, 1908; Age 23; Buried
       March 29; Rev. J. B. Weimer, Minister

252   WEBER, EMIL JOSEPH   April 16, 1928; Age 61, Born December 28,
       1866; Germany, Origin; Married Mary Schreiber; Died of heart
       disease; Buried April 16 at Old Catholic Cemetery; Rev. P. M.
       Lennartz, Minister

330   WEBER, MRS. (E. J.) MARY (nee Schreiber)   February 12, 1947;
       Age 81, Born July 28, 1865; Galveston, Origin; Died at
       Nursing Home at 1826 Ave I; Buried February 13 at Old
       Catholic Cemetery, Malloy; Rev. A. M. Maechler, Minister

197   WEBER, ROBERT JOHN   January 31, 1921; Age 5½, Born July 29, 1915; Alex John Weber and Catherine Breen, Parents; Buried February 2 at Calvary Cemetery; Rev. P. M. Lennartz, Minister

22   WEHMEYER, CATHERINE   November 22, 1902; Age 71; Convert; Buried November 23; Rev. J. B. Weimer, Minister

WEIMER, BARBARA CATHERINE see Mrs. Barbung #117

100   WEIMER, VERY REV. JOHN BAPTIST, V. G.   September 30, 1911; Age 64, Born July 17, 1847; Low Hattemar, Nassua Germany, Origin; Frank Weimer and Charlotte Catherine Malz, Parents; Came to the USA as student for this diocese by the Most Rev. Bishop Dubois; Ordained by bishop Dubois at Cathedral in Galveston in 1871; Pastor of Mentz 1873 - 1891; Thansferred to St. Joseph's in 1891; Made Vicar General by Bishop N. A. Gallagher wich office he held to his death; Buried October 4 in the presence of the Bishop of the diocese, and the clergy and a great concourse of people, at Calvary Cemetery; Rev. P. M. Lennartz, Minister

142   WEINBERGER, ALOYSIUS   April 13, 1916; Age 52, Born May 13, 1864; Deggendorf, Bavaria, Origin; Immigrant in September 9, 1916; Died in accident; Buried April 15 at Calvary Cemetery; Rev. P. M. Lennartz, Minister

88   WERDEHAUSEN, WILLIAM   September 9, 1909; Age 47; Married; Buried September 10; Rev. J. B. Weimer, Minister

263   WICKES, GEORGIA VERONICA   February 4, 1930; Age 27, Born December 22, 1902; Harry M. Wickes and Lena Theresa Leinbach, Parents; Died in New York of heart trouble; Buried February 8 at Old Catholic Cemetery; Rev. P. M. Lennartz, Minister

171   WIESCHKA, FRANK FREDERIC CHARLES   October 1, 1918; Age 28, Born June 30, 1890; Erfurt, Germany, Origin; Single; Frank Wieschka and Mary Louise Helbig, Parents; Buried October 2 at Calvary Cemetery; Rev. P. M. Lennartz, Minister

WILD, MARY see Mrs. Winker #4

320   WILLIAMS, MRS. EVA   May 26, 1942; Age 75, Born December 28, 1866; Widow; New Orleans, La., Origin; Buried May 28 at Calvary Cemetery, Malloy; Rev. A. M. Maechler, Minister

4   WINKER, MRS. MARY (nee Wild)   January 23, 1901; Widow; Age 75; Westphalia, Origin; Buried January 24; Rev. J. B. Weimer, Minister

119   WOLFF, MRS. ROSE (nee Hornung)   August 7, 1913; Age 55, Born March 16, 1858; Belheim, Germany, Origin; Married Frederic Wolff; Buried August 8 at Calvary Cemetery; Rev. P. M. Lennartz, Minister

YOUNG, ANNA see Mrs. Gilbert #190

71   ZACHARKO, OLGA   September 12, 1907; Age 1 month; John Zacharko and Anna Hnatio (sic), Parents; Buried same day; Rev. G. J. Dane, S. J., Minister

253   ZAERKE, OSCAR   November 7, 1928; Age 4, Born July 23, 1924; Oscar Zaerke and Myrthle Buckley, Parents; Died of child's sickness; Buried November 8 at Calvary Cemetery; Rev. P. M. Lennartz, Minister

BAPTISMAL RECORDS
1860 - 1900

William Leroy Harry ABBOTT - Henry ABBOTT and Rebecca MILLICH, Parents; Mathilda ADDINGTON, Godparent; Born March 4, 1899; Baptized April 1, 1899; #1948

Margaret Pauline ABELS - Henry Abels and Olive WILSON, Parents; Pauline ABELS and John WILSON, Godparents; Born December 29, 1874; Baptized June 6, 1875; #752

August Herman John ALBERT (Name could be ELBERT) - John ALBERT and Elizabeth DWANE, Parents; Herman SCHOKE and Christina MARKS, Godparents; Born December 12, 1887; Baptized January 29, 1888; #1370

Mary Gertrude ALDRIDGE - ... ALDRIDGE and Helen SPANN, Parents; Bessy SPANN, Godparent; Baptized May 23, 1866 (Private); Born ...

Caroline Nicholas ALFSON and Josephine Anna ALFSON - Chas. ALFSON and Cath. EISEN, Parents; Nicholas EISEN and Magdalen GENGLER, Godparents; Born January ..., 1872; Baptized January 28, 1872; #611

Frederick James ALLEN - James ALLEN and Leora MORTON, Parents; L. W. SENECHAL, Godparent; (Convert); Born September 15, 1862; Baptized April 8, 1900; #1984

William Henry ALLEN (Convert); Baptized September 14, 1867; #371

Mary Helen ALMERAS - Peter ALMERAS and Mary Ann McPHILIPS, Parents; Joseph VIGNE and Mary Vigne, Godparents; Born January 4, 1863; Baptized May 10, 1863; #109

Rose Ann Elisa ALMERAS - Peter ALMERAS and Mary Ann McPHILIPS, Parents; Alex MESTRALE and Julianne Mary DESERA, Godparents; Born December 14, 1860; Baptized March 24, 1861; #37

Cath. Alley AMADO - Ignatius AMADO and Louise VITTER, Parents; Frederic SCHMIDT and Emily ROSE, Godparents; Born August 14, 1892; Baptized September 11, 1892; #1578

Lyddie Nellie AMADO - Ignatius AMADO and Louise VITTER, Parents; Victor VITTER and Louise RICHARDS, Godparents; Born September 12, 1895; Baptized October 27, 1895; #1735

William James ANDERSON - Olivar ANDERSON and Helen LYONS, Parents; Edward McSWEENEY and Anna BILLS, Godparents; Born March 15, 1871; Baptized July 2, 1871; #591

Caroline Elizabeth Eloine ANDERSON - Theophilo ANDERSON and Rosa BOCK, Parents; Caroline WENDEL and Robert NIPERT, Godparents; Born October 5, 1886; Baptized November 28, 1886; #1290

Frank Edward ANDERSON - Theophilo ANDERSON and Rosa BOCK, Parents; Lillie BOCK (by proxy) and Cora HALLIEN (?), Godparents; Born August 23, 1888; Baptized September 30, 1888; #1490

John Andrew ANDERSON - Theophilo ANDERSON and Rosa BOCK, Parents; Theophil F. HEIGEL and Mary HEIGEL, Godparents; Born March 24, 1885; Baptized May 21, 1885; #1161

Ethel Elizabeth ANDREWS - Victor ANDREWS and Elizabeth SULLIVAN, Parents; Elizabeth BELL and Rudolph BIEHLER, Godparents; Born July 13, 1894; Baptized February 22, 1895; #1702

Anna Catherine ANELLO - Frank ANELLO and Mary GATES, Parents; Joseph TARACE and Ann BUFFA, Godparents; Born January 20, 1886; Baptized January 30, 1886; #1213

John Robert ANELLO - Frank ANELLO and Mauly GATES, Parents; William FREDERICKS and Mrs. Pat. THIERNAM, Godparents; Born September 11, 1888; Baptized December 8, 1889; #1462

N. N. ANONYMOUS; Convert in Hospital; #376

N. N. ANONYMOUS; Infant; #377

N. N. ANONYMOUS; Convert in hospital; #378

N. N. ANONYMOUS; Convert in hospital; #379

N. N. ANONYMOUS; Convert in hospital; #380

Catherine ANONYMOUS - Susanna (Slave), Mother; Age 5 months; Baptized
May 10, 1864; Laura GREEN, Godparent; #154

Elizabeth ANONYMOUS - Selim ANONYMOUS and Sara FLAKE, Parents; Elizabeth
JOCKUSCH, Godparent; Born June 13, 1874; Baptized September 5, 1874;
#722

Charles ANONYMOUS; Convert in hospital; Baptized November 4, 1867; #384

Emil Leon ANONYMOUS - Charles ANONYMOUS and Elizabeth COERS, Parents;
... LEINBACK and Mary GERHARDT, Godparents; Born September 16, 1873;
Baptized September 16, 1874; #726

Francis ANONYMOUS - George ANONYMOUS and Lydia (Slaves), Parents;
Carolina M. SPANN, Godparent; Born October 1860; Baptized March 16, 1861;
#33

Frank ANONYMOUS - Henry ANONYMOUS and Fannie (Slaves) Parents; Laura
GREEN, Godparent; Age 15 months; Baptized May 10, 1864; #152

James ANONYMOUS - Samuel ANONYMOUS and Nanny (Slaves?), Parents; Laura
GREEN, Godparent; Age 14 months; Baptized May 10, 1864; #153

Joan ANONYMOUS; ... PHILIPPS and Magdalen GREYENBUEHL, Godparents;
Baptized April 12, 1873; Convert; #659

Laura Mary ANONYMOUS; Mary McVOLTY, Godparent; Baptized May 8, 1886;
#1236

Louise ANONYMOUS; Age 5 months; Amanda (Slave), Parent; Sara E. PEARSON,
Godparent; Baptized May 10, 1864; #155

Mary Helen ANONYMOUS; Emma Joan SMITH, Godparent; Baptized November 21,
1885; #1200

Moses ANONYMOUS - Lydia (Slave), Parent; Sara E. PEARSON, Godparent;
Age 5 months; Baptized May 10, 1864; #156

Robert ANONYMOUS; Orphan; Private in hospital; Baptized November 1, 1865;
#246

Joseph Frederic APPEL - Frederic APPEL and Ann WIGARD, Parents; Joseph
WIGARD and Mary MEYER, Godparents; Born November 21, 1885; Baptized
March 28, 1886; #1221

William Henry APPEL - Frederic William APPEL and Ann VIGARD, Parents;
Henry WEYER and Elizabeth ABELS, Godparents; Born April 21, 1880;
Baptized April 3, 1882; #962

Alphonso Aloysius ARNOLD - Isidor ARNOLD nad Mary Ann HUG, Parents;
John REMY and Laeticia MEAUME, Godparents; Born April 24, 1890;
Baptized May 25, 1890; #1492

Cecillia ARNOLD - Isidor ARNOLD and Mary Ann HUG, Parents; Henry
JOHNSON and Cecillia KING, Godparents; Born July 23, 1892; Baptized
1892; #1577

Edmund Beauregard ARNOLD - Isidor ARNOLD and Mary Ann HUG, Parents;
Gustav ARNOLD and Margaret ABELS, Godparents; Born May 5, 1896;
Baptized May 24, 1896; #1829

Rosina Mathilda ARNOLD - Isidore ARNOLD and Mary Ann HUG, Parents;
J. J. KRAUS and Mathilda Mary WEBER, Godparents; Born October 30, 1887;
Baptized November 27, 1887; #1365

Mary Ann Alice ARNOLD - Pauline ARNOLD, Parent; Frank CROTTY and Mary
Ann SCHULZ, Godparents; Born June 1, 1865; Baptized May 20, 1866; #288

Douglas Benjamin ARTO - Louis J. ARTO and Caroline ELBERT, Parents;
Benjamin ELBERT and Caroline ELBERT, Godparents; Born July 31, 1884;
Baptized September 29, 1884; #1097

Julia Joan (?) ARTO - Louis Joseph ARTO nad Caroline ELBERT, Parents;
James ARTO and Joan FLECK, Godparents; Born October 22, 1894; Baptized
August 1, 1895; #1726

Caroline Mary AUGSTEN - Wenceslans AUGSTEN and Mary Ann BLUMERING,
Parents; John Fred MICHELS and Mary Magdalen MICHELS, Godparents;
Born October 24, 1860; Baptized November 30, 1865; #250

Frank Anthony AUL - Anthony AUL and Theresa STUDER, Parents; Adopted;
Born May 21, 1894; Baptized July 6, 1894; #1670

James David AUL - David AUL and Minna WASSMUS, Parents; James MOSS and
Dora KEMPE, Godparents; Born October 12, 1885; Baptized October 25, 1885;
#1197

Joseph David AUL - David AUL and Minna WASSMUS, Parents; Pericles
LEGATOS and Cecil LEGATOS, Godparents; Born March 19, 1893; Baptized
April 29, 1893;

Mary Lillian AUL - David AUL and Minnie WASSMUS, Parents; Charles AUL
and Mary MOOR, Godparents; Born July 9, 1884; Baptized August 17, 1884;
#1090

Mary Theresa Antionette AUL - David AUL and Minna WASSMUS, Parents;
Frank Anthony AUL and Theresa AUL, Godparents; Born March 17, 1895;
Baptized April 6, 1895; #1710

Frederic Andrew AUL - Joseph AUL and Ann VULETICH, Parents; Frederic
AUL, Godparent; Born October 27, 1898; Baptized January 29, 1899;
#1937

George Andrew AUL - Joseph AUL and Catherine DESALM, Parents; Anthony
AUL and Mary AUL, Godparents; Born September 28, 1865; Baptized October
12, 1865; #231

James George AUL - Joseph AUL and Catherine DESALM, Parents; Edward
FUCHS and Agatha ARNOLD, Godparents; Born July 25, 1863; Baptized
August 14, 1863; #120

Philip AUL - Joseph AUL and Catherine DESALM, Parents; Joseph AUL and
Mary AUL, Godparents; Born July 4, 1861; Baptized July 14, 1861; #49

Joseph Vincent AUL - Joseph Vincent AUL and Emily WALKER, Parents;
Mrs. ABELS, Godparents; Born January 15, 1875; Baptized January 27, 1875;
#744

Mary Magdalen AUL - Joseph AUL and A. WALKER, Parents; G. SCHOCKE and
Emily GOUGAT, Godparents; Born September 1873; Baptized September 14,
1873; #680

Antonia Netta AUL - Nichols AUL and Lena MEYER, Parents; Anthony
RAPHAEL and Catherine AUL, Godparents; Born February 15, 1899; Baptized
April 2, 1899; #1960

Catherine Josephine AUL - Nicholas AUL and Lena MEYER, Parents; Bernard MAIR and Mary LESMANN, Godparents; Born June 16, 1881; Baptized July 10, 1881; #934

Elizabeth AUL - Nicholas AUL and Lena MEYER, Parents; Adolph DESALME and Catherine MEYER, Godparents; Born September 25, 1883; Baptized October 7, 1883; #1026

Magdalen (Lena) AUL - Nicholas AUL and Lena MEYER, Parents; Joseph AUL and Mary AUL, Godparents; Born May 5, 1892; Baptized May 14, 1892; #1562

Mary Balthosara AUL - Nicholas AUL and Lena MEYER, Parents; Catherine AUL and Henry GREEN, Godparents; Born January 6, 1895; Baptized January 24, 1895; #1700

Mary Cath. Regina AUL - Nicholas AUL and Caroline MEYER, Parents; Charles NOUS and Mary AUL, Godparents; Born February 18, 1886; Baptized February 25, 1886; #1218

Mary Magdalen AUL - Nicholas AUL and Caroline MEYER, Parents; Catherine AUL, Godparent; Born September 28, 1884; Baptized October 6, 1884; #1099

William Nicholas - William Nicholas AUL and Caroline MEYER, Parents; William MEYER and Mary SOMMER, Godparents; Born August 10, 1889; Baptized August 22, 1889; #1446

Bernard Julius BAEHR - Bernard BAEHR and Mary BAEHR, Parents; Julius THEVENOE and Catherine SPATEO, Godparents; Born February 4, 1893; Baptized March 5, 1893; #1596

George Bernard - Leonard BAEHR and Mary BAEHR, Parents; Elenora EWALD, Godparent; Born August 1, 1896; Baptized November 8, 1896; #1859

George Douglas BAKER - Daniel M. BAKER and Mary W. MURPHY, Parents; Born August 16, 1867; Baptized September 16, 1867; #372

Mary BAKER - William (nc) BAKER and Sophy SPIEKER, Parents; Mary BALDRY, Godparent; Born January 1, 1887; Baptized March 25, 1887; #1325

Anna Catherine BARLEMANN - Charles BARLEMANN and Theresa RICKE, Parents; Pierre Firmin DOLEAC and Catherine MAY, Godparents; Born March 3, 1888; Baptized April 15, 1888; #1388

Joseph Martin BARLEMANN - Charles BARLEMANN and Theresa RICKE, Parents; Joseph BEST and Mary HARTWIGT, Godparents; Born January 30, 1885; Baptized February 14, 1886; #1216

John Boniface BARLEMANN - Charles BARLEMANN and Theresa RICKE, Parents; John RICKE and Regina MUELLER, Godparents; Born May 14, 1883; Baptized May 20, 1883; #1009

Mary Magdalene Leocordina BARLEMANN - Charles BARLEMANN and Theresa RICKE, Parents; Violetta Leocordina RICKE, Godparent; Born December 20, 1893; Baptized January 1, 1894; #1638

William Charles BARLEMANN - Charles BARLEMANN and Mary Anna CARL, Parents; Emma BADER, Godparent; Born September 20, 1881; Baptized June 22, 1882; #970

William Frederic Christian BARLEMANN - Charles BARLEMANN and Theresa RICKE, Parents; William RICKE, Godparent; Born December 10, 1893; Baptized January 1, 1894; #1637

Mary Clementine BAROUX - John Bapt. BAROUX and Mary Evelyn BAUDENON, Parents; Frank GILLET and Mary Catherine V. BAROUX, Godparents; Born April 3, 1862; Baptized May 15, 1862; #78

Frank Vincent BARROW - Richard BARROW and Emily MONTEANT, Parents; Mary KING, Godparent; Born March 13, 1890; Baptized May 16, 1890; #1484

Charles Leo BARRY - Emil BARRY and Coralia ROBERT, Parents; Thomas SOHEN per August BLONDEAU and Elenora SOHEN, Godparents; Born December 30, 1865; Baptized January 24, 1867; #335

Mary Helen BARRY - Robert H. BARRY and Mathilda WEBER, Parents; George JOYCE and Mary ARNOLD, Godparents; Born July 14, 1891; Baptized August 22, 1891; #1528

John BARTHEL - Peter (nc) BARTHEL and Sara ALLEN, Parents; John H. COERS and Sara ALLEN, Godparents; Born August 25, 1886; Baptized May 1, 1886; #1232 (Private)

Peter Joseph BARTHEL - Peter (nc) BARTHEL and Sara ALLEN, Parents; Claude ALLEN and Sara ALLEN, Godparents; Born January 23, 1885; Baptized February 17, 1885; #1127

Frank Joseph BARTHOLMANS - Christian BARTHOLMANS and Joan TSCHOECKE, Parents; Joseph William RUECKE and Carolina RUECKE, Godparents; Born October 31, 1864; Baptized November 1, 1868; #425

Susan Joan BATEMAN - Charles BATEMAN and Odilia ROCK, Parents; Joan CREARY, Godparent; Born July 21, 1869; Baptized March 3, 1870; #549

Frank BATTI - Anthony BATTI and Mary CHRISTI, Parents; Jos. BIAGINI and Margaret LERA, Godparents; Born November 19, 1883; Baptized January 20, 1884; #1038

Mary Eugenia BATTI - Anton BATTI and Mary CHRISTI, Parents; Cajetan MARTINELLI and Eugenia MARTINELLI, Godparents; Born October 21, 1885; Baptized November 29, 1885; #1202

Catherine Caroline BAUHANS - George BAUHANS and Elizabeth RITZLER, Parents; Valentin RITZLER and Catherine MICHELS, Godparents; Born April 1, 1866; Baptized May 27, 1866; #291

Elizabeth BAUHANS - George BAUHANS and Elizabeth RITZLER, Parents; Valentin RITZLER and Elizabeth BECKERT, Godparents; Born October 18, 1868; Baptized December 20, 1868; #499

George BAUHANS; Private; Baptized July 2, 1872

Henry BAUHANS - George BAUHANS and Elizabeth RITZLER, Parents; Susanne SCHOBER, Godparent; Born December 29, 1857; Baptized May 7, 1865; Conditional; #199

James BAUHANS - George BAUHANS and Elizabeth RITZLER, Parents; Conditional; Susanne SCHOBER, Godparent; Born June 24, 1861; Baptized May 7, 1865; #201

Sophy Cath. Susan BAUHANS - George BAUHANS and Elizabeth RITZLER, Parents; F. W. WINDMEYER and Sophy FUNK, Godparents; Born August 25, 1863; Baptized November 8, 1863; #131

Valentine BAUHANS - George BAUHANS and Elizabeth RITZLER, Parents; Valentine RITZLER and Catherine BEST, Godparents; Born February 7, 1878; Baptized April 1, 1878; #841

William BAUHANS - George BAUHANS and Elizabeth RITZLER, Parents; Conditional; Susanne SCHOBER, Godparent; Born June 24, 1859; Baptized May 7, 1865; #200

Claude Oliver BAUMAN - Charles Ingomer BAUMAN and Catherine Rosa MUELLER, Parents; Larey LARSEN and Edna Christine ROHDE, Godparents; Born December 25, 1887; Baptized February 12, 1888; #1373

Anna Theresa BAUMANN - Christian BAUMANN and Agnes BROKOFF, Parents; Ann PEINE and William WINKLER, Godparents; Born April 11, 1893; Baptized May 7, 1893; #1604

Mary Magdalene BAUMANN - Christian BAUMANN and Agnes BROCKHOFF, Parents; John SCHOLZ and Sophy Mary EHLERT, Godparents; Born April 10, 1896; Baptized April 26, 1896; #1822

Maurice BAUMANN; Convert; Baptized April 6, 1890

Rose Barbara BAUMANN - Christian BAUMANN and Agnes BROKOFF, Parents; George DIEHL and Rose PICTURE, Godparents; Born November 3, 1888; Baptized November 11, 1888; #1415

William Maurice BAUMANN - Frederic Maurice (nc) BAUMANN and Ann (nc) BAUMANN, Parents; George Leonard BOHN and Victor ROTHENFLUEH, Godparents; Born December 1, 1887; Baptized March 9, 1890; #1475

Stephen BAUMANN; Convert; Baptized May 26, 1898

Emil Theodore Wenceslaus BAUMGART - Ernest BAUMGART and Frances ELLENBUERGER, Parents; Wenceslaus JUERSIG and Elizabeth JUERSIG, Godparents; Born May 19, 1864; Baptized July 17, 1864; #166

Mary L. BAYERTT - Frank BAYERTT and Julia DURONS, Parents; Bartholomew BIBO and Rosalee BIBO, Godparents; Born August 23, 1878; Baptized October 20, 1878; #868

Helen BEARD - John BEARD and Catherine BEARD, Parents; Emily SPANN, Godparent; Born March 14, 1865; Baptized April 19, 1865; #197

Joan Catherine BEARING - Edward J. (nc) BEARING and Joan (nc) SATTLER, Parents; William STUMPF, Godparent; Born October 8, 1886; Baptized April 1, 1888; Note; Name could be BIERING; #1383

Christopher Columbus BEAVINS; Conditional; Herman KRAUS, Godparent; Born January 6, 1842; Baptized January 10, 1885; #1121

Agnes Ann BECK - Louis BECK and Henrietta (nc) BOSER, Parents; Mary LANG nad Mrs. ARNOLD, Godparents; Born December 22, 1879; Baptized May 10, 1894; #1664

Hedwig Theresa BECK - Louis BECK and Henrietta BOSA, Parents; Conditional; Mrs. Marianna BALDRY, Godparents; Born January 3, 1877; Baptized October 19, 1889; #1453

Frank Jos. Lothar BECKER - Lothar BECKER and Amelia DOERR, Parents; Frederic Otto BECKER and Maggie BECKER, Godparents; Born July 17, 1887; Baptized July 23, 1887; #1354

Frank Louis BECKETT - John BECKETT and Elizabeth Joan ANDERSON, Parents; Catherine GIBERT, Godparent; Born January 21, 1861; October 31, 1861; #58

Abrasia Louise BECKMANN - Louis BECKMANN and Elizabeth STECHMANN, Parents; Abrose MONTFORT and Margaret STECHMANN, Godparents; Born January 13, 1891; Baptized February 22, 1891; #1515

August William BECKMANN - Louis BECKMANN and Elizabeth STECHMANN, Parents; Charles STECHMANN and Joan MONFORD, Godparents; Born January 7, 1889; Baptized March 24, 1889; #1426

Barbara Louise BECKMANN - Louis C. BECKMANN and Ann Elizabeth STECHMANN, Parents; Barbara STECHMANN and August STECHMANN, Godparents; Born January 2, 1884; Baptized January 27, 1884; #1039

Cecil Alberta BECKMANN - Louis BECKMANN and Elizabeth STECHMANN, Parents; August STECHMANN and Alberta STECHMANN, Godparents; Born September 23, 1893; Baptized October 29, 1893; #1626

Charles Andrew BECKMANN - Charles BECKMANN and Theresa RICKE, Parents;
Joseph RICKE and Mary RICKE, Godparents; Born November 10, 1800;
Baptized November 23, 1880; #911

Christian Louis BECKMANN; August STECHMANN Sr., Godparent; Born August
11, 1859; Baptized April 30, 1887;

Joseph William BECKMANN - Louis Charles BECKMANN and Elizabeth
STECHMANN, Parents; Josephine B. STECHMANN and Louis Hy. BECKMANN,
Godparents; Born July 18, 1899; Baptized August 16, 1899; #1961

Louis August BECKMANN - Louis BECKMANN and Elizabeth STECHMANN, Parents;
Henry and Margaret STECHMANN, Godparents; Born May 7, 1886; Baptized
June 11, 1886; #1252

Louise Ida BECKMANN - Louis BECKMANN and Mary RICKE, Parents; Ida RICKE,
Godparents; Born January 3, 1881; Baptized January 12, 1881; #915

Mary Magdalene BECKMANN - Louis BECKMANN and Elizabeth STECHMANN,
Parents; Henry STECHMANN and Mary STECHMANN, Godparents; Born August
25, 1896; Baptized September 6, 1896; #1847

Adelaide BEERMANN - John BEERMANN and Mary Ann HEIMANN, Parents;
Ottilia HEIMANN, Godparents; Born January 19, 1853; Baptized May 20,
1866; #286

Benjamin BEERMANN - John BEERMANNand Mary Ann HEIMANN, Parents; Anto
HEIMANN and Sarah ELLEN, Godparents; Born March 29, 1855; Baptized
May 20, 1866; #286

Henry Thomas BEERMANN - John BEERMANN and Mary Ann HEIMANN, Parents;
Conditional; Thomas McGUIRE and Elizabeth THORBES, Godparents; Born
April 29, 1865; Baptized April 15, 1866; #282

John BEERMANN; ca 50 years old; Baptized April 15, 1866; #280

Peter BEERMANN - John BEERMANN and Mary Ann HEIMANN, Parents; Peter
LASSEN by Elizabeth LASSEN, Godparents; Born October 18, 1856; Baptized
May 20, 1866; #287

Magdalene BEHR - Bernard* BEHR and Mary ..., Parents; John BEHR and
Lena SCHOCKE, Godparents; Possible BAEHR; Born June 27, 1891; Baptized
August 2, 1891; #1527

Anna Mary BENDIXEN - George BENDIXEN and Mary HAEHNLEIN, Parents;
Anna HAEHNLEIN and Mathius GASHEN, Godparents; Born April 20, 1888;
Baptized June 10, 1888; #1398

George Adolph BENDIXEN - George BENDIXEN and Mary HAEHNLEIN, Parents;
Mary BOHL, Godparent; Born September 8, 1891; Baptized October 11, 1891;
#1537

George Thomas BENDIXEN - Geo. Chris. BENDIXEN and Mary A. HAEHNLEIN,
Parents; Thomas BRICK and Helen HAEHNLEIN, Godparents; Born August 23,
1886; Baptized October 24, 1886; #1279

Mary Ann Elizabeth BEERMANN (Alias Smith, adopted by John BEERMANN
and Mary Ann HEIMANN); Born January 17, 1849; Baptized April 15, 1866

Catherine BERBERICH - Stephen BERBERICH and Joan BRENNAN, Parents;
John ERELLY and Ellen WOODS, Godparents; Born August 1, 1860; Baptized
August 19, 1860; #14

Lawrence Chas. BERBERICH - Stephen BERBERICH and Joan BRENNAN, Parents;
Thomas CURPHEY and Joan CURPHEY, Godparents; Born May 6, 1862; Baptized
May 18, 1862; #80

Mary Wilhelmina BERCHMAN - William BERCHMAN and Mary McNEY, Parents; William DOM and Minnie SEIBERT, Godparents; Born December 24, 1891; Baptized December 25, 1891; #1547

Joseph Nicholas BERGMANN - William BERGMANN and Mary MASSONET, Parents; Jos. PEINE Sr. and Eugenia HOLDEMANN, Godparents; Born October 29, 1892; Baptized July 16, 1893; #1614

Magdalen Lydia Josephine BERNARD; Convert; Baptized March 20, 1865; #193

Addell Rosale BERTHIN - Frank BERTHIN and Alida CHAPELLE, Parents; Gustave LANNE and Antonia LANNE, Godparents; Born November 2, 1885; Baptized December 25, 1885; #1211

Frank Peter BERTIN - Frank BERTIN and Alice CHAPPELLE, Parents; Emil Louis CHAPELLE and Mary MASSE, Godparents; Born December 28, 1886; Baptized March 28, 1887; #1326

Ernest Lawrence BESSENELLI - John BESSENELLI and Odilia WHITE, Parents; Maybe BACINELLI; Catherine FOLEY, Godparent; Born July 30, 1895; Baptized February 20, 1896; #1807

Agnes Joan BEST - Louis BEST and Anna TSCHAEKE, Parents; John MOSER, Godparent; Born July 1874; Baptized July 23, 1874; #715

Ann Catherine BEST - Louis BEST and Anna TSCHAEKE, Parents; William BEST and Caroline RICKE, Godparents; Born December 1, 1867; Baptized December 22, 1867; #391

Anna Margaret Louise BEST - Louis BEST and Anna TSCHAEKE, Parents; Joseph BEST and Ann Margaret BEST, Godparents; Born August 25, 1881; Baptized September 17, 1881; #940

Catherine Margaret BEST - George BEST and Hester (nc) NELSON, Parents; John NELSON and Catherine BEST, Godparents; Born January 23, 1885; Baptized March 29, 1885; #1147

Charles Louis BEST - Louis BEST and Anna JAEKE, Parents; John BOEDECKER and Mary VOEBNER, Godparents; Born December 5, 1870; Baptized January 8, 1871; #577

Evelyn Louise BEST - Maximus BEST and Alice MANNING, Parents; Ella Nora BEST, Godparents; Born July 25, 1894; Baptized September 5, 1894; #1679

George BEST - William BEST and Catherine RITZLER, Parents; Conditional; Susanne SCHOBER, Godparent; Born December 21, 1858; Baptized May 7, 1865; #202

Joseph William BEST - Louis BEST and Ann TSCHAEKE, Parents; Joseph RICKE and Catherine BEST, Godparents; Born July 27, 1866; Baptized August 12, 1866; #309

Louis John BEST - Louis BEST and Anna TSCHAECKE, Parents; John RICKE and Joan MOSER, Godparents; Born September 29, 1869; Baptized October 17, 1869; #531

Margaret BEST - William BEST and Catherine RITZLER, Parents; Susanna SCHOBER, Godparents; Born March 14, 1860; Baptized May 7, 1865; #203

Mary Catherine BEST - Louis BEST and Anna TSCHAECKE, Parents; Mrs. BEST, Godparent; Born August 15, 1872; Baptized August 25, 1872; #632

William Frank BEST - Louis BEST and Anna TSCHAECKE, Parents; Joseph RICKE and Rose GRUENROTH, Godparents; Born October 9, 1883; Baptized November 4, 1883; #1032

Anthony Frank Emil Cavior BICOCCHI - Anthony BICOCCHI and Ada BLARDON,
Parents; Frank GIOZZA and Emily GIOZZA, Godparents; Born December 16,
1883; Baptized April 27, 1884; #1064

Mary Magdalen BIEHLER - Francis BIEHLER and Magdalen KAISER, Parents;
Rosina SAMMET, Godparent; Born January 22, 1863; Baptized March 8, 1863;
#102

Catherine Pearl BIERMANN - Peter BIERMANN and Catherine MUELLER (?),
Parents; Adelin WARNER, Godparent; Born January 31, 1881; Baptized
May 7, 1881; #922

James Edward BIERMANN - Henry BIERMANN and Elenore BAKER, Parents;
Mary DRNDULL, Godparent; Born February 26, 1884; Baptized April 15,
1884; #1059

John Emil Mary BIERMANN - Henry BIERMANN and Lena HAGEMANN, Parents;
Emil LEINBACH and Mary LEINBACH, Godparents; Born February 15, 1878;
Baptized July 21, 1878; #854

Pearl Mary BIERMANN - Peter BIERMANN and Catherine MUELLER, Parents;
Mary Ann BIERMANN, Godparent; Born September 5, 1882; Baptized May 13,
1883; #1007

Peter Charles BIERMANN - Peter BIERMANN and Catherine MUELLER, Parents;
Catherine KEEGAN, Godparent; Born February 21, 1884; Baptized October
11, 1884; #1102

Leo BILLEBAULT - Prosper BILLEBAULT and Josephine DAHE, Parents; John
Leo FOURNIER and Martha PETER, Godparents; Born February 9, 1878;
Baptized May 15, 1882; A#968

Prosper BILLEBAULT - Prosper BILLEBAULT and Josephine DAHE, Parents;
John Leo FOURNIER and Martha PETER, Godparents; Born August 22, 1880;
Baptized May 15, 1882; B#968

Anthony Victor BILLET - Anton BILLET and Lina FLAKE, Parents; Victor
BAULARD and Mary RINKER, Godparents; Born October 2, 1866; Baptized
June 13, 1867; #353

Frances Wilhelmina Carolina BILLET - Anthony BILLET and Caroline FLAKE,
Parents; William KRONE and Caroline CROMER, Godparents; Born December
23, 1861; Baptized June 20, 1863; #114

Fabian William BLANCHET - Peter Constantin BLANCHET and Caroline
KIMLING, Parents; Fabian KIMLING and Walburga KIMLING, Godparents;
Born September 25, 1866; Baptized October 11, 1866; #322

Mary Anna Augusta BLANK; Conditional; Henrietta SINGER, Godparent;
Born July 4, 1885; Baptized May 24, 1886; #1245

Ann Agnes BLEICKE (BLEIKE); Baptized August 25, 1875; #768

Emil Albert BLEIKE - William BLEICKE and Sophy POPULIER, Parents; Adolph
MULLER and Carolina WOLLFGANG, Godparents; Born October 17, 1877;
Baptized December 23, 1877; #825

Frank Joseph BLEICKE - Frederic BLEICKE and Teresa BERGENBUSCH, Parents;
Charles MOSER and Josephine BLEICKE, Godparents; Born April 12, 1865;
Baptized May 14, 1865; #24

Helen BLEICKE - William T. BLEICKE and Julia BLEICKE, Parents; Charles
BLEICKE and Lizzie WALSH, Godparents; Born October 19, 1889; Baptized
January 8, 1890; #1469

Helen Theresa Mary BLEICKE - William BLEICKE and Mary Sophy POPELIER,
Parents; Anthony POPELIER and Ernestine BRINK, Godparents; Born February
1, 1872; Baptized March 6, 1872; #613

Joseph Bernard BLEICKE - William T. BLEICKE and Julia GONZALES,
Parents; Nicholas B. ... and Theresa JAAS, Godparents; Born October 9,
1886; Baptized November 28, 1886; #1291

Joseph William Marion BLEICKE - Joseph BLEICKE and Frances BERGENBUSCH,
Parents; William BLEICKE and Mary FLAKE, Godparents; Born October 16,
1860; Baptized November 10, 1860; #24

Laura BLEICKE - William BLEICKE and Sophy BLEICKE, Parents; E. CRAWFORD
and Mary Eugenia POPULLEAR, Godparents; Born in 1874; Baptized May 3,
1874; #702

Lillie Louise BLEICKE - William H. BLEICKE and Julia Louise GONZALES,
Parents; William BLEICKE and Mary Elizabeth BLEICKE, Godparents; Born
April 29, 1881; Baptized June 5, 1881; #929

Louise Anna BLEICKE - Frederic BLEICKE and Theresa BERGENBUSCH, Parents;
Frederic BLEICKE Jr. and Theresa BLEICKE, Godparents; Born April 24,
1863; Baptized May 17, 1863; #110

Mary Caroline Josephine BLEICKE - William BLEICKE and Sophy POPULIER,
Parents; John JILLETT and Carolina WOLFGANG, Godparents; Born December
21, 1861; Baptized January 11, 1862; #64

Mary Elizabeth BLEICKE - William BLEICKE and Sophy POPULIER, Parents;
Anthony POPULIER and Gertrude BERKENBUSCH, Godparents; Born February 7,
1867; Baptized February 24, 1867; #336

Mary Theresa BLEICKE; Anna BLEICKE, Godparent; Born August 24, 1875;
Baptized August 25, 1875; #767

Roger Mills BLEICKE - Joseph F. BLEICKE and Hedwig LAUVE, Parents;
Frederic H. LAUVE and Mary H. LAUVE, Godparents; Born August 18, 1893;
Baptized January 10, 1894; #1640

Sophy Mary Ernestine BLEICKE - William BLEICKE and Sophy POPULIER,
Parents; Ernestine BRINK, Godparents; Born November 22, 1863; Baptized
November 29, 1863; #134

Winona Johnson BLEICKE - William T. BLEICKE and Julia L. GONZALES,
Parents; Louise SOMMER and Charles JOHNSON, Godparents; Born December
3, 1882; Baptized March 11, 1883; #993

William Joseph Frank BLEICKE - William T. BLEICKE and Julia Louise
GONZALES, Parents; Frank PURGETTE and Sophy BLEICKE, Godparents; Born
October 23, 1884; Baptized November 30, 1884; #1113

Ella Ruby BLAGGE - Henry M. BLAGGE and Mary Alicia HELMER, Parents;
E. H. COMPTON and James COMPTON, Godparents; Born January 24, 1897;
Baptized August 30, 1900; #2000

Leonida Alice BLOOMLEY - George William BLOOMLEY and Elizabeth Walsh
DAVEY, Parents; Mildred Frances SEIBERT and James L. WALKER, Godparents;
Born July 17, 1895; Baptized September 12, 1895; #1731

Agnes BOCK - Peter BOCK and Susanna GENGLER, Parents; Joseph BORTEEN
and Agnes GENGLER, Godparents; Born May 27, 1866; Baptized August 12,
1866; #307

Oscar Peter BOCK - Peter BOCK and M. SCHWERTFEGER, Parents; Peter BOCK
and Lena GENGLER, Godparents; Born May 29, 1876; Baptized June 1876;
#774

Sarah Emma BOCK - Peter BOCK and Susan GENGLER, Parents; Sarah BOCK,
Godparent; Born September 17, 1873; Baptized December 5, 1873; #690

Susanna Julia BOCK - Peter BOCK and Susanna GENGLER, Parents; David
HERZOG and Susanna SCHWERTFEGER, Godparents; Born November 8, 1862;
Baptized December 10, 1862; #95

Erin Susan Margaret BOCKELMANN - Adolph BOCKELMANN and Mary BUHL,
Parents; Frederic CASHEN and Susan BOCKELMANN, Godparents; Born April
6, 1895; Baptized May 5, 1895; #1713

Ethel May Louise BOCKELMANN - Adolph BOCKELMANN and Mary BUHL, Parents;
Louise BOCKELMANN and Edwin GASCHEN, Godparents; Born June 21, 1898;
Baptized July 31, 1898; #1922

Julius Adolph BOCKELMANN - Adolph BOCKELMANN and Mary BUHL, Parents;
Julius THEVENOT and Margaret BUHL, Godparents; Born August 22, 1892;
Baptized October 9, 1892; #1580

Charles Frederic Henry BODEN - Lambert BODEN and Pauline REISNER,
Parents; M. WAPPNER, Godparent; Born January 12, 1869; Baptized May 30,
1869; #521

Agnes Frances BOEDECKER - Frank BOEDECKER and Mary FALTEMEYER, Parents;
William BLEICKE and Margaret BALFOUR, Godparents; Born February 3, 1878;
Baptized February 10, 1878; #832

Angela BOEDECKER - Louis BOEDECKER and Elizabeth WINKELHANS, Parents;
L. BOEDECKER and Angela BOEDECKER, Godparents; Born February 20, 1875;
Baptized March 20, 1875; #745

Edgar Vincent Marion BOEDECKER - Joseph BOEDECKER and Caroline BAILING,
Parents; Charles ENGELKE (by proxy) and Louis CUMMINGS, Godparents;
Born July 19, 1884; Baptized August 10, 1884; #1085

James Rock Cornelius BOEDECKER - John BOEDECKER and Elizabeth WINKELHAHN,
Parents; Joseph BOEDECKER and Ernestine BRINK, Godparents; Born August
16, 1883; Baptized September 6, 1883; #1021

John Francis BOEDECKER - Francis BOEDECKER and Mary FALTENMAGER, Parents;
Charles BOEDECKER and Mary MEYER, Godparents; Born February 5, 1871;
Baptized February 12, 1871; #576

Joseph Anthony Ferdinand BOEDECKER - John BOEDECKER and Elizabeth
WINKELHAHN, Parents; Elizabeth BOEDECKER and William BOEDECKER, Godparents; Born January 27, 1878; Baptized February 20, 1878; #834

Joseph Leonard BOEDECKER - F. R. BOEDECKER and Mary FALTEMEYER, Parents;
Born July 3, 1872; Baptized July 3, 1872; #631

Kavier Claude BOEDECKER - Frank BOEDECKER and Mary FALTEMEYER, Parents;
John Frank BOEDECKER and Mary DECKELMAYER, Godparents; Born June 10,
1884; Baptized June 30, 1884

Caroline Mary BOEHME; Conditional; Mr. MENZEL, Godparent; LENZ and
WOLF, Witnesses; #1999

Alfred Joseph BOHN - William BOHN and Ann BROCKHOFF, Parents; Ann
MARSAISE, Godparents; Born September 26, 1893; Baptized March 18, 1894;
#1654

Anna BOHN - Nicholas BOHN and Meda TRENBEHL, Parents; Ann STALLER,
Godparents; Born March 3, 1892; Baptized October 30, 1892; #1582

Anna Margaret BOHN - George L. BOHN and Julia OEHRING, Parents; Anna
Margaret SATTLER, Godparent; Conditional; Born February 26, 1889;
Baptized May 12, 1889; #1432

Cecilia BOHN - Nicholas BOHN and Meta (nc) TRENTWEHL, Parents; Cecil
BOHN, Godparent; Born May 7, 1889; Baptized June 22, 1889; #1438

Ernest Martin Joseph BOHN - Emil (nc) BOHN and Mary RICKE, Parents;
Martin RICKE and Carolina RICKE, Godparents; Born March 4, 1888;
Baptized March 15, 1888; #1379

George Augustine BOHN - George L. BOHN and Julia (nc) OEHRING, Parents;
Rev. Jac. F. LAUTH, Godparents; Born August 28, 1886; Baptized October
24, 1886; #1280

Joan BOHN - George L. BOHN and Julia E. E. (nc) OEHRING, Parents;
Caroline RICKE (by proxy), Godparent; Born August 9, 1882; Baptized
July 29, 1883; #1017

Mary Elizabeth BOHN - William BOHN (nc) and Anna PROKOP, Parents; Louise
BILD, Godparent; Born March 2, 1883; Baptized April 14, 1883; #1000

Mary Hedwig BOHN - Emil BOHN and Mary RICKE, Parents; Bernard BOHN and
Elizabeth RICKE, Godparents; Born October 18, 1889; Baptized October 31,
1889; #1454

Nicholas BOHN - Nicholas BOHN and Meta (nc) TRENTWEHL, Parents; John
MAURER and Elizabeth COUCH, Godparents; Born February 2, 1886; Baptized
March 6, 1887; #1316

Nicholas Leonard BOHN - George L. BOHN and Emma E. J. OEHRING, Parents;
Nicholas BOHN and Meta BOHN, Godparents; Born May 26, 1897; Baptized
October 3, 1897; #1891

Robert John BOHN - George Leonard BOHN and Emma Ernestine J. OEHRING,
Parents; John J. GOTTLOB and Catherine BOHN, Godparents; Born September
8, 1893; Baptized November 5, 1893; #1630

Theresa Mary BOHN - Emil (nc) BOHN and Catherine RICKE, Parents; John
RICKE and Theresa SCHOCKE, Godparents; Born May 6, 1886; Baptized May
23, 1886; #1244

William James BOHN - William BOHN and Anna BROCKHOF, Parents; James
THOY and Theresa DELZ, Godparents; Born September 7, 1890; Baptized
August 9, 1891; #1532

William Emil Blasa BOLLERT - Frank (nc) BOLLERT and Catherine FRANZ,
Parents; William KOEHLER and Emma DIRCKS, Godparents; Born June 21,
1886; Baptized July 31, 1886; #1260

August Charles BOLTON - John BOLTON and Ann FAPAN, Parents; August
CASTAY and Lena CASTAY, Godparents; Born December 30, 1878; Recorded
by Rev. J. N. Leonard

Clifford Marc BOLTON - Charles BOLTON and Theresa MILLICH, Parents;
Valentina SCHANTZ, Godparents; Born November 29, 1899; Baptized
February 24, 1900; #1968

Gertrude BONN - Henry BONN and Catherine FITZPATRICK, Parents; William
HARVEY and Rosa REED, Godparents; Baptized November 9, 1867; #385

Sara Renetta BOOTH; Henry HARRIS and Sara HARRIS, Godparents; Born
October 8, 1865; Baptized December 5, 1886; #1294

Elma Elizabeth BOSS - William BOSS and Margaret RITZLER, Parents;
August BOSS and Elizabeth BAUHHENS, Godparents; Born November 21, 1899;
Baptized January 7, 1900; #1972

Theresa Marie BOTTE - Anthony BOTTE and Margaret CHRISTO, Parents;
Peter LERAT and Mary RIPETA, Godparents; Born December 26, 1887;
Baptized April 15, 1888; #1389

Catherine Elizabeth BOYD - H. H. BOYD and Wilhelmine POLVOGT, Parents;
M. G. KEEFE and Christine DOBBERT, Godparents; Born April 1, 1881;
Baptized April 24, 1881; #920

Francis Frederic BOYD - Henry William BOYD and Wilhelmina BOLWOGD, Parents; Jerome FLYNN, Godparent; Born October 31, 1878; Baptized November 24, 1878; #873

Louise Josephine BOYD - William H. BOYD and Wilhelmine POLVOGT, Parents; Joseph RICKE and Louise POLVOGT, Godparents; Born September 22, 1883; Baptized October 14, 1883; #1029

Mary Letty BOYD; Mr. and Mrs. Humphrey BOYD, Godparents; Conditional; Age 26; Baptized December 31, 1899; #1971

William BOYD; Convert; Baptized September 26, 1866; #317B

William Henry BOYD - William BOYD and Wilhelmina POLVOGT, Parents; Mary MORGAN, Godparents; Born November 27, 1890; Baptized December 25, 1891; #1510

Julia Agnes BOYDELL - William BOYDELL and Agnes CALLAHAN, Parents; Patrick KELLY and Isabel PENDERGAST, Godparents; Born June 10, 1884; Baptized September 21, 1884; #1095

Theresa BRAEKELMAN - Joseph BRAEKELMAN and Caroline HESS, Parents; Theresa BLEICKE, Godparents; Born August 11, 1860; Baptized March 3, 1861; #32

Bertha BRAENDLER - Edward BRAENDLER and Pauline KIRSCH, Parents; Charles NOLT, Godparent; Born September 3, 1883; Baptized October 10, 1883; #1028

Anthony Henry BRAUEUTIGAM - William BRAEUTIGAM and Henrietta HEINZE, Parents; Henry TUCKER, Godparent; Born June 20, 1890; Baptized October 23, 1890; #1506

Edward BRAEUTIGAM - Peter W. BRAEUTIGAM and Henrietta M. (nc) HEINSOHN, Parents; Joan POPLIER, Godparent; Born January 29, 1889; Baptized June 22, 1889; #1437

Helen BRAEUTIGAM - Peter BRAEUTIGAM and Henrietta HEINSOHN, Parents; Christian BAUMANN, Godparent; Baptized January 19, 1894; #1646

Louise Mary Agnes BRAEUTIGAM - Peter BRAEUTIGAM and Henrietta HEINSOHN, Parents; Mary Agnes BAHR, Godparent; Born November 7, 1897; Baptized January 22, 1899; #1935

Robert Joseph BRAEUTIGAM - Peter William BRAEUTIGAM and Henrietta HEINSOHN, Parents; Robert BYRNES, Godparents; Born December 14, 1894; Baptized May 12, 1895; #1714

William Henry BRAKER - Joseph BRAKER and Theresa GLASOT, Parents; Henry FRISBY and Mary TAYLOR, Godparents; Born September 10, 1878; Baptized November 17, 1878; #872

Albert Peter BRAMMER - Albert (could be BRAMER or BRAMMAR) BRAMMER and Mary SCHOCKE, Parents; Theresa SCHOCKE, Godparent; Born June 24, 1890; Baptized July 13, 1890; #1501

Christian James BRAMMER - Albert BRAMMER and Mary SCHOCKE, Parents; Henry SCHOCKE and Theresa SCHOCKE, Godparents; Born September 15, 1886; Baptized October 11, 1886; #1274

Gertrude Magdalene Antonia BRAMMER - Albert BRAMMER and Mary SCHOCKE, Parents; Magdalene Antonia VISCOVICH, Godparents; Baptized November 5, 1893; #1627

Herman Albert BRAMMER - Albert BRAMMER and Mary SCHOCKE, Parents; Herman SCHOCKE and Christian SCHOCKE, Godparents; Born June 25, 1891; Baptized July 19, 1891; #1522

James Albert Charles BRAMMER - James BRAMMER and Mary SCHOCKE, Parents; Theresa SCHOCKE, Godparent; Born February 7, 1888; Baptized March 14, 1888; #1378

Mary Odilia Julian BRAMMER - Albert BRAMMER and Mary SCHOCKE, Parents; Odilia SCHOCKE, Godparent; Born January 20, 1898; Baptized February 13, 1898; #1902

Peter Christian BRAMMER - Albert BRAMMER and Mary SCHOCKE, Parents; James BRAMMER, Godparent; Born August 22, 1896; Baptized September 6, 1896; #1848

Mary Bernardine BRANDES; Convert; ca. 1843; Baptized June 3, 1860; Mary BENNETT, Godparent; #8

Otto BRANDLER - Edward BRANDLER and Pauline KIRSCH, Parents; Charles NOLT, Godparent; Born September 3, 1883; Baptized October 10, 1883; #1027

Stephen Leonard BRAUN - Leonard BRAUN and Theresa KOPP, Parents; Stephen SCHIHULSKI and Jōsfa SCHIHULSKI, Godparents; Born December 11, 1894; Baptized December 17, 1894; #1695

Catherine Theresa BRAUN - Leonard BRAUN and Theresa KOPP (Bavaria), Parents; John EVERLING and Joseph RAENDEL, Godparents; Born January 13, 1893; Baptized January 22, 1893; #1595

Emma Sara Sophy Josephine BRAUN - Julius August BRAUN and Mary Josephine BOCK, Parents; Charles Joseph THUSSING and Sara BOCK, Godparents; Born February 25, 1870; Baptized May 14, 1870; #557

Ophilia Blanch BRAUN - Michael BRAUN and Carolina HOLM, Parents; Mary Ophilia MOLKATA, Godparents; Baptized April 30, 1890; #1482

Alice Susan Orene BREEN - Martin BREEN and Catherine LANG, Parents; Miles BREEN and Susan HAHN, Godparents; Born January 17, 1894; Baptized February 25, 1894; #1649

Catherine BREEN - Martin BREEN and Catherine LANG, Parents; Miles BREEN and Mrs. Lena MUELLER, Godparents; Born June 28, 1889; Baptized June 30, 1889; #1439

Mary Agnes BREEN - Martin C. BREEN and Catherine LANG, Parents; Henry MUELLER and Mary MUELLER, Godparents; Born January 5, 1884; Baptized February 10, 1884; #1042

Katherine Sara BREEN - Martin BREEN and Katherine LANG, Parents; John William MUELLER and Magdalen MUELLER, Godparents; Born March 29, 1882; Baptized May 2, 1882; #965

Susan Elizabeth BREEN - Martin BREEN and Catherine LANG, Parents; Henry LANG and Susan HAHN, Godparents; Born April 14, 1885; Baptized June 6, 1885; #1165

Henry William BREITLING - Frederic BREITLING and Josephine WALTER, Parents; Lawrence NUESE and Catherine LANG, Godparents; Born August 4, 1860; Baptized October 14, 1860; #22

Alpha Mary BRIGGS; nee HUDSON from Beaumont; Private; Age 19; Baptized March 15, 1866

Joseph BRIGGS - Joseph BRIGGS and Mary Alpha HUDSON, Parents; Anton HEIMAN and Elizabeth THORBES, Godparents; Born March 5, 1866; Baptized April 1, 1866; #276

Cornelius BRINK - Cornelius BRINK and Joan Elizabeth WOLF (nee POPULAR), Parents; Joseph PEINE and Mary PEINE, Godparents; Baptized October 25, 1896; #1851

Charles Edward BROCKELMANN - Charles Joseph BROCKELMANN and Anna EDWARDS, Parents; Mary BROCKELMANN, Godparent; Born July 21, 1893; Baptized October 23, 1893; #1624

Corina BROCKELMANN - Charles Joseph BROCKELMANN and Ann Cecile EDWARDS, Parents; Caroline DICKS, Godparent; Born December 4, 1895; Baptized March 23, 1896; #1815

Frances Josephine BROKOF - Frank BROKOF and Lena (nc) HARMS, Parents; Rose BILD and Henry PUELLE, Godparents; Born February 24, 1884; Baptized March 19, 1884; #1051

Augusta Mary Wilhelmina BROSIG; Baptized April 5, 1874

Carolina Henrietta Victoria BROSIG - Hugo BROSIG and Louise DAENA (BLAVIER), Parents; J. BROSIG, Godparent; Born December 18, 1871; Baptized January 21, 1872; #608

Charles Albert Andrew BROSIG - Hugo BROSIG and Louise BLAVIER, Parents; Catherine ALFSON and Charles Albert DUEBNER, Godparents; Born October 12, 1872; Baptized November 3, 1872; #636

Charles Theodore Mary BROSIG - Charles BROSIG and Mary Louise KOESTER, Parents; Patrick Theodore BROSIG and Margaret PAINPARE, Godparents; Born December 4, 1867; Baptized February 23, 1868; #404

Charles Theodore Albert BROSIG - Hugo BROSIG and Louise BLAVIER, Parents; Charles BROSIG and Margaret PAINPARE, Godparents; Born February 28, 1867; Baptized April 21, 1867; #343

Emma Wilhelmine Josephine BROSIG - Hugo BROSIG and Louise BLAVIER, Parents; Joseph BROSIG and Wilhelmine RUDOLF, Godparents; Born July 11, 1877; Baptized March 24, 1878; #840

Emily Catherine Henriette BROSIG - Charles BROSIG and Mary Louise KOESTER, Parents; Hugo BROSIG and Catherine MOELLER, Godparents; Born December 1, 1866; Baptized January 20, 1867; #332

James Joseph Hugo BROSIG - Hugo BROSIG and Louise BLAVIER, Parents; Oscar PAINPARE and Margaret GENGLER, Godparents; Born June 23, 1864; Baptized August 12, 1864; #168

Laura BROSIG; Baptized April 5, 1874

Louise Joan Augusta BROSIG - Charles BROSIG and Louise Mary KOESTLER, Parents; Mrs. SCHNEIDER and Hugo BROSIG, Godparents; Born December 25, 1870; Baptized January 21, 1872; #607

Theodore Louis Herman BROSIG - Hugo BROSIG and Louise BLAVIER, Parents; Theodore BRINKHOFF and ... SANDERS, Godparents; Born January 20, 1870; Baptized February 27, 1870; #548

Agnes Mary BROWN - Michael BROWN and Caroline (nc) HOLM, Parents; Francis SEIDEL, Godparent; Born December 6, 1887; Baptized March 5, 1888; #1376

Elenore Antonia BORWN - Michael BROWN and Carolina HAHN, Parents; Mary BENDIXEN, Godparent; Born June 6, 1894; Baptized July 25, 1895; #1671

Martha Caroline BORWN - Michael BROWN and Caroline (nc) HOLM, Parents; Catherine KRAUS (by proxy), Godparent; Born March 24, 1886; Baptized May 13, 1886; #1239

Myrtle Cecil BROWN - Michael BROWN and Caroline HOLM, Parents; Martin SCHMITT and Mary SOMMER, Godparents; Born May 10, 1892; Baptized May 26, 1892; #1565

Wilhelmina BROWN - Michael BORWN and Caroline (nc) HOLM, Parents;
Catherine KRAUS (by proxy), Godparent; Born March 24, 1886; Baptized
May 13, 1886; #1240

William Henry John BROWN - Caroline .., Parents; Baptized June 30, 1896;
#1838

Frank BRUECHER - Joseph BRUECHER and Caroline HEIMANN, Parents; Frank
SOMMER and Catherine KRAUS, Godparents; Born January 22, 1862; Baptized
January 26, 1862; #66

Catherine BRUENNEMAN - Catherine BRUENNEMAN and (Louis HUEBKERT),
Parents; Mrs. C. H. VAUTIER and Victor MASTRAL, Godparents; Born
July 15, 1885; Baptized July 22, 1885; #1177

Francis George BRUNNER - Francis George BRUNNER and Mary CARLOS,
Parents; Francis KOCH and Mary KOCH, Godparents; Born August 28, 1871;
October 22, 1871; #601

Frank George Louis BRUNNER - Charles BRUNNER and Agnes KALLUS, Parents;
John George PFLUEGER and Elizabeth PFLUEGER, Godparents; Born July 28,
1873; Baptized September 20, 1873; #682

Charles James BRUNNER - Charles BRUNNER and Agnes (KALLUS) CARLOS,
Parents; John MAURER and Alizabeth MAURER, Godparents; Baptized
December 1874; #738

Mary Anna BRUNNOM - John BRUNNOM, Parent; Margaret Ann CLOCHER and
Frederic JAEGER, Godparents; Born October 1872; Baptized November 3,
1872; #637

Jerome BRODARICK - Pat BRODARICK and Elizabeth BRODARICK, Parents;
Margaret BRODARICK, Godparent; Born December 5, 1881; Baptized December
22, 1881; #950

John BRYAN - John BRYAN and Carolina PATERSON, Parents; Peter REILLY
and Mary KELLY, Godparents; Born September 27, 1872; Baptized November
11, 1872; #645

Cornelius Joseph BUCKERT - Anthony BUCKERT and Joan Mary HEIMANN,
Parents; Cornelius BRINK and Sophy BLEICKE, Godparents; Born in 1872;
Baptized October 27, 1872; #633

James Marion BUCKLEY - Ed. BUCKLEY and Aemilia SPANN, Parents; John S.
SPANN and Caroline KENISON, Godparents; Born June 16, 1867; Baptized
January 23, 1868; #334

Louise Margaret BUDD - Henry (nc) BUDD and Mary CASSIDY, Parents; Joan
CASSIDY, Godparent; Born August 13, 1885; Baptized November 12, 1885;
#1199

Henry BUELLEY - Henry BUELLEY and Cecile NUTT, Parents; Herman BUELLE,
Godparent; Born November 4, 1877; Baptized February 23, 1878; #835

Augusta Agnes BUERGER - Frank W. BUERGER and Gertrude BERKENBUSCH,
Parents; Augusta WINKELBACH, Godparents; Born December 9, 1887;
Baptized March 11, 1888; #1377

Agusta Mary BUERGER - George BUERGER and Mary KEIS, Parents; Augusta
KEIS, Godparent; Born August 2, 1895; Baptized August 8, 1895; #1727

Bertha Joan BUERGER - Frank William BUERGER and Gertrude BERKENBUSCH,
Parents; Joan MOSER, Godparent; Born March 27, 1881; Baptized April 3,
1883; #998

Frank Joseph Theodore BUERGER - Frank BUERGER and Gertrude BERKENBUSCH,
Parents; Born September 31, 1874; Baptized March 14, 1875; #742

Frank William BUERGER - Frank William BUERGER and Gertrude BERKENBUSCH,
Parents; T. H. H. MOSER and Anne PHILIP, Godparents; Born March 3, 1871;
Baptized May 7, 1871; #586

George Adalbert Alois BUERGER - Frank BUERGER and Gertrude BERKENBUSCH,
Parents; George HOURNAY, Godparent; Baptized February 2, 1873; #653

George William BUERGER - Geroge BUERGER and Mary THEIS, Parents;
Mathilda BUERGER, Godparent; Born October 3, 1896; Baptized March 26,
1897; #1874

Gertrude BUERGER - Frank W. BUERGER and Gertrude BERKENBUSCH, Parents;
William BUERGER and Theresa BLEIKE, Godparents; Born October 3, 1889;
Baptized October 10, 1889; #1452

Grace Theresa BUERGER - Frank W. BUERGER and Gertrude BERKENBUSCH,
Parents; George BUERGER and Theresa WEBER, Godparents; Born October 3,
1889; Baptized October 10, 1889; #1451

Laura Mathilda BUERGER - Frank William BUERGER and Gertrude BERKENBUSCH,
Parents; Lawrence NUESE and Teresa WEBER, Godparents; Born January 2,
1879; Baptized June 5, 1880; #902

Leo Aloysius BUERGER - Frank William BUERGER and Gertrude BERKENBUSCH,
Parents; Caroline BIERMANN, Godparent; Born September 7, 1883; Baptized
November 18, 1883; #1034

Rudolph BULLASCHER - Rudolph BULLASCHER and Mary HERMANN, Parents;
Mathias HERMANN and Rose MITCHELL, Godparents; Born July 25, 1873;
Baptized June 15, 1874; #709

Clara Therese BULLASCHER - Rudolph BULLASCHER and Mary HERMANN, Parents;
David HERMANN and Clara BULLASCHER, Godparents; Born August 4, 1871;
Baptized April 1, 1872; #615

Gertrude Louise BULLASCHER - Rudolph BULLASCHER and Mary HERMANN,
Parents; Walter R. REIFEL and Minnie WENZEL, Godparents; Born August
17, 1887; Baptized September 18, 1887; #1359

Henrietta Hendricks BULLASCHER - Rudolph BULLASCHER and Mary HERMANN,
Parents; Alexander MUSGROVE and Mary MICHELS, Godparents; Private;
Born November 10, 1884; Baptized November 29, 1884; #1112

Joseph Grover Cleveland BULLASCHER - Rudolph BULLASCHER and Mary HERMANN
Parents; James HOGAN and Laura ANTONOVICH, Godparents; Born November 10,
1884; Baptized November 29, 1884; #1111; Private

Lilly Elizabeth BULLASCHER - Rudolph BULLASCHER and Mary HERMANN,
Parents; Margaret BULLASCHER and Elizabeth STRAUBE, Godparents;
Born February 9, 1886; Baptized April 27, 1886; #1331

Margaret Mary Josephine BULLASCHER - Rudolph BULLASCHER and Mary HERMANN,
Parents; G. W. V. HIBBERT and Mary BOEDECKER, Godparents; Born May 5,
1870; Baptized August 28, 1870; #563

Mary Laura Augusta BULLASCHER - Rudolph BULLASCHER and Mary HERMANN,
Parents; H. BULLASCHER and Mary KELLY, Godparents; Born June 28, 1875?;
Baptized January 1, 1876; #771

Theresa BULLASCHER - Rudolph BULLASCHER and Mary HERMANN, Parents;
John F. CROZIER and Pauline FEINLATRE, Godparents; Born July 16, 1881;
Baptized August 14, 1881; #937

Pauline BULLASCHER - Rudolph BULLASCHER and Mary HERMANN, Parents;
John F. CROZIER and Pauline FEINLATRE, Godparents; Born July 16, 1881;
Baptized August 14, 1881; #937A

Anne Therese BULLINGTON; Convert; Theresa Mary STUMPF, Godparent; Baptized April 23, 1900; #1989

Antoinette Catherine BURATOVICH - Marion BURATOVICH and Pearl (nc) GONDEMANN, Parents; Louis HARRISON and Miss GONDEMANN, Godparents; Born May 11, 1989; Baptized July 20, 1898; #1921

Marcelle Catherine BURKE - John Edward BURKE and Brigid HACKETT, Parents; Catherine DUFF, Godparent; Born March 8, 1870; Baptized June 20, 1873; #670

Daniel Walter BURKETT - John BURKETT and Catherine BLAKE, Parents; Thomas BUCKLEY and Elsie EDWARDS, Godparents; Born June 19, 1882; Baptized August 19, 1882; #973

Dorothy BURKHART - John BURKHART and Dorothy RETTBERG, Parents; Clara GERST, Godparent; Born May 18, 1864; Baptized October 4, 1864; #176

Gustave BURKHART - John BURKHART and Dorothy RETTBERG, Parents; Born March 28, 1861; Baptized October 4, 1864; #178

Joan BURKHART - John BURKHART and Dorothy RETTBERG, Parents; Private; Conditional; Born October 14, 1859; Baptized October 4, 1864; #177

Henry John BURKITT (Possibly BURKHART) - John Thomas BURKITT and Louise M. STEVENS, Parents; John Theodore NICHOLAS and Lottie NAVE, Godparents; Born May 14, 1895; Baptized July 14, 1885; #1723

Mary Catherine BUSCH - C. BUSCH and Mary MEIDHOF, Parents; Mrs. KOEHLER and Mrs. KRAUS, Godparents; Born June 4, 1871; Baptized May 5, 1878; #850

John Leonard Thomas BUSCH - Charles BUSCH and Catherine HARRINGTON, Parents; Thomas BURNS and Leonida MOUDOVILLE, Godparents; Born December 3, 1896; Baptized February 3, 1897; #1865

Anne BUSH; Joan MOSER, Godparent; Baptized April 12, 1873; #662

Caroline BUSH; Anna BEST, Godparent; Baptized April 12, 1873; #661

Anna CALLISHAW - James CALLISHAW and Margaret MOORE, Parents; Herman KRAUS and Catherine KRAUS, Godparents; Born July 6, 1894; Baptized July 31, 1894; #1673

Julius Celestian CANBEIHL (possibly CAMBEIHL) - Michael CANBEIHL and Louise WILMETTE, Parents; Celestian LAGNET and Elizabeth BOUCHET, Godparents; Born November 25, 1885; Baptized July 1, 1886; #1255

Louis Frank CANBEIHL - Michael CANBEIHL and Louise WILMETTE, Parents; Frank GIOZZA and Emily GIOZZA, Godparents; Born November 15, 1884; Baptized July 1, 1886; #1256

Hazel Ann Caroline CARLYLE - James CARLYLE and Augusta Theresa DOM, Parents; Bella POIRRIERS and William DOM, Godparents; Born September 19, 1897; Baptized October 31, 1897; #1895

Minna Lucy CARLYLE - James CARLYLE and Anna DOM, Parents; George J. LEINBACH and Mary WAGONER, Godparents; Born February 1, 1894; Baptized April 15, 1894; #1661

Frank Theodore CARROLL - John CARROLL and Anna SOMMER, Parents; Theodore SCHWARZBACH and Mary SCHWARZBACH, Godparents; Born April 11, 1894; Baptized May 20, 1894; #1665

John Gustaphus CARROLL - J. M. CARROLL and Anna Marie SOMMER, Parents; J. A. WILDE and Mrs. Lena SOMMER, Godparents; Born November 20, 1887; Baptized January 1, 1888; #1368

Pauline Antoinette CARROLL - John M. CARROLL and Anna M. SOMMER, Parents; Cecil E. SOMMER and Anthony P. SOMMER, Godparents; Born October 14, 1899; Baptized November 12, 1899; #1967

Catherine Charlotte Isar CASSENTINI - Salvatore CASSENTINI and Cherubina ROMANINI, Parents; Christopher CASSENTINI and Charlotee DOMATI, Godparents; Born May 10, 1893; Baptized July 16, 1893; #1613

Frank Brigido CASTILLO - Frank CASTILLO and Centeero CASTILLO, Parents; John MAURER and Caroline HOFFMAN, Godparents; Born October 7, 1894; Baptized September 18, 1895; #1741

Mary Ann CHAMBARD - John Claud CHAMBARD and Caroline CONRAD, Parents; Ferdinard MARCHAND and Mary Teresa LEROUGE, Godparents; Born March 19, 1868; Baptized January 27, 1868; #401

Rosale Hortense CHAPELLI - Gustave CHAPELLI and Clementine GIRARDIN, Parents; Felix GIRARDIN and Hortense PARKER, Godparents; Born November 16, 1882; Baptized October 5, 1886; #1272

Benjamin CHAUDY - Benjamin CHAUDY and Emily MARCOS, Parents; Ulysses BELLOW and Elizabeth BELLOW, Godparents; Born January 2, 1875; Baptized April 18, 1875; #753

Mary Catherine CHOCK - Christian CHOCK and Mary ODINOT, Parents; Louise CIMBEYH, Godparent; Born June 8, 1893; Baptized June 9, 1893; #1610

Elizabeth Joan CHRISTIANS - Charles CHRISTIANS and Catherine SABLE, Parents; Mary SABLE, Godparents; Born March 28, 1876; Baptized April 8, 1877; #802

Aloysius CLONE - Michael CLONE and Mary GREEN, Parents; James LYNCH and Annie GREEN, Godparents; Born January 2, 1868; Baptized March 1, 1868; #407

Frank Emil COCADAGE - John COCADAGE and Alexanderia BARRERE, Parents; Frank Joseph GIOZZA and Emily GIOZZA, Godparents; Born November 27, 1884; Baptized April 5, 1885; #1149

James John COLLINS - James COLLINS and Margaret PATE, Parents; John McGRAW and Clara McGRAW, Godparents; Born December 11, 1894; Baptized August 8, 1895; #1725

James John Maclin COMPTON - Eugene H. COMPTON and Ella SANDERSON, Parents; Mr. and Mrs. J. P. HENNESSY, Godparents; Born April 13, 1888; Baptized July 27, 1900; #1994

Agnes Ruby COMTON - E. H. COMTON and Ellis ANDERSON, Parents; Convert; Henry Aloysius CURRAN, Godparent; Baptized April 19, 1900; #1987

Anna Cecilia CONLEY - Pat CONLEY and Mary GENT, Parents; Charles DEDRICK and Anna GILLET, Godparents; Born September 19, 1868; Baptized May 15, 1869; #518

William CORTE - Ulric CORTE and Bertha SCHLENDER, Parents; John Joseph KRAUS and Catherine KRAUS, Godparents; Born January 27, 1894; Baptized July 29, 1894; #1672

Adelina Barbara Betty CONROY - James CONROY and Antonia JUNG, Parents; Augusta LEWIS, Godparent; Born November 14, 1896; Baptized July 3, 1897; #1881

Henry James CONROY - James CONROY and Antonia JUNG, Parents; Henry BALIMANN and Lena JUNG, Godparents; Born September 1, 1898; Baptized November 27, 1898; #1930

Mary Irene COWEN - Timothy COWEN and Catherine O'MARA, Parents; Pat WALSH and Mary HUTZ, Godparents; Born August 21, 1867; Baptized March 1, 1868; #406

Helen Burke CRAIG - John Henry CRAIG and Althea Gabriella DERRICK, Parents; At Clear-Creek; Elizabeth MITCHELL and Joseph ANSTAETT, Godparents; Born April 27, 1863; Baptized May 8, 1865; #206

William Henry CRAIG - John Henry CRAIG and Althea Gabriella DERRICK, Parents; Elizabeth M. MITCHELL and Joseph ANSTAETT, Godparents; Born January 6, 1860; Baptized May 8, 1865; #205

Alice CRAIGEN - Edward CRAIGEN and Helen SCHICKSCHNEIDER, Parents; Edward CAROTHER and Asa BROUSSARD, Godparents; Born September 5, 1885; Baptized July 22, 1886; #1258

John CRAY; Private; Elizabeth YOUNG, Godparent; Born October 10, 1874; Baptized October 17, 1874; #728

Mary Agnes CROSS - Charles Wells CROSS and Rose LENZ, Parents; Thebaud WOLFF and Mary LENZ, Godparents; Born October 9, 1895; Baptized November 18, 1895; #1738

Rose Helen Elizabeth CROSS - Charles Wells CROSS and Rose LENZ, Parents; Anthony LENZ and Rosa WOLFF, Godparents; Born October 9, 1897; Baptized November 15, 1897; #1896

Thomas Littel Valentine CROSS - Charles Wells CROSS and Rose E. LENZ, Parents; Thomas L. CROSS and Anna Mary MENZEL, Godparents; Born February 14, 1900; Baptized March 14, 1900; #1980

Agnes Laura CROSSMAN - William CROSSMAN and Mary Ann PESK, Parents; Frederic PESK and Ann HIBBERT, Godparents; Born July 17, 1867; Baptized September 8, 1867; #368

William CROSSMAN - Robert CROSSMAN and Rachel (JOHNSON) DAVIS, Parents; Convert; Born October 1, 1843; Baptized May 29, 1866; #292

George Hartley CUSSENS - Thomas Howard CUSSENS and Lydia STRIPLING, Parents; George F. HARTLEY and Elizabeth THORBES, Godparents; Born April 13, 1863; Baptized October 9, 1864; #181

Thomas Howard CUSSENS - Thomas Howard CUSSENS and Lydia STRIPLING, Parents; George F. HARTLEY and Elizabeth ALLEN, Godparents; Born September 27, 1861; Baptized October 9, 1864; #180

Anna Jemine DAHN - Louis P. (nc) DAHN and Anna DAHN, Parents; James GENGLER and Mary BUDD, Godparents; Born February 8, 1890; Baptized February 23, 1890; #1473

Caroline Mathilde Dorothy Wilhelmina DAHN - Louis P. (nc) DAHN and Anna KAMPE, Parents; William KAMPE and Dorothy KAMPE, Godparents; Born February 21, 1885; Baptized March 8, 1885; #1134

Lucille Catherine DAHN - Louis P. (nc) DAHN and Anna KAMPE, Parents; Michael MAURER and Catherine OLFSEN, Godparents; Born July 27, 1892; Baptized August 14, 1892; #1575

Mathilda Freda Josephine DAHN - Louis P. (nc) DAHN and Anna KAMPE, Parents; Charles KAMPE and Carolina JIBBS, Godparents; Born January 21, 1888; Baptized February 5, 1888; #1372

Elizabeth Estelle DAYLE - Charles DAYLE (probably DAILY) and Delia BUTTERLY, Parents; Charles DAYLE Jr. and Helen Elizabeth FARRELL, Godparents; Born February 19, 1885; Baptized March 12, 1885; #1142

Walter Miles DAYLE - Charles DAYLE (Probably DAILY) and Delia BUTTERLY,
Parents; Miles BREEN and Catherine LANG, Godparents; Born May 28, 1883;
Baptized June 17, 1883; #1019

Elizabeth DAILY - Michael, Parent; Pat CONNELLY and Mary BLONDEAU,
Godparents; Born September 2, 1867; Baptized October 14, 1867; #382

Margaret Jessie DAILY - Charles (?) DAILY and Odile BUTTERLY, Parents;
Margaret BUND, Godparent; Born April 1, 1881; Baptizted April 24, 1881;
#919

Eugene DALIEN - William DALIEN and Alice PHILLIPS, Parents; Joan
PHILLIPS, Godparent; Born August 18, 1875; Baptized October 7, 1875;
#761

Augusta Helen Barbara DALIER; Baptized May 20, 1877; #810

Cecil Anastasia BALLMER - Gregory DALLMER and Mary Ann SCHAUB, Parents;
Scholastica ELBERT, Godparents; Born July 11, 1870; Baptized January 1,
1871; #569

Ernest August DALLMER - George DALLMER and Ann Mary SCHAUB, Parents;
Ernest August ENGELKIN and Sophia DALLMER, Godparents; Born March 14,
1862; Baptized April 20, 1862; #73

Ernestine Rosina DALLMER - George DALLMER and Ann Mary SCHAUB, Parents;
Ernest ENGELKE and Rosina SCHREIBER, Godparents; Born March 13, 1864;
Baptized July 3, 1864; #164

Gregory DALLMER - George DALLMER and Anna Mary SCHAUB, Parents; Private;
Born August 31, 1866; Baptized September 6, 1866; #313

Joseph Henry DALLMER - George DALLMER and Mary Ann SCHAUB, Parents;
Joseph ELBERT and Mary DALLMER, Godparents; Born September 29, 1867;
Baptized December 29, 1867; #392

Mary Corinne DALLMER - Henry Joseph DALLMER and Elizabeth SCHLINGHART,
Parents; Charles F. JAEGER and Cora JAEGER, Godparents; Born October 11,
1893; Baptized October 29, 1893; #1625

Peter Albert DALLMER - George DALLMER and Ann Mary SCHAUB, Parents;
Peter BOCKET and Mary KOEHLER, Godparents; Born April 8, 1860; Baptized
September 16, 1860; #20

Clara Anna DAM - Christian DAM and Wilhelmina SMITH, Parents; Anna
LEINBACH and Clara FLAGG, Godparents; Born September 15, 1882; Baptized
October 29, 1882; #985

William Herman DAM - Christopher DAM and Wilhelmina SCHMIDT, Parents;
E. CONN and Mary MATHEY, Godparents; Born September 8, 1877; Baptized
October 16, 1877; #814

Genovieve Henrietta DANGELESEN - Henry DANGELESEN and Henrietta
WERDEHAUSEN, Parents; James DREW and Caroline LANG, Godparents; Born
July 23, 1884; Baptized September 21, 1884; #1227

Mary Heneritta Josephine DANGELESEN - Henry DANGELESEN and Heneritta
WERDEHAUSEN, Parents; James COYLE and Carolina McRAE, Godparents; Born
February 19, 1886; Baptized April 25, 1886; #1228

Claud Elmer D'ANGIER - Henry Claud D'ANGIER and Emma Ethel BROOKS,
Parents; Albert LAINE and Ann LAINE, Godparents; Born July 10, 1897;
Baptized January 22, 1899; #1936

Catherine Anita DANGLER - Henry DANGLER and Henrietta WERDENHOUSEN,
Parents; James DREW and Mary BLEIKE, Godparents; Born January 12, 1888;
Baptized July 8, 1888; #1401

James Mary Aloysius DARGAN - Philip DARGAN and Sarah BYRNE, Parents;
Nicolas WELCH and Catherine HICKEY by Mary HALL, Godparents; Born
July 24, 1866; Baptized October 28, 1866; #324

John Anthony DAU - Frederick DAU and Mary SCHMITZ, Parents; Joseph
WINDMEYER and Carolina STANLY, Godparents; Born September 21, 1897;
Baptized January 30, 1898; #1901

John Frederick DAU - Frederick DAU and Mary SCHMITZ, Parents; Frederica
HAMMER and Mary D. P. CET, Godparents; Born July 8, 1895; Baptized
September 20, 1895; #1732

Martha DAU - Frederick DAU and Mary SCHMITZ, Parents; George DAU,
Godparents; Born November 21, 1893; Baptized January 16, 1894; #1645

Mary Selina Theodora Joan DAU - Frederick DAU and Mary SCHMITZ, Parents;
Selina MELODUE, Godparents; Born August 24, 1892; Baptized October 2,
1892; #1579

Mary Augusta Margaret Angela DAU - Frederick (nc) DAU and Mary Catherine
SCHMITZ, Godparents; Born November 2, 1889; Baptized December 8, 1889;
#1461

Julia Catherine DEALY - Michael DEALY and Mary GREGG, Parents; John
DOOLEY and Mary McDONELL, Godparents; Born October 16, 1868; Baptized
January 17, 1869; #504

James John DELANEY - Frank DELANEY and E. BARK, Parents; M. BARK,
Godparents; Born August 28, 1872; Baptized October 3, 1873; #683

Joseph William O'Neale DELANY - John Joseph DELANY and Helen CRIAGEN,
Parents; William O'NEIL and Elizabeth O'NEIL, Godparents; Born August
23, 1887; Baptized November 7, 1890; #1507

Agnes Josephine DELZ - Michael DELZ and Theresa BROKOF, Parents; Joseph
BROKOF and Augusta BAUMANN, Godparents; Born July 15, 1887; Baptized
September 30, 1888; #1411

Anna Christine DELZ - Michael DELZ and Theresa BROKOF, Parents;
Christian BAUMANN and Louise PICTURE, Godparents; Born February 24,
1884; Baptized September 30, 1888; #1410

Hazel Elizabeth Dora DELZ - John Joseph DELZ and Mary LEUTCH, Parents;
W. VANDERPOOL and F. W. HAIDEMANN, Godparents; Born October 4, 1896;
Baptized November 4, 1896; #1858

Mildred Theodora Louise DELZ - John DELZ and Mary LEUTSCH, Parents;
Theodore LEUTSCH and Louise LEUTSCH, Godparents; Born February 19, 1894;
Baptized March 18, 1894; #1656

Bernard Charles DERNI - Philip DERNI and Stephani HOLD, Parents; Joan
SPIZA and Bernard SPIZA, Godparents; Born October 4, 1872; Baptized
November 4, 1872; #638

Mary Caroline DESALME - Joseph DESALME and Rosina BUSER, Parents;
Matthias HERRMANN and Mary AULL, Godparents; Born May 30, 1860;
Baptized June 24, 1860; #11

Catherine DE VILLAS (nee HAMMER) - Marc HAMMER, Parent; Convert;
Catherine BARBOUG and Caterine KRAUS, Godparents; Baptized June 24,
1896; #1835

Valerie Emily Clara Margaret DE VILAS - Victor DE VILAS and Catherine
HAMMER, Parents; Victor DE VILAS and Emily ECKERSKORN, Godparents;
Born January 20, 1892; Baptized January 26, 1896; #1803

Marh Martha Philomene DICKSON - Elias DICKSON and Priscilla DICKSON,
Parents; Philomene LEROUGE and John WILSON, Godparents; Born March 29,
1862; Baptized July 22, 1866; #298

William Frank DILLON - John Martin DILLON and Mary Anna ROBERTSON, Parents; William HALLEY and Heneritta SEARLE, Godparents; Private; Born October 22, 1886; Baptized November 19, 1886; #1283

Albert DIRKS - Frank DIRKS and Catherine FRANKEN, Parents; Rev. J. GONNARD, Godparent; Born June 17, 1860; Baptized May 22, 1862; #82

Herman John DIRCKS - Theodore DIRCKS and Emma FRANZ, Parents; John KOEHLER and Helen SCHWARZBACH, Godparents; Born March 28, 1886; Baptized April 25, 1886; #1226

Joseph DIRKS - Frank DIRKS and Catherine FRANKEN, Parents; Rev. J. GONNARD, Godparent; Born May 6, 1858; Baptized May 22, 1862; #81

Josephine DIRKS - Frank DIRKS and Catherine FRANKEN, Parents; Charles HOFBECK, Godparent; Born June 12, 1864; Baptized July 23, 1866; #299

Philip DIRKS - Frank DIRKS and Catherine FRANKEN, Parents; Teresa DIRKS, Godparent; Born February 15, 1866; Baptized July 23, 1866; #300

Theodore Carl DIRCKS - Theodore DIRCKS and Emma FRANZ, Parents; Catherine VIOLET, Godparents; Born August 16, 1888; Baptized September 8, 1888; #1407

Abraham DIXON - Vincent DIXON and Lizzie DIXON, Parents; Born March 29, 1866; Baptized July 30, 1866; #304

Adam DOERR - Adam DOERR and Agatha PLANEY, Parents; Philipp DOERR and Mary SABELL, Godparents; Born October 24, 1877; Baptized December 2, 1877; #823

Edward Blaney BOERR - Adam DOERR and Agnes BLANEY, Parents; Edward BLANEY and Julia HACTER, Godparents; Born January 30, 1883; Baptized September 17, 1883; #1022

Robert James DOM - Christian DOM and Minna SMITH, Parents; Robert C. BALSAM and Ella DELAGRANGE, Godparents; Born November 3, 1898; Baptized March 5, 1899; #1944

Ruth Magdalen DOM - Christian DOM and Isabelle Wilhelmina SMITH, Parents; Ruth STENZEL, Godparents; Born August 8, 1894; Baptized September 2, 1894; #1678

Pauline Aline DONALLA - Ambrose DONALLA and Mary WENDER, Parents; Theodore DONALLA by Dominic DONALLA and M. BONG, Godparents; Born March 28, 1874; Baptized October 9, 1874; #719

Herman William DORECK - Laurence DORECK and Josephine SCHNEIDER, Parents; Herman SCHREIBER and Mary HAINE, Godparents; Born May 9, 1865; Baptized December 3, 1865; #251

Laurence DORECK - Laurence DORECK and Josephine SCHNEIDER, Parents; Theresa FERBERNE, Godparent; Born November 16, 1859; Baptized January 16, 1864; #138

Theresa Margaret DORECK - Lawrence DORECK and Josephine SCHNEIDER, Parents; Teresa FERBERNE and Dorothy JUNEMANN, Godparents; Born December 3, 1861; Baptized January 16, 1864; #139

Albert DORIAN - George DORIAN and Eugenia GEAY, Parents; Joseph GEAY and Blanche REILLY, Godparents; Born May 21, 1887; Baptized May 25, 1887; #1349

Charles John DOULISNE - Adolph DOULISNE and Agatha ARNOLD, Parents; Carl John BAUER and M. KOEHLER, Godparents; Born October 3, 1870; Baptized February 6, 1871; #572

Lilly Elizabeth DOUROUX - Lucien DOUROUX and Isabel Rosalie GLEEN, Parents; Henry STRERIK and Margaret GENGLER, Godparents; Born January 23, 1895; Baptized June 2, 1895; #1717

Lucie DOUROUX - M. C. DOUROUX and Margaret CLARE, Parents; Private; Born September 18, 1890; Baptized September 23, 1890; #1505

Laura Martha DOYLE - Patrick (Murphy) DOYLE and Martha CUSSICK, Parents; Patrick O'REILLY and Laura GREEN by Mary BOLTON, Godparents; Born March 18, 1861; Baptized May 12, 1864; #158

Laura Mary DOYLE - Pat (Murphy) DOYLE and Martha CUSSICK, Parents; Patrick O'REILLY and Laura GREEN by Mary BOLTON, Godparents; Born April 28, 1858; Baptized May 12, 1864; #157

Athleen Agnes DREW - James Joseph DREW and Caroline Margaret LANG, Parents; Henry DENGELEISEN and Mary Louise HEIDET, Godparents; Born December 29, 1895; Baptized February 9, 1896; #1806

Cedric Edward DREW - James DREW and Caroline LANG, Parents; James COYLE and Mary POUEIGH, Godparents; Born November 7, 1891; Baptized December 20, 1891; #1546

Jones Robert DREW - James J. DREW and Caroline M. LANG, Parents; Robert PHILIPSON and Bernardine WERDEHAUSEN, Godparents; Born August 27, 1886; Baptized October 17, 1886; #1276

Maurelius Stephen DREW - James DREW and Caroline LANG, Parents; James DREW and Mary COYLE, Godparents; Baptized December 3, 1893; #1634

Viola Louise DREW - James DREW and Caroline LANG, Parents; Joseph LANGE and Catherine DREW, Godparents; Born December 24, 1887; Baptized January 29, 1888; #1371

Catherine Elizabeth DRIAKER - Theodore DRIAKER and Elizabeth TRINSIK, Parents; Mathias HERMANN and Catherine DRIAKER, Godparents; Born July 24, 1874; Baptized September 6, 1874; #723

Joseph DRIAKER - Joseph DRIAKER and Elizabeth HEYMANN, Parents; William Theodore DRIAKER and Elizabeth DRIAKER, Godparents; Born August 6, 1876; Baptized September 6, 1876; #777

Susan DRIAKER; #796

William DRIAKER; Private; Baptized April 23, 1872; #616

William George DRIAKER - Theodore DRIAKER and Elizabeth SCHMIDT, Parents; Private; Elsie CONNOR, Godparent; Born February 22, 1877; Baptized March 24, 1877; #807

Arthur Joseph DRUED - James DRUED and Caroline LANG, Parents; Thomas PHILIPSON and Catherine PHILIPSON, Godparents; Born November 1889; Baptized December 15, 1889; #1464

Frederic DUBOIS - Frederic DUBOIS and Mary MAUS, Parents; John HASLON and Bessy HUGHES, Godparents; Born July 10, 1879; Baptized September 21, 1882; #982

Clara DUBREE - Louis DUBREE and Hanna ..., Parents; Private; Born December 5, 1872; Baptized June 20, 1890; #1497

Magdalen Hortense DUCO - Leon DUCO, Parent; William TRINCKS and Hortense FEDGES, Godparents; Baptized July 23, 1893; #1615

Mary Ann ERHOLD - Joseph ERHOLD and Mary JUNG, Parents; Lena JUNG and George SCHWEBEL, Godparents; Born September 27, 1895; Baptized February 13, 1898; #1903

Mary Louise Josephine ERHOLD - Joseph ERHOLD and Mary JUNG, Parents;
Louise SCHWEBEL and Ferdinand JUNG, Godparents; Baptized July 30, 1893;
#1616

Chas. Aloysius ESCHENBERG - Conrad ESCHENBERG and Anna VOGT, Parents;
Aloysius MARX and Mary GIMINSKI, Godparents; Born May 4, 1882; Baptized
June 4, 1882; #969

Federic Herman ESDERS - Herman ESDERS and Mary HEIMANN, Parents;
Joseph RICKE, Godparent; Born June 26, 1898; Baptized April 26, 1899;
#1952

Mary Magdalen Heneritta EMIS - Christian EMIS and Alice Mary DETTMER,
Parents; Michael SINGER and Henrietta SINGER, Godparents; Born April
21, 1885; Baptized April 26, 1885; #1156

Sophie Susan EMIS - Christian EMIS and Alice Mary DETTMER, Parents;
Susan FUNK, Godparent; Born October 3, 1877; Baptized October 21, 1877;
#819

George Joseph ERHOLD - Joseph ERHOLD and Mary JUNG, Parents; George
SCHWEBEL and Laura SCHWEBEL, Godparents; Born December 24, 1897;
Baptized February 13, 1898; #1904

Henrietta Sophie ERHOLD - Joseph ERHOLD and Mary JUNG, Parents; Sophie
FALKENHAGEN and Louise SCHWEBEL, Godparents; Born October 26, 1899;
Baptized July 22, 1900; #1995

Joseph ELSLER - Benjamin ELSLER and Frances FRANKE, Parents; Richard
ELSNER and Adelle ELSNER, Godparents; Born January 24, 1888; Baptized
July 22, 1900; #1391

Martha ELSLER - Benjamin ELSLER and Frances FRANKE, Parents; Ernest
MARTIN, Godparent; Born February 16, 1890; Baptized February 18, 1890;
#1471

Ignatius EMATO and Louise VITTER, Parents; J. TARRAS and Anna BUFFIA,
Godparents; Born April 5, 1887; Baptized June 19, 1887; #1352

John EMIS - Christine EMIS and Alice Mary DETTMER, Parents; Mrs. MAURER,
Godparents; Born August 7, 1874; Baptized August 30, 1874; #721

Mary ELLSWORTH - John ELLSWORTH and Louise BLONDEAU, Parents; Mary
Philomene BLONDEAU and August BLONDEAU, Godparents; Born November 28,
1869; Baptized July 3, 1870; #559

Mary Beulah Va. ELLSWORTH - John (nc) ELLSWORTH and Louise BLONDEAU,
Parents; Elizabeth O'NEIL, Godparent; Born December 9, 1880; Baptized
April 16, 1885; #1151

Mary Frances Ernestine ELLSWORTH - John (nc) ELLSWORTH and Louise
BLONDEAU, Parents; Agnes DILLON, Godparent; Born February 6, 1884;
Baptized December 11, 1884; #1115

Benjamin ELZLER - Benjamin ELZLER and Frances FRANKE, Parents; Charles
BARLEMANN and Caroline BOESMUELLER, Godparents; Born September 29, 1886;
Baptized February 13, 1887; #1310

Emma Mary ELLINGER - Marc ELLINGER and Mary KINDSFATER, Parents;
Herman REIKE and Mary OBACK, Godparents; Born August 23, 1874; Baptized
October 11, 1874; #731

Josephine ELLINGER - Maximilian ELLINGER and Ann P. KINDSVATER, Parents;
Josephine FRENCH and Ann P. KINDSVATER, Godparents; Born September 18,
1868; Baptized January 3, 1869; #502

Wilhelmina Margaret ELLINGER - Marc ELLINGER and Mary Ph. KINDSFATER,
Parents; M. ELLINGER and L. KINDSFATER, Godparents; Born October 22,
1871; Baptized December 24, 1871; #604

Laura Gabrielle ELLSWORTH - John ELLSWORTH and Louise BLONDEAU, Parents;
Virginia BLONDEAU and Emily BARRY, Godparents; Born December 16, 1866;
Baptized Arpil 4, 1867

Mabel Cecil EKERT - William EKERT and Elizabeth DUNE, Parents; Frank
THIELEN and Mary THIELEN, Godparents; Born July 8, 1897; Baptized
July 26, 1897; #1885

Catherine Margaret ELBERT - John C. ELBERT and Margaret MONKS, Parents;
Benjamin ELBERT and Catherine ELBERT, Godparents; Born October 20, 1876;
Baptized November 26, 1876; #784

Louis Charles ELBERT - August ELBERT and Wilhelmina DWANE, Parents;
John WENDL and Rose ANDERSON, Godparents; Born January 31, 1886;
Baptized March 14, 1886; #1220

Theresa Anna ELBERT - Joseph ELBERT and Margaret MONKS, Parents;
Andrew KIMISCH and Mary SCHREIBER, Godparents; Born July 24, 1878;
Baptized August 18, 1878; #861

Clara Emily EICHLER - William EICHLER and Catherine MANYON, Parents;
William EICHLER and Emily CASEY, Godparents; Born February 1, 1878;
Baptized September 29, 1878; #866

Geo. Edward EISENBACH - Edward EISENBACH and Helen (nc) TEICHMANN,
Parents; Geo. EISENBACH (by proxy Augusta b. DALIEN), Godparent;
Born March 8, 1883; Baptized June 11, 1883; #1010

William Max EISENBACH - B. L. Edward EISENBACH and Lena (nc) TEICHMANN,
Parents; Mary PEINE and Mary GEIRLEADE, Godparents; Born July 10, 1887;
Baptized November 27, 1887; #1366

Peter Constantine EISIC - William EISIC and ... BLANCHET, Parents;
Fabian KIMLING and Carolina BLANCHET, Godparents; Born November 9, 1871;
Baptized June 2, 1872; #622

Charles William Frederic EHLERT - Charles Henry EHLERT and Sophie W.
WEIER, Parents; John Frederic MICHELS and Mary Magdalen MICHELS,
Godparents; Born February 15, 1880; Baptized May 23, 1892; #1563

Joan Rosalee Eulalia EHLERT - Charles Henry Adolph EHLERT and Sophy W.
WEYER, Parents; George L. BOHN and Elizabeth HAGEMANN, Godparents;
Born February 12, 1875; Baptized May 23, 1892; #1560

John August EHLERT - Charles H. A. EHLERT and Sophie Winfired WEIER,
Parents; George Leonard BOHN and Elizabeth HAGEMANN, Godparents; Born
May 31, 1877; Baptized May 7, 1892; #1559

Rose Magdalen Justin EHLERT - Charles Henry A. EHLERT and Sophie W.
WEIER, Parents; John Frederick MICHELS and Mary Magdalen MICHELS,
Godparents; Born July 24, 1884; Baptized May 23, 1892; #1564

George Frank EGGERT - Edward EGGERT and Mary GARIBALDE, Parents; Frank
PLACIDUS and Elizabeth EGGERT, Godparents; Born June 17, 1898; Baptized
April 30, 1899; #1954

Theresa EGGERT - Theodore EGGERT and Rosalee BENZEL, Parents; Charles
Ferdinand FOGY and Theresa BUNZEL, Godparents; Born January 17, 1880;
Baptized July 7, 1880; #903

Sophie Mary Christina EHBERT - Charles Henry Adolph and Sophie WEYER,
Parents; Christian EMIS and Thecla BRUCKHOF, Godparents; Born May 5,
1873; Baptized June 1, 1880; #673

Ann EHLERT - Adolph (nc) EHLERT and Sophie WEYER, Parents; Anna SMITH,
Godparents; Born August 14, 1882; Baptized July 26, 1883

Mary Ann EDWARDS - William EDWARDS and Mary GREEN, Parents; Catherine
PHILLIPSON and John TREW, Godparents; Born March 6, 1878; Baptized
May 26, 1878; #851

William Goldwin EDWARDS - William EDWARDS and Mary GREEN, Parents;
Catherine PHILLIPSON and John TREW, Godparents; Born July 25, 1871;
Baptized December 4, 1871; #603

Mary EGEN - Mary EGEN and Frances ..., Parents; J. B. SLAVERY and
Elleen SHOLDERS, Godparents; Born June 10, 1869; Baptized June 20, 1869;
#524

Emma EGGERT - Theodore EGGERT and Rosalee BUNZEL, Parents; Martin
BUNZEL, Godparent; Born May 16, 1871; Baptized May 26, 1871

Elizabeth EDWARDS - Henry EDWARDS and Anna BERGMANN, Parents; Mary
Magdalen BERGMANN, Godparent; Born August 16, 1871; Baptized September
17, 1871; #598

John Henry Goulding EDWARDS - William G. EDWARDS (nc) and Mary GREEN,
Parents; Anna MELVILLE, Godparent; Born March 16, 1884; Baptized
February 26, 1885; #1129

Mary Agnes EDWARDS - Mr. EDWARDS and Louise ..., (colored), Parents;
Agnes MOSER, Godparent; Born January 3, 1890; Baptized April 13, 1890;
#1480

Mary Ann EDWARDS - Henry EDWARDS and Anna BERGMANN, Parents; Mary
HEIMANN and Herrman MARWITZ, Godparents; Born July 1865; Baptized
August 20, 1865; #225

Agla Josephine Lagat EDWARDS - John Fulton (nc) EDWARDS and Agla
DENNY, Parents; George EDWARDS and Leontine EDWARDS, Godparents; Born
January 25, 1883; Baptized May 19, 1883; #1008

Anna EDWARDS - Henry EDWARDS and Anna BERGMANN, Parents; Frank SOMMER
and Anthony BERGMANN, Godparents; Born January 16, 1869; Baptized
April 18, 1869; #514

August EDWARDS - Henry EDWARDS and Anna BERGMANN, Parents; Anthony
HEIMANN and Odilia HEIMANN, Godparents; Born November 8, 1863; Baptized
January 31, 1864; #141

Clinton Noel EDWARDS - Sue ..., Parent; William RICKE and Agnes MOSER,
Godparents; Born March 4, 1887; Baptized April 5, 1887; #1330

Elizabeth Rosalee ECKENFELS - Henry ECKENFELS and Catherine BAUHENS,
Parents; Henry Louis HERMANN and Elizabeth BAUHENS, Godparents; Born
December 18, 1893; Baptized January 21, 1894; #1647

Henry Laurence ECKENFELS - Henry ECKENFELS and Catherine BAUHENS,
Parents; Henry RITZLER and Sophie Lott BAUHENS, Godparents; Born
November 17, 1888; Baptized December 25, 1888; #1421

Sarah Helen EDMISTON - Robert EDMISTON and Helen HINRICHS, Parents;
Mary HINRICHS (by proxy), Godparent; Born June 14, 1887; Baptized
July 11, 1887; #1353

John EDMUNDSON - Louis E. EDMUNDSON and Mary Joan HARDIN, Parents;
Born June 9, 1865; Baptized September 30, 1866; #318

Cecil Wilhelmina FRANKLIN - Joseph FRANKLIN and Theresa STRUCK, Parents;
Joseph ENGELKE and Mary FUNK, Godparents; Born March 18, 1880; Baptized
April 18, 1880; #895

Joseph August FRANKLIN - Joseph FRANKLIN and Theresa STRUCK, Parents;
August RAMMACHER and Mary Augusta RAMMACHER, Godparents; Born February
19, 1877; Baptized March 19, 1877; #800

Rosina Isabella FRANZ - Herman FRANZ and Frances KUHN, Parents; Isabel EDGEWARE, Godparent; Born January 30, 1895; Baptized March 10, 1895; #1707

William Valentine FRANZ - Herman FRANZ and Frances KUHN, Parents; Herman FRANZ and Frances KUHN, Godparents; Born November 3, 1896; Baptized February 14, 1897; #1867

Eugene Hamilton FRANK - August Bernard FRANK and Ann Genevieve RIORDAN, Parents; William FOWLKS and Mary RIORDAN, Godparents; Born October 4, 1893; Baptized October 15, 1893; #1623

Mary Laura FRANK - Anthony FRANK and Mary Frances FRANK, Parents; John Joseph FRANK and Mary Frances FRANK, Godparents; Born July 21, 1884; Baptized July 27, 1884; #1084

Romuald Abbot FRANK - August Bernard FRANK and Ann Genevieve RIORDAN, Parents; John Robert RIORDAN and Mary FRANK, Godparents; Born July 3, 1895; Baptized July 27, 1884; #1722

Edward FABY - Edward Sumty FABY and Elizabeth FROHNE, Parents; Sophie FROHNE, Godparents; Born December 14, 1883; Baptized September 17, 1884; #1093

Mary Mathilde Clara FARIG - Frederick FARIG and Anna HUEBNER, Parents; Theresa WEBER, Godparents; Born January 30, 1896; Baptized May 13, 1877; #793

Charles Leo FARRELL - P. W. FARRELL and Katherine THOMPSON, Parents; William THOMPSON and Mary NEWELL, Godparents; Born October 29, 1884; Baptized April 4, 1887; #1328

Clara FELSMANN - Richard FELSMANN and Martha WEISE, Parents; Meta WEIZER and Clara GAARTZ, Godparents; Born December 23, 1895; Baptized August 16, 1896; #1845

Anthony FREDE - Frank Joseph FREDE and Theresa MERKEL, Parents; Private; Anthony MERKEL, Godparent; Born August 20, 1865; Baptized October 8, 1865; #232

William Granderson FRENCH - Robert Danforth FRENCH and Josephine ..., Parents; M. EHLINGER and Mary LOUIS, Godparents; Born October 30, 1869; Baptized December 25, 1869; #536

Clara FRESIMER - Charles FRESIMER and Gertrude SOELLNER, Parents; Susanna BOCK, Godparent; Adopted by Gustaf DUVIRNOY and Dorothy SOELLNER; Born November 5, 1851; Baptized December 28, 1862; #96

Frederic John FROBOESEN - Frederic FROBOESEN and Leopoldine MUEHE, Parents; Conditional; John RICKE, Godparents; Born December 20, 1859; Baptized January 16, 1870; #540

Theresa Mary Caroline FUNK; Theresa FRANKLING, Godparent; Baptized June 14, 1876; #773

Wilhelmina Elizabeth FUNK - Joseph Frank FUNK and Sophia SEEL, Parents; Elizabeth WANDERS, by Mary WINDEMEYER, Godparent; Born January 21, 1868; Baptized March 22, 1868; #411

George Henry FUGGERSON - H. FUGGERSON and Isadora RYAN, Parents; Josephine DIRKS, Godparent; Born May 24, 1870; Baptized May 5, 1872; #618

William FUGGERSON - Robert FUGGERSON and Mary Ann HUSSEY, Parents; Catherine HUSSEY and Henry SHIELDS, Godparents; Born December 16, 1872; Baptized February 25, 1873; #654

Caroline Sophia Susanna FUNK - Joseph FUNK and Sophia SEEL, Parents;
Susanna SCHABER, Godparent; Born June 21, 1862; Baptized August 3, 1862;
#89

Laura Bertha FLAKE - Otto FLAKE and Laura Emily HOFFMANN, Parents;
John HAGEMANN and Catherine ECKSTEIN, Godparents; Born August 9, 1886;
Baptized September 12, 1886; #1269

Emma FIESEL - August FIESEL and Antonio TCHIEDEL, Parents; William
FESSEL and Mary REYMOND by Antonio YOUNG, Godparents; Born September
28, 1889; Baptized November 17, 1889; #1456

Emma J. ___; Convert; Baptized November 28, 1865; #249

Peter FINK - Peter FINK and Catherine CREMER, Parents; Private; Peter
GENGLER and Lena FINK, Godparents; Baptized December 4, 1870; #568

Anna Amelia FLAKE - Otto FLAKE and Laura Emily HOFFMANN, Parents; Emil
WEBER and Theresa WEBER, Godparents; Born November 19, 1884; Baptized
December 28, 1884; #1117

Stewart John FERGISON - Robert FERGISON and Mary Ann HUSSE, Parents;
M. P. HUSSE and Anna HUSSE, Godparents; Born October 9, 1868; Baptized
November 1, 1868; #426

Anna FESSEL - August FESSEL and Antonia FESSEL, Parents; Edmund
LAWRENCE and Antonio YOUNG, Godparents; Born February 2, 1891; Baptized
May 10, 1891; #1520

Elizabeth Caroline TICKLE - Joseph TICKLE and Theresa MAURER, Parents;
Caroline MAURER and James TICKLE, Godparents; Born June 21, 1895;
Baptized June 30, 1895; #1721

Alexander Ferdinand FIEBEL - Leopold FIEBEL and Elizabeth MARCHAND,
Parents; Jeremiah LORDAN and Mary LORDAN, Godparents; Born November 8,
1886; Baptized November 21, 1886; #1286

Elise Clara FELSMANN - Richard FELSMANN and Martha WEISE, Parents;
Martha WEISSE, Godparents; Born September 21, 1893; Baptized October 1,
1893; #1620

Frieda Martha FELSMANN - Richard FELSMANN and Martha WEISE, Parents;
Paul WEISSE, Godparent; Born September 27, 1890; Baptized October 1,
1893; #1619

Richard Paul William FELSMANN - Richard FELSMANN and Martha WEISE,
Parents; Paul WEISSE, Godparent; Born February 12, 1899; Baptized
October 1, 1899; #1963

Emma Catherine FERBERNE - Andrew FERBERNE and Theresa HILLEBRAND,
Parents; Rosina LEMKE, Godparents; Born August 4, 1863; Baptized
November 8, 1863; #132

Conrad William FLUELSER - George FLUELSER and Rosina FLEULSER, Parents;
Conrad HOLZWERTH and Anna GENGLER, Godparents; Born November 13, 1872;
Baptized January 19, 1873; #650

Clara Helen FLYNN - John FLYNN and Catherine HARRIS, Parents; Daniel
HARRIS and Sara HARRIS (by proxy), Godparents; Born February 1, 1887;
Baptized March 9, 1887; #1317

Robert Walker FLYNN - John FLYNN and Catherine HARRIS, Parents; Sara
Helen HARRIS, Godparent; Born September 9, 1885; Baptized December 12,
1885; #1203

Andrew FOERSTL - Bernard FOERSTL and Eve Barbara SCHELLHORN, Parents;
Andrew SCHELHORN and Elizabeth HERRMANN, Godparents; Born August 5,
1867; Baptized August 25, 1867; #365

Laurence William FLAKE - Otto FLAKE and Laura Emily HOFFMANN, Parents;
Rose FLUEHR and Henry ODELL, Godparents; Born July 28, 1891; Baptized
August 15, 1891; #1533

Mabel Pauline FLAKE - Adolph FLAKE and Laura Emily HOFFMAN, Parents;
Edward MCCARTHY and Pauline MCCARTHY, Godparents; Born October 14,
1892; Baptized November 27, 1892; #1589

Philip Sayers FLAKE - Otto FLAKE and Laura Emily HOFFMANN, Parents;
John ANDERSON and Katerine SOMMERS, Godparents; Born December 27, 1898;
Baptized January 29, 1899; #1939

John Henry FLUEHLE - George FLUEHLE and Lillie (?) SCHREIBER, Parents;
Mrs. Katerine CHITTENDEN, Godparent; Born September 5, 1878; Baptized
May 14, 1879; #887

Elenore Ethel Maud FLAKE - Otto FLAKE and Laura Emily HOFFMANN, Parents;
John SCHULTE and Mauly A. KELLY, Godparents; Born October 14, 1889;
Baptized November 4, 1889; #1455

John Gerald FLAKE - Otto FLAKE and Laura Emily HOFFMANN, Parents; John
Baptist MALIA and Amelia PAULEY, Godparents; Born May 11, 1888; Baptized
June 3, 1888; #1396

Joseph Osborn FLAKE - Otto FLAKE and Laura Emily HOFFMANN, Parents;
Emil Martin FLAKE and Frances Mary PAULEY, Godparents; Born March 12,
1883; Baptized April 8, 1883; #999

William Jennings Bryan FRANK - August Bernard FRANK and Ann Genevieve
RIORDAN, Parents; John J. POWELL and Ellen Sarah POWELL, Godparents;
Born January 9, 1897; Baptized January 24, 1897; #1864

Anthony Robert FOWLER - John FOWLER and Mary HEYMAN, Parents; Baptized
before July 23, 1875; #765

Jacobina Catherine FOWLER - James FOWLER and Mary HEYMANN, Parents;
James JACOBS and Catherine JACKSON, Godparents; Born March 19, 1875;
Baptized May 2, 1875; #747

Lydia Christina FOX - Valentin FOX and Sophie STIEFEL, Parents;
Christian FRENCH and Dorothy FRENCH, Godparents; Born September 17,
1863; Baptized August 7, 1864; #167

Emma FRANKE; Louise Mathilda MASSE, Godparent; Baptized May 31, 1884;
#1070

Michael FORD - Frank FORD and Mary MURRAY, Parents; Edmund QUIRK and
Ann MURRAY, Godparents; Born October 14, 1867; Baptized November 1,
1867; #383

Albert Frederic FORDES - Joseph FORDES and Ella Sara CRACKNEN, Parents;
George Felix ALMERAS and Carmen M. ALMERAS, Godparents; Born August 13,
1882; Baptized March 29, 1891; #1519

George John FOSTNER - John FOSTNER and Mary HOFBECK, Parents; Catherine
KRAUS, Godparent; Born April 6, 1862; Baptized May 25, 1862; #84

Clara (FOUNDLING); Mary Antonia MARCHAND, Godparent; Baptized September
1, 1870; #564

Oliver Raymond FOLEY - Pat FOLEY and Catherine KERWIN, Parents; Louis
ALBERTI and Sealy FOLEY, Godparents; Born January 23, 1894; Baptized
February 18, 1894; #1650

Frank George FOLLET - Frank FOLLET and Catherine FRANZ, Parents; Louis
ALBERTI and Sealy FOLEY, Godparents; Born March 31, 1878; Baptized
April 23, 1878; #845

Anthony Francis FORD - Frank FORD and Mary MURRAY, Parents; Anthony HEIMANN, Jr. and Elizabeth THORBES, Godparents; Born September 25, 1863; Baptized November 15, 1863; #133

John FORD - Frank FORD and Mary MURRAY, Parents; Private; Born June 12, 1866; Baptized June 12, 1866

Josephine Julian FUNK - Joseph FUNK and Sophia Ann SEEL, Parents; Julia FRANKLIN, Godparents; Born September 27, 1881; Baptized November 20, 1881; #947

Theresa Anna Mary Antonia FUESSEL - August (nc) FUESSEL and Antonia TSCHIEDEL, Parents; Theresa MAURER, Godparent; Born March 24, 1885; Baptized May 10, 1885; #1281

August Charles FUESSEL - August FUESSEL and Antonia TSCHIEDEL, Parents; Could be FUHSEL.; Frank J. RESSEL and Mary JUNGE, Godparents; Born March 24, 1885; Baptized May 10, 1885; #1159

Mary Agnes FUESSENHAUSER - Frederic FUESSENHAUSER and Mary FUESSENHAUSER, Parents; Mary GLENDENIN, Godparent; Born September 20, 1887; Baptized March 24, 1888; #1382

Joseph Frank Xavier Stephen FUGGER - Joseph FUGGER (THARENET) and Ann SOMMERS, Parents; Michael LANG and Susanna LANG, Godparents; Born July 7, 1866; Baptized July 29, 1866; #303

John Joseph FROBOESEN - Frederic FROBOESEN and Leopoldine MUEHE, Parents; John RICKE, Godparent; Born December 14, 1862; Baptized January 16, 1870; #540B

Sophie FROHNE - Charles FROHNE and Caroline DIRR (DIRKS?), Parents; Ahha FROHNE, Godparent; Born December 12, 1868; Baptized May 9, 1869; #517

Anne Mary Margaret FRONY - Charles FRONY and Wilhelmina KLAUSEN, Parents; Rose EHLERT and Margaret JONSEN, Godparents; Born December 9, 1896; Baptized March 8, 1897; #1872

Catherine FROSCH - George FROSCH, Parent; Private; Baptized June 18, 1864; #163

Anna Estelle GUBEL - H. A. GUBEL and Mavoza O'DONNELL, Parents; John M. ROSAR and Sarah A. JUNES, Godparents; Born April 11, 1876; Baptized November 5, 1876; #783

Charles August GUNTZ - August GUNTZ and Augusta SCHRADER, Parents; Charles HELBLING and Sophy BEST, Godparents; Born February 5, 1900; Baptized April 1, 1900; #1983

Eugene Gustav GUNTZ - August GUNTZ and Augusta SCHRADER, Parents; Aloysia JACHUSCH and Gustav KAHN, Godparents; Born February 10, 1896; Baptized March 15, 1896; #1813

John Frederic GRUENROD - Henry GRUENROD and Fides ELBERT, Parents; Caroline ELBERT and Henry GRUENROD, Godparents; Born December 21, 1873; Baptized December 28, 1873; #691

Edward GAD - August GAD and Dorothy STOPPELBURG, Parents; John SCHMIDT and Mary Elizabeth SCHMIDT, Godparents; Born December 1, 1878; Baptized January 19, 1879; #878

Ambrose Frank GAERTNER - Frank GAERTNER and Mary A. O'FARRELL, Parents; William RICKE, Godparent; Born January 22, 1887; Baptized February 20, 1887; #1311

Rose Marie GAERTNER - Frank GAERTNER and Mary O'FARRELL, Parents;
John MALLET and Rose MONROE, Godparents; Born September 3, 1884;
Baptized September 21, 1884; #1096

Anna GARTNER - John GARTNER and Mary BADER, Parents; John George
GRIESENBERG and Josephine FISCHER, Godparents; Born February 12, 1872;
Baptized March 31, 1872; #614

Pauline Elizabeth Mary GARTNER - John GARTNER and Barbara MEULLER,
Parents; Pauline MORRIS, Godparent; Born September 28, 1875; Baptized
November 6, 1875; #757

Frederic Mathias GASCHEN - Mathias GASCHEN and Helen HAENLEIN, Parents;
Born September 28, 1880; Baptized March 4, 1881

James ___ - Ellen GALVES, Parent; Slave; James was 8 years old; Laura
GREEN, Godparent; Baptized May 10, 1864; #151

Margaret Joan GARCIA - Manuel GARCIA and Eugenia NEVARES, Parents;
John GARCIA, Godparent; Born November 7, 1899; Baptized February 23,
1899; #1977

John GARNER - John GARNER and Barbara MUELLER, Parents; James O'TOOLE
and Mary CUNINGHAM, Godparents; Born January 15, 1878; Baptized March
3, 1878; #836

Georginia Evangeline Dorothy GARTH - August E. GARTH and Dorothy
Augusta STOPELBERT, Parents; George LEINBACH and Mary Evangeline
COLLINS, Godparents; Born April 11, 1889; Baptized May 12, 1889; #1433

Augusta Catherine GALHON - John GALHON and Mary COMPTON, Parents;
Wilhelmina TAM, Godparent; Born November 27, 1877; Baptized April 14,
1878; #844

Myrtil Anna GALLAGHER - Mentor GALLAGHER and S. E. STUART, Parents;
Mrs. Emma GEORGE, Godparent; Born March 18, 1887; Baptized November 3,
1887; #1361

Chile Corinne Margaret GALLOPINI - Anthony GALLOPINI and Ernestine
CATOZZI, Parents; Paul TOLOMEY and Catherine FOWLER, Godparents; Born
March 24, 1892; Baptized June 25, 1893; #1611

Mary Augusta GALNY - Gustav GALNY and Tesse STEPHANUS, Parents; Mary
SAYLOR and James H. DOLAN, Godparents; Born November 9, 1894; Baptized
March 3, 1895; #1704

Anthony GABRIEL - Frank GABRIEL and Cecile PUCHINTZKI, Parents; John
SELENSKI and Elizabeth GETZ, Godparents; Born September 10, 1893;
Baptized September 16, 1893; #1618C

Clara Margaret GENGLER - Peter GENGLER and Theresa SCHULTE, Parents;
John GENGLER and Clara SCHULTE, Godparents; Born September 2, 1894;
Baptized October 7, 1894; #1685

Henry Charles GENGLER - Peter M. GENGLER and Theresa SCHULTE, Parents;
Henry C. SCHAEFER and Helen SOMMER, Sr., Godparents; Born September 26,
1899; Baptized October 15, 1899; #1964

Herman GENGLER - John GENGLER and Margaret SCHREIBER, Parents; Herman
SCHREIBER and Anna Mary SCHAEFER, Godparents; Born September 1, 1862;
Baptized September 28, 1862; #92

Frank Louis GAY - Theobold GAY and Mary Henrietta CLASSEN, Parents;
Peter BORDELAIRE and Adele DALLAS, Godparents; Born March 26, 1873;
Baptized December 15, 1873; #692

Margaret Armantina GAY - Frank GAY and Theresa FROTE, Parents; Armantina
PRADIER, Godparent; Born May 28, 1895; Baptized June 16, 1895; #1719

Anthony GEMENSKY - Anthony GEMENSKY and Agnes DOMBROWSKI, Parents;
Not married; Born January 3, 1873; Baptized January 7, 1873; #647

Robert GEMSKE - Michael GEMSKE and Agatha .., Parents; Born April 22,
1874; Baptized June 14, 1874; #708

Josephine Ann Martha GASCHEN - Mathias (nc) GASCHEN and Helen
HAEHNLEIN, Parents; Ann HAEHNLEIN, Godparent; Born March 19, 1890;
Baptized April 20, 1890; #1481

Henry Hedwig GASCHENRAT - Mathias GASCHENRAT and Helen HAENLEIN,
Parents; Helen HAENLEIN, Godparent; Born March 11, 1882; Baptized
October 21, 1882; #984

Charles Edward GAY - Frank GAY and Theresa FROTE, Parents; Edward
HOLLAND and Anna HOLLAND, Godparents; Born March 21, 1893; Baptized
April 23, 1893; #1600

Elizabeth Josephine GAY - Tibur GAY and Mary Henrietta CLOSSON, Parents;
William O'KELLY and Elizabeth BLEICKE, Godparents; Born March 28, 1869;
Baptized July 25, 1869; #526

John Louis Emil GARTH - A. E. GARTH and Dora Augusta STOPELBERT, Parent;
J. T. HEUNEBERG and Emily LALEADIE, Godparent; Born May 20, 1887;
Baptized June 12, 1887; #1351

Margaret GERSHEN - Mathias GERSHEN and Helen HENLEIN, Parents; Mrs.
Margaret BUHL, Godparent; Born January 31, 1885; Baptized May 9, 1885;
#1158

John Marion GHINAUDO - Frank Ghin GHINAUDO and Philippine Lucia
GHINAUDA, Parents; Peatro BERA and Margaret BERA, Godparents, Hitchcock,
Texas; Born October 6, 1885; Baptized May 9, 1885; #1470

Angelina GIARATANO - Marion GIARATANO and Rose CANGELOSI, Parents;
Cosimo CANADELLA and Antonia BRANDA, Godparents; Born July 10, 1894;
Baptized September 9, 1894; #1680

Peter John GENGLER - John GENGLER and Margaret SCHREIBER, Parents;
Peter BOCK and Mary Eve KOEHLER, Godparents; Born September 24, 1865;
Baptized October 29, 1865; #245

Peter Mathew Joseph GENGLER - Peter GENGLER and Theresa Mary SCHULTE,
Parents; Jos. John SCHULTE and Helen Theresa SOMMER, Godparents; Born
March 15, 1898; Baptized April 3, 1898; #1911

Frances Henrietta GERBER - Christian GERBER and Louise RICHARD, Parent;
Jos. ANSTAETT and Catherine FOX, Godparents; Born October 30, 1862;
Baptized January 29, 1863; #98

John Edward GERHARD - James GERHARD and Mary MAHONY, Parents; Mary
JOHNSON, Godparent; Born June 13, 1869; Baptized January 30, 1870; #541

James GENGLER - John GENGLER and Margaret SCHREIBER, Parents; Sarah
BOTH and James BOTH, Godparents; Born November 14, 1870; Baptized
January 1, 1871; #570

John GENGLER - Peter GENGLER and Agnes FINK, Parents; John GENGLER and
Anna FINK, Godparents; Born August 9, 1860; Baptized September 16, 1860;
#21

Mathias GENGLER - Peter GENGLER and Agnes FINK, Parents; Mathias
GENGLER and Magdalen FINK, Godparents; Born May 4, 1865; Baptized
July 89, 1865; #221

Peter GENGLER - John GENGLER and Margaret SCHREIBER, Parents; Peter
GENGLER and Amalia KALLUS, Godparents; Born February 18, 1868; Baptized
March 15, 1868; #409

William GENAR - William GENAR and Sarah FITZPATRICK, Parents; Joe
KRAUS and Rosina SCHREIBER, Godparents; Born November 13, 1868; Baptized
December 8, 1868; #498B

Louis Paul GLASS - Paul (nc) GLASS and Elizabeth MEYER, Parents; Michael
LANG, Jr., Godparent; Born April 19, 1889; Baptized May 23, 1889; #1435

Norman Paul GLASS - Paul GLASS and Elizabeth MAYER, Parents; Mary Anna
MAYER, Godparents; Born June 23, 1896; Baptized June 29, 1896; #1837

Mary Antonia GLEICH - August GLEICH and Mary O'CONNOR, Parents; Robert
PHILIPSON and Mary Helen DELANEY, Godparents; Born March 27, 1884;
Baptized October 5, 1884; #1098

Stephen GLOECKNER - Anton GLOECKNER and Teresa HAUSER, Parents; Stephen
LANGE and Mary GLOECKNER, Godparents; Born May 5, 1860; Baptized May
27, 1870; #6

Rosa Josephine Emily GIOZZA - Frank GIOZZA and Emily BLARDONE, Parents;
J. B. AGULO and Rose DALIEN, Godparents; Born January 13, 1886; Baptized
May 8, 1886; #1237

Mary GIRARDIN - Felix G. GIRARDIN and Mary LEROUX, Parents; Pauline
LEROUX, Godparent; Born February 23, 1893; Baptized February 23, 1893;
#1595

Mary Cecile GIRARDIN - Victor GIRARDIN and Mary FOURNIER, Parents;
Jos. LABADIE and Cecile de BALAND, Godparent; Born December 24, 1867;
Baptized February 16, 1868; #402

Joseph Louis GLASER - Louise GLASER, Parent; T. Jos. KRAUS and Caroline
KRAUS, Godparents; Born June 9, 1861; Baptized June 18, 1861; #47

William GIBBS - Hugh GIBBS and Mina SANDOV, Parents; Mrs. Catherine
KRAUS, Godparent; Born August 19, 1884; Baptized September 11, 1889;
#1448

William GILBERT - Thomas D. GILBERT and Anna CRAYCROFT, Parents;
Catherine PHILIPSON, Godparent; Born January 14, 1885; Baptized February
1, 1885; #1122

Magdalen GIMMINSKI - Mary GIMMINSKI, Parent; Anastasia GIMMINSKI,
Godparent; Born March 10, 1885; Baptized September 29, 1885; #1187

Augusta Antoinette GIOZZA - Frank GIOZZA and Emilia BLARDONE, Parents;
Charles DALIAN and Augusta DALIAN, Godparents; Born January 22, 1878;
Baptized April 7, 1878; #842

Anna Christina Theresa GERHARDT - John GERHARDT and Mary SCHNEIDER,
Parents; John Albert BAKEL and Theresa GUTTE, Godparents; Born
December 25, 1876; Baptized January 28, 1877; #795

Margaret Cecil GREEN; 25 years old; Baptized in 1875; #760

Mary Magdalene GOTTLOB - John GOTTLOB and Mary (nc) FRIEDERICH,
Parents; Frank GOTTLOB, Godparent; Born July 1, 1891; Baptized
July 26, 1891; #1524

Mary Wilhelmina GOTTLOB - John GOTTLOB and Mary (nc) FRIEDERICH,
Parents; John MAURER and Caroline MAURER, Godparents; Born June 28,
1889; Baptized July 14, 1889; #1442

Theodore GOTTLOB - John GOTTLOB and Mary (nc) FRIEDRICH, Parents;
Theodore GOTTLOB and Anna MARIAN (by proxy), Godparents; Born
January 14, 1888; Baptized January 20, 1888; #1369

James Lawrence Moor GOURLEY - Robert M. GOURLEY and Mary Isabel CRANE, Parents; Lawrence NUESE and Caroline DAVIS, Godparents; Born January 27, 1885; Baptized March 1, 1885; #1132

Hedwig Clementine Theresa GOMBERT - John B. GOMBERT and Hedwig LACHMANN, Parents; Theresa LACHMANN, Godparent; Born December 6, 1890; Baptized January 4, 1891; #1512

Harrison GORDON; Convert; Baptized December 19, 1867; #390

Cecil Gertrude GOTTLOB - John GOTTLOB and Mary FRIEDERICH, Parents; Theodore GOTLOBB and Minne GOTLOBB, Godparents; Born January 21, 1900; Baptized February 11, 1900; #1975

John Rudolph GOTTLOB - Jos. John GOTTLOB and Mary FRIEDRICH, Parents; Rudolph BOENING and Caroline HUNN, Godparents; Born November 4, 1893; Baptized November 26, 1893; #1631

William Anthony GLOECKNER - Anthony GLOECKNER and Wilhelmina ILGEN, Parents; Adam A. BERNAL, Godparent; Born February 12, 1863; Baptized March 25, 1864; #144

Louis GOHM - Gibhard GOHM and Louise LOHRE, Parents; Herman SCHARF and Theresa HIRTH, Godparents; Born January 16, 1897; Baptized March 7, 1897; #1871

Julia Georgia GOMAN - Adam GOMAN and Theresa GOMEN, Parents; George HAGENS and Julia LAZARO, Godparents; Born May 13, 1899; Baptized May 14, 1899; #1956

Florence Dolly Margaret GOMBERT - Andrew T. GOMBERT and Estelle Mary BUERGER, Parents; Mathilde BUERGER, Godparent; Born September 14, 1895; Baptized November 9, 1895; #1737

Joseph John GRUENROD - Henry GRUENROD and Fides ELBERT, Parents; Benjamin ELBERT and S. ELBERT, Godparents; Born April 14, 1878; Baptized April 28, 1878; #848

Rosa Mary GRUENROD - Henry GRUENROD and Fides ELBERT, Parents; Jos. ELBERT and Rose ELBERT, Godparents; Born November 14, 1867; Baptized January 5, 1868; #395

Edmund Aloysius GRUENROTH - Henry GRUENROTH and Fides ELBERT, Parents; George LEINBACH and Mary LEINBACH, Godparents; Born June 21, 1883; Baptized July 8, 1883; #1015

Mary Margaret Louise GROSS - Kilian GROSS and Mary METZ, Parents; Margaret GROSS, Godparent; Private; Born August 1, 1883; Baptized August 4, 1883; #1018

Frances Augusta GROY - William GROY and Carolina JUNG, Parents; Elizabeth HAGEMANN, Godparents; Born November 18, 1870; Baptized March 25, 1862; #72

Henry Joseph GRUENROD - Henry GRUENROD and Fides ELBERT, Parents; Joseph ELBERT and Scholastica ELBERT, Godparents; Born January 30, 1870; Baptized March 13, 1870; #551

Christian Nicholas GREINER - Christian GREINER and Emma SCHRAMM, Parents; Nicholas GREINER and Margaret PUHL, Godparents; Born November 3, 1881; Baptized April 16, 1882; #964

Nicholas Joseph GREINER - Christian GREINER and Emma SCHRAMM, Parents; Nicholas GREINER and Mary A. KELLY, Godparents; Born July 27, 1885; Baptized August 16, 1885; #1182

Charles Euguen GRIMALDE - Joseph GRIMALDI and Helen JESSEL, Parents;
J. B. BARELLI and Eulalia BARELLI, Godparents; Born December 19, 1859;
Baptized August 1861; #53

Frank Joseph Anthony GROSS - Kilian GROSS and Mary METZ, Parents;
Private; Margaret GROSS, Godparents; Born August 12, 1884; Baptized
October 10, 1884; #1101

Geraldine GRAHAM - John M. GRAHAM and Elenora LAVERY, Parents; P. I.
LAVERY and M. E. M. GONZALEZ, Godparents; Born February 8, 1885;
Baptized October 18, 1885; Baptized October 18, 1885; #1193

John Lavery GRAHAM - John M. GRAHAM and Lenora LAVERY, Parents; Mary
MICHELS, Godparent; Born July 24, 1883; Baptized December 8, 1884;
#1114

Gertrude Frances GRAS - Frederic William GRAS and Mary HAUSLER, Parents;
Ernest Julius GERY and Frances GERY, Godparents; Born October 13, 1898;
Baptized November 6, 1898; #1928

Barbara Margaret HAAG - Emil HAAG and Anna Mary MERTHEL, Parents;
Margaret WENTZEL, Godparent; Born January 20, 1870; Baptized June 23,
1872; #625

John Nicholas HAAG - Emil HAAG and Anna Mary MERTHEL, Parents; Margaret
WENTZEL, Godparent; Born March 3, 1872; Baptized June 23, 1872; #626

Ann Mary HAEHNLEIN - Henry HAEHNLEIN and Helen HILDEBRAND (HILLENBRAND),
Parents; Appollonia HILDEBRAND, Godparent; Born March 16, 1867; Baptized
July 15, 1867; #257

Ann Mary HAEHNLEIN - Henry HAEHNLEIN and Helen HILDEBRAND, Parents;
Margaret ADAM, Godparent; Born September 25, ...; Baptized January 2,
1874; #693

Anna Ursula HAEHNLEIN - Henry HAEHNLEIN and Helen HILDEBRAND, Parents;
Ursula FORKERSSEN, Godparent; Born May 18, 1871; Baptized August 1, 1871;
#593

Frances HAEHNLEIN - Henry HAEHNLEIN and Helen HILDEBRAND, Parents;
Matilda BOEHLING, Godparent; Born April 29, 1865; Baptized October 3,
1865; #230

Helen HAEHNLEIN - Henry HAEHNLEIN and Helen HILDEBRAND, Parents;
Scholastica ELBERT, Godparent; Born June 24, 1863; Baptized August 9,
1863; #119

Henry Christopher HAEHNLEIN - Henry HAEHNLEIN and Helen HILDEBRAND,
Parents; Frank B. HILLENBRAND and Appolonia HILLENBRAND, Godparents;
Born December 24, 1868; Baptized February 2, 1869; #508

Charlotte Louise Elizabeth HAGEMAN - John HAGEMAN and Elizabeth HERZOG,
Parents; Theodore ECKSTEIN and Elizabeth HAGEMAN, Godparents; Born
July 17, 1876; Baptized September 6, 1876; #801

Catherine Susan HAHN - Frank HAHN and Mary LANG, Parents; Peter MUELLER
and Catherine LANG, Godparents; Born November 1, 1877; Baptized November
18, 1877; #822

Estelle Mary HAHN - Frank D. HAHN and Mary LANG, Parents; John H.
MUELLER and A. G. FINN, Godparents; Born April 18, 1881; Baptized
June 11, 1881; #930

Louise Catherine Mary HAIDE - Frank Joseph HAIDE and Margaret
WERDEHAUSEN, Parents; George Frank HAIDE and Mary Catherine WERDEHAUSEN,
Godparents; Born December 23, 1874; Baptized February 19, 1875; #739

Clara Caroline Emily HAINE - William HAINE and Mary COERS, Parents;
Emil LAINBACH and Caroline HAGEMANN, Godparents; Born August 5, 1866;
Baptized Janaury 1, 1867; #330

Brigid Ottilia HALEY - Matthew HALEY and Anne DELANEY, Parents; Pat
KELLY and Margaret HALEY, Godparents; Born August 13, 1867; Baptized
November 24, 1867; #387

Mary Ann HAMMER - John HAMMER and Anne SCHULTE (nee SCHUCHARD),
Parents; Mary Magdalene MICHELS, Godparent; Born August 9, 1883;
Baptized February 2, 1885; #1124

John Henry HAMMOND; Convert; Born July 12, 1835; Baptized September 23,
1864; #175

Henry HAMMOND - Henry HAMMOND and Louise BLONDEAU, Parents; Private;
Born June 9, 1864; Baptized July 6, 1864; #165

Alfred HANSEN - Alfred HANSEN and Rosina BAUMANN, Parents; Joseph
MAURER and Theresa MAURER, Godparents; Born June 29, 1891; Baptized
August 2, 1891; #1529

Catherine Barbara HANSEN - Alfred HANSEN and Rosina BAUMANN, Parents;
Catherine KRAUS, Godparent; Born September 30, 1893; Baptized November
5, 1893; #1629

Herman Hy. Peter HANSEN - Alfred HANSEN and Rosina BAUMANN, Parents;
Herman KRAUS and Catherine KRAUS, Godparents; Born July 8, 1888;
Baptized August 16, 1888; #1404

Joseph Frederic HANSEN - Alfred HANSEN and Rosina BAUMANN, Parents;
Emma HERMANN, Godparents; Born December 8, 1895; Baptized January 18,
1896; #1801

Anna Josephine HANSEN - Alfred HANSEN and Rosina BAUMANN, Parents;
Herman KRAUS and Catherine KRAUS, Godparents; Born July 27, 1886;
Baptized August 19, 1886; #1264

Theodore Henry HANSEN - Alfred HANSEN and Rosina BAUMANN, Parents;
Anna HAUSINGER, Godparents; Born February 17, 1898; Baptized March 23,
1898; #1908

Emma Antonia Gertrude HARDIN - William HARDIN and Frances BLEICKE,
Parents; Gertrude BERKENBUSCH, Godparent; Born October 2, 1866; Baptized
October 16, 1866; #323

Henry HARREL; Private; Age 25; Baptized January 8, 1863; #97

Joseph HARRINGTON - Alfred HARRINGTON and Mathilda MONTEAUT, Parents;
Augusta ABADIE, Godparent; Born March 8, 1890; Baptized June 21, 1890;
#1498

Ann Elizabeth HARRIS - A. C. HARRIS and Ann Elizabeth WOOD, Parents;
Anthony REHRMANN and Theresa REHRMANN, Godparents; Born March 5, 1850;
Baptized March 22, 1863; #106

... HARRIS; Convert; Baptized October 1867; #381

Mary Theresa HARTWIGT - Charles HARTWIGT and Leopoldine MUEHE, Parents;
John RICKE and Theresa SCHOEKE, Godparents; Born June 15, 1871; Baptized
July 16, 1871; #592

Joseph HASSIN - Charles HASSIN and Sophie SPIEKER, Parents; Theodore
SPIEKER and Theresa RICKE, Godparents; Born January 1, 1881; Baptized
May 8, 1881; #923

Ethel Cecil HAUSINGER - Henry George HAUSINGER and Ann MAURER, Parents;
Joseph ..., Godparent; Born November 26, 1898; Baptized December 18,
1898; #1933

155

Irene Margaret HAUSINGER - Henry HAUSINGER and Ann MAURER, Parents;
John MAURER and Anne HOLLAND, Godparents; Born July 2, 1895; Baptized
July 29, 1895; #1724

John Felix Matthew HEALY - John Matthew HEALY and Mary SCHEBALM,
Parents; Felix SCHEBALM and Elizabeth HAGEMANN, Godparents; Born
February 3, 1886; Baptized May 16, 1886; #1242

Charles HECK - Martin HECK and Catherine WOLLBAUM, Parents; Charles D.
BRAUN and Caroline LUTZ, Godparents; Born March 5, 1893; Baptized
March 6, 1893; #1597

Dennis HECK - Martin HECK and Barbara FISCHER, Parents; Dennis FOLEY,
Godparent; Born June 22, 1894; Baptized June 30, 1894; #1668

Mary HECK - Martin HECK and Catherine WOLLBAUM, Parnents; William MEES
and Barbara MEES, Godparents; Born August 1, 1899; Baptized August 8,
1899; #1960

Joseph Herman HECK - Martin HECK and Catherine WOLLBAUM, Parents; Joseph
MEES and Amelia SOMMER, Godparents; Born November 30, 1897; Baptized
January 16, 1898; #1899

Robert Caspar HECK - Martin HECK and Catherine WOLLBAUM, Parnents;
Caspar SELENKE and Mary SCHULTE, Godparents; Born February 26, 1896;
Baptized March 29, 1896; #1817

Leona Theresa HEER - William J. HEER and Emma VERBERNE, Parents; T. J.
CONNERLY and Carrie ELBERT, Godparents; Born April 14, ...; Baptized
May 4, 1890; #1483

Mary Louise HEER - William HEER and Emma VERBERNE, Parents; Michael
BURKE and Mary BURKE, Godparents; Born October 2, 1884; Baptized
October 26, 1884; #1107

Joseph HEFFINGER - Sebastian HEFFINGER and Anna PETER, Parents; Martina
PETER, Godparent; Born October 30, 1880; Baptized December 7, 1880; #913

Ann Mary Barbara HEIMANN - Anton HEIMANN and Ottilia BURTSCHELL, Parents;
Frnak SAMMET and Barbara BALLHORN, Godparent; Born April 20, 1866;
Baptized May 10, 1866; #284

Alice Othilia HEIMANN - Anthony HEIMANN and Augusta BIEHLER, Parents;
Othilia HEIMANN, Godparent; Born September 7, 1882; Baptized February
28, 1883; #989

Alva Marie HEIMANN - George HEIMANN and Mary CARR, Parents; Mrs. Mary
CGEST, Godparent; Born January 17, 1887; Baptized May 25, 1887; #1348

Caroline Mary HEIMANN - Anthony HEIMANN and Augusta BIEHLER, Parents;
Othilia HEIMANN, Godparents; Born August 27, 1884; Baptized January 7,
1885; #1120

Catherine Cecil HEIMANN - Henry HEIMANN and Elizabeth HUGHES, Parents;
Theresa POPULAR, Godparent; Born November 20, 1886; Baptized May 21,
1887; #1346

Charles Thaddeus HEIMANN - George HEIMANN and Mary CARR, Parents;
John HEIMANN and Mrs. Emily HEIMANN, Godparents; Born December 31, 1888;
Baptized June 16, 1889; #1436

Forest Nicholas HEIMANN - William HEIMANN and Henrietta MC CORMICK,
Parents; George HEIMANN, Godparent; Born August 21, 1881; Baptized
December 2, 1881; #949

Frances Stella HEIMANN - Henry HEIMANN and Elizabeth HUGHES, Parents;
Frances HEIMANN and Rev. Jac. F. LAUTH, Godparents; Born December 16,
1882; Baptized July 2, 1884; #1079

Francis HEIMANN - Anthony HEIMANN and Odelia BURTSCHELL, Parents; Frank HUDSON and Elizabeth THORBES (HEIMANN), Godparents; Born May 12, 1863; Baptized June 14, 1863; #112

Heram Walter HEIMANN - Walter HEIMANN and Dathula MC CORMICK, Parents; Frances HEIMANN and Rev. Jac. F. LAUTH, Godparents; Born October 26, 1883; Baptized July 2, 1884; #1078

Ida HEIMANN - Henry HEIMANN and Elizabeth HUGHES, Parents; Henry HEIMANN and Mary HEIMANN, Godparents; Born September 1, 1885; Baptized May 5, 1886; #1233

Joseph Wesley HEIMANN - George HEIMANN and Mary CARR, Parents; Alice CARR, Godparent; Born February 2, 1894; Baptized April 28, 1894; #1662

Laurence HEIMANN - Walter HEIMANN and Decathula MC CORMICK, Parents; Julius RUIZ and Theresa RUIZ, Godparents; Born December 16, 1889; Baptized May 23, 1890; #1490

Martha Laura HEIMANN - William HEIMANN and Heneritta MC CORMICK, Parents; Frances HEIMANN and Rev. Jac. F. LAUTH, Godparents; Born October 16, 1883; Baptized July 2, 1884; #1080

Mary Ophelia Augustine HEIMANN - Anton HEIMANN and Ottilia BURTSCHELL, Parents; Jacob DABNEY and Mrs. M. O. Augusta MILLER, Godparents; Born January 19, 1861; Baptized April 7, 1861; #40

Mercedes HEIMANN - William HEIMANN and Henrietta MC CORMICK, Parents; Frances HEIMANN, Godparent; Born March 5, 1886; Baptized May 5, 1886; #1235

Robert Louis HEIMANN - Walter HEIMANN and Dathula MC CORMICK, Parents; Frances HEIMANN and Rev. Jac. F. LAUTH, Godparents; Born December 18, 1880; Baptized July 2, 1884; #1077

Sara Elizabeth HEIMANN - Walter HEIMANN and Dathula MC CORMICK, Parents; Edward BARTELS and Sara E. BARTELS, Godparents; Born September 26, 1895; Baptized June 29, 1895; #1720

Walter Adam HEIMANN - Henry HEIMANN and Elizabeth HUGHES, Parents; Anthony POPULAR and Agnes POPULAR, Godparents; Born July 20, 1889; Baptized December 5, 1889; #1460

Walter Mary HEIMANN - Walter HEIMANN and Mary MC CORMICK, Parents; Margaret BARTELS, Godparent; Born September 6, 1895; Baptized August 28, 1897; #1889

William Anthony HEIMANN - Anthony HEIMANN and Augusta BIELER, Parents; Othilia HEIMANN, Godparent; Born October 31, 1878; Baptized April 18, 1879; #885

Mathias HEIMANN and Augusta EGGERT, Parents; Private; Baptized November 1872; #646

John Clyde Cleveland HEIMANN - George HEIMANN and Mary CARR, Parents; Theresa POPULAR, Godparent; Born May 6 (?), 1885; Baptized June 27, 1885; #1174

Charles Henry HEINE - William HEINE and Mary COERS, Parents; Henry HAGEMANN and Louise HOHORST, Godparents; Born February 9, 1865; Baptized November 21, 1865; #247

Elizabeth Augusta Joan HEINE - William HEINE and Mary COERS (KOURS), Parents; Theodore V. GRUNDNER and Elizabeth HAGEMANN, Godparents; Born January 29, 1868; Baptized May 2, 1869; #516

John Frederic William HEINE - William HEINE and Mary COERS, Parents; John COERS, Godparent; Born June 2, 1861; Baptized October 10, 1861; #57

Anna HEINZE - Germanicus HEINZE and Mary GRUENROD, Parents; B. GRUENROD, Godparent; Born March 15, 1874; Baptized May 25, 1874; #809

Henry HEINZE - Germanicus HEINZE and Mary GRUENROD, Parents; Bernard GRUENROD, Godparent; Born February 22, 1877; Baptized May 25, 1877; #808

Pauline HEINZE - Emmanuel HEINZE and Lena HAGEMANN, Parents; George LEINBACH and Pauline LEINBACH, Godparents; Born July 28, 1892; Baptized November 20, 1892; #1586

Sophie Elise Mary HEINZE - Emmanuel August HEINZE and Caroline BIERMANN (nee HAGEMANN), Parents; Caroline LEINBACH and Elizabeth HAGEMANN, Godparents; Born December 17, 1888; Baptized March 26, 1889; #1427

Elizabeth Helen HELFENSTEIN - John HELFENSTEIN and Elizabeth SCHREIBER, Parents; Mary WEBER, Godparent; Born August 8, 1893; Baptized September 16, 1893; #1618B

George John HELFENSTEIN - John? HELFENSTEIN and Elizabeth SCHREIBER, Parents; Theresa FLUHR and George FLUHR, Godparents; Born July 6, 1891; Baptized August 8, 1891; #1530

Louise HELFENSTEIN - William HELFENSTEIN and Anna WORDENBAUM, Parents; Henry WORDENBAUM and Ellen HELFENSTEIN, Godparents; Born December 6, 1891; Baptized February 7, 1892; #1549

Louise Helen HELFENSTEIN - John HELFENSTEIN and Elizabeth SCHREIBER, Parents; Rose FLEUHR, Godparents; Born January 21, 1890; Baptized February 19, 1890; #1472

Margaret HELFENSTEIN - John HELFENSTEIN and Elizabeth SCHREIBER, Parents; Helen HELFENSTEIN, Godparent; Baptized November 4, 1896; #1860

Mary Elizabeth HELFENSTEIN - John HELFENSTEIN and Elizabeth SCHREIBER, Parents; Emil WEBER and Mary SCHREIBER, Godparents; Born November 24, 1888; Baptized January 6, 1889; #1423

Mary Ellen HELFENSTEIN - William D. HELFENSTEIN and Anna WORDENBAUM, Parents; Catherine HELFENSTEIN and Isidor ARNOLD, Godparents; Born November 30, 1889; Baptized December 22, 1889; #1466

Mary Isabelle HELFENSTEIN - John HELFENSTEIN and Elizabeth SCHREIBER, Parents; Isabelle PENDERGAST and Gabriel MONFORT, Godparents; Born February 27, 1895; Baptized April 7, 1895; #1712

Sophie Ellen HELFENSTEIN - William HELFENSTEIN and Anna WORDENBAUM, Parents; Ellen THOMPSON, Godparent; Born November 30, 1897; Baptized March 6, 1898; #1905

William Joseph HELFENSTEIN - William HELFENSTEIN and Anna WORDENBAUM, Parents; Helen HELFENSTEIN, Godparent; Born September 16, 1894; Baptized October 28, 1894; #1689

William Adam HELMBOLD - John HELMBOLD and Theresa HAGEMANN, Parents; Henry HAGEMANN and Elizabeth HAGEMANN, Godparents; Born March 14, 1862; Baptized May 14, 1862; #77

Mary Joan Caroline HELMBOLD - John HELMBOLD (LEINBACH) and Teresa HAGEMANN, Parents; John HAGEMANN and Caroline HAGEMANN, Godparents; Born November 1, 1867; Baptized January 1, 1868; #394

Albert Martin HELMER - John E. HELMER and Mary Louise UNDERWOOD, Parents; Martin HELMER and Augusta DOM, Godparents; Born Arpil 16, 1884; Baptized May 24, 1885; #1164

Cecil HELMER - John P. HELMER and Mary UNDERWOOD, Parents; K. F. FAZENDO and Cecil FAZENDO, Godparents; Born March 20, 1890; Baptized August 10, 1890; #1503

George Daniel HELMER - John E. HELMER and Mary L. UNDERWOOD, Parents; Daniel MC BRIDE and Mary MC BRIDE, Godparents; Born March 8, 1886; Baptized December 6, 1886; #1295

Alfred HENKEL - George HENKEL and Emily TAQUART, Parents; Joseph TAQUART and Anna HENKEL, Godparents; Born October 28, 1892; Baptized December 25, 1892; #1593

August Mathias HERMANN - Mathias HERMANN and Augusta EGGERT, Parents; Mathias HERMANN Jr. and Clara BULLACHER, Godparents; Born September 17, 1888; Baptized November 9, 1888; #1414

Catherine Henrietta HERMANN - Henry Theodore HERMANN and Anna L. FLANDERS, Parents; Henry ECKENFELS and Catherine ECKENFELS, Godparents; Born October 28, 1892; Baptized May 7, 1893; #1602

Cecil HERMANN - David HERMANN and Laura BLOODGOOD, Parents; Cecil BESEN, Godparent; Born July 13, 1886; Baptized December 17, 1886; #1299

David Matthew HERRMANN - David HERRMANN and Laura BLOODGOOD, Parents; Mathias HERRMANN and Elizabeth TRIAKER, Godparents; Born March 6, 1881; Baptized November 13, 1881; #944

Elenore Frances HERRMANN - Henry Theo. HERRMANN and Ann Louise FLANDERS, Parents; John MC MARTHY and Frances Elenore MC MARTHY, Godparents; Born August 16, 1890; Baptized May 7, 1893; #1603

Emily Mathilda HERRMANN - Mathias HERRMANN and Augusta EGGERT, Parents; David HERRMANN and Mathilda EGGERT, Godparents; Born June 2, 1874; Baptized August 13, 1874; #720

Ernest Martin Theo. HERRMANN - Mathias HERRMANN and Augusta EGGERT, Parents; Theodore EGGERT, Godparent; Born August 3, 1886; Baptized September 9, 1886; #1267

Frank HERRMANN - Mathias HERRMANN and Mary BECKER, Parents; Frank SOMMER and Anna BERGMANN, Godparents; Born February 20, 1860; Baptized April 29, 1860; #3

Frederic Charles HERRMANN - Anthony HERRMANN and Wilhelmina HERRMANN, Parents; Charles KOERNER and Anna MUELLER, Godparents; Born November 9, 1872; Baptized December 19, 1872; #657

Henry Ferdinand HERRMANN - David HERRMANN and Laura BLOODGOOD, Parents; Henry Ferdinand FAZEND and Cecile FAZEND, Godparents; Born September 7, 1883; Baptized April 3, 1884; #1054

John Baptist HERRMANN - Mathias HERRMANN and Mary BECKER, Parents; John B. BULLACHER and Teresa SOMMER, Godparents; Born March 9, 1865; Baptized May 18, 1865; #213

Joseph HERRMANN - Mathias HERRMANN and Mary BECKER, Parents; Joseph SOMMER and Elizabeth RATHENFELX, Godparents; Born April 15, 1862; Baptized May 24, 1862; #83

Margaret HERMANN - David HERMANN and Laura BLOODGOOD, Parents; Rudolph BOLOCK and Margaret WENZEL, Godparents; Born March 29, 1877; Baptized October 16, 1877; #816

Mary HERRMANN - David HERRMANN and Laura (Clara) BLOODGOOD, Parents; Mathias HERRMANN and Mary POLASCHE, Godparents; Born December 12, 1879; Baptized October 24, 1880; #909

Otto John HERRMANN - John HERRMANN and Mary Louise UNDERWOOD, Parents;
Frank THIELEN and Mary Agnes THIELEN, Godparents; Born December 27,
1896; Baptized March 28, 1897; #1875

Pearl Agnes HERRMANN - David HERRMANN and Laura BLOODGOOD, Parents;
Margaret BULLASCHER, Godparent; Born November 21, 1884; Baptized
February 9, 1885; #1125

Rudolph Mathias HERRMANN - Mathias HERRMANN and Augusta ECKERT, Parents;
Rudolph BULLASCHER and Margaret WENZEL, Godparents; Born September 29,
1876; Baptized January 1, 1877; #829

Josephine HERRGOTT - August HERRGOTT and Cecil ..., Parents; Saraphina
ROBENREID and Theresa J. LEINBACH, Godparents; Born November 7, 1863;
Baptized March 27, 1864; #145

Bernard William HERZOG - David HERZOG and Mary BRANDES, Parents;
Wilhelmina STRUBE, Godparent; Born January 22, 1878; Baptized July 29,
1878; #855

Frank Thomas HERZOG - David HERZOG and Mary Bernardine BRANDES,
Parents; Theresa Julia STRUVE, Godparent; Born March 7, 1883; Baptized
June 25, 1883; #1012

Fridolin Frederic HERZOG - David HERZOG and Mary BRANDES, Parents;
Peter HELFRICH (by Frederic SCHILETTER), Godparent; Born March 1, 1873;
Baptized May 31, 1873; #669

Jacob HERZOG - David HERZOG and Mary Bernardine BRANDES, Parents;
... HERZOG (Proxy, John KRAUS) and Susanna BOCK, Godparents; Born
July 23, 1862; Baptized August 10, 1862; #90

Jacob Augustine HERZOG - David HERZOG and Mary Bernardine BRANDES,
Parents; James HERSEY and Catherine FRANZ, Godparents; Born August 20,
1880; Baptized July 3, 1881; #932

Joseph HERZOG - David HERZOG and Mary BRANDES, Parents; Henry KOCH
and Anna RINK, Godparents; Born July 22, 1866; Baptized September 2,
1866; #311

Julia HERZOG - David HERZOG and Mary BRANDES, Parents; Margaret
SCHLITTLER, Godparent; Born July 17, 1868; Baptized May 19, 1869; #519

Laurence David HERZOG - David HERZOG and Mary Dina BRANDES, Parents;
Laurence THROAN and Elizabeth BRAUS, Godparents; Born September 17,
1870; Baptized February 6, 1871; #573

Mary Elizabeth HERZOG - David HERZOG and Mary Bernardine BRANDES,
Parents; Mathias GENGLER and Elizabeth STRUBE, Godparents; Born August
17, 1861; Baptized October 9, 1864; #182

Anthony HEYMANN - John HEYMANN and Augusta BIEHLER, Parents; Catherine
HEYMANN, Godparent; Born February 4, 1875; Baptized April 4, 1875; #743

Anthony Alexander HEYMANN - Anthony HEYMANN and Wilhelmina KOERNER,
Parents; Alexander ROSPOLER and Mary MC DERMOTT, Godparents; Born
December 23, 1877; Baptized April 28, 1878; #849

Odelia Frances HEYMANN - Anthony HEYMANN and Augusta BUEHLER, Parents;
Frank SOMMER and Odelia HEYMANN, Godparents; Born July 9, 1876;
Baptized August 20, 1876; #775

Mary Lawrence HIEGEL - Ferdinand HIEGEL and Sophie ANDERSON, Parents;
Joseph ANDERSON and Catherine ANDERSON, Godparents; Born March 25, 1878;
Baptized April 27, 1878; #846

Hedwig BERTHA HILGEN - Bertha HILGEN, Parent; William HILGEN, Godparent; Born July 6, 1887; Baptized September 10, 1887; #1358

Florentine Louise HILL - William (Melvin) HILL and Anna STEINHARDT, Parents; Theresa DINTER, Godparent; Born August 25, 1884; Baptized January 3, 1885; #1118

Joseph Malvin HILL - Malvin HILL and Caroline WERDEHAUSEN, Parents; Joseph WERDEHAUSEN and Henrietta WERDEHAUSEN, Godparents; Born February 15, 1873; Baptized May 8, 1873; #663

Louise Mary Theresa HILL - Malvin HILL and Caroline WENDEL, Parents; Henry LEWIS and Mary Louise WERDEHAUSEN, Godparents; Born July 15, 1875; Baptized November 6, 1875; #758

Mary Julian Frances HINLOWSKY - Peter HINLOWSKY and Frances JAEGGERTS, Parents; Frances WICOKSKY and Mary Julia STAULER, Godparents; Born December 29, 1872; Baptized January 19, 1873; #648

Bertha Elizabeth HOCH (HOCK) - Henry HOCH (HOCK) and Augusta STAGEROWSKI, Parents; Elizabeth SCHMIDT, Godparent; Born April 9, 1893; Baptized May 25, 1893; #1605

Martin George HOCH - Henry HOCH and Augusta STAROSKI, Parents; Martin RICKE and Mary RICKE, Godparents; Born June 28, 1884; Baptized October 26, 1884; #1108

Olga Joan HOCH - Adam HOCH and Lena KOEHLER, Parents; Joan KOEHLER, Godparent; Born June 16, 1894; Baptized July 26, 1894; #1672A

Charles Louis HOECKER - Oscar HOECKER and Laura ETIE, Parents; Louis ETIE and Clara HOECKER, Godparents; Born August 24, 1881; Baptized October 9, 1881; #943

John HOEHMANN - Anton HOEHMANN and Wilhelmina KOERNER, Parents; Private; Born March 24, 1864; Baptized October 5, 1864; #179

Ann Margaret HOFBECK - John HOFBECK and Caroline TROST, Parents; Herman TROST and Margaret PEINE, Godparents; Born March 3, 1870; Baptized March 13, 1870; #552B

Anna Mary Theresa HOFBECK - John HOFBECK and Caroline TROST, Parents; Anna Mary TROST, Godparent; Born April 15, 1861; Baptized April 18, 1861; #43

Caroline Josephine HOFBECK - John HOFBECK and Caroline TROST, Parents; Herman TROST and Mary RICKE, Godparents; Born May 23, 1867; Baptized June 9, 1867; #352

John Herman HOFBECK - John HOFBECK and Caroline TROST, Parents; Herman TROST and Margaret PEINE, Godparent; Born March 3, 1870; Baptized March 13, 1870; #552A

Mary Margaret HOFBECK - John HOFBECK and Caroline TROST, Parents; Herman TROST and Margaret PEINE, Godparent; Born December 19, 1864; Baptized January 1, 1865; #186

Theresa HOFBECK - John HOFBECK and Caroline TROST, Parents; Theresa REHRMANN, Godparent; Born January 14, 1863; Baptized February 12, 1863; #99

Joan Mary HOGAN - John HOGAN and Mary CREDO, Parents; Margaret STECKMANN, Godparent; Born November 16, 1881; Baptized July 15, 1884; #1083

Jessie Lee HOLLAND - Christopher HOLLAND and Mary THOMPSON, Parents; Victoria GREEN, Godparent; Born January 28, 1882; Baptized March 18, 1884; #1049

Walter Lee HOLLAND - Christopher C. HOLLAND and Mary THOMPSON, Parents; Elenore BIERMANN, Godparent; Born March 13, 1884; Baptized April 15, 1884; #1060

Wilhelmina Evelyn HOLLAND - Christopher C. HOLLAND and Mary THOMPSON, Parents; Elenore BIERMANN, Godparent; Born January 6, 1879; Baptized April 15, 1884; #1061

Albert Julius HOWE - Adolph HOWE and Clara KALUSA, Parents; Clara HOWE, Godparents; Born September 27, 1893; Baptized December 3, 1893; #1633

Charles Henry HOWE - Adolph HOWE and Clara KALUSA, Parents; Charles MUELLER, Godparent; Born November 14, 1886; Baptized December 9, 1886; #1296

Clara HOWE - Adolph HOWE and Clara KALUSA, Parents; Christine MUELLER, Godparent; Born January 31, 1885; Baptized March 18, 1885; #1144

Gertrude Ann HOWE - Adolph HOWE and Clara KALUSA, Parents; Annie C. PEDERSON and Charlie BROSIG, Godparents; Born October 23, 1891; Baptized November 8, 1891; #1543

Henry Christian HOWE - Adolph HOWE and Clara KALUSA, Parents; Elise SEVERIN, Godparent; Born July 13, 1888; Baptized August 14, 1888; #1403

Katherine Ellen HOWE - Adolph HOWE and Clara H. KALUSA, Parents; Catherine MILLER, Godparent; Born Arpil 22?, 1890; Baptized June 10, 1890; #1495

Walter Otto HOWE - Adolph HOWE and Clara KALUSA, Parents; Joan MUELLER, Godparent; Born February 20, 1896; Baptized June 6, 1896; #1830

Ruth Margaret HOPE - Louis HOPE and Anna CORDUA, Parents; Sinclair CORDUA and Delia CORDUA, Godparents; Born May 16, 1897; Baptized August 16, 1897; #1888

Adolph Alexander HOPF - Adolph HOPF and Mary WAGER, Parents; Mrs. Clara FISHER, Godparent; Born November 30, 1887; Baptized June 3, 1888; #1397

Walter James HUBBELL - Sydney HUBBELL and Mary SANDERSON, Parents; James COMPTON, Godparent; Born February 26, 1898; Baptized April 19, 1900; #1988

Alma Ray HUEBNER - Joseph HUEBNER and Mary BERGMANN, Parents; Ray M. DOBSON, Godparent; Born May 27, 1885; Baptized September 5, 1885; #1883B

Joseph Walter HUEBNER - Joseph HUEBNER and Mary BERGMANN, Parents; Ferdinand JUNG and Anthony KAPER, Godparent; Born December 29, 1883; Baptized March 23, 1884; #1052

Laura Helen HUEBNER - Joseph HUEBNER and Mary BERGMANN, Parents; August JAEGER and Mary EDWARDS, Godparents; Born October 13, 1881; Baptized February 19, 1882; #956

Margaret Mary HUEBNER - Rudolph M. HUEBNER and Antonia M. SCHNEIDER, Parents; John FRANKE and Theresa J. MOELLER, Godparent; Born January 31, 1900; Baptized February 18, 1900; #1976

William Oswald HUEBNER - Joseph HUEBNER and Mary BERGMANN, Parents; William BLAKEMAN and Anna EDWARDS, Godparents; Born in 1886; Baptized May 6, 1887; #1341

Helen Agnes HUGHES - Henry HUGHES and Emily HEIMANN, Parents; George HEIMANN and Frances HEIMANN, Godparents; Born February 14, 1886; Baptized May 5, 1886; #1234

Elizabeth HUGHES - Samuel HUGHES and Martha Frances FELTIN, Parents;
Mary HEIMANN, Godparent; Born Born in 1854; Baptized July 2, 1884; #1081

William HUGHES; In hospital; Baptized November 9, 1867; #386

Lillian Martina HUNTER - Louis Martin HUNTER and Mary HARINGTON,
Parents; John HUNTER and Lillian HUTNER, Godparents; Born March 18,
1878; Baptized April 28, 1878; #847

Michael HUSSEY - Michael HUSSEY, Parent; Born September 8, 1867;
Baptized September 13, 1867; #370

Louis Arminius (Herman) HUTTER - Charles HUTTER and Theresa ...,
Parents; L. Antonie ROSE and Margaret PEMBERG, Godparents; Born April
15, 1860; Baptized May 6, 1860; #4

Eva Elizabeth HUTTER (married Peter Charles BOERGERSHAUSEN) - Peter
HUTTER and Anna Mary ZUBER, Parents; Gustave WIESE and Catherine
Rose BURATIN, Godparents; Born March 31, 1876; Baptized February 18,
1899; #1943A

Mary Theresa IFFINGER - Sebastian IFFINGER and Anna PETER, Parents;
Mary KOEHLER, Godparent; Born August 28, 1877; Baptized March 25, 1879;
#880

Hortense ILLEY - John ILLEY and Louise BLANDEAU, Parents; Charles
LEICAMP and Augustine DARRAS, Godparents; Born December 26, 1870;
Baptized April 9, 1871; #584

Alice Mary IRVIN - William Henry IRVIN and Augusta MUNDT, Parents;
Antonio COOK and Andrew PETERSON, Godparents; Born September 25, 1886;
Baptized December 25, 1886; #1304

Ottilia JACOBS - James JACOBS and Emilia (FRANZ?), Parents; Anton
HEIMAN and Mrs. Anton HEIMAN, Godparents; Born May 20, 1874; Baptized
June 28, 1874; #711

John JANEY - James JANEY and Fannie SENON, Parents; Elizabeth MUELLER,
Godparent; Born October 29, 1872; Baptized May 11, 1873; #667

John JAMISON; Private; Baptized May 23, 1867; #350

Anthony William Theodore JANSEN - John JANSEN and Frances JUERSIG,
Parents; Anthony HOERLING and Wilhelmina HOERLING, Godparents; Born
November 18, 1863; Baptized January 3, 1864; #136

Charles Robert JANSEN - John JANSEN and Frances TURSCHIG (JUERSIG?),
Parents; Charles TURSHIG and Rose ELBERT, Godparnets; Born November 2,
1868; Baptized January 31, 1869; #507

Frances Helen JANSEN - John JANSEN and Frances JUERSIG, Parents; Henry
GRUENWALD and Fides ELBERT, Godparnets; Born December 3, 1865; Baptized
March 25, 1866; #275

John JANSEN - John JANSEN and Frances JUERSIG, Parents; John Anthony
HOERLING and Wilhelmina HOERLING, Godparents; Born June 25, 1861;
Baptized July 22, 1861; #50

Leo JANSSEN - Edward JANSSEN and Mellie MC MALLVILLY, Parents; Mrs.
SCHNEIDER, Godparents; Baptized December 21, 1896; Private; #1862

Michael Edward Oscar JANSEN - John JANSEN and Elizabeth SOMMER, Parents;
Michael LANG and Susanna LANG, Godparents; Born April 19, 1866;
Baptized July 29, 1866; #290

John Anthony JAY - Theobold JAY and Henrietta CLOSSON, Parents; John
Anthony SCHERFFINS and Ann SCHERFFINS, Godparents; Born April 30, 1866;
Baptized May 24, 1866; #290

Elizabeth Mary JEFFERSON - William A. JEFFERSON and Caroline DUROLF
(nee KLAUBERG), Parents; John WILSON and Helen WILSON, Godparents;
Born March 3, 1884; Baptized September 8, 1884; #1092

Theresa Mary JELLINECK - Joseph JELLINECK and Mary Theresa HASBUTZKY,
Parents; Charles BRUNNER and Caroline HASBUTZKY, Godparents; Born
June 4, 1872; Baptized July 14, 1872; #630

James Joseph JENT - William Henry Harrison JENT and Eloise SPADES,
Parents; Charles STECHMANN and Mary STEGMANN, Godparents; Born
September 26, 1867; Baptized May 3, 1894; #1663

Anthony JERSIG - Joseph JERSIG and Pauline KOENIG, Parents; John
JANSSEN and J. JANSSEN, Godparents; Born November 26, 1891; Baptized
January 27, 1892; #1548

Charles John JERSIG - Joseph JERSIG and Pauline KOENIG, Parents;
William JANSSEN and Anna TOEBELMANN, Godparents; Born August 27, 1885;
Baptized August 1, 1887; #1355

Dorothy Elizabeth JERSIG - Charles JERSIG and Dorothy ERTZKUS, Parents;
H. CROWLEY and Elizabeth TOEBELMANN, Godparents; Born October 14, 1877;
Baptized October 20, 1877; #818

Elizabeth Magdalen JERSIG - Joseph JERSIG and Pauline KOENIG, Parents;
Rose GREENROTH, Godparent; Born March 11, 1890; Baptized July 11, 1890;
#1500

Joseph Rudolph JERSIG - Joseph JERSIG and Pauline KOENIG, Parents;
John JANSEN, Godparents; Born July 2, 1888; Baptized April 14, 1889;
#1429

Louis Frederic JOCKUSH - John William JOCKUSH and Elisa MOELLER,
Parents; Frederic William WAGNER and Louise Clara KAUFMANN, Godparents;
Born May 4, 1860; Baptized July 15, 1860; #12

Catherine Elizabeth Clementine JOHNSON - John JOHNSON and Elizabeth
SUMMERS, Parents; Clementine GUENARD, Godparent; Born February 10, 1860;
Baptized June 14, 1860; #9

Charles Robert JOHNSON - John JOHNSON and Augusta MUND, Parents; Mary
BAYLOR, Godparent; Born December 10, 1882; Baptized March 25, 1883;
#996

Claudia Camilla JOHNSON - Alphonso JOHNSON and Ann ANDERSON, Parents;
Rene James MUELLER and Camilla ARMSTRONG, Godparents; Born August 24,
1895; Baptized June 24, 1896; #1834

Henry Josephine JOHNSON - John JOHNSON and Elizabeth SOMMER, Parents;
Henry MUELLER and Joan MUELLER, Godparents; Born August 1, 1868;
Baptized March 28, 1869; #512

Lamar Thomas Fisher JOHNSON - Lamar Henry JOHNSON and Margaret
Elizabeth FISHER, Godparents; Born April 6, 1898; Baptized April 24,
1898; #1915

Margaret JOHNSON - Lamar JOHNSON and Margaret Elizabeth FISHER, Parents;
Charles MORSE and Mary JOHNSON, Godparents; Born May 7, 1899; Baptized
June 1, 1899; #1958

Margaret JOHNSON - William JOHNSON and Sophy FROHNE, Parents; Elizabeth
FROHNE, Godparent; Born September 3, 1887; Baptized April 5, 1888; #1385

Peter William Geroge JOHNSON - James JOHNSON and Elizabeth SOMMER,
Parents; John SOMMER and Margaret RICHARDSON, Godparents; Born January
2, 1863; Baptized September 20, 1863; #124

Helen JORDAN - Christian JORDAN and Mary KRAMER, Parents; Caroline
KRAMER, Godparent; Born October 21, 1886; Baptized November 26, 1886;
#1288

Elnora JOSEPH - Frank JOSEPH and Mary Ann RECHETLOCK, Parents; Fannie
WATSON, Godparent; Born September 10, 1868; Baptized September 16, 1868;
#424

Mary Frances JUFFS - Benjamin JUFFS and Mary CLARKE, Parents; B.
WILLINGER, Godparent; Born September 9, 1891; Baptized January 14,
1900; #1974

Frances Anna JUNEMANN - Francis JUNEMANN and Caroline HESS, Parents;
Theresa BLIECKE and Anna HESS, Godparents; Born January 25, 1859;
Baptized March 3, 1861; #31

Infant; Gustave JUNG and Frances SCHNEIDER, Parents; Born December 18,
1865; Baptized December 28, 1865; #255

Caroline JUNG; Conditional; Baptized April 21, 1862; #75

Louis JUNG - August JUNG and Frances SCHNEIDER, Parents; Conditional;
Frank MARKE and Elizabeth FLEGER, Godparents; Born December 13, 1855;
Baptized April 27, 1865; #198

Theresa Helen Christina JUNG - Ferdinand JUNG and Ann .., Parents;
Mary BERGSTROM, Godparent; Born October 12, 1894; Baptized November
25, 1894; #1691

Anna JUNGE - Ferdinand JUNGE and Anna .., Parents; Frank SOMMERS and
Anna EDWARD, Godparents; Born September 12, 1870; Baptized December 4,
1870; #567

Albert Bernard William JUNKER - William JUNKER and Julia MEURY, Parents;
Rose FLEUHR, Godparent; Born February 22, 1895; Baptized April 7, 1895;
#1711

Mary Myrtle Clarence JUNKER - William Peter JUNKER and Julia MUERY,
Parents; Clarence POPLAR, Godparent; Born May 28, 1896; Baptized June
14, 1896; #1832

Wilhelmina JUERGENS; Convert; Baptized April 16, 1868; #417

Catherine Elizabeth KRASSMANN - Robert KRASSMANN and Elenore COVENY,
Parents; Mary WILLIAMS, Godparent; Born June 17, 1881; Baptized August
2, 1881; #936

John KRAUS - Francis KRAUS and Catherine KIRCHGAESSNER, Parents; Michael
TIX and Caroline BRUECHER, Godparents; Born October 31, 1860; Baptized
November 11, 1860; #25

John Frederic KRAUS - Frank KRAUS and Catherine KIRCHGAESSNER, Parents;
Catherine MOORE, Godparent; Born June 13, 1862; Baptized June 29, 1862;
#86

Pauline KRAUS - Frank KRAUS and Catherine KIRCHGAESSNER, Parents; Helen
BERTRAUD (nee KRAUS), Godparent; Born November 28, 1866; Baptized
December 9, 1866; #327

William KRAUS - Frank Joseph KRAUS and Elizabeth BUSCH, Parents; Herman
KRAUS and Catherine KRAUS, Godparents; Baptized in Cathedral; Born
September 16, 1879; Baptized April 16, 1885; #1151A

Frederic Cornelius KRAUS - Frederic John KRAUS and Amelia Emily CASEY,
Parents; C. C. CASEY and Theresa POPLAR, Godparents; Born October 3,
1887; Baptized November 6, 1887; #1362

Ira Julia KRAUS - John KRAUS and Lily HEIMANN, Parents; J. J. KRAUS and Catherine KRAUS, Godparents; Born August 20, 1895; Baptized October 27, 1895; #1734

John Lawrence KRAUS - John KRAUS and Lilly HEIMANN, Parents; Charles POPLIER and Catherine KRAUS, Godparents; Born February 18, 1887; Baptized March 27, 1887; #1327

John Sidney KRAUS - John KRAUS and Lillian HEIMANN, Parents; John KOEHLER and Rosina BAUMANN, Godparents; Born September 20, 1884; Baptized October 12, 1884; #1104

Linus Thaddeus KRAUS - John KRAUS and Mary Lily (HEIMAN), Parents; John Jos. KRAUS and Josephine KRAUS, Godparents; Born November 21, 1892; Baptized December 18, 1892; #1592

Maud Mary Celestine KRAUS - John KRAUS and Mary HEIMANN, Parents; Julius FRIBAUT and Theresa POPULAR, Godparents; Born February 15, 1889; Baptized March 31, 1889; #1428

Mary Viola KRAUS - John F. KRAUS and Emily E. CASEY, Parents; J. J. KRAUS and Mrs. L. C. CASEY, Godparents; Born June 23, 1885; Baptized July 12, 1885; #1176

Henry Herman KRAUS - Joseph KRAUS and Catherine KIRCHGEYMER (?), Parents; John RICKE and M. KOEHLER, Godparents; Born February 26, 1871; Baptized March 26, 1871; #580

Joseph Lawrence Edward KRAUS - Joseph KRAUS and Elizabeth BUSCH, Parents; John LUTZ and Mary LUTZ, Godparents; Born September 15, 1891; Baptized October 31, 1891; #1539

Mary Elizabeth KRAUS - Joseph KRAUS and Elizabeth BUSCH, Parents; E. KRAUS, Godparent; Born April 21, 1872; Baptized May 25, 1872; #619

Emma Marie KRESSEL - Arnold KRESSEL and Theresa BUNZEL, Parents; Martin RICKE and Mary EGGERT, Godparents; Born October 24, 1882; Baptized April 15, 1884; #1062

John Camillus Marion KRETZSCHMAR - John Louis KRETZSCHMAR and Joan Christina SETZOG, Parents; Convert; Dresden, Saxony; Born in 1832; Baptized March 9, 1862; Convert; #62

David KRIEGER - George KRIEGER and ..., Parents; George KRIEGER, Jr., Godparent; Born January 19, 1877; Baptized December 18, 1885; #1207

George KRIEGER - George KRIEGER, Parents; Born May 12, 1881; Baptized October 1, 1885; #1188

Henry KRIEGER - George KRIEGER, Parent; Born July 3, 1882; George KRIEGER, Jr., Godparent; Baptized December 18, 1885; #1208

Herman KRIEGER - George KRIEGER, Parent; George KRIEGER, Jr., Godparent; Conditional; Born December 11, 1874; Baptized December 18, 1885; #1206

William KRIEGER - George KRIEGER, Parent; John MAGUIRE, Godparent; Conditional; Born June 6, 1872; Baptized December 18, 1885; #1205

Bernard KRONE - Bernard KRONE and Joan MEYERS, Parents; Carolina KRAMER, Godparent; Born May 22, 1859; Baptized July 21, 1863; #116

John KRONE - Bernard KRONE and Joan MEYERS, Parents; John Henry WESTERLAGE and Caroline KROMER, Godparents; Born January 28, 1862; Baptized July 21, 1863; #117

David KRONE - Dyonisius KRONE and Sara SEARS, Parents; Sara BARTHEL and Peter BARTHEL, Godparents; Born February 16, 1884; Baptized June 22, 1884; #1075

Anthony KROPP - Anthony KROPP and Verona STOCK, Parents; Joseph PESCHKE, Godparent; Born April 5, 1870; Baptized April 10, 1870; #556

Elizabeth KUEHNE - Theo. KUEHNE and Elizabeth Catherine REIN, Parents; Margaret PEINE, Godparent; Born August 23, 1860; Baptized September 2, 1860; #15

John Henry Frank KUEHNE - Theodore KUEHNE and Catherine Elizabeth REIN, Parents; John JANSEN and Theresa REHRMANN, Godparents; Born March 8, 1866; Baptized April 22, 1866; Conditional; #283

Wilhelmina Sophy KUEHNE - Theodore KUEHNE and Elizabeth RHEIN, Parents; Wilhelmine HOERLING, Godparent; Born October 7, 1863; Baptized August 22, 1864; #169

Elenor Wilhelmina Ormyeb KUNTZ - George (nc) KUNTZ and Catherine JUNG, Parents; Ormye WITTER and Wilhelmina PFLUEGER (by proxy), Godparents; Born December 13, 1884; Baptized April 12, 1885; #1150

Catherine Helen KUNTZ - George KUNTZ and Catherine JUNG, Parents; Oliver LORENZO and Henrietta LORENZO, Godparents; Born December 7, 1886; Baptized April 24, 1887; #1333

Edwena Ernestine Josephine KUNTZ - Joseph KUNTZ and Anna LUMNIEL (KUMMEL), Parents; Edward MUELLER and Ernestine SIMPSON, Godparents; Born February 15, 1881; Baptized April 18, 1881; #926

Irene Frances Mary Anna LADD - Oscar Edward LADD and Sara Elizabeth FLYNN, Parents; Mary BUTLER, Godparent; Born March 10, 1896; Baptized May 7, 1896; #1828

Mary Symphorosa LAGATHES - Peracles LAGATHES and Cecil AULL, Parents; Anthony AULL and Catherine AULL, Godparents; Born July 13, 1871; Baptized September 10, 1871; #597

Dionysius LAGATOUS - Pericles LAGATOUS and Catherine AULL, Parents; Anthony AULL, Godparent; Born November 18, 1877; Baptized December 23, 1877; #827

Mary Theresa LAHRSEN - Henry LAHRSEN and Joan KOENIG, Parents; Theresa KUHLE (by proxy), Godparent; Born June 2, 1889; Baptized June 30, 1889; #1440

Joseph LAIBHAHN - John LAIBHAHN and Agnes SCHLACHTER, Parents; Joseph FOLEY and Margaret SELENKI, Godparents; Baptized January 13, 1895; #1699

Albert George LAINE - Albert LAINE and Anna HENLEIN, Parents; Mary HENLEIN, Godparent; Born July 28, 1893; Baptized September 10, 1893; #1618A

Charles Linus LAINE - Albert LAINE and Anna HENLEIN, Parents; Charles LAINE and Lena GASCHEN, Godparents; Born August 30, 1894; Baptized October 14, 1894; #1687

Clara Mathilde LAKHART - John LAKHART and Caroline RATISEAU, Parents; Rosa MARTINEZ and Alfred RATISEAU, Godparents; Born March 23, 1878; Baptized August 25, 1878; #863

Laura Ernestine LANG - Charles LANG and Clara (nc) MASSEY, Parents; Susan HAHN, Godparent; Born August 24, 1878; Baptized May 30, 1886; #1247

Anna Agnes LANG - George LANG and Catherine PATSON, Parents; Jos. GALKIN and Ch. Ch. GREYENBUEHL, Godparents; Born January 8, 1876; Baptized November 11, 1876; #799

Elenore Hernina Aurelia LANG - H. V. LANG and Catherine SEIBERT, Parents; Ellen HODGKISS, Godparent; Born October 19, 1877; Baptized December 4, 1887; #1367

Joseph Herbert LANG - Herman LANG and Caroline SEIBERT, Parents; Joseph BELBAZ and Pauline BELBAZ, Godparents; Private; Born May 21, 1885; Baptized June 12, 1885; #1167

Anna Edelgard LANG - Herman Victor LANG and Martha FREY (widow JENSEN), Parents; Anna SCHWERTFEGER and Ernest SCHWERTFEGER, Godparents; Born December 14, 1893; Baptized January 7, 1894; #1639

Caroline Notina Edelgarde LANG - Herman Victor LANG and Caroline Elizabeth SEIBERT, Parents; Caroline SEIBERT (by proxy), Godparent; Born February 26, 1884; Baptized March 23, 1884; #1053

Felicitas Philomina Edelberta LANG - Herman Victor LANG and Catherine SEIBERT, Parents; Susan HAHN (by proxy), Godparent; Born July 8, 1886; Baptized August 8, 1886; #1261

Margaret Catherine LANG - Herman Victor LANG and Martha FREY, Parents; Michael REEB and Catherine ECKSTROM, Godparents; Born April 2, 1896; Baptized April 26, 1896; #1823

Martha Helen Ida LANG - Herman Victor LANG and Martha FREY, Parents; Otto Jos. JORDAN and Ida FRANCO, Godparents; Born November 30, 1899; Baptized December 31, 1899; #1970

John Frank Henry LANG - John LANG and Ida Emily KUMKE, Parents; Peter MUELLER and Frank LANG, Godparents; Born January 31, 1878; Baptized August 24, 1878; #862

Edward Louis Henry LANG - John H. LANG and Ida Emily (nc) HUMKE, Parents; Henry E. LANG and Catherine LANG, Godparents; Born October 1, 1883; Baptized August 14, 1884; #1087

Anthony John LANG - Michael LANG and Catherine PEIFFER, Parents; Michael Anthony KIMLEY, Godparent; Born August 21, 1882; Baptized September 17, 1882; #977

Catherine Susan LANG - Michael LANG and Catherine PFEIFFER, Parents; Susan HAHN, Godparent; Born May 29, 1886; Baptized June 20, 1886; #1254

Herman Carl LAND - Michael LAND and Caroline PEIFFER, Parents; Herman LANG and Carl LANG (by proxy), Godparents; Born January 25, 1888; Baptized May 8, 1888; #1390

Joseph Henry LANG - Michael LANG and Catherine PFEIFFER, Parents; Michael John Herman LANG and Mary LANG, Godparents; Born November 24, 1895; Baptized December 22, 1895; #1794

Susan Catherine LANG - Michael LANG and Catherine PFEIFFER, Parents; Susan HAHN, Godparent; Born April 24, 1885; Baptized May 19, 1885; #1160

William Charles LANG - Michael LANG and Catherine PFEIFFER, Parents; William John MUELLER, Godparent; Born March 28, 1884; Baptized April 27, 1884; #1065

Lilian Josephine LANG - Michael J. H. LANG and Nelly Lilian BROUSSARD, Parents; Lucy CARRAGUE and Joseph Henry LANG, Godparent; Born February 10, 1900; Baptized March 4, 1900; #1979

Michael Edward Joseph LANG - Victor LANG and Martha FREY, Parents; Michael LANG and Catherine LANG, Godparents; Born March 24, 1895; Baptized February 22, 1895; #1708

George Joseph LANGE - Stephen LANGE and Helen STEHLING, Parents;
Ferdinand MARCHAND and Octavia MARCHAND, Godparents; Born March 1, 1863;
Baptized March 19, 1863; #105

Mary Caroline LANGE - Stephen LANGE and Mary WERDEHAUSEN, Parents;
Philip WERDEHAUSEN and Caroline WERDEHAUSEN, Godparents; Born August 6,
1867; Baptized August 25, 1867; #366

Anna LATER - Andrew LATER and Rose RISTOE, Parents; Florentine RISTOE,
Godparent; Born December 4, 1858; Baptized September 9, 1860; #18

Mary LATER - Andrew LATER and Rose RISTOE, Parents; Florentine RISTOE,
Godparent; Born May 20, 1860; Baptized September 9, 1860; #19

John LAUBEGGER - Christopher LAUBEGGER and Margaret SAMMET, Parents;
Rosina SAMMET, Godparent; Born November 10, 1858; Baptized October 9,
1866; #321

Frank Vincent LAUSTALOTTE - Justin LAUSTALOTTE and Mary Alice ARRINGTON,
Parents; Frank FOSSEY and Adelaid FOSSEY, Godparents; Born April 10,
1885; Baptized April 21, 1885; #1153

Mary Josephine ....; Baptized April 23, 1896; #1827

Arthur Demetrius LAWSON - Anthony LAWSON and Louise BUEHLE, Parents;
Demetrius ANTON and Mary BUEHLE, Godparents; Born July 6, 1880;
Baptized September 12, 1880; #904

Julia Louise LAWSON - Anthony LAWSON and Louise BUEHLER, Parents;
Dorothea RUTHFORD and Louise LAWSON, Godparents; Born June 7, 1878;
Baptized December 8, 1878; #874

Anna Louise LEATHERN - Louis LEATHERN and Mary AULL, Parents; Patrick
NOLAN and Ann KENNEDY, Godparents; Born June 1, 1880; Baptized December
5, 1880; #912

Anna Louise LEATHERN - Louis LEATHERN and Mary AULL, Parents; Mary
LEATHERN, Godparent; Born September 2, 1888 (Born April 7, 1888);
Baptized April 7, 1888 (Baptized September 2, 1888); #1406

Louis LEATHERN - Louis (nc) LEATHERN and Mary AULL, Parents; Cecil
MOOR, Godparent; Born October 5, 1885; Baptized October 6, 1886; #1189

Robert LEATHERN - Louis LEATHERN and Mary Elizabeth AULL, Parents;
David CLEMENT and Leona EDWARDS, Godparent; Born April 15, 1882;
Baptized September 11, 1882; #975

Joseph Isadore LECLERC - Isadore LECLERC and Mary Theresa VALLE, Parents;
Joseph O. MENARD and Susan MENARD, by proxy, Godparents; Born October
8, 1863; Baptized October 11, 1863; #127

Theophilo Joseph LECONTE - Emil LECONTE and Mary Barbara LEHMANN,
Parents; Theophilo ZINGG and Frances ZINGG, Godparents; Born March 19,
1885; Baptized May 24, 1885; #1162

Henrietta Elizabeth LEDWINKA - Frederic LEDWINKA and Ann Mary BURKHARD,
Parents; Born March 19, 1867; Baptized August 26, 1867; #367

Nicholas Peraclis LEGART - Peraclis LEGART and Cecilia AULL, Parents;
M. AULL, Godparent; Born April 17, 1876; Baptized August 10, 1876; #772

Elenora Louisa LEGATOS - Christopher LEGATOS and Virginia WERNERT,
Parents; Louis PAQUE and Mary LEGATOS, Godparents; Born November 7, 1877;
Baptized June 27, 1880; #899

Mary Theresa LEGATOS - Christopher LEGATOS and Virginia WERNERT, Parents;
George PAQUE and Albertina PAQUE, Godparents; Born May 19, 1876;
Baptized June 27, 1880; #900

Nicholas Andrew LEGATOS - Christopher LEGATOS and Virginia WERNERT, Parents; Demetrius MATHEWA and Louise MATHEWA, Godparents; Born September 8, 1879; Baptized June 27, 1880; #899

Pericletes Diomisius LEGATOS - Christopher LEGATOS and Virgina WERNERT, Parents; Michael BAROMI and Mary PRADIER, Godparents; Born July 29, 1881; Baptized October 26, 1881; #941

Joseph Philip LEGAY - Thiboud LEGAY and Henricka CLOSSON, Parents; James CLOSSON and M. CLOSSON, Godparents; Born March 2, 1871; Baptized April 2, 1871; #581

Charles William LEINBACH - Emil LEINBACH and Pauline KASSEL, Parents; Charles P. DECKELMAYER and Helen BURKE, Godparents; Born January 9, 1884; Baptized February 24, 1884; #1043

George Emil LEINBACH - Emil LEINBACH and Pauline CASSEL, Parents; George Anthony LEINBACH and Clara Emily HEINE, Godparents; Born June 1880; Baptized in 1881; #918

Henrietta Catherine LEINBACH - George LEINBACH and Emily LEINBACH, Parents; George LEINBACH and H. WESENDORFF, Godparents; Born June 17, 1870; Baptized May 22, 1871; #589

Joan Caroline Augusta LEINBACH - George LEINBACH and Emily LEINBACH, Parents; .. HAGEMANN and M. HAGEMANN, Godparents; Baptized February 2, 1873; #652

Francis Joseph LEINMULLER - Francis LEINMULLER and Margaret FAINT, Parents; ... SAMMET, Godparents; Born August 13, 1869; Baptized February 20, 1870; #545

Frank William LEINMUELLER - Frank LEINMUELLER and Margaret FANT, Parents; Frank SAMMET and Mary SAMMET (by Helen BERTRAUD), Godparents; Born January 13, 1868; Baptized February 23, 1868; #405

Mary Catherine LEIODES - Pericles LEIODES and Cecile AULL, Parents; Catherine AULL and Nic. AULL, Godparents; Born October 30, 1873; Baptized November 12, 1873; #688

Frances Ward LEMAN - Charles Henry (nc) LEMAN and Regina REYNAUD, Parents; Frances KEENAN, Godparent; Born September 28, 1881; Baptized March 5, 1883; #992

William LEMPKE - William LEMPKE and Mary STEVENS, Parents; Rose LEMPKE, Godparent; Born October 23, 1885; Baptized May 8, 1886; #1238

Aloysius Herman LENZ - Anthony LENZ and Elizabeth HORNUNG, Parents; Herman KRAUSS and Mrs. A. Mary MENZEL, Godparents; Born August 6, 1887; Baptized September 5, 1887; #1357B

Joseph Christian LENZ - Anthony LENZ and Elizabeth HORNUNG, Parents; John LENZ and Ann Mary MENZEL, Godparents; (Civil marriage - Decree of Nullity May 5, 1953 #67/53 DF married Mrs. Cath M. LEFLEUR - Cathedr- May 6, 1953); Born November 12, 1884; Baptized February 5, 1885; #1128

Mary Theresa LENZ - Anthony LENZ and Elizabeth HORNUNG, Parents; Frederic WOLF and Mary JACOBS, Godparents; Born January 31, 1878; Baptized July 7, 1878; #853

Rose LENZ - John LENZ and Mathilda Christina HABILD, Parents; Charles WOLFE and Rosa LENZ, Godparents; Born December 28, 1893; Baptized August 2, 1894; #1677

Victor Anthony Frank LENZ - John LENZ and Mathilda Christina HALBILD, Parents; Elizabeth LENZ, Godparent; Born November 6, 1895; Baptized September 4, 1896; #1846

Ursula Mary Amelia LENZ - John Peter LENZ and Mathilda Christina HALBILD, Parents; Joseph LENZ and Mary MENZEL, Godparents; Born November 4, 1897; Baptized May 2, 1898; #1916

Frank St. Clair LEONARD - Charles H. LEONARD and Adeline B. REILLY, Parents; Ada LEONARD and Laura LEONARD, Godparents; Born August 6, 1865; Baptized August 22, 1865; #227

Joseph Percy LEONARD - Charles H. LEONARD and Adeline B. REILLY, Parents; Ada LEONARD and Laura LEONARD, Godparents; Born August 6, 1865; Baptized August 22, 1865; #226

Emma Charlotte LERA - Alfred LERA and Minicucci PARMIRA, Parents; C. DONATI and C. CASENTINI, Godparents; Born July 2, 1891; Baptized November 1, 1891; #1541

Justin LERA - Alfred LERA and Minicucci PARMIRA, Parents; Peter LERA and Margaret LERA, Godparents; Born April 24, 1890; Baptized November 1, 1890; #1542

Mary Justine LERA - Alfred LERA and Palmyra MANICHUCCI, Parents; Born April 24, 1890; Baptized April 30, 1890 (?); #1489

Thomas LERA - Alfred LERA and Palmira MENICUCCI, Parents; August MENICUCCI and Mary CALLAHAN, Godparents; Born July 24, 1892; Baptized June 8, 1893; #1607

Emma LERA - Orlando LERA and Constance MENECUCCI, Parents; Maddie WILSON, Godparent; Born February 10, 1896; Baptized March 27, 1896;

Justina LERA - Orlando LERA and Constance MENICUCCI, Parents; John PIOTTI and Acquilina PIOTTI, Godparents; Born November 9, 1892; Baptized June 8, 1893; #1609

Thomas LERA - Orlando LERA and Constance MENICUCCI, Parents; Jeromine MENICUCCI and Michael LERA, Godparents; Born September 25, 1891; Baptized June 8, 1893; #1608

Ann Auleika LEWIS - John LEWIS and Anna HOLBEIN, Parents; Margaret MORRISON, Godparent; Born October 1, 1878; Baptized March 9, 1885; #1139

Anna LEWIS; Wife of John LEWIS; (nee HOLBEIN); Private; Mary HANSON, Godparent; Born in 1849; Baptized March 9, 1885; #1140

James Louis LEWIS - James (nc) LEWIS and Catherine REAGAN, Parents; Frederic WEINDEMANN and Emma LEUTSCH, Godparents; Born January 9, 1887; Baptized January 30, 1887; #1306

John Fitzhugh Lee LEWIS - John LEWIS and Anna HOLBEIN, Parents; Jeo. F. LAUTH, Godparent; Born March 11, 1876; Baptized March 9, 1885; #1135

Mary Henrietta LEWIS - John LEWIS and Anna HOLBEIN, Parents; Elizabeth MASON, Godparent; Born May 12, 1874; Baptized March 9, 1885; #1138

Mathilda Irene LEWIS - John LEWIS and Anna HOLBEIN, Parents; Sara MORRISON, Godparent; Born December 4, 1874; Baptized March 9, 1885; #1137

Violet Alice LEWIS - John LEWIS and Anna HOLBEIN, Parents; Mary HANSON, Godparent; Born October 26, 1869; Baptized March 9, 1885; #1136

Helen Catherine LEYMULLER - Francis Joseph LEYMULLER and Margaret FOEHN, Parents; Helen BERTRAM, Godparent; Born July 21, 1871; Baptized October 22, 1871; #600

Geo. Joseph LIENARD - Able LIENARD and Louise PERRIN, Parents; Feridnand MARCHAND and Theresa FROTE, Godparents; Born November 19, 1863; Baptized December 20, 1863; #135

George Frank LIENHART - George LIENHART and Julienne BRINKHART, Parents; Frank SCHWALM and Joan PETRA SCHWALM, Godparents; Born September 6, 1860; Baptized October 18, 1860; #23

Henrietta Louise LOBENSTEIN - Louis LOBENSTEIN and Magdalen DINTER, Parents; Henry HILL and Anna HILL, Godparents; Born May 11, 1886; Baptized June 3, 1886; #1248

Henry Louis Paul LOBENSTEIN - Louis LOBENSTEIN and Magdalen DINTER, Parents; Pauline DINTER, Godparent; Born December 7, 1881; Baptized June 3, 1882; #954

Paul Michael Louis LOBENSTEIN - Louis (nc) LOBENSTEIN and Magdalen DINTER, Parents; Michael MAURER and Pauline LOBENSTEIN, Godparents; Born September 26, 1884; Baptized November 15, 1884; #1110

Daniel Baptist LORDAN - Jeremiah LORDAN and Hortense MARCHAND, Parents; John Baptist BAUDINAU and Clementine BAUDINAU, Godparents; Born November 13, 1888; Baptized December 16, 1888; #1420

Joseph LORDAN - Jeremiah LORDAN and Hortense MARCHAND, Parents; Theresa GAY, Godparent; Private; Born March 2, 1884; Baptized March 6, 1884; #1046

Mary Hortense LORDAN - Jeremiah LORDAN and Mary Hortense MARCHAND, Parents; Leopold FIEBEL and Elizabeth FIEBEL, Godparents; Born February 5, 1885; Baptized February 27, 1885; #1130

Ellen Gertrude LORDAN - Jerry LORDAN and Hortense MARCHAND, Parents; Charles DORINGER and Gertrude TRIBUT, Godparents; Born July 17, 1891; Baptized September 13, 1891; #1536

Louis Richard LOSSOW - Louis John LOSSOW and Cecilia KING, Parents; Paul Richard LOSSOW and Anna SCHAEFFER, Godparents; Born December 29, 1896; Baptized February 21, 1897; #1868

Rose Mary Margaret LOSSOW - Louis John LOSSOW and Rose HENKELDEI, Parents; Mathias GENGLER and Anna SCHAEFFER, Godparents; Born August 15, 1895; Baptized September 1, 1895; #1730

Ferdinand Charles LOTHRINGER - Ferdinand LOTHRINGER and Catherine DREYER, Parents; Charles DALIAN and Rose WOLFF, Godparents; Born October 22, 1877; Baptized December 23, 1877; #828

Mary Elizabeth LOTHRINGER - Ferdinand LOTHRINGER and Catherine DREYER, Parents; Victor LOTHRINGER and Adele LOTHRINGER, Godparents; Born October 17, 1886; Baptized December 9, 1886; #1297

Augustine LOTT - Frederic William LOTT and Sophy BAUHANS, Parents; Catherine ECKENFELS, Godparent; Born January 13, 1891; Baptized March 1, 1891; #1517

Clarence Henry LOTT - Frederic William LOTT and Sophy BAUHANS, Parents; Henry RITZLER and Elizabeth BAUHHEUS, Godparents; Born August 10, 1895; Baptized September 29, 1895; #1733

Elise Wilhelmina LOTT - Frederic William (nc) LOTT and Sophy BAUHANS, Parents; Otto H. LOTT and Elizabeth BAUHANS, Godparents; Born November 13, 1887; Baptized February 14, 1888; #1374

William LOTT - William LOTT and Sophy BAUHANS, Parents; William BAUHANS and Mrs. FRERIT, Godparents; Born October 9, 1889; Baptized December 8, 1889; #1463

Edward Julius LOUBAT - Oscar LOUBAT and Alida Estelle THEONOT, Parents; Julius THEONOT and Hill LOUBAT, Godparents; Born May 24, 1886; Baptized September 5, 1886; #1266

Christina Margaret LOUIS - Henry LOUIS and PFANNENSTILL, Parents;
Julia FRANKLIN, Godparent; Born September 9, 1877; Baptized April 8,
1878; #843

Eugenia Elenora LOUSTALOTTE - Justin LOUSTALOTTE and Mary Alice
ARRINGTON, Parents; Leo DE HABEN and Eugenia ROSS, Godparents;
Born October 17, 1883; Baptized April 21, 1885; #1154

Mary Ann MABUS - William MABUS and Rose S. CONNELL, Parents;
John COFFEE and Fannie COFFEE, Godparents; Born November 15, 1894;
Baptized (private) December 15, 1894; #1896

Louise Margaret MACERA - Julius MACERA and Mary CLIFTON, Parents;
J. ARMSTRONG and Augusta VAN BENTHUYSEN, Godparents; Born March 13,
1900; Baptized April 15, 1900; #1985

Greenville MAC KENA - P. E. MAC KENA and Isabel LATTI, Parents;
Magdalen GREYENBUEHL, Godparent; Born August 23, 1871; Baptized
April 14, 1872; #671

Peter Edward MAC KINA - Peter MAC KINA (MACKENA) and Isabel
LATTI, Parents; Mary FERGUSON, Godparent; Born October 3, 1868;
Baptized January 23, 1868; #505

Laura Joan MADDEN - John MADDEN and Frances BULLACHER, Parents;
Christian FRENCH and Mary PESKE, Godparents; Born August 26, 1862;
Baptized May 16, 1865; #212

Sara Elizabeth MAGRUDER - Albert Greenville MAGRUDER and Mary E.
DELANY, Parents; Mary Ann JOHNSON, Godparent; Born March 13, 1876;
Baptized April 26, 1899; #1952

Verena Ethel MAGUIRE - George MAGUIRE and Kunigunde MARX; Louis ORY,
Godparent; Born November 17, 1890; Baptized (private) November 17,
1890; #1509

Henry Thomas MALLIA - John Baptist MALLIA and Winifred MITCHELL,
Parents; Thomas QUINN and Helen CONWAY, Godparents; Born January 25,
1868; Baptized March 17, 1868; #410

Catherine MALLOY - Joseph Peter MALLOY and Mary HOULAHAN, Parents;
John Silvester MALLOY and Catherine BUTTENDORF (by proxy), Godparents;
Born September18, 1886; Baptized November 28, 1886; #1289

Mary Antoinette MALLYE - John B. MALLYE (MALLIA) and Winifred
MITCHEL, Parents; Dominic LANG and Carolina LANG, Godparents;
Born April 24, 1878; Baptized June 13, 1878; ---

Anna Elizabeth MANGLIER - Otto John MANGLIER and Rose KREASTA,
Parents; George Leonard BOHN and Anna POMEROY, Godparents; Born
May 23, 1892; Baptized June 19, 1892; #1568

William MANOWITCH - Martin MANOWITCH and Bulah HOXETT, Parents;
Rev. George APEL, Godparent; Born July 2, 1892; Baptized August 7,
1892; #1574

Leo Anthony Henry MANGLIER - Otto MANGLIER and Rose KRESTA, Parents;
Frank MILLER and Anna SULLIVAN, Godparents; Born September 13,
1889; Baptized October 13, 1889; #1450

Cecil MANNING - Thomas MANNING and Joan KANE, Parents; Anthony
AULL and Theresa STUDER, Godparents; Born June 16, 1881; Baptized
August 28, 1881; #939

John Marion MANTEAU - Emil MANTEAU (MONTEAU) and Elvira BARROW,
Parents; John BATTEB and Clothilde MC NEAL, Godparents; Born
December 23, 1891; Baptized January 3, 1892; #1594

Lydia MANTEAU - Valerian MANTEAU and Louise TIBORDEAUX, Parents;
Peter TIBORDEAUX and Cecil ABADIE, Godparents; Born November 14,
1894; Baptized April 1, 1895; #1709

Roman MARCHAL - John MARCHAL and Emma SCHLEICHER, Parents; Catherine
OSTERMEIER, Godparent; Born October 27, 1891; Baptized February 16,
1892; #1550

Margaret Louise MARCHALL (MARCHAND) - Ferdinand MARCHALL (MARCHAND)
and Lillie RENSCH, Parents; Leopold FIVEL and Margaret FIVEL,
Godparents; Born February 26, 1895; Baptized March 1, 1897; #1870

Ferdinand Henry MARCHAND - Ferdinand MARCHAND and Lillie RETNSCH,
Parents; Jerome Michael LORDAN and Ottance LORDAN, Godparents;
Born October 20, 1892; Baptized December 4, 1892; #1590

Octavia Angela MARCHAND - Ferdinand MARCHAND and Octavia GITREY,
Parents; Ferdinand MARCHAND and Octavia MARCHAND, Godparents;
Born October 23, 1886; Baptized November 21, 1886; #1285

Octavia Veronica MARCHAND - Ferdinand MARCHAND and Octavia LIENHART,
Parents; Stephen LAND and Helen STEHLIN, Godparents; Born February 14,
1861; Baptized April 17, 1861; #42

Peter George MARCHAND - Ferdinand MARCHAND and Octavia LIENHART,
Parents; Stephen LANG and Helen LANG, Godparents; Born October 27,
1862; Baptized November 30, 1862; #94

George William MARCHAND - George Peter MARCHAND and Clara WESTERLEDGE,
Parents; John LORDAN and Hortense LORDAN, Godparents; Born July 20,
1885; Baptized December 19, 1885; #1209

Ernest Michael MARCHAND - Julius MARCHAND and Mary FIVEN, Parents;
Frank GAY and Mrs. Theresa GAY, Godparents; Born September 28,
1894; Baptized October 7, 1894; #1684

David Martin MARINOVITCH - F. MARINOVITCH and Ann TRADENVITCH,
Parents; Nicholas RAEVEVITCH and Idalen SCAPULINDA, Godparents;
Born June 15, 1891; Baptized September 5, 1891; #1535

Frances Sophie MARKE - Frank Joseph MARKE and Ann Mary G. FAHNE,
Parents; Ernest PARISOT and Frances JUNG, Godparents; Born September 3,
1855; Baptized April 25, 1861; #44

Margaret Lilly MARSHALL - Haslem MARSHALL and Mary Elizabeth
MILSAPS, Parents; Anne BYRNE, Godparent; Born April 25, 1865;
Baptized June 3, 1865; #218

Paul Haslem MARSHALL - Haslem MARSHALL and Mary Elizabeth MILSAPS,
Parents; Anna BYRNE, Godparent; Born November 3, 1861; Baptized
June 3, 1865; #216

Peter MARSHALL - Haslem MARSHALL and Mary Elizabeth MILSAPS, Parents;
Anna BYRNE, Godparent; Born November 3, 1861; Baptized June 3, 1865;
#217

Antonia MARSHALL - John MARSHALL and Emma SCHLEICHER, Parents;
Andrew RICHMERS and Antonia MIDDLEGGER, Godparents; Born June 7,
1886; Baptized June 10, 1886; #1252

John MARSHALL - John MARSHALL and Emma SCHLEICHER, Parents; Henry
WEIER and Joan MOSER, Godparents; Born October 27, 1881; Baptized
November 27, 1881; #948

John MARSHALL - John MARSHALL and Emma (n.c.) SCHLEICHER, Parents;
Andrew RICHMERS and Antonia MIDDLEGGER, Godparents; Born July 28,
1884; Baptized June 10, 1886; #1250

Joseph MARSHALL - John MARSHALL and Emma SCHLEICHER, Parents;
Mary ALLEN, Godparent; Born June 17, 1890; Baptized June --, 1893;
#1612

Laura Ellen MARSHALL - John MARSHALL and Emma SCHLEICHER, Parents; .
George SWANN and Laura SWANN, Godparents; Born May 12, 1890;
Baptized June 13, 1890; #1496

Mary MARSHALL - John MARSHALL and Emma SCHLEICHER, Parents; Nora
ALBIN, Godparent; Born November 25, 1895; Baptized January 11,
1896; ---

Robert MARSHALL - John MARSHALL and Emma (n.c.) SCHLEICHER, Parents;
(MARSHALL, Roman--see MARCHAL); Andrew RICKMERS and Antonia MIDDLEGGER,
Godparents; Born January 4, 1883; Baptized June 10, 1886; #249

Anna Ernestine MARTIN - John MARTIN and Ernestine STEINBACH,
Parents; --, Godparents; Born September 2, 1883; Baptized October 21,
1883; #1030

Mathilde MARTIN - John MARTIN and Ernestine STEINBACH, Parents;
Catherine KRAUS (by proxy), Godparent; Born July 25, 1886; Baptized
August 18, 1886; #1236

Martin MATEYOWSKI - Henry MATEYOWSKI and Mary RUZICKA, Parents;
Martin HERBAK, Godparent; Born May 4, 1885; Baptized June 20, 1885;
#1171

Henry MATIZKI - Stanislav MATIZKI and Catherine GORIZKI, Parents;
Joseph LENZ and Lillie LIBERTO, Godparents; Born May 14, 1897;
Baptized June 4, 1897; #1878

Mary Caroline MAURER - James MAURER and Wilhelmina BENDER, Parents;
Michael MAURER and Theresa MAURER, Godparents; Born January 27,
1884; Baptized February 10, 1884; #1040

Anna MAURER - John MAURER and Caroline SCHERR, Parents; Anthony
SCHERR and Anna Margaret SCHERR, Godparents; Born April 30, 1874;
Baptized May 10, 1874; #704

Mary Caroline MAURER - John MAURER and Caroline SCHEIER, Parents;
James MAURER and Mary EDWARDS, Godparents; Born March 24, 1882;
Baptized March 29, 1882; #957

Mary Caroline MAURER - John MAURER and Caroline SCHAER, Parents;
Martin RICKE and Mary RICKE, Godparents; Born January 27, 1884;
Baptized February 10, 1884; #1041

Theresa MAURER - John MAURER and Caroline SCHERF, Parents; Stephen
SCHERT and Theresa SELTENREICH, Godparents; Born May 12, 1872;
Baptized May 19, 1872; #620

Anthony Bennett MAURER - Michael MAURER and Mary TISCHENDORF,
Parents; Joseph Bennett TICHLE and Caroline TISCHENDORF, Godparents;
Born --; Baptized January 28, 1894; #1648

Caroline Wilhelmina MAURER - Michael MAURER and Mary Frances
TISCHENDORF, Parents; John MAURER and Wilhelmina MAURER, Godparents;
Born May 4, 1889; Baptized May 19, 1889; #1434

Claude Joseph MAURER - Michael MAURER and Frances TISCHENDORF,
Parents; Joseph MAURER and Clara TISCHENDORF, Godparents; Born
October 10, 1891; Baptized October 25, 1891; #1538

George Michael MAURER - Michael MAURER and Mary Frances TISCHENDORF,
Parents; George TISCHENDORF and Anna Mary MAURER, Godparents;
Born October --, 1895; Baptized November --, 1895; #1736

Wendel James MAURER - Michael MAURER and Mary Frances TISCHENDORF,
Parents; James MAURER and Ida TISCHENDORF, Godparents; Born April 25,
1887; Baptized May 4, 1887; #1340

Caroline Mary MAURER - Peter MAURER (adopted by); --, Godparents;
Born --; Baptized April 14, 1861 (conditional); #41

Anna Mary Elizabeth MAYER - Bernard MAYER and Anna Mary DRESINGER,
Parents; Catherine J. MAYER and Mary Elizabeth MAYER, Godparents;
Born January 15, 1870; Baptized March 20, 1870; #555A

Catherine Josephine MAYER - John Bernard MAYER and Anna Mary
DRESINGER, Parents; Catherine Josephine MAYER and Mary Elizabeth
MAYER, Godparents; Born January 15, 1870; Baptized March 20, 1870;
#555

John Clifford MAYER - John M. MAYER and Sophronia E. JOHNS, Parents;
Mary MAYER, Godparent; Born July 8, 1881; Baptized July 10, 1881;
#933

Thomas Jefferson MAYNARD - Charles D. MAYNARD and Mary MEYERS,
Parents; Leona SCHWALM, Godparent; Born March 11, 1861; Baptized
April 3, 1866; #277

Caroline MC AVENEY - Edward MC AVENEY and Mary HOFBECK, Parents;
Caroline HOFBECK, Godparent; Born March 17, 1888; Baptized July 20,
1889; #1443

John D. MC AVENEY - Edward MC AVENEY and Mary HOFBECK, Parents;
Theresa REHRMANN, Godparent; Born July 17, 1886; Baptized May 29,
1887; #1350

Mary Magdalen MC AVENEY - Edward MC AVENEY and Mary HOFBECK, Parents;
Helen MC AVENEY (by proxy), Godparent; Born February 4, 1885;
Baptized April 24, 1885; #1155

William Edward MC AVENEY - Edward MC AVENEY and Mary HOFBECK,
Parents; Caroline HOFBECK, Godparent; Born February 7, 1883;
Baptized March 22, 1883; #995

Mary MC CAILEY - John MC CAILEY and Ellen MC CAILEY, Parents;
John COURBEY and Mary Anna COURBEY, Godparents; Born November 20,
1872; Baptized December 8, 1872; #641

Henry MC CARTHY - Arthur MC CARTHY and Elizabeth TAYLOR, Parents;
--, Godparents; Born April 19, 1867; Baptized April 25, 1867; #345

Edward William MC CARTHY - Edward MC CARTHY and Pauline Helen
BRAUN, Parents; T. H. R. MC CARTHY and Bertha ABELS, Godparents;
Born December 7, 1881; Baptized February 12, 1882; #955

Joseph MC CARTHY - Edward MC CARTHY and Pauline BRAUN, Parents;
Joan SHEPPARD, Godparent; Born October 11, 1885; Baptized October 11,
1885 (private); #1212

Julia Lee MC CARTHY - William MC CARTHY and Blanche REILLY, Parents;
Emily CALLUM and Mattie PRADIER, Godparents; Born May 14, 1894;
Baptized August 14, 1894; #1676

Richard MC CARTHY - William Richard MC CARTHY and Blance RILEY,
Parents; Richard MC CARTHY and Margaret BAVHI, Godparents; Born
December 31, 1895; Baptized March 22, 1896; #1814

David Crockett MC CRAKEN - David MC CRAKEN and Mathilda HEINES,
Parents; David Crockett JOURDEN and Wilhelmina BOYDT, Godparents;
Born January 24, 1896; Baptized March 8, 1896; #1809

Laura MC CUBBINS - G. J. MC CUBBINS and Mary MONTEUMRY, Parents;
Anna BOURGES, Godparent; Born July 22, 1880; Baptized October 8,
1880; #907

Malcome Joseph MC DONALD - Angus MC DONALD and Catherine BOULTON,
Parents; Ronald MC DONALD and Mrs. G. SMITH (by proxy), Godparents;
Born April 9, 1888; Baptized May 27, 1888; #1394

Emma Martha MC DONALD - Michael MC DONALD and Catherine MURRAY,
Parents; Elizabeth STEGEMANN, Godparent; Born June 8, 1876;
Baptized September 20, 1876; #803

Anna MC KAWENE - Edward MC KAWENE and Mary HOFBECK, Parents;
Theresa ROEHRMOND, Godparent; Born April 23, 1890; Baptized
February 26, 1891; #1516

Josephine MC KENNA - Peter E. MC KENNA and Isabel LATTA, Parents;
Huth MC CORMICK and Margaret MC KENA, Godparents; Born May 13,
1873; Baptized December 23, 1878; #876

Rudolph MC KENNA - Peter E. MC KENNA and Isabel LATTA, Parents;
E. O'ROURKE and John KILPATRICK, Godparents; Born April 20, 1876;
Baptized December 23, 1878; #377

Joan (Jane) MC LEROY - William MC LEROY and Mary DEIGEN, Parents;
Mary CABAZOS, Godparent; Born December 15, 1861; Baptized February 11,
1862; #67

Daniel MC MULLEN - James MC MULLEN and Elizabeth (n.c.) HERTHAN,
Parents; Catherine FOWLER, Godparent; Born September 2, 1883;
Baptized December 23, 1886; #1303

Mary MC NALLEY - James MC NALLEY and Louise Ernestine WECKERT,
Parents; Frank MELLEN and Helen DREW, Godparents; Born March 7,
1886; Baptized April 18, 1886; #1224

Thomas Cleveland MC NALLY - James MC NALLY and Louise WECKERT,
Parents; John MC NALLY and Theresa RAMAKER, Godparents; Born
March 4, 1885; Baptized March 25, 1885 (private); #1146

William John MC NAMARA - -- MC NAMARA and Jane MOORE, Parents;
John HOOK, Godparent; Born November 17, 1869; Baptized November 28,
1869; #533

Walter Marion MC NELLY - James MC NELLY and Louise BECKE (convert),
Parents; Martin MC NELLY and Catherine MC NELLY (by proxy),
Godparents; Born September 15, 1889; Baptized November 23, 1889;
#1458

Adelaide Mary MC RAE - Norman (n.c.) MC RAE and Caroline WERDEHAUSEN,
Parents; James COYLE and Mary COYLE, Godparents; Born July 25, 1885;
Baptized April 25, 1886; #1230

Norman Alexander MC RAE - Norman (n.c.) MC RAE and Caroline
WERDEHAUSEN, Parents; James COYLE and Mary COYLE, Godparents;
Born January 25, 1883; Baptized April 25, 1886; #1229

Isacc Thomas MC WATER - Isacc Thomas MC WATER and Oneida S. B.
LEWIS, Parents; Alexander MC WATERS and Helen MC WATERS, Godparents;
Born September 14, 1886; Baptized November 15, 1886; #1287

George Martin MEES - Adam MEES and Anna ERNST, Parents; George
ERNST and Marie E. KOEHLER, Godparents; Born March 16, 1900; Baptized
March 25, 1900; #1982

John William MEIER - Bernard MEIER and Mary LESSMANN, Parents;
--, Godparents; Born -- 14, 1873; Baptized June 1, 1873; #674

Edward (conditional) MEINECKE - Born 24 years old; Baptized April 18,
1864; #147

Mary Frances MELLEN - George MELLEN (MILLIANI) and Mary Frances --,
Parents; Frank MELLEN and Louise MC NALLY, Godparents; Born
January 21, 1889; Baptized February 10, 1889; #1424

Irene Mary MELVILLE - William MELVILLE and Dora EICHLER, Parents;
George KIRSCHNER and Alice EICHLER, Godparents; Born January 1,
1885; Baptized February 1, 1885; #1123

John Mary (Ainslie) MENDARD - Adolph P. MENDARD and Emma Gertrude
STILES, Parents; Isadore LECHLERC and Mary LECLERC, Godparents;
Born November 9, 1861; Baptized March 24, 1862; #71

Santos MENDEZ - Peter MENDEZ and Mary CARENA, Parents; Andrew
BARGA and Joan BARGA, Godparents; Born November 1, 1888; Baptized
December 8, 1888; #1419

Ida Rosaline MENZEL - Charles MENZEL and Anna Mary HORNUNG,
Parents; Frederic WOLFF and Rosa WOLFF, Godparents; Born January 6,
1877; Baptized September 23, 1877; #811

Mary Elizabeth MENZEL - Charles (n.c.) MENZEL and Anna Mary
HORNUNG, Parents; Anthony LENZ and Elizabeth HAGEMANN, Godparents;
Born February 6, 1883; Baptized January 6, 1884 (private); #1037

August Anthony MENZEL - John MENZEL and Mary Ann SCHULTZ, Parents;
Anton BERGMANN and Bertha -- (prot.), Godparents; Born November 22,
1863; Baptized February 19, 1865; #190

Charles William MENZEL - William BARNES and Elizabeth LENZ, Godparents;
Born February 9, 1878; Baptized January 1, 1882; #951

Otto Frederic MENZEL - Frederic BOYLE and Frederica STIGHORST
(by Mary STIGHORST), Godparents; Born July 25, 1881; Baptized
January 1, 1882; #952

Frederic August METZGER - Jacob August METZGER and Frederica
RHEIN, Parents; Frederic August METZGER, Godparent; Born October 14,
1860; Baptized December 25, 1860; #27

Thecla Joan METZGER - Joseph METZGER and Mary BUCKHOF, Parents;
Germanicus TROST by Frank BUCKHOF and Thecla BUCKHOF, Godparents;
Born October 28, 1874; Baptized November 29, 1874; #735

Celil Lewrener MEURI - Henry (n.c.) MEURI (from Aargan Seitzerland)
and Anna SCHREIBER, Parents; Frank LEWRENER, Godparent; Born
August 2, 1893; Baptized September 3, 1893; #1618

John Louis MEYER - John MEYER and Mary Joan HAMMILL, Parents;
John GROTHGAR and Alice GROTHGAR, Godparents; Born November 14,
1883; Baptized December 9, 1883; #1036

Frank Adolph MICHELS - Frank MICHELS and Susan SCHOEN, Parents;
Adolph MICHELS and Catherine RITZLER, Godparents; Born June 4,
1869; Baptized April 9, 1871; #583

Anna Emma MICHELS - Runold MICHELS and Anna DANNLER, Parents;
Catherine DIRKS, Godparent; Born November 24, 1872; Baptized July 16,
1873; #677

John Edward MICHELS - William (n.c.) MICHELS and Catherine MANION,
Parents; George KIRSCHNER and Isabel MELVILLE, Godparents; Born
June 7, 1883; Baptized September 30, 1883; #1024

Frank Adolph MILLAN - Joseph MILLAN and Caoline WAGNER, Parents;
Adolph WIEL and Wilhelmina BONG (prot.), Godparents; Born November 25,
1866; Baptized December 9, 1866; #326

Mary Ethel (MILLIS) MILLER - Charles MILLER and Helen GROSSMANN (married Albert GOODNIGHT, Incarnate Word, San Antonio June 12, 1912), Parents; Catherine BURKITT and Thomas MC DONALD, Godparents; Born March 25, 1892; Baptized October 28, 1894; #1688

James (private) MILLER - Robert MILLER and Mary --, Parents; --, Godparents; Born September 22, 1864; Baptized September 22, 1864; #174

Joseph MILLEY - John MILLEY and Margaret SWEENEY, Parents; John FORT and Margaret BUM, Godparents; Born September 6, 1878; Baptized September 6, --; #778

Felix MILLIA - John Baptist MILLIA and Winny MITCHELL, Parents; Catherine HENRICKS, Godparent; Born August 24, 1869; Baptized February 13, 1870; #547

Elizabeth MILLICH - Vincent MILLICH and Rosina GAZZEAU, Parents; Natalus TONETTI and Elizabeth PAPINI, Godparents; Born March 4, 1884; Baptized April 13, 1884; #1058

Margaret Emma MILLIGAN - John G. MILLIGAN and Sophie G. DEARY, Parents; William CRONE and Alberta DAVIDSON, Godparents; Born December 13, 1865; Baptized May 23, 1887; #1347

Anna Clara MISCIEVICZ - Joseph MISCIEVICZ and Constantine WASKO, Parents; Frank BROKOF and Thecla BROKOF, Godparents; Born May 6, 1884; Baptized July 12, 1884; #1082

Frank Patrick MITCHELL - Frank D. MITCHELL and Anna Emma KIMLE, Parents; Patrick BARRY and Margaret BULLASCHER, Godparents; Born January 9, 1887; Baptized March 20, 1887; #1323

Anna James MITCHELL - James MITCHELL and Elizabeth GRIFFIN, Parents; -- CONCHE (MESTIER) by -- MITCHELL, Godparents; Born June 1, 1863; Baptized May 8, 1865 (at Clear Creek); #207

Elizabeth (MITCHELL) - Paul and Laura MITCHELL, slaves of James MITCHELL, Parents; --, Godparents; Born October 9, 1864; Baptized May 8, 1865 (at Clear Creek); #210

James (MITCHELL) - Paul and Laura (MITCHELL), slaves of James MITCHELL, Parents; --, Godparents; Born December 24, 1862; Baptized May 8, 1865 (at Clear Creek); #209

John (MITCHELL) - Paul and Laura (MITCHELL), slaves of James MITCHELL, Parents; --, Godparents; Born April 7, 1861; Baptized May 8, 1865 (at Clear Creek); #208

John Peter MOELLER (MUELLER) - John Peter MOELLER (MUELLER) and Caroline RADEMACHER, Parents; Mathias WEBER and wife, Godparents; Born September 1, 1862; Baptized September 21, 1862; #91

Hazel Theresa MONFORT - Gabriel Leo MONFORT and Theresa Helen FLEUHR, Parents; Ambrose Alphonse MONFORT and Lena SCHMIDT, Godparents; Born March 22, 1899; Baptized April 23, 1899; #1951

Elizabeth MONI - Adolph MONI and Rebecca (n.c.) LEUCKAU, Parents; Joseph MARERO and Blanche GRUBER, Godparents; Born December 1, 1882; Baptized March 9, 1884; #1044

Elizabeth (Amelia) MONI - Adolph MONI and Rebecca (n.c.) LICHAW, Parents; I. F. MICHELS, Godparent; Born January 1, 1886; Baptized June 12, 1886; #1253

Mathilde Rosina MONI - Adolph MONI and Rebecca LUGAN, Parents; Abel Thomas LEWELLYN and Rosina HORNUG, Godparents; Born September 26, 1880; Baptives November 20, 1881; #945

Rose MONI - Adolph MONI and Rebecca (n.c.) LEUCKAU, Parents;
Joseph MARERO and Blanche GRUBER, Godparents; Born December 6,
1883; Baptized March 9, 1884; #1045

Helen Magdalen MONIVICZ - Martin MONIVICZ and Beulah HAWKSHEAD,
Parents; Pat WHELTON and Augustine DEVOTI, Godparents; Born
August 16, 1886; Baptized October 17, 1886; #1277

Richard Samuel MONTAUT (married Ruby HEINTSCHELL, June 19, 1951
Sacred Heart--Galveston) - Emil MONTAUT (MONTEAU) and Elvera BARROW,
Parents; Charles FLYDER and Anna BARROW, Godparents; Born May 11,
1894; Baptized August 17, 1894; #1674

Elizabeth MONTAUT (MONTEAUT) - Neuville MONTAUT (MONTEAUT) and
Celestina (MOTT), Parents; Frederick HARRINGTON (absent) and
Clatilda GUEDRY, Godparents; Born July 27, 1887; Baptized February 2,
1888; #1373 A

Mary Olivia MONTEAU (MONTEAUT) - Nevil MONTEAU (MONTEAUT) and
Clestina MOTT, Parents; Desire HERBERT and Melanie NEBOU, Godparents;
Born December 11, 1891; Baptized June 4, 1892; #1566

Clara MONTEAUT (MANTEAU) - Nevil MONTEAUT (MANTEAU) and Celestine
MOTT, Parents; Mary KING, Godparent; Born December 31, 1889;
Baptized June 21, 1890; #1499

Jesse Edward MOOLD - Edward Frank MOOLD and Mary Christine (n.c.)
ROTHEIMER, Parents; John GRAY and Alice MC LAUGHLIN (by proxy),
Godparents; Born January 28, 1887; Baptized March 23, 1887; #1324

Anna Lorraine Cornida MOOLT - Edward MOOLT and Mary Ann ROTHAMMER,
Parents; John YOUNG and Anna YOUNG, Godparents; Born December 17,
1891; Baptized February 18, 1895; #1701

John Michael MOOR - Henry MOOR and Mary Elizabeth AULL, Parents;
Anthony AULL and Magdalen HAGEMANN, Godparents; Born December 31,
1873; Baptized January 4, 1874; #694

Joseph Albert MOTH (married Juanita E. COOK, Houston, June 12,
1918) - James Samuel MOTH and Leontine DANTIN, Parents; Eugene
Edward PAYSSE and Clementine PAYSSE, Godparents; Born November 21,
1895; Baptized January 5, 1896; #1799

Julia Alice MOTH - James Samuel MOTH and Leontine DANTIN, Parents;
Bernard RUBION and Julia DANTIN, Godparents; Born February 20,
1888; Baptized April 8, 1888 (Eagle Pass); #1387

Joseph Henry MOOR - Henry MOOR and Mary Elizabeth AULL, Parents;
Joseph AULL and Catherine AULL, Godparents; Born April 21, 1872;
Baptized June 9, 1872; #624

Mary Magdalen Elizabeth MOOR - Henry MOOR and Elizabeth AULL,
Parents; Catherine AULL and Anthony AULL, Godparents; Born
September 15, 1870; Baptized November 2, 1870; #566

Andrew MOORE - A. J. MOORE and Catherine HOLLINGSHAEUSER, Parents;
Catherine KRAUS, Godparent; Born February 1, 1864; Baptized February 6,
1864; #142

Mary Ann MOORE - Andre Jackson MOORE and Catherine HOLLINGSHAUS,
Parents; Mary Ann FINK, Godparent; Born January 15, 1866; Baptized
February 27, 1866; #269

Mary Cecil MOORE - Louis MOORE and Anna PORTER, Parents; Robert
MOORE and Anna MOORE, Godparents; Born July 29, 1891; Baptized
August 30, 1891; #1534

Henry William MOORE - Thomas MOORE and Dora KAMPE, Parents; William KAMPE and Julia LEMPKE, Godparents; Born February 9, 1894; Baptized April 1, 1894; #1659

Edward John MOORS - Edward MOORS and Mary SAMMET, Parents; John JONES and Margaret MUELLER, Godparents; Born October 2, 1878; Baptized November 17, 1878; #871

Frank Louis MOORS - Edward M. and Mary SOMMER, Parents; Frank SAMMET and Margaret HAHN, Godparents; Born March 11, 1883; Baptized April 29, 1883; #1005

Cecil Catherine MOOR - Henry MOOR and Mary AULL, Parents; Theodore GRUNDNER and Cecil AULL, Godparents; Born April 11, 1869; Baptized April 25, 1869; #515

Mary Pauline MORRISON - Hugh Allison MORRISON and Cora M. WILLIAMS, Parents; August GAY and Theresa GAY, Godparents; Born August 24, 1897; Baptized March 5, 1899; #1945

Joseph Arthur Sidney MORSE - Bleeker MORSE and Lucia JOHNSEN (JOHNSON), Parents; Signey JOHNSEN and Adeline LEUVE, Godparents; Born August 13, 1891; Baptized March 20, 1892; #1553

Gladys Lincoln Anne MOSER (OSER) - George William MOSER (OSER) and Mary Ann ARNOLD, Parents; Mary ann BALDRE and August SCHULTZ, Godparents; Born January 20, 1899; Baptized April 2, 1899; #1949

Ursula Ann Elizabeth MOSER - John MOSER and Agnes NIEDENFUEHR, Parents; John H. ROEMER and Anne MOSER, Godparents; Born October 3, 1888; Baptized October 14, 1888; #1412

Hilda Josephine Rose MOSER - John H. MOSER and Agnes Mary NIEDENFUEHR, Parents; John B. ROEMER and Agnes Hyacintha ROEMER, Godparents; Born November 9, 1887; Baptized November 13, 1887; #1364

Innocent Hubert Marion MOSER (married Theresa REAVERS, St. Patricks, Galveston, February 19, 1912) - John H. MOSER and Agnes NEIDENFUEHR, Parents; George LEINBACH (by proxy) and Emma NEIDENFUEHR, Godparents; Born November 18, 1886; Baptized November 18, 1886; #1282

Agnes Jos. Terese MOSER - Peter Hyacinth MOSER and Elizabeth SCHUMACHER, Parents; Anton RICKE and Joan RICKE, Godparents; Born March 16, 1866; Baptized March 24, 1866; #274

Ann Mary Emma Terese MOSER - Peter Hyacinth MOSER and Elsie Frederika SCHUMACHER, Parents; Lawrence NUESE and Theresa NUESE, Godparents; Born October 27, 1868; Baptized November 15, 1868; #427

Ann Pauline Augusta MOSER - Peter Hyacinth MOSER and Elizabeth SCHUMACHER, Parents; John HEBBERT and Anne HEBBERT, Godparents; Born October 17, 1863; Baptized October 25, 1863; #128

Josephine Agnes Hyacinth MOSER - Peter Hyacinth MOSER and Elizabeth SCHUMACHER, Parents; Anne TSCHAEKE and Jos. ANSTAETT, Godparents; Born August 20, 1861; Baptized August 25, 1861; #52

Caroline Clara MOSER - Theodore Hyacinth MOSER and Elsie Frederika SCHUMACHER, Parents; Caroline RICKE, Godparent; Born June 26, 1872; Baptized July 14, 1872; #629

Leonida Angelina MOTH (married James Walter CARROLL, S. Heart, Galveston, May 14, 1919) - James Samuel MOTH and Leontine DANTIN, Parents; James CORDERO and Angelina CORDERO, Godparents; Born October 4, 1893; Baptized December 24, 2894; #1636

Michael Victor MOTH (Married Cornelia RINGER, June 6, 1916, Houston)
James Samuel MOTH and Leontine DANTIN, Parents; Victor DANTIN and
Eugene DANTIN, Godparents; Born September 6, 1889; Baptized
December 25, 1889; #1467

James Samuel MOTH (married Ann Elizabeth CLARK, St. Patricks,
Galveston, September 2, 1914) - Samuel MOTH and Leontine DANTIN,
Parents; Catherine DANTIN, Godparent; Born January 15, 1892;
Baptized March 11, 1892; #1552

Mary Henrietta -- - Christine Elizabeth MOTZEN, Parent; Henry
GOTTWALD and Martha MARTIN, Godparents; Born May 21, 1867; Baptized
September 22, 1867; #374

Joseph MOUNT - Joseph MOUNT, SR. and Anna HAWKS, Parents; Catherine
HARRIS, Godparent; Born January 28, 1867; Baptized February 24,
1867; #337

Edward Anthony MUELLER - Charles (n.c.) MUELLER and Dorothy DRONE,
Parents; Michael KELLY and Margaret KELLY (by proxy), Godparents;
Born December 11, 1884; Baptized June 25, 1885; #1173

Joseph John MUELLER - Charles (n.c.) MUELLER and Dorothy KRONE,
Parents; Margaret KELLY, Godparent; Born August 11, 1886; Baptized
October 3, 1886 (Baptist; private); #1271

Germanicus Anthony MUELLER (PULLE) - Germanicus MUELLER (PULLE) and
Cecil NUTT, Parents; M. SCHWENDINGER, Godparent; Born April 10,
1876; Baptized Arpil 17, 1876; #770

Bertha MUELLER - Henry MUELLER and Regina BARLEMAN, Parents;
Henry SCHULTE and Bertah WITING, Godparents; Born September 4,
1880; Baptized December 26, 1880; #914

William Edward MUELLER - Henry MUELLER and Joan GORMAN, Parents;
Joseph FERBER and Catherine BREEN, Godparents; Born February 11,
1868; Baptized March 22, 1868; #412

Theresa Josephine MUELLER - John Peter MUELLER and Magdalen LANG,
Parents; Michael GREEN and Mary Josephine PEINE, Godparents;
Born April 12, 1881; Baptized June 3, 1881; #927

Anna Mary MUELLER - Peter MUELLER and Caroline RADEMACHER, Parents;
Clara WEBER and Wilhelmina WEBER, Godparents; Born September 10,
1866; Baptized September 23, 1866; #315

Anthony Joseph MUELLER - Peter MUELLER and Caroline RADEMACHER,
Parents; Anton RICKE and Caroline RICKE, Godparents; Born November 18,
1864; Baptized December 4, 1864; #185

Catherine MUELLER - Peter MUELLER and Magdalene LANG, Parents;
Henry SCHULTE and Catherine LANG, Godparents; Born January 8,
1871; Baptized February 12, 1871; #575

Henry Peter MUELLER - Peter MUELLER and Margaret LANG, Parents;
Mrs. HEBBERT and F. HEBBERT, Godparents; Born September 2, 1872;
Baptized --, 1872; #639

Joan Emma MUELLER - Peter MUELLER and Magdalen LAND, Parents;
John MOSER, Godparent; Born September 27, 1878; Baptized May 29,
1879; #888

John William MUELLER - Peter MUELLER and Magdalen LAND, Parents;
John W. LANG and Mary LANG, Godparents; Born July 29, 1869;
Baptized August 15, 1869; #527

Magdalene MUELLER - Peter MUELLER and Magdalen LANG, Parents; Frank
LANG, Godparent; Born October 5, 1876; Baptized October 6, 1876;
#776

Mary Elizabeth MUELLER - Peter MUELLER and Margaret LANG, Parents;
W. WEBER and Mary LANG, Godparents; Born September 14, 1871;
Baptized October 24, 1874; #730

Charles MUELLER - R. A. MUELLER and Frances BLEIKE, Parents;
Elizabeth WINKELBERG, Godparent; Born May 25, 1878; Baptized
March 27, 1879; #882

Lillie Elizabeth MUELLER - R. A. MUELLER and Frances BLEIKE,
Parents; Elizabeth WINKELBERG, Godparent; Born November 2, 1876;
Baptized March 27, 1879; #883

George Rudolph MUELLER - Rudolph MUELLER and Frances BLEIKE,
Parents; William BLEIKE and Anna BIEHLER, Godparents; Born January 28,
1874; Baptized July 12, 1874; #714

Charles William MUELLER - William MUELLER and Theresa BLEICKE,
Parents; Foseph BLEICKE and Carolina ELBERT, Godparents; Born
November 29, 1876; Baptized February 28, 1877; #794

Rosina Mary Scholastica MUELLER - William Henry (n.c.) MUELLER
and Regina BARLEMANN, Parents; Charles BARLEMANN and Mary RICKE,
Godparents; Born February 10, 1884; Baptized March 16, 1884; #1048

Anna Agnes MUERI - Henry (n.c.) MUERI and Anna SCHREIBER, Parents;
Mary PRENDERGAST, Godparent; Born October 6, 1883; Baptized March 15,
1884; #1047

Edna Lillie Theresa MUERI - Henry MUERI and Ann SCHREIBER, Parents;
Lillie SMIDT, Godparent; Born March 5, 1886; Baptized May 19, 1886;
#1234

Heneritta Margaret Joan MUERI - Henry MUERI and Anna SCHREIBER,
Parents; John KRAUSE and Margaret SCHREIBER, Godparents; Born
April 4, 1881; Baptized July 24, 1881; #935

Julia Mary Elizabeth MUERI - Henry MUERI and Anna SCHREIBER, Parents;
Elizabeth SCHREIBER, Godparent; Born October 17, 1877; Baptized
March 23, 1878; #839

Heneritta MULLEN - James MULLEN and Helen MORETTI, Parents; Mary
MUNCIE, Godparent; Born November 20, 1867; Baptized September 26,
1885; #1185

Josephine MULLEN - James MULLEN and Helen MORETTI, Parents; Helen
WILLES, Godparent; Born May 18, 1874; Baptized October 17, 1885;
#1195

Rufus MULLEN - James MULLEN and Helen MORETTI, Parents; Helen
WILLES, Godparent; Born March 3, 1878; Baptized October 18, 1885;
#1194

John Patrick MULLEN - John Patrick MULLEN and Mathilde Laura
BUERGER, Parents; John Bernard NOLAN and Mrs. Mary NOLAN, Godparents;
Born April 7, 1899; Baptized May 14, 1899; #1955

Anna Mary MURRAY - Richard James MURRAY and Josephine BOCK, Parents;
James BOCK and Anna GENGLER, Godparents; Born August 30, 1874;
Baptized December 8, 1874; #737

John Nelson NAGLE - John NAGLE, Parent; James NAGLE, Godparent;
Born --, Baptized February 25, 1866; #267

Catherine Dorris NAVE - John NAVE and Louise VURKOTT, Parents;
John B. WILSON and Mary VURKOTT, Godparents; Born December 7, 1893;
Baptized January 14, 1894; #1642

Josephine NEBOUT - John NEBOUT and Menalie MONTEAU, Parents;
Joseph BAT and Clothilde ABADIE, Godparents; Born May 18, 1888;
Baptized December 2, 1888; #1418

Anna Margaret NEIS - James NEIS and Margaret KIRCHEN, Parents;
Louis BEST and Anna BEST, Godparents; Born March 4, 1885; Baptized
April 5, 1885; #1148

Henry James NEISS - James NEISS and Margaret KIRCHEM, Parents;
James WITTEIER and Louise HALER, Godparents; Born September 1, 1874;
Baptized October 25, 1874; #732

John Nicholas NEIS - James NEIS and Margaret KIRCHEM, Parents;
Peter GENGLER and M. COOPER, Godparents; Born February 15, 1882;
Baptized March 26, 1882; #959

Fanny (Frances) NEITSCH - Theodore NEITSCH and Augusta OESTREICH,
Parents; Born, December 24, 1859; Baptized August 24, 1867; #364

Charles NELSON - Severin (n.c.) NELSON and Elizabeth KALUSA, Parents;
Charles MUELLER, Godparent; Born June 5, 1885; Baptized October 25,
1885; #1196

George NELSON - Severin NELSON and Elizabeth KALUSA, Parents;
Catherine MILLER, Godparent; Born February 22, 1889; Baptized
June 10, 1890; #1494

Henry Andrew NELSON - Severino NELSON and Elise KALOSA, Parents;
Henry BRUSE and Clara HOWE, Godparents; Born May 12, 1887; Baptized
August 6, 1887; #1357 A

Julia (nee HALL) NELSON - Thos. Jefferson HALL and Nancy ROBERTSON,
Parents; Born November 15, 1833; Baptized November 19, 1866 (convert);
#325

Louis NELSON - Louis NELSON and Frances KOBITZA, Parents; Peter
HELFRICH, Godparent; Born December 26, 1872; Baptized January 23,
1873; #649

Henrietta Rhea NICHOLS - John Theodore NICHOLS and Mary BURKETT,
Parents; Mary Alva NICHOLS and Henry Andrew CARSTENS, Godparents;
Born February 13, 1896; Baptized April 12, 1896; #1819

Mary Emma NICHOLS - E. B. NICHOLS and Catherine PHILIPSON, Parents;
Roseann TRUCHARD, Godparent; Born June 24, 1892; Baptized August 8,
1892; #1573

John Baptist NIEDERGANG - Anthony NIEDERGANG and Catherine TRICKER,
Parents; John Baptist WENZ and Rose Mary TRICKER (by proxy),
Godparents; Born May 3, 1887; Baptized May 6, 1887; #1345

August NIEDERHOEFER - George NIEDERHOEFER and Frances MUELLER,
Parents; Mary HERRMANN, Godparent; Born November 8, 1859; Baptized
May 28, 1865; #215

John NIEDERHOEFER - George (n.c.) NIEDERHOEFER and Frances MUELLER,
Parents; Mary HERRMANN, Godparent; Born September 27, 1857; Baptized
May 28, 1865; #214

Mary Ann NEUHAUS - James NEUHAUS and Mary Ann KUHN, Parents;
Joan MC GINNIS, Godparent; Born March 19, 1885; Baptized February 8,
1887; #1308

Carolina Josephine Vincentia NEUMANN - Thomas NEUMANN and Mary
CALAHAN, Parents; Maurice WALTER and Vincentia MONFRIN, Godparents;
Born February 4, 1882; Baptized October 9, 1886; #1273

Margaret Augusta NEUMANN - Gugust (n.c.) NEUMANN and Augusta BOEHNKE, Parents; Frank BECK and Mary C. RUSSEL, Godparents; Born March 31, 1884; Baptized April 13, 1884; #1057

Lilian Mary NONN - Charles NONN and Aminda IRVIN, Parents; Theresa AULL, Godparent; Born May 14, 1894; Baptized May 30, 1898; #1919

Joan Caroline NONNENMACHER - Anton NONNENMACHER and Frances JAEGE, Parents; Jos. NONNENMACHER and Caroline STOLZ, Godparents; Born June 23, 1861; Baptized June 30, 1861; #48

Joseph NONNENMACHER - Anton NONNENMACHER and Frances JAECH, Parents; August NIEBLE and Mary HERRMANN, Godparents; Born September 4, 1863; Baptized September 13, 1863; #123

August Carl OBER - Albert OBER and Amilia (n.c.) BERGMANN, Parents; Augusta DOM, Godparent; Born June 23, 1886; Baptized October 23, 1886; #1278

Henry John OBER - Albert OBER and Emily BERGMAN, Parents; Nora RUNTZ, Godparent; Born August 5, 1891; Baptized April 3, 1892; #1555

Thomas Keatz OBER - Alfred C. OBER and Emily BERGMANN, Parents; Lillian KEATS, Godparent; Born October 29, 1893; Baptized March 18, 1894; #1657

Edward ODELL - Edward ODELL and Margaret TIFE, Parents; Theresa ROEHRMANN, Godparent; Born May 23, 1873; Baptized June 1, 1873; #672

Edward OELRICH - George OELRICH and Catherine HEWLI, Parents; Baptized August 24, 1867; #363

George Aust OELRICH - George OELRICH and Catherine HEWLI, Parents; Baptized August 24, 1867; #362

Sophy OELRICH - G. A. OELRICH and Catherine HEROLD, Parents; Charlotte GRISHAM, Godparent; Born October 29, 1860; Baptized November 3, 1861; #60

Mary Elizabeth Ella OHNSTEIN - Martin (n.c.) OHNSTEIN and Dalia MANNING, Parents; Mary ARNOLD, Godparent; Born October 5, 1889; Baptized November 19, 1889; #1457

Catherine O'KEEFE - Michael O'KEEFE and Mary Anna HILL, Parents; Mary HILL and Cornelius HILL, Godparents; Born December 28, 1877; Baptized January 13, 1878; #830

Cornelius John O'KEEFE - Michael O'KEEFE and Anna HILL, Parents; Cornelius HILL and Julian HILL, Godparents; Born September 11, 1870; Baptized September 25, 1870; #565

Algeda Joan OPDENWEYER - Charles OPDENWEYER and Mary Catherine OPDENWEYER, Parents; Charles LAUTZ, Godparent; Born November 3, 1876; Baptized February 18, 1877; #804

Henry Charles Gustave OPPERMANN - Gustave OPPERMANN and Mary Ann KNODELL, Parents; Louise HOHORST and Henry HOHORST, Godparents; Born September 20, 1867; Baptized December 16, 1867; #389

Joseph Theodore OPPERMANN - Gustave OPPERMANN and Mary Ann KNODELL, Parents; Jos. ANSTAETT and John PHILIPPS, Godparents; Born April 6, 1866; Baptized May 31, 1866; #294

Thomas John O'ROURKE - John O'ROURKE and Mathilda RIESNER, Parents; Rudolph BULASHER and Mary BULASHER, Godparents; Born November 10, 1895; Baptized April 26, 1896; #1824

Adolph OSBURG - George OSBURG and Augusta LESE, Parents; Catherine KRAUS, Godparent; Born December 23, 1867; Baptized January 19, 1868; #398

Charles OSBURG - George OSBURG and Augusta LOSE, Parents; Jos. KRAUS and Catherine KRAUS, Godparents; Born November 23, 1863; Baptized September 23, 1866; #317 A

Daniel OSBURG - George OSBURG and Augusta LESE, Parents; Catherine KRAUS, Godparent; Born May 24, 1866; Baptized May 30, 1866; #293

Mary Augusta OSBURG - George OSBURG and Augusta LOSE, Parents; Jos. KRAUS and Catherine KRAUS, Godparents; Born April 22, 1861; Baptized September 23, 1866; #316

George William OSER - George William OSER and Mary Ann ARNOLD, Parents; Gabrielle M. REYBOUD and August SCHULTZ, Godparents; Born June 5, ----; Baptized April 24, 1894; #1666

Mildred Merrow Frances OSER - George Wm. OSER and Mary Ann ARNOLD, Parents; Chas. ARNOLD and Angelina ARNOLD, Godparents; Born December 1, 1897; Baptized December 26, 1897; #1898

Gladys Lincoln Ann OSER - (See under MOSER - #1949)

Osmund Oswald OSER - George Wm. OSER and Mary Ann ARNOLD, Parents; Joseph Philip ARNOLD and Ann Oser STOCKTON, Godparents; Born April 2, 1896; Baptized April 26, 1896; #1825

John Amandus O'SHEA - Michael O'SHEA and Margaret TINTORE, Parents; T. GONZALES and Donata TOSER, Godparents; Born May 5, 1872; Baptized October 25, 1872; #634

Ottilia OSWALD - Theodore OSWALD (Stuttgart, Wurtemberg) and Teresa GRAEN (Hildesheim, Hannover), Parents; William OPPERMANN and Rosina CHAMBARD, Godparents; Born September 3, 1861; Baptized July 20, 1865; #222

Elizabeth OSWALD - Theodore OSWALD (Stuttgart, Wurtemberg) and Teresa GRAEN (Hildesheim, Hannover), Parents; William OPPERMANN and Rosina CHAMBARD, Godparents; Born November 23, 1863; Baptized July 20, 1865; #223

Adolph Jeremiah OTTERBECK - Adolph OTTERBECK and Mary CALLAHAN, Parents; Jos. ATKINS and Julia RILEY, Godparents; Born November 10, 1864; Baptized April 18, 1865; #195

Germanus Henry PAISSE - Edward Eugene PAISSE and Clemence RILLS, Parents; Bernard ROUBION and Mrs. Bernard BOUBION, Godparents; Born October 16, 1894; Baptized December 9, 1894; #1693

George William PAPP - Conrad PAPP and Margaret Victoria KERRY, Parents; Magdalen KERRY, Godparent; Born November 12, 1876; Baptized February 2, 1877

George John PAQUET - George PAQUET and Alberta WERNERT, Parents; John HAGEMANN and Theresa ROEHMANN, Godparents; Born February 21, 1874; Baptized July 13, 1874; #713

Louis Philip PAQUET - George PAQUET and Albertina VERNETT, Parents; Mary SAMMET, Godparent; Born September 4, 1869; Baptized October 9, 1869; #530

Anna Louise PATRICK - Clinton Clay PATRICK and Octavia MARCHAND, Parents; Leopold FIEVER and Elisa FIEVER, Godparents; Born April 21, 1885; Baptized July 6, 1885; #1875

William Edward PAYNE - J. T. PAYNE and Frances BAUERS, Parents;
Mr. and Mrs. GRAS, Godparents; Born June 13, 1899; Baptized July 16,
1899; #1959

Louise Helen PAYSSE - Henry PAYSSE and Addie DUNHAM, Parents;
Mrs. PAYSEE and John PAYSEE, Godparents; Born June 18, 1900; Baptized
August 12, 1900; #1997

Joseph Herrmann PEINE - Joseph PEINE and Margaret ROSE, Parents;
Herman TROST and Caroline RICKE, Godparents; Born April 13, 1862;
Baptized April 27, 1862; #76

Martin PEINE - Joseph PEINE and Margaret ROSE, Parents; John
HOFBECK, Godparent; Born November 3, 1864; Baptized November 13,
1864; #183

Mary Josephine PEINE - Joseph PEINE and Margaret ROSE, Parents;
Joseph RICKE and Mary RICKE, Godparents; Born June 3, 1867;
Baptized June 16, 1867; #354

Francis PEITZ - August PEITZ and Mary Ann KALT, Parents; Catherine
COLEMANN, Godparent; Born December 25, 1884; Baptized March 13,
1887; #1318

Frederic August PEITZ - August PEITZ and Mary KALT, Parents;
Conrad ESCHENBERG, Godparent; Born September 23, 1882; Baptized
April 1, 1883; #997

Mary PEITZ - August PEITZ and Mary KALT, Parents; Otto PEITZ,
Godparent; Born August 6, 1887; Baptized May 27, 1888; #1393

Julia PENDERGAST - William PENDERGAST and Joan CONDEY, Parents;
Alfred D. SMITH and Julia PENDERGAST, Godparents; Born June 25,
1889; Baptized August 17, 1889; #1445

John PERRY (Calcasieu Pa., La) six years - Boyer PERRY and Margaret
PERRY (slaves of Captain Green), Parents; Laura GREEN, Godparent;
Baptized May 10, 1864; #149

Laura PERRY (Calcasieu Pa., La) eight years - Boyer PERRY and
Margaret PERRY (slaves of Captain Green), Parents; Laura GREEN,
Godparent; Baptized May 10, 1864; #150

Clementine Mary PERTHUIS - Julius PERTHUIS and Cecile RICKE,
Parents; Martin RICKE and Mary RICKE, Godparents; Born October 16,
1883; Baptized April 15, 1884; #1063

Felix PERTHUIS - Julius PERTHUIS and Cecile RICKE, Parents; Martin
RICKE and Mary RICKE, Godparents; Born October 20, 1885; Baptized
February 14, 1886; #1217

Hyppolite Joseph PERTHUIS - Emil PERTHUIS and Mary RICKE, Parents;
Joseph RICKE and Margaret OPITZ, Godparents; Born August 22, 1885;
Baptized April 18, 1886; #1223

Theresa PERTHUIS - Emil PERTHUIS and Mary RICKE, Parents; Theodore
EGGERT and Theresa EGGERT, Godparents; Born March 4, 1894; Baptized
March 27, 1894; #1658

Constantine Chas. PESSARRA - Frederrick PESSARRA and Louise TROST,
Parents; John LANG and Catherine KRAUS, Godparents; Born February 17,
1848; Baptized April 16, 1896 (convert); #1820

Augustine PETERS - John PETERS and Louise EBERHART, Parents; John
Claud EBERHART and Cecile DENOIS, Godparents; Born June 18, 1859;
Baptized May 13, 1860; #5

John PETRO - John PETRO and Anastasia SCHUBERT, Parents; Antoine KROSS, Godparent; Born October 14, 1872; Baptized December 29, 1872; #644

Tyra Elizabeth PETSON - Charles PETSON and Catherine EISEN, Parents; Elizabeth GILLET and N. EISEN, Godparents; Born --; Baptized October 12, 1873; #684

Carolina Catherine PFLUEGER - George PFLUEGER and Elizabeth SCHNEIDER, Parents; George NELSON and Carolina YOUNG, Godparents; Born February 3, 1882; Baptized March 12, 1882; #958

Caroline Louise PFLUEGER - Geo. PFLUEGER and Elizabeth SCHNEIDER, Parents; France JUNG, Godparent; Born September 7, 1863; Baptized November 5, 1863; #130

Henrietta Leopoline PFLUEGER - Geo. PFLUEGER and Elizabeth SCHNEIDER, Parents; Leopoldine FROBOESEN, Godparent; Born January 22, 1870; Baptized March 6, 1870; #550

John George PFLUEGER - George PFLUEGER and Elizabeth SCHNEIDER, Parents; John SCHNEIDER and Dorothy WALLSTEIN, Godparents; Born October 11, 1865; Baptized December 3, 1865; #252

Mary Frances PFLUEGER - George PFLUEGER and Elizabeth SCHNEIDER, Parents; Frances JUNG (YOUNG), Godparent; Born January 31, 1868; Baptized March 15, 1868; #408

Rose Alberta PFLUEGER - George PFLUEGER and Anna LIEBLING, Parents; Anna FLUER, Godparent; Born January 4, 1874; Baptized April 17, 1874; #700

Theresa Margaret PFLUEGER - George PFLUEGER and Rose FLUEGER, Parents; Theresa WEBER, Godparent; Born September 18, 1876; Baptized December 12, 1876; #780

Frank Joseph PHILIBERT - Henry PHILIBERT and Catherine MC GOVERN, Parents; Frances MC GOVERN, Godparent; Born April 27, 1863; Baptized September 26, 1865; #229

Julius PHILLIP - Daniel PHILLIP and Joan OPPERMANN, Parents; Bernard TIERNAN and Elizabeth MASON, Godparents; Born September 18, 1866; Baptized October 4, 1866; #319

Catherine PHILLIPSON - Robert PHILLIPSON and Catherine QUERR, Parents; Magdalin GREYENBUEHL, Godparent; Born April 6, 1870; Baptized October 20, 1873; #686

Robert PHILLIPSON - Robert PHILLIPSON and Catherine QUERR, Parents; Magdalin GREYENBUEHL, Godparent; Born February 8, 1873; Baptized October 20, 1873; #687

Thomas PHILLIPSON - Robert PHILLIPSON and Catherine QUERR, Parents; Magdalen GREYENBUEHL, Godparent; Born August 20, 1868; Baptized October 20, 1873; #685

Mary Virginia POKER - John POKER and Mary AULL, Parents; Theresa AULL, Godparent; Baptized March 3, 1876; #769

Elizabeth POLASCHE - Born June 9, 1880; Baptized (private) June 9, 1880

Anthony William POPULAR - Anthony POPULAR and Mary Joan HEIMANN, Parents; Joseph KRAUSS and Ida RICKE, Godparents; Born December 12, 1875; Baptized December 14, 1875; #763

Charles Anthony POPULAR - Anthony POPULAR and Mary Joan HEIMANN, Parents; William PLAICE and Ernestine BRINK, Godparents; Born May 25, 1868; Baptized June 14, 1868; #422 A

Clarence Rudolph POPULAR - Anthony POPULAR and Joan HEIMANN, Parents;
Chas. PAPLIER and Mary BLEIKE, Godparents; Born August 23, 1884;
Baptized September 14, 1884; #1094

Louise Adelaide POPULAR - Anton POPULAR and Joan HEIMANN, Parents;
John BOEDECKER and Louise MAILAND, Godparents; Born January 3,
1887; Baptized February 20, 1887; #1312

Mary Fredice POPULAR - Anthony POPULAR and Mary Joan HEIMANN,
Parents; John Frederic KRAUSE and Mary STOPPLEBERG, Godparents;
Born August 2, 1881; Baptized August 28, 1881; #938

Julius Werner PORITZ - Max PORITZ and Apollonia JASINSKI, Parents;
Geo. ENGLISH and Wener von den SCHULENBURG, Godparents; Born
August 17, 1899; Baptized October 29, 1899; #1966

Frank Xavier Louis PICTURE - Wm. (n.c.) PICTURE and Louise VIEWEGER,
Parents; Louise NASCHKE, Godparent; Born August 28, 1884; Baptized
October 16, 1884; #1106

Rosale Helen PICTURE - Wm. Henry PICTURE and Louise VIEWEGER,
Parents; Henry PICTURE and Rosale VIWGER, Godparents; Born June 7,
1871; Baptized August 13, 1871; #594 B

Frank Joseph PILLE - Henry PILLE and Cecil NUTT, Parents; Francis
BROKOF, Godparent; Born March 24, 1879; Baptized June 14, 1879;
#889

Edward PLITT - George PLITT and Anna Mary PLITT, Parents; George
PLITT and Anna Mary PLITT, Godparents; Born January 3, 1864;
Baptized October 5, 1887 (convert); #1360

Victor Emanuel Maxenthius PORITZ - Maseuti PORITZ and Apollonia
JARSINSKY, Parents; Anna ANTRISKY, Godparent; Born November 11,
1897; Baptized March 20, 1898

Walter POWELL - Lawrence POWELL and Joan DUFF, Parents; Sarah
TIERNAN, Godparent; Born July 11, 1867; Baptized January 7, 1868;
#397

William POWELL - Lawrence POWELL and Joan DUFF, Parents; Dionysius
CALLAHAN and Sarah DUFF, Godparents; Born February 19, 1865;
Baptized March 3, 1865 ("Clear Creek"); #191

Augustina PRADIER - August PRADIER and Armantia HENACH, Parents;
Robert JACOVLEF and Mary Louise BLEINDEAU, Godparents; Baptized
April 7, 1861; #39

Joseph Ferdinand PRAGNER - Joseph PRAGNER and Theresa GLASER,
Parents; Ferdinand SOMMER and Elizabeth MAURER, Godparents; Born
March 27, 1877; Baptized May 27, 1877; #806

Albert Louis PRAULI - Conrad Paul PRAULI and Caroline MUELLER,
Parents; Born July 17, 1879; Baptized June 6, 1880; #895

Leona Agnes PRENDERGAST (?) - William PRENDERGAST (?) and Joan
Jane CUDDY (?), Parents; Edward CUDDY and Elizabeth LENZ, Godparents;
Born February 6, 1894; Baptized August 8, 1896; #1841

Alice Barbara PRESTON - Chas. Henry PRESTON and Margaret STECHMANN,
Parents; Mrs. Barbara STECHMANN and Patrick KELLY, Godparents;
Born April 5, 1900; Baptized April 29, 1900; #1991

Henry Martin PREUS - John H. PREUS and Henrietta RICHTER, Parents;
Ellen MC MANUS, Godparent; Born October 9, 1876; Baptized December 18,
1878; #875

Henry PRUESER - Henry PREUSER and Margaret HARMS (n.c.), Parents;
John LORDAN, Godparent; Baptized May 6, 1887; #1344

Lilie Helen PRUESER - Henry PRUESER and Mary HARMS (n.c.), Parents;
Mary ARNOLD, Godparent; Born June 25, 1882; Baptized April 22, 1887;
#1332

William Moreau PRUESER - Henry PRUESER and Margaret HARMS (n.c.),
Parents; John LORDAN, Godparent; Baptized May 6, 1887 (conditional),
#1343

Louis Henry Rudolph PURGET - Frank PURGET (Hitchcock, Texas; also
PURJET today) and Sophy MARTIN, Parents; Mary MARTIN and Louis
MARTIN, Godparents; Born June 9, 1888; Baptized January 2, 1890;
#1468

Virginia Nora PURGET - Frank PURGET and Sophy MARTIN, Parents;
Michael DIROUX and Virginia HELWIG, Godparents; Born December 19,
1890; Baptized August 9, 1891; #1531

Agnes Grace QUESTED - Walter QUESTED and Mary KELLEY, Parents;
Sarah HOYLE, Godparent; Born February (?) 14, 1895; Baptized
July 27, 1896; #1839

Elizabeth Leonida QUESTED - Walter QUESTED and Mary KELLEY,
Parents; Agnes QUESTED, Godparent; Born May 18, 18--; Baptized
July 27, 1896; #1840

Elizabeth Leonida QUESTED - Walter QUESTED and Mary KELLEY, Parents;
Sarah HOYLD, Godparent; Born May 10, 1894; Baptized July 27, 1896
(private); #1843

Mary Ida QUESTED - Walter D. QUESTED and Mollie KELLEY, Parents;
Mollie QUESTED, Godparent; Born February 17, 1891; Baptized August 1,
1891; #1525

Catherine Eliz. QUINLEN - John QUINLEN and Joan WOLLES, Parents;
Margaret JONSON, Godparent; Born June 14, 1869; Baptized June 18,
1869; #525

Mary Eve QUINN - Robert QUINN and Elizabeth HILL, Parents; Joseph
KESSLER, Godparent; Born October 30, 1895; Baptized September 25,
1895; #1797

Eugenia Josephine Adolphine QUINTARO - Camillus QUINTARO and
Eugenia PERDEL, Parents; Peter TARGARONA and Adolphine BERKENBUSCH,
Godparents; Born September 19, 1869; Baptized January 30, 1870;
#542

Dennis Patrick RADLEY (married Mary Helen BURNETTE, St. Mary's,
Temple, Texas, 4/27/20) - Dennis RADLEY and Catherine MC CAULEY,
Parents; William WINKLER and Helen MOORE, Godparents; Born February 4,
1894; Baptized March 4, 1894; #1561

Mary Magdalen RAKE - Adolph RAKE and Anna LANG, Parents; Lillie
SCHREIBER, Godparent; Born December 25, 1876; Baptized October 13,
1877; #813

Frida Anita Joan RAKEL - Herman RAKEL and Ann VAGENBRET (n.c.),
Parents; Albert RAKEL and Anna VAGENBRET, Godparents; Born September 22,
1889; Baptized October 6, 1889; #1449

Herman Henry RAKEL - Gerhardt RAKEL and Mary SCHNEIDER, Parents;
Herman RAKEL and Benigna EKERT, Godparents; Born January 17, 1878;
Baptized February 10, 1878; #833

Mary Eliz. Theresa RAKEL - Gerhard RAKEL and Mary SCHNEIDER,
Parents; Albert RAKEL, Godparent; Born January 27, 1879; Baptized
June 27, 1880; #901

August Chas. Henry RAMACHER - Theodore RAMACHER and Clementine
STRUCK, Parents; Henry HAGEMANN and Sophie DALLMER, Godparents;
Born November 12, 1862; Baptized April 3, 1864; #146

Charles William RAMACHER - Theodore RAMACHER and Catherine STRUCK,
Parents; Charles MOSER and Fides ELBERT, Godparents; Born October --,
1860; Baptized December 25, 1861; #63

Louis Chas. Leonard RAMACHER - Theodore RAMACHER and Clementine
STRUCK, Parents; Charles BROSIG and Anna MARKE, Godparents;
Baptized November 26, 1865; #248

Catherine Anita RAPP - Adam RAPP and Emily CRISTOPH, Parents;
Anita RINKER, Godparent; Born August 5, 1877; #----

Anna RATISSEAU - Alfred RATISSEAU and Augusta GUNDERMANN, Parents;
Anthony SOMMER and Anna KIMELE, Godparents; Born Arpil 23, 1870;
Baptized June 5, 1870; #558

Felix Alfred Chas. August Anselm RATISSEAU - August Anselm RATISSEAU
and Joan Mary Camille Stephanie KRETZSCHMAR, Parents; Alfred P.
RATISSEAU and Carolina LUCKHEART, Godparents; Born February 26,
1863; Baptized August 16, 1863; #121

Louis William RATISSEAU - Alfred Peter RATISSEAU and Augusta
GUNDERMANN, Parents; John Baptist RATISSEAU and Augusta RATISSEAU,
Godparents; Born May 23, 1863; Baptized August 16, 1863; #122

Mary Emily RATISSEAU - Alfred RATISSEAU and Emily GUNDERMANN,
Parents; Henry WEYERS and Sophie WEYERS, Godparents; Born December 10,
1865; Baptized March 18, 1866; #271

Rosalie RATISSOT - August RATISSOT and Camille KRETCHMER, Parents;
J. B. RATISSOT, Godparent; Born October 5, 1866; Baptized December 25,
1866; #329

Joan RAY - Diongs RAY and Katherine CONWAY, Parents; John RAY and
Barbara RAY for Katherine RAY, Godparents; Born August 21, 1876;
Baptized August --, 1876; #779

Isaac RECTOR - Baptized March 30, 1886 (private)

Anna REILLY - Patrick REILLY and GAFFRY, Parents; Pat HUGHES,
Godparent; Born August 3, 1873; Baptized February 8, 1874; #696

Mary Joan REILLY - Patrick REILLY and Mary GEFNEW, Parents;
Frederick PLAIGE and Theresa PLAIGE, Godparents; Born May 3, 1868;
Baptized May 10, 1868; #421

Ella Valeria RENT - John Wm. RENT and Mary SPRINGER, Parents;
Catherine ANDERSON, Godparent; Born March 7, 1897; Baptized June 3,
1897, #1879

Alice Anna RESSEL - Frank Joseph RESSEL and Caroline TSCHIEDEL,
Parents; Anthony SOMMER and Anna SOMMER, Godparents; Born November 7,
1886; Baptized December 5, 1886; #1293

Charles Engelbert RESSEL - Frank Joseph RESSEL and Caroline
TSCHIEDEL, Parents; Engelbert GEIGER and Mrs. LUDVIG, Godparents;
Born July 15, 1888; Baptized August 26, 1888; #1405

Walter Raphael REYNOLDS - Charles R. REYNOLDS and Sara GIRARD,
Parents; Adolph DROUET and Helen WAINRIGHT, Godparents; Born
August 7, 1868; Baptized April 12, 1868; #415

Charles Forest RHUBOTTOM - Charles Forest RHUBOTTOM and Emily HERMANN,
Parents; Anthony POPULAR and Mary Lillie HEIMANN, Godparents;
Born August 30, 1881; Baptized October 2, 1881; #942

Joseph RIAT (RIOT) - John RIAT (RIOT) Baptist and Joan MENNAE, Parents; Elias DUIROS and Mary Frumetia DUIROS, Godparents; Born September 9, 1866; Baptized May 26, 1867; #351

John Joseph Pora RIAT (RIOT) - John RIAT (RIOT) Baptist and Joan MENNAE, Parents; Eugenia STANWOOD, Godparent; Born August 22, 1880; Baptized March 11, 1885; #1141

Mary Frieda RICAVY - Wenceslaw RICAVY and Mary PARTEL, Parents; Robert MALEK and Frieda MALEK, Godparents; Born July 11, 1892; Baptized August 6, 1892; #1572

Edward RICE - Baptized September 11, 1861; #54

Joseph RICHTER - Joseph RICHTER and Catherine FRIETSCH, Parents; Frank CHRIST and Magdalen ANDERS, Godparents; Born April 25, 1867; Baptized May 14, 1867; #348

Anna RICKE - Martine RICKE and Ida RICKE, Parents; John MAURER and Elizabeth Pauline MAURER, Godparents; Born June 10, 1875; Baptized June 20, 1875; #751

Anna Elizabeth RICKE - Martin RICKE and Anna M. HOCK, Parents; Elizabeth RICKE, Godparent; Born June 16, 1885; Baptized August 6, 1885; #1879

Ann Leopoldine RICKE - John RICKE and Mary MUEHE, Parents; Anton RICKE and Leopoldine FROBOESE, Godparents; Born May 3, 1869; Baptized May 26, 1869; #520

Anna Magdalen RICKE - Martin RICKE and Anna Mary HOCK, Parents; Augusta HOCK and Martin HOCK, Godparents; Born June 12, 1897; Baptized July 26, 1897; #1886

Ann Mary RICKE - Martin RICKE and Mary HOCK, Parents; Ann Mary SCHUETZ, Godparent; Born November 2, 1892; Baptized November 21, 1892; #1587

Anthony Herman RICKE - Anton RICKE and Joan TSCHAEKE, Parents; Herman TSCHAEKE and Techa BRUCKHOF, Godparents; Born February 23, 1873; Baptized March 16, 1873; #655

Bertha Caroline RICKE - Anton RICKE and Joan JENSKY, Parents; John RICKE and Caroline RICKE, Godparents; Born March 4, 1867; Baptized March 17, 1867; #339

Charles August RICKE - Anthony RICKE and Joan TSCHAEKE, Parents; Joseph RICKE and Caroline RICKE, Godparents; Born November 5, 1868; Baptized December 6, 1868; #428

Charles Joseph RICKE - Martin RICKE and Mary HOCK, Parents; Carl Joseph HOCK and Mary Christine HOCK, Godparents; Born November 14, 1886; Baptized November 29, 1886; #1292

Elizabeth Frigata RICKE - John RICKE and Mary MEUHE, Parents; J. JACOBS and Anna BEST, Godparents; Born November 15, 1871; Baptized November 26, 1871; #609

Ida RICKE - Martin RICKE and Ida RICKE, Parents; Baptized May 3, 1874; #703

Ida RICKE - Martin RICKE and Anne Mary HOCK, Parents; Mary Frances MAURER, Godparents; Born September 11, 1898; Baptized October 9, 1898; #1926

John Henry RICKE - Anthony RICKE and Anna LANG, Parents; Magdalen GREYENBUEHL and John Hy. LIMMER, Godparents; Born December 20, 1873; Baptized January 15, 1874; #695

Joan Odilia RICKE - Anthony RICKE and Joan JENSKI, Parents;
Martin RICKE and Ida RICKE, Godparents; Born March 13, 1871;
Baptized April 2, 1871; #582

John RICKE - Martin RICKE and Ida MESPIL, Parents; Born November 28,
1872; Baptized December 5, 1872 (private); #640

John Adam RICKE - Martin RICKE and Ida MESPIL, Parents; John KRAUSE,
Godparents; Born June 8, 1879; Baptized June 18, 1879; #890

John Joseph RICKE - John RICKE and Maria MUEHE, Parents; Joseph
RICKE and Sophie TSCHAEKE, Godparents; Born October 8, 1865;
Baptized October 22, 1865; #244

Joseph William RICKE (adopted, orphan) - Joseph RICKE and Caroline
TSCHAEKE (foster parents); John RICKE and Sophie TSCHAEKE, Godparents;
Baptized October 22, 1865; #233

Louis RICKE - Martin RICKE nad Ann Mary HOCK, Parents; Charles
Joseph HOCK, Godparent; Born September 2, 1894; Baptized September 23,
1894; #1682

Martin Edward RICKE - Martin RICKE and Ida MESPIL, Parents; Joseph
RICKE and Theresa RICKE, Godparents; Born October 4, 1877; Baptized
October 16, 1877; #817

Martin Joseph RICKE - Martin RICKE and Mary HOCK, Parents; Joseph
RICKE, Godparent; Born Feburary 28, 1888; Baptized March 18, 1888;
#1380

Mary RICKE - John RICKE and Mary MUEHE, Parents; Joseph RICKE and
Caroline RICKE, Godparents; Born January 14, 1864; Baptized
January 24, 1864; #140

Mary Margaret RICKE - Martin RICKE and Anna Mary HOCK, Parents;
Mary KOEHLER, Godparent; Born November 10, 1889; Baptized November 30,
1889; #1459

William Theodore RICKE - John RICKE and Mary RICKE, Parents;
William SCHOCKE and Anna WIEGARD, Godparents; Born April 15, 1874;
Baptized April 26, 1874; #701

Grover Joseph REID - REID and JOHNSON, Parents; Born November 6,
1891; Baptized November 13, 1891 (private); #1544

Mary Aloysia RIEGER - William RIEGER and Josephine HOLZMANN,
Parents; John OBENDOERFER and Bertha OBENDOERFER, Godparents;
Born January 3, 1897; Baptized Setpember 12, 1897; #1890

Frank Louis RIGNEY - Thomas RIGNEY and Elizabeth MAYS (n.c.),
Parents; John WILSON and Mrs. WILSON, Godparents; Born December 3,
1883; Baptized August 29, 1886 (private); #1265

Anna RINKER - Selim RINKER and Mary BUCHOLZ, Parents; Anna FLAKE,
Godparent; Born October 1, 1870; Baptized August 15, 1878; #856

Anthony Selim RINKER - Selim RINKER and Mary FLAKE, Parents;
Anthony BILLET and Mary Ann BUTLER, Godparents; Born December 28,
1866; Baptized April 3, 1867; #341

Ewohan RINKER - Selim RINKER and Mary BUCHOLZ, Parents; Anna
FLAKE, Godparent; Born October 10, 1877; Baptized August 15, 1878;
#860

Henry RINKER - Selim RINKER and Mary BUCHOLZ, Parents; A. FLAKE,
Godparent; Born November 1, 1872; Baptized August 15, 1878; #859

Nellie RINKER - Selim RINKER and Mary BUCHOLZ, Parents; Anna FLAKE,
Godparent; Born January 2, 1869; Baptized August 15, 1878; #857

William RINKER - Selim RINKER and Mary FLAKE, Parents; John G.
JOCKUSCH and -- BAER, Godparents; Born September 24, 1865; Baptized
December 7, 1865; #253

Anna Mary Louise RIPKE - Henry Frederick RIPKE (n.c.) and Mary
RATH, Parents; Mary BRAMER, Godparent; Born January 26, 1887;
Baptized April 10, 1887; #1331

Carolina Elenore RIPKE - Frederick Henry RIPKE and Mary RATH,
Parents; Caroline DORIAN and Joan Antonia DORIAN, Godparents;
Born July 13, 1897; Baptized October 23, 1897; #1892

Frank Irvin RIPKE - Henry RIPKE and Mary RATH, Parent;s Frank RATH
and Emma LEUTSCH, Godparents; Born November 18, 1894; Baptized
March 4, 1895; #1705

George Henry John RIPKE - George Henry (n.c.) RIPKE and Mary RATH,
Parents; Patrick FLYNN and Jane HAUL, Godparents; Born December 18,
1888; Baptized February 17, 1889; #1425

Henry Patrick Robert RIPKE - Henry F. RIPKE and Mary RATH, Parents;
Patrick BARRY and Rose RIPKE, Godparents; Born December 15, 1891;
Baptized February 28, 1892; #1551

Emma RISLEY - 18 years; Baptized December 9, 1872 (private)

Albert William RITTER - William RITTER and Margaret HEIGEL,
Parents; Catherine KRAUS, Godparent; Born April 17, 1879; Baptized
October 12, 1885; #1190

Charles RITTER - William (n.c.) RITTER and Margaret HEIGEL,
Parents; Rosina BAUMANN, Godparent; Born January 28, 1881; Baptized
October 12, 1885; #1191

Ida Helen RITTER - William (n.c.) RITTER and Margaret HEIGEL,
Parents; Catherine KRAUS, Godparent; Born November 9, 1876;
Baptized October 12, 1885; #1192

Alice RITTMUS - Mary BUHL, Godparent; Baptized June 12, 1885; #1166

Helen RITZLER - Valentine RITZLER and Catherine MICHELS, Parents;
Thomas COLLINS and Helen COLLINS, Godparents; Born November 16,
1871; Baptized December 24, 1871; #605

Helen Charlotte RITZLER - Henry RITZLER and Mary GEBBERT (GEBART?),
Parents; Charles Jos. SHARKE and Pauline MUEHE, Godparents; Born
November 14, 1899; Baptized January 14, 1900; #1973

Henerietta Joan RITZLER - Henry RITZLER and Mary GIBBERT (GEBART?),
Parents; Henry ECKENFELS and Joan ECKERT, Godparents; Born
September 16, 1891; Baptized November 1, 1891; #1540

Henry Valentine RITZLER - Valentine RITZLER and Catherine MICHELS,
Parents; Henry MICHELS and Elizabeth BAUHANS, Godparents; Born
July 28, 1867; Baptized September 22, 1867; #373

James RITZLER - Valentine RITZLER and Catherine MICHELS, Parents;
Catherine BEST, Godparent; Born December 22, 1869; Baptized February 6,
1870; #544

Louis Valentine RITZLER - Henry RITZLER and Mary GEBBERT, Parents;
Valentine BAUHENS, Godparent; Born December 24, 1895; Baptized
February 9, 1896; #1805

Margaret Josephine RITZLER - Henry RITZLER and Mary GEBBERT, Parents;
Joseph BEST and Margaert RITZLER, Godparents; Born September 4,
1893; Baptized October 15, 1893; #1621

Sophy RITZLER - Valentin RITZLER and Catherine MITCHELS, Parents; Catherine BAUHENS, Godparent; Born May 10, 1881; Baptized May 10, 1881; #924

Susan Wilhelmina RITZLER - Valentin RITZLER and Catherine MICHELS, Parents; Susan Wilhelmina MULLER, Godparent; Born November 21, 1877; Baptized December 23, 1877; #824

Joseph Jefferson Davis ROACH - Jacob ROACH and Kessia SILVESTER, Parents; Mary MC KAY, Godparent; Born July 1, 1861; Baptized July 15, 1862; #88

Mary Loretta ROACH - Thomas ROACH and Anne HEALY, Parents; Mrs. Margaret HEALY, Godparent; Born July 19, 1885; Baptized August 2, 1885; #1183 A

John Ross ROANE - James ROANE and Sophie TRUIBAUT, Parents; Helen MC MANUS, Godparent; Born January 5, 1888; Baptized April 14, 1888; #1451

Frederick Marshall ROBERTSON - Emmet Marshall ROBERTSON and Maggie ROBERTSON, Parents; Mary Philomene MAYNA ?, Godparents; Born August 20, 1880; Baptized July 2, 1881; #931

Henry C. (ROBERTSON) (presumed) - Henry C. ROBERTSON (presumed) and Mary Anne KIRSCH, Parents; Regina KIRSCH, Godparent; Born December 27, 1887; Baptized July 1, 1888; #1399

Lillian Louise ROBINSON - Henry C. ROBINSON and Mary Anne DEER, Parents; Regina KIRSCH, Godparent; Born August 11, 1892; Baptized December 14, 1892; #1591

Mary Joan Louise Alexandra ROBIRO - Anthony ROBIRO and Irene INLUX, Parents; Aloysius ROBIRO and Mary TROSCLAIS, Godparents; Born December 27, 1868; Baptized February 14, 1869; #510

Augusta ROEPER - Frank Jos. ROEPER and Emily FUNK, Parents; Joseph KRONE and Frances BLEIKE, Godparents; Born December 13, 1860; Baptized March 31, 1861; #38

Joseph Henry ROHDE - Louis Geo. ROHDE and Sophy Louise WINDMEYER, Parents; Joseph WINDMEYER and Terese WINDMEYER, Godparents; Born November 26, 1898; Baptized March 19, 1899; #1946

Louis George ROHDE - Louis Geo. ROHDE and Sophy WINDMEYER, Parents; Joseph WINDMEYER, Godparent; 2 years 15 days; Baptized August 21, 1898; #1924

Charles ROHLEDER - Valentin ROHLEDER and Eve Magdalen ABB, Parents; Rev. Chas. PADEY (Sponsor); Born October 24, 1855; Baptized March 22, 1861; #35

Frederic ROHLEDER - Valentine ROHLEDER and Eve Magdalene ABB, Parents; Catherine HARRIS, Godparent; Born September 16, 1852; BAptized April 13, 1868; #416

John Joseph ROHLEDER - Damian ROHLEDER and Mary LETZ, Parents; John HOFBECK and Caroline HOFBECK, Godparents; Born December 3, 1868; Baptized December 6, 1868; #498 A

Magdalen ROHLEDER - Valentine ROHLEDER and Eve Magdalen ABB, Parents; Rev. Charles PADEY (Sponsor); Born February 4, 1860; Baptized March 22, 1861; #36

Alexander Adolph ROHLING - Frank John ROHLING (ROLLING, ROLING) and Helen SPEYER, Parents; Alexander KUHLMANN and Dorothy EICHLER, Godparents; Born September 15, 1877; Baptized December 23, 1877; #826

Carolina Cecil ROHLING - Frank John ROHLING and Helen SPEYER,
Parents; John PARKER and Anna HILL, Godparents; Born March 12,
1875; Baptized July 2, 1875; #755

Catherine ROHLING - Frank John ROHLING and Helen SPEYER, Parents;
Herman RACKEL and Catherine WALKER, Godparents; Born July 7, 1882;
Baptized September 24, 1882; #983

Joseph Paul ROHLING - Frank John ROHLING and Helen SPEYER, Parents;
Margaret HAHN and Paul SCHNEE, Godparents; Born December 18, 1879;
Baptized October 31, 1880; #910

John Ernest ROHMBIEL - John Ernest ROHMBIEL and Mary LEATHERN
(LEATHON?), Parents; Josephine KRAUSS, Godparent; Born February 27,
1891; Baptized March 12, 1891; #1518

Charles ROSE (BOSE) - Richard ROSE (BOSE) and -- FAUSTE, Parents;
K. HUSSEY, Godparent; Born September 21, 1870; Baptized July 1,
1871; #595

Josephine Mary ROTH - Maximilian Jos. ROTH and Catherine WILHELM,
Parents; Argau Augusta ROBERTSON, Godparent; Born April 21, 1891;
Baptized March 12, 1896; #1811

Maximiliam Joseph ROTH - Maximilian Jos. ROTH and Catherine WILHELM,
Parents; Argau Augusta ROBERTSON, Godparent; Born January 8, 1893;
Baptized March 12, 1896; #1812

John Henry ROTTER - John August ROTTER and Mary Ann FERI, Parents;
Frank SAROTELLI, Godparent; Born June 15, 1894; Baptized March 7,
1896; #1808

Bernard Eugene ROUBION - Bernard ROUBION and Ann PAYSSE, Parents;
Edward Eugene PAYSSE and Eugenia DOUGHERTY, Godparents; Born May 26,
1892; Baptized July 10, 1892; #1570

Henerietta ROUBION - Bernard ROUBION and Ann PAYSSE, Parents;
Sede DANTIN and Frank PAYSSE, Godparents; Born July 15, 1893;
Baptized August 6, 1893; #1617

William Albert ROURKE - John ROURKE and Mathilda RIESENER, Parents;
William WOOD and Minnie JAEGER, Godparents; Born September 1, 1897;
Baptized December 4, 1898; #1932

Bernice Joan ROWAN - James ROWAN and Sophie FREBOESIUS, Parents;
William ROWAN and Joan FREBOESIUS, Godparents; Born October 13,
1886; Baptized December 12, 1886; #1298

Margaret Joan ROWAN - William ROWAN and Catherine WALLSTEIN,
Parents; Martha BARRITT and Clemens MARTIN, Godparents; Born April 15,
1896; Baptized June 7, 1896; #1831

Eugene William RUDA - Florian RUDA and Ann JERIE, Parents; Henry
SKARKE, Godparent; Born December 13, 1894; Baptized December 25,
1894; #1897

Agnes Caroline RUECKE - Martin RUECKE and Ida MISBL, Parents;
John RUECKE and Caroline RUECKE, Godparents; Born January 16,
1869; Baptized February 7, 1869; #509

Bernard RUEHL - G. Bernard (n.c.) RUEHL and Edwarda P. SHAW, Parents;
Henry SCHAEFER and Anna SCHAEFER, Godparents; Born May 18, 1887;
Baptized March 9, 1894; #1653

Julius Charles RUIZ - Julius W. RUIZ and Emily POPULAR, Parents;
Charles POPULAR and Sophie BLEIKE, Godparents; Born July 6, 1890;
Baptized September 14, 1890; #1504

Laura Evelyn RUMBUEHL - Henry RUMBUEHL and Anna GILLET, Parents;
Paul BAULARD and Amelia BARONA, Godparents; Born June 14, 1874;
Baptized September 13, 1874; #724

John Robert RUMBUEHL - Ernest RUMBUEHL and Mary LEATHON, Parents;
Augusta AULL and Henry PASCHETHE, Godparents; Born May 13, 1892;
Baptized June 26, 1892; #1569

Wilhelmina Eliz. RUMBUEHL - Ernest RUMBUEHL and Mary MOORE, Parents;
Charles H. CASSEL and Augusta AUL, Godparents; Born October 11,
1894; Baptized December 2, 1894; #1692

John Charles RUPPERT - Joseph RUPPERT and Agnes LANGHAUSEN, Parents;
Charles BARLEMANN and Mathilda MONI, Godparents; Born November 23,
1893; Baptized December 12, 1893; #1635

Blanche (Private) SALE - Levi SALE and Christine BRAMM, Parents;
Virginia BLANDEAU and August BLANCEAU, Godparents; Born December 11,
1866; Baptized May 9, 1866; #347

Anna SANDERSON - Oliver SANDERSON and Nellie LYONS, Parents;
Mary LYONS, Godparent; Born September 3, 1868; Baptized June 17,
1869; #523

Ann Elizabeth SANDERSON - James SANDERSON and Ada TERHENN, Parents;
Pauline SOMMER and Frank SOMMER, Godparents; Born July 8, 1859;
Baptized January 5, 1868; #396

Henry SCHAEFER - Christine (n.c.) SCHAEFER and Mary WONDER, Parents;
Philippine SHAW, Godparent; Born (Septmeber) --, 1853; Baptized
September 3, 1860; #16

Cecil Emma SCHMIDT - Frederic SCHMIDT and Joan VITTER, Parents;
Anthony AMADO and Emma LEROSE, Godparents; Born May 26, 1895;
Baptized August 11, 1895; #1728

Estelle Marie SCHMIDT - Buchanan SCHMIDT and Lillie SCHREIBER,
Parents; Gabriel MONFORT and Theresa FLEUR, Godparents; Baptized
June 28, 1894; #1669

George Buchanan SCHMIDT - Buchanan (n.c.) SCHMIDT and Lillie
SCHREIBER, Parents; Elizabeth SCHREIBER, Godparent; Born November 17,
1886; Baptized March 1, 1887; #1315

George William SCHMIDT - Buchanan (n.c.) SCHMIDT and Lillie
SCHREIBER, Parents; Frank SCHREIBER and Rosa FLUEHR, Godparents;
Born May 29, 1885; Baptized December 17, 1885; #1204

Frederic Sebastian SCHLITTLER - N. N. Anonymous and N. N. Anonymous,
Parents; F. FALTENMEYER, Godparent; Baptized Arpil 12, 1873; #660

Nicolas William SCHLITTLER - Fridolm SCHLITTLER and Margaret
BINSBACHER, Parents; William WEBER and Teresa REHRMANN, Godparents;
Born September 11, 1867; Baptized December 1, 1867; #388

Albert Henry SCHMIDT - Buchanan SCHMIDT and Lilian MEURI, Parents;
Mary MEURI, Godparent; Born May 15, 1895; Baptized June 12, 1895;
#1718

Anna Louise SCHMIDT - Frederic SCHMIDT and Joan VITTER, Parents;
Victor VITTER and Louise AMADO, Godparents; Born September 15,
1896; Baptized June 11, 1897; #1883

John Henry (Foundling) - Parents unknown; Christian and Wife
SCHAEFER, Adopted; Christine SCHAEFER and Philippine SHAW, Godparents;
Born August 27, 1860; Baptized September 3, 1860; #17

Ferdinand SCHAER - Stephen SCHAER and Anna CHRISTIAN, Parents;
Ferdinand YOUNG and Ann EDWARDS, Godparents; Born October 3, 1874;
Baptized October 25, 1874; #729

Joseph SCHAER - Stephen SCHAER and Ann (n.c.) CHRISTIANSEN, Parents;
John MAURER and Caroline MAURER, Godparents; Born May 26, 1884;
Baptized June 1, 1884; #1072

Ernest Raymond SCHARF - Herman SCHARF and Theresa HIRTH, Parents;
Adolph ZAEPFEL and Anna HERTWICK, Godparents; Born January 4, 1895;
Baptized February 3, 1895; #1703

Herman Charles SCHARF - Herman SCHARF and Theodora SHIRK, Parents;
Gebhard GOHM and Louis GOHM, Godparents; Born November 30, 1898;
Baptized January 29, 1899; #1938

Anna Musline SCHERER - Ferdinand SCHERER and Elizabeth GREEN,
Parents; Josephine ALBERTI and Frederic PALEGLAW, Godparents;
Born September 24, 1896; Baptized February 21, 1897; #1869

Henry Joseph SCHIRMER - Henry SCHIRMER and Anna PETIT, Parents;
Anna HAENLEIN, Godparent; Born April 5, 1890; Baptized May 22, 1890;
#1488

Eva SCHLICK - James SCHLICK and Elizabeth MALTA, Parents; Elizabeth
SELENSKY and C. W. BARNES, Godparents; Born November 22, 1895;
Baptized December 22, 1895; #1793

Alma Emma SCHNEIDER - Charles SCHNEIDER and Theresa LOFFERRS,
Parents; Helen SOMMER and Emma SCHNEIDER, Godparents; Born June 25,
1877; Baptized March 20, 1893; #1598

Anna SCHNEIDER - Adolph SCHNEIDER and Josephine Adolphine GRUENDEL,
Parents; Conrad VOGT and Anna GRUEN, Godparents; Born March 19,
1865; Baptized August 27, 1865; #228

Carolina Josephine SCHNEIDER - William Adolph SCHNEIDER and Josephine
GRUENDEL, Parents; John Peter MUELLER and Caroline ---, Godparents;
Born June 5, 1861; Baptized March 23, 1862; #70

Charles William SCHNEIDER - Henry Geo. SCHNEIDER and Anna CALLAHAN,
Parents; William CALLAHAN and Catherine SCHNEIDER, Godparents;
Born -- 15, --; Baptized November 3, 1872; #635

Corinne Sarah Anna SCHNEIDER (married ole Richard ANDERSON--annuncia-
tion--Houston 6/21/1919) - Henry SCHNEIDER and Corinne MICKE,
Parents; Christian Chas. BECKER and Sara BECKER, Godparents;
Born March 29, 1895; Baptized March 26, 1898; #

Frederic Peter SCHNEIDER - Wilhelmina SCHNEIDER and Adolphina
GRUENDEL, Parents; Peter MAURER and Louise MAURER, Godparents;
Born November 23, 1857; Baptized April 29, 1860; #1

Gladys Lilian Aloysia SCHNEIDER - Henry SCHNEIDER and Corinne MICKE,
Parents; Mrs. MILLER (by proxy) and Anna SCHNEIDER, Godparents;
Born June 9, 1896; Baptized March 26, 1898; #1909

Herman SCHNEIDER - Adolph SCHNEIDER and Adolphine GRUENDEL, Parents;
Lucy MAURER (by proxy) and Herman MAURER, Godparents; Born
October 12, 1867; Baptized January 19, 1868; #399

Peter SCHNEIDER - Wm. Adolph SCHNEIDER and Adolphina GRUENDEL,
Parents; Peter BOCK and Susanna BOCK, Godparents; Born September 1,
1859; Baptized April 29, 1860; #2

Theresa Josephine SCHNEIDER - Adolph SCHNEIDER and Adolphina
GRUENDEL, Parents; Thersa LEINBACH, Godparent; Born November 4,
1863; Baptized January 14, 1864; #137

Gottlieb Amadius Louis SCHNITTGER - Gottlieb SCHNITTGER and Emma
WIEGOND, Parents; Herman Louis KRAUS, Godparent; Born August 25,
1883; Baptized October 5, 1883

Alma Theresa SCHOCKE - John SCHOCKE and Catherine (n.c.) MC GRAW,
Parents; Theresa SCHOCKE, Godparent; Born November 1, 1883; Baptized
December 1, 1883; #1035

Mary Helen Spier SCHMIDT - John I. SCHMIDT and Bertha GALLASHAW,
Parents; James GALLASHAW (by proxy) and Helen ROSS, Godparents;
Born April 10, 1885; Baptized April 16, 1885; #1152

Paul Ernest SCHMIDT - Peter SCHMIDT and Catherine THEILACKER,
Parents; Rosa BILD, Godparent; Born March 17, 1883; Baptized June 18,
1883; #1011

William Raymond SCHMIDT - John SCHMIDT and Nothburga C. WILZ,
Parents; William BLUM and Victoria SCHMIDT, Godparents; Baptized
May 11, 1871; #591 B

Alice Cecile SCHMIDT - Bauk SCHMIDT and Lily SCHREIBER, Parents;
Agnes MEURI, Godparent; Born August 2, 1896; Baptized September 7,
1896; #1849

Helen SCHMIDT - Buchanan (n.c.) SCHMIDT and Lily SCHREIBER,
Parents; Mary SCHREIBER, Godparent; Born May 19, 1883; Baptized
July 1, 1883; #1013

James Buchanan SCHMIDT - Buchanan SCHMIDT and Lillie SCHREIBER,
Parents; Julia MARI, Godparent; Born June 6, 1892; Baptized
August 15, 1892; #1576

John SCHMIDT (convert) - Valentine RITZLER and -- SCHUBERT, Godparents;
26 years; Baptized December 24, 1868; #500

Ludmilla SCHMIDT - John WCHMIDT and Teresa KUBICK, Parents; Joseph
MANOWSKI and Anna WINKLER, Godparents; Born 1867; Baptized May 14,
1867; #349

Ann Teresa SCHOCKE - Christian SCHOCKE and Teresa MUEHE, Parents;
Mary RICKE, Godparent; Born March 30, 1866; Baptized April 12,
1866; #279

Anna Wilhelmina SCHOCKE - John SCHOCKE and Othilia HAHNREITER,
Parents; Wilhelmina HENKEL and Elizabeth SCHOCKE, Godparents;
Born January 29, 1894; Baptized March 4, 1894; #1652

Anthony Frederic SCHOCKE - William Frederic SCHOCKE and Theresa
REIHMANN, Parents; Anthony SOMMER and Anna SHAEFER, Godparents;
Born September 9, 1882; Baptized September 19, 1882; #980

Bertha Emma SCHOCKE - Herman SCHOCKE and Christian MARX, Parents;
Albert BRAMMER and Emma MARX, Godparents; Born March 21, 1892;
Baptized April 17, 1892; #1556

Elizabeth Agnes SCHOCKE - John SCHOCKE and Theresa MAY, Parents;
Theresa ROEHRMAN, Godparent; Born July 14, 1874; Baptized July 26,
1874; #716

Henry Joseph SCHOCKE - Herman SCHOCKE and Christina MARX, Parents;
Elizabeth SCHOCKE, Godparent; Born August 3, 1889; Baptized
August 11, 1889; #1444

Herman Maurice SCHOCKE - Christian SCHOCKE and Theresa MUEHE,
Parents; Herman TROST and Mary RICKE, Godparents; Born October 15,
1860; Baptized November 11, 1860; #26

Joseph Louis SCHOCKE - Herman SCHOCKE and Christine MARX, Parents;
Joseph RICKE and Valeriana RICKE, Godparents; Born October 21, 1893;
Baptized November 5, 1893; #1628

Catherine SCHOCKE - John SCHOCKE and Catherine (n.c.) MC GRAW,
Parents; Herman SCHOCKE and Elise SCHOCKE, Godparents; Born
December 24, 1885; Baptized January 31, 1886; #1214

Cecilia SCHOCKE - John SCHOCKE and Catherine MC GRAW, Parents;
Herman SCHOCKE and Theresa SCHOCKE, Godparents; Born July 3, 1887;
Baptized July 19, 1891 (conditional); #1523

Christian SCHOCKE - Chas. SCHOCKE and Theresa MUEHE, Parents;
Christina SCHOCKE and Theresa FINN, Godparents; Born March 17,
1821; Baptized January 27, 1898 (conditional); #1900

Clara Margaret Joan SCHOCKE - William SCHOCKE and Theresa HOCKMANN,
Parents; August GENGLER, Godparent; Born July 9, 1896; Baptized
July 9, 1896; #1842

Leona Marie SCHOCKE - John SCHOCKE and Catherine (n.c.) MC GRAW,
Parents; Mary SCHOCKE (Mary Eliz. see TSCHOCKE), Godparent; Born
August 5, 1882; Baptized April 19, 1883; #1004

William Blasius SCHOCKE (married Anna Lee WILLIAMS, 7/2/1913,
St. Patrick, Galveston) - William SCHOCKE and Theresa ROEHRMANN,
Parents; William KRONE and Theresa SCHOCKE, Godparents; Born
February 3, 1885; Baptized February 17, 1885; #1126

Henry SCHOELLER - N. N. Anonymous and N. N., Parents; Jac. F. LAUTH,
Godparent; Born April 2, 1859; Baptized March 23, 1885 (conditional);
#1145

Walter William SCHOELLMANN (married Grace Loretta MALONE, St. Mary's,
Temperanceville, Ohio, 28 July 1914) - Wm. F. SCHOELLMANN and
Philippine WINDMEYER, Parents; William WINDMEYER and Cecil KING,
Godparents; Born December 10, 1892; Baptized March 19, 1893; #1599

Bernard August SCHOENBERG - John Bernard August SCHOENBERG and
Bell Joan Augusta Louise ? BROSIG, Parents; Charles BROSIG and
Mary BROSIG, Godparents; Born April 20, 1895; Baptized December 1,
1895; #1739

Julius Andrew SCHOENBERG - August Julius SCHOENBERG and Louise
BROSIG, Parents; Julius SCHUELKE and Ann PETERSON, Godparents;
Born September 4, 1898; Baptized November 6, 1898; #1929

Elizabeth SCHREIBER - Herman SCHREIBER and Rosina FLUEHE, Parents;
John GENGLER and Elizabeth HAGEMANN, Godparents; Born January 9,
1865; Baptized March 12, 1865; #192

Francis Herman SCHREIBER - Herman SCHREIBER and Rose FLUEHE, Parents;
Francis SOMMER and Catherine KRAUS, Godparents; Born April 8, 1868;
Baptized April 22, 1868; #419

Frank Herman SCHREIBER - Herman Frank SCHREIBER and Ida CASTELLO,
Parents; Born June 11, 1892; Baptized June 12, 1892; #1567

Herman John SCHREIBER - Herman John SCHREIBER and Rosina FLUEHE,
Parents; John GENGLER and Rosina SAMMET, Godparents; Born February 6,
1863; Baptized March 1, 1863; #101

Margaret Frances SCHREIBER - Henry Herman SCHREIBER and Rosina
FLUEHE, Parents; Frank SAMMER and Margaret GENGLER, Godparents;
Born August 28, 1861; Baptized September 22, 1861; #55

Mary SCHREIBER - Herman SCHREIBER and Rosina FLUEHE, Parents;
Mary KOEHLER, Godparent; Born July 30, 1866; Baptized September 16,
1866; #314

Anna Elizabeth SCHUCHARDT - N. N. Anonymous and N. N., Parents; Mary
BUHL, Godparent; Baptized February 27, 1855; #1131

Inez Marie SCHULER - Adolph SCHULER and Catherine SCHREMPP, Parents;
Bernard SCHREMPP and Amelia Mary GARTH, Godparents; Born December 21,
1898; Baptized February 8, 1899; #1942

Nelly Fredericka SCHULER - Adolph SCHULER and Catherine SCHREMPP,
Parents; Margaret Fredericka BREUDLER and Bernard SCHREMPP, Godparents;
Born December 15, 1896; Baptized February 8, 1899; #1941

-- SCHULTE - Henry SCHULTE and Clara WEBER, Parents; John RIKE,
Godparent; Baptized May 4, 1873; #665

Herold Alphonse Peter SCHULTE - Jos. John SCHULTE and Aloysia
VIEHMANN, Parents; Peter GENGLER and Theresa GENGLER, Godparents;
Born October 10, 1897; Batpized October 24, 1897; #1894

Mary Theresa SCHULTE - Henry SCHULTE and Clara WEBER, Parents;
John WEBER and Theresa WEBER, Godparents; Born April 25, 1875;
Baptized May 5, 1875; #748

Peter Henry SCHULTE - Henry SCHULTE and Clara WEBER, Parents;
Peter MULLER, Godparent; Born February 14, 1872; Baptized February 25,
1872; #612

Albert Raphael SCHULTZ - Henry (n.c.) SCHULTZ and Anna Eliz.
SCHUCHARDT, Parents; Jac. F. LAUTH, Godparent; Born January 14,
1879; Baptized June 17, 1885; #1170

Augustine SCHULTZ - August SCHULTZ and Mary ARNOLD, Parents;
Pauline ARNOLD, Godparent; Born June 15, 1860; Baptized July 25,
1860; #13

Ernest Gabriel SCHULTZ - Henry (n.c.) SCHULTZ and Ann Eliz.
SCHUCHARDT, Parents; Jac. F. LAUTH, Godparent; Born March 18, 1874;
Baptized June 17, 1885; #1169

August Theodore SCHWARZBACH - Theodore SCHWARZBACH and Mary VOGT,
Parents; Frank SAMMET and Helen SCHWARZBACH, Godparents; Born
March 11, 1886; Baptized April 25, 1886; #1225

Henry Joseph Eugene SCHWENDINGER - Joseph SCHWENDINGER and Mary
NUTT, Parents; Anna PEINE, Godparent; Born August 14, 1875; Baptized
October 3, 1875; #759

Cora SEAWELL - James SEAWELL and Josephine AYRES, Parents; Mary
MOSCHINI, Godparent; Born March 27, 1878; Baptized April 28, 1887;
#1337

Cordelia SEAWELL (married Romeo ROMAN, Holy Rosary, Galveston,
2/4/1915) - James SEAWELL and Josephine AYRES, Parents; Lillie
SEAWELL, Godparent; Born August 31, 1882; Baptized April 28, 1887;
#1338

James Joseph SEAWELL - N. N. Anonymous and N. N., Parents; Joseph
POPLIER and Mary MOSCHIM, Godparents; Born October 18, 1870;
Baptized February 27, 1887; #1314

Leo SEAWELL - James SEAWELL and Josephine AYRES, Parents; Chas.
BEE and Mary MOSCHINI, Godparents; Born October 4, 1875; Baptized
April 28, 1887; #1335

Lillie Temora SEAWELL - James SEAWELL and Josephine AYRES, Parents;
Mary MOSCHINI, Godparent; Born June 27, 1868; Baptized April 28,
1887; #1336

Herman SEBASTIAN (Alta Loma) - John SEBASTIAN and Regina ZEILER,
Parents; Margaret POICHET, Godparent; Born June 10, 1899; Baptized
September 12, 1899; #1962

Rosa Stephania SEBASTIAN - John SEBASTIAN and Regina FEILER,
Parents; Catherine FOWLER and Nicholas MOLSAM, Godparents; Born
December 18, 1894; Baptized January 2, 1895; #1698

Susan Regina Wilhelmina SEEL - Louis SEEL and Regina DIRKS, Parents;
L. FUNK and W. A. FUNK, Godparents; Born September 6, (1875);
Baptized March 2, 1866; #797

John Louis SEGNANOVICZ (married Loys REIMSCHISAEL, Cathedral,
Galveston, 12/2/1919) - Nicholas SEGNANOVICZ and Magdalen LEONTON,
Parents; John KIRKER and Helen KIRKER, Godparents; Born January 12,
1885; Baptized March 15, 1885; #1143

Anna SELENKI - John SELENKI and Margaret LENZ, Parents; Christian
BAUMANN and Anna TERRY, Godparents; Born November 18, 1895;
Baptized December 8, 1895; #1740

Ann Mary SELENSKI - Peter SELENSKI and Catherine SCHLACHTER,
Parents; Anthony GABRIEL and Ann Mary WOLFE, Godparents; Born
March 14, 1894; Baptized March 18, 1894; #1655

Irene Stella Mary SIEFFERT - Robert SIEFFERT and Emma ARDISSON,
Parents; Elizabeth HAGEMANN, Godparent; Born November 25, 1880;
Baptized May 11, 1881; #925

Elenora Mary SEEL - Louis SEEL and Regina DIRKS, Parents; Mary
THORMOLEN, Godparent; Born April 4, 1879; Baptized March 3, 1883;
#990

Louise Barbara SEEL - Louis SEEL and Regina DIRKS, Parents; Barbara
KAHMER and G. WINDMEYER, Godparents; Born February 29, 1872;
Baptized June 2, 1872; #623

Sophie Mary Josephine SEEL - Louis SEEL and Regina DIRKS, Parents;
Michael TICKS and Sophie FUNK, Godparents; Born November 1, 1869;
Baptized February 20, 1870; #546

Catherine SELENSKI - Caspar SELENSKI and Margaret OTTWALD, Parents;
Catherine KRAUS, Godparent; Born November 2, 1894; Baptized
November 18, 1894; #1894

August Herman SELLER - Herman SELLER and Mary ST. LERER, Parents;
August SCHULTZ by Theresa SCHULTZ, Godparents; Born May 4, 1873;
Baptized May 28, 1873; #668

Frank Joseph SELLERS (married Cath. Brigid BROWN, St. Patrick,
Galveston, 3/3/1919) - Sylvester SELLERS and Sarah MEYER, Parents;
Mary Ann ---, Godparent; Born November 2, 1898; Baptized December 21,
1898; #1934

John Bernard SELLERS - Sylvester SELLERS and Sara MEYER, Parents;
Bernard WILLINGER and Mary Eva KOEHLER, Godparents; Born September 2,
1896; Baptized September 23, 1896; #1850

Sylvester Frederic Henry SELLERS - James SELLERS and Elizabeth
SELLERS, Parents; Anna MAYER, Godparent; Born July 8, 1871; Baptized
May 15, 1900; #1992

Aloysia Mary Fides SENECHAL - Louis SENECHAL and Rose GREENROD,
Parents; Mary PEINE and Peter GENGLER, Godparents; Born May 21,
1891; Baptized June 21, 1891; #1521

Harriette Rose Leocadia SENECHAL - Louis Wm. SENECHAL and Rose
GRINROOD, Parents; Henry GRINROOD and Fides GRINROOD, Godparents;
Born December 9, 1896; Baptized January 24, 1897; #1863

Geronina Josephine SERRA - Joseph SERRA and Anna MORGENTHALER,
Parents; Emmanuel STURLESS and Anna BUTSCHER, Godparents; Born
January 23, 1885; Baptized October 30, 1885; #1198

Arthur Alexander SHAW - Frank D. SHAW and Mary Catherine THOMAS,
Parents; Agnes Cecil DOERR, Godparent; Born January 5, 1879;
Baptized March 18, 1879; #379

Camille Roland SHAW - Frank Michael and Mary Catherine THORMAN,
Parents; M. SABELL and Frank BLANEY, Godparents; Born July 27,
1874; Baptized September 17, 1874; #727

Catherine Margaret SHAW - Michael SHAW and Anna Catherine MEYER,
Parents; Henry C. SHAFER and Mary MEYERS, Godparents; Born March 22,
1879; Baptized June 5, 1881; #928 B

Charles Leonard SHAW - Michael SHAW and Anna MEYER, Parents;
Florence IVY, Godparent; Born -- 22, 1882; Baptized August 14,
1884; #1088

Daniel Henry Pallais SHAW - Frank D. SHAW and Catherine THOMAS,
Parents; Henry SCHAEFER and Philippine BRUCH, Godparents; Born
May 12, 1866; Baptized July 29, 1866; #301

Joseph SHAW - Michael Frank SHAW and Mary Catherine THOMAS, Parents;
T. BLUM and Philippine BLUM, Godparents; Born September 18, 1877;
Baptized November 13, 1877; #821

Marshal William Werner SHAW - Michael SHAW and Ann Catherine
MEYER, Parents; Henry C. SHAEFFER and Mary MEYER, Godparents;
Born July 25, 1880; Baptized June 5, 1881; #928 A

Mary Magdalen SHAW - F. R. SHAW and Mary Catherine THOMAS, Parents;
M. SHAW and Mary VALAIS, Godparents; Born May 28, 1873; Baptized
June, 1873; #671

Philippine Margaret SHAW - Francis SHAW and Mary THOMAS, Parents;
Philippine BLUM, Godparent; Born September 12, 1880; Baptized
October 24, 1880; #908

William Thomas Augustine SHAW - Michael SHAW and Anna MEYER,
Parents; Florence IVY, Godparent; Born June 13, 1884; Baptized
August 14, 1884; #1089

Susan Elizabeth SHETLEY - William SHETLEY and Ada TERHENN, Parents;
John H. STONER and Helen STONER, Godparents; Born January 1, 1866;
Baptized September 8, 1867; #369

William F. SHETLEY (convert) - Baptized April 17, 1868; #418 A

Cecil Ada SHETLEY (convert) - Baptized April 17, 1868; #418 B

Martin SILENSKI (Arcadia, Texas) - Peter SILENSKI and Catherine
SCHLACHTER, Parents; Frieda HECK, Godparent; Born September 14,
1899; Baptized October 22, 1899; #1965

Ann Mary SKARKE - Charles SKARKE and Ann MALCHER, Parents; Mary
HENRICH and Frank BOENING, Godparents; Born August 4, 1898;
Baptized August 18, 1898; #1923

Charles Frederic SKARKE - Chas. Jos. SKARKE and Ann MELCHER,
Parents; Carl SKARKE and Mary SKARKE, Godparents; Born November 11,
1895; Baptized December 25, 1895; #1796

John SKRENIG - John SKRENIG and Ann BOLAG, Parents; Joseph KELLER,
Godparent; Born March 29, 1861; Baptized May 19, 1861; #45

Adolph August SMITH - C. P. SMITH and Elizabeth ALLEN, Parents;
Elizabeth PARKER, Godparent; Born December 22, 1886; Baptized
March 13, 1887; #1319

Apollonia Martina SMITH - James SMITH and Josephine Louise ENGEL,
Parents; Martin GLYNN and Apollonia GOYES, Godparents; Born January 3,
1886; Baptized February 28, 1886; #1219

Edward August SMITH - Buchanan SMITH and Lillie SCHREIBER, Parents;
Edward SMITH, Godparent; Born September 28, 1890; Baptized January 30,
1891; #1514

Frank Joseph SMITH - Buchanan SMITH and Caroline SCHREIBER, Parents;
Emil WEBER and Rosina FLUEHR, Godparents; Born November 15, 1888;
Baptized January 6, 1889; #1422

Helen Frances SMITH - Frank SMITH and Ella EKERT, Parents; Elizabeth
BARTHAL, Godparent; Born August 22, 1896; Baptized March 22, 1897;
#1873

Robert Clarence SMITH - Buchanan SMITH and Lillie SCHREIBER, Parents;
Mary MEURY, Godparent; Born November 27, 1897; Baptized April 10,
1898; #1912

Sarah Louise SMITH - Geo. James SMITH and Louise ENGELHARDT,
Parents; Anthony SOMMER and Frieda ENGELHARDT, Godparents; Born
September 5, 1897; Baptized April 19, 1898; #1914

Thomas Frank SMITH - John SMITH and Emma --, Parents; V. GURY,
Godparent; Born July 24, 1887; Baptized August 22, 1887 (private);
#1356

William Henry SMITH - James SMITH and Mary INGRAM, Parents; William
MURPHY and Mary ALBERTI, Godparents; Born January 6, 1897; Baptized
February 14, 1897; #1866

August Thomas SOLAN - Thomas SOLAN and Elnora BLANDEAU, Parents;
August BLANDEAU and Louise ELSWORTH, Godparents; Born January 22,
1871; Baptized August 13, 1871; #594 A

Frances Elizabeth SOLAN - Thomas SOLAN and Elnora BLANDEAU, Parents;
Leopold BLANDEAU and Emily BAUDENON, Godparents; Born January 20,
1869; Baptized September 2, 1871; #596

Julia Marie SOLAN - Thomas SOLAN and Lenora BLANDEAU, Parents;
Felix BESIER and Alex WHITE, Godparents; Born August 29, 1873;
Baptized September 3, 1873; #680 B

Aleine Ruth SOMMER - Jos. SOMMER and Odilia HEIMANN, Parents;
Rudolph KETTELER and Theresa SOMMER, Godparents; Born September 8,
1894; Baptized October 14, 1894; #1686

Amelia Theresa SOMMER - Ferdinand SOMMER and Anna GLASER, Parents;
August SOMMER and Amelia PILLURTZ, Godparents; Born August 28,
1877; Baptized October 16, 1877; #815

Ann Mary SOMMER - Frank SOMMER and Theresa SCHRADER, Parents;
Ferdinand SOMMER and Antonio BERGMANN, Godparents; Born January 4,
1869; Baptized January 31, 1869

Anna Theresa SOMMER - Ferdinand SOMMER and Ann GLASER, Parents;
Ferdinand JUNG and Theresa DELZ, Godparents; Born October 25,
1885; Baptized November 22, 1885; #1201

Anthony Peter SOMMER (married Lutie SPECHT, Holy Trinity, Dallas,
June 7, 1914) - Anthony SOMMER and Helen GENGLER, Parents; Peter
GENGLER and Anna SCHAEFER, Godparents; Born January 8, 1887;
Baptized February 13, 1887; #1309

Caroline Sophy SOMMER - Ferdinand SOMMER and Anna GLASER, Parents;
Joseph PRAKEL and Caroline RESSEL, Godparents; Born July 17, 1884;
Baptized August 10, 1884; #1086

Cecil Emma SOMMER - August SOMMER and Mary HERRGOTT, Parents;
Anthony SOMMER and Anna SOMMER, Godparents; Born May 6, 1884;
Baptized May 25, 1884; #1067

Elizabeth Amalia SOMMER - August SOMMER and Mary HERGOTT, Parents; Frank ROESSLER and Mary SOMMER, Godparents; Born August 16, 1889; Baptized September 22, 1889; #1447

Helen Theresa SOMMER - Anthony SOMMER and Helen GENGLER, Parents; John CROZIER and Theresa SCHOCKE, Godparents; Born December 30, 1880; Baptized January 30, 1881; #916

Henry Charles SOMMER - Anthony SOMMER and Helen GENGLER, Parents; Chas. SOMMER and Anna SCHAEFER, Godparents; Born October 2, 1878; Baptized November 3, 1878; #870

John Baptist SOMMER - Frank SOMMER and Theresa KRAUS, Parents; Stephen LANGE and Mary HERRMANN, Godparents; Born January 26, 1862; Baptized February 23, 1862; #68

Mary SOMMER - Ferdinand SOMMER and Anna YOUNG, Parents; Anthony KAPER and Anna FITSCH, Godparents; Born February 18, 1873; Baptized June 15, 1873; #675

Mary Agnes SOMMER - Anthony SOMMER and Helen GENGLER, Parents; Ferdinand RESSEL and Mary SOMMER, Godparents; Born April 16, 1883; Baptized May 6, 1883; #1005

Mary Louise SOMMER - August SOMMER and Mary HERGOTT, Parents; Charles SOMMER and Louise Sara KEVENY, Godparents; Born December 11, 1878; Baptized April 16, 1879; #884

Mathilda Anna SOMMER - Ferdinand SOMMER and Anna CLOSSEN, Parents; Charles SOMMER and Anna GENGLER, Godparents; Baptized April 25, 1875; #746

Theresa Gabriel SOMMER - August SOMMER and Mary HERGOTT, Parents; Charles SOMMER and Theresa SOMMER, Godparents; Born June 26, 1891; Baptized August 2, 1891; #1526

Sara Mary SPANN (slave) - Elenor SPANN, Parent; C. M. PRICE, Godparent; 45 years; #46

Carolina SPIKER - Theodore SPIKER and Mary --, Parents; Caroline WOLFGANG, Godparent; Born April 25, 1873; Baptized June 25, 1874; #710

Joan Lucy SPIZA - Anthony SPIZA and Inez BARCELO, Parents; Joan SPIZA and Bernard SPIZA, Godparents; Born June 2, 1875; Baptized September 12, 1875; #762

William STANZER - Otto STANZER and Anna GERHOLD, Parents; William STANZER and Helen HAENLEIN, Godparents; Born December 31, 1877; Baptized March 20, 1878; #838

Anna Barbara STECHMANN - August STECHMANN and Barbara HILLER, Parents; Herman KRAUS and Ann MAURER (by proxy), Godparents; Born June 2, 1885; Baptized June 13, 1885; #1168

August Rudolf STECHMANN (Hanover, Germany) - Marriage fixed up with Barbara HILLER; Jac. F. LAUTH, Godparent; Born September 7, 1836; Baptized September 6, 1884

Barbara Josephine STECHMANN (married Wm. L. STANFORD, S. Heart, Galveston, October 8, 1912) - August STECHMANN and Barbara HILLER, Parents; Rovert MC NAMORA and Margaret STECHMANN, Godparents; Born January 24, 1888; Baptized February 19, 1888; #1375

Clara Josephine STECHMANN - Chas. Wm. STECHMANN and Jeanette Leona MONFORD, Parents; Chas. PRESTON and Theresa Helen MONFORD, Godparents; Born January 21, 1900; Baptized March 25, 1900; #1981

Edna Barbara STECHMANN - Chas. STECHMANN and Joan MONFORD, Parents;
August STECHMANN and Barbara STECHMANN, Godparents; Born August 17,
1893; Baptized October 15, 1893; #1622

George Joseph STECHMANN - August STECHMANN and Barbara HILLER,
Parents; Elizabeth STECHMANN, Godparent; Born April 23, 1874;
Baptized May 10, 1874; #705

James William STECHMANN - Chas. Wm. STECHMANN and Joan Antonia
MONFORD, Parents; Ambrose MONFORD and Bertha Elizabeth MONFORD,
Godparents; Born November 24, 1895; Baptized December 22, 1895;
#1795

Louise Josephine STECHMANN - August STECHMANN and Barbara HILLER,
Parents; Louise BECKMANN and Elizabeth STECHMANN, Godparents;
Born March 19, 1882; Baptized April 9, 1882; #963

Chas. Ambrose STEGMANN - Chas. Wm. STEGMANN and Janette MONFORD,
Parents; Edmund MONFRED and Margaret STEGMANN, Godparents; Born
February 28, 1892; Baptized April 24, 1892; #1558

Anna STENZEL - Charles STENZEL and Joan HAZELHORST, Parents;
Helen HAEHNLEIN, Godparent; Born March 31, 1860; Baptized June 15,
1864; #160

Charles Joseph STENZEL - Charles STENZEL and Joan HAZELHORST,
Parents; Wilhelmine HOERLING, Godparent; Born February 1, 1856;
Baptized September 8, 1864; #172

Clara STENZEL - Jos. Chas. STENZEL and Joan HASSELHORST, Parents;
Apollonia HILDEBRANDT, Godparent; Born March 25, 1866; Baptized
August 12, 1866; #308

George STENZEL - Chas. STENZEL and Joan HAZELHORST, Parents;
Helen HAEHNLEIN, Godparent; Born December 1, 1862; Baptized
June 15, 1864; #161

Helen STENZEL - Charles STENZEL and Adalaid GOEDECKE, Parents;
Helen HAENLEIN, Godparent; Born November 10, 1869; Baptized
December 26, 1869; #537

Mary STENZEL - Charles STENZEL and Joan HAZELHORST, Parents;
Helen HAEHNLEIN, Godparent; Born January 12, 1864; Baptized June 15,
1864; #162

Otto STENZEL - Charles STENZEL and Joan HAZELHORST, Parents;
William HOERLING, Godparent; Born January 5, 1854; Baptized
September 8, 1864; #171

William STENZEL - Charles STENZEL and Joan HAZELHORST, Parents;
Helen HAEHNLEIN, Godparent; Born January 8, 1858; Baptized June 15,
1864; #159

Frank Ernest STEPHENSON - E. N. STEPHENSON and Clara EVANS, Parents;
Mrs. H. H. HARMAN and Aloysius COMPRE (absent), Godparents; Born
July 10, 1885; Baptized August 9, 1885; #1180

Carolina STERNE - Frank STERNE and Mary HAUS, Parents; Nelly CLARK,
Godparent; Born November 10, 1877; Baptized September 21, 1882;
#981

Elizabeth Georgian STEWART - John L. STEWART and Henrietta PFLUEGER,
Parents; Mina PFLUEGER and Charles PFLUEGER, Godparents; Born
February 6, 1890; Baptized April 6, 1890; #1476

Elizabeth STOPPELBERG - Chas. Fr. STOPPELBERG and Mary Eliz.
WEBER, Parents; Caroline HOFBECK, Godparent; Baptized August 8,
1866 (private; ceremonies supplied October 7, 1866); #306

John STOPPELBERG - Carol Frederic STOPPELBERG and Mary Eliz. WEBER,
Parents; Mary KOEHLER, Godparent; Born January 20, 1864; Baptized
March 5, 1864; #143

Mary Elizabeth STOPPELBERG - Frederic STOPPELBERG and Eliz. WEBER,
Parents; Mary KOEHLER, Godparent; Born September 29, 1861; Baptized
November 2, 1861; #59

John William STONER - John Henry STONER and Helen HART, Parents;
Michael DUNCAN and Margaret HART, Godparents; Born February 22,
1867; Baptized March 9, 1867; #340

Mary Agnes STORK - Henry STORK and Anna FINK, Parents; Peter
GENGLER and Agnes GENGLER, Godparents; Born July 6, 1867; Baptized
August 11, 1867; #358

Robert Leo STRECKFUS - Henry Aloysius STRECKFUS and Theresa Mary
SCHOTT, Parents; Jos. SCHOTT and Emma SIEK, Godparents; Born
December 20, 1895; Baptized April 2, 1896; #1818

Mary Bertha Teresa Elizabeth STRUBE - Adolph STRUBE and Elizabeth
COERS, Parents; Teresa LEINBACH, Godparent; Born November 30,
1864; Baptized April 18, 1865; #196

Teresa Elizabeth STRUBE - Adolph STRUBE and Elizabeth COERS,
Parents; John Henry COERS and Teresa PRICE, Godparents; Born
October 8, 1866; Baptized January 1, 1867; #331

Wilhelmina Elizabeth STRUBE - Adolph STRUBE and Elizabeth COERS,
Parents; Elizabeth COERS, SR., Godparent; Born January 1, 1861;
Baptized October 10, 1861; #56

William STRUCK - N. N. Anonymous and Theresa STRUCK, Parents;
Frank RUETHER and Mary WERDEHAUSEN, Godparents; Born February 14,
1862; Baptized April 20, 1862; #74

Anna Catherine STUMPF - Wm. STUMPF and Mary SATTLER, Parents;
Adam SATTLER and Catherine SATTLER, Godparents; Born April 11,
1882; Baptized May 14, 1882; #967

Charles Ignothius STUMPF - William STUMPF and Mary (n.c.) SATTLER,
Parents; John KOEHLER and Mary KOEHLER, Godparents; Born August 7,
1884; Baptized August 31, 1884; #1091

Frances Mary STUMPF - Wm. STUMPF and Mary SATTLER, Parents; Theresa
KOCH, Godparent; Born August 7, 1878; Baptized August 31, 1878;
#864

Frank Adam William STUMPF (Baden, Germany) - Wm. STUMPF and Mary
SATTLER, Parents; F. R. WISSE and Catherine SATTLER, Godparents;
Born April 24, 1873; Baptized May 11, 1873; #664

Frank Joseph STUMPF - N. N. Anonymous and Theresa STUMPF (Nee?),
Parents; Mary Barbara BALIBESEH, Godparent; Baptized September 9,
1876; #782

John SULLIVAN - Wm. SULLIVAN and Ellen MC GILL, Parents; -- MEREDITH,
Godparent; Born July 9, 1870; Baptized August 7, 1870; #562

Adolph Henry TACQUARD - James TACQUARD and Julia JACOB, Parents;
Leo BROSSIER and Mary BROSSIER, Godparents; Henry BEGUIN and
Louise BEGUIN, Proxies; Born January 25, 1868; Baptized February 20,
1868; #403

Julia Emily TACQUARD - James TACQUARD and Julia JACOB, Parents;
Charles BOUTHERY and Zoe BOUTHERY, Godparents; Born August 7, 1881;
Baptized August 17, 1882; #972

Julius Leroy TACQUART - Julius TACQUART and Hedwig HENKEL, Parents;
George HENKEL and Leonida TACQUART, Godparents; Born March 23,
1896; Baptized June 21, 1896; #1833

Sadie Pauline TACQUART - Julius TACQUART and Hedwig HENKEL, Parents;
Charles HENKEL and Sarah BOCK, Godparents; Born June 19, 1894;
Baptized September 11, 1894; #1681

Julia (TUQUARD) TAQUARD - Henry E. TAQUARD and Martha PERRY,
Parents; Peter BRAEUTIGAN, Godparent; Born January 1, 1889; Baptized
July 21, 1890; #1502

Joan (Jeanne) TARGARONA - Peter TARGARONA and Isabel TAIT, Parents;
T. FONTAINE and -- NUESSE, Godparents; Born April 18, 1863;
Baptized January 30, 1870 (conditional; in Shreveport, La., Red
River); #543 B

Peter TARGARONA - Peter TARGARONA and Isabel TAIT, Parents; C.
QUINTARO, Godparent; Born January 3, 1861; Baptized January 30,
1870 (conditional; in Shreveport, La. Red River); #543 A

Elizabeth TARPY - Michael TARPY and Brigid COLYNAN, Parents;
Philip SAVAGE and Joan HUSSEY, Godparents; Born October 3, 1867;
Baptized January 25, 1868; #400

Wallace Anthony Lee TEUBUSCH - Stephen TEUBUSCH and Emma HEIMANN,
Parents; Anthony HEIMANN and Odilia HEIMANN, Godparents; Born
August 16, 1892; Baptized October 23, 1892; #1581

Anna THOMAS - Adam THOMAS andBarbara DUNKEN, Parents; Joseph
ANSTAETT, Godparent; Born October 22, 1845; Baptized September 24,
1863 (conditional); #126

Mary Catherine THOMAS - Adam THOMAS and Barbara DUNKEN, Parents;
Rev. Joseph ANSTAETT (sponsor), Godparent; Born November 10,
1843; Baptized September 24, 1863; #125

Anna Alice THOMPSON - William THOMPSON and Mary E. TEALE, Parents;
Albert DIEZ and Mrs. Anna RUEMBUEHL, Godparents; Born October 17,
1887; Baptized April 8, 1888; (in Chambers County); #1386

Ferris Eugene THOMPSON - William THOMPSON and Frances GERBER,
Parents; Angelina GOYES and Camille ODINOT, Godparents; Born
June 18, 1892; Baptized July 24, 1892; #1571

Guy Bernard THOMPSON - Guy B. (n.c.) THOMPSON and Mary I. QUINN,
Parents; Henry VOSS and Margaret MC DONALD, Godparents; Born
May 1, 1885; Baptized August 15, 1886; #1262

Adolph Paul THORMAHLEN - Adolph THORMAHLEN and Mary PLASECKA,
Parents; M. MUELLER, Godparent; Born August 20, 1878; Baptized
September 30, 1878; #867

Arnold Wm. Chas. THORMAHLEN - Arnold E. (n.c.) THORMAHLEN and
Mary Helen PIASECKA, Parents; Rev. Jac. F. LAUTH and Louise SEEL
(by proxy), Godparents; Born September 10, 1883; Baptized June 12,
1884; #1074

Mary Isabel Regina THORMAHLEN - Arnold E. THORMAHLEN and Mary
PIASECKA, Parents; Regina SEEL, Godparent; Born February 23, 1880;
Baptized March 3, 1883; #991

Charles Henry THRINGER - August THRINGER and Anna FAHRENBACH,
Parents; Rev. Ch. Ch. GREYENBUEHL (sponsor), Godparent; Born
June 2, 1869; Baptized January 23, 1872; #610

Rose May TICKLE (Eliz. Caroline see after FESSEL) (married Fred. Jos.
Kreft, St. Patricks, Galveston, April 24, 1950) - Joseph Mich.
TICKLE and Theresa MAURER, Parents; Ann HAUSINGER, Godparent; Born
October 2, 1898; Baptized October 30, 1898; #1927

Sara Elizabeth TILLEMANN - Frank TILLEMANN and Sophie DE MEERBERGER,
Parents; Rose GAMBERT, Godparent; Born September 9, 1876; Baptized
October 22, 1877; #820

Mary Frances TISCHENDORF - N. N. Anonymous and N. N., Parents;
Theresa MAURER, Godparent; Born October 14, 1867; Baptized December 24,
1885 (conditional); #1210

Anthony Joseph TIX - Michael TIX and Margaret WESER, Parents;
John Joseph KRAUS and Christina BRINK, Godparents; Born October 28,
1861; Baptized December 15, 1861; #61

Mary Davida Ada TOCK - David TOCK and Ann MONTEGUE, Parents;
Anna DOYLE, Godparent; Born January 31, 1869; Baptized March 18,
1869; #511

Frances Celina (Helenr) TOLKOWSKI - Frank TOLKOWSKI and Frances
MAINA, Parents; Theophile ZINGG and Frances ZINGG, Godparents;
Born December 30, 1884; Baptized May 24, 1885; #1163

Marion John Hy. TOMFOHRDEN - Alexander TOMFOHRDEN and Cath. FREY,
Parents; Joan KOENIG, Godparent; Born September 18, 1884; Baptized
October 16, 1884; #1105

Martha TOMFOHRDEN - Alexander TOMFOHRDEN and Catherine FREY,
Parents; Martha FREY, Godparent; Born February 10, 1886; Baptized
May 30, 1886; #1246

Henry Emil TOMFOHRDEN - Alexander TOMFOHRDEN and Catherine FREY,
Parents; Emily ZUBER, Godparent; Born September 22, 1887; Baptized
November 13, 1887; #1363

Frances Odilia TONIS - Emil TONIS and Anna ELSLER, Parents; Hedwig
ELSLER, Godparent; Born December 28, 1896; Baptized June 2, 1897;
#1877

Frederic Anton TOUEIGH - Theophilo TOUEIGH and Marian DREW, Parents;
Robert PHILIPSON and Catherine PHILIPSON, Godparents; Born April 8,
1888; Baptized May 27, 1888; #1395

Mary Elizabeth TOWSEY - -- TOWSEY and Elizabeth HALL, Parents;
Victor GURY and Mary HALL, Godparent; Born April 23, 1858; Baptized
August 2, 1865; #224

Frank TRAVA - Frank TRAVA and Wilhelmina SHAK, Parents; Frank
GIOZZA, Godparent; Born June 7, 1878; Baptized October 29, 1878;
#869

Mary Margaret TRENT - Thomas TRENT and Mary MAYER, Parents;
Born April 17, 1861; Baptized July 1, 1862; #87

Charles Jesse TRIACKER - Joseph TRIACKER and Elizabeth HEIMANN,
Parents; Frederic JAEGER and Catherine TRIACKER, Godparents;
Born January 8, 1887; Baptized February 20, 1887; #1313

Jesse Charles TRIACKER - Theodore TRIACKER and Elizabeth SMITH,
Parents; William JERSICH and Catherine CONZALES, Godparents;
Born January 6, 1883; Baptized March 18, 1883; #994

Julia Isabel TRIACKER - Joseph TRIACKER and Elizabeth HEIMANN,
Parents; Joseph TRIACKER and Catherine GONZALES (by proxy),
Godparents; Born December 16, 1882; Baptized February 11, 1883;
#988

Joseph TRIACKER - Theodore TRIACKER and Elizabeth SMITH, Parents;
Joseph TRIACKER and Josephine BLEICKE, Godparents; Born December 11,
1870; Baptized March 19, 1870; #554

(Sarah) Ottilia STRIACKER - Joseph TRIACKER and Elizabeth HEIMANN, Parents; Othilia HEIMANN, Godparents; Born September 9, 1884; Baptized November 2, 1884; #1109

Mary Helen TRIACKER - Theodore TRIACKER and Elizabeth SMITH, Parents; Mary HERRMANN, Godparent; Born January 3, 1887; Baptized January 9, 1887; #1305

Odilia Josephine TRIACCAR (see also DRIAKER) - Joseph TRIACCAR and Elizabeth HEIMANN, Parents; Odilia HEIMANN, Godparent; Born October 12, 1879; Baptized December 28, 1879; #892

Anna Marie Cecil TROST - Herman TROST and Sophie WIND, Parents; Henry PATTOF and Mrs. Caroline RICKE per Magd. GREYENBUEHL, Godparents; Born November 22, 1872; Baptized December 8, 1872; #643

Bernardine Josephine TROST - Herman TROST and Sophie WEDEMAIER, Parents; -- HOFBECK and Bernardine C. RICKE, Godparents; Born July 25, 1868; Baptized August 16, 1868; #423

Henry Louis TROST - Herman TROST and Sophie WEDEMAIER, Parents; Joseph PEINE and Caroline TSCHAECKE, Godparents; Born December 6, 1880; Baptized February 27, 1881; #917

Germanicus Morris TROST - Germanicus TROST and Sophie WEDEMAIER, Parents; John RICKE and Anna WEDEMAIER, Godparents; Born September 19, 1875; Baptized October 3, 1875; #764

John Francis TROST - Herman TROST and Sophie WEDEMAIER, Parents; John HOFBECK and Mary RICKE, Godparents; Born February 16, 1871; Baptized March 26, 1871; #579

Martin Louis TROST - Herman TROST and Sophia WEDEMAIER, Parents; Martin RICKE and Caroline HOFBECK, Godparents; Born February 21, 1879; Baptized May 11, 1879; #886

Mary Sophie TROST - Herman TROST and Sophie WEDEMAIER, Parents; Joseph PEINE and Caroline HOFBECK, Godparents; Born April 2, 1867; Baptized April 28, 1867; #346

Peter Alysius TROST - John TROST and Sophie WEDEMAIER, Parents; Peter Mathew GENGLER, Godparent; Born June 21, 1882; Baptized July 2, 1882; #971

Sophie TROST (nee WEDEMAIER, wife of Herman TROST) (convert) - Henrion DEICON, Godparent; Born October 26, 1844; Baptized December 23, 1869; #534

Sophie Theresa TROST - Herman TROST and Sophie WEDEMAIER, Parents; Theresa REHRMAN and Frederic WEDEMAYER, Godparents; Born October 2, 1869; Baptized October 31, 1869; #532

Mary Josephine TROUETTE - John A. TROUETTE and Louise CHABEAU, Parents; C. WISSNIGER, Godparent; Born June 30, 1883; Baptized July 2, 1883; #1014

Mary TRUCHARD - John TRUCHARD and Hedwig DEHNISCH, Parents; Peter LASSAIGNE and Mary TRUCHARD, Godparents; Born November 8, 1897; Baptized December 19, 1897; #1897

Mary Elizabeth (SCHOCKE) TSCHOCKE - Christian TSCHOCKE and Theresa MUEHE, Parents; Mary Eliz. MUEHE, Godparent; Born November 3, 1862; Baptized November 21, 1862; #93

Louis TURNER - N. N. Anonymous and N. N., Parents; Baptized August 8, 1866 (U.S. Military Hospital); #305

John Anthony VAGLIENTI - John VAGLIENTI and Theresa SERACO, Parents; John VIOTTO, Godparent; Born August 28, 1893; Baptized June 2, 1895; #1716

Joseph Alexander VARGA - N. N. Anonymous and N. N., Parents; Baptized September --, 1876; #785

Elizabeth VARNELL - James (n.c.) VARNELL and Mechaelina GUSSMANN, Parents; Joseph HESSLER and Catherine KESSLER, Godparents; Baptized December 6, 1896; #1861

Clara Henrietta VAN DEN ENDE - Wm. VAN DEN ENDE and Mary (n.c.) BECKMAN, Parents; Henry SCHULTE and Clara SCHULTE, Godparents; Born September 1, 1886; Baptized September 12, 1886; #1268

Elizabeth VAN DEN ENDE - Wm. Simen Hubert VAN DEN ENDE and Mary (n.c.) BECKMANN, Parents; Elizabeth MARTIN and Emma M. A. VAN DEN ENDE, Godparents; Born January 25, 1874; Baptized April 15, 1883; #1002

Emma Mary Augusta VAN DEN ENDE - Wm. Simen Hubert VAN DEN ENDE and Mary (n.c.) BECKMAN, Parents; Eliz. MARTIN and Emma M. A. VAN DEN ENDE, Godparents; Born January 8, 1870; Baptized April 15', 1883; #1001

John Arnold VAN DEN ENDE - Wm. Simen Hubert VAN DEN ENDE and Mary (n.c.) BECKMANN, Parents; Eliz. MARTIN and Emma M. A. VAN DEN ENDE, Godparents; Born November 14, 1876; Baptized April 15, 1883; #1003

William Henry VAN DEN ENDE - Wm. VAN DEN ENDE and Mary BECKMAN, Parents; Henry MUELLER and Margaret MUELLER, Godparents; Born September 2, 1880; Baptized September 26, 1880; #906

Joseph Louis VAN STRUVE (convert) - Born November 21, 1840; Baptized May 7, 1865; #204

Joan Lennon VAUGHN (Bolivar Point) - Daniel VAUGHN and Anna VAUGHN, Parents; Chas. WARREN and Allen (Helen) WARREN, Godparents; Born December 2, 1887; Baptized April 2, 1888; #1384

Anna Mary VEICHT - Nicholas VEIGHT and Anna MAUKA, Parents; Conrad ESCHENBERG and Mary LEINBRIG, Godparents; Born December 23, 1881; Baptized January 15, 1882; #953

Agnes Josephine Elizabeth VERBERNE - John VERBERNE and Margaret MUELLER, Parents; John MEALEY and Elizabeth MEALEY, Godparents; Born January 21, 1887; Baptized March 19, 1887; #1320

Andrea Mary VERBERNE - John VERBERNE and Margaret (n.c.) MUELLER, Parents; Henry GRUENROTH and Emma HEER (by proxy), Godparents; Born August 18, 1883; Baptized August 27, 1883; #1020

Camille Mary VERBERNE - John VERBERNE and Margaret MUELLER, Parents; Thomas COUSINS and Mary DIRCK, Godparents; Born March 30, 1890; Baptized May 18, 1890; #1487

Gertrude Catherine VERBERNE - John VERBERNE and Margaret MUELLER, Parents; Peter BIERMANN and Catherine BIERMANN, Godparents; Born March 30, 1890; Baptized May 18, 1890; #1486

Henry William VERBERNE - John VERBERNE and Emma HERR, Parents; William HERR and mother, Godparents; Baptized March 31, 1894; #1660

Joseph Louis VERBERNE - John VERBERNE and Margaret MUELLER, Parents; Louis KOCH and Catherine BIERMANN (by proxy), Godparents; Born March 17, 1885; Baptized June 25, 1885; #1172

William Joseph VERBERNE - Andrew VERBERNE and Teresa HILDEBRAND, Parents; Jos. ELBERT and Scholastica ELBERT, Godparents; Born August 3, 1866; Baptized October 7, 1866; #320

Louis Joseph VILLENEUVE - John VILLENEUVE and Anna BONN, Parents;
Josephine MARRERO, Godparent; Born November 24, 1884; Baptized
January 2, 1885; #1119

Mary Ann Margaret VIOTTO - John VIOTTO and Angelina LERA, Parents;
Marino GELUSSIKE and Ann GELUSSIKE (second marriage (to I'SPOSSO)
to Stewart J. SHAW, St. Patrick's, (here) September 21, 1955),
Godparents; Born July 19, 1894; Baptized October 30, 1894; #1683

Thomas VIOTTO - John VIOTTO and Angelene LERRA, Parents; Peter
LERRA, Godparent; Born May 27, 1892; Baptized November 27, 1892;
#1588

Mary Emelda Anna VICOVICH - Anton VICOVICH and Magdalen BUSS, Parents;
Ann MARCOVICH, Godparent; Born October 28, 1896; Baptized April 26,
1897; #1876

Anna Antonia VISCOWITCH - Anthony VISCOWITCH and Magdalen BUSS,
Parents; Vido MARCOVICH and Catherine FOWLER, Godparents; Born
May 28, 1894; Baptized June 24, 1894; #1667

Herman Andrew VOGT - Conrad VOGT and Dorothy OSTERMANN, Parents;
Herman SCHREIBER and Mary HERRMANN, Godparents; Born October 10,
1860; Baptized January 13, 1861; #29

Louise Frances VOGT - Conrad VOGT and Dorothy OSTERMANN, Parents;
Frank SOMMER and Loiuse BECKER, Godparents; Born April 6, 1862;
Baptized May 25, 1862; #85

Margaret VOGT - Conrad VOGT and Henrietta MICCA, Parents; Mary
SAMMET, Godparent; Born March 3, 1871; Baptized January 5, 1872;
#606

Margaret Rosina VOGT - Conrad VOGT and Dorothy OSTERMANN, Parents;
Rosina SAMMET, Godparent; Born August 8, 1866; Baptized September 2,
1866; #312

Mary Rosina VOGT - Conrad VOGT and Dorothy OSTERMANN, Parents;
Rosina SAMMET, Godparent; Born April 15, 1864; Baptized July 2,
1865; #219

Paul VOIGT - Charles (n.c.) VOIGT and Margaret KOLB, Parents;
Jac. F. LAUTH, Godparent; Born February 28, 1881; Baptized October 29,
1883; #1031

Emma Wilhelmina VOLLERT (married Lawrence L. BONATZ, Holy Rosary,
Houston, April 22, 1922) - Francis (n.c.) VOLLERT and Catherine
FRANZ, Parents; William KOEHLER and Emma FRANZ (by proxy), Godparents;
Born December 9, 1882; Baptized February 11, 1883; #986

Andrew WAGER - Andrew WAGER and Elizabeth ANDREANS, Parents;
Josephine WAGER, Godparent; Born October 3, 1876; Baptized October 4,
1876; #786

Alice Wilhelmina WAGNER - Theodore WAGNER and Clara MOELLER, Parents;
John William JOCKUSCH and Elise JOCKUSCH, Godparents; Born October 16,
1860; Baptized February 10, 1861; #30

Anna Catherine WAGNER - John WAGNER and Catherine EISEL, Parents;
Caroline HAGEMANN and Emily LEINBACH, Godparents; Born February 2,
1869; Baptized May 22, 1871; #588

Arthur Butler Chas. WAGNER - Theodor WAGNER and Clara MOELLER,
Parents; August von BUTTLAR and Caroline WAGNER, Godparents;
Born January 27, 1867; Baptized June 27, 1867; #356

Henry WAGNER - John WAGNER and Catherine EISEL, Parents; Henry
HAGEMANN and Caroline HAGEMANN, Godparents; Born November 15, 1869;
Baptized May 22, 1871; #587

Cora Ann WAINRIGHT - Fred WAINRIGHT and Ellen MC CARTHY, Parents;
Michael WALSH and Margaret WALSH, Godparents; Born March 7, 1868;
Baptized June 14, 1868; #422 B

Catherine Mabel WALLACE - John WALLACE and Caroline (n.c.) BURNS,
Parents; John WHITBURN and Augusta REDDY, Godparents; Born November 30,
1885; Baptized July 18, 1886; #1257

John WALLIS - John Arthur WALLIS and Carrie (n.c.) BURNS, Parents;
Martin PEINE and Mary MARTIN, Godparents; Born August 21, 1889;
Baptized March 30, 1890; #1477

Mary Ellen (WALZ) WALSH - Pat WALSH and Margaret WALDSCHMIDT,
Parents; John WALSH and Catherine COWEN, Godparents; Born
November 4, 1868; Baptized January 1, 1869; #501

Magdalen Agnes WALTER - August WALTER and Josephine BROWE, Parents;
Margaret PORCHET, Godparent; Born December 29, 1894; Baptized
May 17, 1895; #1715

Louise Brigid (WALSH) WALZ - T. WALZ and Louise DINGLOTHEN,
Parents; James CARROL and Louise DINGLOTHEN, Godparents; Born
November 10, 1870; Baptized January 29, 1871; #571

Francis Joseph WARE - Frank WARE and Joan REITH, Parents; Louis
HAPTKEM and Charles LEIMANN, Godparents; Born April 16, 1868;
Baptized January 10, 1869; #503

Mary Dewey WARNELL - James WARNELL and Mikela GUSMAN, Parents;
Mary MENZEL, Godparent; Born April 30, 1898; Baptized June 4,
1898; #1920

Laura Campbell WARREN - Charles WARREN and Helen DUNSHIE, Parents;
Barbara PARKER, Godparent; Born October 4, 1884; Baptized October 7,
1884 (private); #1100

August Mathew Henry WARTH - August WARTH and Anna Margaret FORD,
Paretns; Joseph Henry HUEBNER and Anthony KAPER, Godparents;
Born October 4, 1880; Baptized September 3, 1882; #974

Mary Louise WARTH - August WARTH and Anna FORD, Parents; Mary
LUDWIG and Frank GREY, Godparents; Born August 31, 1878; Baptized
June 13, 1880; #897

Catherine WASNA - Michael WASNA and Victoria MADALUISKA, Parents;
Joseph FIBULSKI and Anna ENDRGSK, Godparents; Born April 21, 1896;
Baptized May 2, 1896; #1826

Mary Monterey WATKINS (nee CONDRA) (convert) - Mr. and Mrs. DELOMEL,
Godparents; 26 years old; #1969

Alexander John WEBER - August WEBER and Mary PENDERGAST, Parents;
Alexander John WEBER and Catherine SWEENEY, Godparents; Born
October 5, 1888; Baptized November 4, 1888; #1413

Antonia Elenore WEBER - William Jos. WEBER and Antonia STEFFIERS,
Parents; Mary WEBER, Godparent; Born November 3, 1892; Baptized
November 4, 1892; #1583

August WEBER - William WEBER and Theresa SCHULTE, Parents; John
WEBER and Catherine WEBER, Godparents; Born July 25, 1861; Baptized
August 4, 1861; #51

Clara Catherine WEBER - William WEBER and Nettie (n.c.) STEVENS,
Parents; Emil FLAKE and Catherine FLAKE, Godparents; Born September 11,
1884; Baptized October 12, 1884; #1103

Clarence Thompson WEBER - Emil J. WEBER and Marie SCHREIBER, Parents;
Mary THOMPSON, Godparent; Born March 30, 1900; Baptized April 29,
1900; #1990

Elizabeth WEBER - August A. WEBER and Mary PRENDERGAST, Parents;
Isabel PRENDERGAST, Godparent; Born July 25, 1885; Baptized July 25,
1885 (private); #1178

Emil WEBER - William WEBER and Teresa SCHULTE, Parents; P. MILLER
and Clara WEBER, Godparents; Born December 28, 1866; Baptized
January 23, 1867; #333

Emil Peter -- - Emil Joseph -- and Mary SCHREIBER, Parents;
Peter M. GENGLER and Theresa SCHULTE, Godparents; Born February 8,
1892; Baptized March 27, 1892; #1554

Helen Catherine WEBER - John WEBER and Petronella INGERMANN,
Parents; Daniel INGERMANN and Catherine WEBER, Godparents;
Born February 18, 1863; Baptized March 15, 1863; #104

Herman Frank WEBER - Emil Joseph WEBER and Mary SCHREIBER, Parents;
Frank SCHREIBER and Rose FLEUHR, Godparents; Born April 23, 1897;
Baptized June 12, 1897; #1880

John Emil WEBER - Mathias WEBER and Clara MUELLER, Parents; John
WEBER and Catherine ABELS, Godparents; Born November 9, 1864;
Baptized November 21, 1864; #184

Louis William WEBER - Alysius WEBER and Mary PRENDERGAST, Parents;
Louis RIBAUX and Caroline RIBAUX, Godparents; Born October 22,
1892; Baptized November 20, 1892; #1585

Mary Emily Theresa WEBER - William WEBER and Nettie (n.c.) STEPHEN,
Parents; August WEBER and Theresa WEBER, Godparents; Born November 20,
1882; Baptized February 11, 1883; #987

Peter WEBER - Mathias WEBER and Clara MUELLER, Parents; Peter
MUELLER, Godparent; Born December 13, 1860; Baptized January 6,
1861; #28

Peter Alexander WEBER - John WEBER and Petronilla INKERMANN,
Parents; Peter MILLER and Theresa WEBER, Godparents; Born
October 17, 1865; Baptized January 7, 1866; #266

Theresa Henrietta Louise WEBER - William WEBER and Nettie LIDEKE,
Parents; Henry SCHULTE and Theresa SCHULTE, Godparents; Born
May 12, 1887; Baptized June 5, 1887; #1351 A

Vivian WEBER - August John WEBER and Marian PRENDERGAST, Parents;
Elizabeth HELFENSTEIN, Godparent; Born December 19, 1890; Baptized
January 17, 1891; #1531

William Otto WEBER - Mathias WEBER and Clara MILLER, Parents;
William WEBER and Catherine WEBER, Godparents; Born January --,
1863; Baptized February 15, 1863; #100

Philip WECHSLER - Philip WECHSLER and Helen MAUDOWN, Parents;
Mrs. HUSSEY, Godparent; Born April 3, 1875; Baptized June 12,
1875; #750

Louise Ernestine WECKERT (conditional) - N. N. Anonymous and N. N.,
Parents; Mary BUEHL, Godparent; Baptized September 16, 1885; #1184

Agnes Louis WERDEHAUSEN - William WERDEHAUSEN and Agnete SMITH,
Parents; J. H. SMITH and Emma SMITH, Godparents; Born October 1,
1888; Baptized November 11, 1888; #1416

Joseph Philip WERDEHAUSEN - Philip WERDEHAUSEN and Bernardine
NEUMAN, Parents; Catherine WEBER, Godparent; Born May 8, 1860;
Baptized June (24), 1860; #10

Lucille Ursula WERDEHAUSEN - William WERDEHAUSEN and Agnes SMITH,
Parents; J. M. SMITH and Laura RUEHBUEHL, Godparents; Born June 22,
1900; Baptized July 22, 1900; #1996

Magdalen Edna WERDENHAUSEN - William WERDENHAUSEN and Agnes SMITH,
Parents; Henry MC GRAY and Joseph WERDENHAUSEN, Godparents; Born
April 18, 1892; Baptized May 15, 1892; #1561

William Frederic Joseph WERDEHAUSEN - Philip WERDEHAUSEN and
Bernardine HEIMANN, Parents; William OPPERMANN and Theresa COERS,
Godparents; Born January 29, 1863; Baptized March 8, 1863; #103

Catherine Margaret BRUEGGEMANN (nee BRUEGGEMANN, convert) - Henry
BRUEGGEMANN and Anna BARLACH, Parents; Catherine KRAUS, Godparent;
Born January 16, 1831; Baptized May 21, 1896; #1836

Mary Agnes Alice WEISNER - Aloysius WEISNER and Elizabeth RISENBERG,
Parents; Dominic LANG and Joan ASCHER, Godparents; Born September 26,
1886; Baptized October 14, 1886; #1275

Bertha Theresa WEISS - Joseph WEISS and Anna LEINBACH, Parents;
Lena WICKS, Godparent; Born November 12, 1895; Baptized March 9,
1896; #1810

John WEISS - James WEISS and Margaret KIRCHRUN, Parents; M. OTT,
Godparent; Born October 19, 1876; Baptized November 12, 1876; #798

William George James WEISS - George WEISS and Angelica CARDINES,
Parents; James GENGLER and Anna GENGLER, Godparents; Born February 3,
1884; Baptized May 3, 1884; #1066

Aloysia Josephine WELLS - William WELLS and Eugenia BECKETT,
Parents; Louis PAQUET and Albertina VERNERT, Godparents; Born
November 18, 1880; Baptized September 17, 1882; #979

Francis Hillary WELSCH - Patrick WELSCH and Catherine CORYHAN,
Parents; Born March 9, 1873; Baptized August 8, 1873; #678

John Joseph WENDELL - John WENDELL and Mary Caroline HELZEL,
Parents; Charles FOGGE and Louise ERHOLD, Godparents; Born October 8,
1876; Baptized December 25, 1876; #788

Andrew Henry WENZEL - Louis WENZEL and Margaret HERMANN, Parents;
Henry EDWARDS and ANN EDWARDS, Godparents; Born May 10, 1874;
Baptized May 16, 1874; #717

Louis Davidson WENZEL - Louis WENZEL and Margaret HERMANN, Parents;
David HERMAN and Charlotte MERTHL, Godparents; Born November 26,
1870; Baptized March 23, 1872; #613 C

Mary Louise WENZEL - Louise WENZEL and Margaret HERMAN, Parents;
Mary HERMAN, Godparents; Born April 20, 1869; Baptized September 5,
1869; #528

Miriam Margaret WERNER - Frederic WERNER and Minnie FUNK, Parents;
William WINDMEYER and Julia FUNK, Godparents; Born September 24,
1897; Baptized August 27, 1898; #1925

Alexander Bernard WEYER - Henry WEYER and Mary KLEINMANN, Parents;
John HAGEMANN and Elizabeth MOSER, Godparents; Born April 17,
1874; Baptized May 17, 1874; #706

Anna Mary WEYER - Henry WEYER and Mary KLEINMANN, Parents; John
Baptist ROEMER and Paula MOSER, Godparents; Born January 26, 1882;
Baptized April 3, 1882; #961

Henry WEYER - Henry WEYER and Mary KLEINMANN, Parents; John
KLEINMANN and Sophie WEYERS, Godparents; Born January 7, 1873;
Baptized February 2, 1873; #651

Joseph Patrick WEYER - Henry WEYER and Mary KLEINMANN, Parents;
Joseph BROKHOF and Mary GRAEGOFT, Godparents; Born February 14,
1878; Baptized March 9, 1878; #837

Louis George WEYER - Henry WEYER and Mary KLEINMANN, Parents;
John MOSER and Anna MOSER, Godparents; Born October 18, 1883;
Baptized April 9, 1884; #1055

Mary WEYER - Henry WEYER and Mary KLAUS (?), Parents; George
LEINBACH and Hyacintha (MOSER?), Godparents; Born November 21,
1876; Baptized November --, 1876; #787

Sophie Elizabeth WEYER - Henry WEYER and Mary Dorothy KLEINMANN,
Parents; John MOSER and Joan MOSER, Godparents; Born September 15,
1871; Baptized October 15, 1871; #599

Henry Edward Anthony WICKES - Henry M. WICKES and Lena LEINBACH,
Parents; Theresa LEINBACH and Percy WICKES, Godparents; Born
December 31, 1897; Baptized May 12, 1898; #1917

Mary Frances WICKES - Henry WICKES and Lena LEINBACH, Parents;
George LEINBACH and Ann LEINBACH, Godparents; Born October 17, 1893;
Baptized November 27, 1893; #1632

Ursula Theresa WICKES (married Anthony E. RAHE, S. Heart, Galveston,
February 7, 1918) - Henry WICKES and Lina Theresa LEINBACH, Parents;
George LEINBACH and Catherine MC CREA, Godparents; Born September 28,
1895; Baptized December 18, 1895; #1742

Josephine Wilhelmina Mary WIEGMANN - William WIEGMANN and Sophie
HAGEMANN, Parents; H. HARVITZ and Wilhelmina WIEGMANN (by U.
HAGEMANN), Godparents; Born 1876; Baptized September 22, 1876; #781

Louisa Anna WILD - Henry WILD and Anna Susan KIMLEY, Parents;
Alexander DUFAURE and Ann Barabara KIMLEY, Godparents; Born
March 1, 1873; Baptized May 11, 1873; #666

Anna Mary WILLINGER (married Wm. HERING, St. Joseph's, San Antonio,
May 12, 1914) - Bernard WILLINGER and Mary MEYER, Parents; Elizabeth
GLASS and John MEYER, Godparents; Born July 26, 1895; Baptized
August 18, 1895; #1729

Rose Martha WILLINGER (married Willis H. MILLER, St. Joseph's,
San Antonio, 4/7/1920) - Bernard WILLINGER and Mary MEYER, Parents;
Anna ANDRSKY and John Paul MEYER, Godparents; Born October 3, 1897;
Baptized October 24, 1897; #1893

Stephen WILLIS - Hugo WILLIS and Margaret DIVINE, Parents; Wilhelmina
HOERLING, Godparent; Born April 10, 1862; Baptized June 30, 1863;
#115

John August WILSON - Thomas WILSON and Charlotte --, Parents;
William RICKE and Emma NIEDENFUEHR, Godparents; Born October 25,
1886; Baptized April 5, 1887; #1329

Mary WILSON - Charles WILSON and Olive WESLEY, Parents; G. GREYENBUEHL,
Godparent; Born February 27, 1875; Baptized June 18, 1875; #749

Mary Anna WILSON - N. N. Anonymous and N. N., Parents; Theresa
MAURER, Godparent; Born December 31, 1871; Baptized May 31, 1884;
#1071

Walter WILSON - Charles WILSON and Helen LYNCH, Parents; Walter
HELT and Elizabeth LYNCH, Godparents; Born October 17, 1889;
Baptized May 25, 1890; #1891

Elizabeth Frances Augusta WINKELBACH - Henry WINKELBACH (WINKELBERG)
and Eliz. Theodora BLEICKE, Parents; August WINKELBACH and Frances
BLEIKE, Godparents; Born August 16, 1873; Baptized September 14,
1873; #681

Mary Aline WINKELBACH - Henry WINKELBACH and Elizabeth BLEICKE,
Parents; M. CROSSEN, Godparent; Born December 31, 1876; Baptized
February 6, 1877; #790

Caroline WINKELBERG - H. WINKELBERG and Elizabeth BLEIKE, Parents;
Catherine BILLET, Godparent; Born February 17, 1879; Baptized
March 27, 1879; #881

Joseph Amador WINDMEYER - William (n.c.) WINDMEYER and Mary SEEL,
Parents; Joseph Amador SANCHEZ, Godparent; Born May 27, 1883;
Baptized March 19, 1884; #1050

Josephien Caroline Sophie WINDMEYER - William WINDMEYER and Mary
SEEL, Parents; Joseph FUNK and Sophie FUNK, Godparents; Born July 29,
1866; Baptized August 26, 1866; #310

Philippine Cecil Susan WINDMEYER - William WINDMEYER and Mary SEEL,
Parents; Philippine BRUCH, Godparent; Born August 1, 1867; Baptized
September 29, 1867; #375

William WINDMEYER - William WINDMEYER and Mary SEEL, Parents;
Sophie Susan FUNK, Godparent; Born September 12, 1873; Baptized
December 10, 1873; #689

William Louis Hy. WINDMEYER - William WINDMEYER and Mary SEEL,
Parents; William SCHELMER and Wilhelmina SCHELMER, Godparents;
Born July 14, 1871; Baptized October 22, 1871; #602

Henry Stephen WISRODT - August (n.c.) WISRODT and Philippine
ENGELKE, Parents; Charles ENGELKE and Mary KOEHLER, Godparents;
Born December 26, 1876; Baptized December 29, 1879 (conditional);
#893

Charles PHILIP WOLF (WOLFF) - Frederic WOLF and Rose LERCH, Parents;
Charles LERCH and Catherine LERCH, Godparents; Born September 27,
1874; Baptized November 9, 1874; #733

John WOLF (WOLFF) - Ferdinand WOLF and Eve BRAUNNAGEL, Parents;
Born November 23, 1895; Baptized November 26, 1895; #1798

Elizabeth Alice WOLFEN - Frederic WOLFEN and Mary WALSH, Parents;
Daniel WALSH, Godparent; Born May 30, 1867; Baptized June 18,
1867 (private); #355

Frederica Elizabeth WOLFF - Frederic (n.c.) WOLFF and Rose HORNUNG,
Parents; John LENZ and Elizabeth LENZ, Godparents; Born September 2,
1884; Baptized March 6, 1885 (private); #1133

Frederic WOLFF - Frederic WOLFF and Rose HORNUNG, Parents; Anthony
LENZ and Elizabeth LENZ, Godparents; Born October 20, 1878; Baptized
December 25, 1879; #891

George Joseph WOLFF - Frederic WOLFF and Rosa HORNUNG, Parents;
Joseph GORRANDONA and Louise LEWELLYN, Godparents; Born May 14,
1881; Baptized November 20, 1881; #946

Benie Angelica Collins (orphan) WOFFORD - Edward S. GARTH and Mary
KOEHLER, Godparents; Born August 23, 1896; Baptized March 26, 1899;
#1947

Joseph James WOODSON - Joseph WOODSON and Elizabeth FORHNE, Parents;
William RICKE and Sophie FROHNE, Godparents; Born September 19,
1886; Baptized December 20, 1886; #1302

John Calhoun WRITT - John Calhoun WRITT and Mary Athenis BONIFAY,
Parents; Anna Catherine STUMPF, Godparent; Born August 12, 1896;
Baptized August 19, 1896; #1844

Ernest Adolph YILGE - N. N. Anonymous and Bertha YILGE, Parents;
John EMES and Mary EMES, Godparents; Born December 25, 1883;
Baptized December 19, 1886; #1301

Frank Charles Otto YILGE - N. N. Anonymous and Bertha YILGE,
Parents; Christian BAUMANN and Mary EMES, Godparents; Born
August 13, 1882; Baptized December 19, 1886; #1300

Charles Clement YOFFIN - Clement George YOFFIN and Clementine
GRIEYER, Parents; Clemence GRIEYER and Mary GRIEYER, Godparents;
Born April 14, 1876; Baptized April 1, 1877; #805

Anthony YOUNG - Anthony YOUNG and Anthonia SCHUELL, Parents;
Frank BROCKELMANN, Godparent; Born November 5, 1876; Baptized
January 30, 1877; #789

Carolina YOUNG - Ferdinand YOUNG and Anna TSCHILL, Parents; Carolina
MAURER, Godparent; Born June 2, 1878; Baptized June 17, 1878; #852

Ferdinand YOUNG - Ferdinand YOUNG and (Anna TSCHILL), Parents;
Stephen SHAW and Mary LIEBREICH, Godparents; Born February 2, 1875;
Baptized February 21, 1875; #740

Francis YOUNG - Gustaf YOUNG and Frances SCHNEIDER, Parents;
J. ANSTAETT, Godparent; Born March 14, 1861; Baptized April 8,
1863; #108

Francis Catherine (JUNG) YOUNG - Gustaf YOUNG and Frances SCHNEIDER,
Parents; Elizabeth SCHNIEDER and Frank SCHNEIDER (by proxy),
Godparents; Born June 11, 1863; Baptized November 5, 1863; #129

Louise YOUNG - Gustaf YOUNG and Frances SCHNEIDER, Parents;
J. ANSTAETT, Godparent; Born November 1, 1858; Baptized April 8,
1863; #107

Mary YOUNG - Ferdinand YOUNG and Anna TSCHILL, Parents; Antoine
KARPER and Anna FRITCH, Godparents; Born -- 28, 1873; Baptized
March 2, 1873; #658

Wilhelmina Emily Margaret ZUBER - William ZUBER and Emily GELPKE,
Parents; James NEISE and Margaret NEISE, Godparents; Born
December 14, 1880; Baptized December 13, 1891; #1545

---, Agatha 151
---, Amanda (slave) 120
---, Anna 62, 98, 165
---, Barbara 76
---, Bertha 178
---, Caroline 134, 198
---, Cecil 160
---, Celestine 1
---, Charlotte 216
---, Clara Laura 2
---, Daniel, Ven Sr. M.
    51
---, Edward 71
---, Elisabeth, Ven
    Sisters 57
---, Elizabeth, Ven Sr. M.
    59, 60
---, Emma 204
---, Emma J. 147
---, Fannie (Slave) 120
---, Frances 145
---, Hanna 142
---, Ignatius, Sister 22
---, Irene 54
---, James 150
---, Joachin 33
---, Joseph 155
---, Josephine 146
---, Josephine Cath. 12
---, Justice Ven. Sr. M.
    51
---, Louis 71
---, Louise 37, 145
---, Lucas, Mrs. 54
---, Lydia (slave) 120
---, M. Peloyia, Sister
    36
---, Mabel 67
---, Marcus 71
---, Mary 37, 95, 125,
    178, 205
---, Mary Ann 202
---, Mary Frances 178
---, Mary Henrietta 182
---, Mary Josephine 169
---, Mary, Sister 22, 35,
    36, 47
---, Mary, Sr. M. 53
---, Michael 139
---, Michel 58
---, Nanny (slave) 120
---, Nicholas B. 128
---, Ottilia 105
---, Pius, Ven Sister 57
---, Robert 71
---, Sue 145
---, Susana (slave) 120
---, Theophile 21
---, Theresa 163
---, Theresa Margaret 36
---, Veronica, Sister 2
---, Wilhelmine, Sr. M.
    64
---elfrich, Peter 21
AARENSDORF, Sophie 55
ABADIE, August 66
    Augusta 155
    Cecil 174
    Cecile 66
    Clothilde 184
    Leah 66
ABB, Eve Magdalen 195
    Eve Magdalene 195
ABBOTT, Henry 119
    William Leroy Harry
    119
ABEL, Bertha 2
ABELS, -- Mrs. 121

ABELS (cont.)
    Bertha 176
    Carolije Agnes 5
    Caroline 13
    Catherine 214
    E. 21
    Elizabeth 120
    Henry 21, 91, 119
    Margaret 121
    Margaret Pauline 119
    Pauline 119
    Peter 96
ABLER, Henry 26
ADAM, Margaret 154
ADAMS, Susan 65
ADDINGTON, Mathilda 119
AGULO, J. B. 152
AHER, Mary 27
AHL, Catherine 60
AHRENS, Terese 15
AHREUS, August 21
    Augusta 21
    Joseph Emanuel 21
AIGNER, Mary 67
ALBERT, August Herman
    John 119
    Fides 91, 99
    John 119
ALBERTI, Josephine 198
    Louis 148
    Mary 204
ALBERTSON, Charles 21
ALBIN, Nara 175
ALDRIDGE, -- 71, 119
    Mary Gertrude 119
ALFSON, Caroline Nicholas
    119
    Cath. 119
    Catherine 41, 133
    Chas. 119
    Charles 21
    Josephine Anna 119
ALLEN, C. J. 21
    Elizabeth 1
    F. J. James 7
    Claude 123
    Elizabeth 203
    Fred Guy 47
    Frederick James 119
    James 119
    Mary 175
    Sara 123
    Sarah 2
    William Henry 119
    William John 47
ALLWOOD, Mary 60
    Sidney 60
ALMERAS, Carmen M. 148
    George Felix 148
    Mary Helen 119
    Peter 119
    Rose Ann Elisa 119
AMADEO, Cecil 71
    Ignatius 71
AMADO, Anthony 197
    Cath. Alley 119
    Ignatius 119
    Louise 197
    Lyddie Nellie 119
AMARO, Josephine Rosario
    66
AMBROSE, Andrew 53
    Naska 53
AMBRUSTER, Anthony 21
AMSEHL, Florian 59
ANDERS, Magdalen 192
    Paul Robert 47
    Raul Robert 4

ANDERSDATTER, Anna
    Christine 61
ANDERSON, Andrew 51
    Ann 164
    Burt Wilbur 47
    C. B. 24, 43
    Caroline Elizabeth
    Eloine 119
    Catherine 21, 160, 191
    Elizabeth Christine 51
    Elizabeth Joan 124
    Ellis 137
    Frank Edward 119
    James Henry 47
    John 21, 148
    John Andrew 119
    John Oscar 47
    John P. 47
    Joseph 2, 160
    Joseph William 21
    Martha 62
    Mary 67
    Mina 36
    O. A. 91
    Olivar 119
    Richard 198
    Rose 144
    Sarah, Mrs. 91, 108
    Sophie 160
    Theopile 21, 119
    W. 21
    William James 71, 119
ANDLER, Ferdinand 2
ANDRASCHKA, Barbara 63
    Mary 63
ANDREA, Dora 14
    Dora Eliz. 7
ANDREANS, Elizabeth 212
ANDREWS, Ethel Elizabeth
    119
    John Benjamin 47
    Victor 119
    Thm. Peter 47
ANDRSKY, Anna 216
ANDRYCRYK, Ann 36
ANGLEHOFFER, Chas. 25
ANELLO, Anna Catherine
    119
    Frank 119
    John Anello 119
ANNELLO, Crocifisca 34
ANNON, Parker 32
ANONYMOUS, -- 71
    Catherine 120
    Charles 120
    Edward 71
    Elizabeth 120
    Emil Leon 120
    Francis 120
    Frank 120
    George (slave) 120
    Henry (slave) 120
    James 120
    Joan 120
    Laura Mary 120
    Louis 71
    Louise 120
    Marcus 71
    Mary Helen (slave) 120
    Moses 120
    N. N. 120, 197, 200,
    201, 207, 209, 210,
    211, 214, 216, 217,
    218
    Robert 71, 120
    Samuel (slave) 120
    Selim 120
ANSEN, Amalia 76

ANSTAETT, E. 25
  J. 218
  J. B. 30, 34
  Jos. 151, 181, 185
  Joseph 138, 208
  Jos., Rev. 21, 22, 23,
    24, 25, 26, 27, 28,
    29, 30, 31, 32, 33,
    34, 35, 36, 37, 38,
    39, 40, 41, 42, 43,
    71, 72, 73, 74, 75,
    78, 77, 78, 79, 80,
    81, 82, 83, 84, 85,
    86, 87
  Joseph, Rev. 208
ANTON, Demetrius 169
  Rudolf. 52
ANTONIA, Mary Adelaide 1
ANTONOVICH, Ann Elis. 4
  Laura 135
  Lazarus 21
ANTRISKY, Anna 189
APEL, Geo., Rev. 75, 77,
  80
  George, Rev. 23, 30,
    35, 173
  Veronica 30
APPEL, Anna 71
  Frederic 120
  Joseph Frederic 120
  William Henry 120
ARDISSON, Emma 202
ARMSTRONG, Camilla 164
  J. 173
ARNOLD, --, Mrs. 124
  Abbott Laurence 53
  Agatha 25, 121, 141
  Alphonse Alois 14
  Alphinse Aloysius 7,
    120
  Angelina 13, 186
  Angelina Genevieve 6
  Anna Mary 101
  Anton 25
  Bian J. 53
  Catherine 67
  Cecillia 120
  Chas. 186
  Edmund Beauregard 121
  Gustav 12
  Isidor 36, 71, 120,
    121, 158
  Joseph 36
  Joseph Philip 5, 186
  Mary 21, 123, 185, 190
  Mary Ann 4, 36, 71, 82,
    91, 181, 186
  Mary Ann Alice 121
  Mary Edna 53
  Pauline 32, 43, 121,
    201
  Rosina Mathilda 71,
    121
  Thomas 42
ARRINGTON, Mary Alice 169,
  173
ARTIQUE, Martha 37
ARTISAN, Josephine 32
ARTO, Caroline, Mrs. 91,
  96
  Douglas Benjamin 121
  James 121
  Julia Joan 121
  Louis J. 121
  Louis Joseph 121
ASCHER, Joan 215
ATKINS, Jos. 186
AUCLAIR, Cyril 71
AUCOIN, Euola 63
AUERBACH, Paul A. 42
AUGSTEN, Caroline Mary 121
  Wenceslans 121
AUGUSTINE, Jenny 63

AUGUSTINE (cont.)
  Salvatore 63
AUGUSTINEE, Theresa 33
AUL, Anthony 121
  Antonia Netta 121
  Augusta 197
  Catherine 121, 122
  Catherine Josephine
    122
  Charles 121
  David 121
  Elizabeth 122
  Frank Anthony 121
  Frederic 121
  Frederic Andrew 121
  George Andrew 121
  James David 121
  James George 121
  Joseph 121, 122
  Joseph David 121
  Joseph Vincent 121
  Magdalen Lena 122
  Mary 121, 122
  Mary Balthosara 122
  Mary Cath. Regina 122
  Mary Lillian 121
  Mary Magdalen 121, 122
  Nicholas 122
  Nichols 121
  Mary Theresa
    Antoinette 121
  Philip 121
  Theresa 121
  William Nicholas 122
AULL, Anthony 1, 21, 31,
  167, 173, 180
  Anton 38
  Catherine, Mrs. 91
  Augusta 197
  Cathererine 21, 167,
    170, 180
  Cecil 167, 181
  Cecile 1, 170
  Cecelia 169
  David 21
  Elizabeth 180
  George Andrew 4
  James George 71
  Joseph 1, 4, 180
  M. 169
  Mary 38, 140, 169,
    181, 188
  Mary Elizabeth 1, 169,
    810
  Mary Magdalen 4
  Nic. 170
  Theresa 38, 185, 188
AULL-NOUN, William 4
AULLS, Mary 25
AUXIN, Joseph 4
AVINEY, E. E. 21
AYMES, Henry 15
AYRES, Josephine 201
BABACKI, Agnes 54
  Geo. 54
BABIK, Simon 47
BACINELLI, -- 126
BACKENBUSH, Gertrude 28
BADER, Emma 122
  Mary 150
BAEHR, -- 68
  Audrey 15
  Audrey Agnes 8
  Bernard 122
  Bernard Julius 122
  Edna 14
  Edna Agnes 7
  Ellerine 8, 15
  George Bernard 122
  Leonard 122
  Mary 122
BAER, -- 194
  Anna 41

BAGBY, Cecile King 91
BAHR, Mary Agnes 131
BAHRENBERT, L., Dr. 55
BAIL, Mary 71
BAILEY, Mary 59
BAILING, Caroline 129
BAK, Mary 52
BAKEL, John Albert 152
BAKER, Daniel M. 21, 122
  Elenore Nellie 22
  George Douglas 122
  Mary 122
  William 122
BALACLAS, J. B., Rev. 27
BALCET, Frederic Robert
  43
  Louis 43
BALDERACHI, John Jos. 5
BALDRE, Mary Ann 181
BALDRI, Mary Anna, Mrs.
  91
BALDRY, Marianna, Mrs.
  124
  Mary 122
BALEZ, Octavius 4
BALFOUR, Margaret 129
BALIBESEH, Mary Barbara
  207
BALIMANN, Henry 137
BALLHORN, Barbara 156
BALLINGTON, Anna Mary 64
BALLIS, James 36
BALLMER, Cecil Augusta
  139
  Gregory 139
BALSAM, Robert G. 141
BANACH, Marianore 54
BANNER, Anna 64
BANTIN, James 13
BARBONA, Kate 66
BARBONG, Barbara
  Catherine, Mrs. 91
  Catherine 61
BARBOUG, Catherine 140
BARBUNG, Barbara
  Catherine, Mrs. 116
BARCELO, Inez 205
BARELLI, Eulalia 154
  J. B. 154
BARGA, Andrew 178
  Joan 178
BARGONG, Catherine 47
  Mrs. Cath. 47
BARK, E. 140
  M. 140
BARLACH, Anna 215
BARLEMANN, Anna Catherine
  54, 122
  Anne 14
  Anne Cecile 7
  Charles 21, 54, 91,
    122, 143, 183, 197
  Charles Andrew 91
  John 13
  John Alois 91
  John Boniface 122
  Joseph 14
  Joseph Aloysius 7
  Joseph Martin 122
  Louise Joseph 6
  Mary 15, 54
  Mary Magdalen
    Lescordina 122
  Mary Terese 8
  Regina 182, 183
  William 15, 54
  Wm. Aloysius 8
  William Charles 122
  William Frederic 91
  William Frederic
    Christian 122
BARLERMARER, Charles 97
  Charles, Mrs. 97

BARMANN, Frederic 21
BARNES, C. W. 198
    William 178
BAROMI, Michael 170
BARON, Anna 67
BARONA, Amelia 197
BARONCINI, Ippolito 47
    John Anton Th. 47
BAROUX, John Bapt. 122
    Mary Catherine V. 122
    Mary Clementine 122
BARRERE, Alexandria 137
BARRITT, Martha 196
BARROW, Anna 180
    Elvera 180
    Elvira 173
    Frank Vincent 123
    Richard 123
    Verna 91
BARRY, Charles Leo 123
    Emil 123
    Emily 144
    Frances McCarthy 54
    John McCarthy 54
    Mary Helen 123
    Patrick 179, 194
    Robert H. 123
BARTELS, Edward 157
    Margaret 157
    Sara E. 157
BARTHAL, Elizabeth 204
BARTHEL, John 123
    John Cornelius 4
    Peter 123, 166
    Peter Joseph 123
    Sara 166
BARTHELME, August 47
    Ludwig 47
BARTLEMANN, Theresa 30
BARTHOLMANS, Frank Joseph
    123
    Christian 123
BARWIK, Minnie 55
BASHNAL, L. J., Rev. 58
BASMAISON, Gilbert 47
    Pierre 47
BASTIT, Joan 33
BAT, Joseph 184
BATEMAN, Charles 123
    Susan Joan 123
    Margaret 26
BATES, John Mifflin 47
    Joseph Thomas 47
BATJE, Dietrich 22
    Otto 22
    Rebecca 22
BATTEB, John 173
BATTI, Anton 123
    Anthony 123
    Frank 123
    Margaret, Mrs. 71
    Mary Eugenia 123
BATZLER, Margaret 30
BAUDENON, Clemence 24
    Emily 204
    Mary Evelyn 122
BAUDINAU, Clementine 172
    John Baptist 172
BAUER, August John 3
    Carl John 141
    Flora 91, 93
BAUERS, Frances 187
BAUHANS, -- 71
    Cath. 56
    Catherine 53, 96
    Catherine Caroline 123
    Elizabeth 34, 110, 123,
        130, 194
    Elizabeth, Mrs. 91
    Geo. 91
    George 123
    Henry 123
    James 2, 91, 123

BAUHANS (cont.)
    Sophie 2, 32, 34
    Sophy 26, 172
    Sophy Catherine Susan
        123
    Valentine 123
    William 123, 172
BAUHENS, Catherine 195
    Elizabeth 145, 172
    Sophie Lott 145
    Valentine 194
    William George 92
BAUHHANS, Catherine 25
    John 25
BAULARD, Paul 197
    Victor 127
BAUMAN, Charles Ingomer
        123
    Claude Oliver 123
BAUMANN, Anna Theresa
        124
    Anne 5, 124
    August 140
    Christian 22, 71, 124,
        131, 140, 202, 218
    George 22
    Frederic Maurice 124
    Mary Magdalen 71, 124
    Maurice 5, 124
    Rose Barbara 124
    Rosina 28, 61, 92,
        100, 155, 166, 194
    Stephen 124
    William Maurice 124
BAUMGART, Emil Theodore
        Wenceleus 124
    Ernest 124
BAUTSCH, Frank Charles
        47
    Henry 47
BAUTTE, Cecile 9
    Leona 9
BAVHI, Margaret 176
BAYERTT, Mary L. 124
    Frank 124
BAYLOR, Mary 164
BEARD, Helen 124
    John 124
    Catherine 124
BEARING, Joan Catherine
        124
    Edward J. 124
BEARMANN, Mary 28
BEAVINS, Christopher
        Columbus 124
BECK, Agnes 13
    Agnes Ann 124
    Agnes Elizabeth 6
    Frank 18
    Hedwig 5
    Hidwig Theresa 124
    Louis 124
BECKE, Louise 177
BECKER, Adolf C. 48, 65
    Catherine 42
    Christian Chas. 198
    Frank Jos. 124
    Fred Henry 68
    Leonard John 48
    Lothar 124
    Louise 67, 212
    Maggie 124
    Mary 39, 159
    Mildred, Mrs. 68
    Sara 198
BECKERT, Elizabeth 123
BECKETT, Eugenia 215
    Frank Louis 124
    John 124
BECKER, Fred Richard 48
    Fred William Richard
        48
    Frederic Otto 124

BECKER (cont.)
    John 71
    John Fred Hy. 48
    Latharius 22
BECKMAN, Louis, C. 22
    Mary 211
BECKMANN, Abrasia Louise
        124
    August William 124
    Barbara 14
    Barbara Louise 124
    Cecil Alberta 124
    Charles Andrew 125
    Christian Louis 4,
        125
    Dorothea 42
    John 71
    Joseph William 125
    Louis 92, 124
    Louis August 125
    Louis C. 124
    Louis Charles 125
    Louis Hy. 125
    Louis Joseph 7
    Louise 14, 206
    Louise Cecile 7
    Louise Ida 125
    Mary 25, 66, 211
    Mary Magdalene 125
BEE, Charles Louis 4
    Chas. 201
BEEKMANN, Barbara Agnes 6
BEERMANN, Adelaide 125
    Benjamin 125
    Henry Thomas 125
    John 125
    Mary Ann Elizabeth 125
    Peter 125
BEGUIN, D. H. 41
    Henry 207
    Louise 207
BEHR, Bernard 125
    John 125
    Magdalene 125
    Theresa 52
BEHRENS, Louise 64
BEHRINGER, Amalia 32
BELBAZ, Joseph 168
    Pauline 168
BELBAZE, Bertha 8
BELL, Elizabeth 119
BELLOW, Elizabeth 137
    Ulysses 137
BENDER, Marg. 22
    Mina 34
    Minna 82
    Peter 36
    Wilhelmin 80, 175
BENDIXEN, Ann Antonia 7
    Anna 52, 56
    Anna M. 61
    Anna Mary 60, 107, 125
    Anna Mary Catherine 92
    Anne 14
    George 60, 125
    George A. 71
    George Adolph 125
    Geo. Chris. 125
    George Christian 22
    Mary 133
    Mary, Mrs. 92, 99
    Pauline 60
    George 71
    George Thomas 71, 125
BENETT, Anna Mary 41
BENGELSDORF, Christine 68
BENNETT, Mary 132
BENNOT, Albert 54
    Olive G. 54
BENSCOVA, Frances 55
BENSEL, Anna M. 39
BENZEL, Rosalee 144
    Theresa 144

BERA, Margaret 151
    Peatro 151
BERBERICH, Catherine 125
    Lawrence Chas. 125
    Stephen 125
BERCHMAN, Mary Wilhelmina
    126
    William 126
BERGEN, James 71
BERGENBUSCH, Alophone 1
    Frances 72, 128
    Gertrude 1, 128
    Teresa 127
    Theresa 128
BERGER, Erick, Mrs. 53
    George 92
    Joseph 53
    Lena 53
    Margaret, Mrs. 113
    Marquerite, Mrs. 92
BERGERON, Betty Ann 17
    Jasper 16
BERGINIUS, Mary 61
BERGMAN, Emily 185
BERGMANN, Amilia 185
    Anna 26, 34, 80, 145,
    159
    Anthony 26, 71
    Anton 26, 178
    Antonia 2
    Antonio 204
    August 71
    John 22, 48
    Joseph Nicholas 126
    Mary 2, 162
    Mary Magdalen 145
    Robert Jos. 48
    William 22, 126
BERGSTROM, Mary 165
BERKENBUSCH, Adolphine 33,
    190
    Gertrude 35, 134, 135,
    155
BERKENHURST, Gertrude 94
BERLETH, Mary 24
    Theresa 24
BERNAL, Adam A. 153
BERNARD, August 41
    Johanna 92
    Lydia 40
    Magdalen Lydia 1, 126
    Martha 40
    Martha, Mrs. 92, 115
BERNER, Catherine 50
    Ferdinand 63
    Ferdinand C. 92
BERRMANN, Benjamin 2
BERTHET, G., Rev. 79
BERTHIN, Adell Rosale 126
    Frank 126
BERTIN, Frank Peter 126
BERTRAM, Helen 171
BERTRAUD, Helen 165, 170
BESEN, Cecil 159
BESIER, Felix 204
BESKA, Mary 93
BESSENELLI, Ernest
    Laurence 126
    John 126
BEST, --, Mrs. 126
    Agnes Joan 126
    Ann Margaret 26, 126
    Anna 136, 184, 192
    Anna Margaret Louise
    126
    Catherine 4, 123, 126,
    194
    Catherine Margaret 126
    Charles Louis 3, 126
    Ella Nora 126
    Evelyn Louise 126
    George 126
    John George 22

BEST (cont.)
    John Joseph 22
    Joseph 122, 126, 194
    Joseph William 126
    Loius 22, 71, 126,
    184
    Louis John 71, 126
    Margaret 126
    Mary Catherine 126
    Maximilian 22
    Maximus 126
    Sophy 149
    William 22, 126
    William Frank 126
BETHSCHEIDER, Nicholas
    Edw. 92
BEYER, Theresa 65
BIAGINI, Jos. 123
BIBO, Bartholomew 124
    Rosalee 124
BICOCCHI, Anthony Frank
    Emil Cavior 127
    Anthony 127
BIEHLER, Anna 183
    Augusta 30, 40, 156,
    157, 160
    Francis 127
    M. 30
    Mary Magdalen 127
    Rudolph 119
BIERING, Catherine 14,
    58
    Catherine Mary 6
    E. J. 58
BIERMANN, Caroline 56,
    135, 158
    Catherine 211
    Catherine Pearl 127
    Elenore 162
    H. 28
    Henry 22, 127
    James Edward 127
    John Emil Mary 127
    Mary Ann 127
    Peter 127, 211
    Peter Charles 127
    Pearl Mary 127
    Peter 22, 127
BIGAT, John 40
    John, Rev. 21
BIGGS, Dorothy 52
BILD, Loiuse 130
    Rosalie Helen 3
    Rosa 199
    Rose 133
BILHARTS, Xavier 25
BILLEBAULT, Leo 127
    Prosper 127
BILLET, Anthony 127, 193
    Anthony Victor 127
    Anton 127
    Catherine 217
    Frances Wilhelmina
    Carolina 127
BILLIGMANN, Frederic 72
BILLS, Anna 119
BINAR, August 92
BINEBACHER, Margaret 197
BINTIGER, Rose 107
BIRON, Mary 60
BITTEL, Anna C. 36
    Frank Hos. 36
    Stephan 36
BLACK, Emily, Mrs. 55
    Frank 55
BLAGGE, Ella Ruby 128
    Henry M. 128
BLAKE, Cath. 73
    Catherine 136
BLAKEMAN, William 162
BLANCHEAU, August 197
BLANCHET, -- 144
    Caroline 144

BLANCHET (cont.)
    Fabian William 127
    Peter Constantin 127
BLANDEAU, August 204
    Elnora 204
    Lenora 204
    Leopold 204
    Louise 163
    Virginia 197
BLANEY, Agnes 141
    Edward 141
    Florence 92, 101
    Frank 203
BLANK, Mary Anne Augusta
    4, 127
BLANTZ, Elizabeth 92, 107
BLARDON, Ada 127
BLARDONE, Emily 152
BLASCHKA, Pauline 113
BLASOVIC, Martha 62
BLASSKIEWICZ, Antonia 57
    Jos. 57
BLASVITZ, Anna 58
    Martha 58
BLAVIER, Louise 133
BLATZ, Catherine 85
BLEICK, Theresa 135
BLEICKE, Ann Agnes 127
    Anna 128
    Caroline 72
    Charles 127
    Elizabeth 1, 43, 151,
    216
    Eliz. Theodora 216
    Frank Joseph 127
    Frances 29, 155, 183,
    195
    Fred 29
    Frederic 127
    Frederic, Jr. 128
    Frederic Peter 92
    Helen 127
    Helen Theresa Mary 127
    Jos. 72
    Joseph 72, 127, 128,
    183
    Joseph Bernard 128
    Joseph F. 128
    Joseph G. M. 71
    Joseph William Marion
    128
    Josephine 127, 209
    Julia 127
    Laura 128
    Lillie Louise 128
    Louise Anna 128
    Mary 25, 139
    Mary Caroline Josephine
    128
    Mary Elizabeth 128
    Mary Theresa 128
    Rogers Mills 128
    Sophy 25, 128, 134
    Sophy Mary Ernestine
    128
    Theodore 72
    Theresa 128, 131, 165,
    183
    Wilhelmina 41
    Wilhelmine 72
    William 25, 127, 128,
    129, 183
    William H. 128
    William Joseph Frank
    128
    William I. 127, 128
    William Johnson 128
BLEIKE, Ann Agnes 127
    Ann Louise 2
    Elizabeth 217
    Emil Albert 127
    Frances 24, 216
    Frederic 2

BLEIKE (cont.)
  Josephine 1
  Laura Mary 4
  Mary 189
  Sophie 196
  Terese 1
BLEINDEAU, Mary Louise
  189
BLOCKE, Jacob 22
BLONDEAU, August 123, 143
  Emily 34
  Eugene 34
  Leopold 2
  Louise 143, 155
  Mary 139
  Mary Philomeme 34, 143
  Laura 29
  Philomine 143
  Virginia 144
BLOODGOOD, Clara 160
  Laura 159, 160
BLOOMLEY, George William
  128
  Leonida 128
BLOVIAR, Louise 72
BLUM, Jos. 25, 26, 31, 38
  Joseph 22, 42
  M. 38
  Philippine 203
  T. 203
  William 199
BLUME, Agnes 51
  Neal 48
  Virgil, Mrs. 51
  Virgil Albert n.c. 48
BLUMERING, Mary Ann 121
BOCARD, Anthony 22
BOCK, -- 72
  Agnes 128
  James 183
  Josephine 183
  Lillie 119
  Mary Josephine 131
  Oscar Peter 128
  Peter 22, 28, 72, 128,
    129, 151, 198
  Peter, Jr. 22
  Rosa 119
  Rose 21
  Sara 132
  Sara Isabelle 3
  Sarah 128, 208
  Susanna 146, 160, 198
  Susana Julia 129
BOCKET, Peter 139
BOCKELMAN, Adolph 22, 92,
  129
BOCKELMANN, Adolf Hy 48
  Adolf Julius 48
  Erin Susan Margaret 129
  Ethel May 48
  Ethel May Louise 129
  Herman Charles 92
  Julius Adolph 129
  Louise 129
  Mary Bohl, Mrs. 92
  Susan 129
BOCKLING, Caroline 30
BODDEKER, Angelina 72
  Joseph Leonard 72
BODEKER, Charles 36
  Francis 23
  Jos. 23
BODEN, Charles Frederic
    Henry 129
  Lambert 23, 129
BOEDDEKER, Charles 1
BOEDECKER, Agnes Frances
  129
  Angela 129
  Charles 129
  Edgar Vincent Marion
    129

BOEDECKER (cont.)
  Elizabeth 129
  F. T. 129
  Francis 129
  Frank 129
  James Rock Cornelius
    129
  John 126, 129, 189
  John Francis 129
  John Frank 129
  Joseph 129
  Joseph Anthony
    Ferdinand 129
  Joseph Leonard 129
  Kairer Claude 129
  L. 129
  Louis 129
  Mary 135
  Mary Angela 4
  Viola 16
  William 129
BOEHLING, Mathilda 154
BOEHM, Anna 65
BOEHME, Caroline Mary 129
BOEHNKE, Augusta 185
BOENING, Frank 23, 48,
    92, 203
  Frank A. 48
  Henry 48
  Marian 16
  Mary 65
  Mary Amalia, Mrs. 92,
    105
  Mary Rose 92
  Raymond 92
  Rudolph 23, 92, 153
  Rudolph A. 50
  Rudolf Alfred 48, 92
  W. I. 92
  William Paul 48
BOERGERHAUSEN, Eve Eliz.
  Mary 6
  Peter Charles 163
  Peter Chas. Jos. 6
BOESMUELLER, Caroline 143
  Caroline Anna Ant. 3
  Hedwig Mary 3
  Mary Caroline Seraphine
    4
BOGUSKI, Casimir 48
  Marcel 48
BOHL, Mary 125
BOHN, Agnes 7
  Alfred Joseph 129
  Ann Margaret 129
  Anna 7, 129
  Anne Marg. 14
  Bernard 130
  Catherine 130
  Cecil 129
  Cecilia 129
  Emil 23, 130
  Ernest Marten Joseph
    130
  George 14
  George Augustine 130
  George Frank 7
  George L. 129, 130, 144
  George Leonard 48, 124,
    130, 144, 173
  Henry William 131
  Joan 130
  Joan Mary 6
  John 13
  Louise 13
  Louise Ida 59, 92
  Louise Mary 6
  Lula Louise 104
  Mary Elizabeth 130
  Mary Hedwig 130
  Meta 130
  Nicholas 93, 129, 130
  Nicholas Leonard 130

BOHN (cont.)
  Robert 15
  Robert John 48, 130
  Robert Joseph 8
  Theresa Mary 130
  William 129, 130
  William James 130
BOKEN, Ann Joan 56
BOLLARD, V. G. 38
BOLLER, George Carl 48
  William 48
BOLLERT, Frank 130
  William Emil Blasa 130
BOLOCK, Rudolph 159
BOLTON, August Charles
  130
  Charles 130
  Clifford Marc 130
  John 130
  John Henry 61
  Mary 142
  Mary Elizabeth 61
BOLWOGD, Wilhelmina 131
BONATZ, Laurence L. 212
BONG, Dorothy 72
  M. 141
  Wilhelmina 178
BONIFACE, Catherine 31
BONIFAY, Mary Athenis 217
BONN, Daisy Falconiere 4
  Gertrude 3, 130
  Henry 72, 130
BONNO, John 49
BOOTH, Sararenet 29
  Sara Renetta 130
BORDELAIRE, Peter 150
BORE, Margaret 109
BOREN, Lenis T. A. 49
  William Archic 49
BORIC, Jos. 49
BORIK, Frank 49
BOSA, Henrietta 124
BOSE, Charles 196
  Richard 196
BOSER, Henrietta 124
BOSMEMBREN, Mary 47
BOSS, August 130
  Emma Elizabeth 130
  William 130
BOTH, James 151
  Sarah 151
BOTTE, Anthony 130
  Theresa Marie 130
BOUCHER, Alice 39
BOUCHET, Elizabeth 136
BOUDREAUX, Joseph Oscar
  49
  Theodor 49
BOULTON, Catherine 177
BOUNCIL, Rosale 72
BOUGEOIS, Odilon 49
  Wilfred 49
BOURGES, Anna 177
BOURYES, Charles 26
BOUSE, Evelyn 63
  Evelyn Aleen 9
  John 63
BOUTHERLY, Loe 207
BOUTHERY, Charles 207
  Faustine 41
BOUTTE, Leona 49, 57
BOWDEN, Catherine 72
  Quirin 72
BOWLER, Ammabell 49
BOWLES, John Henry 49
BOWMAN, George 93
  Helen, Mrs. 93, 98, 99
BOYD, Catherine Elizabeth
  130
  Francis Frederic 131
  H. H. 130
  Humphrey 131
  Humphrey, Mrs. 131

BOYD (cont.)
　Laetitia Mary 7
　Louise Josephine 131
　Mary Letty 131
　William 131
　William H. 131
　William Henry 131
BOYDELL, Julia Agnes 131
　William 131
BOYDT, Wilhelmina 176
BOYKEN, Augusta 29
BOYLE, Frederic 178
BOYORSKA, Marianne 54
BRADEN, Martha 33
BRADFORD, J. D. 49
　Percy Aulcie 49
BRACKELMANN, Joseph 131
　Theresa 131
BRAENDLER, Bertha 131
　Edward 131
BRAEUTIGAM, Anthony 23
　Edward 72, 131
　Helen 131
　Henrietta 72
　Louise Mary Agnes 131
　Peter 72, 131
　Peter W. 23, 131
　Peter William 131
　Robert Joseph 131
　William 23, 131
BRAEUTIGAN, Peter 208
BRAKER, Joseph 131
　William Henry 131
BRAMER, Mary 194
BRAMM, Christine 197
BRAMMAR, Albert 131
BRAMMER, Albert 14, 72,
　131, 132, 199
　Albert Joseph 7
　Albert Peter 131
　Christian James 131
　Gertrude 15
　Gertrude Agnes 8
　Gertrude Magdalene
　　Antonia 131
　Herman Albert 131
　James 14, 132
　James Albert Charles
　　132
　James Anthony 7
　Peter 72
　Peter Christian 132
BRANDA, Antonia 151
BRANDES, Bernadine 29
　Mary 160
　Mary Bernadine 160
　Mary Dina 160
　Mary Bernadine 132
BRANDLER, Edward 132
　Otto 132
BRANDSTETTER, Leopold 93
BRANDT, Alice 35
BRANN, Moritz 96
BRAUEUTIGAM, Anthony
　Henry 131
BRAUN, Catherine Theresa
　132
　Charles D. 156
　Emma Sara Sophy
　　Josephine 132
　John 23
　Julius August 132
　Leonard 132
　Michael 132
　Ophilia Blanch 132
　Pauline 176
　Stephen Leonard 132
BRAUNNAGEL, Eva 43
　Eve 217
　Joseph 43
BRAUNS, Albert N. 36
BRAUS, Elizabeth 160
BREEKMANN, Antonia 66

BREEN (cont.)
　Agnes 14
　Agnes Margaret 6
　Alice 60
　Alice Susan Orene 132
　Catherine 116, 182
　Catherine Magdalen 93,
　　104
　Elisabeth 14
　Elizabeth Anne 6
　Katherine Sara 132
　Martin 23, 60, 93, 132
　Martin C. 93, 132
　Martin Charles 93
　Martin Chas. 93
　Mary Agnes 132
　Mary Magdalen 93
　Miles 132, 138
　Miles Frances 93
　Miles Frank 4
　Sarah 13
　Sarah Catherine 6
　Susan Elizabeth 132
BREENROOD, Joseph Ignatius
　5
BREITLING, Frederic 132
　Henry William 132
BREITSCHOPF, Emmanuel 49
　Henry A. 49
　William 49
BRENDLE, Hedwig 52
BRENDLER, Herman Joseph 4
BRENNAN, Joan 125
　Michael 23
BREUDLER, Margaret
　Fredericka 201
BRICE, Catherine 93, 113
BRICK, Catherine U. 59
　Jerry C. 59
　Thomas Dubois 59
BRICKS, Thomas 35, 125
BRIDGES, Anna 66
BRIGGS, Alpha Mary 132
　Fred William 53
　Frederic William 49
　Harry 49
　Joseph 132
　Josephine 8, 15
　Josephine Catherine
　　53, 93, 97
　W. H. 97
　William Harry 53
　Willie 8, 15
BRINK, Charles 30
　Christina 209
　Cornelius 23, 132, 134
　Ernestine 72, 127, 128,
　　129, 188
BRINKHOF, Theodore 2
BRINKHOFF, Theodore 133
BROCK, Anthony 31
　Chas. 40
BROCKHARD, Elizabeth 58
BROCKHOF, Anna 130
BROCKHOFF, Agnes 71
　Ann 129
BROCKELMANN, Charles
　Edward 133
　Charles Joseph 133
　Corina 133
　Frances 218
　Mary 133
BRODARICK, Elizabeth 134
　Jerome 134
　Margaret 134
　Pat 134
BROECKELMANN, Theresa 72
BROERS, Henry 8
BROKHOF, Anne 2
　Frank 72, 133, 179
　Thecla 72, 179
BROKOF, Agnes 22
　Francis 189

BROKOF (cont.)
　Frances Josephine 133
　Joseph 22, 72, 140,
　　215
　Theresa 140
BROOKE, Caroline Marie,
　Mrs. 93
BROKOFF, Agnes 124
BROOKS, Eddie 23
　Emma Ethel 139
　Flora, Mrs. 17, 91, 93
　George Herrick 23
BROS, Francis 49
BROSIG, Augusta Cecile 5
　Augusta Mary
　　Wilhelmina 133
　Bell Joan Augusta
　　Louise 200
　Caroline Celestine 5
　Carolina Henrietta
　　Victoria 133
　Chas. 72
　Charles 133, 191, 200
　Charles Albert Andrew
　　133
　Charles Theodore Albert
　　133
　Charles Theodore Mary
　　133
　Charlie 162
　Emily Catherine
　　Henrietta 72, 133
　Emma Wilhelmine
　　Josephine 133
　Hugo 133
　J. 133
　James Joseph Hugo 133
　Joseph 133
　Laura 133
　Louise 2, 200
　Louise Joan Augusta
　　133
　Mary 200
　Mary Gertrude 5
　Patrick Theodore 133
　Theodore Louis Herman
　　133
BROSING, Augusta 72
BROSSIER, Leo 207
　Mary 207
BROWN, Agnes Mary 133
　Elenore Antonia 133
　Mary Caroline 133
　Myrtle Cecil 133
BROSING, Hugo 72, 73
BROSOVIC, Mary 65
BROSSIVE, Mary 52
BROUSSARD, Aaron 64
　Alpha 49
　Alphie 64
　Asa 138
　Eljie? 9, 64
　Eloge 49, 64
　Jas., Rev. 95
　Joseph Aaron 9, 49
　Marie 48
　N. D. 65
　Nellie Lillian 33
　Nelly Lilian 168
　Paul 9
　Rila 9
BROWE, Josephine 213
BROWN, Cath. Brigid 202
　Glennon Downey 50
　Marg. 54
　Marck C. 50
　Marion J. 50
　Marion J., Mrs. 50
　Mary 110
　Michael 23, 133, 134
　Thomas 63
　Wilhelmina 134
　William Henry John 134

BROWNING, Ann T. 27
BROWNS, Albert Michael 3
BRUCH, Otto 23
  Philippine 203, 217
BRUCKHOF, Techa 192
  Thelca 144
BRUECHER, Caroline 27,
  165
  Frank 134
  Frank Edward 2
  Jos. 27
  Joseph 134
BRUEGGEMANN, Catherine
  Margaret 215
  Henry 215
BRUENING, Herman John 93
  Pauline, Mrs. 93
BRUENNEMAN, Catherine 134
BRUNNER, Charles 23, 134,
  164
  Charles James 134
  Francis George 134
  Frank G. M. 3
  Frank George Louis 134
BRUNNOM, John 134
  Mary Anna 134
BRUNTON, Birdie, Mrs. 50
  James 50
  John Joseph 50
BRUSE, Henry 184
BRYAN, John 134
BUCHMANN, Hedwig 30
  Joseph 73
BUCHOLTZ, Elizabeth 39
BUCHOLZ, Mary 193
BUCK, Ellis 16
  Mary Isabelle 16
BUCKERT, Anthony 134
  Cornelius 134
BUCKHOF, Frank 178
  Mary 178
  Thecla 178
BUCKLEY, Ed. 134
  Edward 73
  James 73
  James Marion 134
  Mildred 68
  Myrtle 68
  Thomas 68, 136
BUDD, Henry 134
  Louise Margaret 134
  Mary 138
BUECHNER, Chas. Fred. 93
  Wilhelmina, Mrs. 93,
  115
BUEHL, Guido 28
BUEHLE, Louise 169
  Mary 169, 214
BUEHLER, Augusta 160
  Louise 169
BUELLE, Herman 134
BUELLY, Henry 134
BUERGER, Augusta Agnes
  134
  Augusta Mary 134
  Bertha Joan 134
  Estelle Mary 153
  Frank 134, 135
  Frank Joseph Theodore
  134
  Frank Theodor 4
  Frank W. 73, 134, 135
  Frank William 134, 135
  Frederic 73
  Frederic Wm. 3
  Geo. Adalbert Alois 3,
  135
  George 134, 135
  George William 135
  Gertrude 73, 135
  Grace Theresa 135
  Joseph Marion 3
  Laura Mathilda 135

BUERGER (cont.)
  Leo Aloysius 135
  Loe 93
  Mathilda 35, 135, 153
  William 35, 135
BUESMUELLER, Charles
  Joseph 3
BUFFA, Ann 119
BUFFIA, Anna 143
BUGERON, Wallace 16
BUHL, Fritz 93
  Margaret 129
  Margaret, Mrs. 93, 151
  Mary 3, 22, 35, 92,
  129, 194, 200
  Mary Marg. 48
BUJAN, Jane ?
BULASHER, Mary 185
  Rudolph 185
BULLACHER, Clara 159
  Frances 173
  John B. 159
  Rudolph 23
BULLASCHER, Clara 135
  Clara T. E. 3
  Clara Therese 135
  Gertrude Louise 135
  H. 135
  Henrietta Hendricks
  135
  Joseph Grover
  Cleveland 135
  Lilly Elizabeth 135
  Margaert C. 3
  Margaret 135, 160, 179
  Margaret Mary
  Josephine 135
  Mary Laura Augusta 135
  Pauline 135
  Rudolph 135, 160
  Rudolf Alois 5
  Theresa 135
BULLASHER, Mary Gertrude
  5
BULLINGTON, Anna Theresa
  41, 136
  Jaspar William 41
BUM, Margaret 179
BUND, Margaret 139
BUNZEL, Martin 145
  Rosale 32, 74, 145
  Theresa 32, 166
BURATIN, Catherine Rose
  163
BURATOVICH, Antoinette
  Catherine 136
  Marion 136
BURDA, John Frank 93
  John 93
BURG, Catherine 49
BURGER, Estella 28
  Frank William 37, 43
  Fred William 94
  Frederic William 28
  George Adalbert
  Aloysius 94
  Helen 8, 15
BURGESS, John Edward 50
BURIC, John 50
  Joseph 50
BURKE, Catherine 62
  Helen 170
  John Edward 136
  Marcelle Catherine 136
  Mary 32, 156
  Michael 156
  T. A. 26
BURKETT, Daniel Walter 136
  John 136
  Mary 184
BURKHARD, Ann Mary 169
BURKHART, Dorothy 136
  Gustave 136

BURKHART (cont.)
  Henry John 136
  Joan 136
BURKITT, Andrew John 73
  Catherine 179
  Henry John 136
  John Thomas 73, 136
BURLINGTON, Anna 93, 114
  Anna Theresa 114
BURNER, Newton B. 23
BURNETT, Claud 13
  Claud Ignatius 5
BURNETTE, Mary Helen 190
BURNS, Alice 30
  Caroline 213
  Carrie 213
  Joseph 23
  Thomas 136
BUROSSE, --, Dr. 55
BURSUM, Henry Sigfried 50
  Herman 50
BURTSCHELL, Odelia 157
  Ottilia 156, 157
BUSCH, Anne 136
  C. 136
  Charles 136
  Elizabeth 32, 165, 166
  Frank 32
  John Leonard Thomas 136
  Margaret 73
  Mary Catherine 136
BUSER, Rosina 140
BUSH, Caroline 136
BUTCHER, Hubert Alois 3
BUSS, Magdalen ?
BUTLER, Mary 167
  Mary Ann 193
BUTTENDORF, Catherine 173
BUTSCHER, Anna 202
BUTTERLY, Delia 138, 139
  Odile 139
BYRNE, Anne 174
  C. E., Rev. 9
  Joan 31
  John 31
  Sarah 140
  Timothy 73
BYRNES, Robert 131
BYRON, Francis Mary 3
CABAZOS, Mary 177
CADAN, Anton 62
  Julia 62
CADDOUE, Julia 34
CALAHAN, Mary 184
CALLAHAN, Agnes 131
  Anna 198
  Dionysius 189
  Mary 171, 186
  William 198
CALLISHAW, Anna 136
  James 136
CALLUM, Emily 176
CAMPBELL, Florence 48
CAMBEIHL, Julius Celestian
  136
CANADELLA, Cosimo 151
CANBEIHL, Julius Celestian
  136
  Louise Frank 136
  Michael 136
CANCELOSI, Rose 151
CANINENBERG, J. P. John 7
CANNON, Andrew 50
  Andrew John 94
  Frederic Joseph 50
  John 50
  John Marion 50
CAP DE VILLE, J. B. 33
CAPDE VILLE, John 31
CAPPADONA, Fred 68
CARDINES, Angelica 215
CARENA, Mary 178
CAREY, Emily E. 94, 103

CARKER, Wm. John 16
CARL, Mary Anna 122
CARLESON, Oscar M. 50
CARLOS, Agnes 134
    Mary 134
CARLYLE, Hazel Ann
        Caroline 136
    James 136
    Minna Lucy 136
CARNEKOSWRSA, Louise 57
CAROTHER, Edward 138
CARR, Alice 157
    Mary 156, 157
CARRAGIN, Lucie 33
CARRAGUE, George 50
    John Joseph 50
    Lucy 168
    Marguerite 50
CARROLL, Anna Mary, Mrs.
        113
    Anna S., Mrs. 94
    Emily 101
    Emily Irwin 94
    Frank 8, 15
    Frank Theodore 136
    Herman Helen 52
    James 8, 52
    James Walter 181
    John 14, 136
    John Gustaphus 136
    J. M. 136
    John James 6
    John M. 52, 94, 137
    Pauline A. 66
    Pauline Antoinette 137
CARSCH, Augusta 29
CARSON, Mrs. 27
CARSTEN, Elizabeth 50
    Frieda 50
    Henry ?
CQASTENS, Henry Andrew 184
CARTER, A. H. 50
    James Louis 50
    Sam 34
    Sydney Ernest 50
CARTLER, Catherine 58
CARTWELL, Margaret 57
CARTWRIGHT, Mary 122
CASANEK, Frances 67
    Joseph 67
CASENTINI, C. 171
CASEY, Amalia Elenore 32
    Amelia Emily 165
    C. C. 165
    Emily 51, 144
    Emily E. 166
    L. C., Mrs. 166
CASSEY, Corleius J. 94
CASHEN, Frederic 129
CASSEL, Charles H. 197
    Pauline 170
CASSENTINI, Catherine
        Charlotte Isar 137
    Christopher 137
    Salvatore 137
CASSIDY, James 31
    Joan 134
    Mary 134
CASTAY, August 130
    Lena 130
CASTELLO, Ada 39
    Ida 200
CASTILLO, Centerro 137
    Frank 137
    Frank Brigido 137
CASTLES, Catherine 58
CATAZZI, Ernestine 150
CAULKING, John 14
    John Joseph 7
CAVANAUGH, Anice 54
CAVITT, Clara Veronica 5
CERING, Agnes 48
CET, Mary D. P. 140

CGEST, Mary, Mrs. 156
CHABEAU, Louise 210
CHALKE, Mary 50
CHALKER, Mary 68
CHAMBARD, John Claud 137
    Mary Ann 137
    Rosina 186
CHAMBODUT, L. C. M., Rev.
        72, 73, 78, 83
CHAMBOUDUT, L. C. M. 36
CHAMPAGNE, Catherine 9
    Enis T. 55
    Eugene 16
    Hazel 16
    J. E. 63
    Mary Louise 16
    Natalie 9, 49
    Paul 49
    Paul, Mrs. 94
    Rose 56
CHAPELLI, Rosale Hortense
        137
    Gustave 137
CHANDLER, P. H. 24
CHAPIN, O. B. 42
CHAPPELLE, Emil Louis 126
    Alice 126
CHARLOTTE, Peter 73
CHASSANIOL, Delores M. 66
    Edna 58, 103
    George 58
CHAUDY, Benjamin 137
CHEVARRI, Eamon 24
CHIEDEL, Antonia 48
CHIFTON, L. E. E. 26
CHITTENDEN, Katerine, Mrs.
        148
CHOCK, Christian 137
    Mary Catherine 137
CHOJNOSKA, Frances 48
CHOKADA, Catherine 67
CHRIST, Frank 192
CHRISTI, Mary 123
CHRISTIAN, Anna 198
CHRISTIANS, Anna 38
    Charles 137
    Elizabeth Joan 137
CHRISTIANSEN, Ann 198
CHRISTO, Margaret 130
CHWOSTEK, Frank 65
CICMNOCZLOWSKA, Mary Anna
        36
CIMBEYH, Louise 137
CLAIR, Catherine 21
CLAIRE, Margaret 73
CLARE, Margaret 142
CLARK, Ann Elizabeth 182
    Clara A. 47
    Elizabeth 22
    Neely 206
CLARKE, Helen Agnes 2
    Mary 165
CLASSEN, Mary Henrietta
        150
CLAVIKOVA, Anna 67
CLEER, Joseph 30
    Mary 30
CLEMENT, David 169
CLEVELAND, Catherine
        Elizabeth 49
    O. D. 49
CLIFTON, Mary 173
CLINTON, Anna 33
CLOCHER, Margaret Ann 134
CLONE, Aloysius 137
    Michael 137
CLOSSEN, Anna 205
    Henricka 170
    Henrietta 163
    James 170
    John 24
    M. 170
    Mary Henrietta 151

CLOVER, --, Mrs. 67
CLUEN, Alice Edwards 34
COCADAGE, Frank Emil 137
    John 137
COERS, Elizabeth 120, 207
    John 157
    John H. 123
    John Henry 29, 207
    Mary 29, 156, 157
    Theresa 215
COFFEE, Fannie 173
    John 173
COHALEN, Mary 55
COLEMAN, Catherine 187
    Charles Wm. 4
COLLEGER, Sara 36
COLLINS, Helen 194
    James 137
    James John 137
    Mary Evangline 150
    Rose Anne 4
    Thomas 194
COLOMBO, Nick, Mrs. 57
COLSBERG, William Henry 5
COLYNAN, Brigid 208
COMEAUX, Arnold 16, 56
    Bernadette 9
    Delano 51
    Gertrude 9
    James 9
    Janet Marie 9
    Leroy Anthony 9, 17
    Warren 16
    Warren Jerome 51
    Yvonne 9
COMPRE, Aloysius 206
COMPTON, E. H. 128
    Eugene H. 137
    James 128, 162
    James John McClin 137
    Mary 150
    Perle 35
COMTON, Agnes Ruby 137
    E. H. 137
CONBOY, Agnes 59, 105, 106
CONCEAUX, Arnold James 9
    Autonices 9
    Joseph 9
    Warren Jerome 9
CONCHE, -- 179
CONDEY, Joan 187
CONDRA, Mary Monterey 213
CONLEY, Anna Cecelia 137
    Cornelius 24, 33
    Pat 137
CONLIN, Frank 63
    Mattie 63
CONN, E. 139
CONNELL, Rose S. 173
CONNELLY, Pat 139
CONNERLY, T. J. 156
CONNOR, Elsie 142
    Margaret Louise 73
    Sara 40
CONRAD, --- 73
    Caroline 137
CONROY, Adelina Barbara
        Betty 137
    Henry James 137
    James Conroy 137
CONWAY, Katherine 191
CONSTANTINE, Conrad 52
    Conrad C. 51, 57
    Delores M. 52
    Evailna, Mrs. 94
    John 57
    John C. 52, 94
    Mary 57
    Mary Margaret 52
    Rose Ann 57
CONWAY, Emma 58
    Helen 173
    Mary Ann 64

COOK, Anita 58
  Antonio 163
  Geo. 58
  Juanita E. 180
  Mary 39
  May 58
COONEY, Thomas Frank 73
COOPER, Henry 94
  M. 184
  Rebecca Rubi 94
  W. S. 24
CORBET, Margaret 30
CORCA, Grace Marie 63
  Joseph 63
CORDERO, Angelica 13
  Angelica Ignatia 6
  Angelina 181
  James 181
CORDRAY, Alice Louise 53
  Caroline Magdalen, Mrs.
    94, 101
  Carrie 51
  Edith Cath. 50
  George C. 51
  Thomas J., Sr. 53, 94
  Thomas Jules 51
CORK, Angelis 73
CORKER, Wm. John 16
CORNEAUX, Janet 16
CORNELIUS, William 51
CORNETT, James 60
  Willewa Mary 60
CORTE, Ulric 137
  William 137
CORYHAN, Catherine 215
COSSMAN, Caroline 52
COSTELLA, Ada 94, 104
COUCH, Elizabeth 130
COUDAGE, Angeline Mary 5
COURAGE, Josephine 96
  Margaret Jean 94
COURBEY, John 176
  Mary Anna 176
COUSINS, Joseph 24
  Thomas 24, 211
COVENY, Elenore 165
COWAN, Catherine 42, 213
COWEN, Mary Irene 138
  Timothy 138
COX, Catherine 27
COYLE, James 142, 177
  Mary 142, 177
CRACKNEN, Ella Sara 148
CRAIG, Helen Burke 138
  John Henry 138
  William Henry 138
CRAIGEN, Alice 138
  Edward 138
  Helen 140
CRANE, Mary Isabel 153
CRAWFORD, E. 128
CRAWPER, James 94
CRAY, John 138
CRAYCROFT, Anna 152
CRAYEROFT, Anna 52
CREARY, Joan 123
CREDO, Mary 161
CREMER, Catherine 147
COYLE, James 24, 139
CRISSMANIK, Anna 62
CRISTOPH, Emily 191
CRITTENDEN, Alice Bell 53
  Frank 95
  Laura 14
  Laura Agnes 7
  Laura V. 94
  Leona Josephine, Mrs.
    95, 113
  Lillian Leona 67
  Sadie L. 51
CORDUA, Anna 162
  Delia 162
  Sinclair 162

CROFT, Daniel Heller 95
  Fred 8
  Rosalie 56
  St. John 95
CROMER, Caroline 127
CRONE, William 179
CRONHOLM, Carl Reuben 51
  Gustave 51
CROOK, Rosina 49
CROSS, Agnes 15
  Charles Lee 51
  Charles Wells 138
  Charles Welsh 24
  George 51
  Mary Agnes 51, 138
  Rosa, Mrs. 51
  Rosa Lenz, Mrs. 95
  Rose Helen Elizabeth
    138
  Thomas 24
  Thomas L. 138
  Thomas Littel
    Valentine 138
CROSSEN, M. 216
CROSSMAN, Agnes Laura 138
  John 53
  Robert 138
  William 138
  William J. 24
CROTHERS, Lois M. 50
  Samuel 51
  William Harrison 51
CROTTY, Frank 121
CROWLEY, H. 164
CROZIER, John F. 135, 205
CRY, James 24
CRYACKER, Joseph 1
CUDDY, Edward 189
  Jane (Joan) 189
CUENARD, Caroline
    Clementine 24
CUMMINGS, Louis 129
CUNINGHAM, Mary 150
CURPHEY, Joan 125
  Thomas 125
CURRAN, Henry Aloysius
    137
CURTIS, Hanna 25
CUSHAMAN, W. D. 24
CUSSENS, George Hartley
    138
  Thomas Howard 138
CUSSICK, Martha 142
CZERKAS, Branislav 51
  Clement 51
DABANO, Mary 51
DABNEY, Jacob 157
DAEHNE, Anna 53
  Louis 53
  Lucille Catherine 53
DAENA, Louise 133
DAFONTE, Benito 51
  Ramon 51
DAHE, Josephine 127
DAHM, Mary Anna 21
  Selina Anna 21
DAHN, Anna 138
  Anna Jemine 138
  Anna Josephine, Mrs.
    95, 102
  Caroline Mathilde
  Dorothy Wilhelmina
    138
  Louis 95
  Louis P. 138
  Lucille Catherine 138
  Mathilda Freda
    Josephine 138
DAILEY, John S. 51
  Percy Arond 51
DAILY, Charles 138, 139
  Elizabeth 138, 139
  Harold 55

DAILY (cont.)
  Margaret Jessie 139
DALIAN, Augusta 152
  Charles 152
DALIEN, Augusta B. 144
  Augusta Bertha 2
  Eugene 139
  Rose 152
  William 139
DALIER, Augusta Helen
    Barbara 139
DALLAS, Adele 150
DALLMER, Ann Mary 73
  Ernest A. 73
  Ernest August 139
  Ernistine Rose Da 2
  Ernestine Rosina 139
  George 73, 139
  Gregory 73, 139
  Henry Joseph 139
  James 42
  Mary 139
  Mary Corinne 139
  Mary Eva 95, 103
  Peter Albert 73, 139
  Sophie 42, 86, 191
  Sophia 139
DALMER, Elisabeth 2
DALNEY, Elizabeth, Mrs.
    57
DAM, Christian 139
  Christopher 24, 139
  Clara Anna 139
  William Herman 139
DAMANI, Helen Carol 95
  Helen Caroline 95
  Lawr. Francis 95
DANA, Catherine 60
DANE, G. J., Rev. 105
DANGELESEN, Henry 139
  Genovieve Henrietta
    139
  Henry Andrew 24
  Mary Heneritta
    Josephine 139
DANIEL, James Lynn 51
  James Thomas 51
  Viola, Mrs. 95, 104
D'ANGIER, Claud Elmer 139
  Henry Claud 139
DANGLER, Catherine Anita
    139
  Henry 139
DANNLER, Anna 178
DANTIN, -- 51
  Catherine 182
  Edwin 15
  Emil Michael 5
  Eugene 182
  James 28
  James Leo Alois 5
  Julia 35, 180
  Leontine 35, 81, 180,
    181, 182
  Lucia 13
  Lucia Catherine 6
  Ruthe 15
  Sede 196
  Victor 38, 51, 182
DARGAN, James Mary
    Aloysius 140
  Philip 140
DARLITZ, Mary 58
DARNEY, Maurice 24
  Patrick, F. 24
DARRAS, Augustine 163
  Eelicitas 65
  Felicitas 52
  George 52
  George Hector 51
  Julius 52, 65
  Peter 52
DARRIS, Joseph 34

DAU, Augusta 24, 43
  Frank Leonard 24, 43
  Fred Leonard 95
  Frederic 95
  Frederick 140
  George 140
  John Anthony 140
  John Frederick 140
  Jurgen 24, 43
  Marg. Frederice 7, 14
  Martha 140
  Mary Augusta Angela
    140
  Mary Selina Theodora
    140
DAVENPORT, James Robt. 58
  Lorraine 58
DAVEY, Elizabeth Walsh
    128
DAVIDSON, Alberta 179
  Henry 24
DAVIE, E., Mrs. 58
DAVIS, B. D. 26
  Birschie Scott 95
  Caroline 153
  Mary Magdalen 2
  Mathilda B. 73
  Rachel 138
  Sophie 59
  Ursula Mary Emily, Mrs.
    95, 105
DAVY, Martin 24
DAXBERGER, Helen Caroline,
    Mrs. 95
  John 95
DAY, Celeste 58
  Joseph Paul 3
  Mary Agnes 3
DAYLE, Charles 138, 139
  Charles, Jr. 138
  Elizabeth Estelle 138
  Thomas John 3
  Walter Miles 139
DEALY, Julia Catherine
    140
  Michael 140
DEAN, Lizzie 94
DE BALAND, Cecile 152
DE BARBIERIS, Mary 73
DEBNER, Theodore 25
DECKELMAYER, Charles P.
    170
  Mary 129
DECOITO, Casimir 52
  Joseph 16, 52, 56
  Mary Ann 56
  Rosetta, Mrs. 95
  Thomas 16
DECROS, Eli 73
  Frumentia 73
DEDRICK, Charles 137
DEER, Mary Anne 195
DEGE, Arthur 33
DEGEN, James 26
DE HABEN, Leo 173
DEHNISCH, Hedwig 210
DEICON, Henrion 210
DEIGEN, Mary 177
DEIKS, Philippine 25
DE JESU, Rita Maria 52
DELAFONTE, Cecelia 9
  Patricia Ann A. 9
  Ella 141
DELAHUNTY, Maggie 29
DELANEY, Anne 155
  Frank 140
  James John 140
  Mary Helen 152
DELANY, John 140
  Joseph William O'Neale
    140
  Mary E. 173
DELOMEL, --, Mr. 213

DELOMEL (cont.)
  --, Mrs. 213
  P. Sarah 7
DELTZ, Augusta 24
  John 25, 43
DELZ, Agnes Josephine 140
  Anna Christine 140
  Hazel Dorothy Louise
    73
  Hazel Elizabeth Dora
    140
  John Joseph 25, 140
  Michael 25, 140
  Mildred 8, 15
  Mildred Theodora
    Louise 140
  Theresa 204
  Theresa, Mrs. 95, 109,
    130
DE MEERBERGER, Sophie 209
DEMESY, -- 74
DEMONET, Albert 2
  Mary 2
DENGELEISEN, Henry 142
DENIKA, Avalina 51
DENIKE, Elizabeth, Mrs.
    58
DENKE, Edward 49
DENNY, Agla 145
DENOIS, -- 24
  Cecile 187
DE PAZZIK, --, Sr. M. 55
DERNI, Bernard Charles
    140
  Philip 140
DEROUX, Clara 74
DERRICK, Althea Gabriella
    138
DESALM, Catherine 121
DESALME, Adolph 122
  Joseph 140
  Mary Caroline 140
DESERA, Julianne Mary 119
DESOMIEARY, Genevieve 16
DESORMEAUX, Gertrude 17
DETTMER, Alice Mary 143
DEUTSCHER, Charles 52
  Joseph 52
DEVER, Felix 32
DE VILAS, Valerie Emily
    Clara Margaret 140
  Victor 140
DE VILLAS, Catherine 140
DEVOTI, Augustine 180
  Mary Martha Marg. 16
DEVITO, Mary Martha Marg.
    16
DICKSON, Elias 140
  Mark Martha Philomine
    140
  Priscilla 140
DIEHL, George 22, 124
DIERS, Carolina 27
DIEZ, Albert 208
DILLON, Agnes 143
  John Martin 141
  William Frank 141
DINA, Anna 41
DINGLOTHEN, Louise 213
DINTER, Emma 74
  Germanicus 2
  Herman 74
  John 13
  John Herman 25
  John Joseph 6
  Magdalen 172
  Mathilda Caroline 2
  Pauline 172
  Theresa 161
DIRCK, Mary 211
DIRCKS, Angelina 14
  Angelina Josephine 8
  Angelina Mary Catherine

DIRCKS (cont.)
  Angelina Mary
    Catherine 95
  Anna Mary 74
  Caroline 133, 149
  Cecile 15, 63
  Emma 95, 130
  Frances 2
  Henry 2
  Herman 14
  Herman John 6, 52, 95,
    141
  Philomene 1
  Teresa 2, 141
  Theodore 141
  Theodore Carll 141
  Theodore George 95, 96
  Tho. Geo. 52
DIRKS, Albert 141
  Catherine 178
  Frank 32, 141
  George 74
  Joseph 74, 141
  Josephine 25, 141, 146
  Mary Ann 74
  Mary Catherine 74
  Philip 141
  Regina 202
  Theodore 25
  Theresa 27
  Wilhelmina 32
DIROUX, Michael 190
DIRR, Caroline 149
DISUBADORA, Alice V. 38
DITTMAN, Clara Victoria,
    Mrs. 96, 99
  Francis 96
DIVANE, Helen 4
DIVINE, Margaret 216
DIXON, Abraham 141
  Lizzie 141
  Vincent 141
DOBBERSTEIN, Paul 52
DOBBERT, Christine 130
DOBSON, Ray M. 162
DOEBBNER, Josephine 39
DOEMMERMUTH, Ann 37
  Nicholas 37
DOERFLER, Andrew 52
  Robert Aloysius 52
DOERR, Adam 141
  Agnes Cecil 203
  Amelia 124
  Edward Blaney 141
  Philipp 141
DOIL, J. A. 23
DOLAN, James H. 150
  James Herman 5
  Ruth 15
DOLEAC, Pierre Firmin 122
DOM, Anna 136
  Augusta 158, 185
  Augusta Terese 3
  Augusta Theresa 136
  Christian 141
  Josephine 7, 14
  Robert James 141
  Ruth 15
  Ruth Magdalen 141
  Ruth Teresa 8
  William 126, 136
DONAGHAN, Catherine 112
DOMAINE, Anice 55
DOMATI, Charlotte 137
DOMBROWSKI, Agnes 151
DONALLA, Ambrose 141
  Dominic 141
  Pauline Aline 141
  Theodore 141
DONATI, C. 171
DONEVAN, Margaret 31
DONOHOE, Catherine 27
DONOVAN, Catherine 112

DOODMAN, Callie Pearl 57
DOOLEY, Mary Catherine
  140
ROAN, Charles 41
DORECK, Emma 96, 105
  Frank 25
  Frank Hubert 25
  Fraon (Frank?) 43
  Herman William 141
  Laurence 25, 43, 141
  Josephine 74
  Theresa Margaret 141
DOREE, Charles James 52
  Jacob 52
DORIAN, Albert 141
  Caroline 194
  Charles B. 57
  George 141
  Joan Antonia 194
  Lenora Catherine 57
DORINGER, Charles 172
DORNHOFF, Mary 99
DORNIACK, Pauline 74
DOROTHY, Rosaline 62
DORTHY, Edmund 62
DOUGHERTY, Eugenia 196
DOULDING; Sarah 30
DOULISNE, Adolph 141
  Charles John 141
DOUROUX, Aldia Clara 4
  Lillian 96
  Lilly Elizabeth 142
  Lucian 96, 142
  Lucie 142
  M. C. 142
  Paschalis 13
DOWDY, James Thomas 52
  Nicholas 52
DOWLEY, John 24
DOWNEY, John William 52
  William A. 52
DOYLE, Anna 27, 209
  Chs. Wm. 4
  Elis. Terese 5
  Eugenia 59
  John Daniel 3
  Laura Martha 142
  Laura Mary 142
  Mary 30
  Mary Joan 4
  Pat
  Patrick 142
  Thomas 25
  William Joseph 4
DRAMMAN, Albert 74
DREARY, Sophie G. 179
DRESCHER, Edw. 8, 15
DRESINGER, Anna Mary 176
DREW, Athleen Agnes 142
  Caroline 36
  Catherine 142
  Cedric Edward 142
  Helen 177
  Helen Christine 3
  James 24, 36, 139, 142
  James J. 25, 142
  James Joseph 142
  Jones Robert 142
  Marian 209
  Mary Ann 36
  Maurelius Stephen 142
  Richard 40
  Viola Louise 142
  William 96
DREYDOPPEL, Anna, Mrs. 99
  Annie, Mrs. 96
  Chas. Edw. 96
  Charles 52
  Charles E. 96
  Eva Louise 96
  Eve 15
DREYER, Catherine 172
DRIAKER, Catherine 142

DRIAKER (cont.)
  Catherine Elizabeth
    142
  Elizabeth 142
  Joseph 142
  Odilia Josephine 210
  Susan 142
  Theodore 142
  William 142
  William George 142
  William Joseph 142
DRNDULL, Joseph 22
  Mary 22, 127
DRONE, Dorothy 182
DROUET, Adolph 191
  Anne 39
DRUED, Arthur Joseph 142
  James 142
DRYAKER, Theodore 31
DUBOIS, Frederic 74, 142
  Israel 66
  Most Rev. Bishop 116
  Thelessia 66
DUBREE, Clara 142
  Louis 142
DUBUIS, C. M., Rt. Rev.
    1, 2
  Claud M., Rt. Rev. 1
  D. M. (C. M.), Rt.
    Rev. 22, 34, 36
DUCASSE, Mary 37
DUCO, Leon 142
  Magdalen Hortense 142
DUCROS, Elias 25
DUEBNER, Charles Albert
    133
DUERR, Louis 23, 25
DUES, Anthony John 53
  Clara 8
  Edward Herman 53
  George H. 53
DUFARE, Alexander 25, 216
DUFF, Catherine 136
  Joan 189
  Sara 189
DUFFARD, Alexander 25, 43,
    47
  Ann Mary Barb. 3
  Cecile 47
  Emma 25, 43
  Frederic 68
  Mich. Alex. Aug. 4
  Michael 25, 43
DUFFY, Agnes 60
  Brigid 63
DUFOURE, -- 34
DUGAS, Elodie Rita 16
  John 16
  Lola, Mrs. 96
DUGUS, Cecile 9
  Elodie 9
DUIROS, Elias 192
  Mary Frumetia 192
DULEY, Frida 8, 15
DULY, Emily 68
DUMESNEY, Joseph Paul 1
  William Adolph 25
DUMSCHEN, Catherine 59
DUMONT, P. M. 38
DUNCAN, Michael 207
DUNE, Elizabeth 144
DUNHAM, Addie 187
DUNKEN, Barbara 208
DUNKLACKER, William P. 25
DUNN, Delia 41
DUNSHIE, Helen 213
DUPLANTIS, Armabell 49
DUROLF, Caroline 164
DURONS, Julia 124
DURST, Fridolin 25
DUVIRNOY, Gustaf 146
DVORAK, Veronica 50
DWANE, Elizabeth 119

DWANE (cont.)
  Helen 4
  Wilhelmina 144
DYDA, Ilko 53
  Jos. 53
DYDER, Ieko 53
EARLS, John 62
EBERHART, John Claud 187
  Louise 187
EBNER, Anna 29
EBOURG, William 30
ECKENFELS, Catherine 159,
    172
  Elizabeth Rosalee 145
  Henry 25, 34, 53, 56,
    96, 145, 159, 194
  Henry Anthony 7
  Henry Laurence 14, 53,
    145
  Laurence 25
  Lillian Eliz. 8, 15
  Rosalie Mary 56
ECKERSKORN, Emily 140
  Joseph 25
  Patrick 25
ECKERT, Augusta 160
  Joan 194
ECKSTEIN, Catherine, Mrs.
    96, 108, 147
  Theodore 96, 154
ECKSTROM, Catherine 33,
    168
ECRET, Margaret 16
EDDY, Almeda 60
  Helen 23
EDGEWARE, Isabel 146
EDHISTON, Sarah Helen 145
  Robert 26, 145
EDMUNDSON, John 145
  Louis E. 145
EDWARD, Anna 165
EDWARDS, --, Mr. 145
  Agla Josephine Legat
    145
  Ann 1, 198, 215
  Ann Cecile 133
  Anna 24, 133, 145, 162
  August 145
  Clinton Noel 145
  Elizabeth 74, 145
  Elsie 136
  George 145
  George Joseph 3
  J., Mrs. 49
  John Fulton 145
  John Henry Goulding
    145
  Henry 26, 145, 215
  Joseph 74
  Josephine, Mrs. 96
  Leona 169
  Leontine 145
  Mary 162, 175
  Mary Agnes 145
  Mary Ann 145
  William 145
  William G. 145
  William Goldwin 145
EGEN, Mary 145
EGGELING, Erick 62
EGGERS, Walter 65
EGGERT, -- 74
  Augusta 29, 56, 101,
    157, 159
  Edward 144
  Elizabeth 144
  Emma 74, 145
  George Frank 144
  Mary 166
  Mathilda 159
  Rosalie 96
  Teresa Ferdinanda 13
  Terese Ferd. Mary 5

EGGERT (cont.)
    Theodore 4, 32, 74,
        144, 145, 159, 187
    Theodore Rudolph 74
    Theresa 144, 187
EHBERT, Charles Hy.
    Albert 26
    Charles Henry Adolph
        144
    Sophie Mary Christian
        144
EHLERT, Adolph 144
    Ann 144
    Charles H. A. 144
    Charles Henry 144
    Charles Henry A. 144
    Charles Henry Adolph
        144
    Charles John 5
    Charles William
        Frederic 144
    Joan Rosalee Eulalia
        144
    John 13, 57
    John August 144
    Mary Sophie 57
    Rose 13, 149
    Rose Agnes 6
    Rose Magdalen Justin
        144
    Sophy Mary 124
EHLINGER, M. 146
    Mary 24
EHRENDS, Mabel, Mrs. 58
EHRHOLD, Joseph 26
EICHLER, Alice 32, 178
    Clara Emily 144
    Dora 178
    Dorothy 195
    William 32, 144
EIMER, Anna 53
    Blase 53
    Martin 53
EISEL, Catherine 212
EISEN, Catherine 21
    Josephine 24
    N. 188
    Nicolas 24, 119
    Theresa 21
EISENBACH, B. L. Edward
        144
    Balthasar Louise
        Edward 96
    E. 26
    Edward 26, 144
    Geo. 144
    Geo. Edward 144
    George Edward 74
    John 96
    Louis Ed. 74
    Max 14, 47, 64
    Max Aloysius 7
    William Max 144
EISIC, Peter Constantine
        144
    William 144
EISNER, Ann 26
EKERT, Benigna 190
    Ella 204
    Mabel Cecil 144
    William 144
ELBERT, --, Mrs. 26
    August 144
    B. H. 29
    Benjamin 26, 121, 144,
        153
    Carolina 183
    Caroline 2, 26, 91, 96,
        121, 149
    Carrie 156
    Catherine 1, 144
    Catherine Margaret 144
    Charles 58

ELBERT (cont.)
    Christina 74
    Fides 28, 55, 99, 149,
        153, 163, 191
    Ida 58
    John 74, 119
    John C. 144
    Jos. 153, 211
    Joseph 1, 28, 139,
        144, 153
    Joseph, Jr. 28
    Joseph, Sr. 28
    Louis Charles 144
    Margaret 2
    Nicholas 26
    Rose 1, 26, 153, 163
    S. 153
    Scholastica 1, 28,
        139, 153, 154, 211
    Theresa Anna 144
ELFSTROM, John 37
ELIA, Estelle 97, 98
ELLEN, Sarah 125
ELLENBUERGER, Frances 124
ELLINGER, Emma 74
    Emma Mary 143
    G. 74
    Josephine 143
    M. 143
    Marc 143
    Maximilian 143
    Wilhelmina Margaret
        143
ELLSWORTH, John 143
    Laura Gabrielle 144
    Mary 143
    Mary Beulah Va. 143
    Mary Frances Ernestine
        143
ELSLER, Anna 209
    Benjamin 74, 143
    Elisabeth Anne 5
    Hedwig 209
    Joseph 74, 143
    Martha 143
ELSNER, -- 6
    Adelle 143
    Hedwig 13
    Richard 143
    Richard Joseph 3
ELSWORTH, Louise 204
ELZLER, Benjamin 143
ELZNER, Benjamin 75
    Frances 97
EMATO, Ignatius 143
EMES, Christian 3
    Joan 22
    John 4, 217
    Mary 3, 217, 218
EMILIANI, Josephine 75
    Joseph 75
EMIS, Christian 26, 143,
        144
    Christine 143
    John 34, 143
    Mary Magdalen
        Henrietta 143
    Sophie Susan 143
ENDRGSK, Anna 213
ENGEL, Josephine Louise
        204
    Sophie Magd. 86
ENGELHARDT, Frieda 204
    Loiuse 204
ENGELKE, Benno Aloysius 7
    Benno Joseph 14
    Charles 129, 217
    Ernest 139
    Helen Margaret 3
    Joseph 145
    Julia 97, 105
    Louise 13
    Louise Joseph 6

ENGELKE (cont.)
    Philipine 217
ENGELKIN, Ernest August
        139
ENGELKING, Chas. 47
ENGLAND, George 26
ENGLEHARDT, Louise 40
    Werner 40
ENGLISH, Geo. 189
ENOCH, Armance 36
EPP, Barbara 56
ERDMAN, Mary Jane 47
ERELLY, John 125
ERHOLD, George Joseph 143
    Henrietta Sophie 143
    Joseph 97, 142, 143
    Louise 97, 215
    Mary Ann 142
    Mary Louise Josephine
        143
    Michael 75
ERICKSON, Dorothy 38
ERNST, Anna 177
    George 177
EROUAN, Catherine 38
ERTZKUS, Dorothy 164
ERVIN, Mary 47
ERWIN, Curtis 16
ESCHENBURG, Chas. Aloysius
        143
    Conrad 143
ESCHER, Georgia 41
ESDERS, Frederic Herman
        143
    Herman 143
ETIE, Laura 161
    Louis 161
EUCUDI, Basil 26
EULIE, Pluff 33
EVANS, Clara 206
EVE, Mary Terese 3
EVERETT, Anthony, Jr. 17
EVERLING, John 131
    Mary Louise Josephine
        97
EVERS, Clemence 42
EWALD, Elenora 122
EYT, M. 75
EYTH, --, Mrs. 31
    Eugenia Stanley 31
FABER, Emma 36, 39
FABIAN, --, Mrs. 41
    John 41
FABY, Edward 146
    Edward Sumty 146
FAGAN, Anna 61
    Stanislaus 26
FAGES, Mary 4
FAHNE, Ann Mary G. 174
FAHRENBACH, Anna 208
FAINT, Margaret 170
FALCO, Joseph 32
    Philomina 32
FALDERMEYER, Barbara 75
FALESKY, Barbara 38
FALKE, Louise 75
FALKENHAGEN, Sophie 143
FALLON, Leorge F. 26
    Mary 26
FALTENMAGER, Mary 129
FALTEMEYER, Mary 129
    F. 197
FANT, Margaret 170
FAPAN, Ann 130
FARIG, Frederick 146
    Mary Mathilde Clara
        146
FARK, John 22
FARMER, Josephine 37
FARRELL, Charles Leo 146
    Helen Elizabeth 138
    P. W. 146
FARREN, Elizabeth 75

FAUSTE, -- 196
FAZEND, Cecile 159
  Henry Ferdinand 159
FAZENDO, K. F. 159
  Cecil 159
FEDGES, Hortense 142
FEICHMANN, August 26
  Helen 26
  Julius 26
  L. 26
FEILER, Regina 202
FEINLATRE, Pauline 135
FELINK, Joseph 26
FELSMANN, Clara 146
  Elise Clara 147
  Frieda Martha 147
  Richard 146, 147
  Richard Paul William
    147
FELTIN, Martha Frances
    163
FENETY, Carl Lester 53
  Edward W. 53
FERBER, Joseph 182
FERBERNE, Andrew 147
  Emma Catherine 147
  Teresa 141
  Theresa 141
FERGISON, Robert 147
  Stewart John 147
FERGUSON, Anna Belle 68
  Mary 173
FERI, Mary Ann 196
FERIC, Anna 38
  William 38
FERNANDEZ, Louise 97
FERRA, Jos. 31
  Joseph 21
FESCHINGER, Barbara 49
FESSEL, Anna 147
  Antonia 147
  August 147
  Eliz. Caroline 208
  William 147
FIAKE, Mary Aloysia 5
FIBULSKI, Joseph 213
FIDELI, Mary 13
  Mary Magdalen 5
FIEBEL, Alexander
    Ferdinand 147
  Elizabeth 172
  Ernest 2
  Leopold 147, 172
FIELDS, Roy Howard 53
  William Harrison 53
FIESEL, --, Mrs. ?
  Anna 48
  Antonia, Mrs. 97, 115
  August 14, 48, 65, 147
  Augustine Alois 7
  Emma 14, 48, 65, 147
  Mary 14, 64
  Mary Ellen 65
  Mary Josephine 7
FIESSEL, Emma Agnes 7
FIEVER, Elisa 186
  Leopold 186
FIGOSKI, W. 61
FINCH, Emma J. 33
FINCLAIR, Lorraine 35
  W. H. 35
FINDLING, Frederic 41
FINK, Agnes 151
  Amalia 2, 75
  Anna 151, 207
  Anthony 26
  Lena 147
  Magdalene 26, 151
  Mary Ann 75, 180
  Peter 26, 147
FINN, A. G. 154
  James W. 53
  James Walter 53

FINN (cont.)
  Patrick 26, 53, 97
  Robert 8, 15
  Robert W. 64
  Robert William 53
  Theresa 97, 200
  Thomas 15, 26, 47
  Thomas P. 53, 67, 68
FISCHEL, Theresa 36
FISCHER, Agatha 25
  Anthony 75
  Barbara 156
  Gertr. 54
  Josephine 150
FISHER, Clara, Mrs. 162
  John J. 75
  Margaret Elizabeth 164
FITZMORRIS, Kate 49
FITZPATRICK, Catherine
    130
  Lizzie 37
  Sarah 152
FIVEL, Alexander F. 75
  Elizabeth 75
  Ernest 15
  Ernest Aloysius 8
  Leopold 75, 174
  Magdalen 13
  Magdalen Eliz. 6
  Margaret 174
  Mary 80
FIVEN, Mary 174
FLACK, Gordon Rex 53, 97
  Josephine Catherine,
    Mrs. 93, 97
  Thomas Jefferson 53
FLAGG, Clara 139
FLAIG, Clara Mary 3
  Frederic Wm. 3
FLAKE, Adolf 97
  A. 193
  Adolph 148
  Anna 13, 58, 193
  Anna Amelia 147
  Anne Mary 6
  Caroline 127
  Catherine 213
  E. 43
  Elenore Ethel Mand 148
  Emil 213
  Emil Martin 148
  Ethel 14, 50
  Ethel Marg. 7
  John Gerald 148
  Joseph 13
  Joseph Osborn 148
  Joseph Peter 6
  Laura Bertha 75, 147
  Laura Emma 97, 100
  Laurence, William 148
  Lina 127
  Mabel 15
  Mabel Cecile 8
  Mabel Pauline 148
  Martin Henry 2
  Mary 34, 128, 193, 194
  Otto 26, 58, 97, 147,
    148
  Philip Sayers 148
  Sara 120
FLANDERS, Anne L. 159
  Anne Louise 159
FLANIGAN, Anna 31
FLECK, Joan 121
FLECKENSTEIN, Rosa 62
FLEGER, Elizabeth 165
FLEIDER, -- 59
  Caroline 59
FLEUHR, Rosa 39
  Rose 158, 214
  Terese Helen 5
FLEUR, Rosina 29
  Theresa 197

FLEURY, E. Rev. 22, 26,
    27, 38
  Em., Rev. 79, 83
  Louis Emil 21
FLIEHLER, Leo 13
FLIELLER, Leo Jos. Alois
    5
FLOECK, Catherine
  Rosalie 2
FLORA, Beatrice 6
FLORES, Adele 53
  Dionysius 53
FLORS, Abraham 53
FLUEGEL, George 33
FLUEGER, Rose ?
FLUEHE, Rose 200
  Rosina 200
FLUEHLE, George 148
  John Henry 148
FLUEHR, Conrad 75
  George 27, 32, 97, 112
  George Conrad 3
  Rosa 97, 197
  Rose 148, 165
  Rose Magdalene 3
  Rosina 204
  Rosina, Mrs. 97, 112
  Theresa Helen 179
  William John 3
FLUELSER, Conrad William
    147
  George 147
  Rosina 147
FLUER, Anna 188
FLUHR, George 158
  Theresa 158
FLYDER, Charles 180
FLYNN, Clara Helen 147
  Jerome 131
  John 147
  John W. 27
  Patrick 194
  Robert Walker 147
  Sara Elizabeth 167
FOEHN, Margaret 171
FOERSTL, Andrew 147
  Bernard 147
FOGGE, Charles 215
FOGLER, Mathias 40
FOGY, Ferdinand 144
FOLDEMAYER, Mary 23
FOLEY, Catherine 126
  Dennis 156
  Joseph 167
  Oliver Raymond 148
  Pat 148
FOLLET, Frank 148
  Frank George 148
FOLEY, Sealy 148
FONTAINE, T. 208
FORD, Anna 27, 213
  Anna Margaret 213
  Anthony Francis 149
  Frank 148, 149
  Hugo 27
  John 149
  Mathias 27
  Michael 148
FORDER, Ellen Leontine 66
  Fred Alb. 66
FORDES, Albert Frederic
    148
  Joseph 148
FOREST, Edwin 27
  R. 29
FORHNE, Elizabeth 217
FORKERSSEN, Ursula 154
FORT, John 179
FOSSEY, Adelaid 169
  Frank 169
FOSTER, Mary 32
  W. K. 23
  William 4

FOSTNER, George John 148
    John 148
FOUNDLING, Clara 148
    John Henry 75, 197
FOURBEY, John 47
    Mary Agnes 47
FOURNIER, John Leo 127
    Mary 152
FOWLER, Anthony Robert
    148
    Catherine 150, 177,
        202, 212
    Catherine J. 31
    Catherine Lucie 3
    James 31, 148
    Jacobina Catherine 148
    John 148
FOWLKS, William 146
FOX, Catherine 51, 151
    Lydia Christina 148
    Valentin 148
FOYTIK, Agnes 50
FRANCES, Mary 22
FRANCISCO, Emmanuel 27
FRANCO, Ida 168
FRANK, Anton, Rev. 108
    Anthony 146
    August Bernard 146,
        148
    Eugene Hamilton 146
    Ignaz Frank 54
    John Joseph 146
    Joseph, Mrs. 59
    Joseph Philip 54
    Mary 146
    Mary Frances 146
    Mary Laura 146
    Mathilda 95
    Minnie 98
    Walter 54
    William Jennings Bryan
        148
    Winiford 98
FRANKE, -- 75
    Emma 148
    Emma Clara 3
    Frances 74, 143
    John 162
    Mary 25
    Mathilda 31, 48
FRANKEN, Catherine 32,
    141
FRANKLIN, -- 75
    Cecil Wilhelmina 145
    Joseph 27, 145
    Joseph August 145
    Julia 149, 173
    Mary Catherine 74
FRANKLING, Theresa 146
FRANZ, Catherine 86, 130,
    148, 160, 212
    Edw. Aloysius 7
    Edwin 52
    Emilia 163
    Emily 52
    Emma 25, 52, 95, 141,
        212
    Herman 27, 146
    Leona 15
    Rosina Isabella 146
    William 27
    William Valentine 146
FREBOESIUS, Joan 196
    Sophie 196
FREDE, Anthony 146
    Frank Joseph 146
FREDERICKS, William 119
FREEMAN, Patrick 75
    Thomas 96
FREI, Anna 28
    Paul 75
FREISTERNEN, Theresa 30
FRENCH, Christian 97, 148,

FRENCH (cont.)
    Christian (cont.) 173
    Dora 97
    Dorothy 148
    Josephine 143
    Robert Danforth 146
FRERICH, John G. 23
FRERIT, Mrs. 172
FRESIMER, Charles 146
    Clara 146
FREUDENBURG, Charles R.
    87
    Henry Aug. 54
    Henry August 54
    Marie M., Mrs. 97
FREY, Anthony 33
    Cath. 209
    Catherine 30, 209
    Martha 33, 168, 209
FRIBAUT, Julius 166
FRICKER, Catherine 36
FRIEDEL, Anna 34
FRIEDENBURG, Charles 54
    Henry 54
FRIEDERICH, Marie 59
    Mary 61, 65, 99, 152
FRIEDRICH, Louise 28
    Mary 28
FRIESER, Mary 68
FRIETSCH, Catherine 192
FRISBY, Henry 131
FRITCH, Anna 218
    Anne 55
    Frederic 55
FRITSCH, Anna 205
FROBOESE, Leopoldine 192
FROBOESEN, Frederic 146,
    149
    Frederic John 146
    John Joseph 146
    Leopoldine 188
FROBOSEN, Leopoldine 29
FROEBER, Anna 78
    Anna Barbara 32, 68
FROEHLICH, Ernestine 97
    Joseph 97
    Mary 97
    Pauline 97
    Theresa, Mrs. 98
FROHNE, Ahha 149
    Ann Margaret Mary 75
    Caroline 98
    Charles 27, 149
    Elizabeth 146, 164
    Sophie 78, 146, 149,
        217
    Sophy 164
FRONY, Anne Mary
        Margaret 149
    Charles 149
FROSCH, Catherine 75, 149
    George 75, 149
FROTE, Theresa 150, 151
FRUGE, Norma Sue 16
    Ollie Ruth 16
FUCHS, Adam 53, 54, 63,
        65, 98
    Adam J. 54, 57
    Agnes 53
    Edward 121
    Agnes, Mrs. 63
    Henry 54
    Jacob 62
    James 14, 50, 54, 65
    James Aloysius 7
FUENTES, Dolores 49
    Luziano 49
FUESSEL, Anne 15
    Anne Marg. 8
    August 149
    August Charles 149
    Theresa Anna Mary
        Antonia 149

FUESSENHAUSER, Frederic
    149
    Mary 149
    Mary Agnes 149
FUGGER, (Thavenet),
        Joseph 27, 149
    Joseph Frank Stephen
        Xavier 149
FUGGERSON, George Henry
    146
    H. 146
    Robert 146
    William 146
FUHSEL, -- 149
FUNDENBERG, Stanley B. 27
FUNDLING, Catherine 35
FUNK, Caroline Sophia
        Susanna 147
    Emily 195
    Frank 43
    Frank Charles 27
    Joseph 217
    Joseph Frank 27, 146,
        147, 149
    Josephine Julian 149
    L. 202
    Mary 75, 145
    Julia 215
    Minnie 215
    Sophie 202, 217
    Sophie Susan 217
    Sophy 123
    Susan 143
    Theresa Mary Caroline
        146
    W. A. 202
    Wilhelmina Elizabeth
        146
FURBY, Elsa, Mrs. 58
FURWAGEN, Louise 102
GAARTZ, Clara 146
GABRIEL, Anthony 150, 202
    Frank 150
GAD, August 149
    Edward 149
GAELLWEILER, N., Rev. 21,
        23, 24, 26, 27, 28,
        29, 31, 32, 33, 39,
        42, 71, 74, 78, 79,
        80, 81, 83, 84, 85,
        86, 87
GAELWEILER, Nicholas 36
GAERTNER, Charles 75
    Ambrose Frank 149
    Frank 149, 150
    Rose Marie 150
GAESCHEN, Frederic -
        Matthew 98
GAFFEY, -- 191
GALHON, Augusta Catherine
    150
    John 150
GALKIN, Jos. 167
GALLAGHER, Mentor 150
    Myrtil Anna 150
    N. A., Rt. Rev. 3, 4,
        5, 7, 8, 116
GALLASHAW, Bertha 39, 199
    Brigid 39
    James 199
GALLOPINI, Chili Corinne
        Margaret 150
    Anthony 15
GALNY, Gustave 150
    Mary Augusta 150
GALVES, Ellen 150
GALVIN, John 27
GAMBERT, Rose 209
GAMBLE, Paul, Mrs. 61
GANE, Patrick 1
GANGI, Jo Ann 68
    Jos. C. 68
GARCIA, Elbadocia 51

GARCIA (cont.)
  Elvira 49
  John 150
  Manuel 150
  Margaret Joan 150
GARDASE, Mary Ann 58
GARDET, August 42
GAREY, Anna F. 53
GARIBALDE, Mary 144
GARINGS, Jerry Joseph 54
  Joseph Jeremiah 54
GARLAND, Peter 54
  Thos. J. Bartholomew
    54
GARMAN, Theodore 76
GARMANN, James 76
GARNER, John 150
GARNIER, George 27
GARRESSOM, H. D., Capt.
  24
GARRIE, Alice Mary 17
  Mary 60
GARTH, A. E. 76, 151
  Amelia Mary 201
  August E. 150
  Edward S. 217
  Georginia Evangeline
    Dorothy 150
  John Louis Emil 76
  Dorothy Augusta, Mrs.
    76
  John Louis Emil 151
GARTHAR, May 54
GARTNER, Anna 150
  Pauline Elizabeth Mary
    150
GARVEY, Andrew Michael 58
GARY, Alice Marie 9
  Angela 9
  Cecile 9
  Erville 60
  Mabel Marie 60
  Phelsie Julia 9
GARTH, Edw. Sebastian 5
GASCHEN, -- 67
  Clara 13, 67, 98, 115
  Clara Cath. 6
  Edwin 129
  Estelle, Mrs. 97, 98
  Frederic Mathias 150
  Helen, Mrs. 98
  J. 52
  Josephine Ann Martha
    151
  Lena 167
  Magdalen 62
  Magdalen Josephine 7,
    14
  Mathias 150, 151
  Matthew 56, 93
  Mattie 56, 98, 100
GASHEN, Mathias 125
GASCHENRAT, Henry Hedwig
  151
  Mathias 151
GATES, Mary 119
  Mauly 119
GAUTIER, Bernard Peter 3
  Elis. Mary 5
GAY, August 181
  Charles Edward 151
  Elizabeth Josephine 151
  Frank 150, 151, 174
  Frank Louis 150
  Henrietta 43
  Margaret Armantia 150
  Mary 13
  Mary Agnes 6
  Terese 13
  Terese Margaret 6
  Theobold 150
  Theresa 172, 181
  Theresa, Mrs. 174

GAY (cont.)
  Tibur 151
GAYTON, Henry 40
GAZZEAU, Rosina 179
GEAY, Eugenia 141
  Joseph 141
GABART, Mary 194
GEBBERT, Frances 38
  Mary 38, 83, 194
GEBNEY, John 27
GEFNEW, Mary 191
GEILFUSS, Ferdinand 38
GEIGER, Engelbert 191
GEIRLEADE, Mary 144
GELPKE, Christian 25
  Emily 218
GELUSSIKE, Ann 212
  Marino 212
GEMENSKY, Anthony 151
GEMSKE, Michael 151
  Robert 151
GENAR, William 152
GENARD, Louis 26
GENGLER, Agnes 128, 207
  Anna 21, 31, 40, 147,
    183, 205, 215
  Anna Susan 111
  Anne 2
  Annie Susan 38, 98,
    111
  August 200
  Catherine 76
  Cecile Eliz. Magd. 3
  Clara Margaret 150
  Helen 40, 58, 85, 98,
    114, 204, 205
  Henry 98
  Henry Charles 150
  Herman 150
  James 4, 27, 138, 151,
    215
  John 27, 40, 76, 150,
    151, 200
  Lena 38, 123
  Magdalen 119
  Margaret 26, 132, 142,
    200
  Mary Ann 75
  Mathias 151, 160, 172
  Nicholas 76
  Peter 40, 98, 147, 150,
    151, 184, 201, 202,
    204, 207
  Peter John 151
  Peter M. 98, 150
  Peter Matthew 27, 210
  Peter Matthew Joseph
    151
  Susan 28, 128
  Susana 128, 129
  Theresa 201
  Theresa Mary, Mrs. 98,
    113
GENT, Mary 137
GEORGE, Emma, Mrs. 150
GERALD, Desomeaux 16
GERBER, Christian 151
  Frances Henrietta 151
  Frances 208
GERBNER, John 28
GERE, Charles Burkhart
  54
  Jules Ernest 54
GERHARD, James 151
  John Edward 151
GERHARDT, Anna Christina
  Theresa 152
  Henry 28
  John 152
  Mary 120
GERHOLD, Anna 205
GERSHEN, Margaret 151
  Mathias 151

GERST, Clara 136
GERTNER, Peter 76
GERY, Charles 13
  Charles Aloysius 6
  Ernest Julius 154
  Frances 154
GETZ, Elizabeth 150
GHEYER, Reneker 57
GHINAUDO, Frank Ghin 151
  John Marion 151
  Philippine Lucia 151
GIARATANO, Angelina 151
  Marion 151
GIBBERT, Mary 194
GIBBS, Anne Elis. 5
  Hugh 152
  William 152
GIBERT, Catherine 124
GILBERT, -- 98
  Anna, Mrs. 98, 116
  Catherine 98
  David Thomas 98
  Don 98
  Elizabeth 52
  Elizabeth Frances 98
  Frank 8
  John 13, 52
  John Joseph 6
  Mary 4
  Mary Ellen 98
  Rose 52, 56
  Rosetta 95
  Thomas 52
  Thomas D. 98, 152
  Thomas David 98
  John J. 98
  Wilfred 8, 15
  William 13, 152
  Wm. Frank 6
GILLES, Eliz. 37
GILLET, Anna 137, 197
  Caroline 43
  Elizabeth 188
  Frank 122
  Pearl Evelyn 52
  Victor Andrew 52
  Victor W. 52
GILLETT, Victor 39
GILMAN, Frederic Herbert
  54
  Geo. L. 54
GIMBEL, Emma 57
GIMINSKI, Marie 22
  Mary 143
GIMMINSKI, Anastasia 152
  Magdalen 152
  Mary 152
GINGLER, Herman 76
GIOZZA, Augusta Antoinette
  152
  Emily 127, 136, 137
  Frank 127, 136, 152,
    209
  Frank Joseph 137
  Rosa Josephine Emily
    152
GIRARD, Sara 191
GIRARDIN, Clementine 137
  Felix 137
  Felix G. 152
  Mary 152
  Mary Cecile 152
GITREY, Octavia 174
GITTRY, Corinne Agnes 53
GLABACK, Anna 56
GLASER, Ann 204
  Anna 40, 204
  Joseph Louis 152
  Louise 152
  Theresa 189
GLASS, Anna 40
  Caroline 28
  Elizabeth 216

GLASS (cont.)
  Louis 28
  Louis Paul 152
  Norman Paul 152
  Paul 28, 152
GLASSER, Anna 31
GLEEN, Isabel Rosalie 142
GLEICH, August 76, 152
  Augustin 99
  Frederic Caesar 4
  John 76
  Julia 13
  Julia Elizabeth 6
  Julia Maud 99
  Mary 13
  Mary Antonia 152
  Mary Terese 6
GLENN, Roselle Isabel 96
GREBHART, Mary 110
GLOCKNER, Julia 62
GLOECKNER, -- 76
  Anthony 28, 153
  Anton 152
  Christine 40
  Mary 31, 79, 152
  Stephen 152
  William Anthony 153
GLOGER, Regina 101
  Rose 115
  Rudolph 52
GLOSOT, Theresa 131
GLOWACKI, Felix 54
  Vincent 54
GLYNN, L. Rev. 34
  Martin 204
GNESIK, Ed. 35
GOEDECKE, Adalaid 206
  Charles Oscar Emil 28
GOETZ, Caroline 40
GOHM, Gebhard 198
  Gibhard 153
  Louis 153, 198
GOLDEN, Anna 37
  Geo. 35
  Timothy 37
GOLKE, Louise 99
GOMAN, Adam 153
  Julia Georgia 153
GOMBERT, Andrew T. 153
  Andrew Thomas 28
  Catherine, Mrs. 99
  Florence Dolly
    Margaret 153
  Hedwig Clementine
    Theresa 153
  John B. 28, 153
  M. Theodore 28
GOMEN, Theresa 153
GONDEMANN, -- Miss 136
  Pearl 136
GONNARD, J., Rev. 141
GONZALES, Catherine 209
  Julia 128
  Julia L. 128
  Julia Louise 128
  T. 186
GONZALEZ, M. E. M. 154
GOODMAN, Caroline, Mrs.
    99, 100
  Oscar J. 54
  Oscar John 99
GOODNIGHT, Albert 179
GORDON, Harrison 153
  John Bertrand A. 55
  John Ralph 55
GORIZKI, Catherine 175
GORMAN, Joan 182
  Margaret 23
  Mary 23, 25
GORRANDONA, Joseph 217
GORSEN, Henry 29
GOTLOB, Mary, Mrs. 7
GOTTLOB, Anton 99

GOTTLOB (cont.)
  Cecile 8, 15, 65
  Frank 152
  John 15, 28, 59, 61,
    65, 67, 152, 153
  John Anton 99
  John J. 130
  John Paul 8
  John Rudolph 153
  Jos. John 153
  Mary 14, 23, 48
  Mary Agnes 7
  Mary Frances 61
  Mary Gertrude 48
  Mary Magdalene 152
  Mary Wilhelmina 152
  Minna 14
  Minnie 54, 55, 153
  Theodore 14, 28, 152,
    153
  Theodore Aloysius 7
  Wilhelmine Caroline 59
  Wilhelmine Cecile 7
GOTTSELIG, Allard Barkal
    55
  Ida 55, 67
  John 55, 67
  Leo 99
  Michael 99
GOTTWALD, Henry 42, 182
GOUGAT, Emily 121
GOURLEY, James Laurence
    Moor 153
  Robert M. 153
GOYES, Adolf 4
  Angelina 208
  Angeline Mary Justine
    3
  Apollonia 204
GRABINGER, J. Rev. 5, 38,
    40, 42, 72, 73, 74,
    79, 80, 85
GRABSCH, Amalia 76
  Charles 76
GRAEGOFT, Mary 215
GRAEN, Teresa 186
GRAHAM, Geraldine 154
  John Lavery 154
  John M. 154
GRAHM, John 21
GRANGUARD, Mary 14
  Mary Aline 6
GRAS, -- Mr. 187
  -- Mrs. 187
  Frederic William 154
  Gertrude Frances 154
GRASSMUCK, Linda Melanie,
    Mrs. 99
  W. H. 99
GRAY, Caroline 76
  John 76, 180
  William 76
GRAYCROFT, Anna 98
GREE, Clara Victoria 96,
    99
GREEN, -- Captain 187
  Annie 137
  Elizabeth 198
  Henry 122
  June E. 61
  Laura 120, 142, 150,
    187
  Margaret Cecil 152
  Mary 137, 145
  Michael 182
  Samuel 28
  Victoria 161
  William 28
GREENROD, Rose 202
GREENROOD, Edmund 13
  Edmund John 6
GREENROTH, Rose 164
GREGG, Mary 140
GREINER, Christian 153

GREINER, Christian 153
  Christian Nicholas 153
  Nicholas 153
  Nicholas Joseph 153
GRENRODD, Rose 48, 63
GRENROOD, Edward Aloysius
    99
  Fides, Mrs. 91, 99
  Laura Bessie, Mrs.
    99, 102
  Rose 113
GREY, Frank 213
  Francis Augusta 3
GREYENBUEHL, Ch. Ch. Rev.
    21, 22, 23, 24, 25,
    26, 27, 28, 29, 30,
    31, 32, 34, 35, 36,
    38, 59, 41, 43, 71,
    72, 74, 75, 76, 77,
    78, 79, 80, 81, 82,
    83, 84, 85, 86, 87,
    167, 208
  G. 216
  M. 21, 27, 34
  Magd. 210
  Magdalen 120, 173, 188,
    192
  Magdalin 188
GREENBUHL, Magdalene 34,
    36, 41, 43
GRIESENBURG, John George
    150
GRIEYER, Clemence 218
  Clementine 218
  Mary 218
GRIFFIN, Elizabeth 179
GRIFFITH, Indiana 28
GRIFFON, Ella 65
GRIMALDE, Charles Eugen
    154
  Joseph 154
GRIMSHAW, Mary 47
GRINRODD, Joseph J. 55
GRINROOD, Fides 202
  Henry 55, 99, 202
  Rose 202
GISHAM, Charlotte 185
GRONE, Mary 23
GROSS, Barbara 25
  Charles 8
  Frank Joseph Antohny
    154
  Kilian 153, 154
  Kilien 28
  Margaret 153, 154
  Mary A. 22
  Mary Magaret Louise
    153
GROSSMANN, Helen 179
GROTE, Anthony 26
GROTHGAR, Alice 178
  John 178
GROY, Frances Augusta 153
  William 153
GRUBER, Blanche 179, 180
GRUEN, Anna 198
GRUENDEL, Adolphina 198
  Aldophine 84, 198
  Josephine 198
  Josephine Adolphine
    198
GRUENINGN, James 36
GRUENROD, B. 158
  Bernard 158
  Henry 149, 153
  Henry Joseph 153
  John Frederic 149
  Joseph John 153
  Mary 158
  Rosa Mary 153
GRUENRODD (GRUENROOD?),
    Henry 28
  Rose 40

GRUENROOD, Henry O. 28
    Mary 76
GRUENROTH, Edmund
        Aloysius 153
    Fides 4
    Henry 153, 211
    John Frederic 3
    Rose 126
GRUENWALD, Henry 163
GRUNDELL, Joseph 28
GRUNDNER, Theo. Rev. 30,
    35, 41, 42, 72, 73,
    75, 76, 78, 79, 81,
    82, 83
    Theodore 181
    Theodore V. 157
GRUNKNER, Theo. Rev. 26
GUBBERT, Mary 49
GUBEL, Anna Estelle 149
    H. A. 149
GUEDRY, Clatilda 180
GUENARD, Clementine 164
GUERIN, Blanche 38
GUIDRY, Alb. 55
    Angela A. 49
    Anthony 55
    Antoine 66
    Dell William 17
GULDEN, Timothy 21
GULHANIK, Jos. 35
GULLET, Anna 38
GULOTTA, Gabrile 63
GUMINISKI, Bruno 76
GUNDERMANN, Augusta 191
    Emily 191
GUNTER, Edith, Mrs. 99,
    107
    H. 99
GUNTZ, August 149
    Charles August 149
    Eugene Gustav 49
GUOKAS, Anthony 55
    Anton 55
GURY, V., Rev. 5, 21, 22,
    23, 24, 25, 28, 29,
    30, 34, 35, 36, 37,
    39, 41, 43, 71, 72,
    73, 74, 75, 76, 77,
    78, 79, 80, 81, 84,
    85, 204
    Victor 209
GUSMAN, Mikela 213
GUSSMANN, Mechaelina 211
GUTTE, Theresa 152
HAAG, Barbara Margaret
    154
    Emil 154
    John Nicholas 154
HAAR, Frances 54
HACKEL, Mary 62
HACKER, Amalia 55
    Frank 55
    Gottlieb 55
    Michael 55
    Oswald Paul 55
HACKETT, Brigid 136
HACTER, Julia 141
HAEHNLEIN, -- 76
    Ann 151
    Ann Mary 154
    Anna 104, 125
    Anna Ursula 154
    Frances 154
    Helen 151, 154, 206
    Helen Mary 2, 125
    Henry 154
    Henry Christopher 154
    Lena 67
    Mary 71, 125
    Mary A. 125
    Mary Anna 22
    Mary Appollonia 22
HAEKNLEIN, Anne Catherine

HAEKNLEIN, Anne Catherine
    3
HAENLEIN, Anna 33, 52,
    96, 99, 198
    Anna Ursula 76
    Annie 96
    Emma 96
    Helen 56, 76, 92, 99,
        150, 151, 205, 206
    Helen, Mrs. 99
    Henry 33, 52, 76
    Mary 92, 99
HAGEDORN, Catherine 53
HAGEMANN, -- 29, 170
    Caroline 1, 22, 56,
        100, 155, 158, 212
    Charlotte Louise
        Elizabeth 154
    Elizabeth 99, 144,
        153, 154, 156, 157,
        158, 178, 200, 202
    H. 170
    Henry 56, 76, 157,
        158, 191, 212
    John 2, 147, 154, 158,
        186
    Lena 23, 25, 100, 101,
        127, 158
    Magdalen 180
    Sophie 216
    Teresa 158
    Theresa 21, 99, 104,
        158
    U. 216
HAGENS, George 153
HAGERMANN, Caroline 33
HAGGERTI, Mary 38
HAHAN, William 28
HAHN, Carolina 133
    Catherine Susan 154
    Estelle Mary 13, 154
    Estelle Mary Eliz. 5
    Eva, Mrs. 104
    Eve, Mrs. 100
    Frank 100, 154
    Frank D. 154
    Frank James 5
    Margaret 181, 196
    Susan 132, 167, 168
    Susan Mary 5
HAHNREITER, Anthony 39
    Othilia 199
    Ottilia 39, 100, 112
HAIDE, Frank Joseph 154
    George Frank 154
    Louise Catherine 154
HAIDEMANN, F. W. 140
HAINE, Clara Caroline
    Emily 155
    Mary 63, 141
    William 155
HALBILD, Mathilda
    Christina 170, 171
HALER, Louise 184
HALEY, Brigid Ottilia 155
    Margaret 155
    Margaret Josephine 2
    Matthew 155
HALFMAN, Laura Emma 97,
    100
HALL, Julia 184
    Laura 40
    Elizabeth 209
    Mary 140, 209
    Thos. Jefferson 184
HALLER, Martha 30
HALLEY, William 141
HALLIEN, Cora 119
HALSHORN, Caroline 40
HAMBURG, Gertrude 76
    Henry 76
HAMELIN, Inez Eloise 60
HAMILTON, Amize 106

HAMILTON (cont.)
    Anice 100
HAMMER, Catherine 140
    Frederica 140
    John 155
    Marc 140
    Mary Ann 155
HAMMERLE, Emily 59
HAMMILL, Mary Joan 178
HAMMOND, Henry 155
    John Henry 155
HAMPEL, Mary 47
HAMPLON, -- 59
HANCOCK, Joan 56
HAND, Robert 55
HANS, A., Mrs. 24
    Theresa 47
    W. 24
HANSA, Mathilds 53
    Wenzel 53
HANSCHETT, Elizabeth 55
HANSEN, Alf. Christina 61
    Alfred 28, 155
    Alfred Christina 100
    Anna Josephine 61,
        100, 109, 155
    Anne 14
    Catherine Barbara 76,
        155
    Herman Hy. Peter 155
    Joseph Frederic 155
    Neil 55
    Rosina, Mrs. 92, 100
    Theodore Henry 155
    William Herman Towald
        55
HANSON, Emma Th. 64
    Mary 171
HAPTHEM, Louis 213
HARDIN, Emma Antonia
        Gertrude 155
    Mary Joan 145
    William 155
HARDING, L. J. 55
HARDKING, Frederic
        Jackson 55
HARDWIG, Mary 77
HARINGTON, Mary 163
HARK, Martha 31
HARMAN, H. H. 206
HARMS, Lena 133
    Margaret 189, 190
    Mary 190
HARREL, Henry 155
    Hugh 56
    Taylor 56
HARRINGTON, Alfred 155
    Catherine 136
    Frederick 180
    Joseph 155
    Mary Winifred (alias
        Murphy) 21
HARRIS, -- 155
    A. C. 155
    Ann Elizabeth 155
    Anna Elizabeth (widow)
        31
    Anne Elisabeth 77
    Annie 8
    Catherine 147, 182, 195
    Catherina A. 27
    Daniel 147
    Daniel J. 29
    Elizabeth 27
    Elizabeth M. 35
    Henry 130
    Henry F. 29
    Sara 29, 35, 130, 147
    Sara Helen 147
HARRISON, Louis 136
HARRY, -- 67
HARRYMAN, T. G. 56
    Virgil 56

HARSTMAN, Marg. 115
HART, Maggie 58
HARTEZ, Nora 65
HARTMAN, Andrew 29
    Ethel Nell 55
    Roger John 55
    T. 55
HARTMANN, Frances 36
    P. 42
HART, Helen 41, 207
    Margaret 207
HARTING, Mary 36
HARTWIG, Charles 77
    Mary Magdalen 3
HARTWIGHT, Charles 4
HARTWIGT, Charles 29, 155
    Mary Theresa 155
HARVEY, Mary 100
    Mary Theresa 100
    William 130
HARVITZ, H. 216
HASBUTKY, Caroline 164
HASBUTZKY, Mary Theresa
    164
HASLON, John 142
HASELHORST, Joan 206
HASSELHORST, Joan 85
HASSELMEIER, Fred Maury
    56
    Gale 16
    Gasehen 16
    Louis Geo. 16, 56, 100
    Mary Agnes, Mrs. 100,
      105
    Pauline 68, 103
HASSELMEYER, Fred. M. 100
    Fred Maury 61
    Lillian 61
    Mattie 61, 98
    Mattie, Mrs. 100
    William 56
HASSET, Joan 35
HASSIN, Charles 155
    Joseph 155
HAUER, Charles Borromes
    100
    Leopold 100
HAUL, Jane 194
HAUS, Mary 206
HAUSEN, Anne Mary 6
HAUSER, Teresa 152
HAUSINGER, Ann 208
    Anna 155
    Ethel 8
    Ethel Cecil 155
    Geo. Henry 50
    George Henry 48
    Henry 155
    Henry George 155
    Irene Margaret 50, 156
HAUSLER, Mary 154
HAUSSINGER, Irene Marg.
    8, 15
HAVARTY, Mary 27
HAWKS, Anna 182
HAWKSHEAD, Beulah 180
HAYMANN, Anton 56
    Anton A. 56
HAXTHAUSEN, Helen 8, 15
HAY, Minnie 50
HAZE, Anna 101
HAZELHORST, Joan 40, 206
HEALY, Ann 41
    John Felix Matthew 156
    John Matthew 56
    Margaret, Mrs. 195
HEBBERT, --, Mrs. 182
    Anne 181
    F. 182
    John 181
HECK, Charles 37, 156
    Dennis 156
    Frederice 13

HECK (cont.)
    Frederice Cecile 5
    Frederice Mary 13
    Frieda 203
    Joseph Herman 156
    Martin 43, 156
    Mary 156
    Michael 13
    Michael Aloysius 5
    Robert Caspar 156
HECTOR, Cecile 52
HEDWIG, Anna 38
HEER, Emma 211
    Leona Theresa 156
    Mary Louise 156
    William 29, 156
    William J. 156
HEFFINGER, Joseph 156
    Sebastian 156
HEIDET, Frank 77
    Frank John 29
    Margaret 23
HEIDT, Mary Louise 142
HEIGEL, Jos. 21
    Margaret 194
    Mary 119
    Theophil F. 119
HEIMAN, Anna 41
    Anton 100, 132, 163
    Anton, Mrs. 163
    Anthony 40
    Emily 52, 101
    Emily E. 100
    Lissie 115
    Odilia 40
    Ottilia, Mrs. 100
HEIMANN, A. 31
    Alice 77
    Alice Othilia 156
    Alva Marie 156
    Amalia 1, 31
    Ann Mary Barbara 156
    Anthony 34, 77, 145,
      156, 157, 208
    Anthony, Jr. 36, 149
    Anto 125
    Anton 156, 157
    Bernardine 215
    Caroline 37, 43, 134
    Caroline Mary 156
    Catherine Cecil 156
    Charles Thaddeus 156
    Elizabeth 157, 209,
      210
    Emily 162, 191
    Emily, Mrs. 156
    Emma 208
    Emma Augusta 4
    Ernestine 30
    Forest Nicholas 156
    Frances 156, 157, 162
    Frances Stella 156
    Frank 77
    George 156, 157, 162
    Henrietta 4
    Henry 29, 36, 156, 157
    Henry, Sr. 29
    Heram Walter 157
    Ida 157
    Joan 189
    Joan Mary 134
    John 1, 100, 156
    John Clyde Cleveland
      157
    Joseph 1
    Joseph Wesley 157
    Laurence 157
    Lillian 166
    Lillie 32
    Lilly 166
    Lily 166
    Martha Laura 157
    Mary 1, 29, 31, 36,

HEIMANN (cont.)
    Mary (cont.) 143, 145,
      157, 163, 166
    Mary Ann 125
    Mary Joan 36, 37, 188,
      189
    Mary Lillie 191
    Mary Lily 166
    Mary Ophelia Augustine
      157
    Mathias 157
    Mercedes 157
    Monroe Julius 4
    Odelia 34
    Odile Agnes 5
    Odilia 145, 204, 208,
      210
    Othilia 156, 157, 210
    Ottilia 47, 125
    Robert Louis 157
    Sara Elizabeth 157
    Walter 29, 157
    Walter Adam 157
    Walter Mary 157
    William 13, 29, 156,
      157
    William Anthony 157
    William Laurence 3
    Wm. Jos. 5
HEIMER, Mary 28
HEINE, Charles Henry 157
    Clara Emily 170
    Elizabeth Augusta Joan
      157
    John Frederic William
      157
    Mary 28, 63
    William 29, 157
HEINKELE, Joseph 100
    Rosa 100
    Rudolph Adalbert 100
HEINLEIN, Mary 60
HEINRICH, Joseph 65, 100
    Joseph P. 56
    Mary 65
    Victor 15
    Victor Bernard 8, 100
HEINS, Albert William 56
    Charles 56
    Charlotte 56
    George 56
    Paul 23
HEINSOHN, Frederic 23
    Henrietta 23, 131
    Henrietta M. 131
    William 23
HEINTZE, Caroline, Mrs.
    100
    Martin Emm. 99
HEINTZ, Caroline 54
    Daniel 56
    George 56
HEINZ, Eugenia 55, 67
HEINZE, -- 100
    Anna 158
    Anne 3
    Augusta 30
    Augusta H. 21
    Emmanuel 56, 100, 101,
      158
    Germanicus 158
    Henry 158
    Henrietta 131
    Pauline 100, 158
    Robert 56
    Sophie 14, 101
    Sophie Cecile 7
    Sophie Elise Mary 158
HEINZELMANN, Michael, Rev.
    22, 23, 26, 30, 37,
    38, 39, 41, 43, 73,
    75, 78, 84
HELBIG, Mary Louise 116

HEBLING, Charles 149
HELD, Bernard Bohn 4
HELFENSTEIN, Catherine
  158
  Elizabeth 77, 214
  Elizabeth Helen 158
  Ellen 158
  George John 158
  Helen 158
  Helen Rose 7, 14
  John 29, 77, 158
  Louis 29
  Louise 158
  Louise Helen 158
  Margaret 158
  Mary Elenore 7, 14
  Mary Elizabeth 77, 158
  Mary Isabelle 158
  Mary Ellen 158
  May Belle 15
  Sophie Ellen 158
  William 158
  William D. 158
  William Joseph 158
  Wm. 15
  Wm. Peter 8
HELFERICH, John 29
HELFRICH, Mary Elisabeth
  2
  Peter 160, 184
  Philip 2, 160
HELMBOLD, John 158
  Mary Joan Caroline 158
  William Adam 158
HELMER, Albert Martin 158
  Cecil 159
  Cecile 7, 14
  George Daniel 159
  John E. 158, 159
  John Edward 101
  John P. 159
  Martin 158
  Mary Alicia 128
HELMERN, Albert Magnus 101
HELMICH, Martha 52
HELT, Walter 216
HELWIG, Virginia 190
HELZEL, Mary Caroline 215
HEMMES, Peter 77
HENACH, Armantia 189
HENCKEL, Chas. 41
  Frederic 41
  Frederic Thomas 3
  George Alfred 3
  Hedwig 41
  Mary Amalia 4
HENDEL, Max James 5
HENDERSON, Margaret 32
HENDREN, Ann 31
HENDRICK, Mary 23
HENDRICKS, Catherine 179
HENKEL, Charles Jos. 5
  Alfred 159
  Anna 159
  Charles 208
  George 159, 208
  Hedwig 208
  Hedwig Mary 3
  Martha Agnes 3
  Wilhelmina 199
HENKELDEI, Rose 172
HENLEIN, Anna 167
  Helen 151
  Mary 167
HENNESSY, J. P. ?
  J. P., Mrs. 137
HENRICH, Mary 203
HERBAK, Martin 175
HERBERT, Desire 180
  John J. 29
HERBST, Julius 51
HERGOT, Edward 2
  Mary 2

HERGOTT, Mary 66, 104,
  205
HERING, Wm. 216
HERMAN, Albert 9
  Anne 9
  Charles Howard 9
  David 215
  Margaret 215
  Mary 215
  Mildred Ruth 9
HERMANN, August Mathias
  159
  Catherine Helen 66
  Cecil 159
  Catherine Henrietta
  159
  David 2, 29, 101, 135,
  159
  David Matthew 159
  Ferdinand 66
  Henry Louis 145
  Henry Theodore 159
  John 2
  Margaret 215
  Mary 1, 23, 135
  Mathias 29, 77, 135,
  159
  Mathias, Jr. 159
  Matthias 56, 142
  Rudolf Matthias 56
  Susan 33
HEROLD, Catherine 185
HERR, Emma 211
  William 13, 211
  William Joseph 6
HERRGOTT, August 77, 160
  Cecil 77
  Cecile 77
  Josephine 77, 160
  Mary 101, 114, 204
HERRMANN, Anthony 1, 159
  Catherine 22, 42
  David 159, 160
  Elenore Frances 159
  Elizabeth 147
  Emily Mathilda 159
  Ernest Martin Theo.
  158
  Frank 158
  Frederic Charles 159
  Henry Ferdinand 159
  Henry Theo. 159
  John 160
  John Baptist 159
  Joseph 77, 159
  Margaret 39, 159
  Mary 37, 43, 159, 184,
  185, 205, 210, 212
  Mathew 1
  Mathias 39, 159, 160
  Matthias 140
  Otto John 160
  Pearl Agnes 160
  Rudolph Mathias 160
  Wilhelmina 159
HERSCHGAENSNER, Catherine
  104
HERSEY, James 160
HERTH, Raymond 38
  Theresa 38
HERTHAL, Frances 58
HERTHAN, Elizabeth 177
HERTWICK, Anna 198
HERWIG, Mina 39
HERZOG, -- 160
  Bernard William 160
  David 29, 129, 160
  Elizabeth 154
  Frank Thomas 160
  Fridolin Ferderic 160
  Geo. 37
  Jacob 160
  Jacob Augustine 160

HERZOG (cont.)
  Joseph 29, 160
  Julia 160
  Laurence David 160
  Mary Elizabeth 160
HESLOP, Frank 56
  Frances 56
HESS, Anna 165
  Caroline 131, 165
HESSLER, Joseph 211
HEUMAN, Caroline M. 53
  Caroline Magdalen 94,
  101
  Charles Howard 16, 50
  Edith Catherine 50
  Lillian 53
  Mildred Ruth 16
HEWLI, Catherine 185
HEYERMAN, Caroline 54
HEYMAN, Anthony 30
  John Albert 30
  Mary 148
HEYMANN, Anna 77
  Anthony 160
  Anthony Alexander 160
  Augusta Mary Olive 2
  Catherine 160
  E. 28
  Elizabeth 142
  J. T. H. 30
  John 160
  Mary 148
  Mary Elisabeth 2
  Odelia 160
  Odelia Frances 160
HIBBERT, Ann 138
  G. W. V. 135
HICKEY, Catherine 140
HICKNER, Caroline 67
  Frank 67
HIEGEL, Fedinand 160
  Mary Lawrence 160
HIFFINGER, Louis 77
HIFINGER, Anna 39
  Sebastian 39
HIL, Angelica 34
HILDEBRAND, Appolonia
  154, 206
  Helen 154
  Teresa 211
  Theresa 42
HILDEBRANDT, Helen 52
  Lena 33
HILDENBRAND, Franz Bernard
  77
HILGEN, Bertha 161
  Hedwig Bertha 161
  William 161
HILL, Anna 172, 185, 196
  Cornelius 185
  Elizabeth 190
  Florentine Louise 161
  Henry 172
  Jacob 30
  Joseph Malvin 161
  Julian 185
  Louise Mary Theresa
  161
  Malvin 161
  Mary 185
  Mary Anna 185
  Melvin 30, 161
  William 161
HILLEBRAND, Theresa 147
HILLENBRAND, Appolonia
  154
  Helen 154
HILLER, Ann Barbara 37
  Barbara 205, 206
HILLERS, Anton 57
  Fred Henry Marion 57
HILLS, Mary 101, 114
HINDS, Walters Robert 57

HINLOWSKY, Mary Julian
   Frances 161
   Peter 161
HINRICKS, Helen 145
   Mary 145
   Helen 26
HINSEY, Elizabeth 50
HIRTH, Theresa 153, 198
HNATIO, Anna 116
HOBBS, Omah 56
HOCH, Adam 161
   Anna 25, 37
   Bertha Elizabeth 161
   Henry 161
   Martin George 161
   Martin Joseph 6
   Olga Joan 161
HOCK, Ann Mary 193
   Anna M. 192
   Anna Mary 101, 110,
     192, 193
   Anne Mary 192
   Augusta 192
   Bertha Elizabeth 161
   Carl Joseph 192
   Charles 34
   Charles Joseph 193
   George 29, 110
   Henry 161
   Margaret 29
   Martin 13, 192
   Martin Rud. Chas. Jos.
     4
   Mary 37, 47, 56, 110,
     192, 193
   Mary Christine 192
HOCKMANN, Theresa 200
HODGKISS, Ellen 168
HOECKER, Charles Louis
   161
   Clara 161
   Oscar 161
HOEDL, Julianne 59
HOEFER, Bridid Ann 7
HOEHMANN, Anton 161
   John 161
HOERLING, Anthony 163
   John Anthony 163
   Wilhelmina 163, 167,
     216
   Wilhelmine 206
   William 206
HOERMANN, Theresa 31
HOERNER, Charles 30
HOFBECK, -- 77, 210
   Ann Margaret 161
   Anna Mary Theresa 161
   Caroline 176, 195, 206,
     210
   Caroline Josephine 101,
     161
   Charles 141
   John 30, 77, 161, 187,
     195, 210
   John Herman 3, 161
   Mary 21, 81, 148, 176,
     177
   Mary Margaret 161
   Michael 30
   Theresa 25, 30, 161
HOFBEK, Terese 2
HOFF, Marguerite 64
HOFFMAN, Caroline 137
   Laura 97
HOFFMANN, Anna 36
   Christine 28
   Emily 3
   Laura 34
   Laura Emily 147
   Louise Josephine 3
   Margaret Anna 31
HOFFSCHILD, Mary 22
HOGAN, Catherine 3

HOGAN (cont.)
   James 135
   Joan Mary 161
   John 161
   Patrick 30
   Thomas 30
HOHORST, Henry 185
   Louise 157, 185
HOLBEIN, Anna 171
HOLD, Stephani 140
HOLDEMANN, Eugenia 126
HOLLAND, Anna 151
   Anne 156
   Christopher 161
   Edward 151
   Christopher C. 162
   Jessie Lee 161
   Walter Lee 162
   Wilhelmina Evelyn 162
HOLLINGHAUS, Joseph 1
HOLLINGSHAUS, Catherine
   180
HOLLINGSHAEUSER,
   Catherine 180
HOLLWEG, Elizabeth 57
HOLM, Carolina 23, 132,
   133, 134
HOLMES, Flora 54
   Mary Agnes 66
HOLZMANN, Josephine 193
HOLZWERTH, Conrad 147
HOLZWORTH, Charles 66
HOMANN, Cath. 56
HOMBURG, Henry 24
   Wilhelmin 24
HOMRIGHANS, Christian 30
HONCHERA, John 57
   Stanislaus 57
HOOK, John 177
HOPE, Louis 162
   Ruth Margaret 162
HOPF, Adolf 14, 162
   Adolph Alexander 162
   Adolph Joseph 7
HOPKINS, John 47
HORACK, Frank 57
   Leopold 57
HORN, Catherine 80, 104
HORNER, Arkley 57
   Lester George 57
HORNUG, Rosina 179
HORNUNG, Alsace 68
   Anna Mary 35, 178
   Cressy 31
   Elizabeth 24, 48, 170
   Elizabeth Mary 101
   Mary 104, 105
   Mary Anna 64
   Mary Eliz. 107
   Mary Elizabeth 101
   Rosa 217
   Rose 68, 101, 217
HORT, Bartholomew 54
   Mary Ann 54
HOSPAEKY, Theresa 26
HOULAHAN, Mary 173
HOURIGAN, J. 35
HOURNAY, George 135
HOWARD, -- 57
   Benjamin Harrison 30
   John Maurice 52
   Roger 57
   Walter Earl 57
HOWE, Adolph 162
   Albert Julius 162
   Charles Henry 162
   Clara 162, 184
   Gertrude Ann 162
   Henry Christian 162
   Katherine Ellen 162
   Walter Otto 162
HOWLETT, Robert H. 30
HOXETT, Bulah 173

HOYLD, Sarah 190
HOYLE, Clara 30
   George Edward 30
   Richard 30
   Sarah 190
HUBBELL, Sydney 162
   Walter James 162
HUBELE, Henry 36
HUCH, Anna Mary, Mrs. 91
HUCK, Anna Mary, Mrs. 101
HUDNALL, Eliz. 9
   Eliz. Sue 16
   James 9, 16
   Jane Lois 9
   Joseph 9
   Lois Jane 16
   Magdalen 9
   Mary Catherine 17
   Michael 9
   Patrick 9
   Pat Walton 17
   Teresa 9
HUDSON, Alpha Mary 132
   Frank 157
   Mary Alpha 132
HUEBELE, Emily 58
HUEBERT, Frank 101
   John 101
HUEBKERT, Louis 134
HUEBNER, Alma Ray 162
   Anna 146
   Joseph 162
   Joseph Henry 213
   Joseph Walter 162
   Laura Helen 162
   Margaret Mary 162
   Rudolph M. 162
   Rudolph Michael 30
   Theodore 30
   William Oswald 162
HUEHOLD, Emily 38
HUENEBERG, J. T. 151
HUEPERS, August Edward
   57
   Geo. William 57
HUG, Mary Ann 36, 120, 121
HUGHES, Bessy 142
   Elizabeth 29, 156, 157,
     163
   Emelene E. 101
   Emily E., Mrs. 100
   Francis 9
   Helen Agnes 162
   Henry 162
   Henry Samuel 30
   James 9
   James L. 48
   James Leslie 57
   Laurence 57
   M. Elizabeth 55
   Mildred 55
   Pat 191
   Samuel 163
   William 55, 163
   William Laur. 57
HULLETT, Flora 56
HUMKE, Ida Emily 168
HUMMEL, Caroline 66, 101
HUND, Elizabeth 59
   Henry 59
HUNGERFORD, Agnes 9
   Willie May, Mrs. 9
HUNN, Caroline 153
HUNTER, John 163
   Lillian Martina 163
   Louis Martin 163
HULBERTO, George 49
HURY, Leo 13
   Leo Bernard 6
HUSSE, Anne 147
   M. P. 147
   Mary Ann 147
HUSSEY, Catherine 146

HUSSEY (cont.)
--, Mrs. 214
Joan 208
K. 196
Mary Ann 146
Michael 77, 163
Michael, Jr. 77
HUTCHINS, Pauline 24
HUTCHISON, Anna 77
HUTNER, Lillian 163
HUTTER, Charles 163
Eva Elizabeth 163
Herman 163
Louis Arminius 163
Louis Herman 77
Peter 163
HUTZ, Mary 77
HUVER, Anna 63
Frances 63
IFFINGER, Mary Theresa
163
Sebastian 163
ILGEN, Gottlieb 28
Wilhelmine 27, 153
ILLEY, Hortense 163
John 163
IMHOFF, Jos. Sebastian 5
INGERMANN, -- 42
Alexander 42
Daniel 214
Petroniela 42, 214
INGRAM, Mary 204
INKERMANN, Petronilla 214
INLUX, Irene 195
IRVIN, Alice Mary 163
Aminda 185
William Henry 163
I'SPOSSO, -- 212
IRWIN, Emily 101
IVEY, Florence, Mrs. 92,
101
IVY, Florence 203
IZAGMIRE, Ramona 94
JAAS, Theresa 128
JACHUSCH, Aloysia 149
JACKSON, Anne 32
Catherine 148
John 30
JACOB, James 52
Julia 207
JACOBER, Joseph 77
JACOBS, Clara Josephine
52
J. 21, 27, 192
J. J. 32
Jacob 31
James 148, 163
Jeanette Celestine 7
Joanette E. 55
John 55, 101
Lester Emil 101
Mary 170
Ottilia 163
JACOVLEF, Robert 189
JAECH, Frances 185
JAECKEL, Henrie 61
JAEGER, August 162
Charles F. 139
Cora 139
Frederic 134, 209
Mary Elizabeth 31
Minnie 196
JAEGGERTS, Frances 161
JAEKA, Otilla 24
JAEKE, Anna 126
JAGER, Walter H. 31
JAMISON, John 78, 163
JANCE, Otto Albert 3
JANEK, Frank 59
Louise 59
JANEY, James 163
John 163
JANSEN, Anthony William

JANSEN (cont.)
Anthony William
Theodore 163
Charles Robert 78, 163
Frances 78
Frances Helen 163
Joan Wilhelmine
Aemilia 78
John 78, 163, 164, 167
Michael Edward Oscar
163
Edward 163
J. 164
John 2, 164
Leo 163
William 164
JANSSENS, William Godfrey
Henry 101
JARMANN, Mary 1
JARSINSKY, Apollonia 189
JASINKA, Apollonia 36
Thomas 36
JAY, John Anthony 163
Theobald 163
JEDLIKE, Anton 59
Antonia 59
JEFFERSON, Elizabeth Mary
164
William A. 164
JELLINECK, Theresa Mary
164
JELLINICK, Joseph 164
JENKENS, J. P. 35
JENSKI, Joan 193
JENSKY, Joan 37, 192
Joan Ricke 1
Thecla 22
JENSON, Singar 36
JENT, James Jos. 13
James Joseph 6, 164
William Henry Harrison
164
JERSICH, William 209
JERIE, Ann 196
JERRY, Charles Burkhart
54, 57
JERSIG, Anthony 164
Charles 78, 164
Charles John 164
Dorothy Elizabeth 164
Elizabeth Magdalen 164
Frances 78, 101, 102
John 78
Joseph 2, 164
Joseph Rudolph 164
JESSEL, Helen 153
JETZELSPERGER, Joseph 55
Theresa 55
JIBBS, Carolina 138
JILLET, John 128
JINKENS, Jenny 63
JOBESON, Evailna 94
JOCKUSCH, Elise 212
Elizabeth 120
John G. 194
John William 212
JOCKUSH, John William 164
Louis Frederic 164
JOERGENS, Augusta 78
JOHNS, Sophronia E. 176
JOHNSEN, Lucia 181
Sidney 181
JOHNSON, -- 78, 102, 193
Alphonso 164
Catherine Elizabeth
Clementine 164
Charles 33, 128
Charles Robert 164
Christine 51
Claudia Camilla 164
Evadna 51
Emma 40
Evanda 52

JOHNSON (cont.)
Evadna Dean 57
Fanny Mary 5
Frances, Mrs. 101, 102
Geo. William 68
H. I. 16
Henry 120
Henry Josephine 164
Ida E. 49
James 164
John 164
Joseph Charles 102
Josephine 35
Lamar 164
Lamar Henry 164
Lamar Thomas Fisher
164
Lucia 181
Luella 16
Lucille Rose 68
Margaret 164
Mary 151, 164
Mary Ann 173
May 54
Peter William George
164
Rachel 138
Sophie 78
William 54, 164
JOHNSTON, James F. 40
James Frank 31, 102
Rosalie, Mrs. 102, 109
Thomas, J. Rev. 23
William Henry 31
JONES, -- 28
Edgar Harding 57
Emmat 50
John 181
Lottie 33
Walter 28
William B. 57
William P. 57
William Penn 57
JONSEN, Margaret 149
JONSON, Margaret 190
JORDAN, C., Mrs. 103
Christian 31, 78, 165
Helen 25, 165
Mary, Mrs. 102
Otto Aloysius 7
Otto Jos. 60, 168
Otto Joseph 14
R. 29
JOSEPH, Frank 78, 165
Elenora 165
Elenore Josephine 78
G. T. 41
JOUNG, Antonia Helen 5
JOURDEN, David Crockett
176
JOYCE, George 123
JUENGER, Anna 49
JUERGENS, Wilhelmine 2
JUERGERSEN, Anna Mary 65
JUERSIG, Charles 1
Elizabeth 124
Frances 163
Magdalen 78
Wenceslaus 124
JUETTE, Terese 2
JUFFS, Benjamin 165
Mary Frances 165
JULIA, Emma Ernestine 48
JUNEAU, Louise Marg. 68
JUNEMANN, Dorothy 141
Frances Anna 165
Francis 165
JUNES, Sarah A. 149
JUNG, Anna, Mrs. 102, 115
Antonia 137
August 165
Carolina 153
Caroline 1, 165

JUNG (cont.)
  Catherine 167
  Ferdinand 102, 143,
    162, 165, 204
  Ferdinand Jos. 4
  Frances 174, 188
  Francis Catherine 218
  Gustave 78, 165
  Lena 137, 142
  Louis 78, 165
  Mary 26, 142, 143
  Mary Ann Magd. 3
  Severus 28
  Teresa 8
  Terese 15
  Theresa Helen
    Christina 165
JUNGE, Anna 165
  Ferdinand 165
  Mary 97, 149
  Richard 102
  Theresa 102
JUNKER, Albert Bernard
    William 165
  Anita 50
  Anita Mary 66
  Bernard 15
  Bernard John 8
  Florence 8, 15
  Florence Frances 47
  Julia, Mrs. 102, 107
  Julia Mary, Mrs. 50
  Mary Myrtle Clarence
    165
  Ruth Catherine 50
  T. William 66
  W. T. 102
  William 165
  William P. 50
  William Peter 47, 165
JUERGENS, Wilhelmina 165
JURGENS, William 78
KAHLA, Anna Laura 64
  Cecile 9
  Cecile Warren 17
KAHLENBERG, Frederica 32
KAHLENBERGER, Catherine
    63
  Cecil W. 55
  Frank W. 55
  Ida Mae 9, 55
KAHMER, Barbara 202
KAHN, Gustav 149
KAINER, -- 23
  Henry 23
  Mary 23, 65, 100
KAIS, Charles 14
  Charles Joseph 57
  John Joseph 57
KAISER, Barbara Helen
    Mary 3
  George 51
  Magdalen 127
KAIST, Ida 50
KALA, Aloysius 58
KALBEY, August 58
  Charles 58
KALOE, Catherine 2
KALLUS, Agnes 2, 23, 134
  Amalia 2, 26, 151
  Philip 26
KALOKOVSKI, Catherine 54
KALOSA, Elise 184
KALT, Mary Ann 187
KALUSA, Clara 162
  Clara H. 162
  Elizabeth 184
KAMEYER, Anna, Mrs. 102,
    114
  Anne 16
  Catherine 8
  Catherine F. 53
  F., Jr. 58

KAMEYER (cont.)
  F. W. 58
  Fred 8
  Fred Wm. 53
  Frederic W. 58
  Frederic William 102
  Frederic William, Sr.
    102
  Frederick 58
  Hermann 58
  Marie Theresa 53
KAMIKOVA, Frances 60
KAMPE, Alfert 15
  Anna 137
  Anna Josephine 53, 95,
    102
  Charles 31, 95, 137
  Chas. Joseph 4
  Dora 181
  Dorothy 138
  George 48
  Josephine 8, 15
  Mathilde Emily 48
  William 3, 31, 138,
    181
  William Herman 102
  Willie 8, 15
KANDER, Frank Nicholas
    31
KANE, Joah 173
KANEWSKI, Augustin Henry
    58
  Sylvester 58
KANYSER, Mathilde 25
KAPER, Anthony 162, 208,
    213
KAPROLAT, Augusta 66
  Fred 66
KARINKOVA, -- 67
  Frances 67
KARLINE, Mary 24
KARLOVITZ, Paul 58
  Catherine 58
KARPER, A. 28
  Antoine 218
KASINSKI, Constantain 51
  Sophie Cath. 51
KASSEL, Evelyn 51
  Pauline 170
KASSMEIER, George 31
KAUDER, Frances M. 77
  Frank Nicholas 78
KAUFFMANN, Lena 41
KAUFMANN, Caroline 62
  Louise Clara 164
KEAGHEY, Kellie 102
KEATS, Lillian 185
  Odilia Mary 5
  Thomas 39
KECCHEROVA, Mary 59
KEEFE, M. G. 130
KEEGAN, Catherine 127
  Catherine Cecile 3
  Mary Elisabeth 3
KEENAN, Frances 170
KEHNE, Charles 31
  Fred. 31
KEILER, Elizabeth 59
KEIS, Augusta 134
  Mary 94, 134
  Minnie 58
KEISS, John 31
  John, Sr. 31
KELLEGHEN, Philip 31
KELLER, Joseph 203
  L. Ph. Rev. 24, 28,
    33, 34, 38, 39, 40,
    80, 81
  Phil., Rev. 59
KELLERMEIER, John 4
KELLEY, Ann Elisabeth 4
  Catherine 30
  Christopher 99

KELLEY (cont.)
  John I. 31
  Margaret Mary 3
  Mary 134, 190
  Mollie 190
KELLY, C., Mrs. 102
  John T. 102
  Margaret 182
  Mary 135
  Mary A. 153
  Mauly A. 148
  Michael 182
  Pat 155
  Patrick 131, 189
  Richard 102
KELSE, Sara 39
KEMPE, Dora 121
KENISON, Caroline 134
KENNA, Mary 26, 38
KENNEDY, Ann 169
KEPPLER, Joseph 54, 66
KERNER, Wilhelmina 31
KERPEL, Louis 62
KERRY, Magdalen 186
  Margaret Victoria 186
KERWIN, Catherine 148
KESSAN, E. M. 24
KESSL, Henry 48
KESSLER, Catherine 211
  John Joseph 31
  Joseph 190
  Philip Walter 78
  Joseph 78
KETTELER, Rudolph 204
KETTLER, Ferdinand 102
  Frederic 31
  Rudolph 31, 102
KETTNER, Elizabeth 36
KEVENY, Louise 114
  Louise Sara 205
KIERNAN, Patrick 47
KIKS, Regina 39
KILLEEN, Helen Cecile 4
KILLIAN, Michael N. 31
KILPATRICK, John 177
KIMELE, Anna 191
KIMISCH, Andrew 144
KIMLE, Anna Emma 179
KIMLEY, Anna 37
  Anna Susan 43, 216
  Ann Barbara 216
  Anne 1
  August 31, 78
  Caroline 1
  Caroline Marie 25
  Emma Anne 2
  George 78
  Louise Caroline 78
  Mary 78, 79
  Michael 78
  Michael Anthony 168
KIMLING, Caroline 127
  Fabian 127, 144
  Walburga 127
KIMMECK, Andrew 79
KIMMELE, Joseph 103
KIMMELEY, Anna Barbara
    103
KIMMICK, Andrew James 79
KIMMLE, Caroline 47
  Emma 68
  George Michael 68, 103
KIMMLEY, Geo. M., Mrs.
    103
  George Michael 103
KINDSFATER, L. 143
  Mary 143
KINDSVATER, Ann P. 143
KINDT, Emma 13
  Emma Aloysia 5
KING, Cecil 200
  Cecillia 120
  Mary 123, 180

KINSEY, Peter 63
KIRCHEM, Margaret 82, 108, 184
  Mathilde 14
  Mathilde Eliz. 7
KIRCHEN, Margaret 184
KIRCHER, Caroline 1
  John 1
KIRCHGAESSNER, Catherine 79, 165
KIRCHGEYMER, Catherine 166
KIRCHRUN, Margaret 215
KIRK, Elizabeth, Mrs. 103, 108
  Flora 62
  Margaret 110
  Margaret Elizabeth 62
  Q. P. 26
  Thomas Joseph 62, 103
KIRKER, Adelaide Mary 4
  Emily Angela 2
  John 79, 202
  Helen 202
KIRKPATRICK, Alma 55
  Anna H. 47
  Clinton 79
  Clinton Leopold 79
  H. A. 55
KIRSCH, Mary Anne 195
  Pauline 131
  Regina 195
KIRSCHNER, George 32, 178
  Mary 32
KIRZ, Anna 62
KISSINGER, John Charles 58, 103
  John James 58
KITTY, Jacob (Rickett) 27
KLAUBERG, Caroline 164
KLAUS, Mary 216
KLAUSEN, Wilhelmina 149
KLEIBER, Al Alphonse 21
KLEIMAN, Mary 42
KLEINECKE, August 43
  Herman Emil 58
  Lena 43
KLEINMANN, John 215
  Mary 1, 32, 215, 216
  Mary Dorothy 216
KLENECKE, Hermann Ferd. 58
KLENK, Frederic Michael 32
KLOEPPER, -- 79
KNIGHT, Juliette 42
KNODELL, Mary Ann 185
KNOPIER, John 79
KNOPP, Claude 68
  Claude C. 103
  Claudia 103
  Claudia Ann 68
  Paul J., Sr. 103
  Pauline, Mrs. 103
KOBITZA, Frances 184
KOCH, Adam 79, 103
  Anna 79
  Emma 79
  Francis 134
  Frank Anthony 2
  Henry 32, 79, 160
  Joseph 103
  Louis 211
  Louis David 32
  Margaret 103
  Mary 23, 50, 103, 134
  Martin Bruno 79
  Theodore 30
  Theresa 207
  William 23
  Wilma Anita 103
KOEBELEN, Emil 47
  Theresa 47

KOEHLER, -- 79
  --, Mrs. 136
  Joan 161
  John 25, 103, 141, 166, 207
  Lena 161
  Lina 103
  M. 141, 166
  Marie E. 177
  Mary 1, 139, 163, 193, 200, 207, 217
  Mary Agness 2
  Mary Eva 202
  Mary Eva, Mrs. 95
  William 39, 130, 212
KOELLER, George 31
KOENIG, Joan 32, 167, 209
  Pauline 164
KOERNER, Alice 4
  Anna 4
  Charles 159
  Minnie 30, 56
  Wilhelmina 160, 161
KOESTER, John 32
  Joseph 32
  Mary Louise 72
  Wilhelmine Caroline 79
KOESTLER, Louise Mary 133
KOHLA, Cecil Warren 9
  Paul 9
KOLB, Margaret 212
KONECNY, James 58
  John 58
KOPECKY, J. 68
KOPP, Theresa 132
KORTE, William 8, 15, 103
KOSE, Mathilde 38
KOSS, Eliz. 56
KOURS, Mary 157
KOUS, Mary 62
KOUTILA, Theresa 58
KOVACS, Joseph 62
  Theresa 62
KOVAL, John 55
  Mary 55
KOVIS, Martin Mitchell 55
KRAEMER, Anton 103, 107
  Mary 26, 103
KRAHN, Victor 27
KRAMER, Carolina 166
  Caroline 165
  Mary 31, 47, 165
KRASIVIZ, Mark 64
  Mary 64
KRASSMANN, Catherine
  Elizabeth 165
  Robert 163
KRATZER, Anthony 32
  David 32
KRAUS, --, Mrs. 136
  Caroline 152
  Catherine 13, 27, 28, 32, 79, 133, 134, 136, 137, 140, 148, 155, 165, 166, 175, 180, 186, 187, 194, 200, 202, 215
  Catherine, Mrs. 152
  Catherine Agnes 6, 57
  E. 166
  Edward Laurence 57
  Elizabeth 47
  Elizabeth, Mrs. 103
  Emily E., Mrs. 94, 103
  F. Joseph 32
  Francis 165
  Frank 79, 104, 165
  Frank Cornelius 79
  Frank Joseph 103, 104, 165

KRAUS (cont.)
  Fred 15, 51
  Frederic 2, 51
  Frederic Cornelius 165
  Frederic John 79, 165
  Helen 165
  Henry Herman 166
  Herman 30, 32, 124, 136, 155, 165, 205
  Herman Louis 199
  Ira Julia 166
  J. J. 121, 166
  Joe 152
  John 104, 160, 165, 166
  John F. 165
  John Fred 103
  John Frederic 165
  John Jos. 166
  John Joseph 27, 32, 137, 209
  John Laurence 166
  John Sidney 166
  Joseph 1, 166
  Joseph J. 28
  Joseph Laurence Edward 166
  Josephine 5, 166
  Linus Thaddeus 166
  Mary 104, 105
  Mary Eliz. 3
  Mary Elizabeth 166
  Mary Helen 79
  Mary Viola 166
  Maud Mary Celestine 166
  Paul 36
  Pauline 165
  Sidney 67
  T. Jos. 152
  Theresa 85, 205
  Viola 95, 104
  Viola Mary 51
  William 165
KRAUSE, Antonia 41
  B. 41
  John 25, 32, 183, 193
  John Frederic 32, 189
  Theresa 40
KRAUSS, Herman 170
  John Joseph 2
  Joseph 188
  Josephine 196
KRAUSSE, Mary 37
KREASTA, Rose 173
KRECOVA, Jos. 68
  Lida 68
KREFT, Fred Jos. 208
KREMER, Catherine 26
  John 26
KREPE, Arnold 32
KRESSEL, Arnold 166
  Emma Marie 166
KRESTA, Anton 34
  Rose 34
KRETZSCHMAR, Joan Camille
  F. Mary 37
  Joan Camille Stephanie 191
  John Camillus Marion 166
  John Louis 166
KRETCHMER, Camille 191
KRIEGER, David 166
  George 32, 166
  George, Jr. 166
  George, Sr. 4, 166
  Henry 166
  Herman 4, 166
  William 4, 166
KRIGER, George, Jr. 4
KROMER, Caroline 166
  Thomas 32

KRONE, Bernard 166
    Catherine 79
    David 166
    Dorothy 182
    Dyonisius 166
    John 30, 166
    Joseph 195
    William 32, 127, 200
KROPP, Anthony 167
KROSS, Antoine 188
KRUEGER, Lillian 95
KRYENEN, Petronella 104
KUBAN, Mary 68
KUBICK, Teresa 199
KUEBELER, Joseph Alphonse
    104
KUEHNE, Elizabeth 167
    John Henry Frank 167
    Theo. 167
    Theodore 79, 167
    Wilhelmina Sophy 167
KUEMELY, Caroline 25, 43
KUEMLIN, Caroline
    Walburga 79
KUEMMELE, Michael 32
KUFFNER, Francis Xavier
    79
KUHALOVA, Barbara 60
KUHENS, Rose 25
KUHLE, Theresa 167
KUHLHANECH, Cecil 35
KULHMANN, Alexander 195
KUHN, Frances 27, 146
    John William 27
    Mary Ann 36, 184
KULIKOWSKA, Frances 61
KUMKE, Ida Emily 168
KUMMEL, Anna 167
KUNTZ, Catherine 34
    Catherine Helen 167
    Edwena Ernestine
        Josephine 167
    Elenor Wilhelmina
        Ormyeb 167
    George 167
    Joseph 167
KUPAA, Joseph 26
KURPITEZ, Louis 79
KYLE, Grace Elizabeth 64
LABADIE, Jos. 152
    Nicholas D. 79
LA BAUVE, Junior 17
    Wilbur 17
LACHINE, George 58
LACHMANN, Hedwig 153
    Theresa 153
LACHMUND, Mr. 28
    Hedwig 28
    Mary Terese 3
    Ricka 28
LADD, Irene Frances Mary
    Anna 167
    Oscar Edward 167
LAGATHES, Mary Symphorosa
    167
    Peracles 167
LAGATOUS, Dionysius 167
    Pericles 167
LAGLER, Cecile 62
    Henry 58, 62
    Stephan 58, 62
LAGNET, Celestian 136
LAHNEN, Joan 58
LAHRRSEN, George Frederic
    58
    Henry 58
LAHRSEN, Henry 32, 167
    Mary Theresa 167
LAIBHAHN, John 167
    Joseph 167
LAINE, Albert 33, 79,
    104, 139, 167
    Albert George 167

LAINE (cont.)
    Ann 139
    Anna 52
    Charles 167
    Charles Joseph 8
    Charles Linus 167
    Ossemy 33
LAKHART, Clara Mathilde
    167
    John 167
LALEADIE, Emily 151
LAMATHE, Alto 33
LAMERS, Frank 33
LAMMER, August 104
    Louise 104, 114
    Theresa 102
LAND, Herman Carl 168
    Helen 174
    Magdalen 182
    Madeline 35
    Michael 168
    Stephen 174
LANDRY, Benita 48
    Malvin 16
    Nicholas 48
LANCTON, Peter Joseph 2
LANE, Charles Linus 48
    Mattie 63
LANG, Ann 13
    Anna 190, 192
    Anna Agnes 167
    Anna Edelgard 168
    Anthony John 168
    Carl 168
    Carolina 173
    Caroline 24, 139, 142
    Caroline M. 25, 139,
        142
    Caroline Margaret 142
    Caroline Notina
        Edelgarde 168
    Cath. 93
    Cath. Magd. 93
    Catherine 1, 23, 28,
        60, 80, 102, 132,
        139, 154, 168, 182
    Catherine Magdalen 93,
        104
    Catherine Susan 168
    Charles 1, 167
    Dominic 173, 215
    Edelgard 15, 55
    Edelgard Cath. 8
    Edward Louis Henry
        168
    Elenore Hernina
        Aurelia 168
    Elizabeth 80
    Eva 104
    Eve 100
    Fay Mary 6
    Felicitas 55
    Felicitas Philomina
        Edelberta 168
    Frank 104, 168, 182
    George 24, 43, 167
    H. V. 168
    Henry 132
    Henry E. 168
    Herman 7, 14, 55, 168
    Herman, Jr. 55
    Herman Charles 80
    Herman Victor 1, 33,
        168
    Jay 14
    John 13, 168, 187
    John Frank Henry 168
    John George 6
    John H. 168
    John W. 182
    Joseph 2, 40
    Joseph Henry 168
    Joseph Herbert 168

LANG (cont.)
    Katherine 132
    Laura Ernestine 167
    Lilian Josephine 168
    Louis 104
    Magdalen 182
    Magdalene 182
    Margaret 182, 183
    Margaret Catherine 168
    Martha 33
    Martha Helen Ida 168
    Mary 1, 13, 124, 154,
        168, 182, 183
    Mary Caroline 83
    Mary Catherine 6
    Michael 1, 28, 33, 37,
        38, 47, 80, 104,
        149, 163, 168
    Michael Edward Joseph
        168
    Michael J. H. 168
    Michael, Jr. 152
    Michael John 5
    Michal John Herman 168
    Peter A. 33
    Stephen 28, 80
    Susan 14
    Susan Catherine 47,
        168
    Susan Mary 6
    Susanna 149, 163
    Victor 168
    William Charles 168
LANGE, Catherine, Mrs.
    104
    Frank 33
    George Joseph 169
    Helen 80
    Joseph 142
    Mary 24
    Mary Caroline 169
    Stephen 33, 152, 169,
        205
LANGHAUSEN, Agnes 197
LANGLINAIS, Aspasie 49
LANNE, Antonia 126
    Gustave 126
LAPAT, Regina 62
LARSEN, Larey 123
LARSON, Frank D. 58
    John 58
LASALINIER, Chas., Mrs.
    53
LASERRE, Lily Mary Eliz.
    14
LASSAIGNE, Peter 210
LASSEN, Mrs. 30
    Elizabeth 125
    Joseph Charles 104
    Louise 8, 15
    Louise Ida, Mrs. 92
    Lula Louise, Mrs. 104
    Otto Godfrey 59
    Peter 125
LASSERRE, John Peter 22
    Louis 33
    Mary Cathr. 7
LASSIN, Mary 16
    Mary L. K. 16
LASSOW, Louis Richard 80
LATER, Andrew 169
    Anna 169
    Mary 80, 169
LATTA, Isabel 177
LATTI, Isabel 173
LAUBEGGER, Christopher
    169
    John 169
LAUBENGEIGER, Margaret 28
LAUIE, Charles 15
LAUSTALOTTE, Frank Vincent
    169
    Justin 169

LAUTH, Jac. F., Rev. 3,
   4, 79, 130, 156,
   157, 208
  Jac. F. 200, 201, 205,
   212
  James, Rev. 21, 22,
   23, 24, 25, 26, 27,
   28, 29, 30, 31, 32,
   33, 34, 35, 36, 37,
   38, 39, 40, 41, 42
  Jeo. F. 171
LAUTZ, Charles 185
LAUUIER, Bernadette 9
  Loretta Marie 9
LAUVE, Adine Mary 4
  Aline Mary 4
  Frederic H. 128
  Hedwig 128
  Mary H. 128
LAVERDY, Joseph 30
LAVERY, Elenora 154
  Lenora 154
  P. I. 154
LAWRENCE, Edmund 147
LAWSON, Anthony 169
  Arthur Demetrius 169
  Julia Louie 169
  Louise 169
LEANTAND, Anthony 33
LEATHEREN, Louis 33
LEATHERN, Anna Louise 169
  John 80
  Louis 80, 169
  Mary 169, 196
  Robert 169
LEATHON, Mary 196, 197
LEBLANI, -- 27
LEBEAUF, Melanie 60
LECHLERC, Isadore 178
LECK, Ferdinand 27
LECLERC, Isadore 169
  Joseph Isadore 169
  Mary 178
LECONTE, Emil 169
  Theophilo Joseph 169
LECROSE, Theresa 25
LEDWINKA, Frederic 169
  Henrietta Elizabeth
   169
LEFLEUR, Cath. M., Mrs.
  170
LEGART, Nicholas Peraclis
  169
  Peraclis 169
LEGATOS, Cecil 121
  Charles 33
  Christopher 169, 170
  Elenora Louisa 169
  Mary 169
  Mary Theresa 169
  Nicholas Andrew 170
  Pericles 121
  Pericletes Diomisius
   170
LEGAY, Joseph Philip 170
  Thiboud 170
LEGGITT, Jessie 49
LEHMANN, Mary Barbara 169
LEICAMP, Charles 163
LEIMANN, Charles 213
LEIMER, Brobett 16
  Ferdinand 59
  Frank 16
  Helen 15
  Michael 59
LEINBACH, Ann 216
  Anna 43, 139, 215
  Anne C. H. 3
  Caroline 158
  Charles William 170
  Elizabeth 80
  Emil 2, 127, 155, 170
  Emily 170, 212

LEINBACH (cont.)
  Geo. 4
  George 150, 153, 158,
   170, 181, 216
  George Anthony 170
  George Emil 170
  George J. 136
  Henrietta Catherine
   170
  Joan Caroline
   Augusta 170
  John 21, 104, 158
  Lena 216
  Lena Theresa 116
  Lina Theresa 216
  Magdalen 43
  Mary 21, 40, 43, 126,
   153
  Pauline 158
  Terese Carol Elis. 3
  Theresa 99, 207, 216
  Theresa J. 160
  Theresa, Mrs. 104
  Thersa 198
LEINBACK, -- 120
LEINBRIG, Mary 211
LEINMUELLER, Francis 170
  Francis Joseph 170
  Frank 170
  Frank William 170
LEIODES, Mary Catherine
  170
  Pericles 170
LELSZ, Ivonetta 16
  Murk 59
  Peter 59
LEMAIRE, Sarah 65
LEMAN, Charles Henry 170
  Frances Ward 170
  Martha I. C. 3
  Rosalie Mary 3
LEMPKE, Julia 181
LEMKE, Rose 170
  Rosina 28, 147
  William 170
LEMMAL, Henrietta 21
LENGAUER, Cath. 93
LENNARTZ, P. M., Rev.
  47, 48, 59, 50, 51,
  52, 53, 54, 55, 56,
  57, 58, 59, 60, 61,
  62, 63, 64, 65, 66,
  67, 68
LENTZ, Charles 38
LENZ, -- 129
  Ada, Mrs. 94, 104
  Aloysius Herman 170
  Anthony 24, 138, 170,
   178, 217
  Anton 64, 104, 105
  Arthur 48
  Charles 13
  Charles A. 104
  Charles Michael 5
  Elizabeth 63, 170,
   178, 189, 217
  Elizabeth Mary, Mrs.
   101, 105
  Ernestine M. 105
  Herman 14
  Herman Anton 7
  John 48, 105, 170,
   217
  John, Mrs. 105
  John Peter 3, 105
  Joseph 13, 171, 175
  Joseph Anthony 6
  Joseph Christian 170
  Louisa 47
  Margaret 202
  Mary 24, 48, 92, 138
  Mary Amalia 92, 105
  Mary Elis. 5

LENZ (cont.)
  Mary Theresa 170
  Rosa 51, 170
  Rosalie 4, 15
  Rose 24, 138, 170
  Rose E. 138
  Ursula Mary Amelia
   171
  Ursula Mary Emily 95
  Victor Anthony Frank
   170
  Victor Frank 105
LEONARD, Ada 171
  Charles H. 171
  Frank St. Clair 171
  Henry 33
  J. J., Rev. 21, 22,
   24, 25, 26, 28, 31,
   32, 34, 35, 38, 39,
   41, 42, 43
  J. N., Rev. 79, 130
  Joseph Percy 171
  Laura 171
  Louis 14
  Louis Aloysius 8
  Mary 24
  Sophie 15
LEONTON, Magdalen 202
LEOTAND, John 47
LEPEYRE, J. M. 21
LEPFEL, Adolph 38
LERA, Alfred 59, 171
  Angelina 212
  Emma 171
  Emma Charlotte 171
  Justin 171
  Justina 171
  Margaret 123, 171
  Mary Justine 171
  Michael 171
  Orlando 170
  Peter 8, 15, 171
  Thomas 59, 171
LERAT, Peter 130
LERCH, Catherine 217
  Charles 217
  Rose 217
LEROSE, Emma 197
LEROUGH, Mary Teresa 137
  Philomene 140
LEROUS, Donatus Clement
  Victor 3
LEROUX, Cecile Clementine
  4
  Mary 152
  Pauline 152
  Pauline Ambrosia 3
LERRA, Angelene 212
  Peter 212
LESE, Augusta 82, 186
LESMANN, Mary 122
LETZ, Mary 195
LETZNICH, Theresa 47
LEUCKAU, Rebecca 179, 180
LEUTSCH, Adolph 25, 33
  Adolph John 4
  Ann Mary 4
  Edward 13
  Edward John 6
  Emma 25, 96, 171, 194
  Emma, Mrs. 96, 105
  Mary 25, 140
LEUVE, Adeline 181
LEVERING, Mary 61
LEWELLYN, Abel Thomas 179
  Louise 217
LEWIS, Anna 171
  Augusta 137
  Henry 161
  James 33, 171
  James Louis 171
  John 171
  John Fitzhugh Lee 171

LEWIS (cont.)
  Mary Ann 27
  Mary Henrietta 171
  Mathilda Irene 171
  Pauline 40
  Thomas H. 105
  Violet Alice 171
LEWRENER, Frank 178
LEYMULLER, Francis
    Joseph 171
  Helen Catherine 171
LIAB, Helen 67
LIBERTO, Lillian 13
  Lillian Veronica 6
  Lillie 175
LICHAW, Rebecca 179
LIDEKE, Nettie 214
LIEBISCH, David 111
  Helen 111
  Mathilde 105, 111
LIEBLING, Anna 188
LIEBREICH, Albert 34
  Mary 218
LIEFRICH, Margaret 22
LIENARD, Able 171
  Geo. Joseph 171
LIENHART, George 172
  George Frank 172
LIMKE, Julia, Mrs. 105
  Henry 105
LIMLEY, Caroline 40
LIMMER, John Hy. 192
LINK, Adam 29
LINKE, Julia, Mrs. 97
LINNETT, Anna 32
LINNMANN, Catherine 79
LINTNER, Frank 59
LIPSCOMB, Natalie 48
LITTLE, Susan 27
LIZA, Frank 105
  Joseph 105
  Mary 105
LOBENSTEIN, Henrietta
    Louise 172
  Henry Louis Paul 172
  Louis 172
  Paul Michael Louis 172
  Pauline 172
LOCE, August 37
  Leonida 37
LEONRING, Henry 30
LOEPZ, Earl 17
LOESCHLER, Charles 34
LOEWING, Henry 42
LOFFERRS, Theresa 198
LOGRE, Edmund, Jr. 24
LOHRE, Louise 153
LOISELLE, P. 43
  Peter 39
LONG, John George 34
  Susan 80
LOPEZ, Vincent 55
LORDAN, Daniel Aloysius 7
  Daniel Baptist 14, 172
  Ellen Gertrude 172
  Ethel Mary Gertrude 7
  Ferdinand Aloysius 5
  George 13
  George Joseph 6
  Gertrude 14
  Gertrude Mary 7
  Hortense 174
  Jeremiah 80, 147, 172
  Jerome 13
  Jerome Michael 174
  Jerome Stephen 6
  Jerry 172
  John 174, 189, 190
  John Joseph 4
  Joseph 172
  Mary 147
  Mary Hortense 80, 172
  Ottance 174

LORENTZ, Hugh 59
LORENZO, Henrietta 167
  Oliver 167
LOSE, Augusta 186
LOSSOW, Louis John 172
  Louis Richard 172
  Paul Richard 172
  Rose Mary Margaret 172
LOTHRINGER, Adele 172
  Adele Catherine 7
  Ferdinand 172
  Ferdinand Charles 172
  Ida 68
  Mary Elizabeth 172
  Victor 172
  Victor Joseph 3
LOTT, Augustine 172
  Clarence Henry 172
  Elis. Wilhelmine 14
  Elise Wilhelmina 172
  Eliz. Wilhelmine 7
  Frederic W. 34
  Frederic William 172
  Otto H. 25, 172
  Valeninte, Mrs. 56
  William 26, 172
LOUBAT, Edward Julius 172
  Hell 172
  Oscar 172
LOUIS, Christina Margaret
    173
  Henry 173
  Mary 146
LOUSTALOTTE, Eugenia
    Elenora 173
  Justin 173
LOUSTAUNAU, Sidney
    Eugene 4
LOWENSTEIN, Julia 63
LOWRY, Lloyd 59
  Charles C. 59
LOYAN, Elizabeth 96
LAZARO, Julia 153
LTZNICH, August 47
LUCAT, Wilhelmine 66
LUCKHEART, Carolina 191
LUDVIG, --, Mrs. 191
LUDWIG, Anna 80
  Mary 213
LUEDIGE, Christian 34
  Henrietta 34
LUELKE, Elizabeth 37, 43
LUGAN, Rebecca 179
LUMNIEL, Anna 167
LUTHER, Andrew 106
  William Louis 106
LUTZ, Adam 40
  Caroline 156
  John 105, 166
  Margaret 40
  Mary 166
  Mary, Mrs. 104, 105
  Theresa 43
LYLE, Ethel Mae 60
  Frank 60
LYNCH, Elizabeth 216
  Helen 216
  James 137
  Wilhelmine E. 43
LYON, Laura 63
LYONS, Helen 119
  Mary 56, 197
  Mary Agnes 100, 105
  Nellie 197
  Nelly 84
  Thomas J. 34
  William George 105
MABUS, Mary Ann 173
  William 173
MACERA, Camille Mary 5
  Edward Aloyius 5
  James 34
  Julius 34, 173

MACERA (cont.)
  Louise Margaret 173
MACHIN, Josephine, Mrs.
    105, 106
MACIK, Louis 66
  Moli 66
MACK, Joseph J., Rev. 68,
    105, 109
MAC KENA, Greenville 173
  P. E. 173
MAC KINA, Peter 173
  Peter Edward 173
MADALINSKI, Voctoria 86
MADALUISKA, Victoria 213
MADDEN, John 173
  Laura Joan 173
MADISON, J. B. 25, 43
MADUCIA, Anna 60
MAECHLER, A. M., Rev. 9,
    16, 17, 48, 49, 50,
    51, 52, 53, 55, 56,
    57, 60, 61, 62, 63,
    64, 65, 66, 67, 68,
    91, 92, 93, 94, 95,
    96, 97, 98, 99, 101,
    102, 104, 105, 106,
    107, 108, 109, 110,
    111, 112, 113, 114,
    115, 116
MAGADIEN, Paul 34
MAGGARTHY, Anna 27
MAGKONSKY, Elizabeth M.
    27
  Sophie 27
MAGNA, Joan 34
  Joseph 34
  Michael 34
MAGNANI, Julus 60
  Sisie 60
MAGRUDER, Albert
    Greenville 173
  Sara Elizabeth 173
MAGUIRE, Verena Ethel 173
  George 173
  George M. 34
  John 166
MAHONEY, John E. 42
MAHONY, Mary 151
MAHR, Albert Joseph 59
  Philip 59
MAIER, Catherine 50, 92
  Charlotte 50
MAILAND, Louise 189
MAINA, Frances 209
MAINDHOFF, Margaret 110
MAIR, Bernard 122
MAIRBOUR, E. 21
MAITRI, Rosalina 83
MALCHER, Ann 203
  Anna 113
MALEK, Frieda 192
  Robert 192
MALIA, John Baptist 148
MALLET, John 150
MALLIA, Henry Thomas 173
  John B. 173
  John Baptist 173
MALLOY, Ann 13
  Ann Mary 6
  Catherine 14, 173
  Catherine Cecile 7
  John Silvester 173
  Joseph Peter 173
MALLYE, John B. 173
  Mary Antoinette 173
MALONE, Grace Loretta 200
MALSAM, Nicholas 43
MALTA, Elizabeth 198
MALZ, Charlotte Catherine
    116
MALZBURGER, Catherine 80
MANGELIERS, Otto John 3
MANGLIER, Anna Elizabeth

MANGLIER (cont.)
  Anna Elizabeth 173
  Henry 34
  Leo Anthony Henry 173
  Otto 34, 173
  Otto John 173
MANION, Catherine 178
MANICHUCCI, Palmyra 171
MANNAGHAN, Thaddeus 38
MANNING, Alice 126
  Cecil 173
  Dalia 185
  Thomas 173
MANOWITCH, Martin 173
  William 173
MANOWSKI, Joseph 199
MANSER, Mary 80
MANTEAU, Clara 180
  Emil 173
  John Marion 173
  Lydia 174
  Nevil 180
  Valerian 174
MANYON, Catherine 144
MARCHAL, John 174
  Roman 174, 175
MARCHALL, Ferdinand 174
  Margaret Louise 174
MARCHAND, Elizabeth 75,
    147
  Ernest 80
  Ernest Michael 174
  Ferdinand 33, 80, 137,
    169, 171, 174
  Ferdinand Henry 80,
    174
  George Peter 174
  George William 174
  Hortense 172
  Julius 80, 174
  Margaret Louise 174
  Mary Antonia 148
  Mary Hortense 172
  Octavia 79, 169, 174,
    186
  Octavia Angela 174
  Octavia Veronica 174
  Peter George 174
MARCION, Mary 65
MARCOS, Emily 137
MARCOVICH, Ann 212
  Vido 212
MARERO, Joseph 179, 180
MARHOLD, Caroline 38
MARI, Julia 199
MARIAN, Anna 152
MARINOVITCH, David Martin
    174
  F. 174
MARKE, Anna 191
  Ann, Mrs. 80
  Frances Sophie 174
  Frank 165
  Frank Joseph 174
MARKI, Lanira 50
MARKOVICH, Louise 105
MARKS, Christina 119
MARRATT, Ernest 65
MARSAISE, Ann 129
MARSCHNER, Florence 59
MARSHAL, Laura 93
MARSHALL, Antonia 174
  Haslam 174
  John 174, 175
  Joseph 175
  Laura Ellen 175
  Margaret Lilly 174
  Mary 175
  Paul Haslem 174
  Peter 174
  Robert 175
  Roman 175
MARTIAL, M. Hortense 80

MARTIN, Agnes Ernestine
    105
  Ambrose 31
  Anna Ernestine 175
  Caroline Elizabeth 105
  Catherine 47
  Clemens 196
  Clemens Paul 5
  Clement 13
  Dorothy 16
  Eliz. 211
  Elizabeth 211
  Ernest 143
  John 59, 65, 106, 175
  Louis 59, 105, 106, 190
  Louis Daniel 106
  Louis Joseph 59
  Marguerite 106
  Martha 182
  Mary 26, 31, 65, 114,
    190, 213
  Mary Victoria 5
  Mathilde 175
  Sophie 190
  William 53
MARTINELLI, Cajetan 123
  Eugenia 123
MARTINEZ, Rosa 167
MARTINI, Louise 13
  Louise Mary 6
MARULLO, Jo Ann 68
MARVITZ, Bertha 26
  Herman 26
MARWITZ, Herrman 145
MARX, Aloysius 143
  Anthony 36, 39
  Christian 199
  Christina 39, 199
  Christine 199
  Christine Mary 3
  Cunigunde 34, 39
  Emma 4, 34, 199
  Kerney 36
  Kunigunde 173
  Rose Mary 3, 36
MARY, Maria 33
MASAR, -- 59
  Divis 59
MASEY, Evelyn 67
MASON, Elizabeth 171
MASONET, John Michael 22
  Marie 22
MASSE, Louise Mathilda 3,
    148
  Mary 126
MASSEY, Clara 167
MASSONET, Mary 126
MASTRAL, Victor 134
MATELA, Ignatius 60
  Joseph 60
MATELSKY, Frank 60
  Henry Herman 60
MATEYOWSKI, Henry 175
  Martin 175
MATHEWA, Demetrius 170
  Louise 170
MATHEWS, Henry 33
MATHEY, Mary 139
MATHIS, Louise 47
  Ludwig 47
MATHISON, Melvin 80
MATIZKI, Henry 175
  Stanislav 175
MATT, Jos. 40
  Joseph 2, 51, 80, 106
MATTE, Wilson 60
MATYOWSKI, -- 60
  Henry 60
  Theodore 60
MATYSEK, Charles 60, 67
  Frank 60
MAUBAULES, Edna Louise 17
  Ethel Mary 106

MAUBAULES (cont.)
  Jacklin Cecile 106
  Johnny Fay 106
MAUDOWN, Helen 214
MAUMANN, Mary Rose 32
MAURATH, Crescentia 43
MAURER, --, Mrs. 143
  Alizabeth 134
  Amize, Mrs. 106
  Anice, Mrs. 100
  Ann 41, 155, 156, 205
  Anna 48, 50, 175
  Anna Mary 175
  Anthony Bennett 175
  Carolina 218
  Caroline 1, 42, 115,
    147, 152, 198
  Caroline, Mrs. 106,
    112
  Caroline Cecil 7
  Caroline Mary 176
  Caroline Wilhelmine 14,
    175
  Clarence 15
  Clarence Anthony 8
  Claude Joseph 175
  Elizabeth 189
  Elizabeth Pauline 192
  Frederic 80
  George 8, 15, 106
  George Michael 175
  Herman 198
  James 34, 80, 175, 176
  John 2, 34, 41, 60,
    67, 80, 106, 115,
    130, 134, 137, 152,
    156, 175, 182, 198
  Joseph 106, 155, 175
  Joseph Michael 4, 50
  Louise 81, 198
  Lucia 80
  Lucie 81
  Lucy 198
  Mary Caroline 175
  Mary Frances 4, 192
  Mary Terese 3
  Michael 3, 32, 34, 106,
    138, 172, 175, 176
  Minna 36
  Peter 80, 81, 176, 198
  Terese 4
  Theresa 41, 147, 149,
    155, 175, 209, 216
  Theresa Marie 106
  Theresa Mary, Mrs. 115
  Wendel James 176
  Wendelin 106
  Wendolin 14, 81
  Wendolin Joseph 7
  Wilhelmina 175
MAURERE, Anna Mary 3
  Joseph M. 60
MAUS, Mary 142
MAUSER, F. 21
MAY, Catherine 122
  Theresa 199
MAYER, Andrew 1, 27, 34,
    105
  Anna Mary Elizabeth 176
  Barbara 75
  Bernard 176
  Catherine J. 176
  Catherine Josephine 176
  Eliz. 105
  Elizabeth 27, 28, 152
  Elizabeth, Mrs. 106
  Fridolin 28, 81
  John 1
  John Baptist 34
  John Bernard 176
  John Clifford 176
  John M. 176
  Josephine 105, 106

MAYER (cont.)
  Mary 176, 209
  Mary Ann 34
  Mary Anna 152
  Mary Elizabeth 176
  William 81
  Xavier 34
MAYNA, Mary Philomine 195
MAYNARD, Charles D. 176
  Thomas Jefferson 176
MAYS, Elizabeth 193
MAZZARA, Mary Josephine
  9, 16
  Vincent 9, 16
MC ALISTER, Elizabeth 54
MC ARDLE, Jos., Rt. Rev.
  94
MC AVENEY, Caroline 176
  Edward 176
  Helen 176
  John D. 176
  Mary Magdalen 176
  William Edward 176
MC BRIDE, Daniel 159
  Helen 22
  Mary 159
MC CAILEY, Ellen 176
  John 176
  Mary 176
MC CARRON, Gilbert 34
  Henry 34
MC CARTHY, Arthur 176
  Edw. Ignatius 5
  Edward 13, 148, 176
  Edward William 176
  Ellen 36, 213
  Henry 176
  Joseph 176
  Julia Lee 176
  Pauline 148
  Richard 176
  Ruth 16
  T. H. R. 176
  William 16, 176
MC CAULEY, Anastasia 4
  Catherine 190
  Helen Mary 4
MC CLEERY, Jennie Louise
  61
  Samuel 61
MC CLUSKY, John 24
MC CORMICK, Dathula 29,
  157
  Decathula 157
  Henrietta 29, 156, 157
  Huth 177
  Mary 157
MC CRACKEN, Anne 13
  Anne Veronica 6
  David 176
  David Crockett 176
MC CREA, Catherine 216
MC CUBBINS, G. J. 177
  Laura 177
MC DERMOTH, Martin 40
  Mary 160
  Mary E. 40
MC DONALD, Agnes 40
  Angus 177
  Emma Martha 177
  James 32, 34
  Malcome Joseph 177
  Margaret 208
  Michael 177
  Ronald 177
  Thomas 179
  Virginia 65
MC DONELL, Mary 40
MC GILL, Ellen 207
MC GINNIS, James Joseph 4
  Joan 184
MC GORIGAN, Ann 27
MC GOVERN, Catherine 188

MC GOVERN (cont.)
  Frances 188
MC GOWAN, Bridgett, Mrs.
  106
MC GRAW, Catherine 39,
  199, 200
  Clara 137
  John 137
  Joseph 39
MC GRAY, Henry 215
MC GREAL, Anna 24
MC GRUDER, George H. 23
MC GUIRE, Catherine
  Frances 4
  George 36
  Thomas 125
MC INERNEY, Daniel B. 60
  Edward 60
MC KAWENE, Anna 81, 177
  Edward 81, 177
MC KAY, Mary 195
MC KENA, Margaret 177
MC KENNA, Casey 42
  Josephine 177
  Peter E. 177
  Rudolph 177
MC KESSON, David 39
  Emma 39
MC LAUGHLIN, Alice 180
MC LEROY, Jane 177
  Joan 177
  William 177
MC MALLVILLY, Mellie 163
MC MANUS, Alice 4
  Ellen 189
  Helen 195
  Thomas 35
MC MARTHEY, Frances 159
  John 159
MC MULLEN, Daniel 177
  James 177
  Mollie 24
MC NAB, Joan Frances 35
MC NALLEY, James 177
  Mary 177
MC NALLY, James 13, 35,
  177
  James Aloysius 6
  John 14, 177
  John Joseph 6
  Louise 178
  Louise Ernestine 4
  Mary 13
  Thomas Cleveland 177
  Mary Helen 6
MC NAMARA, -- 177
  William John 177
MC NAMORA, Rovert 205
MC NEAL, Clothilde 173
MC NELLY, Catherine 177
  James 177
  Martin 177
  Walter Marion 177
MC NEY, Mary 126
MC RAE, Adelaide Mary 177
  Carolina 139
  Norman 177
  Norman Alexander 177
MC SWEENEY, Edward 119
MC VOLTY, Mary 120
MC WATER, Isaac Thomas 177
MC WATERS, Alexander 177
  Helen 177
  Mary 3
MEALY, Elizabeth 211
  John 211
MEAUME, Laeticia 120
MECKI, Edward 28
MEES, Adam 177
  Barbara 156
  Frank Clement 7
  George Martin 177
  Joseph 156

MEES (cont.)
  Mary Anne 13
  Marg. Catherine 7
  Mary Terese 6
  William 156
MEGSON, William 4
MEIBACH, Charles 81
MEIDHOF, Mary 136
MEIER, Bernard 177
  John William 177
  Joseph 81
  Josephine 21
MEIERS, Eugene 106
  Eugene Fred 60
  Louis Lyl 60
MEINECKE, Edward 177
MEITHOF, Margaret 29
MELCHER, Anna 84
MELLEN, Frank 177, 178
  George 178
  Mary Frances 178
MELODUE, Selina 140
MELVILLE, Anna 145
  Belle 34
  Elisabeth 4, 64
  Irene Mary 178
  Isabel 178
  William 178
MENARD, Adolph P. 178
  John Mary 178
  Joseph O. 169
  Susan 169
MENDEZ, Peter 178
  Santos 178
MENECUCCI, Constance 171
MENGEL, Cora Terese 5
MENICUCCI, August 171
  Jeromine 171
  Palmira 59, 171
MENNAE, Joan 192
MENTZEL, Charles 64
  Mary 48, 51
  Mary Elizabeth 64
MENZEL, --, Mr. 129
  A. Mary, Mrs. 170
  Ann Mary 170
  Anna Mary 138
  August Anthony 178
  Charles 35, 107, 178
  Charles William 178
  Chs. Philip 5
  Edith 99, 107
  Ida 61
  Ida Rosalie 5
  Ida Rosaline 178
  John 178
  Mary 13, 17, 213 -
  Mary Catherine 6
  Mary Elizabeth 178
  Mary Elizabeth, Mrs.
  101, 107
  Otto 13, 38
  Otto Frederic 107, 178
  Otto Michael 6
MERCER, Clara E. 24
  Oscar 24
MEREDITH, -- 207
MERIQUE, Celina 36
MERKEL, Anthony 146
  Theresa 146
MERSINGEN, Edw. Laurence
  60
MERSINGER, Lawrence 60
MERTHEL, Anna Mary 154
MERTHL, Charlotte 215
MESPIL, Ida 193
MESS, Mary Helen 13
  Mary Helen Marg. 6
MESSIA, Frances 66
MESTRALE, Alex 119
MESTIER, -- 179
METTLIKA, Kostilizanna 64
METTNER, Hugo 57

METZ, Mary 153, 154
METZGER, Anton 103, 107
    Frederic August 178
    Jacob August 178
    Joseph 178
    Mary, Mrs. 107
    Mary Ann 80
    Mary Anne 33
    Thecla Joan 178
MEURI, Agnes 13, 199
    Cecil Leurener 178
    Henry 178
    Julia 47
    Lilian 197
    Mary 197
MEURIE, Julia Aloysia 5
MEURY, Julia 102, 107,
    165
    Mary 204
MEYER, -- 28
    Ann Catherine 203
    Anna 107, 203
    Anna Catherine 203
    Ann Catherine 203
    Caroline 122
    Catherine 122
    Elizabeth 152
    H. 42
    John 178, 216
    John Louis 178
    John Paul 216
    Lena 121, 122
    Mary 120, 129, 203,
      216
    Mary, Mrs. 107
    Sara 202
    Sarah 202
    Wm. Joseph 4
    William 122
MEYERS, Joan 166
    Lena 47
    Mary 176, 203
    "Skippy" 17
MEZA, John, Mrs. 107
    John F. 107
    Martha 68
    Olga Inez 107
MICCA, Henrietta 212
MICHALICK, -- 81
MICHALIK, Anton 107
    Vincent 107
MICHEL, Henry 81
    Philip James 81
    William 81
MICHELS, Adolph 178
    Anna Emma 178
    Catherine 2, 38, 123,
      194, 195
    Frank 178
    Frank Adolph 178
    H. 38
    Henry 38, 194
    I. F. 179
    John 22
    John Fred 121
    John Edward 178
    John Frederic 144
    Mary 135, 154
    Mary Magdalen 128, 144,
      155
    Runold 178
    William 2, 178
MICKE, Corinne 198
MICKELS, Rosine Agnes 3
MICOULEAU, Rev. Anthony
    32, 42
MIDDLEGGER, Antonia 174,
    175
MIDLETON, M. 27
MIETHE, Amalia 52
MIHR, Theresa 39
MILES, Anna Mary, Mrs.
    107

MILES (cont.)
    Anan Mary Catherine
      92
    Ben D. 61
    Bennie Bendixen 16
    F. J. 60
    Lawrence A. 61, 107
    Lawrence Abbott 60
    Mary Anne 16, 61
MILKOVA, Hedwig 67
MILLE, Frederic 31
MILLEN, Frank 35
    Frank Adolph 178
    Joseph 178
MILLER, --, Mrs. 198
    Anna 28
    Barbara 28
    Catherine 184
    Charles 179
    Charles August 61
    Clara 214
    Frank 173
    James 179
    Josephine 23
    M. 81
    M. O. Augusta 157
    Mary 81
    Mary Ethel 179
    Nellie 106
    P. 214
    Peter 214
    R. J. 52
    Raymond 65
    Robert 25, 43, 61, 179
    William 38
    Willis H. 216
MILLEY, John 179
    Joseph 179
MILLIA, Felix 179
    John Baptist 179
MILLIANI, Frank J. 35
    Joseph J. 35
MILLIANY, Joseph 2
MILLICH, Catherine
      Elizabeth 179
    Theresa 130
    Vincent 179
MILLIGAN, John G. 179
    Margaret Emma 179
MILLINIANEY (MELLEN),
    George 35
MILLIS, Mary Ethel 179
MILLRICH, Rebecca 119
MILSAP, Mary Elizabeth
    174
MISBEL, Ida 83
MISBL, Ida 196
MISCIEVICZ, Anna Clara
    179
    Joseph 179
MISPEL, Ida 37, 43
    Robert 37, 43
MITCHEL, Winifred 173
MITCHELL, -- 179
    Anna James 179
    Elizabeth 138, 179
    Elizabeth M. 138
    Emma 68
    Frank D. 179
    Frank Patrick 179
    James 179
    John 179
    John E. 35
    Kaniel 1
    Laura 179
    Martha 15
    Paul 179
    Philip 35
    Rose 135
    Winifred 173
    Winny 179
MITCHELS, Catherine 195
MITCHOULI, Agnes 81

MITZ, Mary 28
MOBERG, Hanna C. 51
    Julia 51
MOCK, Anna 99
MOELLER, Catherine 133
    Clara 27, 212
    Elisa 164
    Pauline 41
    John Peter 179
    Theresa J. 162
MOFFETH, Mary 59
    William 28
MOFFETH, Seymour 13
    Seymour Joseph 6
    William 13
    Wm. Aloysius 6
MOHR, A. 30
MOLKATA, Ophilia 132
MONDRIK, Joseph O. 35
MONFORD, Ambrose 206
    Bertha Elizabeth 206
    Evelyn Josephine 15
    Janette 206
    Jeanette Leona 205
    Joan 124, 206
    Joan Antonia 206
    Joan L. 40
    Theresa Helen 205
MONFORT, Ambrose Alphonse
    179
    Gabriel 197
    Gabriel Leo 179
    Hazel Theresa 179
MONFRED, Edmund 206
MONFRIN, Vincentia 184
MONGER, Susan 27
MONI, Adolph 179, 180
    Amelia 13, 179
    Amalia Elnore 6
    Elizabeth 13, 179
    Eliz. Margaret 6
    Mathilda 197
    Rose 13, 180
    Rose Catherine 6
MONIVICZ, Helen Magdalen
    180
    Martin 180
MONKS, Margaret 144
MONOHAN, George 67
MONROE, Rose 150
MONSHAUSEN, Angelina 8
    Anna Angela 52
    Anne Mary 14
    Eliz. 15
    Elizabeth Barbara 53
    Frances 53, 62
    Frances Louise 8, 15
    Joan 8, 15, 52, 62
    Joan Theresa 57
    John 8, 15, 52, 53, 57,
      61, 62, 107
    Mary 107, 109
    Mary Agnes 7
    Mathew 8
    Mathias 8, 15
    Selma, Mrs. 107
MONTAUT, Elizabeth 180
    Emil 180
    Neuville 180
    Richard Samuel 180
MONTEANT, Emily 123
MONTEAU, Eloisa 55
    Emil 173, 180
    Mary Olivia 180
    Menalie 184
    Nevil 180
MONTEAUT, Chlothilde 66
    Clara 180
    Neuville 180
    Mary Olivia 180
    Mathilda 155
    Nevil 180
MONTEGUE, Ann 209

MONTEUMRY, Mary 177
MONTFORT, Abrose 124
  Ambrose 5
  Gabriel 158
  Joan 5
MOOLD, Edward Frank 180
  Jesse Edward 180
MOOLT, Anna Lorraine
    Cornida 180
  Edward 180
MOOR, Cecil 169
  Cecil Catherine 181
  Henry 180, 181
  John Michael 180
  Joseph Henry 180
  Mary 121
  Mary Augusta 3
  Mary Gertrude 3
  Mary Magdalen
    Elizabeth 180
MOORE, A. J. 180
  Andrew 180
  Andrew Jackson 180
  Anna 180
  Catherine 165
  Elizabeth 33
  Helen 190
  Henry William 181
  Jane 177
  Louis 180
  Louise 81
  Margaret 136
  Mary 38, 197
  Mary Ann 180
  Mary Cecil 180
  Nellie 52
  Robert 180
  Thomas 181
  Walter 62
MOORS, Caroline 65
  Edward 181
  Edward John 181
  Frank Louis 181
MORAT, Ellen 35
MORETTI, Helen 183
MORGAN, Dominic 2
  Elizabeth, Mrs. 92,
    107
  Mary 131
  Philip 2
  William 107
MORGANTHALER, Anna 202
MORIARTY, Eugene 35
MORITZ, Frederica 34
MORRIS, Pauline 150
MORRISON, Hugh Allison
    181
  Margaret 171
  Mary Pauline 181
  Sara 171
MORRISSY, Ellen 24
MORSE, Bluker 181
  Charles 164
  Joseph Arthur Sidney
    181
MORTON, B. 64
  Bliss 58
  Leora 119
MOSBAUER, John 81
MOSCHIM, Mary 201
MOSCHINI, Mary 201
MOSER, -- 84
  Agnes 81, 145
  Agnes Jos. Teresa 181
  Agnes Mary 4
  Ann Mary Emma Terese
    181
  Ann Pauline Augusta
    181
  Anna 35, 81, 216
  Anna Caroline 81
  Anne 181
  Caroline 81

MOSER (cont.)
  Caroline Clara 181
  Charles 26, 127, 191
  Elisabeth 2, 62
  Elizabeth 103, 108,
    215
  George William 181
  Gladys Lincoln Anne 181
  Hilda Josephine Rose
    181
  Innocent 14
  Innocent Hubert
    Marion 181
  Innocent John 7
  Hyacintha 216
  Joan 1, 37, 126, 134,
    136, 174, 216
  Joan Henrietta 42
  John 81, 126, 181, 182,
    216
  John H. 35, 181
  John Henry 1, 108
  Josephine Agnes
    Hyacinth 181
  Mary Elisabeth 2
  P. 37
  P. H. 22
  P. K. 37
  Paula 34, 108, 215
  Peter Hyacinth 181
  Peter Hysinth 108
  Philomen 25
  T. H. H. 135
  Theodore Hyacinth 181
  Ursula 81
  Ursula Ann Elizabeth
    181
  William 81
MOSLAM, Nicholas 202
MOSS, James 121
MOSSER, Rosa 68
MOTH, James Samuel 35,
    180, 181, 182
  Joseph Albert 180
  Julia 14, 66
  Julia Alice 180
  Julia Leontine 6
  Leonida Angelina 181
  Leontine 81
  Michael Victor 182
  Samuel 182
MOTT, Celestina 180
  Celestine 180
  Clestina 180
  Ledock Pratt, Jr. 56
MOTZEN, Christine
    Elizabeth 182
MOUDOVILLE, Leonida 136
MOUNT, Joseph 182
  Joseph, Sr. 182
MOUTON, Arthuisue Cecile
    17
  Arthurine Cecile 9
  Darby Joseph 9
  Joseph Darby 17
  Mary 9
  Paul 9
MUCAS, Mathias 51
MUEHE, Elizabeth 81
  Leopoldine 146, 155
  Maria 193
  Mary 30, 83, 192
  Mary Eliz. 210
  Mary Sophie 108, 110
  Pauline 194
  Teresa 199
  Theresa 23, 26, 84,
    111, 199, 200, 210
  William 32, 81
MUEHEL, Henry 81
MUELLER, Agnes 100
  Anna 30, 159
  Anna Mary 182

MUELLER (cont.)
  Anthony Joseph 82, 182
  August 82
  Barbara 150
  Bertha 182
  Carl 15
  Caroline 82, 189
  Catherine 22, 127, 182
  Catherine Mary 3
  Catherine Rosa 123
  Chas. 61
  Charles 162, 182, 183,
    184
  Charles August 61
  Charles John 3
  Charles William 183
  Christine 162
  Clara 39, 86, 108, 113,
    214
  Dorothy Rose 4
  Edward 167
  Edward Anthony 182
  Elizabeth 163
  Frances 184
  Frederic 14
  George Rudolph 183
  Germanicas 182
  Germanicus Anthony 182
  Henry Peter 3, 182
  Henry 108, 132, 164,
    182, 211
  Herman 35
  Joan 162, 164
  Joan Emma 182
  John H. 154
  John Mary 5
  John Peter 35, 179,
    182, 198
  John William 132, 182
  Joseph John 182
  Lena, Mrs. 132
  Lillie Elizabeth 183
  Lula 82
  M. 208
  Magdalen 132, 182
  Margaret 181, 211
  Mary 132
  Mary Elisabeth 3, 4,
    183
  Metha Joan 61
  Peter 35, 82, 154,
    168, 182, 183, 214
  R. A. 183
  Regina 122
  Rene James 164
  Robert 40
  Rosina Mary Scholastica
    183
  Rudolph 183
  Theresa Josephine 182
  William 183
  William Edward 182
  William Henry 183
  William John 3, 168
MUERI, Agnes Mary 6
  Anna Agnes 183
  Henry 183
  Edna Lillie Theresa
    183
  Henrietta Margaret
    Joan 183
  Julia Mary Elizabeth
    183
MULHERN, Terence 82
MULHOLLAND, Marguerite
    108
MULLEN, Claude 35
  Henrietta 183
  James 183
  John 35
  John Patrick 63, 183
  Josephine 183
  Paul Fitton 35

MULLEN (cont.)
  Rufus 183
MULLER, Adolph 127
  Catherine 162
  Edella 53
  Ella 53
  Louis 53
  Peter 201
  Susan Wilhelmina 195
  Wilhelmine 2
MULROY, James P. 35
MUNICE, Mary 183
MUND, Augusta 164
MUNDT, Augusta 163
MUNN, Helen, Mrs. 108
  Margaret 40
  Thomas J. 40
MURPHEE, Harold 8
MURPHY, Mary W. 122
  Pat 142
  Patrick 142
  William 204
MURRAY, Ann 148, 149
  Anna Mary 183
  Catherine 177
  Esther 55
  Julia 66
  Mary 148
  Mary, Mrs. 28
  Richard James 183
MUSGROVE, Alexander 135
MUZAR, Mathias 53, 65
  Matth. 61
MUZUR, Mathias 50
MYLCOVA, Hedwig 60
MYLKOVA, Ignaz 60
NAGLE, James 183
  John 183
  John Nelson 183
  Stephen 82
NAGNIN, Gerald Michael 17
  Hardy 16
  May 16
  Nolia 16
  Paul 16
NAGNOBER, Charles 35
NAHM, Adam 33, 36
NAKWASIL, Paul 58
  Theresa 58
NAQUIM, David Edward 17
NAQUIN, Adam 65
  Amelia 65
  Ursula Ura 65
NASS, Cath 23
NASCHKE, Louise 189
NAUKA, Anna 211
NAVE, Catherine Dorris
  183
  John 183
  Lottie 136
NAVRATIL, August 52
  Stephenie 52
NAYLOR, Kathleen 60
NEBOU, Melanie 180
NEBOUT, John 184
  Josephine 184
NEESE, Lawrence 153
NEIDENFUEHR, Agnes 181
  Emma 181
NEIGEBAUER, Agatha 37
NEIS, Anna Margaret 184
  James 82, 108, 184
  John 108
  John Joseph 3
  John Nicholas 184
  Margaret 3, 13
  Margaret Mary 6
  Marguerite 106, 108
  Pauline 82
  Pauline Celestine 4
NEISE, James 218
  Margaret 216
NEISS, Henry James 184

NEISS (cont.)
  James 82, 184
  Sebastian 5
NEITSCH, Amalia 34
  Fanny 184
  Frances 184
  Henry 34
  Theodore 184
NELSON, Arnold 36
  Bertha 54
  Charles 184
  Christ. 54
  George 184, 188
  Henry Andrew 184
  Hester 126
  John 36, 126
  Julia 184
  Louis 184
  Severin 184
  Severino 184
NENINIZ, Anna 64
NETTELTON, William 40
NEUBAUER, Anna 57
NEUHANS, Joseph 36
NEUHAUS, James 184
  Mary Ann 184
  Mary Anne 4
NEUMANN, Anna 49
  Bernardine 214
  Carolina Josephine
    Vincentia 184
  Gugust 185
  Joseph 49
  Louise 36
  Margaret Augusta 185
  Thomas 184
NEUSTAPA, -- 61
  Matthias 61
NEVARES, Eugenia 150
NEWELL, Mary 146
NICHOLAS, Henrietta Rhea
  184
  John Theodore 136, 184
NICHOLS, Catherine 109
  Catherine, Mrs. 108
  Dorthy 8, 15
  Dottie 59
  E. B. 184
  Helen 8, 108
  Kimey 8
  Kinney 15
  Mary Alva 184
  Mary Emma 184
NIDA, Magdalen 42
NIEBLE, August 185
NIEBLING, August 1
NIEDENFUEHR, Agnes 35,
  108, 181
  Emma 216
NIEDERGANG, Anthony 184
  Anton 36
  John Baptist 184
NIEDERHOEFER, August 184
  George 184
  John 184
NIEDERMANN, Sophie 67
NIEDERREUTHER, Louis 3
NIEMEYER, Josephine 1
NIGHTWINE, Chas. Aug. 61
  Charles Kane 61
NIPERT, Robert 119
NIPP, Margaret 42
NOLAN, John Patrick 183
  Mary 35
  Mary, Mrs. 183
  Patrick 169
NOLT, Charles 131, 132
NONN, Charles 185
  Lilian Mary 185
NONNENMACHER, Anton 185
  Joan Caroline 185
  Jos. 185
  Joseph 185

NONNENMACHER (cont.)
  Rosina 82
NONUS, Emmanuel Jackson
  62
  Lydia Mary 62
NORDMANN, Elizabeth 26
NORDSTROM, John C. 25
NORRIS, Aarace Joseph 9
  Abdon 9
  Abdou 16
  Anna Mae 9, 16, 48, 57
  Anthony 9
  Avnel 49
  Dave 57
  David, Mrs. 63
  Gloria Jean 9
  Horace Joseph 17
  James 9
  John 9
  Joseph 9
  Loveless 49
  Paul 9
  Paul Wylie 49
  Reina 64
  Rena 49
  Reua 16
  Rita 9
  Shirley Marie 9, 17
  Theresa 9
  Uyless Paul 9
NOUN, Theresa 21
NOUS, Charles 122
NOVAK, Mary 51
NOVOSAD, Frances 59
NOWROSKI, Joseph 61
NUESE, Elizabeth 29
  Juese (?) 36
  Lawrence 108, 132,
    135, 181
  Theresa 181
NUESSE, -- 208
  --, Mr. 33
  --, Mrs. 33
  Elizabeth 82
NUTT, Cecil 182, 189
  Cecile 134
  Joseph 26
  Mary 39, 201
O'BACK, Mary 143
OBENDOERFER, Bertha 193
  John 193
OBER, Albert 185
  Alfred C. 185
  August Carl 185
  Henry John 185
  Thomas Keatz 185
OBERLE, Anthony 22, 36,
  82
O'BRIEN, Helen 29
OCHS, Wilhelmine 37
O'CONNELL, Jean 34
O'CONNOR, Brigid 66
  Mary 76, 99, 152
ODELL, Edward 185
  Henry 148
ODINOT, Camille 208
  Mary 137
O'DONNELL, Mavaza 149
O'DONOHOE, Clarence W. 61
  Th. 61
OEHLERT, Maud, Mrs. 108,
  113
OEHLRICH, Edward 82, 185
OELRICH, G. A. 185
  George 185
  George Aust. 185
  Sophy 185
OEHRINE, Emma E. J. 130
  Emma Ernestine J. 130
  Julia 129, 130
  Julia E. E. 130
OELSCHLAEGER, Catherine
  96, 108

OEHLSCHLAEGER (cont.)
    Magdalen 82
OERING, Augusta 23
OESTREICH, Augusta 184
O'FARRELL, Mary 150
    Mary A. 149
OFFER, Frank 37
    Mary 37
OHME, Mary 48
OHNSTEIN, Martin 185
    Mary Elizabeth Ella
    185
O'KANE, Elizabeth Jane 61
O'KEEFE, Catherine 185
    Cornelius 185
    Mary Helen 3
    Michael 185
O'KEELY, William 151
OLAEU, Gabrielle 67
OLESCHLAEGER, Catherine
    42
OLFSEN, Catherine 138
OLLIS, Maurer, Minna 82
    William Frederic 36
OLSEN, Henry 51
O'MARA, Catherine 138
O'MEARA, Eugene 42
O'NEIL, William 140
    Elizabeth 140, 143
ONKEN, Otto 56
OPDENWEYER, Algeda Joan
    185
    Charles 185
    Mary Catherine 185
OPITZ, Margaret 187
OPPERMANN, Amanda 35
    Emily 35
    Gustave 185
    Henry Charles Gustave
    185
    Joan 188
    Jos. 35
    Joseph Theodore 185
    Laura 35
    Mary Ann 1
    William 186
    Wm. Bern. 1
O'REILLY, Patrick 142
O'ROURKE, E. 177
    Thomas John 185
    Vincent Bryan 30
ORTLON, N. N. 108
    Jim 108
    Jim, Mrs. 108
ORY, Ledger 36
    Louis 173
OSBURG, Adolph 186
    Charles 186
    Daniel 82, 186
    George 82, 185
    Mary Augusta 186
ORY, S. Johnson Louis 36
OSER, George Wm. 186
    George William 36, 82,
    181, 186
    Gladys Lincoln Ann 186
    Gladys Lincoln Anne 181
    Mildred Merrow Frances
    186
    Osmund Oswald 186
    William 36
O'SHEA, John Amandas 186
    Michael 186
OSTERMANN, Dorothy 212
OSTERMAYER, Arthur 61
    Louis 61
    Louis Arthur 108
OSTERMEIER, Catherine 174
O'SULLIVAN, Jos., Rev. 97
OSWALD, Elizabeth 186
    Ottilia 186
    Theodore 186
O'TOOLE, James 150

OTTERBACK, Adolph
    Jeremiah 186
OTTERBECK, Adolph 185
OTTWALD, Margaret 202
OVESNEY, Joseph 49
OWENS, Bennie F. 61
    Bennie F., Jr. 61, 67
    Marvin 61
OXMANN, Margaret 43
PASCAL, Aloysius 62
    Mary 62
PADEY, Rev. Charles 195
    Rev. Chas. 195
PAETZ, Chas. J. 17
    Margaret Maiy 17
PAINE, Joseph 35
    Joseph Herman 82
PAINPARE, Margaret 133
    Oscar 133
PAIRIS, Marie Angelice 60
PAISSE, Edward Eugene 186
    Germanus Henry 186
PALEGLAW, Frederic 198
PALERMO, Rosalie 63
PALLA, Anne 57
    Joseph 57
PALLIAS, Mary 38
PAMERI, Francis J. 60
PANS, William 23
PAOLI, Cath. 47
PAPINI, Elizabeth 179
PAPLIER, Chas. 189
PAPP, George William 186
    Conrad 186
PAQUE, Albertina 169
    George 169
    Louis 169
PAQUET, George 186
    George John 186
    Louis 215
    Louis Philip 186
PARHAM, Mary 47
PARIS, Edward 82
PARISOT, Ernest 174
PARKER, Barbara 213
    Elizabeth 203
    Hortense 137
    John 66, 196
    Sarah 51, 91, 108
PARMIRA, Minicucci 171
PARRISH, Mrs. 38
PARTEL, Mary 192
PASCHETHE, Henry 197
PATE, Margaret 137
PATEROVA, Joseph 61
    Sophia 61
PATERSON, Carolina 134
PATRICK, Anna Louise 186
    Clinton Clay 186
PATRON, Peter 67
    Sophie 67
PATSON, Catherine 167
PATTOF, Henry 210
PATTON, Lilly 51
PAUL, Christina 31
PAULA, Anna 65
PAULEY, Amelia 148
    Frances Mary 148
PAULUS, Mary 47
PAVELL, Augusta 13
    Augusta Eliz. 6
PAYNE, J. T. 187
    Thomas 14
    Thomas Henry 7
    William Edward 187
PAYSSE, --, Mrs. 187
    Edward Eugene 196
    Eugene 38
    Eugene Bernard 82
    Frank 196
    Germaine 60
    Germanus 82
    Henry 187

PAYSSE (cont.)
    John 187
    John Bapt. 60
    Joseph 13
    Joseph Aloysius 6
    Louise Helen 187
    Mary Rose 60
PAYSEE, Annie 38
PAYSSE, Bernadette 13, 60
    Bernadette Angelica 6
    Clementine 180
    Edward 180
PEACOCK, Samia 56
PEARSON, Sara E. 120
PECHLER, Philomine 32
PEDERSON, Annie C. 162
PEFFERKORN, H., Rev. 76,
    77, 82, 86, 87
PEIFFER, Catherine 168
PEINE, Ann 124
    Anna 82, 201
    John 39, 60, 108
    John Joseph 2
    Jos., Sr. 126
    Joseph 22, 24, 82, 109,
    132, 187, 210
    Joseph Herrmann 187
    Margaret 82, 161, 167
    Martin 109, 187, 213
    Mary 4, 132, 144, 202
    Mary J. 109
    Mary Josephine 187
PEITZ, August 187
    Francis 186
    Frederic August 187
    Mary 187
    Otto 187
PELERISE, Mary Joseph 1
PELZEL, Ottilia 49
PEMBERG, Margaret 163
PENCE, Bozina 50
    John 50
PENDERGAST, George 27
    Isabel 131
    Isabella 42
    Isabelle 158
    Julia 187
    Leona Agnes 189
    Lillie 58
    Mary 42, 86, 183, 213,
    214
    Thomas 27
    William 187, 189
PERALTA, Emily 55
    John 55
    Manuel 55
PERDEL, Eugenia 190
PEREZ, Rosina 63
PERLE, Miss 38
PERRICONE, Alphonse 66
    Mary Camille 66
PERRIN, Louise 171
PERRY, Boyer 187
    Eunice Louise 57
    John 187
    Laura 187
    Margaret 187
    Martha 208
PERTHUIS, Adolph 49
    Clementine 187
    Clemona 91
    Emil 187
    Felix 187
    H. 41
    Julius 187
    Theresa 187
PERUSINA, J., Rev. 107
    N., Rev. 107
PESCHKE, Joseph 167
PESK, Frederic 138
    Mary Ann 138
PESKE, Henrietta 24
    Mary 173

PESKE (cont.)
Mary Ann 24
PESSARRA, Constantine
Chas. 187
Frederrick 187
PETER, Anna 156, 163
Martina 39, 156
Martha 127
PETERS, Augustine 187
Carl Wm. Chr. 50
Ernestine Mary 50
Henry 109
PETERS, John 187
Anna Josephine, Mrs.
109
Anton Christian 61
Rasmus Chr. 61
PETERSON, Andrew 163
Ann 200
Anne Josephine 106
Anthony Christian 109
Gustave 52
Louise Rebecca 52
Salomon 23
PETIT, Anna 198
PETRO, John 188
PETSON, Charles 188
Tyra Elizabeth 188
PETTERSON, Andrew 36
Erasonic 36
PFANNENSTILL, -- 173
PFEIFER, Catherine 104
PFEIFFER, Catherine 47,
80, 168
PFISTER, Emily 37
PFLUEGER, Agnes Louise 3
Carolina Catherine 188
Caroline Louise 188
Charles 4, 206
Elizabeth, Mrs. 104,
134
Geo. 188
George 109, 188
Henrietta 206
Henrietta Leopoline
188
John George 134, 188
Mary Frances 188
Minna 206
Rose Alberta 188
Wilhelmine Elisabeth
3
PFLUGER, Agnes 57
Charles George 109
Elizabeth 109, 111
George 109
PFLUM, Mary 107, 109
Selma 52, 53, 57, 62
PHILIBERT, Frank Joseph
188
Henry 188
PHILIP, Anne 135
PHILIPPS, Aloysia 2
Victor 2
PHILIPPSON, Robert 109
PHILIPS, Anne 1
PHILIPSON, Catherine 109,
142, 145, 152, 184,
209
Robert 142, 152, 209
Thomas 109, 142
PHILLIP, Daniel 188
Julius 188
PHILLIPS, -- 120
Alice 139
Anna 29
Daniel 29
John 185
Joan 139
Theresa 29
PHILLIPSON, Catherine 188
Robert 188
Thomas 188

PHLUEGER, Geo. 41
Henrietta 41
PIASECKA, Mary 41, 208
Mary Helen 208
PICTURE, Frank 6, 13, 109
Frank Xavier Louis 189
Henry 189
Louise 140
Louise, Mrs. 109
Rosale Helen 189
Rosalia Helen 31
Rosalie 102, 109
Rose 22, 124
Wm. 189
Wm. Henry 189
William H. 109
William Henry 31, 102
PINKENBERG, Fred 109
Theresa Mary, Mrs. 109
PIERCE, Frederic 30
PIERRE, Emma Sophe Rose 2
PIERSEN, Andrew Luke 61
Mary Andrew 61
PIERSON, Marcus 16
PILLE, Frank Joseph 189
Henry 189
PILLURTZ, Amelia 204
PILSEN, Nemera 8
PINK, Minnie 62
PINKENBURG, Frederic 62
Mary 60, 106
Theresa Mary, Mrs. 114
PINTO, Angela 62
PIOTTI, Acquilina 171
John 171
PISTONE, Theresa 68
PLACIDUS, Frank 144
PLAICE, William 188
PLAIGE, Frederick 191
Theresa 191
PLANCHET, Caroline 82
PLANEY, Agatha 141
PLASECKA, Mary 208
PLATTOW, Catherine 34
PLITT, Anna Mary 189
Edward 36, 189
George 36, 189
George William 47
PLUMMER, Douglas 62
James Tucker 62
Vemes Willis 62
PODZEMNY, Joseph 49
POETZ, Leana 64
POHL, Margaret 82
POICHET, Margaret 201
POIRRIERS, Bella 136
POKER, John 188
Mary Virginia 188
POKORSKA, Frank 54
Helen 54
POLASCHE, Elizabeth 83,
188
Mary 159
POLKA, Albert 60
Louisa Ella 60
POLSFUSS, Augusta 106
POLVOGT, Louise 131
Wilhelmine 130, 131
POMEROY, Anna 173
POOLE, Georgia Sybil
Estelle 51
Margaret 82
Ruther, Mrs. 51
POPELIER, Anthony 127
Sophy 127
POPLAR, --, Mr. 30
--, Mrs. 30
Clarence 165
Theresa 165
POPLIER, Anthony 4
Charles 166
Joan 131
Joseph 201

POPLIER (cont.)
Joseph Corn. 3
POPULAR, --, Mr. 37
--, Mrs. 37
Anthony 37, 157, 191
Agnes 157
Agnes Mary 5
Anthony 188, 189
Anthony William 188
Anton 37, 189
Charles 196
Charles Anthony 188
Clarence Rudolph 189
Emily 196
Joan Elizabeth 132
Louise Adelaide 189
M. Joan 37
Mary Fredice 189
Theresa 37, 156, 157,
166
POPULIER, Anthony 36, 128
Rudolph 36
Sophy 127, 128
Wilhelmine 83
POPULLEAR, Mary Eugenia
128
PORCHET, Margaret 213
PORITZ, Herman 36
Julius Werner 189
Maseuti 189
Max 36, 189
Victor Emanuel
Maxenthius 189
PORTERHOUSE, Louise 60
PORTIER, Clement
Stanidaus 2
PORTSCHER, Joseph Anthony
83
POSPICAL, Rosalie 60
POTTER, Leo William 62
William 62
POTTHOFF, Margaret 41
POUEIGH, Mary 142
Theophilo Anton 36
POULSON, Charles 36
POUR, Jaroslav 62
Joseph 62
POWELL, Ella 65
Ellen Sarah 148
John J. 148
Laurence 189
Walter 189
William 189
PRADIER, Armantina 150
August 36, 189
Augusta 36
Augustina 189
Mary 170
Mattie 176
PRAGNER, Joseph 189
Joseph Ferdinand 189
PRAKEL, Joseph 204
PRAKER, Joseph Ferdinand
5
PRATALI, Frederic 48
PRAULI, Albert Louis 189
Conrad Paul 189
PREISS, Elizabeth 83
PRELLWITZ, Gustave 23
PRENDERGAST, Isabel 214
Marian 214
Mary 214
Vivian 14
Vivian Mary 6
PRENIHSL, Theresa 97
PRESTON, Alice Barbara
189
Chas. 205
Chas. Henry 189
Charles Henry 37
Jon 37
PRETS, John 62
John, Mrs. 62

PRETS (cont.)
  Steve 62
  Thomas 62
PREUS, Henry Martin 189
  John H. 189
PRICE, Teresa 207
PRIESMUTH, Charles 14
  Chs. Peter 7
PRILLWITZ, Theresa 64
PRIMROSE, Carrie 78
PROCKHOFF, Theresa 25,
  95, 109
PROKOP, Anna 130
PROSCH, Benard C. 48
PROSPER, Leo Joseph 109
PROUSE, William 64
PRUESER, Henry 189, 190
  Lilie Helen 190
  William Moreau 190
PUCHINTZKIK, Cecile 150
PUCIARELLO, Emil 8
PUELLE, Henry 133
PUGH, Thomas 42
PUHL, Margaret 153
PULLE, Germanicus Anthony
  182
  Germanicus 182
PUPPO, Bartholomew 83
  Dominic 4
  Marietta 13
  Marietta Lucia 6
  Pelego Stephen 5
  Stephen 83
PURGET, Frank 190
  Louis Henry Rudolph
  190
  Virginia Nora 190
PURGETTE, Frank 128
PURJIT, Frank 190
PUSKER, Louis 62
  Michael 62
QUERR, Catherine 188
QUESTED, Agnes 190
  Agnes Grace 190
  Elizabeth Leonida 190
  Helen 41
  Mary Ida 190
  Mollie 190
  Sarah 30
  Walter 41, 190
  Walter D. 190
  William George 30
QUINLEN, Catherine Eliz.
  190
  John 190
QUINN, Frank 42
  Mary A., Mrs. 110
  Mary Eve. 190
  Mary I. 208
  Robert 190
  Thomas 173
QUINTARO, C. 208
  Camillus 190
  Eugenia Joshephine
  Adolphine 190
QUIRK, Edmund 148
QUITSCH, Theodore 23
RACKEL, Herman 196
RADEMACHER, Caroline 35,
  179, 182
  Frank George 35
RADLEC, Elizabeth 55
RADLEY, Dennis 190
  Dennis Patrick 190
RAENDEL, Joseph 132
RAEVEVITCH, Nicholas 174
RAHE, Anthony E. 216
RAIMER, Anna Mary 50
RAKE, Adolph 190
  Mary Magdalen 190
RAKEL, Albert 37, 83, 190
  Frida Anita 190
  Gerhard 190

RAKEL (cont.)
  Gerhardt 37, 190
  Henry 83
  Herman 190
  Herman Henry 190
  Mary Eliz. Theresa 190
RALLEY, Emma 110
RAMACHER, August Chas.
  Henry 190
  Charles William 190
  Louis Chas. Leonard
  190
  T. H. 33
  Theodore 190
RAMACKER, -- 27
  Terese 4
  Theodore 37
  Theresa 177
RAMEAU, John Baptist 37
  Joseph 37
RAMMACHER, August 145
  Mary Augusta 145
RAMMER, Alice 57
  John J. 57
  Margaret 57
RAMSEY, Barbara 36
RANKIN, Myrl 110
RAPHAEL, Anthony 121
RAPP, Adam 191
  Catherine Anita 191
RASNOWSKY, Alois 62
  Vincent 62
RASS, Anthony 8
RATH, Frank 194
  Mary 194
RATHENFELX, Elizabeth 159
RATISEAU, Alfred 167
  Caroline 167
RATISSEAU, Alfred 191
  Alfred P. 191
  Alfred Peter 191
  Anna 191
  August Anselm 37, 191
  Augusta 191
  Felix Alfred Chas.
  August Anselm 191
  John Baptist 191
  Louis William 191
  Mary Emily 191
  Mary Thalia 37
RATISSOT, August 191
  J. B. 191
  Rosalie 191
RATLIFF, Henry Alfred 62
  Leslie 110
  Leslie Alfred 62
  N. N. 110
RATZAMAN, Fred W. 64
RATZMAN, Christine Mar. 64
  Rosalie Wilhelmina 64
RATZMANN, Ernest 15
  Ernest Aloysius 8
  Frank 15
  Rose 14
  Rose Mary 7
RAU, Henrietta, Mrs. 63
RAUBSHAULZ, Louise 62
RAY, Barbara 191
  Diongs 191
  Joan 191
  John 191
  Katherine 191
RAYER, Barbara 62
REAGAN, Catherine 33, 171
  James 54
  John 33
REAVERS, Theresa 181
RECHELTLOCK, Mary Ann 78,
  165
RECTOR, Isaac 191
REDDY, Augusta 213
REEB, Michael 4, 33, 168
REED, Rosa 130

REEVES, Bridig 34
  George 34
REGINI, Eugenia Mary 13
  Eugenia Mary Rosalia
  5
  Louise 13
  Louise Mary 6
REHAK, Anna 62
REHMANN, Theresa 64
REHRMANN, Anthony 83, 155
  Anton 30
  Teresa 197
  Theresa 26, 30, 155,
  161, 167, 176, 210
REICHERZER, Frank Theo. 3
REID, -- 193
  Grover Joseph 193
REIFEL, Ann Louise 94
  Walter R. 135
REIFFEL, Walter 36
REIFFERT, H. Rev. 22, 37,
  72, 83
REIFSCHNEIDER, J. E.,
  Rev. 64
  John Ed., Rev. 52
REIHMANN, Theresa 199
REIKE, Herman 143
REILLY, Adeline B. 171
  Anna 191
  Blanche 141, 176
  Elvira 57
  Mary Joan 191
  Patrick 191
  Peter 134
REIMSCHISAEL, Loys 202
REIN, Anna 110
  Catherine 167
  Elizabeth Catherine
  167
  William 110
REINBUHR, H. 21
REINEKE, Minn. 35
REISINGER, Josephine 53
REISNER, Mathilda 59, 185
  Pauline 129
REISS, -- 83
REISSER, Frances 57
REITH, Joan 213
REITZE, Mary Caroline 83
REMY, John 120
RENANT, Mary Frumentia 25
RENSCH, Lillie 174
RENT, Ella Valeria 191
  John Wm. 191
RENTSCH, Lillie 80
REPOSE, Theresa 62
RESSEL, Adolf Joseph-5
  Alice 14
  Alice Anna 191
  Alice Cecile 7, 48
  Caroline 204
  Caroline, Mrs. 110, 115
  Charles 7, 14, 62
  Charles August 110
  Charles Engelbert 191
  Emma 110
  Ferdinand 205
  Frank 26, 60
  Frank J. 149
  Frank Jos. 110
  Frank Joseph 3, 110,
  191
  Wilhelmine 83
  Wm. John 4
RETNSCH, Lillie 174
RETTBERG, Dorothy 136
REYBOUD, Gabrielle M. 186
REYMOND, Mary 147
REYNAUD, Regina 170
REYNOLDS, Charles R. 191
  Walter Raphael 191
RHEIN, Elizabeth 167
  Frederica 178

RHEINFELD, Wilhelmin 41
RHEINLEENDER, John 32
RHODE, Louis George 37
   Theodore Henry 37
RHODES, Elva 63
RHUBOTTOM, Charles
   Forest 191
RIAT, Joan (Menne) 25
   John 192
   John Baptist 25, 192
   John Joseph Pora 191
   Joseph 191
RIBAUX, Caroline 214
   Louis 214
RICAVY, Mary Frieda 192
   Wenceslau 192
RICE, Edward 192
RICHARD, Elizabeth 27
   Louise 151
   Peter 21
   Peter, Rev. 42
RICHARDSON, Helen (Ellen)
   30
   Margaret 164
RICHERS, Adelle 29
RICHMERS, Andrew 174
RICHMOND, Mary 52
RICHTER, Henrietta 26,
   189
   Henrietta Marie 42
   Joseph 192
RICKE, -- 14
   Agnes 83
   Ann Leopoldine 83
   Anna 15, 83, 192
   Ann Mary 192
   Anna Elizabeth 192
   Anna Magdalen 192
   Anna Mary, Mrs. 101,
   110
   Annie 56
   Anthony 37, 43, 192,
   193
   Anthony Herman 192
   Anton 181, 182, 192
   Bernadine C. 210
   Bertha Caroline 192
   Carolina 130
   Caroline 23, 33, 41,
   42, 126, 130, 181,
   182, 187, 192, 193
   Caroline, Mrs. 210
   Catherine 130
   Cecile 187
   Charles 37, 43
   Charles August 192
   Charles Joseph 192
   Christine M. 47
   Elizabeth 30, 130
   Elisabeth Brigid 3
   Elizabeth Frigata 192
   Ida 2, 8, 83, 125,
   188, 192, 193
   Joan 181, 210
   Joan Odilia 192
   John 4, 29, 30, 59,
   83, 110, 122, 126,
   130, 146, 149, 155,
   166, 192, 193
   John Adam 193
   John Henry 192
   John Joseph 110, 193
   John, Mrs. 59
   Joseph 13, 22, 30, 33,
   37, 39, 42, 125,
   126, 131, 143, 187,
   192, 193, 199
   Joseph, Jr. 23
   Joseph Charles 6, 62
   Joseph William 193
   Louis 193
   Louis Andrew 8
   Louise 15

RICKE (cont.)
   M. 37
   Marg. Catherine 7
   Margaret 14
   Martin 14, 29, 37, 43,
   47, 56, 83, 130,
   161, 166, 175, 187,
   192, 193, 210
   Martin Aloysius 7
   Martin Edward 193
   Martin Joseph 193
   Mary 23, 47, 56, 62,
   83, 125, 130, 161,
   175, 187, 193, 199,
   210
   Mary Eliz. 8
   Mary Magdalen 2
   Mary Margaret 193
   Mary Sophie, Mrs. 108,
   110
   Odilia 83
   Theresa 21, 39, 54, 91,
   122, 125, 155, 193
   Valeriana 199
   Violetta, Leocordina
   122
   William 122, 145, 149,
   216, 217
   William Theodore 193
RICKMERS, Andrew 175
RICKS, William Frederic 4,
   110
RIED, Louise 23
RIEGER, Mary Aloysia 193
   William 193
RIEMER, Heding 52
   Paul 52
RIESEL, George 35
RIESENBACK, George 83
RIESENEE, Mathilda 196
RIESENHUBER, Aloysius
   Frank 110
   Frank 110
   Mary 110
RIESINGER, Mathilda 54
RIETHER, Susan 84
RIGNEY, Frank Louis 193
   Thomas 193
RIKE, John 201
RILEY, Blanche 176
   Julia 186
RILLS, Clemence 186
RING, Josephine 64
RINGELER, Victoria 42
RINGER, Cornelia 182
RINGH, Anna Olga 83
   Charles George 37
   Edward 37
   Ernest 37
   Ernest Godfrey 37
RINK, Anna 160
RINKER, Anna 193
   Anita 191
   Anthony Selim 193
   Ewohan 193
   Mary 127
   Nellie 193
   Selim 193, 194
   Henry 4, 193
RINZ, Emil 37
   Julius 37
   P. W. 38
RIORDAN, Ann Genevieve 146
   John Robert 146
   Mary 146
RIOT, John 192
   John Joseph Pora 192
   Joseph 192
RIPCHI, Louise 54
RIPETA, Mary 130
RIPKE, Aloysia 54
   Anna Mary Louise 194
   Carolina Elenore 194

RIPKE (cont.)
   Frank Irvin 194
   Frederick Henry 194
   George Henry 194
   George Henry John 194
   Henry 194
   Henry F. 194
   Henry Frederick 194
   Henry Patrick Robert
   194
   Rose 194
RISENBERG, Elizabeth 215
RISLEY, Emma 194
RISTOE, Florence 30
   Florentine 169
   Rose 169
RITTER, Albert William 194
   Charles 194
   William 194
RITTMEYER, Geo. A., Rev.
   7, 14, 66
   George A., Rev. 30, 37,
   40, 41
RITTMUS, Alice 194
RITZLER, -- 83
   Catherine 2, 22, 126;
   178
   David 38
   Edna 14, 56
   Edna Catherine 8
   Elizabeth 91, 110, 123
   Ellis 55
   Ellis F. 110
   Helen 8, 15, 194
   Helen Charlotte 194
   Helen Pauline 49
   Henrietta Joan 194
   Henry 25, 38, 49, 50,
   54, 63, 83, 110,
   111, 145, 172, 194
   Henry Valentine 194
   James 194
   Louis Valentin 83
   Louis Valentine 194
   Margaret 5, 130, 194
   Margaret Josephine 83,
   194
   Mary 49
   Sophy 195
   Susan Wilhelmine 83,
   195
   Valentin 194, 195
   Valentine 38, 123, 194,
   199
RITZLES, Elizabeth 25
RIVAUX, George 62
   Louis 62
ROACH, Alice 64, 113
   Arthur 64
   Jacob 195
   Joseph Jefferson Davis
   195
   Lannie 64
   Mary Loretta 195
   Thomas 195
ROANE, James 195
   John Ross 195
ROBENREID, Saraphina 160
ROBERT, Coralia 123
ROBERTS, -- 92
   Evelyn 16
   Evelyn Rita 9
   Gaston 48
   Gaston, Mrs. 66
   Stella 9, 48
   Teresa 9
   Theresa 9
ROBERTSON, Argau Augusta
   196
   Emmet Marshall 195
   Frederick Marshall 195
   Henry C. 195
   Maggie 195

ROBERTSON (cont.)
  Mary Anna 141
  Nancy 184
  Oscar 62
  Samuel 62
ROBINIUS, John Jas. 65
  Martha Mary 65
ROBINSON, Henry C. 195
  Lillian Loiuse 195
ROBIRO, Aloysius 195
  Anthony 195
  Mary Joan Louise
    Alexandra 195
ROCH, Charles 14
  Joseph 14
  Joseph Aloysius 6
ROCK, Odilia 123
RODRIGUES, Phelian 60
RODRIGUEZ, Agnes 63
  Clifton John 63
  Electa 57
  Hubert 63
RODRIQUEZ, Oliveda 49
ROEHMANN, Theresa 186
ROEHRMAN, Theresa 199
ROEHRMANN, Ch. 34
  Mrs. 36
  Theresa 39
ROEHRMOND, Theresa 177
ROEMER, Agnes Hyacinth
    181
  Anna Mary, Mrs. 111
  Frank 8
  J. B. 83
  John B. 84, 181
  John Baptist 215
  John H. 181
  Joseph 83
  Leo Emil 84
ROEPER, Augusta 195
  Euphemia 1
  Frank Joseph 195
ROESSEL, Frank 31
ROESSLER, Frank 205
ROFTOPOLA, John 38
ROGANO, Antonio 111
  Emma, Mrs. 110
  Emma Ralley, Mrs. 111
ROGERS, Carles 63
  E. J. 63
  Howard A. 63
  John M. 38
  Zula 66
ROHDE, Edna Christine 123
  Joe 8, 15
  Joseph Henry 111, 195
  Louis Geo. 195
  Louis George 84, 111,
    195
ROHLEDER, Charles 195
  Damian 195
  E. Magdalene 41
  Frederic 195
  Magdalen 195
  Valentin 195
  Valentine 195
  Victor 84
ROHLING, Alexander Adolph
    195
  Carolina Cecil 196
  Catherine 196
  Frank John 195, 196
  Joseph Paul 196
ROHMBIEL, John Ernest 196
ROHRMANN, Terese 2
ROLING, Frank John 195
ROLLING, Frank John 195
ROMAN, Romeo 201
ROMANINI, Cherubina 137
ROMERO, Leonida 49
ROONEY, Catherine S. 49
  Francis 111
  Walter R. 49

ROSAR, John M. 149
ROSE, Ann Mary 35
  Charles 196
  Emily 119
  L. Antonie 163
  Margaret 82, 108, 187
ROSELLI, Dominic 34
  Lucie 34
ROSENBAU, Bernard 55
  Magdalen 55
  Marie 55
ROSKOPF, Joseph 30
  Rose Margaret 30
ROSPOLER, Alexander 160
ROSS, Eugenia 173
  Helen 39, 1-9
ROSSIGNOL, -- 27
ROTH, Josephine Mary 196
  Maximilian Jos. 196
  Maximilian Joseph 196
ROTHAMMER, Mary Ann 180
ROTHEIMER, Mary Christine
    180
ROTHEMEYER, Anna Mary 30
ROTHENFLUEH, Victor 124
ROTHMUND, Catherine 21
ROTHSPRACK, Fred Wm. 63
  Henry William 63
ROTTER, John August 196
  John Henry 196
ROUBION, Bernard 38, 186,
    196
  Bernard Eugene 196
  Bernard, Mrs. 186
  Henrietta 196
  Henrietta Bernadette 8
  James 38
  John 15
ROURKE, Agnes 54
  Dudley Thomas 59
  J. M. 54
  John 59, 196
  Lillian Etta 59
  Pearl Cecile 54
  William Albert 196
ROWAN, Bernice Joan 196
  James 196
  Margaret Joan 196
  William 13, 196
  Wm. James 6
RUBION, Bernard 180
  Eugene 111
  Henrietta 15
RUDA, Eugene William 196
  Florian 38, 196
  Gottlob 38
RUDER, Susan 38
RUDOLF, Wilhelmine 133
RUECKE, Agnes Caroline 196
  Carolina 123, 196
  John 196
  Joseph William 123
  Martin 196
RUEHBUEHL, Laura 214
RUEHL, Bernard 196
  G. Bernard 196
RUEHRMAN, Theresa 111
RUEMBUEHL, Anna, Mrs. 208
  E. 38
  Henry 38
RUETHER, Frank 207
RUITZ, Mathilda 100
RUIZ, Julius 157
  Julius Charles 196
  Julius W. 196
  Theresa 157
RULOFF, Agnes 54, 57
RUMI, Theresa 95
RUMBUEHL, Ernest 197
  Henry 197
  John Robert 197
  Laura Evelyn 197
RUNFOLA, Gabriel 63

RUNFOLA (cont.)
  Joseph 63
RUNTZ, Nora 185
RUPPERT, John Charles 197
  Joseph 197
RUPPRECHT, Catherine 63
RUSSEL, Mary C. 185
RUSSI, Charles 63
  Michael 63
RUSSO, Alphonsa 49
  Mary 63
RUTHERFORD, Dora 26
RUTHFORD, Dorothea 169
RUTHMAN, J. M., Rev. 76
RUTHMANN, J. William,
    Rev. 40
RUZICKA, Mary 175
RYAN, Georgiana, Mrs. 111
  Isadora 146
  James 9, 16
  Jerome 9
  Margie 16
  Mary Elizabeth 61
RYBOLA, Mary 50
SABATIER, Charles 63, 111
  Jean George Charles 63
  Mary 63
SABATIERE, Elisabeth 16
SABATIMO, Elanor 68
SABELL, M. 203
  Mary 141
SABETIER, Elisabeth 16
SABLE, Catherine 137
  Mary 137
SAESCHEN, Clara 61
ST. LERER, Mary 202
SALE, Blanche 197
  Levi 197
SALUDO, Lucille 49
SAMED, F. 31
SAMMER, Frank 200
SAMMET, -- 170
  Frank 1, 111, 156,
    170, 181, 201
  Margaret 169
  Mary 2, 170, 181, 186,
    212
  Rosina 127, 169, 200,
    212
SAMPSON, Milton George 51
SANASKI, F. 37
  Leo Casia 37
SANCHEZ, Joseph Amador
    217
SANDERS, -- 133
  Rhea 56
  Thelma Lee 66
SANDERSON, -- 84
  Anna 197
  Ann Elizabeth 197
  Ella 137
  James 197
  Mary 162
  Oliver 84, 197
SANDOV, Mina 152
SANDS, A., Mrs. 58
SANTERS, John A. 84
SAROTELLI, Frank 196
SATROW, Manuel T. 62
SATTLER, Adam 207
  Anne Mary Marg. 5
  Catherine 207
  Joan 58, 124
  Margaret 129
  Mary 41, 58, 66, 207
SAUINER, Loretta 16
SAUNDERSON CECIL, Ada 40
SAVAGE, Philip 208
SAVOIS, Laura 65
SAWSON, Louis S. 26
SAWYER, John 29
SAYLOR, Mary 150
SCAPULINDA, Idalen 174

SCARF, Herman 38
  Irvin 38
SCHABER, Susanna 147
SCHAEFER, --, Mrs. 197
  Anna 196, 204, 205
  Anna Mary 150
  Annie Susan, Mrs. 98,
    111
  Christian 111, 197
  Christine 197
  H. 25
  Henry 1, 196, 197, 203
  Henry C. 150
  Henry Charles 111
  Joseph 111
  Mary 84
  Mathilde 105, 111
SCHAEFFER, Anna 172
  Charles 31
  Elizabeth 25
  Henry 39, 41
  Henry C. 38, 203
  Julius 29
  Mary 40
SCHAEPER, Joan 41
SCHAER, Caroline 106, 175
  Ferdinand 198
  Ferdinand Joseph 5
  Joseph 198
  Stephen 198
SCHAN, Henry 38
  Ida 38
SCHANDREIN, Emily 47
  Paul 47
SCHANTZ, Mary Ann 21
  Valentina 130
SCHARF, Herman Charles
  198
  Ernest Raymond 198
  Herman 153, 198
SCHAUB, Ann Mary 139
  Anna Mary 73, 139
  Mary Ann 139
SCHEBALM, Felix 156
  Mary 156
SCHEELE, Anna, Mrs. 111,
  113
  Henry 38
SCHEER, Caroline 60
SCHEIDER, Chas. Wm.
  Henry 3
SCHEIER, Caroline 175
SCHELHORN, Andrew 147
  Eve Barbara 147
SCHELMER, Wilhelmina 217
  William 217
SCHEMBRE, Buehla 8, 15
  Joe 8, 15
SCHER, Caroline 67
  Marcelline 15
SCHERER, Anna Musline 198
  Ferdinand 198
  Lena 41
SCHERF, Caroline 175
SCHERFFINS, Ann 163
  John Anthony 31, 163
SCHERR, Anna Margaret 175
  Anthony 175
  Caroline 175
  Stephen 38
SCHERT, Stephen 175
SCHESTA, Sophie 60
SCHESTAK, Joseph 60
SCHEXNAIDER, Anna 9
  Dalton John 9
  Evelyn, Mrs. 55
  Evelyn Aleen 9, 17
  John 9
  Joseph 9
  P. M. 51
  Wilton Lee Joseph 9
SCHEXNAYDER, Philimier,
  M. 63

SCHEXNAYDER (cont.)
  Romuald 63
SCHICKSCHNEIDER, Helen
  138
SCHIEBEL, Martin 111
SCHIEDAL, Antonia 48, 65
SCHIEDEL, Anna 102
SCHIESSEL, Ignatius 63
  Lawrence 63
SCHIHULSKI, Josfa 132
  Stephen 132
SCHILETTER, Frederic 160
SCHILZ, Helen 52
SCHINDLER, Anton 63
  Thomas 63
SCHIRMER, Henry 198
  Henry Joseph 198
SCHLACHTER, Agnes 167
  Catherine 202, 203
SCHLEHUBER, Dorothy 31
  Frances 31
SCHLEICHER, Emma 174, 175
SCHLENDER, Bertha 137
SCHLICK, Eva 198
  James 198
SCHLINGHART, Elizabeth
  139
SCHLITTER, Frederic
  Sebastian 197
  Fridolm 197
  Margaret 160
  Nicolas William 197
SCHLOSSER, Barbara 56
  Rudolph 22
SCHMALM, Leahr 31
SCHMERBER, Alberta 24
SCHMID, Christine 68
  Elizabeth 41
SCHMIDT, --, Mrs. 27
  Adam William 112
  Adolf Henry 112
  Albert Henry 197
  Alice Cecile 199
  Anna Louise 197
  B. 38
  Bauk 199
  Buchanan 197, 199
  Caroline 38
  Cecil Emma 197
  Elizabeth 142, 161
  Estelle Maria 197
  Frederic 119, 197
  George Buchanan 197
  George William 197
  Helen 199
  James Buchanan 199
  John 2, 149, 199
  John I. 199
  John Joseph 39
  Julia 8
  Julius William 63
  Lena 13, 179
  Lena Terese 6
  Louis 54
  Ludmilla 199
  Marie 97
  Mary Elizabeth 149
  Mary Ellen 112
  Mary Helen Spier 199
  Minnie 58
  Paul Ernest 199
  Peter 199
  Victoria 199
  Wilhelmina 24, 139
  Wilhelmine Mary 4
  William 112
  William G. 38
  William Raymond 199
SCHMITT, Martin 133
SCHMITZ, Anna 24, 43
  Anton 24, 43
  Mary 24, 43, 95, 140
  Mary Catherine 140

SCHMITZ (cont.)
  Nicholas 84
SCHMUCK, Frank 64
  Reinhold 64
SCHNABEL, Cath. 58
SCHNU, Paul 196
SCHNEIDER, -- 84
  --, Mrs. 133, 163
  Adolph 84, 198
  Agatha 67
  Alma 13
  Alma Emma 198
  Alma Helen Ernestine 5
  Anna 198
  Annie 38
  Antonia M. 162
  Antonia Margaret 30
  Carolina Josephine 198
  Caroline 2
  Catherine 198
  Charles 198
  Charles William 198
  Corinne Sarah Anna 198
  Elizabeth 41, 50, 109,
    112, 188, 218
  Emma 198
  Frances 78, 165, 218
  Frank 218
  Frederic Peter 198
  Gladys Lilian Aloysia
    198
  Henry 22, 198
  Henry Geo. 198
  Herman 31, 198
  Jacob 64
  John 112, 188
  Jos. 67
  Joseph 30
  Josephine 25, 43, 74,
    141
  Leo 13
  Leo John 6
  Louise 64
  Mary 83, 152, 190
  Otto 37
  Peter 84, 198
  Theresa Josephine 198
  Theresa Josephin Joan
    84
  Wilhelmina 31, 198
  William Adolph 198
SCHNITTGER, Gottlieb 199
  Gottlieb Amadius Louis
    199
SCHOBER, --, Mrs. 30
  John 84
  Susanne 123, 126
SCHOCKE, Alma Theresa 199
  Ann Teresa 199
  Anna 64
  Anna Wilhelmina 199
  Anthony 13
  Anthony Frederic 199
  Anthony Joseph 6
  Bertha 14, 64
  Bertha Agnes 7
  Bertha Emma 199
  Catherine 200
  Cecilia 63
  Cecile 14, 68
  Cecile Odile 7
  Cecilia 200
  Chas. 200
  Christian 39, 131, 199,
    200
  Christian Charles 112
  Christian Frank 6
  Christina 112
  Clara 15
  Clara Margaret 64
  Clara Margaret Joan
    200
  Elisabeth Mary Magd. 3

SCHOCKE (cont.)
Elise 200
Elizabeth 199
Elizabeth Agnes 199
Florence 8
Florine Lucille 61
G. 121
Helen 112
Helen Terese 4
Herman 14, 31, 112,
131, 199, 200
Herman Aloysius 64
Herman Anthony 7
Herman Maurice 199
Herman Martin 64
J. 39
J., Mrs. 100
John 63, 68, 112, 199,
200
John William 2
Joseph 15, 112
Joseph Aloysius 8
Joseph Louis 199
Leona Marie 200
Leonida 13, 68
Leonida Catherine 6
Lois 61
Lois Marguerite 67
M. Mary 31
Mary 2, 39, 72, 131,
132, 200
Mary Elizabeth ?
Minnie Anna Wilhelmine
63
Norma Lee 67
Odilia 132
Ottilia 63, 112
Theresa 53, 84, 97,
112, 130, 131, 132,
199, 200, 205
Theresa, Mrs. 111
Wilhelmine 8, 15, 111
William 39, 67, 193,
200
William Blasius 200
William Fred 64
William Frederic 112,
199
Wm. F. 61
SCHOECKE, Anthony 39
Christian 23, 26
Elizabeth 23
John 39
Lena 23, 125
Theresa 26, 29, 39
SCHOEKE, Theresa 155
SCHOELLER, Henry 39, 200
SCHOELLMAN, William 39
SCHOELLMANN, Arthur 15
Walter 14
Walter Aloysius 7
Walter William 200
Wm. F. 200
SCHOELMAN, Arthur 55
SCHOELMANN, Walter 59
SCHOEN, Susan 178
SCHOENBERG, August
Julius 200
Bernard August 200
John Bernard August
200
Julius Andrew 200
SCHOER, Caroline 112
SCHOKE, Herman 39, 119
SCHOLIBE, Henry 39
SCHOLZ, John 124
SCHOLZE, John. 112
SCHOMERS, --, Mrs. 59
John 59
Louise 59
Mary 59
SCHORPP, John 65
SCHOTT, Jos. 207

SCHOTT (cont.)
Theresa Mary 207
SCHRADER, Augusta 149
Theresa 204
SCHRAM, Emma 153
SCHREIBER, Anna 178, 183
Anne 2
Caroline 204
El. 38
Elisa 29
Elizabeth 39, 158,
183, 197, 200
Francis Herman 200
Frank 39, 197, 214
Frank Herman 200
Henry Herman 200
Herman 29, 84, 112,
141, 150, 200, 212
Herman Frank 200
Herman John 200
John 84
Lillie 38, 148, 190,
197, 199, 204
Lillie S. 197
Lily 199
Margaret 27, 150, 151,
183
Margaret Frances 200
Marie 213
Mary 29, 42, 112, 115,
144, 158, 199, 200,
214
Rosina 27, 32, 97, 112,
139, 152
SCHREMPP, Bernard 201
Catherine 201
SCHREYER, Mary 84
SCHRINA, Anna 38
SCHROEDER, Agnes 48
James 40
Martha 67
Pauline 58
Teresa 1
Theresa 40
SCHROMER, Mary Elisabeth
2
SCHROTH, George 64
SCHUBERT, -- 199
Anastasia 188
SCHUCHARD, Anne 155
SCHUCHHARDT, Anna Eliz.
201
SCHUCHARDT, Anna Elizabeth
200
SCHUELER, Linas 30
SCHUELKE, Julius 200
SCHUELL, Anthonia 218
Margaret 28
SCHUETZ, A. 43
Ann Mary 192
SCHUG, Clara 50
Fred 50
SCHULER, Adolph 201
Inez Marie 201
Nelly Fredericka 201
SCHULTE, -- 201
Anne 155
Clara 108, 113, 150,
211
H. 84
Henry 27, 39, 42, 84,
113, 182, 201, 211,
214
Herold Alphonse Peter
201
John 21, 84, 113, 148
John Henry 113
John Joseph 3
Jos. John 151, 201
Joseph 27
Joseph J. 39
Louise Aloysia 6
Mary 156

SCHULTE (cont.)
Mary Theresa 201
Peter Henry 201
Teresa 86, 214
Terese Mary 4
Theresa 27, 98, 150,
213, 214
Theresa Mary 98, 113,
151
SCHULTZ, Ann Elizabeth 31
August 36, 181, 186,
201, 202
Augustine 201
Ernest Gabriel 201
Ernest Raphael 4
Henry 2, 201
Mary (alias Arnold) 42
Mary Ann 178
Theresa 202
SCHULTZE, Joseph 39
SCHULZ, Mary Ann 121
SCHUMACHER, Elise
Frederika 181
Elizabeth 108, 181
SCHUPPERT, Susan 84
SCHUTZI, John 84
SCHVIRNN, Susan 29
SCHWAB, Anna 32
Mary 32
SCHWALM, Frank 172
Joan Petra 172
Leona 176
SCHWAN, Clemens 56
SCHWARTZ, Matthias 64
Michael 64
SCHWARTZER, Joseph 113
SCHWARZBACH, August
Theodore 201
Elizabeth 31
Helen 141
Helen, Mrs. 113
Mary 136
Theodore 39, 136, 201
SCHWARZBACK, Cato 31
SCHWATZBACH, Helen 31,
42, 201
SCHWEBEL, George 142, 143
Laura 143
Louise 143
SCHWENDINGER, Henry
Joseph Eugene 201
Joseph 39, 201
M. 182
Mary 31, 102
SCHWERDTFEGER, Henry
Joseph 3
SCHWERTFEGER, Anna 168
Ernest 22, 168
Susan 22
Susana 129
SCOTT, Charles Benjamin
64
Charles Fred 64
Honoria 35
SDANICE, Mary 67
SEALE, Edward George 62
Flora 62
SEARLE, Henrietta 141
SEARS, Sara 166
SEAWELL, Cora 201
Cordelia 201
James 201
James Joseph 4, 201
Leo 201
Lillie 201
Lillie Temora 201
SEBASTIAN, Herman 201
John 201, 202
Rosa Stephanie 202
SEBELL, N. S. 38
SEEL, Anne Mary 43
Elenora Mary 202
Eleonore 13

SEEL (cont.)
  Elenore Mary 6
  John 27
  Louis 39, 84, 202
  Louise 208
  Louise Barb. Wilh. 3
  Mary 27, 86, 217
  Regina 208
  Sophia 146, 147, 149
  Sophie 27
  Sophie Mary Josephine
    84, 202
  Susan Agnes 5
  Susan Regina
    Wilhelmina 202
SEGNANOVICZ, John Louis
  202
  Magdalen 3
  Mary Virginia 4
  Nicholas 202
SEGURA, Dorothy 16
  Dorothy Teresa 9, 56
  Duffy Lee Joseph 9, 17
  Eloi 56
  Ferryline Mary 17
  Joseph 9
  Lillie Mae 16, 56
  Paul 9
  Ralph Paul 9, 17
  Rita 9
SEIBEL, George 64
  Henry 41
  James 64
SEIBERT, Antonia 62
  Caroline 168
  Caroline Elizabeth 168
  Catherine 168
  George W. 39
  Louis 39
  Mildred Frances 128
  Minnie 126
SEIDEL, Francis 133
SEIDELHUFER, Mary 59
SEIDLER, Anna 111, 113
SEIHULSKY, Gabriel 40
  Stephen 40
SEILER, Catherine 49, 53,
    97
  Catherine, Mrs. 93,
    113
  Frederic 113
SEIPELS, Cath. 55
SELENKI, Margaret 167
  Margaret Josepha 5
SELENSKI, Anna 202
  Ann Mary 202
  Anne Mary 6, 43
  Caspar 40, 43, 56, 156,
    202
  Catherine 202
  Frances Cath. 7
  Fanny 14
  George James 8
  John 40, 150, 202
  John Joseph 6
  Jos. Aloysius 7
  Joseph 43
  Margaret 113
  Marquerite 92
  Peter 43, 202
SELENSKY, Elizabeth 198
  George 15
SELLER, August Herman 84,
    202
  Herman 84, 202
  Terese 84
SELLERS, Elizabeth 202
  Frank Joseph 202
  James 202
  John Bernard 202
  Sylvester 202
  Sylvester Frederic
    Henry 202

SELTENREICH, Theresa 175
SELZER, Mary 57
SENA, Delphine 65
  Emmanuel 65
SENECHAL, Aloysia Mary
    Fides 202
  Fides 14, 92
  Fides Wilhelmine 7
  Harriette Rose
    Leocadia 202
  L. W. 119
  L. W. Louis 7
  Louis 48, 202
  Louis W. 40
  Louis Wm. 202
  Louis William 113
  Mary Fides 48
  Rose 15, 48, 63
SENFT, Catherine 27
SENKOVOLWOWIRKI, Paranka
    53
SENESCHAL, Louis Ww.
  Rose Henriette 63
SENON, Fannie 163
SENSEN, Frances Cath. 63
SEPMSON (SEMPSON?),
    Adelaid 21
SERACO, Theresa 210
SERRA, Geronina Josephine
    202
  Joseph 202
SETZOG, Joan Christina 166
SEVERIN, Elise 162
SGITOWICH, Geo. Joseph 5
SHAEFER, Anna 199
SHAFER, Henry C. 203
SHAK, Wilhelmina 209
SHANNON, Joseph
  Cornelius 4
SHASOLM, Leona Josephine
    95, 113
SHAUGHNESSY, Cath.
  Fitzgerald 33
SHAW, Arthur Alexander 203
  Camille Roland 203
  Catherine Margaret 203
  Charles Leonard 203
  Daniel Henry Pallais
    203
  Edwarda P. 196
  F. R. 203
  Francis 203
  Frank 23
  Frank D. 203
  Frank Michael 203
  Joseph 203
  M. 203
  Marshall William
    Henry 203
  Mary Magdalen 203
  Michael 203
  Michael Frank 203
  Philippine 197
  Phillippine 23, 197
  Stephen 218
  Stewart J. 212
  Thomas 65
  William James 113
  William Thomas
    Augustine 203
SHEELE, C. 38
SHEIHAN, William 24
SHELDON, Jos. C. 40
SHEORLAVIN, Barbara 68
SHEPPARD, Joan 176
SHERIDAN, Patrick 38
SHETLEY, Cecil Ada 203
  Cecile Ann 2
  Susan Elizabeth 203
  William 203
  William F. 2, 203
  William Franklin 40
SHIELDS, Henry 146

SHIRK, Theodora 198
SHOLDERS, Elleen 145
SHOTAKOVA, Emily 61
SHOTWELL, Ida May 68
SHOUK, Steve 67
SHUBERT, John 112
SHUKANES, Catherine 64
  Jura 64
  Stephan Andrew 64
SHUKES, Elizabeth 55
SHULTZ, Albert Raphael
    201
SIAHOWICZ, Frances 57
SICKA, Louise 47
SIEBERT, Anna M. 40
SIEFFERT, Irene Stella
    Mary 202
  Robert 202
SIEK, Emma 207
SIGRIST, John 40
SIKICH, Louise 64
  Robert 64
  Walter 64
  Walter Paul 113
SILENSKI, Martin 203
  Peter 203
SILER, Frederic 113
  Laura 113
  Maud 108, 113
SILHANEK, Mary 49
SILVA, Cruasbassia 9
  Jessie 113
  Jesus de la Luz 51
  Juanita 16, 51
  Mary 51
  Rudolph 16
  Rudy 9
SILVESTER, Kessia 195
SIMMONS, May 66
SIMON, Emma 66
SIMONIZ, Mark 64
  Matthias 64
SIMPSON, Charles Neal 64
  Ernestine 167
  Homan 68
  James T. 40
  Neal Cavitt 64
SIMPTON, Ernest Eugene 64
  Leslie Fern 64
  Monica 9
  Rita Marie 9
SINGER, Henrietta 127,
    143
  Michael 143
SIRINGO, Catherine Mary
    Agnes 2
SITZVANZ, Sophie 49
SKARKE, Adele Anna Mary
    113
  Anita 8, 15
  Anna 84
  Ann Mary 203
  Carl 203
  Charles 65, 113, 203
  Charles Jos. 194
  Chas. Jos. 203
  Chas. Joseph 65
  Frederic 113
  Henry 8, 15, 47, 196
  Herbert Oscar 65
  Joseph 113
  Mary 8, 47, 203
  Mary Rosalie 113
SKRENIG, John 203
SKROBANEK, Adolf 65
  John 65
SLAVERY, J. B. 145
SLAVIK, Emily 66
SMETANA, Frank Charles 65
  Joseph 65
SMIDT, Lillie 183
SMITH, Adolph August 203
  Agnes 62, 215

SMITH (cont.)
  Alfred D. 187
  Angela Aloysia 2
  Andrew 65
  Anna 144
  Apollonia Martina 203
  Buchanan 204
  C. P. 203
  Daniel C. 40
  Edward 204
  Edward August 204
  Elis. Anne 4
  Elisabeth 13
  Elizabeth 209, 210
  Elizabeth Agnes 6
  Emma 214
  Emma Joan 120
  Frank 204
  Frank Claud 4
  Frank Joseph 204
  G., Mrs. 177
  Geo. 40
  Geo. James 204
  George 40
  Gustave 63
  Helen Frances 204
  Henrietta 41
  Isabelle Wilhelmina
    141
  J. H. 214
  J. M. 214
  James 63, 203, 204
  Joan 41
  Joe 67
  John 25, 48, 204
  John F. 41
  Margaret 52
  Margaret Louise 63
  Martin 23
  Mary 23
  Mary Ann Elizabeth 125
  Minna 141
  Richard 13
  Richard Aloysius 6
  Robert Clarence 204
  Sarah Louise 204
  Thomas Anthony 204
  Wilhelma 139
  William Henry 204
SNADERS, Geo. Ww. 66
SNEBELEN, Amatus J., Rev.
    8, 13, 61, 67
SNIDER, Catherine 60
SOELLNER, Dorothy 146
  Gertrude 146
SOHEN, Elenora 123
  Thomas 123
SOLAN, August Thomas 204
  Frances Elizabeth 204
  Julia Marie 204
  Thomas 204
SOMMER, A. 38
  A. L., Mrs. 114
  Aleine Ruth 204
  Amelia 156
  Amelia Theresa 204
  Ann 149
  Ann Mary 3, 4, 115,
    204
  Anna 13, 27, 52, 136,
    191, 204
  Anna M. 137
  Anna Marie 136
  Anna S. 94
  Anna Theresa 204
  Anne Elenore 6
  Anthony 1, 14, 40, 84,
    85, 191, 199, 204,
    205
  Anthony Frank 6
  Anthony P. 137
  Anthony Peter 204
  Anton 58

SOMMER (cont.)
  August 1, 40, 66, 114,
    204, 205
  Caroline Sophy 204
  Cecil E. 137
  Cecil Emma 197
  Cecile Agnes 6, 56
  Cecile Emma 13
  Charles 2, 31, 39, 40,
    58, 204, 205
  Charles Joseph 5
  Charles Louis 114
  Chas. 205
  Elisabeth 14
  Elizabeth 163, 164
  Elizabeth Amalia 205
  Elizabeth Cecile 7
  Ferdinand 1, 31, 40,
    189, 204, 205
  Francis 200
  Frank 39, 40, 84, 85,
    114, 134, 145, 159,
    160, 197, 204, 205,
    212
  Helen 13, 28, 98, 114,
    150, 198
  Helen Margaret 5
  Helen Theresa 58, 151,
    205
  Henry Charles 205
  John 164
  John Baptist 85, 205
  Jos. 204
  Joseph 41, 85, 159
  Joseph Anthony 3, 40
  Lena, Mrs. 136
  Louise 56, 104, 114,
    128
  Margaret 36
  Mary 41, 101, 122, 133,
    205
  Mathilda Anna 205
  Mary Agnes 85, 205
  Mary, Mrs. 101, 114
  Mary Louise 205
  Pauline 197
  Sophie 13
  Sophie Cecile 6
  Teresa 159
  Teresa Mary 7
  Terese 14
  Terese Ignatia 5
  Theresa 31, 114, 204,
    205
  Theresa G. 66
  Theresa Gabriel 205
  Tony 38
SOMMERS, Caroline 26
  Catherine 24
  Ferdinand 27
  Frank 165
  Julia 26
  Katerine 148
SONNIER, Dallas Felix 9
  Ollie 65
  Peter 9
  Valcin 65
SOSBY, John 114
SOULNIER, Ollie 65
SPADES, Eloise 164
SPAITH, Leopoldine (alias
    Reissner) 23
SPANN, Aemilia 134
SPALDING, Anna 56
SPANN, Bessy 119
  Carolina M. 120
  Elenor 205
  Emily 73, 124
  Francis Sales 85
  Helen 119
  John 1
  John F. 85
  John S. 134

SPANN (cont.)
  M. C. 42
  Michael 24, 25
  Peter 31
  Sara Mary 205
SPATEO, Catherine 122
SPEAKER, Frederic Joseph
    5
  Josephine 85
  Mary, Mrs. 101, 114
  Theodore 85
SPECHT, Lutie 204
SPEERS, E. A., Mrs. 31
SPETH, -- 85
SPEYER, Helen 195, 196
SPIEKER, Caroline 4
  Helen 2
  Louise Jos. 3
  Sophie 155
  Sophy 122
  Theodore 155
SPIES, Hermine 67
  Joseph 67
SPIKER, Carolina 205
  Theodore 205
SPIZA, Anthony 205
  Bernard 140, 205
  Joan 140, 205
  Joan Lucy 205
SPRINGER, Cajus 65
  Charles 65
  Fred Majus 65
  Mary 191
STACEROWSKI, Augusta 161
STALLER, Ann 129
STANFORD, Wm. L. 205
STANLY, Carolina 140
STANSFILED, Caroline 65
  Charles Bonart 65
  James Ww. 65
STANWOOD, Eugenia 192
STANZER, Otto 205
  William 205
STAROSKI, Augusta 161
STASNI, Caroline 57
STATTON, Esena 53
STAULER, Mary Julia 161
STECHMAN, Albertine 37
  August Ferdinand 37
  Margaret Ann 37
STECHMANN, --, Mr. 22
  --, Mrs. 22
  Alberta 124
  Albertine Cecile 5
  Anna Barbara 205
  Ann Elizabeth 124
  Anna Elizabeth 22
  Anne Cecile 6
  Anne Barbara 13
  Anne Mary 13
  Ann Mary Barbara 5
  Aug. Rudolf Ferd. 3
  August 124, 205, 206
  August, Sr. 125
  August Rudolph 205
  Barbara 124, 206
  Barbara Josephine 205
  Barbara, Mrs. 189
  Carl W. 40
  Charles 124, 125, 164
  Chas. 206
  Chas. Wm. 205, 206
  Clara Josephine 205
  Edna Barbara 206
  Elizabeth 21, 124, 125,
    206
  George Joseph 206
  Henry 125
  Henry Ferdinand 3
  James William 206
  Josephine 14
  Josephine B. 125
  Josephine Cecile 7

STECHMANN (cont.)
  Louise 13
  Louise Josephine 206
  Louise Margaret 6
  Margaret, Miss 40,
    124, 125, 189, 205
  Mary 125
STECKMANN, Margaret 161
STEFFIERS, Antonia 213
STEGEL, Frances 40
  Josepha 40
STEGEMANN, Elizabeth 177
STEGER, Basil 52, 65
  Celia 52
  John 52, 65
STEGMANN, Chas. Ambrose
  206
  Chas. Wm. 206
  Margaret 206
  Mary 164
STEHLE, Maxemilian 85
STEHLIN, Helen 33, 80,
  174
  Sebastian 33, 80
STEHLING, Anna 36
  Helen 169
STEIN, A. 33
  Mary 41
STEINBACH, Ernestine 59,
  65, 106, 175
  Gertrude 35
STEINBRINK, Henry 29
  Lee 8
  Wilbur 8, 15
  William James 31
STEINER, Catherine 64
STEINHARDT, Anna 161
STEINHART, Anna 30
STEINHOFF, Henry 27
  John Henry 40
  McCarte 27
STEINLE, Crescentia 67
STELZEL, John 65, 114
  Mary 114
  Richard Wigand 65, 114
  Susan 50, 64
  Susie 114
STENGLE, Helen 43
STENZEL, -- 85
  Ann 40, 85
  Anna 206
  Charles 40, 206
  Charles Joseph 206
  Chas. 40, 206
  Clara 206
  Geo. 40
  George 206
  Helen 85, 206
  Joan 85
  Jos. Chas. 206
  Mary 40, 206
  Otto 40, 206
  Ruth 141
  William 40, 206
STENZLER, August 41
STEPHANIES, Tesse 150
STEPHENS, Nettie 214
  Nettie A. 42
STEPHENSON, E. J. 51
  E. N. 206
  Frank Ernest 206
  Norma Lee 51
STERIC, Henry 142
STERNE, Carolina 206
  Frank 206
STETTER, Nyman 66
STETTING, Charles Henry
  32
  Elizabeth Margaret 32
STEVENET, Simon Stephen
  85
STEVENS, Louise M. 136
  Mary 170

STEVENS (cont.)
  Nettie 213
  William 60
  William, Mrs. 60
STEWARD, John Lawrence 41
  Peter Wallace 41
STEWART, Elizabeth
  Georgian 206
  John L. 206
  John Lawrence 114
STEYMANN, Mary Elisabeth
  2
STIEFEL, Sophie 148
STIGHORST, Frederica 178
  Mary 178
STILES, Emma Gertrude 178
STINES, Marion Smith 65
  William James 65
STOCK, Louise 52
  Verona 167
STOCKTON, Ann Oser 186
STOLLER, Louise 55
STOLZ, Caroline 185
STONER, Helen 203
  John H. 1, 41, 203
  John Henry 207
  John William 207
STOPELBERT, Dora Augusta
  151
  Dorothy Augusta 150
STOPPELBERG, Charles 85
  Carol Frederic 207
  Chas. Fr. 206
  Dora Augusta 76
  Dorothy Augusta 2
  Elizabeth 206
  Frederic 207
  Henry George 2
  John 207
  Mary 189
  Mary Elizabeth 207
STOPPELBURG, Dorothy 149
STORK, Henry 207
  Mary Agnes 207
STOWEL, Catherine Agnes 57
STRIACKER, Ottilia 210
  Sarah 210
STRAUB, Charles 59
STRAUBE, Elizabeth 135
STRECKFUS, Henry Aloysius
  207
  Robert Leo 207
STRICKLAND, Joseph 65
  Joseph A. 65
STRIPLING, Lydia 138
STRUBE, Adolph 207
  Elizabeth 160
  Mary Bertha Teresa 207
  Teresa Elizabeth 207
  Wilhelmina 160
  Wilhelmina Elizabeth
  207
STRUCK, Catherine 191
  Clementine 191
  Theresa 145, 207
  William 207
STRUVE, Theresa Julia 160
STUART, Chas. William 64
  S. E. 150
STUBBS, Frank Spencer 65
  John Adam 65
STUBENRAUCH, Adam 85
  Louise 85
STUDER, Theresa 121, 173
STUMPF, Anna 13, 102, 114
  Anna C. 53
  Anna Catherine 217
  Anna K. 58
  Anna May 64
  Anna, Mrs. 114
  Anne Agnes 6
  Anna Catherine 58, 207
  Catherine 41

STUMPF (cont.)
  Charles 13
  Charles Aloysius 6
  Charles Ignothius 207
  Emma Wilhelmine 114
  Frances Mary 207
  Frank Adam William 207
  Frank Joseph 207
  J., Mrs. 93
  J. J. Terese Ann 7
  John 114
  John Jos. 114
  John Joseph 41, 62, 64,
    66, 114
  John Jos. Christian 5
  Joseph 114
  Louise Catherine 114
  M. H. 85
  Mary Martha 114
  Mary Theresa 41, 62,
    207
  Theresa 203
  Theresa Mary 109, 114,
    136
  William 41, 58, 62, 66,
    114, 124, 207
  Wm. 85
STURLESS, Ammanuel 202
SULLEY, John 41
SULLIVAN, Anna 173
  Elizabeth 52, 119
  Helen 32
  John 207
  Mary 64
  William 31
  Wm. 207
SUMMERS, Elizabeth 164
SUND, A., Dr. 30
SURNIN, Flora 17
SURRAL, A--- 8
SWANN, George 175
  Laura 175
SWANSON, Frederica 37
SWARBRICK, James 41
SWEAM, Angeline 51
SWEENEY, Catherine 213
  Catherine Elizabeth 3
  D. J. 62
  James Joseph 66
  John Joseph 66
  Margaret 179
  Mary 41
SYMAK, Bertha 53
SZEZUREK, Stanislaus 48
  Victoria 48
TACQUARD, Adolph Henry
  207
  J. 41
  James 207
  Jules Joseph 5
  Julia Emily 207
TACQUART, Henry 41
  Julius 41, 208
  Julius Leroy 208
  Leonida 208
  Sadie Pauline 208
TAIRIER, Rev. 30
TAIT, Charles William 28
  Louise 28
  Isabel 208
  Louise M. 28
TAM, Wilhelmina 150
TANBUSH, Stephan 41
TAQUARD, Henry E. 208
  Julia 208
TAQUART, Emily 159
  Joseph 159
  Jules 13
TARACE, Joseph 119
TARGARONA, Jeanne 208
  Joan 208
  Peter 190, 208
TARPY, Elizabeth 208

TARPY (cont.)
Michael 208
TARRAS, J. 143
TAVENER, Bert E. 50
Evelyn Myrtle 50
TAVENET, Mary 1
TAX, Joe Frank, Jr. 66
Joseph Frank 66
Loretta 66
Nicholas Aloysius 66
TAYLOR, Elizabeth 176
Elizabeth C. 34
J. E. 25
Lydia Mathilda 48
Mary 131
Myrtle 48
Thomas S. 48
TCHAKOVAN, Anna 60
TCHIEDEL, Antonia 147
TEALE, Mary E. 208
TEGADE, Lucinda 47
TEICHMANN, Helen 144
Lena 96, 144
TENGLER, Theresa 34
TERHENN, Ada 197, 203
TERHEUM, H. 42
TERRY, Anna 202
TEUBUSCH, Stephen 208
Wallace Anthony Lee
208
TEUCHMANN, Lena 74
THARENET, Joseph 149
THAVENET, John 85
Joseph 27
Julianne 27
Mary 21
THEILACKER, Catherine 199
THEIMER, Joan 26
THEIS, Mary 135
THELE, August Joseph 66
William 66
THEMANN, Catherine 23
THEOBALD, John 36
Minna 36
THERNAT, Julian 22
THEVENOT, Julius 129
THIBODAUX, Alma 48
Celest 51
THIELEN, Chas. F. 41
Frank 144, 160
Mary 144
Mary Agnes 160
Myrtle 8
THEILMANN, Ann Mary 4
THEONOT, Julius 172
Alida Estelle 172
THEVENOE, Julius 122
THIEM, Emil 66
John 61
Richard 66
THIERNAM, Pat, Mrs. 119
THOMAS, Adam 208
Catherine 203
Mary 203
Mary Catherine 203, 208
THOMFOHRDEN, Alexander 32
Catherine 32
THOMPSON, Anna Alice 208
Earl 8
Ellen 158
Ferris Eugene 208
Guy Bernard 208
Guy B. 208
Katherine 146
Mary 161, 162, 213
William 41, 146, 208
THOMSON, Earl 47
THORBES, Elizabeth 125,
132, 138, 149, 157
THORMAHLEN, Adolph 208
Adolph Paul 208
Arnold E. 208
Arnold Wm. Chas. 208

THORMAHLEN (cont.)
Mary Isabel Regina 208
THORMAHLEY, A. E. 41
THORMOLEN, Mary 202
THOY, James 130
THRINGER, August 208
Charles Henry 208
THROAN, Laurence 160
THUSSING, Charles Joseph
132
TIBORDEAUX, Louise 174
Peter 174
TICHLE, Joseph Bennett 175
TICKLE, Elizabeth Caroline
147
James 41, 147
James, Jr. 41
John 8, 15
Joseph 147
Jos. Mich. 208
Joseph Bennet 114
Joseph Bernard 41
Rose May 8, 208
Theresa Marie, Mrs.
106, 115
TICKS, Michael 202
Regina 1, 84
TIDINGS, Mary 105
TIERNAN, Frank 35
Sarah 189
TIFE, Margaret 185
TILL, Stephan 65
Theresa 65
TILLEMANN, Frank 209
Sara Elizabeth 209
TILLWITZ, Emily 2
TINTORE, Margaret 186
TISCHENDORF, Caroline 101,
115, 175
Clara 175
Constantine 66, 115
Frances 106, 175
George 175
Geo. Constantine 66
Ida 34, 176
Mary 175
Mary Frances 34, 175,
176, 208
TIX, Anthony Joseph 209
Michael 165, 209
TLEHANEK, Victoria 48
TOBLEMAN, Harry Reinhart
66
John Reinhard 66
Norman Clarence 66
TOCK, David 209
Mary Davida Ada 209
TOEBELMANN, Anna 164
Elizabeth 164
TOLKOWSKI, Frances Celina
209
Frank 209
Helenr 209
TOLOMEY, Paul 150
TOMFOHRDEN, Alexander 209
Henry Emil 209
Marion John Hy. 209
Martha 209
TONETTI, Natalus 179
TONIS, Emil 209
Frances Odilia 209
TOOK, Anna 85
David 85
Mary Davida 85
TOSER, Donata 186
TOUEIGH, Frederic Anton
209
Theophilo 209
TOWSEY, -- 209
Mary Elizabeth 209
TRADENVITCH, Ann 174
TRAHAN, Ambrose 63, 66
Duprea 66

TRAHAN (cont.)
Francois 66
Rita Victoria 4
TRAINER, Rosalie 63
TRALLE, Ernest 41
TRAMONTE, Dinah 66
Dominic 66
Sam 66
Joseph J. 66
TRAVA, Frank 209
TRAVERSO, Peter Joseph 5
Rose 15
Rose Eliz. 8
TREACCAR, Alvin Joseph
115
Alvin William 115
Frank William 115
Gertrude Mary 115
Joseph 115
Margaret 115
Theodore 41
TREMELL, Mattie 55
TRENBEHL, Meda 129
TRENT, Mary Margaret 209
Thomas 209
TRENTWEHL, Meta 129, 130
TREVINO, Adele 53
TREVINIO, Mary 4
TREW, John 145
TRIACCAR, Joseph 210
Odilia Josephine 210
William 85
TRIACCER, Joseph, Fr., 5
TRIACKER, Charles Jesse
209
Elizabeth 159
Jesse Charles 209
Joseph 3, 209, 210
Julia Isabel 209
Mary Helen 210
Ottilia 210
Sarah 210
Theodore 209, 210
TRIBOUT, Clementine 33
Jules J. 58
TRIBUT, Gertrude 172
TRICKER, Catherine 184
TRINCKS, William 142
TRINISK, Elizabeth 142
TROLLE, Julius 41
TROLLNEY, --, Mrs. 9
TROSCLAIS, Mary 195
TROST, Anna Marie Cecil
210
Anna Mary 161
Anna Mary Cecil 85
Bernardine Josephine
210
Caroline 30, 161
Germanicus 178, 210
Germanicus Morris 210
Henry Louis 210
Herman 30, 41, 115,
161, 187, 199, 210
John 210
John Francis 210
John Frank 3
Joseph 2
Louis 30
Louise 187
Martin Louis 210
Mary Sophie 210
Peter Alysius 210
Sophie 2, 210
Sophie Theresa 210
TROUETTE, John A. 210
Mary Josephine 210
TROY, John 54
John P. 54
Louise C. 54
TRUBE, H. 21
TRUCHARD, John 210
Mary 4, 210

TRUCHARD (cont.)
  Roseann 184
TRUMP, Arthur 51
  Tralice Norma 51
TSCHAECKE, Caroline 210
TSCHAEKE, Anna 22, 71,
  126
  Anne 1, 181
  Caroline 193
  Frank 22, 42
  Herman 192
  Joan 192
  Josephine Sophie 42
  Sophie 193
TSCHIEDAL, Caroline 83,
  109
TSCHIEDEL, Antonia 149
  Caroline 191
  Caroline T. 191
TSCHIEDL, Anna 102, 114
  Antonia 97, 114
  Caroline 115
TSCHILL, Anna 218
TSCHOCKE, Christian 210
  Mary Eliz. 200
  Mary Elizabeth 210
  William 1
TSCHOECKE, Joan 123
TUCKER, Henry 131
TULAE, Bertha 40
TULIS, Josephine 58
TUPIL, Catherine 53
TURBA, Charles 62
  Julia 62
TURNER, Louis 210
TURSCHIG, Charles 163
  Frances 163
UGER, Mary Frances 22
  Richard 22
UGESDO, Medo 65
UNDERWOOD, Mary 159
  Mary L. 159
  Mary Louise 158, 160
USNARSCH, Bertha 66
VAGENBRET, Ann 190
  Anna 190
VAGLIENTI, John 210
  John Anthony 210
VALAIS, Mary 203
VALENZUELA, Angelo Carlos
  115
  Angelo Carlos, Mrs.
  115
  Ann Marie Marguerite
  115
VALLE, Mary Theresa 169
VALOT, Guadalupe 51
VALUCEK, Moli 66
VALUSEK, Ferdinand 66
  John 66
VAN BENTHUEPEN, Augusta
  173
VAN DEN ENDE, -- 67
  Catholicus 67
  Elizabeth 3, 42, 211
  Emma 25
  Emma M. A. 3, 211
  Emma Mary Augusta 211
  John Arnold 211
  William 25, 42
  William Henry 211
  Wm. 211
  Wm. Simen Hubert 211
VAN DER WERFF, Janieka 59
VANDERPOOL, Elizabeth 25
  William 25
  W. 140
VANEK, Gregory 60, 67
  Martin 67
VANKEE, Frank 58
VANEKER, Wilhelmina 36
VAN ROCHEN, Wilhelmina 93,
  115

VAN STRUVE, Joseph Louis
  211
VARGA, Benjamin 42
  Joseph Alexander 211
  Joseph Henry 42
VARNELL, Elizabeth 211
  James 211
VASLA, Anthony 65
VAUGHN, Anna 211
  Daniel 211
  Joan Lennon 211
VAUTIER, C. H., Mrs. 134
VEHM, Mary 48
VEICHT, Anna Mary 211
  Nicholas 211
VELELS, Anna 61
VERBENA, Andrew 85
VERBERNE, -- 85
  Agnes Josephine 211
  Andrea Mary 211
  Andrew 42, 211
  Camille 85
  Camille Mary 211
  Elizabeth 211
  Emma 29, 156
  Emma Terese Mary 2
  Gertrude Catherine 211
  Henry William 211
  Joan 29
  Joseph Louis 211
  Mary 1, 23
  Theresa 32
  William Joseph 211
VERNERT, Albertina 26,
  186, 215
VEUIL, F. 62
VIATOR, Lola S., Mrs. 63
VICOVICH, Anton 212
  Mary Emelda Anna 212
VIEHL, A., Rev. 16
VIEHMANN, Aloysia 201
  Frederic 39
  Louise 39
VIEWEGER, Charles August
  115
  Louise 109, 189
  Mathilda Louise 31
VIEWERGER, Louise 109
VIGARD, Ann 120
VIGNE, Joseph 37, 123
  Mary 119
VILLENEUVE, Cecile J. 64
  John 64, 212
  Louis Joseph 212
  Mary Margaret 64
VINCENT, Dilta 55
  Eugene 63
  Lucia 9
  Mary Dilta 63
  Rorvena 9
  Rowena Mae 16
VIOLET, Catherine 141
VIOTTO, John 210, 212
  Mary Ann Margaret 212
  Thomas 212
VISCOVICH, Anita 8
  Magdalene Antonia 131
VISCOWITCH, Anthony 212
VITTER, Joan 197
  Louise 71, 119, 143
  Victor 119, 197
VIWGER, Rosale 189
VOEBNER, Mary 126
VOGT, Anna 143
  Caroline 2
  Conrad 42, 198, 212
  Herman Andrew 212
  Louise Frances 212
  Margaret 212
  Margaret Rosina 212
  Mary 39, 201
  Mary Rosina 212
VOIGHT, Charles 212

VOIGHT (cont.)
  Christian 3
VOIGT, Carl Herman 67
  Herman 67
  Paul 212
VOLLERT, Catherine 86
  Emma Wilhelmina 212
  Francis 212
VOLLMER, Christine 35
VON BUTTLAR, August 212
VON DEN ENDEN, Arnold 115
  William Simon Hubert
  115
VON DEN SCHULENBURG,
  Wener 189
VON ROTC, A. 68
VON STIMFORD, Martha
  Baroness 92, 115
VON STRUVE, Louis Joseph
  1
VORAUER, John 67
  Ludwig 67
VOSS, Henry 208
VOULK, Mathilde 105
VRANA, Rev. 95
VULETICH, Ann 121
  Bartholomew 14
  Bartholomew Joseph 6
VURKOTT, Louise 183
  Mary 183
VYORAL, Rosa 47
WACENBRETT, Mathilda 37
WAGENFUEHRER, Frederic 42
WAGER, Andrew 212
  Josephine 212
  Mary 162
WAGNER, Alice H. 61
  Alice Wilhelmina 212
  Anna Catherine 212
  Arthur Butler Chas.
  212
  Barbara 75
  Caroline 178, 212
  Catherine 27
  Catherine M. 68
  Clara, Mrs. 98, 115
  Frederic 29
  Federic William 164
  Henry 68, 212
  John 212
  Joseph 86
  Mary 136
  Paul 67
  Theodor 212
  Theodore 212
  True Eaton 67
  Truitt 61
WAIDHOFER, Joseph 16
WAINRIGHT, Cora Ann 213
  Fred 213
  Helen 191
WAKEFIELD, Mary 37
WALDRON, Richard Lloyd 68
  Ww. Harold 68
WALDSCHMIDT, Margaret 42,
  213
WALKER, A. 121
  Catherine 196
  Emily 12
  Helen 37
  James L. 128
  Lyda 67
WALLACE, Catherine Mabel
  212
  John 212
  Russel L. 52
WALLIS, John 213
  John Arthur 213
WALLSTEIN, Catherine 196
  Dorothy 188
WALSH, Daniel 217
  Ellen 24
  John 213

WALSH (cont.)
Louise Brigid 213
Louise Emma 6
M. J. 39
M. J., Mrs. 39
Margaret 213
Mary 37, 217
Michael 14, 213
Michael Peter 7
Mary Ellen 213
Pat 138, 213
Patrick 42
Patrick August 42
WALTER, Appolonia 33
August 213
Josephine 132
Magdalen Agnes 213
Maurice 184
WALTERS, Mary 36
WALTHERS, Alfred 57
Anita Elizabeth 57
WALZ, Louise Brigid 213
Mary Ellen 213
T. 213
WANDERS, Elizabeth 146
WANNEMACHER, Aloysius 67
Charles 67
WAPPLER, Christina 42
Frederic Theophilus 42
Sophie 86
WAPPNER, M. 129
WARD, Mary Catherine 3
WARE, Francis Joseph 213
Frank 213
WARNE, Mary 63
WARNELL, James 213
Mary Dewey 213
WARNER, Adelin 127
WARREN, Allen 211
Charles 213
Chas. 211
Helen 211
John 42
Laura Campbell 213
Mary 24
WARTH, August 213
August Mathew Henry
213
Mary Louise 213
WASLAVIK, Catherine 60
WASNA, Catherine 86, 213
Michael 86, 213
Victoria 86
Voctoria 86
WASSMUS, Minna 121
WATKINS, Mary Monterey
213
WATSON, Fannie 165
WATT, Joseph 42
WATTS, Adelaide Elis. 4
WATZLAVICK, James 23
WCHMIDT, John 199
WEAVER, Beulah 65
Jimmie Elizabeth 65
Leonard 65
WEBB, Lucy 27
WEBER, --, Mr. 39, 113
--, Mrs. 39
Aemilian 7
Aemilian Peter 14
Alex John 116
Alexander John 213
Alysius 214
Antonia Elenore
Arthur 21
August 2, 42, 213, 214
August A. 213
August John 214
Catherine 213, 214
Clara 14, 182, 201,
214
Clara Catherine 213
Clara M. 39

WEBER (cont.)
Clara Terese 7
Clarence 8, 15
Clarence Thompson 213
E. J., Mrs. 115
Eliz. 207
Elizabeth 214
Emil 42, 147, 158, 204,
213
Emil J. 213
Emil Joseph 115, 214
Emil Peter 214
Emile 29
H. F. 66
Helen 86
Helen Catherine 214
Henry 86
Herman 8, 15
Herman Frank 214
John 2, 42, 58, 201,
213, 214
John Emil 86, 214
Louis William 214
Lillian 58
Mary 86, 112, 115, 158,
213
Mary Eliz. 206, 207
Mary Emily Theresa 214
Mathias 35, 42, 86,
179, 214
Mathilda 21, 123
Mathilda Mary 121
Oscar 86
Peter 214
Peter Alexander 214
Robert John 116
Theresa 86, 135, 146,
147, 188, 201, 214
Theresa Henrietta
Louise 214
Vivian 214
W. 183
Wilhelmina 182
William 42, 86, 197,
213, 214
William H. 42
William Jos. 213
William Otto 86, 214
WEBSTER, Edward 42
Ludon Gerald 68
Thomas 42
WECHSLER, Philip 214
WECKERT, Louise 177
Louise Ernestine 35,
177, 214
WEDEMAIER, Anna 210
Sophia 210
Sophie 210
WEDEMAYER, Frederic 210
WEDEMEYER, Frederic 41
Sophy 41
WEGMER, Wilhelmine 21
WEHMEYER, Catherine 116
Catherine Agnes 6
WEIDEMAN, Emme 33
WEIDENBACH, Catherine 24
WEIDENMANN, Emma 25
WEIDENBACH, John Jos. 24
WEIDMANN, Christopher 25
WEIER, Henry 174
Sophie W. 144
Sophie Winfried 144
WEIHAUSEN, Claus August
67
WEIMER, Barbara 65, 114
Barbara Catherine 91,
115
Frank 116
J. B., Rev. 5, 6, 7, 8,
13, 14, 15, 21, 22,
23, 24, 25, 26, 27,
28, 29, 30, 31, 32,
33, 34, 35, 36, 37,

WEIMER (cont.)
J. B., Rev. (cont.) 38,
39, 40, 41, 42, 43,
47, 48, 49, 50, 51,
52, 53, 54, 55, 56,
57, 58, 59, 60, 61,
62, 63, 64, 65, 66,
67, 68, 69, 70, 71,
72, 73, 74, 75, 76,
77, 78, 79, 80, 81,
82, 83, 84, 85, 86,
87, 91, 92, 93, 94,
95, 96, 97, 98, 99,
100, 101, 102, 103,
104, 105, 106, 107,
108, 109, 110, 111,
112, 113, 114, 115,
116
John Baptist, Very Rev.
116
WEINBERG, Louis 42
WEINBERGER, Aloysius 116
WEINDEMANN, Frederic 171
WEINRECHT, Caroline
(Cora) A. 36
Frederic P. 36
WEINZAEPFLEN, M., Rev.
33, 40, 41
WEISE, Martha 146, 147
WEISNER, Aloysius 215
Mary Agnes Alice 215
WEISS, Bertha Theresa 215
George 215
James 215
John 215
Joseph 215
William George James
215
WEISSE, Martha 147
Meta 146
Paul 147
WEITZMANN, Anna 39
WELCH, Nicolas 140
WELLINGTON, Beatrice
Margaret 47
Thomas 47
WELLS, Aloysia Josephine
205
William 215
WELSCH, Francis Hillary
215
Patrick 215
WILSHANS, Carlotta 101
WEND, Sibyl 72
WENDEL, Caroline 119, 161
John Joseph 4
WENDELL, John 215
John Joseph 215
WENDER, Mary 141
WENDL, John 144
WENIBURG (WEINBURG?), E.
21
WENTZEL, Margaret 154
WENZEL, Alphonse 67
Andrew Henry 215
Ferdinand 67
Louis 215
Louis David 4
Louis Davidson 215
Louise 215
Margaret 159
Mary Louise 215
Minnie 135
WERDEHAUSEN, --, Mrs. 23
Agnes Louis 214
Agnes Louise 62
Bernardine 142
Caroline 1, 33, 42, 80,
161, 169, 177
Henrietta 2, 24, 139,
161
Jos. 25
Joseph 2, 161

WERDEHAUSEN (cont.)
Joseph Philip 214
Lucille Ursula 214
Margaret 1, 29, 154
Mary 33, 42, 169, 207
Mary Catherine 154
Mary Louise 161
Philip 33, 169, 214
William 2, 62, 116, 214
WERDENHAUSEN, Joseph 215
Magdalen Edna 215
Philip 215
William Frederic
Joseph 215
WERDENHOUSEN, Henrietta 139
WERDERHAUSEN, Edna M. 62
Philipp 86
WERLLA, Emma 13
WERNER, Frederic 215
Miriam Margaret 215
WERNERT, Alberta 186
S. 33
Virginia 33, 169, 170
WERTPFAL, Mathilda 48
WERTROP, Florence 59
William 59
WESENDORFF, H. 170
WESER, Margaret 209
WESLEY, Olive 216
WESTERFELD, Carl 62
WESTERLAGE, John Henry 166
WESTERLEDGE, Clara 174
WESTERMEIER, Aloysia 67
WETTENHAUSEN, Carrie 30
WEVERKOVA, Frances 65
WEVLLA, Emma Agnes 6
WEYER, Alexander Bernard 215
Anna 57
Anna Mary 215
Henry 120, 215, 216
Joseph Patrick 215
Louis George 216
Mary 216
Sophie Elizabeth 216
Sophy W. 144
WEYERS, Alexander 2
Henry 191
Henry J. 86
Sophie 1, 26, 36, 86, 191, 215
WEYHER, Alexander Bernard 86
Henry 42
John Henry 86
WHEELING, Catherine 23
WHELTON, Pat 180
WHITBURN, John 213
WHITAKER, M. 22
WHITE, Alex 204
Alice 54
Amelia 56
Chas. 56
France 54
Odilia 126
WHITLEY, E. S. 68
WHITNEY, Anna 24
WHITTY, Robert K. 13
WICKES, Georgia Veronica 116
Harry M. 116
Henry 43, 216
Henry Edward 216
Henry M. 216
Mary 15
May Eliz. 8
Mary Frances 216
Percy 216
Ursula 15
Ursula Theresa 216

WICKS, Georgie 8, 15
Harry 8
Lena 215
Mary 56
WICOKSKY, Frances 161
WIDDEMEYER, Anna 66
WIECHERT, Anna 71
WIESCHKA, Frank 116
Frank Frederic Charles 116
WILDEMANN, Barbara 86
WIEGARD, Anna 193
WIEGESHING, Mary 57
WIEGMANN, Josephine
Wilhelmina Mary 216
Wilhelmina 216
William 216
WIEGOND, Emma 199
WIEL, Adolph 178
WIENERS, Anthony 86
WIESE, Gustaf, Rev. 41
Gustave 163
Guy, Rev. 75
WIGARD, Ann 120
Joseph 120
WIHLANDER, Henry 66
WILD, Charles Henry 43
Henry 216
Louise Anna 216
Mary 116
WILDE, J. A. 136
WILFF, Frederic 43
WILHELM, Catherine 196
Mary 86
WILKE, Florence 8, 15
Xenia 14, 59, 60
Xenia Gertrude 7
WILLES, Helen 183
WILLIAMS, Alice 53
Anna 64
Annie Lee 61, 67
Cora M. 181
Emily 35
Eva, Mrs. 116
Margaret 61
Mary 165
Rachel L. 61
WILLINGER, Anna Mary 216
B. 165
Bernard 202, 216
Rose Martha 216
WILLIS, Hugo 216
Stephen 216
WILLOUGHBY, Elva 60
WILMETTE, Louise 136
WILRYCX, Charles 62
Leona 62, 102
Regina 62
WILRYKS, -- 32
WILSON, --- Mrs. 193
A. Capt. 24
B. 26
Benjamin 67
Catherine 86
Charles 216
George 67
Helen 164
John 119, 140, 164, 193
John August 216
John B. 183
Maddie 171
Mary 216
Mary Ann 3
Mary Anna 216
Olive 21, 26, 119
Paul 67
Thomas 216
Walter 216
WILZ, Nothburga C. 199
WIND, Sophie 210
WINDERMEYER, Mary 146
WINDMEIER, Philippine 39
William 39

WINDMEYER, F. W. 123
Florence William 43
G. 202
Henry 13
Henry Joseph 6
Joseph 13, 140, 195
Joseph Amador 217
Joseph John 6
Joseph Caroline Sophie 86, 217
Philippine 200
Philippine Caroline
Susan 217
Sophie 195
Sophie L. 37
Sophie Louise 111, 195
Sophie Mary 4
Terese 195
Terese Agnes 5
Theresa 37
William 37, 86, 200, 215, 217
William Louis Hy. 217
WINDERWOLF, T., M.D. 50
WINKELBACH, August 43, 216
Augusta 134
Elizabeth Frances
Augusta 216
Henry 43, 216
Mary Aline 216
WINKELBERG, Caroline 217
Elizabeth 183
H. 217
Henry 216
WINKELHANS, Elizabeth 129
Henry 65
Mary 116
WINKLER, Anna 199
William 124, 190
WINN, Anna Butler 40
WINSLOW, Wilhelmine
Elisabeth 2
WIRTH, August 67
Otto 67
WISCINSKI, John 67
Wladislas 67
WISE, Alice 67
WISRODT, August 217
Henry Stephen 217
WISSE, F. R. 207
WISSINGER, C. 210
WITING, Bertah 182
WITTEIER, James 184
WOFFORD, Benie Angelica
Collins 217
WOLCOTT, H. E. 35
WOLF, -- 129
Charles Philip 217
Ferdinand 43, 217
Frederic 170, 217
Joan Elizabeth 132
John 217
Theresa 67
WOLFE, Ann Mary 202
WOLFEN, Frederic 217
Elizabeth Alice 217
WOLFF, Amalie Schlosser 22
Charles Philip 217
Chs. Philip 4
Ferdinand 43
Fred 68
Frederic 35, 68, 178, 217
Frederica Elizabeth 217
Frieda 13, 68
Frieda Mary 6
George 13
George Joseph 6, 68, 217
John 217
Rosa 35, 138, 178

WOLFF (cont.)
  Rose, Mrs. 101, 116
  Theobald 13
  Theobald Frand 6
WOLFGANG, Carolina 128
  Caroline 205
  William 87
WOLKARS, Zoe 38
WOLKEN, Mary 28
WOLLFGANG, Carolina 127
WOLLBAUM, Catherine 156
WOLLES, Joan 190
WONDER, Mary 197
WOOD, Ann Elizabeth 155
  Edna 63
  William 196
WOODMAN, E. C. 54
WOODS, Albert 68
  Ellen 125
WOODSON, Joseph 217
  Joseph James 217
WORDENBAUM, Anna 158
  Henry 158
WUIHL, Apollonia 87
WRITT, John Calhoun 217
WUNDER, Mary Anne 111
YANESKA, Mary 47
YARDEM, Mary 22
YEADACKEN, Earl, Mrs. 59
YEAGER, Isabel Joan 66
YILGE, Adolf Gustave 4
  Bertha Mary 4
  Ernest Adolph 217
  Frank Charles Otto 218
YILLGE, Bertha 217, 218
YOFFIN, Charles Clement
    218
  Clement George 218
YOUNG, -- 87
  Anna 98, 116, 180, 205
  Anthony 218
  Antonio 147
  Carolina 188, 218
  Caroline 76
  Caroline Joan 5
  Catherine Josephine 2
  Elizabeth 138
  F. 38
  Ferdinand 198, 218
  Frances 188
  Francis 218
  Francis Catherine 218
  Gustaf 218
  John 180
  John W. 51
  Louise 2, 218
  Mary 218
  W. 33
YOUNGE, Anna Mary 87
YOUSE, Loretta 51
YURKOVICH, Mark 68
Z---, Andrew 87
ZABEL, Ferdinand 43
ZACHARKO, John 116
  Olga 116
ZACHARKS, Anne Agnes 67
  John 67
  Rosie 67
ZAPFEL, Adolph 198
ZAESKE, Albert 68
  Oscar F. 68, 116
ZARALLA, -- 87
ZCHIEDEL, Ferdinand 87
ZECELICH, John 68
  Mary 68
ZEILER, Regina 201
ZEINMER, August 43
ZEISER, Mary Ann 42
ZEITLER, Frances 38
ZELLER, Cath. 59
  Louis 25
ZERNA, Metha Joan 61
ZIDEK, John 68

ZIEGLER, August Henry 43
ZIMMERMANN, Charles
  Aloysius 6
ZINGELMANN, Louis F. C.
  68
  William 68
ZINGG, Frances 169, 209
  Theophilo 169, 209
ZINK, Martha 53
ZUBER, Anna Mary 163
  Emilia 25
  Emily 209
  Wilhelmina Emily 218
  William 218
ZWICKEL, Paul 87

www.ingramcontent.com/pod-product-compliance
Lightning Source LLC
Chambersburg PA
CBHW021856020426
42334CB00013B/360